Building Literacy *in* Secondary Content Area Classrooms

Thomas G. Gunning

Professor Emeritus
Southern Connecticut State University

Adjunct Professor
Central Connecticut State University

PEARSON

Boston • Columbus • Indianapolis • New York • San Francisco • Upper Saddle River
Amsterdam • Cape Town • Dubai • London • Madrid • Milan • Munich • Paris • Montreal • Toronto
Delhi • Mexico City • São Paulo • Sydney • Hong Kong • Seoul • Singapore • Taipei • Tokyo

Vice President, Editor in Chief:
 Aurora Martinez Ramos
Editor: Erin Grelak
Editorial Assistant: Michelle Hochberg
Executive Marketing Manager: Krista Clark
Production Editor: Paula Carroll

Editorial Production Service: Jouve
Manufacturing Buyer: Megan Cochran
Electronic Composition: Jouve
Interior Design: Carol Somberg
Photo Researcher: Annie Fuller
Cover Designer: Linda Knowles

Credits and acknowledgments borrowed from other sources and reproduced, with permission, in this textbook appear on the appropriate page within text or on page 499.

Many of the designations by manufacturers and sellers to distinguish their products are claimed as trademarks. Where those designations appear in this book, and the publisher was aware of a trademark claim, the designations have been printed in initial caps or all caps.

Library of Congress Cataloging-in-Publication Data
Gunning, Thomas G.
  Building instruction in secondary content area classrooms / Thomas G. Gunning.
    p. cm.
Includes bibliographical references.
  ISBN-13: 978-0-205-58081-1
  ISBN-10: 0-205-58081-5
  1. Reading (Secondary)—United States.   2. Language arts (Secondary)—United States.
3. Content area reading—United States.   4. Interdisciplinary approach in education.   I. Title.

  LB1632.G86 2012
  428.4071'2—dc23

                                                                2011022526

PEARSON

ISBN-13: 978-0-205-58081-1
ISBN-10: 0-205-58081-5

About the Author

Thomas G. Gunning, a former high school and junior high English teacher, has served as an English department head, secondary school reading specialist and lead teacher, and elementary school reading consultant. Gunning is Professor Emeritus, Southern Connecticut State University, where he was department chairperson and director of the Reading Clinic. He is currently an Adjunct Professor, Reading/Language Arts Department, Central Connecticut State University, where he has taught courses in assessment and intervention and content area literacy.

Gunning has been a consultant for elementary and secondary schools in areas ranging from improving the core curriculum, implementing response to intervention, and planning programs for disabled readers. Trained as a Junior Great Books discussion leader, Tom has tried out this approach with students in an urban school.

Gunning has conducted research on group reading inventories, vocabulary assessment, reading disabilities, intervention programs, readability, response to intervention, decoding processes and strategies, and literacy skills needed to cope with high-stakes tests.

Gunning's other books with Pearson include:

- *Creating Literacy Instruction for All Children in Grades Pre-K to 4*, Second Edition © 2013 ISBN: 9780132685818   Coming Soon!

- *Creating Literacy Instruction for All Students*, Eighth Edition © 2013 ISBN: 9780132685795   Coming Soon!

- *Creating Literacy Instruction for All Students In Grades 4-8*, Third Edition © 2012 ISBN: 9780132317443

- *Assessing and Correcting Reading and Writing Difficulties*, Fourth Edition © 2010 ISBN: 9780136100829

- *Developing Higher-Level Literacy in All Students: Building Reading, Reasoning, and Responding* © 2008 ISBN: 9780205522200

- *Closing the Literacy Gap* © 2006 ISBN: 9780205456260

For more information about any of these books, please visit www.pearson highered.com

TO MICHAEL DANIEL MULHALL

who was born just as this book was being completed

Brief Contents

Contents

CHAPTER 1 **Reading and Writing in the Content Areas: An Introduction** 2

CHAPTER 7 **Study Skills and Strategies** **186**

Lessons

Exemplary Teaching

Preface

Goals of This Text

Building Literacy in Secondary Content Area Classrooms presents techniques, strategies, approaches, and materials that will enable you to build the skills students need to become literate in and successfully read and write about topics in the content areas. You will learn how to analyze content area materials in terms of their text characteristics and the demands they make upon the reader. You will then learn how to use this information to plan appropriate instruction. Throughout *Building Literacy in Secondary Content Area Classroooms*, you will be asked to look at a variety of content area texts in terms of organization, vocabulary, and concepts covered and to assess what level of background knowledge, reading competence, and thinking skills students need to comprehend the texts. You will then be shown teaching techniques and student strategies that best enable students to learn from particular kinds of texts.

Given the current focus on standards and high-stakes tests, this textbook emphasizes setting for your students clear objectives that are grounded in accepted content area standards and conducting ongoing assessment that makes sure your students are progressing toward meeting those standards. Using higher-order thinking skills, integrating content areas, using multiple sources, and considering multicultural perspectives are other important topics in this textbook.

Important Features of This Text

Because this is a text on teaching reading and writing in the content areas, techniques and strategies used to learn in the content areas have been incorporated into the text so that you can experience as well as read about them. In the following pages you will get a snapshot of all the main features of this text.

Before reading each chapter you will be asked to complete an **Anticipation Guide**

Anticipation Guide

For each of the following statements, put a check under "Agree" or "Disagree" to indicate your opinion. If possible, discuss your responses with classmates.

	Agree	Disagree
1. Instruction in literacy skills should pay off in increased content area learning.	___	___
2. Students who have superior background knowledge will learn more than students who have superior learning strategies.	___	___
3. Because of differences in subject matter and teaching approaches, it would not be advisable for content area teachers to agree to teach a core of strategies.	___	___
4. It's best to master one or two effective teaching techniques than to try to use six or more techniques.	___	___
5. Content area teachers must take extra steps to help struggling learners.	___	___

and to activate your knowledge by answering the questions in the **Using What You Know** section.

This chapter explores the nature of secondary school reading, most of which is content area reading, along with the factors that enhance literacy skills in the content areas. It also discusses the quiet crisis: the fact that 25 to 40 percent of today's secondary school students have difficulty coping with their textbooks (Alliance for Excellent Education, 2010; Schoenbach, Greenleaf, Cziko, & Hurwitz, 1999; Snow, Burns, & Griffin, 1998). Before reading this chapter, reflect on your knowledge of reading in science, history, and other content areas. In particular, think about these questions:

Using What You Know

You will also be asked to check your reading periodically through **Checkup** questions posed throughout the text and to reflect on your reading after finishing each chapter. You will find motivating and insightful questions in the **Reflection** boxes at the end of each chapter. These are strategies that you will also be teaching your students.

CHECKUP

1. What role do textbooks play in teaching content area subjects?
2. Why is it important that textbooks be written at the appropriate grade level?

Reflection

Return to the Anticipation Guide at the beginning of this chapter. Respond once again to the items. Did your responses change? If so, how and why? What do you think should be the role of content area teachers in fostering literacy in their subjects? What should be the role of content area teachers in helping struggling learners?

Struggling Readers

Reconstructive elaboration and other memory devices have been used successfully with struggling readers and students with learning disabilities who may need more teacher guidance than achieving readers.

English Language Learners

English language learners do especially well in cooperative learning situations because they are more willing to use their developing language skills in a small-group situation and they are more willing to ask for help.

This text carefully considers the nature of student readers. Given the current inclusion movement, this textbook emphasizes instruction that includes *all students*. It suggests how to plan programs and make modifications so that you can provide for struggling learners as well as for achieving students. Approximately 25 percent to 40 percent of today's secondary school students have difficulty coping with the content area texts. Rich and extensive marginal annotations for **Struggling Readers** offer strategies, techniques, and materials especially appropriate for students who are struggling to learn.

For English language learners, stress will be placed on learning academic language and the key technical vocabulary of each major subject matter area. Additional information on how to adapt instruction for ELL students can be found in the **English Language Learners** marginal annotations throughout the text.

Although textbooks are the main source of content area information for most students, *Building Literacy in Secondary Content Area Classroom* advocates the use of trade books, periodicals, and technology. There are numerous Web sites devoted to the content areas. There are also tools available on the Internet or as software that foster learning. These resources, plus other technological advances and the reading and writing skills needed to get the most benefit from the new literacies, are discussed within the chapters as well as in the **Using Technology** annotations.

Because today's students have so much more to learn, this textbook presents study skills in detail. It also includes explanations of some of the study aids that accompany digital texts and highlights writing to learn.

Above all else, *Building Literacy in Secondary Content Area Classrooms* is designed to be a practical guide to helping today's students use reading and writing to learn content area subjects. There are numerous step-by-step sample **Lessons** covering a wide range of key topics such as comprehension, vocabulary, and writing skills, to help students apply these techniques into the classroom.

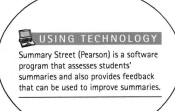

USING TECHNOLOGY

Summary Street (Pearson) is a software program that assesses students' summaries and also provides feedback that can be used to improve summaries.

LESSON 3.3

Introducing the Frayer Model

Step 1: Brainstorming the Concept

In order to involve students and find out what they know about the topic, write the topic word *mollusks* on the board and ask students to tell what they know. List students' responses on the board. If students are unfamiliar with the term, mention some members of the phylum: snails, clams, octopuses.

Step 2: Discussing Examples of the Concept

From the information listed on the board, note examples of mollusks. If there are very few examples, list additional ones.

Step 3: Discussing Relevant Characteristics

Talk over what mollusks have in common; for instance, they have a similar body that includes a foot, gut, and mantle; they are invertebrates, soft-bodied, and cold-blooded; they usually have a shell.

Exemplary Teaching features in all chapters bring teaching techniques to life with real accounts of effective teaching practices garnered from memoirs of gifted teachers, newspaper accounts, or the author's own observations.

Exemplary Teaching

Clarifying Confusing Concepts

Noting that her middle school class of English language learners was having difficulty reading Jane Yolen's (1992) *Encounter*, a fictionalized account of Columbus's arrival in the New World told from the native people's point of view, Carol put a key portion of the text on a transparency and gave students duplicated copies of the segments. As she read the segments, students raised their hands when an unknown word or confusing passage appeared (Harvey, 1998). When students asked about the word *landfall*, Carol asked if anyone knew what the word meant. One student believed that it might mean a place where the land falls off. But on rereading the text with that meaning in mind, he noted that it didn't make sense. A second student thought that it might mean a place where ships land. She explained that if one reread the sentence while keeping that meaning in mind, the text made sense. Pointing to the word on her transparency, Carol explained that the student had made very good use of context and that rereading a sentence containing an unknown word was an excellent way to try to find out what the word might mean. After arriving at a possible definition, it was a good idea to see whether that meaning fit the sense of the sentence and the selection.

As she read and students noted other problems, Carol discussed and demonstrated other strategies that might be used to repair comprehension. Later, students tried applying the strategies independently.

Passages from Books, from textbooks to tradebooks, appear in most chapters to help you see what kinds of reading your pupils are expected to do.

Organization of This Text

The first chapter of *Building Literacy in Secondary Content Area Classrooms* explores the nature of content area literacy and discusses basic principles of content area instruction. Chapter 2 analyzes the kinds of texts that students will be required to read in the content areas and presents ways of assessing the texts and matching readers with texts at the appropriate level. Chapter 3 discusses learning content area vocabulary. Chapters 4, 5, and 6 explore techniques for fostering comprehension. Chapter 7 examines study skills and habits. Chapter 8 discusses writing to learn in the content areas. Chapter 9 considers ways to help all students learn, placing special emphasis on helping those who are struggling. Chapters 10 and 11 highlight techniques that can be used in specific content areas. Chapter 12 highlights the use of trade books, periodicals, and technology. Chapter 13 presents suggestions for evaluating students' progress and looks at assessment issues. Chapter 14 sums up the text and looks at ways to organize and improve literacy instruction in the content areas.

Building Literacy in Secondary Content Area Classrooms provides extensive coverage of a variety of key assessment measures and instructional techniques. Particular emphasis has been placed on assisting struggling readers. The text is designed to help you develop the kinds of literacy skills and strategies that will enable all of your students to learn your content more fully and more efficiently.

Supplements for Students and Instructors

Instructor's Manual with Test Bank   For each chapter, the Instructor's Manual features a series of Learner Objectives, a Chapter Overview, suggestions for Before, After, and During Reading, a list of suggested Teaching Activities, and suggestions for Assessment. The Test Bank contains an assortment of multiple-choice, short essay, and long essay questions for each chapter. This supplement has been written completely by the text author, Tom Gunning.

Pearson MyTest   The printed Test Bank is also available through our computerized testing system, MyTest, a powerful assessment generation program that helps instructors easily create and print quizzes and exams. Questions and tests are authored online, allowing ultimate flexibility and the ability to efficiently create and print assessments anytime, anywhere! Instructors can access Pearson MyTest and their test bank files by going to www.pearsonmytest.com to log in, register, or request access. Features of Pearson MyTest include:

Premium Assessment Content

- Draw from a rich library of assessments that complement your Pearson textbook and your course's learning objectives.
- Edit questions or tests to fit your specific teaching needs.

Instructor-Friendly Resources

- Easily create and store your own questions, including images, diagrams, and charts using simple drag-and-drop and Word-like controls.
- Use additional information provided by Pearson, such as the question's difficulty level or learning objective, to help you quickly build your test.

Time-Saving Enhancements

- Add headers or footers and easily scramble questions and answer choices—all from one simple toolbar.
- Quickly create multiple versions of your test or answer key, and when ready, simply save to Microsoft-Word or PDF format and print!
- Export your exams for import to Blackboard 6.0, CE (WebCT), or Vista (WebCT)!

PowerPoint™ Presentation   Designed for teachers using the text, the PowerPoint Presentation consists of a series of slides that can be shown as is or used to make hand-outs or overhead transparencies. The presentation highlights key concepts and major topics for each chapter. (Available for download from the Instructor Resource Center at www.pearsonhighered.com/irc)

The Power of Classroom Practice

In *Preparing Teachers for a Changing World*, Linda Darling-Hammond and her colleagues point out that grounding teacher education in real classrooms—among real teachers and students and among actual examples of students' and teachers' work—is an important, and perhaps even an essential, part of training teachers for the complexities of teaching in today's classrooms. MyEducationLab is an online learning solution that provides contextualized interactive exercises, simulations, and other resources designed to help develop the knowledge and skills teachers need. All of the activities and exercises in MyEducationLab are built around essential learning outcomes for teachers and are mapped to professional teaching standards. Utilizing classroom video, authentic student and teacher artifacts, case studies, and other resources and assessments, the scaffolded learning experiences in MyEducationLab offer pre-service teachers and those who teach them a unique and valuable education tool.

For each topic covered in the course you will find most or all of the following features and resources:

Connection to National Standards

Now it is easier than ever to see how coursework is connected to national standards. Each topic on MyEducationLab lists intended learning outcomes is connected to the appropriate national standards. All of the activities and exercises in MyEducationLab are mapped to the appropriate national standards and learning outcomes as well.

Assignments and Activities

Designed to enhance student understanding of concepts covered in class and save instructors preparation and grading time, these assignable exercises show concepts in action (through video, cases, and/or student and teacher artifacts). They help students deepen content knowledge and synthesize and apply concepts and strategies they read about in the book. (Correct answers for these assignments are available to the instructor only under the Instructor Resource tab.)

Building Teaching Skills and Dispositions

These learning units help students practice and strengthen skills that are essential to quality teaching. After presenting the steps involved in a core teaching process, students are given an opportunity to practice applying this skill via videos, student and teacher artifacts, and/or case studies of authentic classrooms. Providing multiple opportunities to practice a single teaching concept, each activity encourages a deeper understanding and application of concepts, as well as the use of critical thinking skills.

As part of your access to MyEducationLab.

A+RISE®, developed by three-time Teacher of the Year and administrator, Evelyn Arroyo, gives new teachers in grades K-12 quick, research-based strategies that get to the "how" of targeting their instruction and making content accessible for all students, including English language learners.

A+RISE® Standards2Strategy™ is an innovative and interactive online resource that offers new teachers in grades K-12 just in time, research-based instructional strategies that:

- Meet the linguistic needs of ELLs as they learn content.
- Differentiate instruction for all grades and abilities.
- Offer reading and writing techniques, cooperative learning, use of linguistic and non-linguistic representations, scaffolding, teacher modeling, higher order thinking, and alternative classroom ELL assessment.
- Provide support to help teachers be effective through the integration of listening, speaking, reading, and writing along with the content curriculum.
- Improve student achievement.
- Are aligned to Common Core Elementary Language Arts standards (for the literacy strategies) and to English language proficiency standards in WIDA, Texas, California, and Florida.

Lesson Plan Builder Activities

The Online Lesson Plan builder is a tool that helps familiarize new and prospective teachers with the steps of a lesson plan, providing them a concrete structure that accounts for all the necessary elements, and allowing them quick access to important components including state and national standards.

Look for activities on the MyEducationLab for your course that link directly into the Online Lesson Plan Builder. You'll see video of a classroom and be offered the opportunity to determine a goal and craft a lesson for the group, scaffolded as you do to remember to focus on specific learning outcomes, incorporate standards, and focus on the individual needs of learners.

IRIS Center Resources

The IRIS Center at Vanderbilt University (http://iris.peabody.vanderbilt.edu)—funded by the U.S. Department of Education's Office of Special Education Programs (OSEP)—develops training enhancement materials for pre-service and in-service teachers. The Center works with experts from across the country to create challenge-based interactive modules, case study units, and podcasts that provide research-validated information about working with students in inclusive settings. In your MyEducationLab course we have integrated this content where appropriate.

Simulations in Classroom Management

One of the most difficult challenges facing teachers today is how to balance classroom instruction with classroom management. These interactive cases focus on the classroom management issues teachers most frequently encounter on a daily basis. Each simulation presents a challenge scenario at the beginning and then offers a series of choices to solve each challenge. Along the way students receive mentor feedback on their choices and have the opportunity to make better choices if necessary. Upon exiting each simulation students will have a clear understanding of how to address these common classroom management issues and will be better equipped to handle them in the classroom.

Study Plan Specific to Your Text

A MyEducationLab Study Plan is a multiple choice assessment tied to chapter objectives, supported by study material. A well-designed Study Plan offers multiple opportunities to fully master required course content as identified by the objectives in each chapter:

- **Chapter Objectives** identify the learning outcomes for the chapter and give students targets to shoot for as you read and study.
- **Multiple Choice Assessments** assess mastery of the content. These assessments are mapped to chapter objectives, and students can take the multiple choice quiz as many times as they want. Not only do these quizzes provide overall scores for each objective, but they also explain why responses to particular items are correct or incorrect.

- **Study Material: Review, Practice and Enrichment** give students a deeper understanding of what they do and do not know related to chapter content. This material includes text excerpts, activities that include hints and feedback, and interactive multi-media exercises built around videos, simulations, cases, or classroom artifacts.

Course Resources

The Course Resources section on MyEducationLab is designed to help students, put together an effective lesson plan, prepare for and begin their career, navigate their first year of teaching, and understand key educational standards, policies, and laws.

The Course Resources Tab includes the following:

- The **Lesson Plan Builder** is an effective and easy-to-use tool that students can use to create, update, and share quality lesson plans. The software also makes it easy to integrate state content standards into any lesson plan.

- The **Preparing a Portfolio** module provides guidelines for creating a high-quality teaching portfolio.

- **Beginning Your Career** offers tips, advice, and other valuable information on:
  - *Resume Writing and Interviewing*: Includes expert advice on how to write impressive resumes and prepare for job interviews.
  - *Your First Year of Teaching*: Provides practical tips to set up a first classroom, manage student behavior, and more easily organize for instruction and assessment.
  - *Law and Public Policies*: Details specific directives and requirements teachers need to understand under the No Child Left Behind Act and the Individuals with Disabilities Education Improvement Act of 2004.

- **Longman Dictionary of Contemporary English Online** Make use of this online version of the CD-ROM of the Longman Dictionary of Contemporary English – the quickest and easiest way to look up any word while you are working on MyEducationLab.

Certification and Licensure

The Certification and Licensure section is designed to help students pass their licensure exam by giving them access to state test requirements, overviews of what tests cover, and sample test items.

The Certification and Licensure tab includes the following:

- **State Certification Test Requirements:** Here students can click on a state and will then be taken to a list of state certification tests.

- Students can click on the **Licensure Exams** they need to take to find:
  - Basic information about each test.
  - Descriptions of what is covered on each test.
  - Sample test questions with explanations of correct answers.

- **National Evaluation Series? by Pearson:** Here students can see the tests in the NES, learn what is covered on each exam, and access sample test items with descriptions and rationales of correct answers. They can also purchase interactive online tutorials developed by Pearson Evaluation Systems and the Pearson Teacher Education and Development group.

- **ETS Online Praxis Tutorials:** Here students can purchase interactive online tutorials developed by ETS and by the Pearson Teacher Education and Development group. Tutorials are available for the Praxis I exams and for select Praxis II exams.

Visit *www.myeducationlab.com* for a demonstration of this exciting new online teaching resource.

Acknowledgments

My thanks to Aurora Martínez-Ramos, Vice President, Editor in Chief, Literacy and ELL, at Allyn & Bacon, who provided many helpful suggestions as well as support and encouragement and to Michelle Hochberg, editorial assistant at Allyn & Bacon, for her gracious, competent assistance. As always, I am indebted to my wife Joan for her caring and understanding.

The following reviewers provided helpful insights:

Rosalind Horowitz, The University of Texas–San Antonio
Kelly McNeal, William Paterson University
Cynthia Sharp, Nevada Department of Education
Anne A. Thomas, Wilkes University

I appreciate the time they took to detail specific suggestions for clarifying and improving the text.

Building
Literacy
in
Secondary
Content Area
Classrooms

CHAPTER 1

Reading and Writing in the Content Areas: An Introduction

Using What You Know

This chapter explores the nature of secondary school reading, most of which is content area reading, along with the factors that enhance literacy skills in the content areas. It also discusses the quiet crisis: the fact that 25 to 40 percent of today's secondary school students have difficulty coping with their textbooks (Alliance for Excellent Education, 2010; Schoenbach, Greenleaf, Cziko, & Hurwitz, 1999; Snow, Burns, & Griffin, 1998). Before reading this chapter, reflect on your knowledge of reading in science, history, and other content areas. In particular, think about these questions:

- What steps did your teachers take to help you learn the reading and writing skills necessary for their content area?
- Do you use any special learning strategies to comprehend what you read in the content areas? If so, what are they? How well do they work for you?
- Do you have any problems reading and writing in the content areas?
- How might you improve your comprehension and retention of the material?
- How might you help students improve their reading and writing in the content areas?

Content Area Literacy

Jeremy, a middle school student, is struggling with his science and social studies texts, even though he appears to read at grade level. In elementary school, students have limited experience with **expository text**. Mostly, they read narrative fiction or expository text

■ **Expository text** is designed to explain. Other main types of text are descriptive, narrative, and persuasive.

written in narrative style. As a result, Jeremy is neither experienced nor skilled in reading content area texts. As an observer in Jeremy's social studies class explained,

> Jeremy had encountered text that, for him, was **inconsiderate**. The paragraph from which he read was fifteen sentences long. There were no characters. There was no bold print to draw the reader's attention to important ideas. The subheading "Lexington and Concord" referred to towns that weren't mentioned until the fourth and fifth sentences. Words such as *forestall* and *tactic* weren't defined contextually in the passage. It was a far cry from Beverly Cleary's *Dear Mr. Henshaw*, which Jeremy had recently read: "It wasn't inappropriate for Jeremy to read that text; we all have to tackle inconsiderate text. But Jeremy needed some specific instruction to help him pay attention strategically, to focus on the most important ideas." (Keene & Zimmermann, 1997, pp. 87–88)

When asked to list some important details in the article he had read about the Revolutionary War, Jeremy was at a loss. Further discussion revealed that his comprehension of the article was inadequate to the point of being almost nonexistent. He was able to recite a few minor details, but he could not explain the significance or overall meaning of the article. Jeremy wasn't alone. Many of the other students in his class were also unable to cope with content area texts. As the observer commented, "Many were so disconnected from the meaning of the text, especially expository text, that they were often unaware of the essence of what they were reading" (Keene & Zimmermann, 1997, p. 82). Jeremy and the other students were subsequently taught strategies that included reading to determine the most important information in text, and they made substantial progress in their comprehension.

To get a sense of what content area literacy involves, read the following excerpts from content area books. Which did you find easiest? Which was the most difficult? What background knowledge and skills are required to read each excerpt?

Cytokinesis: How do daughter cells split apart after mitosis?

As a result of mitosis, two nuclei—each with a duplicate set of chromosomes—are formed. All that remains to complete the M phase of the cycle is cytokinesis, the division of the cytoplasm itself. Cytokinesis usually occurs at the same time as telophase. Cytokinesis completes the process of cell division—it splits one cell into two. The process of cytokinesis is different in plants and animals.

> *Cytokinesis in Animal Cells* During cytokinesis in most animal cells, the cell membrane is drawn inward until the cytoplasm is pinched into nearly two equal parts. Each part contains its own nucleus and cytoplasmic organelles.

> *Cytokinesis in Plant Cells* Cytokinesis in plant cells proceeds differently. The cell membrane is not flexible enough to draw inward because of the rigid cell wall that surrounds it. Instead a structure known as the cell plate forms halfway between the divided nuclei. The cell plate gradually develops into cell membranes that separate the two daughter cells. A cell wall then forms in between the two membranes, completing the process. (Miller & Levine, 2009, p. 284)

How Did the Supreme Court React to Reforms?

Roosevelt and his New Deal programs ran into problems with the Supreme Court. Most of the members of the Supreme Court believed some of the New Deal legislation was unconstitutional.

> The Supreme Court declared the National Recovery Act and the Agricultural Adjustment Act unconstitutional. This declaration angered President Roosevelt. He believed that the "nine old men" on the Supreme Court stood in the way of progress. Six of the justices, who had been appointed for life, were over seventy years of age. Roosevelt decided to appoint a new justice for every justice over the age of seventy.

> The six new justices, Roosevelt thought, would assure that New Deal laws would not be **overturned** by the Supreme Court. Roosevelt's decision was not well accepted. Members of Congress **denounced** it as political "court-packing." Many Americans also rejected the plan. (King & Napp, 1998, p. 502)

■ **Inconsiderate text** is text that is difficult for the reader to understand because it has not been written with the reader in mind.

The Sentimentality of William Tavener **by Willa Cather**

One spring night Hester sat in a rocking chair by the sitting room window, darning socks. She rocked violently and sent her long needle vigorously back and forth over her gourd, and it took only a very casual glance to see that she was wrought up over something. William sat on the other side of the table reading his farm paper. If he had noticed his wife's agitation, his calm, clean-shaven face betrayed no sign of concern. He must have noticed the sarcastic turn of her remarks at the supper table, and he must have noticed the moody silence of the older boys as they ate. When supper was but half over little Billy, the youngest, had suddenly pushed back his plate and slipped away from the table, manfully trying to swallow a sob. But William Tavener never heeded ominous forecasts in the domestic horizon, and he never looked for a storm until it broke. (Cather 1990, pp. 353–354)

Although all of these excerpts require basic reading skills, including a good general vocabulary and the overall ability to construct meaning from print, each content area has its own organization and language. The first excerpt, which is drawn from a tenth-grade biology text, has a main idea–detail–sequence organization. In the first paragraph, which describes the general nature of cytokinesis, the main idea of the section is stated in the question: *How do daughter cells split apart after mitosis?* The main idea of the remaining two paragraphs is stated in the last sentence of the first paragraph: *The process of cytokinesis is different in plants and animals.* These paragraphs use a process–sequence organization to describe how cytokinesis occurs in plants and in animals. The excerpt contains a number of aids for the reader. In addition to generous use of illustrations (not shown here), the main ideas are clearly announced. Although the concept of cytokinesis has been explained previously, it is defined in context: *the division of the cytoplasm itself.* Headings clearly signal the main idea for the last two paragraphs, and there is also an explanation of the differences between plant and animal cytokinesis. However, even with these aids, the segment is difficult. Readers must have a firm understanding and recollection of previously presented key concepts and technical words such as *mitosis, cytoplasm, membranes, daughter cells, nucleus, nuclei* as well as general vocabulary words such as *duplicate, flexible, proceeds, rigid.* Coverage of material is cumulative. Students who fail to grasp or forget key concepts will have difficulty with passages such as this one.

The second excerpt, which describes Roosevelt's attempt to "pack" the Supreme Court, has an overall sequential narrative structure. However, it also has a cause–effect substructure that explains why Roosevelt appointed new justices and why many rejected his strategy. In addition to learning such technical terms as *New Deal, legislation,* and *unconstitutional,* readers also need to know the general vocabulary words *declaration, denounced,* and *rejected.* Necessary background knowledge includes information about the Supreme Court, the New Deal, and the National Recovery and Agricultural Adjustment acts. Whereas technical terms used in science tend to have specific, concrete meanings, in history and social studies, many terms—for example, *liberal*—refer to highly abstract concepts and do not lend themselves to easy explanation.

The third excerpt, from a short story by Willa Cather, portrays a conflict between a husband and wife. It has a narrative structure and contains such potentially troublesome words such as *vigorously, agitation, heeded, ominous,* and *domestic.* The story also contains figurative language, such as "never heeded ominous forecasts in the domestic horizon, and he never looked for a storm until it broke." Necessary background information includes understanding family dynamics and knowing what life was like during the late 1800s.

What Content Area Literacy Is

All three excerpts require a fairly sophisticated vocabulary and well-developed comprehension skills. However, each also makes its own unique demands and has its own background requirements. As learning researchers Bransford, Brown, and Cocking (2001) conclude, "Different domains of knowledge, such as science, mathematics, and history, have different organizing properties. It follows, therefore, that to have an in-depth grasp of an area requires knowledge about both the content of the subject and the broader structural organization of the subject" (pp. 237–238).

The first excerpt requires background knowledge of cells; the second, background knowledge of the Great Depression; and the third, background knowledge of personal relationships and literary techniques, as well as the ability to empathize with characters. Having overall competency in reading is not enough. Successful readers of these excerpts also need strategies and understandings specific to each subject. These strategies and understandings are best taught by the subject matter teacher. The theme of this text is that an important element of teaching in the secondary content areas is helping students acquire the skills and understanding necessary to learn a particular body of content.

Content literacy is the "ability to use reading and writing for the acquisition of new content in a given discipline. Such ability includes three principal cognitive components: general literacy skills, content-specific literacy skills (such as map reading in the social studies), and prior knowledge of content" (McKenna & Robinson, 1990, p. 184). We are not all equally literate in each content area.

CHECKUP

1. What does content area literacy involve?

The Constructive Nature of Content Area Literacy

At one time, reading was viewed as a relatively passive process of acquiring the author's message, with information being transferred to the reader in much the same way that data is transferred from one computer to another. Today, reading is viewed as a *constructive* process. The reader doesn't simply grasp the author's meaning, but also uses his personal background of experience to construct meaning based on information the author provides. The meaning does not reside only in the text or in the reader, but in a **transaction** between the two. The reader is changed by the text, and at the same time, the text is changed by the reader, with both coming together in a dynamic transaction (Rosenblatt, 1994).

Readers actively seek meaning and interpret text in the light of their own background of experience. Use your experience to interpret the following passage. What do you think it might be about?

> Every Saturday night four good friends get together. When Jerry, Mike, and Pat arrived, Karen was sitting in her living room writing some notes. She quickly gathered up the cards and stood up to greet her friends at the door. They followed her into the living room but as usual they couldn't agree on exactly what to play. Jerry eventually took a stand and set things up. Finally, they were eager to play. Karen's recorder filled the room with soft and pleasant music. Early in the evening, Mike noticed Pat's hand and the many diamonds. As the night progressed the tempo of play increased. Finally, a lull in the activities occurred. Taking advantage of this, Jerry pondered the arrangement in front of him. Mike interrupted Jerry's reverie and said, "Let's hear the score." They listened carefully and commented on their performance. When the comments were all heard, exhausted but happy, Karen's friends went home. (Anderson, Reynolds, Schallert, & Goetz, 1977, p. 372)

The text, which is deliberately ambiguous, was given to a group of music students and a group of physical education students. The music students tended to interpret the selection as describing a quartet's practice session, whereas the physical education students were more likely to read it as an account of a card game. Most of the students failed to see that the passage was open to interpretation. Only 20 percent of the students realized there were two possible interpretations. The researchers concluded that readers construct meaning in terms of their background knowledge and experience.

Conceptualizing the reader as being an active participant has a number of implications for teaching in the content

■ **Content literacy** is the ability to use reading and writing to acquire information in a subject area.

■ **Transaction** refers to the relationship between the reader and the text in which the text is conditioned by the reader and the reader is conditioned by the text.

areas. It is important that teachers be aware of the knowledge that students bring to the content area, particularly if their information is incomplete or even erroneous. For instance, students may believe it is warmer in summer because the earth is closer to the sun at that time. In order to teach the concept of changing seasons, the teacher must help students overcome this misconception.

Ongoing assessment of students' knowledge is also essential. Unless teachers have some grasp of students' current levels of understanding, they will have difficulty helping them construct coherent concepts. For instance, if the science teacher realizes that students believe that seasons change because the earth is closer to or farther from the sun, he can demonstrate the varying angles of the earth as it orbits the sun and explain how the angle of the sun determines the amount of heat that reaches the earth.

CHECKUP

1. Why is reading called a constructive process?
2. What implications does this have for instruction?

Content Literacy from Sociocultural and Critical Perspectives

Literacy is influenced by our culture and by our interactions with others. Through discussion of texts that we have read or viewed, we gain insight and perspectives from others that we can integrate into our own construction of meaning.

Literacy also involves taking a critical perspective. Critical literacy recognizes that all text is written from a particular perspective, under particular circumstances, and at a particular time, and that these factors need to be taken into account by readers. It considers the underlying meaning of communication, particularly elements such as political, social, and cultural context and the manner in which the text was constructed. Readers are urged to ask critical questions such as: What is the author's social, political, and cultural perceptive? From whose point of view is this text told? Whose point of view, if any, has been left out? What would happen if we viewed this text from multiple perspectives? For example, what if a history of World War II were told from the perspectives of the soldiers who fought the battles instead of those of the generals or politicians?

Readers construct the meaning of a text based on their personal perspective and circumstances. In some approaches, critical literacy is expected to result in social action, equity, and justice. On a larger scale, the whole curriculum might be examined to discern on what beliefs or values it is based and which values it attempts to incalculate. "Power, identity, and agency play important roles in whose social and cultural practices are valued—and thus whose literacy practices are valued and whose are not" (Moje, Overby, Tysvaer, & Morris, 2008, p. 109). Another consideration would be the impact that a differentiated curriculum might have upon struggling students versus students who have well developed proficiency in literacy. A critical literacy approach would address whether some students are more privileged than others (Cadeiro-Kaplan, 2002).

Content Literacy and the New Literacies

The New Literacies, still another perspective on what it means to be literate in the twenty-first century, refer to using the Internet and related media, but the concept goes beyond mere technology. Recognizing that there are many modes of expression (Kist, 2010), the New Literacies encompass other modes of expression, such as drawing, painting, photographing, dancing, designing, or combining images with text. The New Literacies also value group work and cooperative ventures, which, ironically, allow students to more fully express themselves as individuals as they use drawing, clip art, music, and video clips to explore or report on a topic in a unique way. For example, a high school senior created a presentation in which she described her aspirations in words, but also used photos to display her family and friends as well as her cultural background. To illustrate her dream of becoming a professional singer, she included a clip of herself singing the national anthem at a baseball game. She commented that being able to use media allowed her to more fully express herself, particularly ideas and emotions that words would not have conveyed (Alvarez, 2009).

The concept of multiple literacies can change the way we view adolescent learners and also the way they view themselves. As Alvermann (2009) explains, "Because many adolescents growing up in a digital world will find their own reasons for becoming literate—reasons that go beyond reading and writing to acquire academic knowledge—it is important that teachers create opportunities for them to engage actively in meaningful subject matter learning that both extends and elaborates on the literacy practices that they already possess and value" (p. 24).

O'Brien (2003) described a situation in which one disengaged and two underachieving adolescent students were given topics of interest and digital media to use in exploring them. In traditional classrooms these students had been deemed to be "at risk." But when they were given tasks that were interesting and challenging but doable, they became enthusiastic, competent learners.

Making use of students' out-of-school literacy has a number of benefits. As Gutiérrez (Bookshelf, 2010) comments,

> An obvious advantage is the motivation factor. A less obvious one concerns activating prior knowledge—students know pop culture, so you have a chance to build on that knowledge base and, more importantly, engage with it critically. "Critically" meaning evaluating content, yes, but also self-critically, reflecting on one's own literacy skills and goals. And there's an even bigger opportunity here. By definition, "popular" culture is one that's widely shared. That gives students a chance not only to respond to texts, but also to respond in an informed way to each other's responses. After all, that's what their outside-of-school literacies look like anyway—take blog comments as an example. So while today's youth are accustomed to that kind of discourse, as educators we can help them become more aware of their own modes of participation, their own thought processes. Clearly these are skills that can enhance their use of academic language, support them when it comes to writing critical or persuasive pieces, or prepare them for speaking-and-listening activities such as debating.

Content Literacy from a Twenty-First Century Perspective

Commenting on the educational demands of the current century, the National Council of Teachers of English (2008) notes,

> As society changes so, too, does the concept of literacy. Literacy has always been a collection of cultural and communicative practices shared among members of particular groups. . . . Because technology has increased the intensity and complexity of literate environments, the twenty-first century demands that a literate person possess a wide range of abilities and competencies, many literacies. These literacies—from reading online newspapers to participating in virtual classrooms—are multiple, dynamic, and malleable. As in the past, they are inextricably linked with particular histories, life possibilities and social trajectories of individuals and groups.
>
> Twenty-first century readers and writers need to
>
> - Develop proficiency with the tools of technology
> - Build relationships with others to pose and solve problems collaboratively and cross-culturally
> - Design and share information for global communities to meet a variety of purposes
> - Manage, analyze and synthesize multiple streams of simultaneous information
> - Create, critique, analyze, and evaluate multi-media texts.

Although there are many types of literacy, this text will focus on the kinds of literacy that secondary school students need to master in order to be successful in school and that will prepare them for post-secondary education and the world of work. This means exploring techniques and approaches for fostering literacy in the key academic areas in secondary school. It will also explore methods and materials for building the literacy skills of both struggling readers and writers and English language learners. For all students, the text will focus on providing the kind of content that will prepare them well for both postsecondary education and high-quality twenty-first-century jobs.

CHECKUP

1. What is content literacy from a sociocultural and critical perspective?
2. What are the New Literacies?
3. How might students' out-of-school literacies be used to develop their in-school literacy?
4. What are some examples of twenty-first century-literacies?

Providing Challenging Content

ACT researchers (2006a) found that the ability to comprehend complex text provides the best preparation for college. "The clearest differentiator in reading between students who are college ready and students who are not is the ability to comprehend *complex* texts" (pp. 16–17; emphasis in original). The researchers defined a *complex text* as one that had the following six aspects (which can be abbreviated to "RSVP"):

- **Relationships:** Interactions among ideas or characters in the text are subtle, involved, or deeply embedded.
- **Richness:** The text possesses a sizable amount of highly sophisticated information conveyed through data or literary devices.
- **Structure:** The text is organized in ways that are elaborate and sometimes unconventional.
- **Style:** The author's tone and use of language are often intricate.
- **Vocabulary:** The author's choice of words is demanding and highly context-dependent.
- **Purpose:** The author's intent in writing the text is implicit and sometimes ambiguous. (ACT, 2006a, p. 17)

Because the ability to cope with complex text is so important for students' success with college-level reading, ACT researchers recommend that secondary students grapple with complex text in each of their courses. All courses in high school, not just English and social studies, but also mathematics and science must challenge students to read and understand complex texts.

> In most cases, a complex text will contain multiple layers of meaning, not all of which will be immediately apparent to students upon a single superficial reading. Rather, such texts require students to work at unlocking meaning by calling upon sophisticated reading comprehension skills and strategies. (ACT, 2006a, pp. 23–24)

The Alliance for Excellent Education (2009) made a similar recommendation about providing challenging content for all students:

> Regardless of their plans, all of the nation's young people need high-level knowledge and skills to achieve success in a rapidly changing world of technological advances and international competitiveness. And every American has a stake in their success, whether they have school-age children of their own or not . . . All students must learn the advanced skills that are the key to success in college and in the 21st century workplace. Every student should take demanding classes in the core subjects of English, history, science, and math; and no

USING TECHNOLOGY

Alliance for Excellent Education
all4ed.org provides a wealth of information on improving secondary education.

- **Relationships:** Interactions among ideas or characters in the text are subtle, involved, or deeply embedded.

- **Richness:** The text possesses a sizable amount of highly sophisticated information conveyed through data or literary devices.

- **Structure:** The text is organized in ways that are elaborate and sometimes unconventional.

- **Style:** The author's tone and use of language are often intricate.

- **Vocabulary:** The author's choice of words is demanding and highly context dependent.

- **Purpose:** The author's intent in writing the text is implicit and sometimes ambiguous.

student should ever get a watered-down course of study. Further, students should also be given the opportunity to earn industry certification or some college credit while in high school through programs such as Advanced Placement, International Baccalaureate, or those offered through a local college or university. (p. 1)

Realizing that some students will undoubtedly experience difficulty learning challenging content, the Alliance also recommends extra help for those who need it: "Every high school should have a system in place to identify kids as soon as they start to struggle in reading, math, or any core subject, and every school should reserve time and resources for the immediate help those kids need to stay on course." (2009, p. 1)

CHECKUP

1. What are the characteristics of complex text?
2. What is the significance of being able to read complex text?
3. What is involved in reading complex text?

Reading in the Secondary School

USING TECHNOLOGY

The Nation's Report Card nces.ed.gov/nationsreportcard contains detailed information about students' performance in specific content areas.

How well do students in middle and high schools read? They probably read better than they are given credit for, but not as well as they could or should. Media and professional reports typically cite NAEP (National Association of Educational Progress) statistics indicating that only 31 percent of eighth graders and 38 percent of twelfth graders are reading at the proficient level (National Center for Education Statistics, 2010). The implication is that all students should be reading at the proficient level in order to be successful in school. However, results of state and international tests suggest that NAEP's basic level is a more reasonable standard. 75 percent of eighth-grade students and 74 percent of twelfth-grade students reading at the basic level or above on NAEP.

Students' performance on both state and international tests is generally higher than it is on the NAEP. For instance, on the PISA (Program for International Student Assessment), which was last given to 15-year-olds in 2010, students from only 9 out of 64 countries and other entities had higher average scores than U.S. students (Fleischman, Hopstock, Pelczar, & Shelley, 2010). On the 2007 TIMSS (Trends in International Mathematics and Science Study) assessment, U.S. eighth graders scored above average and were ranked eleventh out of 49 countries (Martin et al., 2008). All of these results suggest that the basic level is a more reasonable benchmark than the proficient level for describing most students' performance. This is not to suggest that we should be satisfied with the current level of achievement. We should vigorously pursue a higher standard of achievement.

In addition, some assessments may be masking students' true reading abilities. Both the NAEP and a number of state tests use constructed or written responses to assess reading proficiency. An analysis of students' responses on these tests suggests that some students have difficulty expressing themselves in writing (Gunning, 2006). Even though students might know the answer to a constructed response question and would be able to express it orally, they have difficulty communicating what they know in a written response. The problem is not in their reading comprehension but in their written expression. Calder and Carlson (2002) found that the oral responses of many middle-level students were superior to their written answers and inferred that "for them, deep understandings seemed to evaporate when they tried to wrestle their thoughts to paper. This told us that we had work to do if we wanted to distinguish between assessing understanding and assessing students' ability to communicate their understanding" (p. 2).

Since 1971, when the NAEP reading test was first administered, scores for 13-year-olds have increased by only 4 points. The average reading score for 17-year-olds of 286 in 2008 shows an increase of just one point since 1971 (Rampey, Dion, & Donahue, 2009). Although 13-year-olds have shown limited improvement and 17-year-olds virtually none, it is important to note there has been a significant change in the demographics of students tested. Minority students, who are more likely to come from impoverished circumstances or who may still be learning English and therefore would tend to have lower scores, make up a greater proportion of the secondary school student body than they did in the earlier days of NAEP testing (Grigg, Donahue, & Dion, 2007).

Adolescent literacy is still a cause for concern. About one-third of entering ninth graders are two years below grade level in reading (Balfanz, McPartland, & Shaw, 2002). According to a study conducted by ACT (2005), an estimated 50 percent of students who take the ACT are not prepared for college work. Eleven percent of entering postsecondary school students are enrolled in remedial reading coursework (National Center for Education Statistics, 2003). This lack of preparedness also extends to students who enter the world of work immediately after high school. According to an ACT (2006a) study of skills needed for occupations that do not require a college degree but that provide a living wage, the reading and mathematics skills needed to obtain and hold these jobs are similar to those needed to succeed in college.

The problem of preparedness is more severe for students living in poverty. A survey of urban educators revealed that more than half of incoming ninth graders were reading below grade level (Council of the Great City Schools, 2009). In their work with Talent Development High Schools, Balfanz, McPartland, and Shaw (2002) found that the typical student entering an urban high school was reading between the fifth- and sixth-grade level. In addition, a significant number of secondary school students have severe reading problems. Archer (2010) noted the following reading levels at her urban middle school: 31 percent of students are four to eight years behind in reading; 38 percent are one to three years behind; and only 31 percent are on or above grade level.

Low literacy rates are accompanied by low graduation rates. Nationwide, just over 70 percent of students graduate from high school (Bill & Melinda Gates Foundation, 2009). Graduation rates for African-American, Hispanic, and low-income students are lower still, just slightly above 50 percent. Even with a high school diploma, only half of graduates leave high school prepared to succeed in college, career, and life.

CHECKUP

1. What is the status of literacy in the secondary schools?
2. What are the key indicators that there is a literacy problem in the secondary schools?

Efforts to Improve Adolescent Literacy

The good news is that extensive efforts are being made to improve adolescent literacy. Within the last five years, more than a dozen reports on adolescent literacy have been issued. In addition, a federal program entitled Striving Readers has been initiated. The dual purposes of Striving Readers are to:

- Raise middle and high school students' literacy levels in Title I-eligible schools with significant numbers of students reading below grade-level
- Build a strong, scientific research base for strategies that improve adolescent literacy instruction (U.S. Department of Education, 2009)

In general, Striving Readers takes a two-pronged approach to improving the literacy of secondary students. The first is to embed literacy instruction in the content areas. The second is to provide extra assistance for students reading significantly below grade level. Descriptions of programs for striving secondary readers can be found in Chapter 9.

Helping All Students

Although the focus is now on underachieving secondary students, all students deserve to have fully developed literacy skills. Secondary science teacher Victoria Ridgeway Gillis recalls reluctantly attending a meeting on the topic of reading in the content area

(Alvermann, Phelps, & Gillis, 2010). Satisfied with her teaching, she nevertheless accepted the presenter's challenge to try a few of the strategies discussed and report back on the results. Gillis dutifully tried two of the strategies with her basic class but not with her gifted students. At the end of the unit, she gave the same test to her basic and gifted classes. The results "astounded" her: The basic students outperformed the gifted students. The lesson Gillis learned was twofold. First of all, basic students can learn high-level content, if given support. Secondly, even gifted students can benefit from instruction in useful literacy strategies. Not having been taught the strategies, they underperformed. All students in all classes can benefit from instruction in literacy skills and strategies, which is the theme of this text.

A Question of Equity

One of the biggest recent changes in content area instruction has been the emphasis on equity. In the past, only the best students had access to the most rigorous courses. Today, the focus is on providing all students with a basic education in science, math, and technology so that all are scientifically and technologically literate. To meet this challenging goal, teachers will need to be prepared to teach a wider variety of students and to gear instruction to meet a greater diversity of backgrounds, abilities, and learning styles.

CHECKUP
---

1. What is the literacy crisis?
2. What efforts are being made to solve the literacy crisis?
3. Why is solving the crisis a matter of equity?

Impact of the Standards Movement

Because of widespread dissatisfaction with educational achievement, challenging **standards** have been adopted by every state and every major discipline. The goal in establishing challenging, world-class curriculum standards that are measureable is to support instruction geared to higher achievement. Standards "define our expectations for what's important for children to learn, serve as guideposts for curriculum and instruction, and should be the basis of all assessment" (American Federation of Teachers, 2008, p. 2).

Because standards vary from state to state, The National Governors Association & Council of Chief State School Officers (2010) have created a set of Common Core Standards in English language arts and math. The Common Core Standards "define the knowledge and skills students should have to succeed in entry-level, credit-bearing, academic college courses and in workforce training programs." There are ten anchor standards for reading, writing, language, and content area reading and content area writing. The anchor standards are broad statements of objectives, which are further broken down into more specific grade-specific objectives. The anchor standards are listed on the inside front cover. To find specific standards by grade level, consult the Common Core State Standards for English Language Arts and also Literacy in History/Social Studies, Science, & Technical Subjects at www.corestandards.org/assets/ CCSSI_ELA Standards.pdf. Because of the widespread adoption of Common Core State Standards, this text has incorporated them into appropriate sections. The margin note "CCSS" designates places in the text where suggestions for implementing a particular standard are presented.

Elementary and Secondary Act

Along with the standards movement came high-stakes tests and the No Child Left Behind Act of 2001 (NCLB), a version of the Elementary and Secondary Act, which was enacted in 1965 to bolster the educational development of children living in poverty, The purpose of NCLB was "to ensure that all children have a fair, equal and significant opportunity to obtain a high-quality education and reach, at a minimum, proficiency on challenging state academic achievement standards and state academic assessments" (Sec. 109). More specifically, the goal

■ **USING TECHNOLOGY**
Education World® National and State Standards www.educationworld .com/standards provides information about Common Core State Standards and links to each state so you can examine your state's standards and also links to standards created by each major discipline.

■ **Standards** are statements of what students should know or be able to do.

was that 100 percent of all students reach proficiency at their grade level in state math and reading/language arts by school year 2013–2014. Although criticized because it has led, in many instances, to "teaching to the test," a narrowing of the curriculum, and assessments of English learners before they have had adequate time to learn English, NCLB has succeeded in drawing attention to the most needy students. NCLB, together with Response to Intervention (RTI), have conveyed the conviction that making provision for struggling learners is every teacher's responsibility. A number of provisions are expected to change in the impending reauthorization of the Elementary and Secondary Act, but its current emphasis on preparing every student to be college and career ready will remain the same.

Universal Access

California's concept of Universal Access is an example of an implementation of the Act's goals. As explained in California's *Reading/Language Arts Framework*:

> The ultimate goal of language arts programs in California is to ensure access to high-quality curriculum and instruction for all students in order to meet or exceed the state's English-language arts content standards. To reach that goal, teachers [use] assessment for planning programs, differentiating curriculum and instruction, using grouping strategies effectively, and implementing other strategies for meeting the needs of students with reading difficulties, students with disabilities, advanced learners, English learners, and students with combinations of special instructional needs. Procedures that may be useful in planning for universal access are to:
>
>> Assess each student's understanding at the start of instruction and continue to do so frequently as instruction advances, using the results of assessment for program placement and planning.
>>
>> Diagnose the nature and severity of the student's difficulty and modify curriculum and instruction accordingly when students have trouble with the language arts.
>>
>> Engage in careful organization of resources and instruction and planning to adapt to individual needs. A variety of good teaching strategies that can be used according to the situation should be prepared.
>>
>> Differentiate when necessary as to depth, complexity, novelty, or pacing and focus on the language arts standards and the key concepts within the standards that students must master to move on to the next grade level.
>>
>> Employ flexible grouping strategies according to the students' needs and achievement and the instructional tasks presented.
>>
>> Enlist help from others, such as reading specialists, special education specialists, parents, aides, other teachers, community members, administrators, counselors, and diagnosticians when necessary and explore technology or other instructional devices or instructional materials, such as Braille text, as a way to respond to students' individual needs. (California Department of Education, 2007, p. 263)

FYI

The role of the secondary literacy specialist or coach is to focus on literacy skills. This role often includes working directly with striving readers and also with other specialists and teachers.

CHECKUP

1. What is the standards movement?
2. What are the Common Core State Standards?
3. How is content area instruction affected by the Common Core State Standards?

The Content Teacher's Role

One English teacher sent the following e-mail query to a language arts specialist:

> I encountered a question at a job interview for a high school position that totally caught me off guard. The question was "How would you teach reading?" To be honest, teaching reading never occurred to me.

Content teachers teach content and the literacy processes involved in learning that content.

Source: Fotolia.

As an English teacher, I take it for granted that my students know how to read, especially in regular high school English classes. Am I wrong to assume this? We are so pressured to teach what the state and district requires in a short amount of time. How do we stop to teach students how to read? (NCTE, 2001, p. 10)

The role of content area teachers in fostering literacy is spelled out by the National Governors Association & Council of Chief State School Officers (2009):

While the English language arts classroom has often been seen as the proper site for literacy instruction, this document acknowledges that the responsibility for teaching such skills must also extend to the other content areas. Teachers in the social and natural sciences, the humanities, and mathematics need to use their content-area expertise to help students acquire the discipline-specific skills necessary to comprehend challenging texts and develop deep knowledge in those fields. At the same time, English language arts teachers not only must engage their students in a rich array of literature but also must help develop their students' ability to read complex works of nonfiction independently. (p. 1).

Summarizing a number of reports on adolescent literacy, Fagella-Luby, Ware, and Capozzoli (2009) found that a key recommendation was "enhancing content area instruction for all learners, regardless of literacy level, by targeting elements of instruction that provide relevant literacy skills in specific content areas. In short, content area teachers are asked to help students read like scientists in science classes, historians in social studies classes, and so forth. . . . improving adolescent reading by embedding literacy instruction in content-area instruction for all students is the product of rethinking what and how all content area teachers teach, not solely the purview of the English Department, but rather a shared responsibility among secondary educators" (p. 460).

Content literacy does not require content teachers to instruct students in basic reading and writing skills such as **decoding**, or finding the main idea, or in such basic writing skills as composing a sentence or a paragraph. It does require that content area instructors teach both the content of their subject and the processes involved in learning that content. Thus, content literacy requires that the science teacher instruct students about common science word forms such as *hydro, derma,* and *endo.* It also requires that the science teacher show students how to read science texts critically and with a sense of inquiry and model how to compose lab reports. For the history teachers, it means teaching students how to read maps and charts of various kinds, to compare sources of information about historical events, and to draw conclusions based on primary sources. These are skills needed for an understanding of science and history, and they are best taught in the context of exploring these subject matter areas. In other words, content area teachers are expected to teach those literacy skills needed to read and write about their subject matter area. Content area teachers are asked to teach both the content of their subject and the processes involved in learning that content. After all, who is better equipped to teach students how to learn subject matter than someone who has firsthand experience learning it? To explain the thinking processes necessary to learn a subject, one must possess those processes.

Content area teachers often focus only on presenting their subject matter. When they observe that some students understand very little from their texts, they teach around the texts. They paraphrase or summarize the text or use other methods, such as labs, simulations, or audiovisual aids, to convey the content. As one history teacher explained, "Because you can't rely on students to read, I feel like I'm constantly summarizing the history textbook so kids don't miss the main points. I wish I didn't have to assume that role as much, but I find I do" (Schoenbach et al., 1999, p. 8). The teacher becomes an

■ **Decoding** is using phonics or other word analysis skills to translate print into speech.

enabler. Perceiving that they don't have to read the texts, the students stop reading assigned material. As a result, students fail to learn crucial literacy skills.

There are several obstacles to being a content literacy teacher. Content teachers may be unsure about which reading and writing skills and strategies they should be teaching or they may feel uncomfortable about this task. They also may feel so overwhelmed by the demands of today's ever-expanding curriculum and the challenge of preparing students for high-stakes tests that they don't feel they can take on what they view as an added responsibility (Meltzer, 2002). In actuality, teaching students strategies for learning more effectively means that instruction in content literacy skills holds the potential for enabling students to learn at least some of the content on their own.

Heller and Greenleaf (2007) recommend that "members of every discipline should identify the literacy skills needed to read and write in their area and be responsible for teaching those skills and strategies." As Moje (2008) explains, content literacy also involves understanding how knowledge is both constructed and communicated in a discipline.

> For example, in science, a norm of practice is that researchable problems be carefully defined and systematically and repeatedly studied before claims can be made about phenomena. Particular forms of evidence—typically empirical or observable forms that derive from experimental study—are required to make claims. In history, by contrast, the norms of practice differ. Historians, like natural scientists, study researchable problems systematically, but the means of obtaining evidence and the forms that provide warrant for claims differ. The time period in which a claim is situated matters tremendously to an historian; thus, temporal context is one dimension—among many other dimensions—the reader of historical texts must know, uncover, or examine as she or he reads (Bain, 2000; Wineburg, 1991). Mathematicians engage in what seems like similar practices of questioning, contextualizing, representing, proving, and consulting (Bass, 2008), but the actual practices and forms of representation used to convey concepts in mathematics are radically different from those of history. Mathematicians would not consider themselves investigators, but would rather be seen as problem solvers or proof seekers who work through the logic of a problem context to arrive at claims regarding mathematical abstractions. How mathematicians read texts also differs from the reading practices of other disciplines (Moje, 2008, p. 100).

Because different disciplines have specific ways of constructing and communicating knowledge, their texts differ and involve varying cognitive processes. Teachers in each discipline can most effectively teach the literacy skills and understandings required by their discipline.

To achieve the current goal of providing all students with a high quality education that adequately prepares them for postsecondary education or the world of work, the effort needs to systematic and school wide. "The challenge is to connect reading and writing to the rest of the secondary school improvement agenda, treating literacy instruction as a key part of the broader effort to ensure that all students develop the knowledge and skills they need to succeed in life after high school" (Shanahan & Shanahan, 2008, p. 1).

Embedding Skills and Strategies

Content area teachers should provide or reinforce instruction in the skills and strategies that are particularly effective in their subject areas. This instruction should be coordinated with language arts teachers, other content area teachers, and literacy coaches. By emphasizing the reading and writing practices that are specific to their subjects, teachers can encourage students to read and write like historians, scientists, mathematicians, and other content area experts. Content area teachers should also use teaching aids and devices that will help at-risk students better understand and remember the content they are learning. "Graphic organizers, prompted outlines, structured reviews, guided discussions, and other instructional tactics that modify and enhance curriculum content in ways that promote its understanding and mastery have been shown to greatly enhance student performance—for all students in academically diverse classes, not just students who are struggling" (Biancarosa & Snow, 2006, p. 15).

The Special Role of the English Teacher

English teachers should be prepared to teach comprehension and study skills as well as some advanced word recognition skills such as using the dictionary; using context; and using knowledge of roots, prefixes, and suffixes to develop vocabulary. These skills do not need to be taught separately; they can be taught as part of the language arts curriculum. Because of their expertise in language arts, English teachers have a greater responsibility for instruction in reading and writing than do other content area teachers.

Bereiter and Scardamalia (1987) caution that content area teachers risk the danger of becoming knowledge tellers if they simply dispense information and don't guide students in ways of understanding, organizing, and retaining that knowledge. Students might simply accumulate knowledge without relating it to what they already know or organizing it within their own understanding of the world. Superficially learned, this information is all too readily forgotten because it was never integrated into students' existing core of knowledge. Learning strategies that help students process information so it is more fully understood and more deeply processed, such as summarizing important information, will be explained in this text.

While it is true that achieving students may have been taught learning strategies in earlier grades, or picked up them up on their own, for the most part, underachieving students do not have an adequate grasp of strategies. Even if they have been taught them, they might not be able to apply them. With about 25 to 40 percent of students falling into this category, the importance of teaching students *how* to learn is obvious.

Specialist vs. Content Teacher

One solution to teaching literacy in the content areas is to have the reading specialist or English teacher instruct students in key strategies. The benefit to this approach is that the reading specialist or English teacher has expertise in this area, and the content area teacher would not lose valuable instructional time. However, if this approach is used, content area teachers should work carefully with reading specialists to ensure that they understand the strategies and can help students apply them to each particular content area. Although there are general strategies that apply across content areas, modifications may be necessary for individual subjects. In addition, transfer is a problem: Students who are taught strategies in one context may not apply them to other contexts; they need to be reminded to apply strategies to the content areas. In addition, learning to use a strategy takes a considerable amount of time. Content area teachers must reinforce the strategies that the specialist has introduced and help students when they are having difficulty applying them.

Making Better Use of Time

Pressured by an ever-increasing amount of content to cover—more scientific discoveries are announced each day, and history is being made every moment—and faced with high-stakes tests, content area teachers may believe that they can't take time out to teach literacy skills. However, as mentioned earlier, instruction in content literacy skills actually saves time: If students have acquired the necessary skills, they should be able to learn more of the material on their own and can benefit more from the teacher's guidance. For example, in one chemistry class, a resource teacher who was helping new teachers observed a novice teacher explaining all the material students had been assigned to read for homework—a selection on using moles in measurement (Patton, 1993). Wondering why they hadn't understood the material better, the resource teacher asked students how they had gone about reading the chapter. The students had failed to use any strategies and had merely focused on solving the chapter problems. Because the students did not have or had not applied strategies, the teacher spent virtually the entire period explaining what the students should have been able to learn through their reading and was unable to go on to a higher-level application of the material. Time spent on strategies for reading the chemistry text would have saved valuable instructional time.

CHECKUP

1. What is the content area teacher's role in the teaching of literacy?
2. Why might the language arts teacher have a special role?

Characteristics of Adolescents

Fostering the literacy development of secondary students requires that the techniques and materials employed build on an understanding of adolescence. The popular notion of adolescents as being an out-of-control species has undergone a revision. As Hersch (1999), who studied a group of adolescents intensively, notes,

> It is a popular notion that adolescents career out of control, are hypnotized by peer pressure or manipulated by demons for six years or so, and then if they don't get messed up or hurt or killed, they become sensible adults, that's ridiculous . . . The turbulence of adolescence today comes not so much from rebellion as from the loss of communication between adults and kids, and from the lack of realistic, honest understanding of what the kids' world really looks like. (p. 365)

This is not intended to suggest that adolescence is not without its challenges. All of us undoubtedly have memories of growing up and facing the many difficulties of coping with the teen years. However, being an adolescent today is more difficult than ever. As Christenbury, Bomer, and Smagorinsky (2009) note,

> Today's adolescent . . . faces some challenges that were not part of previous generations: earlier physical maturation and later economic (and possibly emotional) independence. In today's schools, adolescents are the most tested group of young people in history, in most middle-class households the most regulated and scheduled, and a group that, as a whole faces some real insecurity regarding societal stability, expectations, and pressures." (p. 5)

Adolescence is a time of physical, cognitive, psychosocial, and emotional growth. During adolescence, students begin to develop a sense of who they are and who they might become. Identity consists of two factors: self-concept and self-esteem. Self-concept is an individual's perception about attributes such as intelligence, roles in life, and possible goals. Self-esteem pertains to how an individual feels about his or her self-concept (American Psychological Association, 2002). Adolescence is a time for trying on different roles and behaviors to see which ones fit best.

In addition to physical growth spurts, adolescents also experience accelerated growth in their brains, especially in the areas of decision making and higher-level thinking (Strauch, 2003). Adolescents become better able to reason logically and to think abstractly, symbolically, and hypothetically. In their efforts to try out these newly developing capabilities, adolescents may seem confrontational and argumentative, but really they are simply exercising these new skills (American Psychological Association, 2002). Because of their developing ability to think critically, adolescents need opportunities to evaluate and discuss issues; sometimes this takes the form of finding flaws in the reason of others, especially those in authority—including teachers. However, adolescents still need and look to adults for guidance as they encounter difficult situations.

Although adolescents' ability to reason is increasing at an accelerated rate, their decision-making ability may actually decrease during mid-adolescence (American Psychological Association, 2002). Affirmation from adults can provide much needed support for adolescents who are feeling insecure.

Physical changes and the increased demands of school can be especially challenging for students who have learning disabilities. Although they may have been able to cope in elementary school, the increased demands of secondary school might be overwhelming. Adolescents with learning disabilities experience serious emotional distress at two to three times the rate of other students, and they may also resist the support that is provided them (American Psychological Association, 2002).

> Developmental characteristics may result in resistance to instructional support, particularly for adolescents with LD. For example, because adolescents manifest a desire for independence and expression of personal identity, they often resist dependent relationships with adults able to provide needed services and support. On the contrary, these students have a compelling need for peer group acceptance and access to peer social interaction. Teens may reject being singled out in any way from their peers and strive to belong. Perceived social competence, which may be diminished in adolescents with LD, is a reliable indicator of school success and long-term life adjustment and satisfaction. (National Joint Committee on Learning Disabilities, 2008)

As Bateman (2009) notes, peer crowds and cliques can have a profound influence—both positive and negative—on how adolescents respond to school. Cliques and other groups vary in norms and beliefs. In her research Bateman found a strong relationship between a positive and supportive peer culture in school and classroom settings and students' academic, emotional, and social adjustment. Bateman found that students define a supportive peer community as one that:

Shares their values and educational goals

Actively supports their learning needs

Provides a safe and pro-social environment in which adolescents can learn

Values their contributions

Bateman concludes that:

> It is clear that convergent evidence from many different areas of research suggest that peer culture has a very strong influence on students' adjustment to school during adolescence. Given the sensitivity of adolescents to peers, the effects of this informal social organization of the school community in crowds and cliques can surpass and counteract the effects of any formal school norms (such as regular attendance, the importance of academic achievement, and proper conduct). The issue of adolescents belonging to "positive" peer communities that encourage academic engagement and pro-social behavior should therefore become a central point of concern for parents and educators during the period of adolescence. (2009)

Adolescents are frequently heard to comment that school is boring. Despite the negative remarks that adolescents often make about school, school can be a source of safety and stability, especially if the school environment is caring and positive (American Psychological Association, 2002).

> Some of the same qualities that characterize families of adolescents who do well—a strong sense of attachment, bonding, and belonging, and a feeling of being cared about—also characterize adolescents' positive relationships with their teachers and their schools. One additional factor, adolescent perception of teacher fairness, has also been found to be associated with positive adolescent development. These factors, more than the size of the school, the type of school (e.g., public, private), or teacher–pupil ratio, have been found to be strongly associated with whether adolescents are successful or are involved with drugs or delinquency or drop out of school (Resnick et al., 1997; Klein, 1997). (American Psychological Association, 2002, p. 24)

CHECKUP

1. What characteristics of adolescents should be taken into consideration when planning an instructional program?

Characteristics of an Effective Content Area Literacy Program

An effective secondary content area literacy program has a number of components. They include building on students' strengths, fostering cognitive development, fostering principled understanding, integrating domain knowledge and thinking skills, making connections, building academic language, developing literacy competencies, learning with and from others, and fostering motivation and engagement.

Building on Students' Strengths

Reading and writing in the content areas builds on the basic reading and writing skills that students already possess. Content area reading and writing require specific knowledge and vocabulary, in addition to other specialized skills that may be necessary to understand a particular subject (McKenna & Robinson, 1995). The key word here may be *build*. Among the strengths students bring to the content areas are a background of relevant knowledge, the ability to reason, an understanding of language, and the ability to communicate with others (Herber & Herber, 1993). Students frequently have a wealth of knowledge and experience to bring to the content areas, particularly in the sciences. Students have experienced weather of all types; have observed animals, plants, and the stars; and have directly experienced many of the laws of physics.

Fostering Cognitive Development

More than ever, learning in the content area demands higher-order thinking skills:

Doing mathematics involves solving problems, abstracting, inventing, proving . . . .

Doing history involves the construction and evaluation of historical documents . . . .

Doing science includes such activities as testing theories through experimentation and observation. . . . Society envisions graduates of school systems who can identify and solve problems and make contributions to society throughout their lifetime. (Bransford et al., 2001, pp. 132–133)

The vast majority of students can answer questions of a **literal** nature, but in every content area students have difficulty answering questions that require a depth of thinking. For instance, in a national geography assessment, most students were able to answer the following factual question: *Where is the world's largest tropical rain forest?* But only a small percentage of the students were able to answer the application question: *Support the conclusion that tropical rain forests promote wide species variation* (Hawkins, Stancavage, Mitchell, Goodman, & Lazer, 1998). Although in the history assessment most students were able to note that the purpose of a political cartoon was to address the issue of civil rights, only a very small percentage could explain that the cartoon was pointing out the gap between the passage of civil rights legislation and actual change (Hawkins et al., 1998). Therefore, a key element in developing content literacy is building thinking skills, especially those that involve interpreting and applying principles and concepts.

An effective program emphasizes developing students' thinking. Instead of simply acquiring information, students should be learning to evaluate that information and to apply it when appropriate. Developing thinking skills might also entail learning to think like an historian, a scientist, or a mathematician. In traditional science experiments, students learn the procedures for conducting experiments. The experiments have predetermined results and are designed to illustrate scientific principles and to acquaint students with procedures for conducting experiments. Current emphasis is on having students

■ **Literal comprehension** involves understanding stated information but does not include interpretation.

plan and conduct their own experiments much as a scientist would. In literature study, emphasis is also on depth of learning and understanding. For example, after studying the major themes of *Invisible Man* (Ellison, 1952), a teacher led her class in a discussion of their own ethnicities (Langer, 1999).

Fostering Principled Understanding

Given the vast number of media outlets and devices for obtaining information, today's students may have difficulty discerning which information is important or relevant, and accurate or reliable. Ironically, all too often, students' attention is drawn to information that is trivial. They need instruction that helps them "separate the message from the noise that surrounds it" so that they can discover underlying principles (Alexander & Jetton, 2000).

With so much information available now, it is essential that students have some way of organizing it. Unfortunately, much of the information that students take in is fragmented and thus not related to the core concepts and principles that help students attain a principled understanding. In addition to helping students see the relevance of information, a principled understanding also helps them see how information relates to key concepts.

In an approach known as Understanding by Design, the focus is on answering essential questions and teaching for understanding (Wiggins & McTighe, 2006). Planning begins by noting the essential questions that students will be answering and the big idea they will be considering. The essential questions and big idea are used to articulate a coherent curriculum and inform students about goals and requirements for the course. The Strategic Instructional Model (SIM), initially created to help students with special needs who have been placed in inclusion classes, has a similar approach. Course and Unit Planning Routines are used to spell out "the big picture" and to plan a coherent curriculum based on key ideas (Lenz & Deshler, 2004).

In the introduction to the free online text *Biology* (Akre, Brainard, Gray-Wilson, & Wilkin, 2009), the author provides an overall big idea that provides a way of organizing much of the information that students will learn about cells and related topics. The introduction also explains why this particular segment is important to learn:

> Knowing the make up of cells and how cells work is necessary to all of the biological sciences. Learning about the similarities and differences between cell types is particularly important to the fields of cell biology and molecular biology. The importance of the similarities and differences between cell types is a unifying theme in biology. They allow the principles learned from studying one cell type to be applied when learning about other cell types. For example, learning about how single-celled animals or bacteria work can help us understand more about how human cells work. Research in cell biology is closely linked to genetics, biochemistry, molecular biology, and developmental biology.

After students have mastered basic concepts, the teacher should ask thought-provoking questions that require careful consideration of information and involve discerning underlying explanatory or causal principles, such as *why, why not, how, what if, how does X compare to Y,* and *what is the evidence for X*? Students should be trained to ask these questions as they read or listen to lectures or view instructional films. The teacher can use think-alouds that include connections and personal observations and model the process of asking deeper-level questions. Students can exchange and discuss their explanations. In the class discussion, the teacher can explore multiple explanations and perspectives and ask questions that involve the real world and that challenge students' assumptions or beliefs. Pashler and colleagues (2007) suggest conducting activities such as the following:

> Students in a high school chemistry course may be challenged to figure out how to reduce the calcium, chlorine, or pollutants in a water system. They would need to know why such substances are a hazard, how to measure the concentration of the chemicals, and methods for lowering the concentration. Identifying the potential hazards and solutions would motivate some students because it solves a problem in the community and/or may challenge the government, a corporation, or some authority. (p. 31)

Integrating Domain Knowledge and Thinking Skills

Although developing thinking skills and building domain knowledge are often treated as separate categories, they are complementary. Without a degree of content knowledge, students are unable to engage in some types of higher-order thinking skills (Penner, 2000). Fostering content knowledge can also promote cognitive development. As they acquire knowledge, students are better able to see patterns and induce generalizations. Novices in a content area become experts by acquiring extensive knowledge. The knowledge they acquire affects how they organize and interpret that knowledge and how they reason and solve problems (Bransford et al., 2001).

Making Connections

Making connections fosters learning and retention. We understand new ideas better when we can connect them to familiar concepts. The concept of representative democracy becomes more understandable when students can relate it to selecting a class representative for the student government. Understanding is also enhanced when connections are made between concepts learned at different times. United States democracy becomes more understandable when compared with democracy in ancient Greece and the parliamentary form of government in Canada and the United Kingdom. Concepts are further enhanced when connections are made across subject matter areas. Students studying democracy in history class will more fully understand the concept if they make connections with the novel *Johnny Tremain*. In one study of a secondary school that had high test scores despite having a large number of at-risk learners, the researchers found that the teachers were constantly making connections among knowledge, skills, and ideas across lessons, classes, and grades as well as across in-school and out-of-school applications (Langer, 1999). For instance, at Springfield High School, English teacher Suzanna Rotundi helped her students make connections with other works, with tests, and with life when she presented the book, *Invisible Man* by Ralph Ellison:

> My primary goal is to provide them with what I consider a challenging piece of literature that will give them an excellent resource for the AP exam. It fits in well with the works we have studied in that it explores the inner consciousness and makes use of a recurring image/symbol that has been the key to several other literary works . . . that of blindness. It allows them to explore the way a symbol can convey meaning in several literary works.
>
> . . . The ramifications in terms of social psychology with the concept of invisibility apply to so many different life experiences. I try to open the students' appreciation of how this work relates to their own world and it introduces them to the question of identity and how the daily interactions are crucial to identity formation. (Langer, 1999, p. 864)

Descriptions of content curricula typically list key objectives, each of which may be important. However, the individual objectives may not be perceived as part of a larger network of knowledge. "Stress on isolated parts can train students in a series of routines without educating them to understand an overall picture that will ensure the development of integrated knowledge structures and information about conditions of applicability" (Bransford et al., 2001, p. 139).

CHECKUP

1. How can higher-level thinking skills be fostered within the content areas?

Building Academic Language

The hallmark of a content area is the language used to express its major concepts. In addition to a specialized vocabulary, each content area also employs syntactic and rhetorical structures to convey information. Compare the vocabulary and syntactic and rhetorical structures used in the excerpts presented in the beginning of the chapter. The excerpts include technical vocabulary as well as high-level general vocabulary, formal use of language, and a highly

Academic language is the formal language of instruction used in classrooms and texts.

English Language Learners

A list of key academic vocabulary can be found in Chapter 9.

structured organization. Apart from the specialized language of the discipline, content areas also use a formal English that may be more complex and abstract than the language students are used to. Even the language of the classroom lecture may pose problems for some students. This is especially true for **English language learners**, who may have a relatively good grasp of conversational English, but may not be familiar with expressions such as *categorize the following, analyze, compare,* and other terms typically used as part of the language of instruction.

Developing Literacy Competencies

An essential element in learning content concepts is acquiring and implementing the strategies that facilitate learning. For science, this means learning how to read science texts and write lab reports. On a deeper level, it might mean learning how to think like a scientist. For history, it means learning to read and write historical accounts. On a more advanced level, it involves drawing and evaluating conclusions based on historical data. For instance, when writing about social studies issues such as the fairness of the death penalty or the role of the Electoral College, the teacher can walk students through the steps of locating descriptive accounts and opinion pieces and help them distinguish between the two. The teacher can also discuss ways in which the material might be handled. The class might even do a cooperative piece on the role of the Electoral College or the fairness of the death penalty so that students can better understand how to implement needed reading and writing strategies. The teacher and the class can create a set of guidelines, or a **rubric**, for writing the piece. In successful content area programs, teachers break down new or difficult tasks and provide students with step-by-step guidance. The guidance is **metacognitive**: Students are not just given a list of cookbook-type directions; they also learn the reason for the procedures and when and where these procedures are best applied. In this way, students take cognitive control of the strategies so they can adapt them to fit their own working styles. For instance, at Hudson Middle School, teacher Cathy Starr encouraged her students to reflect on their research efforts by asking themselves such questions as: Did you spend time trying to find the information? Did you keep going until you had learned enough to write your report? (Langer, 1999).

Initially, students might follow the teacher's lead as the teacher models strategies and coaches students in their use. Ultimately, students are responsible for adapting strategies to fit their own styles and needs and applying these strategies independently.

CHECKUP

1. How can academic language and literacy competencies be developed?

Learning with and from Others

Much of what we learn takes place through discussion with others or through **scaffolding** offered by adults and more knowledgeable peers. In a cooperative or collaborative learning group, students organize and test their learning when they present their ideas and views. By listening to others, students add to their own understanding and learn to view ideas from multiple perspectives; they gain not only information, but also insight into other ways of thinking. In learning groups, students can both seek clarification for their ideas and help others to understand content area concepts better.

Learning is fostered when students have a sense of being part of a supportive learning community. "Learning seems to be enhanced by social norms that value the search for understanding and allow students (and teachers) the freedom to make mistakes in order to learn" (Bransford et al., 2001, p. 145). There are several factors that have an impact on a classroom community, including peer impressions, grading practices, and culture. In some classes, students may not respond because they fear making mistakes or, conversely,

■ **English language learners** are not native speakers of English, but they are acquiring English.

■ **Rubrics** are descriptions of the traits or characteristics of standards used to judge a process or product.

■ **Metacognitive** refers to the quality of being aware of one's thinking processes.

■ **Scaffolding** refers to the support and guidance provided by an adult or more knowledgeable peer that helps a student function on a higher level.

Exemplary
Programs

Implementing Key Instructional Practices

Herbert Hoover High, open since 1929 and with Ted Williams as one of its most illustrious graduates, had fallen upon hard times. The average score for ninth graders, according to the Gates-MacGinitie, was 5.9. Three years later the average score was 8.2. What accounted for this dramatic growth? Three years of carefully planned and implemented professional development. After reviewing the research, the school's staff development committee recommended the use of seven key instructional practices: anticipatory activities, read-alouds, graphic organizers, vocabulary instruction, writing to learn, structured note taking, and reciprocal teaching, techniques that are discussed in upcoming chapters. Monthly meetings were held to discuss and review strategies; teachers made commitments to use these strategies in their classes, and follow-up meetings were held. The power of the approach was twofold. First of all, highly effective procedures were promoted. Second, and perhaps more importantly, all teachers implemented the procedures. It was a whole-school approach.

Meanwhile on the East Coast, Bullard-Havens, a vocational-technical school, also made dramatic progress after extensive professional development. The percentage of students who achieved proficiency on the demanding state tests increased from 55 percent to 80 percent in the last three years. In a process similar to the training at Hoover High, through extensive professional development, all teachers at Bullard-Havens were trained to develop the literacy skills needed to be successful in their content areas. At Bullard-Havens, teachers implemented SIMS strategies (see Chapter 9) and the Collins writing program (see Chapter 8). Although the approach at Bullard was more structured than that at Hoover, both programs emphasized note taking, graphic organizers, vocabulary, writing to learn, and comprehension strategies. After strategies were introduced, follow-up sessions were held and class observations were made to ensure that the strategies were being taught effectively. Teachers also met regularly in teams to discuss the progress of their students and to plan together. The secret of success for both schools is thorough professional development and sincere whole-school commitment with administrative backing. Although both schools have large numbers of students who are members of minority groups and who live in poverty, these typically underachieving students were able to greatly improve their test scores. These results from both coasts show that, when taught effectively, all students learn.

they may not want to be perceived as being too bright. Highly competitive classes with aggressive grading practices also discourage cooperation. Culture also has an impact on the classroom community. According to their culture, Inuit students are expected to learn by listening and observing; therefore, they are hesitant to speak out in class (Crago, 1992). But in Japan, students learn from the errors of others. Japanese teachers have created a classroom community in which students who have made errors are expected to help their classmates by discussing their thinking (Hatano & Inagaki, 1996).

Fostering Motivation and Engagement

Students' motivation depends, in large part, on their goals. A major goal for some students might be passing tests or pleasing teachers and parents. Some may have a genuine interest in a subject, while others may see that it provides some information that is worth knowing. Goals, of course, can be overlapping. Students can have a genuine interest in a subject and also be concerned about doing well on tests. In his chemistry text, Dickson (1995) motivates readers by making connections between chemistry and their everyday lives. He quotes and discusses a number of familiar statements that use chemical terms:

I'm on a low-sodium diet.

Watch your calories.

This is iodized salt.

Chlorofluorocarbons contribute to the destruction of the ozone layer. (p. 3)

Dickson also motivates students by making the subject understandable and readable. And he shows how chemistry can be applied both to their understanding of other science courses and to their functioning in everyday life.

Students whose learning goals are external are more anxious learners. They are concerned with pleasing teachers and parents, and they measure progress in terms of how well they do in comparison with others. These students tend to be more passive, more reliant on the teachers. They may not use as many strategies, and their learning may lack depth. In contrast, learners who are intrinsically motivated tend to be less anxious and more confident. Since they enjoy learning for its own sake, their knowledge has more depth. In addition to being more confident, they persist in the face of challenge (Nichols, Jones, & Hancock, 2000).

Goals should be specific and attainable. Students may have long-term goals, such as learning basic algebra so that they can take more advanced courses, but they should also have goals that are short-term and immediate, such as being able to solve at least 80 percent of the problems at the end of a chapter or knowing how to use a microscope to examine slides. When students set goals, they put themselves in a position **to monitor** their learning. If they aren't reaching their goals, they can take corrective action. Setting and achieving learning goals fosters both autonomy and a sense of **self-efficacy**. It can also lead to more effective learning. For instance, a student who rereads a chapter in an attempt to increase her understanding of how to solve simultaneous equations may find that simply rereading does not work. However, when she studies the sample equations and works on some practice problems, she begins to understand the procedure. Setting and monitoring her goals has helped her to adopt strategies that enable her to reach her goal.

The way a subject is presented can have an impact on students' learning goals. Downplaying grades, presenting interesting topics, planning discussions and hands-on activities, and highlighting ways in which topics in the content areas apply to students' lives fosters deeper interest and involvement in learning. On the other hand, negative comments, competitive practices, emphasis on grades, threats of failure, homogeneous grouping, negative attitudes toward underperforming students, and giving students little choice or control over their learning may undermine students' motivation (Conley, 1997).

Knowledge about a subject and interest in the subject are interrelated. The more students know about a subject, the greater their interest will be, and the fuller their comprehension is likely to be (Conley, 1997). However, as students grow older, their interest in academic subjects may decline, especially if they are struggling with a subject. What's more, **intrinsic motivation**, which is a powerful force in performance, decreases while **extrinsic motivation**, a much weaker element, increases. If students are struggling, their confidence in their ability as learners also declines, as does their expectancy for success (Guthrie, Alao, & Rinehart, 1997). Struggling learners are left with a diminished sense of competence, particularly when they reach middle school and high school, which have more competitive environments and place a greater emphasis on performance and grades. To make matters worse, all too often, teachers emphasize the performance of top students. By planning instruction and activities so that all students are placed on the path to successful learning and fostering a cooperative rather than a completive spirit, secondary teachers will be developing more fully students' academic skills and the skills needed to be successful in today's global, interconnected society.

Self-Regulated Learning

Academic discipline and motivation are also metacognitive. Students are aware of what the teacher expects, how to meet these expectations, and what to do if problems arise (Conley, 1997). In self-regulated learning, students take control of their learning: They set goals, create plans to meet those goals, and implement the plans and monitor their

---

■ **To monitor** means to be aware of or to check one's cognitive processes.

■ **Self-efficacy** is a belief in oneself as a learner.

■ **Intrinsic motivation** is a natural internal desire, such as curiosity or interest, that leads individuals to engage in an activity.

■ **Extrinsic motivation** is an external reward, such as praise, group approval, or money, that leads individuals to engage in an activity.

progress. They can assess their performance by noting whether the science experiments yield the hypothesized results or whether the answers to the math problems make sense logically. And by reflecting on their progress, self-regulated students are able to see which strategies are working and which need revising.

Because they reflect on what they know, these students are aware of when they understand material, when they need clarification or more information, and which study techniques work for them. With these kinds of awareness, self-regulated learners are able to take charge of their learning.

The two key components that predict future success in high school and college are academic achievement and academic discipline (ACT, 2008). Self-regulated learning can act as a foundation for academic discipline—the degree to which a student is hardworking and conscientious. Academic discipline is evidenced by the amount of effort invested in completing schoolwork and engaging in learning new material. It includes:

> Planning and Organization—thinking about necessary steps and devising plans for achieving objectives. Students skilled in this area have a strong sense of time, organization, and prioritization and use strategic skills to aid in learning new information.

> Follow-Through and Action—engaging in behaviors according to previously set plans and remaining engaged in a task until the objective is accomplished in a timely fashion. Students skilled in this area are able to assess their own progress throughout a task and act accordingly based on this assessment.

> Sustained Effort—maintaining focus on longer-term goals and working to achieve individual elements of these goals. Students skilled in this area persist despite challenges, exhibit on-task behavior, and are able to manage distractions in order to achieve a goal (p. 26). Orderly conduct and relationships with school personnel were also crucial behaviors.

CHECKUP

1. What are the characteristics of motivation?
2. What role does motivation play in learning?
3. What are the characteristics of an effective content area literacy program?
4. Which of the characteristics are most crucial?

Building a Positive Literacy Identity

As Moje and Luke (2009) explain, literacy is more than a set of skills. Literacy is a social practice that results in the construction of identities. "People's identities mediate and are mediated by the texts they read, write, and talk about . . . both what and how one reads and writes can have an impact on the type of person one is recognized as being and on how one sees oneself . . ." (p. 1). Gee (2003) explains that a strong, positive literacy identity is a prerequisite for fully developing literacy abilities:

> All deep learning—that is, active, critical learning—is inextricably caught up with identity in a variety of ways. . . . People cannot learn in a deep way within a semiotic domain if they are not willing to commit themselves fully to the learning in terms of time, effort, and active engagement. Such a commitment requires that they are willing to see themselves in terms of a new identity, that is, to see themselves as the *kind of person* who can learn, use, and value the new semiotic domain. (p. 59)

A lack of a positive literacy identify can hinder students' progress, especially if they are struggling. Some struggling readers will stop participating for fear that others will discover that they are poor readers. As Hall (2008/2009) notes,

> I often hear kids say that they don't want anyone to identify them as poor readers.
> They frequently are ashamed of their perceived weaknesses and will do whatever it takes to cover them up. Sometimes they try to figure out what it takes to be identified as a good reader then try to emulate it. Others simply withdraw from class and from reading, believing that if they do not participate then no one can identify them as poor readers. (p. 352)

Sadly, struggling readers may resist instruction that would help them become better readers because they fear they will be identified as poor readers. On the positive side, Hall's research suggests that instruction will be more effective if teachers relate it to students' sense of identity by asking such questions as "What kind of reader do you want to be?" and helping them set goals that will assist them in constructing a desired identity.

Perhaps, even more than reading, writing is dependent on an individual's identity. As Street (2009) explains, one way of building positive identities is to foster voice and stance in student writing. "Strong voice and stance are most likely to emerge when students care about a subject or topic and have deep knowledge of it." Moje and Luke (2009) conclude, "Strong academic writing, from the academic literacies perspective, depends on knowledge of self and on awareness of one's identity enactments" (p. 24).

Importance of the Teacher

Of all the elements needed to create an effective content area program, the teacher is the one that is far and above the most important.

In his survey of nearly 15,000 secondary school students, Ferguson (2002) found that more than 80 percent of students planned to work hard in their classes and wanted to improve their skills and learn as much as they could. The vast majority of secondary school students want to do well, but many perceive that they lack the literacy skills necessary to be successful. More than 80 percent felt their teachers were supportive and encouraging and treated students with respect. However, many students were concerned about the way teachers would treat them if they made a mistake. Based on his surveys, Ferguson devised a three-legged program known as Tripod, which features "content, pedagogy and relationships: teachers need to understand what they are teaching (content knowledge); they need multiple effective ways of communicating the material to students (pedagogy); and they need to relate to students (relationships) in ways that motivate and enable them." Ferguson concluded, "When teachers have strong content knowledge and are willing to adapt their pedagogies to meet student needs, adding good teacher-student relationships and strong encouragement to the mix may be key. It may help black and Hispanic students seek help more readily, engage their studies deeply and ultimately overcome skill gaps that are due in substantial measure to past and present disparities in family-background advantages and associated social inequities" (p. 4). This text will focus on the pedagogy of literacy integrated with content knowledge, but will also stress the importance of understanding affective factors and providing needed support.

A truly effective program that meets today's challenges desperately needs all three features, but building personal relationships and providing academic and psychological support are especially important. As one student explained, "I find it encouraging when teachers tell me I 'can do it' and when they don't make judgments about why I haven't done something that I was supposed to." Another says, "I find it encouraging when teachers give me full explanations to help me understand things, instead of short 'yes' or 'no' answers." A third student says, "I find it encouraging when teachers stay after school to give me extra help and don't seem like they're in a big hurry to go" (Ferguson, pp. 14–15). On a smaller scale, Lycke (2010) found in her study of a rural high school that students were more highly motivated when they had a relationship with their teachers and when their teachers manifested interest in them by attending events in which the students were participating. A program known as AVID has had dramatic success in preparing underachieving poor and minority students for college by providing the support they needed.

An Effective Teacher in Action

In her observations of Landy, a highly successful chemistry teacher, over a period of two years, researcher Elizabeth Moje (1996) discovered that Landy taught students learning strategies because she cared about them and wanted them to be successful. Landy viewed chemistry as a highly organized, precise body of knowledge, so she taught students a host of reading and writing strategies that would help them organize the principles of chemistry in a precise way. The students perceived the strategies that they were taught and were required to use as evidence that Landy cared about them and was trying to help them. One of the reasons they had faith in the strategies and persisted in their use was because of the positive relationship they had with Landy.

In addition to teaching them highly effective strategies for reading and retaining information from the text, Landy also showed students how to talk about chemistry in a precise and objective fashion. By asking students not only to make observations but also to critique observations, she taught them how to think like scientists. In addition to having them learn the meanings of technical terms, she also asked students to use these terms so that they could incorporate them in their speaking and writing in meaningful ways. To make abstract concepts concrete, she often made analogies between a key concept and some outside activity in which students were engaged. In addition to helping students understand concepts, she showed an interest in them and built relationships with them. These relationships were a key factor in her success with her students. In explaining her approach to teaching, Landy stated:

> When I started teaching I taught very traditionally. I taught my subject. I taught all the facts. But I've learned over the years that I don't teach subjects, I teach students, and so I've geared my teaching toward helping them learn how to learn. (Moje, 1996, p. 186)

Commenting on Landy's effectiveness, Lew, a struggling learner, noted that SQ3R, a study system explained in Chapter 7, helped him cope with his chemistry text:

> SQ3R helps because she has you put the main topics in question form. So throughout your notetaking you should be able to answer the question, so it will give you a better understanding for what you read about. (Moje, 1996, p. 187)

But he also attributed his relative success as a student to Landy's caring attitude:

> She never puts someone down. She keeps them focused and makes them want to do the work more and more and more. . . . That's why I like this class so much even though I'm not an A student in there. She's positive so she keeps me into it so I'll keep trying harder. I'd be flunking chemistry if I didn't have a positive teacher. You need something to keep you going. (Moje, 1996, p. 187)

Effective content area teachers like Landy have a quality known as *teacher efficacy*— the belief that teachers can have a positive influence on students. Teachers with high efficacy stress learning for the sake of learning, use praise rather than criticism, accept students as they are, and have a deep and abiding belief in students' ability to learn. They also use their time effectively and persevere with struggling learners (Eggen & Kauchak, 2001). They teach appropriate strategies and expect learning to require sustained effort (Eisenberger, Conti-D'Antonio, & Bertrando, 2000). Other characteristics that lead to increased learning include the following:

> Students engage in higher-order thinking by synthesizing and explaining information and reaching their own conclusions about the topics they study.

> Teachers introduce students to established branches of learning—accepted facts, concepts, and theories—with enough depth that students develop a complex understanding of the subject matter, including alternative explanations for different phenomena.

> Students interact with the teacher and each other to expand their understanding of existing branches of learning.

> Classroom learning has value beyond the classroom, enabling students to make connections between what they learn and their lives outside school.

> Extra help is provided for those who need it. Students are provided with assistance as soon as they begin to struggle in any of the content areas. (Alliance for Excellent Education, 2009; Newmann & Wehlege, 2000)

The best instruction is the result of a combination of content and teaching knowledge. Content knowledge is necessary for good teaching, but it is not sufficient. Experts are not automatically good teachers. However, even the most gifted teachers need a solid grounding in content. Although there are general principles for effective instruction, some aspects of teaching are content specific. Good teachers know which concepts in their domain are difficult to understand and have devised ways to foster students' understanding of these concepts. Teachers who are able to instruct effectively in more than one discipline are able to do so because they have expertise and experience in more than one discipline (Bransford et al., 2001).

CHECKUP

1. What are the characteristics of an effective content area teacher?

Literacy Standards for Secondary Content Teachers

Just as schools and school systems have standards, so, too, do educational professionals. An overview of the International Reading Association's Standards for Middle and High School Content Classroom Teachers, along with a chart showing the chapters in which the standards are addressed, is printed on the inside back cover of this text. The International Reading Association's Web site at www.reading.org and the text, *Standards for Reading Professionals Revised 2010* (International Reading Association, 2010), show how the standards might be applied by secondary content teachers. The basic purpose of the standards is to specify what secondary content teachers should know and be able to do to teach their students the literacy skills needed in their subject matter areas. The standards are used by the National Council for the Accreditation of Teacher Education (NCATE) to evaluate professional preparation programs as well as to plan the content of Praxis, a professional exam for prospective teachers. Because of the importance and relevance of the standards, *Building Literacy in Secondary Content Area Classrooms* emphasizes them. The text also emphasizes ways in which candidate teachers can demonstrate that they have met the standards. At the end of each chapter, there is a feature entitled "Extension and Application" that highlights activities for showing that you have met the standards emphasized in that chapter.

Summary

Content area literacy is the ability to use reading and writing to acquire new knowledge in a particular discipline. Although general reading and writing skills are needed, each discipline also has its own specific literacy demands. Content area literacy is impacted by sociocultural interaction with others; critical literacy; New Literacies, which offer an expanded view of literacy that includes fuller expression; and the demands of the twenty-first century. Unfortunately, about 25 to 40 percent of students have difficulty reading their content area texts. The content area teacher's role is to teach to all students the reading and writing skills needed to learn a particular subject. Although the reading specialist or English teacher may help, the content area teacher is in the best position to teach content-specific literacy skills. Adolescence is a time of physical, emotional, and psychological changes. Given their quest for self-identity, need for peer relationships, and growing ability to think abstractly, adolescents need caring, committed teachers who take the time to build relationships and understand their concerns. Since career demands are on a par with the demands of college, all students should be challenged by a demanding curriculum but should be provided with any help that they need. The ability to comprehend complex text is regarded as the best preparation for college. Striving Readers and other programs and more than a dozen national reports have brought increased attention to adolescent literacy. Elements of an effective literacy program require building on students' strengths, fostering cognitive development, fostering principled understanding, making connections, building academic language, developing literacy competencies, learning with and from others, and fostering motivation, engagement, self-regulated learning, and positive literacy identity. Equity, universal access, and the impact of the standards movement and the widely adopted Common Core State Standards and federal legislation such as the Elementary and Secondary School Acts are also factors that will influence effective content area programs. When all is said and done, the most important factor in an effective content area program is the teacher. An effective subject matter teacher focuses on students' needs and integrates content and strategies so that students will learn.

Reflection

Return to the Anticipation Guide at the beginning of this chapter. Respond once again to the items. Did your responses change? If so, how and why? What do you think should be the role of content area teachers in fostering literacy in their subjects? What should be the role of content area teachers in helping struggling learners?

Extension and Application

Read Elizabeth Moje's account of Landy, an exceptionally effective content area teacher who, because she cared deeply about her students, taught strategies that she believed would help them learn. This account can be found in Moje, E. (1996). "I teach students, not subjects": Teacher-student relationships as contexts for secondary literacy. *Reading Research Quarterly, 31*, 172–195.

What do you think the role of the content area teacher in your discipline should be? What would be the teacher's role and responsibility for the teaching of literacy skills needed to understand and communicate in the discipline? Write a brief reflection on this topic.

Analyze a current textbook or other text typically used in your subject matter area. What skills and strategies would students need to apply to read it?

Go to Topic 3: Motivation in the MyEducationLab (www.myeducationlab.com) for your course, where you can:

- Find learning outcomes for Motivation along with the national standards that connect to these outcomes.
- Complete Assignments and Activities that can help you more deeply understand the chapter content.
- Apply and practice your understanding of the core teaching skills identified in the chapter with the Building Teaching Skills and Dispositions learning units.

Go to the Topic A+RISE in the MyEducationLab (www.myeducationlab.com) for your course. A+RISE® Standards2Strategy™ is an innovative and interactive online resource that offers new teachers in grades K–12 just-in-time, research-based instructional strategies that:

- Meet the linguistic needs of ELLs as they learn content.
- Differentiate instruction for all grades and abilities.
- Offer reading and writing techniques, cooperative learning, use of linguistic and nonlinguistic representations, scaffolding, teacher modeling, higher-order thinking, and alternative classroom ELL assessment.
- Provide support to help teachers be effective through the integration of listening, speaking, reading, and writing along with the content curriculum.
- Improve student achievement.
- Are aligned to Common Core Elementary Language Arts standards (for the literacy strategies) and to English language proficiency standards in WIDA, Texas, California, and Florida.

CHAPTER 2

The Nature and Assessment of Content Area Texts

This chapter contains the single most powerful procedure for improving reading in the content areas. As simple as it is effective, the procedure consists of matching students with materials that they can read. Have you ever tried to read a text that was simply too difficult for you? How did you feel about it? How did you cope with the situation? Unfortunately, approximately 25 to 40 percent of today's students are being asked to read content area books that are too difficult for them. Balfanz, McPartland, and Shaw (2002) assert:

Using What You Know

> To address student motivation in assigned or self-selected reading, the match with a student's reading skill level and content areas of interest are very important. Often struggling readers are poorly motivated to undertake additional reading, either because they are embarrassed to reveal weaknesses or because they have a history of frustration or failure with reading. Thus it is important to offer reading materials at a level that will not further frustrate student efforts. (p. 17)

This recommendation can be carried out by teachers carefully selecting books and other materials that students can handle. This chapter explores the nature of content area texts, looks at ways of assessing their difficulty levels, and then discusses techniques that can be used to make sure that students are provided with materials that they can read.

The Importance of Content Area Texts

The textbook has been described as the predominant tool in content area instruction (Alvermann & Moore, 1991) and as the "core of the curriculum in many schools" (Duffy et al., 1989, p. 436). In a recent study, 43 percent of U.S. science teachers reported using a textbook as the primary basis of their science lessons; 39 percent used it as a supplement. The international averages were 52 and 34 percent, respectively. Some 20 percent of U.S. teachers assigned textbook reading almost always or all of the time, and 53 percent assigned textbook reading some of the time. The international averages were 35 and 46 percent, respectively (Martin, Mullis, Foy, Olson, Erberber, Preuschoff, & Galia, 2008). In an earlier study, when asked about their **texts**, students replied that they liked those texts best that were interesting and had information that they could relate to and disliked those that were boring or hard to understand (Lester & Cheek, 1997–1998). Almost 50 percent of the students chose literature texts as their favorite, with math and social studies texts rated as the least favorite texts. Student suggestions for improving texts included using more graphics and up-to-date illustrations, featuring interesting topics, and creating texts that are easier to understand. A significant number of students felt that texts should not use "big" words that "nobody understands" (p. 289).

The Problem of Coverage

Although they continue to be a major tool in content area instruction, today's **texts** are so packed with facts that the reader may lose sight of the overall point of a section or chapter. Indeed, many texts jump from topic to topic without fully developing any one idea. Compared to math and science texts used in other countries, U.S. texts cover more topics, but with much less depth. The typical U.S. science text covers between fifty-three and sixty-seven topics. In Germany, the range of topics covered is nine to sixteen, and in Japan, texts cover between eight and seventeen topics (National Science Boards, 2001). As might be expected, key topics were given less coverage in U.S. texts (Science and Engineering Indicators, 2001).

Textbooks are expensive to produce. Thus, to generate maximum sales, textbook publishers include topics that will appeal to the widest possible audience, covering in particular the content standards set by the largest states. When textbooks incorporate the standards of so many states, they run the risk of covering too many topics. In addition, teachers who are pressured by high-stakes tests geared to state standards feel compelled to cover the entire text, even though it includes an excessive number of topics.

The Difficulty Level of Content Area Texts

The difficulty of texts used at each grade level varies considerably as do the reading levels of students. However, at each grade level, except at grade 10, the average difficulty level of texts exceeds the average reading level of students (Metametrics, 2009). Moreover, more than 25% of the texts had a measured readability of one to three years above the target grade level.

In his survey of nearly 15,000 secondary school students, Harvard researcher R. F. Ferguson (2002) asked, "How much of the material that you read for school do you understand very well?" Students could choose one of three answers: "Almost All, A Lot, Half or Less." Fewer than 30 percent of the survey takers chose "Almost All." For African-American students and Hispanic students, the percentages were 15 percent and 14 percent, respectively. Overall, more than 40 percent of students responded that they were unable to understand what they had read more than half the time. The statistics for African-American and Hispanic students who gave this response were 55 and 56 percent, respectively. Text comprehension, then, is an obstacle to academic success for most students, but especially for African-American and Hispanic students. A primary purpose of this book is to explore ways to make secondary school texts accessible to virtually all students.

Comprehension suffers when texts are too difficult. When high school students reading below their grade level were given material on their instructional reading level, their comprehension was adequate. However, when these same below-level readers were given material on their grade level but above their reading level, comprehension plummeted, and a number of students simply gave up (Kletzien, 1991). As one frustrated student commented, "I have no idea what this is talking about; I am just trying to remember anything that I can about Africa" (p. 82).

Texts can be too difficult, even for students reading on grade level. Some middle-grade students who possessed at least grade-level reading ability had difficulty with the condensed language of a long poem and the archaic language in an excerpt from a primary-source diary that were included in their text (Afflerbach & VanSledright, 2001). Although

■ Although the term **text** typically conjures up the image of a book, the term has a broader definition so that text can include "anything that can carry meaning" or "be interpreted" (Moje, Stockdill, Kim, & Kim, 2011, pp. 454–455). This includes books, periodicals, diaries, letters, logs, speeches, classroom discussions, talk, media, and visual images.

the text was on grade level, the adjunct materials were apparently on a higher level. Students also had difficulty integrating information from the main body of the text with these supplementary readings. However, targeted teaching might have been sufficient to help them overcome these difficulties.

Despite the difficulty level of current texts, there is an apparent gap between the reading skills of many high school seniors and the reading demands of college and the workplace (National Governors Association and Council of Chief State School Officers, 2010a). There is also a gap between the materials generally read in high school and those read in college and the workplace. To close both gaps, the Common Core State Standards, have incorporated a feature known as grade bands. The bands include grades 2–3, 4–5, 6–8, 9–10, and 11–12. The difficulty level at every band has been expanded so that by senior year students will be expected to be able to read at or close to college and career level. In other words, the standards call for students to be able to read more challenging material at every grade level beginning with grade 3. Even though Common Core Standards call for having students read more challenging materials, this does not mean that students should be given material that exceeds their reading ability. Giving students material that is too hard is virtually guaranteed to stunt their literacy growth.

CHECKUP

1. What role do textbooks play in teaching content area subjects?
2. Why is it important that textbooks be written at the appropriate grade level?

The Nature of Content Area Texts

Content area texts, which include technical vocabulary and new concepts, are generally more difficult to read than the fiction pieces. In fact, students score significantly lower on assessments of informational text than they do on tests on fictional texts even when the measured readability of the texts is the same (Milone, 2008). As it increases in complexity, expository text also diverges more substantially from oral language and requires that the reader have more advanced text processing skills. Read and compare the following presentations.

Presentation One

As the devastation wrought by the drought and grasshopper infestations worsened, crops failed and cattle and other farm animals sickened and died. As a result, farm income fell drastically.

Presentation Two

In the summer of 1931 there was no rain. The dry weather was bad for the crops, but it was good for the grasshoppers. Hordes of grasshoppers began attacking the crops. They hungrily ate plant after plant. Later more grasshoppers appeared. They ate much of what was left. The crops failed. The grass and the feed corn that the cattle ate dried up. The cattle grew sick and died. Farmers made very little money that year. (Press, 1999, p. 37)

The ideas are the same, but their expression is very different. The first is a written explanation. The second is an oral presentation. The oral presentation requires more words and clauses to say basically the same thing as the written presentation. However, with its step-by-step explanation, the oral presentation is easier to understand. The written passage is more condensed and complex, and it has a great lexical density (Unsworth, 1999). Lexical density is the proportion of content words per clause. Speech has an average of two content words per clause. Written text has a lexical density of four to six content words, but may be higher (Halliday, 1994).

This greater density is achieved through a process of turning action verbs into nouns. The nouns are more abstract than the verbs they replace. The concrete idea of drought ruining crops is turned into the more abstract concept of *devastation*. Hordes of grasshoppers attacking crops becomes the more abstract term *infestation*. *Farm income* replaces the idea of farmers making money. This nominalization of the language, while more abstract, makes it easier for authors to build complex ideas. However, the more language is nominalized, the farther it departs from everyday language and the greater challenge it offers to readers, especially to English language learners. In addition to acquiring the technical vocabulary of a content area, readers must also learn its specialized grammar. As Unsworth (1999) notes, "For many students this does not occur spontaneously. It will need carefully scaffolded experience with written texts and explicit teaching of knowledge about language" (p. 514).

Vocabulary may also need to be scaffolded. As texts become more advanced, the nature of the vocabulary changes. There is an increasing proportion of technical or literary vocabulary and general vocabulary words that may not be familiar to readers (Chall, Bissex, Conard, & Harris-Sharples, 1996).

Complex expository language is not the only element that causes content area text to be more difficult. As students progress through secondary school, the expository texts they encounter increase in difficulty along three other dimensions: background knowledge required, density and difficulty of ideas, and cognitive demands.

Background Knowledge and Difficulty and Density of Ideas

Texts used in advanced grades present a greater number of ideas and more complex and abstract concepts. These texts also require a greater amount of background knowledge. Note the density of ideas in the following passage and the background that a reader would need to fully comprehend it:

> The fifties may have been marred by racism and the threat of nuclear annihilation, but many Americans floated through those years on a cloud of prosperity and family values. An emphasis on marriage, children, and family life prevailed throughout the decade. The thirties had been the era of the Great Depression, when couples could not afford children and lived in crowded shacks, flats, or dilapidated apartments. The forties were war years, when women worked while husbands, fathers, brothers, and boyfriends marched off to battle. Many returned with serious injuries; some never returned at all. By the fifties, Americans had had enough of deprivation and anguish. (Kallen, 1999, p. 52)

Cognitive Demands

Because of their greater density and complexity of ideas, more advanced texts require higher-level reasoning skills. Students may be called upon to analyze a situation, infer causes, compare or contrast solutions, draw conclusions, apply a proposed solution, and evaluate the credibility of information. Note the cognitive skills required to read the following passage. Readers are called upon to compare and contrast Jefferson with Washington and Adams and to predict how Jefferson's beliefs might affect his presidency and the new nation:

> Thomas Jefferson, the victor in the fierce contrast between the Republicans and the Federalists, was quite a different sort of person from the presidents before him, Washington and Adams. Those two Federalists believed in government by an elite of mostly "well born" men who had proved themselves by becoming wealthy. They adopted some of the manners of the British aristocracy, dressing in elegant clothes and holding formal parties at which leading figures from law, business, and government mingled. Thomas Jefferson was a Republican who believed that the strength of the country lay in the vast majority of Americans who owned their own farms. Such people had no bosses over them: in those days, before the secret

ballot, they could vote as they wished, not how a landlord or employer told them to vote. Jefferson had faith that they would elect the most talented and virtuous men available. (Collier & Collier, 1999, p. 18)

All content area texts are not equally difficult. History texts may be a bit easier than science texts because they tell a story and may be written in narrative style. Each content area text makes its own unique demands on the reader. When they are aware of the demands made by a particular subject matter text, teachers are in a better position to help students comprehend material in that area. Following is an overview of the major subject matter areas and the demands their texts make upon readers.

Science

Science texts attempt to build on the readers' background of everyday experience but, increasingly, they allude to unfamiliar concepts. Note how a science text develops the concept of *convection currents:*

> Air begins to move when the sun heats the land and warms the air above. Molecules in the air move faster when they are heated and the air starts to expand. It becomes less dense than the surrounding air. At the same time, cooler, heavier air is drawn in below to replace the rising air. This circulation of air is called convection current. (Morgan, 1996, p. 10)

Reading science requires the ability to follow the chain of reasoning used to explain processes that result in phenomena such as convection currents. Each link in the process must be understood and connected to the next link. Then, when readers encounter the name of the process in future reading, they must remember the process that this name describes.

Readers must be able to deal with a large number of details and engage in some abstract reasoning—for instance, the type of reasoning needed to understand the relationship between the angle of the sun and the temperature on earth. Students must be able to deal with theoretical ideas, particularly in the physical sciences. Life sciences texts (biology, health, ecology) tend to be more explicit, descriptive, and technical, whereas physical sciences texts (physics, astronomy) tend to be more abstract and theoretical, requiring that readers make a greater number of inferences (Chall et al., 1996). Physics texts are usually harder to read and more demanding cognitively than biology texts.

Social Studies

Social studies texts may be narrative or expository. Narrative texts present events in storylike fashion. Expository texts discuss events in terms of causes and effects and the issues involved, requiring more interpretation, analysis, and evaluation of events and ideas (Chall et al., 1996).

Although not as technical a subject as science, history can be very abstract as in the following text.

Passage from Tenth-Grade Text

Enlightenment Ideas. Colonial protests drew upon the liberalism of the Enlightenment. Europe's leading liberal writers included Baron de Montesquieu of France and John Locke of England. They argued that people had divinely granted natural rights, including life, liberty, and property. A good government protected these individual rights. Locke insisted that government existed for the good of the people. Therefore, people had the right to protest any government that violated this "social contract" by failing to protect their rights.

Patrick Henry, a young Virginia representative, used these ideas to draft a radical document known as the Virginia Resolves. He argued that only the colonial assemblies had the right to tax the colonists:

> "Resolved therefore. That the General Assembly of this colony, together with his majesty or his substitutes have, in their representatives capacity the only exclusive right and power to lay taxes and imposts upon the inhabitants of this colony; and that every attempt to vest

such power in any other person or persons whatever than the General Assembly aforesaid is illegal, unconstitutional, and unjust, and has a manifest tendency to destroy British as well as American liberty."

—Patrick Henry, May 29, 1765
(Lapsansky-Werner, Levy, Roberts, & Taylor, 2010, p. 99)

Literature

Readers of popular fiction need to grasp only the surface meaning of the writing. However, reading literature requires going beyond the surface meaning and experiencing the emotional depth of a work. There is a greater intensity of involvement as the reader identifies with complex characters and situations. At higher levels, knowledge of literary conventions and literary language are required, as is the exercise of aesthetic judgment. Compare your reading of the following two selections:

Passage from *Sweet Valley High: Winter Carnival*

It was four o'clock on a rainy Tuesday afternoon, and Elizabeth Wakefield was looking down at her sopping shoes with a rueful smile on her face. It figured that she missed the bus on one of the few rainy days that they had all winter. And it also figured that her twin sister, Jessica, would have taken the Fiat that they shared to run an errand for the cheerleading squad. Elizabeth sighed. There were still four blocks to go before she got home, and at this rate she could practically swim. (William, 1986, p. 1)

Passage from *The Witch of Blackbird Pond*

It took nine days for the *Dolphin* to make the forty-three mile voyage from Saybrook to Wethersfield. As though the ship were bewitched, from the moment they left Saybrook, everything went wrong. With the narrowing of the river the fresh sea breeze dropped behind, and by sunset it died away altogether. The sails sagged limp and soundless, and the *Dolphin* rolled sickeningly in midstream. On one or two evenings a temporary breeze raised their hopes and sent the ship ahead a few miles, only to die away again. In the morning Kit could scarcely tell that they had moved. The dense brown forest on either side never seemed to vary, and ahead there was only a new bend in the river to tantalize her. (Speare, 1958, pp. 14–15)

In addition to a greater richness and originality of language, *The Witch of Blackbird Pond* has a more complex plot and more lifelike characters. It has the power to transport readers to another time and place. It enables them to see the world through the eyes of another person and to experience a wide range of deep emotions. Although readers may enjoy *Sweet Valley High*, they will not have the depth of experience that may be evoked by *The Witch of Blackbird Pond*.

CHECKUP

1. What demands do context area textbooks make on the reader?
2. How do texts from different content areas make different demands on the reader?

Carefully Constructed Texts Make a Difference

In their study of history texts, Beck, McKeown, Sinatra, and Loxterman (1991) found a number of deficiencies that made textbooks difficult to understand. As Armbruster (1996) points out, considerate texts "say a lot about a few ideas rather than a little about many ideas. . . . By sacrificing depth for breadth, textbooks often fail to explain concepts and clarify the relationships among ideas in a way that matches the topic knowledge of the intended audience" (p. 55). Beck and her colleagues (1991) revised a segment of a history text by clarifying confusing elements, elaborating and explaining key events, making connections explicit, and explaining why the groups acted the way they did so readers could understand their motivation. They explained key terms, such as *intolerable*, that are necessary for an understanding of the text but would probably be unfamiliar. They also broke up sentences so that they would be less dense. In addition, they filled in important background information students might lack that would facilitate their understanding of the passage. In making these revisions, they doubled the length of the text. However, comprehension of the reader-friendly passage was dramatically better: Students recalled 25 percent more information and were able to answer nearly twice as many comprehension questions.

A text is reader friendly when authors go out of their way to make their writing as clear and understandable as possible, when they carefully consider their readers as they write. Reader-friendly texts use headings to announce main ideas, define words in context, and give plenty of examples. Notice how the author of a popular book on weather, excerpted below, uses questions, examples, and analogies to make a difficult concept comprehensible. Note, too, that the author does not assume background knowledge that the reader may not possess. He begins by explaining the states of water, an understanding of which is necessary in order to grasp the concept of *humidity*.

Moisture and Humidity

In all my years of teaching and talking about the weather, I have never encountered a concept more difficult to grasp than humidity. If you make it through the next few pages, the rest of the book will be a breeze. [This alerts the reader to read slowly and carefully because a difficult concept is being explained.]

Let's start off by recognizing that water can exist in three different states: solid, liquid, and vapor. All states consist of the molecule H_2O; the only difference concerns the spacing of the molecules. The following figure depicts these different states. As a solid, the water molecules are closest together. As a vapor, the molecules are farthest apart. So, the whole story here hinges on what makes these molecules drift apart, or come together. Any guesses? [The question prompts readers to become active and to predict why molecules drift apart, or come together, something that proficient readers do.]

How about temperature? Think of the molecules as popcorn in a popper. When the heat is first turned on, the kernels are just sitting there, solidly, on the bottom of the popper. But then, as heat is added and the temperature increases, the kernels start popping, and the popped corn starts moving around. Like popcorn, water vapor molecules are bouncing around, thanks to heat in the atmosphere. The water molecules are far enough apart that the vapor is invisible. The vapor itself comes from the water that is evaporated from the earth's surface, including oceans and lakes (Goldstein, 2002, pp. 13–14) . [The use of analogy makes an abstract concept concrete. It also invites the reader to visualize the process, which is an excellent aid to comprehension and retention.]

In subsequent passages, the author uses illustrations, examples, and the analogy of a glass that overflows if too much water is poured into it to explain humidity. Part of what makes the text understandable is that the author took the time to provide a detailed, step-by-step explanation. Some science texts provide a highly condensed version of this process that omits the helpful examples and analogies that make such a difficult concept comprehensible.

Today's texts incorporate a number of features that foster understanding and retention. The Prentice Hall United States History Program, for instance, incorporates Understanding by Design and Essential Questions, which help students focus on key ideas. The traditional text, *Biology* (Miller & Levine, 2009), has a Foundations version; designed for struggling students, this edition has fewer pages, is written at a lower level, and includes learning strategies. Vocabulary is highlighted and previewed; prefixes, suffixes, and roots are explained; and word origins are provided. Each section ends with a check on understanding. Students are directed to use graphic organizers and other devices to foster comprehension of the material. At the end of each section, there is a key question whose response summarizes the main point of that section. Because the answer to the question is included, students should provide their own answer first and then check it against the one given in the text. A workbook of reading strategies accompanies the textbook.

Holt's World Geography Today (Sager, & Helgren, 2008) presents three guide questions to help students set purposes for reading and provides a reading strategy, such as visualizing or using graphic organizers. Technical vocabulary words are defined in context in the text. Reading Checks, which ask questions about key concepts, are presented throughout each chapter. Generous use is made of heads and subheads. Each section ends with a review that contains an exercise designed to have students summarize, organize, and evaluate what they have learned. The tools of the geographer—mapping and graphing—are emphasized.

Electronic Textbooks

Electronic texts have a number of helpful features. *Holt's World Geography Today* (Sager, & Helgren, 2008) is accompanied by video clips, interactive maps, graphic organizers that can be completed online, a grapher, current events features, a researcher tool that allows students to consult other social studies sources, and content updates. In *CK-12 Basic Algebra* (Gloag, Gloag, & Kramer, 2010), film clips are included in which a teacher works out sample problems that illustrate the mathematical operations being discussed. Because digital text is easily updated, the problem of having outdated texts could be eliminated. In addition, e-books are appealing: Students who are reluctant to take a physical text home might be willing to read and respond to an online text. Many online texts also are less expensive to license than it would be to purchase sets of class texts. For these reasons, a number of school districts have switched to e-texts.

Some digital texts, such as FlexBooks, which are digital texts produced free of charge by CK-12 Foundation (www.ck12.org/) can be personalized. Teachers can add features, change content, or even simplify the texts. Digital texts can be easily searched and, if they are presented in a format that permits copying, lend themselves to cut-and-paste note taking. Perhaps best of all, by using a text-to-speech feature, the books can be read aloud to students who have limited reading proficiency. Of course, digital texts aren't as handy to read, but sections can be printed out for students who want a hard copy.

Value of Textbooks

Heavily criticized for proving inclusive but shallow coverage, textbooks have been abandoned or bypassed by many teachers. However, when used with other sources and under the teacher's guidance, textbooks can be a valuable reference and provide a framework for your course. "Helping students learn how to read science and social studies textbooks is an important element of helping them to learn the concepts related to content area instruction" (Fairbanks, Roser, Schallert, 2008, p. 29).

CHECKUP

1. What are some of the characteristics of a carefully constructed text?
2. In what way does a carefully constructed text help the reader?
3. What are some helpful learning features of online texts?

Assessing Texts

Because texts are a key teaching tool in most content area classes and can make a significant difference in students' learning, they should be carefully assessed. It is essential that students be able to read their texts. When assessing the demands made by content area texts, factor in both the author's style and the reading aids that the author includes. Text features that hinder comprehension include: difficult or unfamiliar language, ambiguous

or distant references, failure to provide information that will enable the reader to activate appropriate background knowledge, lack of clear connections between ideas or events, inclusion of irrelevant material, and a high density of ideas.

The difficulty level of material is also influenced by the organization of a text. A text that is well organized and well written is easier to understand. Elaboration, or developing ideas fully, makes a text easier to comprehend (Coleman, 1971), as does repeating key ideas (Kintsch, Kozminisky, Streby, McKoon, & Keenan, 1975). Using comprehension aids also lowers the difficulty level of a text. An introductory overview, headings, and questions placed before and after the text and interspersed within the text can aid comprehension (Zakaluk & Samuels, 1988). Explicitly stating instructional objectives can also foster understanding (Anderson, 1980). Charts, tables, maps, photos, drawings, phonetic respellings of difficult words, defining words in context, and a glossary are other features that aid the reader. Interest is also a factor in estimating the difficulty level of a text. Students may put forth extra effort if they have a strong interest in the text. Table 2.1 contains a number of subjective factors that may be considered when assessing texts.

TABLE 2.1 Subjective Readability Index

TEXT FACTORS			LOW		HIGH	
Content						
Familiarity of concepts	1	2	3	4	5	
Concreteness of concepts	1	2	3	4	5	
Style						
Clarity of writing	1	2	3	4	5	
Elaboration of key concepts	1	2	3	4	5	
Ease of vocabulary	1	2	3	4	5	
Simplicity of sentences	1	2	3	4	5	
Use of anecdotes	1	2	3	4	5	
Relates text to students' background	1	2	3	4	5	
Organization						
Use of heads, subheads	1	2	3	4	5	
Focus on major ideas	1	2	3	4	5	
Logical flow of ideas	1	2	3	4	5	
Exclusion of irrelevant material	1	2	3	4	5	
Features That Enhance Comprehension						
Chapter overview	1	2	3	4	5	
Summary	1	2	3	4	5	
Questions	1	2	3	4	5	
Graphics	1	2	3	4	5	
Film clips & recordings	1	2	3	4	5	
Phonemic respellings	1	2	3	4	5	
Definitions provided in text	1	2	3	4	5	
Glossary	1	2	3	4	5	
Text-to-speech capability	1	2	3	4	5	
Total (The higher the total, the easier the text)						
Reader Factors	1	2	3	4	5	
Background of knowledge	1	2	3	4	5	
Vocabulary	1	2	3	4	5	
Overall reading ability	1	2	3	4	5	
Interest	1	2	3	4	5	
Motivation	1	2	3	4	5	
Study/work habits	1	2	3	4	5	
Total (The higher the number, the better the reader)						

Source: Gunning, Thomas G., *Creating Literacy Instruction for All Students in Grades 4 to 8*, 3rd ed., © 2012. Printed and electronically produced by permission of Pearson Education, Inc., Upper Saddle River, New Jersey.

Subjective Estimate of Readability

Fostering literacy in the content areas requires teachers to be aware of the complexities of the texts that students will be reading as well as the demands that these texts will make on students. A good starting point is to estimate the overall difficulty level of the text. This can be done either subjectively or objectively, or by using a combination of objective and subjective methods. The quickest and perhaps most widely used technique for estimating text difficulty is teacher judgment. Unfortunately, teacher judgment can be inaccurate. In one study, the teachers' judgments differed by as much as six years from estimates yielded by a readability formula (Jorgenson, 1975). Teacher judgment can be greatly improved if guidelines and anchor passages are used to help estimate difficulty levels (Carver, 1975–1976; Chall, Bissex, Conrad, & Harris-Sharples, 1996; Singer, 1975). Listed in Figure 2.1 are science anchor passages arranged in order of difficulty. Passages are provided for grades 4, 6,

---

FIGURE 2.1
Science Anchor Passages

Grade 4

Concepts are concrete and include *disease* and *germs,* which have probably been introduced in school. An estimated 15–20 percent of sixth and seventh graders read at a fourth-grade level or lower. Smaller percentages at levels 8–12 will be reading at this level or lower.

Don't forget to wash your hands! Eat all your vegetables. You'd better clean that cut. It's late; go to sleep! Have you ever heard these reminders? They're all good things for you to do because each can help your body fight disease.

The best way to help your body fight disease is to keep your body healthy. You can do this by eating well, getting regular exercise, and getting enough sleep. These things will help your body stay strong so that it can fight germs. Keeping your body clean will also help keep germs from entering your body. (Badders et al., 1999a, F 54)

Grade 6

Sentences are moderately long and vocabulary is mostly familiar, but include words such as *diet, grains, benefits, sparingly,* and *flexible.* Concepts are somewhat abstract, and some of the content is likely to be unfamiliar. An estimated 25 percent of eighth graders read at a sixth-grade level or lower. Smaller percentages at levels 9 -12 will be reading at this level or lower

Perhaps one of the most important steps in building healthful habits is to learn to eat in a healthful way. If the food you eat isn't healthful or if you eat too much or too little, then your body won't be as healthy as it can be.

Meats and milk products should make up less of your diet than grains, fruits, and vegetables. And some of the foods that many people like best, including sugary and fatty foods, should be eaten sparingly. Some fat is needed in the diet. But generally people take in too much fat, causing them to gain weight. To cut down on fat in your diet, choose lean meats and avoid fatty food.

Generally there is only one way to maintain proper weight—have a healthful diet and get regular exercise. Exercise has other benefits—it promotes a healthy heart, good lungs, strong muscles, a flexible body, and a feeling of well being. (Badders et al., 1999b, G59-60)

Grade 8

Sentences are longer and more complex. Vocabulary is definitely more advanced and includes technical words such as *pathogen, circulatory, respiratory,* and *resistance.* Concepts are becoming more abstract, and density of concepts has increased. More than 25 percent of students in grades 9-12 read at this level or lower.

One way to stay healthy is to avoid contact with pathogens. If someone has an infectious disease, avoid close contact. Wash your hands before handling food and eating. Prepare and store food properly and do not eat food that has spoiled. What are some other ways you can avoid contact with pathogens? Another way to protect yourself against disease is to practice good health habits. Good health habits promote your resistance, or ability to fight pathogens. Studies show that healthful practices begun at an early age make it more likely that you will be a healthy adult. What kind of practices help you stay healthy? First, be sure to get regular exercise. Your heart and blood vessels are strengthened by exercise. Exercise also relieves stress. Stress often lowers your resistance to infection. Second, get enough sleep. Most teenagers require seven to eight hours of sleep each night. Too little sleep can lower your resistance to pathogens. Third, eat a nutritious diet. Start off each day with breakfast. Many teenagers skip breakfast, but your growing body needs three meals a day. . . . It's also important to eat fewer fatty foods, like butter, and fewer foods high in cholesterol, like eggs. These foods contribute to heart and circulatory diseases. Fourth, avoid tobacco and alcohol. By not smoking, you're protecting your body from respiratory disease. By not drinking alcohol, you are protecting your body from many diseases of the heart, stomach, and liver. Fifth, have regular medical checkups. (Warner et al., 1991, p. 477)

Grade 10

Syntax and vocabulary have become advanced. Concept density is high, and vocabulary has become abstract and technical. Readers need a fairly good background in biology in order to comprehend this passage fully.

Although the body is able to manufacture many of the molecules it needs, it must still obtain the materials for this from the food it takes in. The classes of nutrients that are part of any healthy diet are water, carbohydrates, fats, proteins, vitamins, and minerals.

Water

Water is the most important of all nutrients. Water is needed by every cell in our body, and it makes up the bulk of blood, lymph, and other body fluids. Water dissolves food taken into the digestive system. Water in the form of sweat cools the body. Water is lost from the body as vapor in every breath we exhale and as the primary component of urine. If enough water—at least a liter a day—is not taken in to replace what is lost, dehydration can result. This leads to problems with the circulatory, respiratory, and nervous systems. Drinking plenty of pure water is one of the best things you can do to help keep your body healthy. (Miller & Levine, 1998, p. 852)

Grade 12–adult

Sentences are generally long and complicated, and vocabulary is advanced. There is a high proportion of relatively difficult words. Concept density is high, and considerable background knowledge is required.

The health and fitness benefits of physical activity cannot be overstated: Exercise is essential for maintaining cardiovascular fitness, muscle strength, stamina, balance, and joint flexibility. Strength-developing exercise improves overall musculoskeletal health, and stretching maintains flexibility. Physical activity also increases energy level, improves mood, and diminishes anxiety and stress. Exercise can be beneficial in avoiding weight gain and in helping replace fat with muscle.

Moderate exercise performed consistently can prevent or control heart disease and diabetes. Higher levels of physical activity are linked with increased levels of high density lipoprotein (HDL), the "good" cholesterol in the blood. If you are a smoker, increasing your level of physical activity may motivate you to cut down on your smoking. Women who exercise may lessen the debilitating effects of osteoporosis, or avoid the disease altogether. Physical activity is also one of the best means we have of ensuring that we age well and enjoy life more fully. Exercise can even increase life expectancy. (Klag, 1999, p. 33)

8, 10, and 12. Accompanying each text selection is a brief description of the language, background, idea density, and cognitive level of the passage. Using the passages and descriptions as a guide, select the difficulty level from the passages in Figure 2.1 that seem most like the passage you are assessing. If the passage seems to be between two of the scaling passages, place it between the two; if it seems harder than passage 8 but easier than passage 10, place it at level 9. If in doubt, err on the conservative side. If you can't decide between the two levels, choose the higher level. It is better to give students a passage that is a little on the easy side than one that is too difficult. After estimating the difficulty level of the passage, note the skills and knowledge that the average student in that grade would have to bring to the passage to read it successfully. Consider the subjective factors noted in Table 2.1. If you are estimating the difficulty level of a textbook, examine three or four sample passages of about 100 words each and average the results of your estimates.

Teachers can use a number of Web sites to check the readability level of texts.

Source: Ilene MacDonald/Alamy.

The passages in Figure 2.1 can be used to estimate the **readability** of passages in subject matter areas other than science, but they provide the most valid results when used with science passages. A better instrument is the *Qualitative Assessment of Text Difficulty* (Chall et al., 1996). Based on research that indicates that different types of text require different kinds of background and types of strategies, the *Qualitative Assessment of Text Difficulty* has six scales: one for popular fiction, one for literature, one for biographical and narrative history, one for expository history, one for the biological sciences, and one for the physical sciences. Most of the scales contain nine levels and range in difficulty from grade 1 through college. To estimate the difficulty level of a text, the user chooses the most appropriate scale and then selects 100-word samples and compares them with the scaled passages. When teachers used these scales, their judgments were within one year of the quantitative readabilities of texts nearly 100 percent of the time (Chall et al., 1996).

Using Objective Measures to Estimate Readability

Along with subjective measures of readability, you also may use an objective formula. **Readability formulas** have a long history of use for checking the difficulty level of texts. Although there are many factors involved in determining the difficulty level of a text, the two factors that have the highest correlation with text difficulty are sentence complexity and difficulty of vocabulary. Sentence or syntactic complexity is typically assessed through sentence length. Although some short sentences are more complex than some long sentences, on average, the longer the sentence, the more difficult it tends to be. This is also true of words. Although some short words are hard and some long words are relatively easy, on average, the longer the word or the more syllables it has, the more difficult it is. Word length and number of syllables are frequently used as measures of vocabulary difficulty. However, some formulas determine difficulty level by calculating the proportion of words not on a list of easy or high-frequency words or determining the frequency with which the words appear in print.

Syllable Formulas

Because of its ease of use, the Fry Readability Graph is one of the most popular readability formulas. The Fry Graph, shown in Figure 2.2, measures sentence length and the number of syllables in a word. Appearing in a number of popular word processing programs, including Microsoft Word, the Flesch-Kincaid formula is also widely used. It, too, measures sentence length and number of syllables in a word and correlates very highly with the Fry Graph (Fusaro, 1988). In Word, it can be found in Tools: Spelling and Grammar. (You may have to use the Preferences [Options in PCs] menu to activate it. To avoid checking grammar, uncheck all grammar items under Settings.) After spelling and grammar have been checked, click on NO when you get the message: "Word finished checking the selection. Do you want to continue checking the remainder of the document?"

Word List Formulas

A number of readability formulas use the proportion of words not appearing on a word list of familiar words instead of number of syllables as a measure of vocabulary difficulty.

One of the most carefully validated word list formulas is the New Dale-Chall Readability Formula (Chall & Dale, 1995). The New Dale-Chall can be used to estimate the difficulty level

■ **Readability** is the difficulty level of a selection.

■ **Readability formulas** are objective measurements of the difficulty level of reading material. They generally consist of some measure of the average sentence length and the proportion of hard words in a selection.

FIGURE 2.2 Fry Graph for Estimating Readability

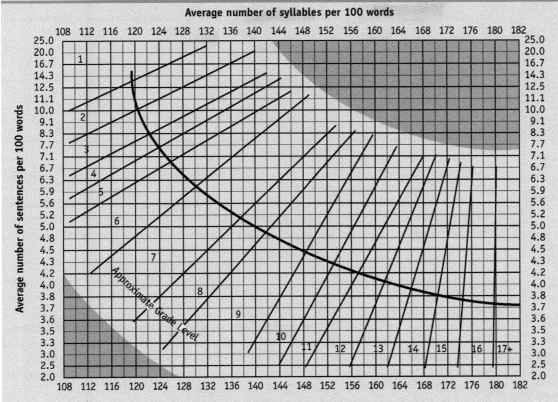

Average number of syllables per 100 words

Expanded Directions for Working Readability Graph

1. Randomly select three (3) sample passages and count out exactly 100 words each, beginning with the beginning of a sentence. Do count proper nouns, initializations, and numerals.

2. Count the number of sentences in the 100 words, estimating length of the fraction of the last sentence to the nearest one-tenth.

3. Count the total number of syllables in the 100-word passage. If you don't have a hand counter available, an easy way is to simply put a mark above every syllable over one in each word, then when you get to the end of the passage, count the number of marks and add 100. Small calculators can also be used by pushing numeral 1, then the + sign for each word or syllable when counting.

4. Enter graph with *average* sentence length and *average* number of syllables; plot dot where the two lines

intersect. Area where dot is plotted will give you the approximate grade level.

5. If a great deal of variability is found in syllable count or sentence count, putting more samples into the average is desirable.

6. A word is defined as a group of symbols with space on either side; thus, *Joe, IRA, 1945,* and *&* are each one word.

7. A syllable is defined as a phonetic syllable. Generally, there are as many syllables as vowel sounds. For example, *stopped* is one syllable and *wanted* is two syllables. When counting syllables for numerals and initializations, count one syllable for each symbol. For example, *1945* is four syllables, *IRA* is three syllables, and *&* is one syllable.

Source: "Fry's Readability Graph: Clarifications, Validity, and Extension to Level 17" by E. Fry, 1977, *Journal of Reading*, 21, p. 249.

of material from grade 1 through grade 16, but it is most valid for materials in the grade 3 to grade 12 range.

Formulas That Require Computers

Three widely used formulas are so complex that they require computers: the Degrees of Reading Power (DRP), the Lexile Scale, and ATOS. The Degrees of Reading Power measures sentence length, number of words not on the Revised Dale List, and average number of letters per word (Touchstone Applied Science Associates, 1994). Most readability formulas report their estimates in grade equivalent scores—for instance, 5.2, 9.7,

TABLE 2.2 **DRP and Lexile Scores**

GRADE EQUIVALENT	DRP SCORE	LEXILE SCORE
2	24–33	400–500
3	34–42	500–700
4	43–49	700–800
5	50–55	800–900
6	56–59	900–1000
7	60–63	1000–1100
8	64–66	1000–1100
9–12	67–70	1100–1300

7–8. However, the Degrees of Reading Power reports its levels in DRP Units. Table 2.2 translates DRP units into grade equivalent scores.

The Lexile Scale is a two-factor formula that consists of a measurement of sentence length and word frequency. It is now the most widely used readability measure. All major standardized reading tests and many popular literacy programs report student reading scores in Lexiles. There are currently Lexile measures for more than 100,000 books and 80 million articles. Some students describe themselves in terms of Lexiles. When interviewed about their perceptions of themselves as readers, many of the students in an intervention class described themselves and their progress in terms of Lexiles, "I moved up 60 Lexiles. I am at Lexile 550" (O'Brien et al., 2009).

ATOS (Advantage-TASA Open Standard) uses number of words per sentence, characters per word, and average grade level of words to analyze the entire text to estimate the readability of a book. The estimate is expressed as a grade-level equivalent. Most ATOS scores are available from Renaissance Learning, at www.arbookfind.com. The organization will also do a readability analysis of texts for which it does not have scores. Table 2.3 presents a comparison of readabilities yielded by the Lexile, ATOS, and DRP.

Estimating Demands Made by Texts

Although it is helpful to know the overall readability level of a text, it is also important to know what demands the text will place on students in the following areas: language complexity, including vocabulary and sentence structure; background knowledge, including general background knowledge and subject-specific knowledge; density and difficulty of ideas; and reasoning skills required to comprehend the text. As you look over a text, ask yourself the question: What does the reader need to bring to the text in order to be able to understand it? The answer will help you select texts that are on the appropriate levels for your students. It will also aid you in providing instruction and strategies that will help your students better understand their texts.

C H E C K U P

1. How should the difficulty level of a textbook be assessed?
2. Why is it important to use both subjective and objective factors?

Making the Match Between Reader and Text

Knowing the difficulty level of a passage is only half the equation. Next, you need to find out what difficulty level of material your students can handle by determining their overall reading levels. A student's reading ability is an estimate of the level of difficulty of the material that he or she will be able to read. A student with a ninth-grade reading ability should be able to read ninth-grade texts with reasonable comprehension. Of course, students' reading ability varies with the kind of text being read, the student's knowledge of the topic, and the student's interest and motivation. Therefore, it is also helpful if you

TABLE 2.3 Comparison of Readability Estimates Yielded by Different Computer Formulas

	LEXILE	ATOS	DRP
Across Five Aprils	1000 (7–8)	6.6	59 (8)
Animal Farm	1130 (9–10)	7.3	60 (9–10)
Banner in the Sky	680 (3)	5.1	51 (4)
Brian's Winter	1140 (9–10)	5.9	54 (6)
Call It Courage	830 (5)	6.2	55 (6)
The Call of the Wild	1140 (9–10)	8.0	62 (9–10)
Catcher in the Rye	790 (4)	4.7	49 (3)
The Chocolate War	790 (4)	5.4	56 (7)
The Fighting Ground	580 (3)	4.2	50 (4)
Flowers for Algernon	910 (6)	5.8	55 (6)
Go Tell It on the Mountain	1030 (7–8)	6.5	59 (8)
The Great Gatsby	1205 (11–12)	7.3	61 (9–10)
Hiroshima	1190 (9–10)	8.4	64 (9–10)
Let the Circle Be Unbroken	850 (5)	5.7	53 (5)
Lord of the Flies	770 (4)	5.0	58 (8)
The Outsiders	820 (5)	5.3	51 (4)
The Pearl	1010 (7)	7.1	58 (8)
The Scarlet Letter	1420 (12+)	11.7	67 (11–12)
A Separate Peace	1110 (9–10)	6.9	59 (8)
Where the Lilies Bloom	920 (6)	5.2	53 (5)

Note: Numbers in parentheses are approximate grade level equivalents of Lexile and DRP scores.

have information about their language ability, background knowledge, reasoning skills, and ability to read the type of text generally used in your content area.

If your class if fairly typical, you will find a wide range of abilities among your students. To estimate the range of reading levels in a heterogeneously grouped class, multiply the average chronological age by 2/3. Thus, if the average age of your tenth-graders is fifteen, then there may be a span of ten reading levels (2/3 × 15 = 10) ranging from grade 5 through grade 15.

There are numerous ways to obtain students' instructional levels. The most valid approach is to administer an **informal reading inventory (IRI)**. In an informal reading inventory, students are asked to read a series of passages that gradually increase in difficulty. The goal is to locate the highest reading level at which the student can read both with and without some assistance by the teacher (**instructional** and **independent** levels). and the level at which the material is simply too difficult

■ **The informal reading inventory** is a placement test that consists of a series of word lists and selections that grow increasingly difficult. The objective of the test is to find the highest levels at which students can read on their own independently and with help.

■ **The instructional** level is the level of material that a student can read with 95 to 98 percent word recognition and 70 to 89 percent comprehension.

■ **The independent level** is the level of material that a student can read with at least 99 percent word recognition and 90 percentage comprehension.

TABLE 2.4 **Commercial Reading Inventories**

NAME	AUTHORS	GRADES
Bader Reading and Language Inventory	Bader & Pearce	1–12 & adult
Burns/Roe Informal Reading	Roe & Burns Inventory	1–12 & adult
Comprehensive Reading Inventory	Cooter, Flynt, & Cooter	1–12
Critical Reading Inventory: Assessing Students Reading and Thinking	Applegate	1–12
Ekwall/Shanker Reading Inventory	Shanker & Ekwall	1–12
English-Espanol Reading Inventory for the Classroom	Flynt & Cooter	1–12
Informal Reading-Thinking Inventory	Manzo, Manzo, & McKenna	1–11
Informal Reading Inventory	Burns & Roe	1–12
Qualitative Reading Inventory IV	Leslie & Caldwell	1–12
READ: Reading Evaluation Adult Diagnosis	Colvin & Root	Adult
Reading Inventory for the Classroom	Flynt & Cooter	1–12

(**frustration** level). A list of commercial inventories that have passages that range from first through twelfth grade is presented in Table 2.4. Unfortunately, administering an informal reading inventory is fairly time consuming because each student must be evaluated individually, so it may not be practical unless you are in a self-contained class or teach small groups of students. Administering IRIs also requires training. However, if you have the training and the time, this is an excellent way to get valid levels and also to get to know your students and their reading abilities better.

Group reading inventories are the next best method for obtaining placement. To administer a group inventory, select a typical passage (about 200 to 300 words long) from a content area text that is of average difficulty. Create a series of eight to ten questions, as shown in Figure 2.3. Most questions should be on a literal level, but ask two or three that require students to make inferences, summarize information, or identify main ideas. The questions may require constructed responses, in which students have to compose answers, or they may be multiple choice. Constructed response questions provide more insight into the students' reasoning processes and writing abilities. Although they are more time consuming to compose, multiple-choice questions are easier to correct. Explain the purpose of the inventory and briefly introduce the passage. Ask a topic-related question that will set the purpose for reading the selection and also provide an opportunity for you to assess students' background knowledge. The Qualitative Reading Inventory-5 (Leslie & Caldwell, 2010) functions as a group inventory. At levels three and higher, it can be given to groups of students.

Once a purpose has been set, observe students as they read. Note especially signs that they are having difficulty with the text, including puzzled expressions, lip movement, frowning, or asking about difficult vocabulary. After they have finished reading the selection, students respond to the questions that you have provided. When all have finished, discuss the selection, starting with the purpose question. During the discussion, note the adequacy of students' comprehension and also their ability to go back over the passage to find verifying information and read it aloud to the class.

After scoring students' responses and considering your observations of their work, note how many were able to handle the text. The criterion is 70 to 75 percent comprehension. For students for whom the text seems too difficult, try one on an easier level. For those who were not challenged, try a more difficult text. You might also retest low-scoring students with an individual informal reading inventory or simply have them read portions of the text aloud. At this point, you want to see whether low comprehension scores are due to poor decoding skills. If lack of decoding is not a problem—if low scores are due to inadequate comprehension—students may need added preparation before reading, more background building, or instruction in effective comprehension strategies.

■ The frustration level is the level at which the student's word recognition is 90 percentage or less or comprehension is 50 percentage or less.

Read "Progress and Reason" and "Two Views of the Social Contract" on pp. 446 and 447. Then answer the questions below.

What contribution did Lavoisier and Priestly make?

What did Jenner discover?

What are natural laws?

What did Enlightenment thinkers believe they could do?

Why do you think this period was given the name Enlightenment?

What did Hobbes believe people were like?

What kind of government did Hobbes believe was necessary?

What did Locke believe people were like?

What kind of government did Locke believe was best?

Whose ideas, Hobbes's or Locke's, were most influential in shaping the government of the United States? Explain your choice.

FIGURE 2.3
Sample Group Reading Inventory

Once you have collected and examined all the data, decide on the text(s) that best fit students' needs. Make adjustments for those for whom the text is too difficult or too easy.

Commercial Group Inventories

Some national tests, such as the Degrees of Reading Power, are designed to yield an instructional level. The Metropolitan Achievement Tests, one of the few sets of norm-referenced standardized tests designed to provide placement information, also provide instructional levels. The Scholastic Reading Inventory, which yields scores in Lexile units, and STAR, a computerized placement test published by Accelerated Reader, also provide estimated reading levels. These estimated reading levels should be verified by noting how well students handle their text.

A quick but efficient way to obtain an estimate of students' reading levels is to administer the Reading-Level Indicator (Pearson AGS). The Indicator is a brief test that contains forty multiple choice items, consisting of twenty vocabulary items (sample shown below) and twenty sentence comprehension items (sample shown below). The Indicator yields estimated instructional and independent reading levels. Tests come in two forms so that they may be used for pre- and post-test assessment. The Indicator can be used with students in the upper elementary grades through college.

The Reading-Level Indicator has a companion version in Spanish. Giving both versions of the test will help you to determine the comparative literacy abilities of students in both

EXAMPLE FOR VOCABULARY	EXAMPLE FOR SENTENCE COMPREHENSION
Ex. Slice the apple.	Ex. Where have you _____ all this time?
_____ a. cut	_____ a. left
_____ b. polish	_____ b. seen
_____ c. sling	_____ c. put
_____ d. deliver	_____ d. been
_____ e. bake	_____ e. done
(Pearson AGS, 2002)	

English and Spanish. You may find that a Spanish-speaking student who obtains a low score on the English version has a high level of reading ability in Spanish. Such a student will become a good reader in English once his knowledge of English improves. A Spanish-speaking student who scores low in both languages will need intensive instruction in reading. Some caution needs to be exercised in interpreting scores. The Spanish version is just a translation of the English version. Therefore, the difficulty of the items in Spanish may not be the same as the difficulty level in English.

FIGURE 2.4 **Sample Cloze Passage**

Standard time. Americans loved speed. And railroads made it _____ for them to race _____ the continent faster than _____ before. The trains that _____ from city to city _____ strange new problems. One _____ that had not been _____ till then was that _____ town had its own _____ set to its own _____ time. The astronomers said _____ it was "noon" when _____ saw the sun reach _____ zenith—the highest point _____ the heavens. Since the _____ was constantly in motion, _____ since the sun rose _____ when you were more _____ the east, then whether _____ was yet noon obviously _____ on *where* you were.

_____ what this meant for _____ railroad! The Pennsylvania Railroad _____ to use Philadelphia time _____ its eastern lines. But _____ was five minutes earlier _____ New York time and five _____ later than Baltimore time. _____ Indiana there were 23 _____ local times. In Illinois _____ were 27, and in Wisconsin 38.

_____ railroads used the local _____ for their arrival in _____ station. In between cities _____ was the greatest confusion. _____ for speeding trains a _____ minutes could make the _____ between a clear track _____ a fatal collision.

Finally _____ was suggested that instead _____ "sun time" they should _____ a new kind of "time" which would be "_____ time."

For the United States _____ a whole, you could _____ off on a map _____ few conspicuous time belts _____ and down the whole _____. You would only need four: _____ time, central time, mountain _____, and Pacific time—each several hundred miles wide. Standard time would be exactly the same for all places within each zone. (Boorstin & Kelley, 2002, p. 415)

Answers:
possible, across, ever, sped, brought, trouble, noticed, every, clocks, particular, that, you, its, in, earth, and, sooner, to, it, depended, imagine, a, tried, on, that, than, minutes, In, different, there, most, time, each, there, yet, few, difference, and, of, use, railroad, standard, as, mark, a, up, country, eastern, time

TABLE 2.5 **Scoring Cloze**

LEVEL	PERCENTAGE
Independent	> 57
Instructional	44–57
Frustration	< 44

■ **Cloze** is a procedure in which the reader demonstrates comprehension by supplying missing words. *Cloze* is short for *closure*, which is the tendency to fill in missing or incomplete information.

Cloze Procedure

Instead of creating questions for a group reading inventory, you can use a fill-in-the-blank device know as cloze. Short for *closure*, **cloze** is a procedure in which students read selections from which words have been deleted. A sample cloze passage is presented in Figure 2.4. In classic cloze, every fifth word is deleted from a 250-word passage, so that there are a total of 50 missing words (see Figure 2.4). The first and last sentences are left intact, and no proper nouns or numbers are removed. Students use their background knowledge, language ability, and reading ability to predict and fill in the missing words. Passages are scored according to how many words students are able to replace. Exact replacements are required; otherwise, scoring becomes too subjective. However, standards are more lenient than those of traditional tests. The **instructional level** is 44 to 57 percent. See Table 2.5.

Some students may be dismayed by the unfamiliar format, so give a few practice passages before using cloze as a placement device. Cloze works best when the passages are close to the students' actual reading levels. On easy passages, students tend to supply synonyms rather than exact replacements, even though their comprehension of the passage may be quite good. The substitutions, of course, are counted as errors and may lead to an underestimation of the students' reading ability (Smith, W. L., 1978). Vocabulary also plays a major role in students' performance. If the replacement word is not a familiar one, students will not be able to supply it. Had they been reading an intact passage, they might have been able to infer the meaning of the unfamiliar word and thus maintained comprehension.

Before administering a cloze test, the teacher explains the nature of cloze, gives tips for completing the exercise, and models the process of completing a cloze activity. Tips may include:

■ Read the whole exercise first.
■ Use all the clues given in a passage.
■ Read past the blank to the end of the sentence. Sometimes the best clues come after a blank.

- If necessary, read a sentence or two ahead to get additional clues.
- Spell as best you can. You lose no points for misspelled words.
- Do your best, but do not worry if you cannot correctly complete each blank. Most readers will be able to fill in fewer than half the blanks correctly.
- After you have filled in as many blanks as you can, reread the selection. Make any changes you think are necessary. (Gunning, 2003)

Students also can be given some practice sessions so that they become familiar with the format. A versatile procedure, cloze is also used to foster comprehension and assess the readability of texts.

Word List Tests

One time-saving way to get a quick estimate of students' instructional levels is to administer a word list test. In a word list test, students read a series of words that gradually increase in difficulty. There is a close correlation between the ability to pronounce words in isolation and overall reading (Manzo & Manzo, 1993), so the results of the word list test can be used to estimate students' instructional reading levels. Of course, because they require only the ability to pronounce words, these tests neglect comprehension and may provide misleading levels for students who are superior decoders but poor comprehenders, or vice versa. Two widely used word list tests are the Wide Range Achievement Test (WRAT) and the Slosson Oral Reading Test (SORT). In a comparison of commercial and teacher-made informal reading inventories with the reading subtest of the WRAT, which requires only the pronouncing of isolated words, the WRAT yielded estimates that were one to two grade levels above the estimates yielded by the inventories (Bristow, Pikulski, & Pelosi, 1983). The Slosson Oral Reading Test, which also seems to overestimate students' reading levels by a year or two, presents twenty words at each grade level from beginning reading (preprimer) through grade 12.

Word Reading Survey

The Word Reading Survey, which is based on the San Diego Quick Assessment created by LaPray and Ross (1969), is a quick and easy-to-use informal word list test. The test consists of a series of graded words that range from beginning first grade through high school (see Figure 2.5). To administer the test, type the words on cards or present them in lists. Start at the beginning and continue to test until the student gets half the words on a level wrong. As the student reads, record his responses. This will provide insights into his word recognition needs. The student's estimated reading level is the highest level at which he can read seven or eight words out of ten. Note that this estimate is based only on the student's ability to pronounce printed words. Neither the ability to read words in context nor comprehension is assessed. The estimated level can be verified by having the student read a passage at that level or by observing the student's performance as he reads materials on his estimated reading level. Make adjustments as necessary.

Data from State or National Objective Tests

Data from state or national objective tests may also be used to indicate students' instructional levels. These tests yield **grade level equivalents**, **stanines**, **percentile ranks**, and **normal curve equivalents**. The grade level equivalent scores are sometimes interpreted as instructional reading levels, but that is incorrect. A grade level equivalent of 9.2 means that the test taker got the same number of items correct as the average ninth grader in the norm group that took the test in October (the second month of the

English Language Learners

Because they have a more limited English vocabulary, English language learners find cloze especially difficult. A modified cloze test such as the STAR or DRP or mazes in which students choose from possible responses would be a better assessment.

Struggling Readers

Despite its obvious limitations, the San Diego Quick Assessment, Word Reading Survey, or a similar word list test can be a useful device for identifying students who have serious word-reading difficulties or who are reading well below grade level.

- A grade level equivalent indicates the score that the average student at that grade level achieved.

- A stanine is a point on a nine-point scale, with 5 being average.

- A percentile rank is the point on a scale of 1 to 99 that shows what percentage of students obtained an equal or lower score. A percentile rank of 75 means that 75 percent of those who took the test received an equal or lower score.

- A normal curve equivalent is the rank on a scale of 1 through 99 that a score is equal to.

FIGURE 2.5 **Word Reading Survey**

1	2	3	4	5	6	7	8	9–12
I	please	branch	reason	escaped	absence	continuously	calculator	administrative
the	never	middle	distant	business	instinct	application	agriculture	spontaneous
we	hour	stronger	lonesome	continue	responsible	incredible	prohibited	molecule
go	climb	picture	silent	obedient	evaporate	maximum	legislation	ritual
hat	field	hunger	wrecked	entrance	convenience	environmental	translucent	recipient
help	spend	several	decided	applause	commercial	accumulate	astronomical	conscientious
coat	side	empty	certainly	government	necessary	geographical	optimistic	infectious
are	believe	since	favorite	celebration	recognition	triangular	narrate	beneficiary
how	happen	impossible	realized	microscope	vertical	pollutant	persuasive	affiliation
work	suddenly	straight	solution	navigate	starvation	currency	obnoxious	paralysis

school year). It doesn't necessarily mean that the student can read ninth-grade material—she may have made some good guesses. However, it does provide a reasonable estimate of what the student's reading level might be. If possible, use an individual inventory to check the students' levels, especially if they had very low scores.

If the test does not provide a grade-level equivalent score, giving only a stanine, percentile rank, and normal curve equivalent score, use these to estimate the student's instructional level. A stanine of 5 and percentile rank and normal curve equivalent of 50 are average, which suggests that the student is probably reading on grade level. A stanine of 4 and a percentile rank between 35 and 50 suggest that the student is probably reading a year or two below grade level. Lower stanines, percentile ranks, and normal curve equivalents indicate more serious underachievement. Stanines above 5 and percentile ranks and normal curve equivalents above 50 suggest above-average achievement.

Students' estimated levels should be verified with a group or individual reading inventory or by observing students' performance as they read their texts. This is especially true if students have low scores. Low scores are very untrustworthy and can be the result of guessing.

CHECKUP

1. Why is it important to match the reader and the text?
2. What are some ways to estimate students' reading levels?

Although matching students with texts that they can understand is complex and time-consuming, it may be the most important step teachers take in implementing an effective content area program. Students who are given texts that are on their level understand them better, work harder, behave better in class, and feel more confident about themselves as learners (R. Anderson, 1990; Gambrell, Wilson, & Gantt 1981).

Because most texts are written on or above grade level, matching below-level readers with materials they can handle poses a problem. Suggestions for making texts more accessible and locating materials for below-level readers are explored in Chapter 9.

Summary

Textbooks are the core of instruction in many content area classes. For as many as 25 to 40 percent of students in a typical secondary school, the textbooks used in their classes may be too difficult. The use of complex expository language, the

amount of background knowledge required, the density and difficulty of ideas, and increasing cognitive demands are the major factors that cause content area texts to be difficult. Although each content area makes its own set of demands on the reader, texts in all areas become more complex and demanding as students move up through the grades. The difficulty of texts can be assessed in a number of ways: objective formulas, comparison with benchmark books or passages, and use of checklists. There are three formulas that can be applied only with the aid of a computer: the DRP, Lexile Scale, and ATOS. Readability estimates of hundreds of content area texts are available on the Web, as are readability estimates of thousands of trade books. Because formulas measure only mechanical elements, the best procedure for assessing the difficulty level of a text is to use both objective and subjective measures.

To match students with texts, it is necessary to know students' reading levels. Students should be given texts in which

they know at least 95 percent of the words and understand at least 70 percent of what they read. Although individual informal reading inventories generally provide the most valid estimate of students' reading levels, group inventories and cloze tests can be used for that purpose. Most norm-referenced group tests do not yield reading levels; they simply tell how students did when compared with the norm group that took the test. However, the DRP and Metropolitan Reading Tests yield estimated levels, as do the Scholastic Reading Inventory, which yields scores in Lexile units, and STAR, a computerized test published by Accelerated Reader. Word list tests and the Reading-Level Indicator can also be used to estimate reading level. Estimated reading levels should be verified by noting how well students handle their texts.

Reflection

Return to the Anticipation Guide at the beginning of this chapter. Respond once again to the items. Did your responses change? If so, how and why? What is the responsibility of the content area teacher in terms of matching readers and texts?

Extension and Application

Examine three textbooks in your content area. What demands do the texts seem to be making on readers? What helpful aids do the textbooks contain?

Using one of the formulas mentioned in the chapter, assess the readability of a content area text. Use the benchmark passages to verify the estimated readability level. Also use Coh-Metrix to analyze text.

Construct and administer a group reading inventory to a content area class or use one of the group inventories or placement tests listed. What is the range of reading levels in the group? What seem to be the group's strengths and weaknesses?

 Where the Classroom Comes to Life

Go to Topic 7: Planning for Instruction in the MyEducationLab (www.myeducationlab.com) for your course, where you can:

- Find learning outcomes for Planning for Instruction along with the national standards that connect to these outcomes.
- Complete Assignments and Activities that can help you more deeply understand the chapter content.
- Apply and practice your understanding of the core teaching skills identified in the chapter with the Building Teaching Skills and Dispositions learning units.
- Examine challenging situations and cases presented in the IRIS Center Resources.

Go to the Topic A+RISE in the MyEducationLab (www.myeducationlab.com) for your course. A+RISE® Standards2Strategy™ is an innovative and interactive online resource that offers new teachers in grades K–12 just-in-time, research-based instructional strategies that:

- Meet the linguistic needs of ELLs as they learn content.
- Differentiate instruction for all grades and abilities.
- Offer reading and writing techniques, cooperative learning, use of linguistic and nonlinguistic representations, scaffolding, teacher modeling, higher-order thinking, and alternative classroom ELL assessment.
- Provide support to help teachers be effective through the integration of listening, speaking, reading, and writing along with the content curriculum.
- Improve student achievement.
- Are aligned to Common Core Elementary Language Arts standards (for the literacy strategies) and to English language proficiency standards in WIDA, Texas, California, and Florida.

CHAPTER 3

Building Content Area Vocabulary

For each of the following statements, put a check under "Agree" or "Disagree" to indicate your opinion. If possible, discuss your responses with classmates.

	Agree	Disagree
1. Most content area texts present too many new words.	_____	_____
2. It is better to teach a few key words in depth than to try to introduce all the new words contained in a content area text.	_____	_____
3. If a content area text contains more new words than students can handle, the teacher should obtain an easier text.	_____	_____
4. Part of the content teacher's responsibility is to teach students strategies and skills for learning new words.	_____	_____
5. The primary tool for learning new words is the dictionary.	_____	_____

Using What You Know

What made reading in the content areas difficult for you? For many students, the sheer number of technical terms to be learned is a challenge. How did you respond to the challenge of becoming proficient in the content vocabulary of your courses? What strategies did you use? How effective were they? What strategies would you teach your students?

Learning the Words

One of the chief barriers to learning in the content areas is posed by the technical vocabulary students must master in each subject. For instance, a section on the brain in a high school biology text contained fifteen technical terms on a single page. Each discipline has a specialized vocabulary used to label major concepts. The key to understanding the discipline is to become proficient in its vocabulary. In neuroscience, this would mean, in part, knowing the terms for the anatomy of the brain. However, what makes learning technical vocabulary especially challenging is that it usually isn't enough to learn a single technical word; it is often necessary to learn a cluster of terms (Nelson-Herber, 1986). For instance, it would be difficult to read even the most basic description of the brain without knowledge of such terms as *cerebral cortex, convolutions convoluted, hemispheres, corpus callosum, frontal, temporal*, and *parietal lobes, cerebrum, cerebellum, limbic system*, and *brain stem*.

The content area teacher must decide which technical terms the students should learn in order to be able to understand and discuss a concept. Current texts are overloaded with technical terms. One popular biology text includes 120 cell-related technical terms in its description of cells. In contrast, *Designs for Science Literacy* recommends just eleven technical terms (American Association for the Advancement of Science, 2001). Prestigious science reform groups fear that students view science as mainly a matter of memorizing technical vocabulary and often substitute memorization for genuine understanding. They recommend fostering understanding and then introducing technical vocabulary:

> Once students can understand that cells get energy from food and use the energy to put together complex proteins, their knowing such terms as "oxidation," "respiration," "mito-chondrion," and "ribosome" can be helpful, but learning the words without the basic notion is empty . . . Although Project 2061 recommends minimizing unnecessary technical terms,

it is committed to expanding students' useful scientific vocabulary. The correct use of technical vocabulary is to be applauded once they understand the meanings (American Association for the Advancement of Science, 2001, pp. 18–19).

In addition to the essential technical vocabulary required by the subject being studied, students should also have a solid general vocabulary. The section on the brain included the following general vocabulary words: *processes, routed, coordinates, efficiently, primary, automatic, response,* and *stimulus*.

Terms that need special attention in the content areas include the following:

Technical terms: Words, terms, and expressions that are peculiar to a particular content area and that are not typically found in general reading: *meridian, temperate*

Figurative terms: pork barrel, cold war, domino theory

Words with multiple meanings: Often, these are words that have a general meaning but also have a particular, sometimes carefully defined, meaning in the content areas: *force, mass, work, energy, cabinet, bill*

Words easily confused with other words: longitude for *latitude, executive* for *execution, principal* for *principle*

Acronyms: OPEC, NATO, WHO (Parker, 2001).

Terms written as formulas: H_2O, $NaCl$, CO_2

Relative Difficulty of Words

Some words are relatively easy to learn. Concrete nouns that label physical objects, such as *kiosk* or *ibu*, are easier to learn than labels for complex processes, such as *oxidation* or *photosynthesis*, or abstract concepts, such as *ecology* or *democracy*. There is also a question of depth of knowledge. For instance, a reader needs to have a working knowledge of the specialized and technical meanings of *resource allocation, profit incentive, demand, supply, consumer*, and *suppliers* in order to understand the following passage.

Prices and the Profit Incentive

In a free market efficient resource allocation goes hand in hand with the profit incentive. Suppose that scientists predicted extremely hot weather for the coming summer. In most parts of the country consumers would buy up air conditioners and fans to prepare for the heat. Power companies would buy reserves of oil and natural gas to supply these appliances with enough power. Since demand would exceed supply, consumers would bid up the price of fans, and power plants would bid up the price of fuel.

Suppliers would recognize the possibility for profit in the higher prices charged for these goods, and they would produce more fans and air conditioners. Oil and natural gas fields would hire workers to pump more fuel for power plants. Eventually, more fans, air conditioners, and fuel would move into the market. The potential heat wave would have created a need among consumers for certain goods, and the rise in prices would have given producers and incentive to meet this need. (Sullivan & Sheffrin, 2010 p. 153)

English Language Learners

In the sciences, many of the technical terms have cognates in a number of languages. That is, they have the same origin and so have similar appearances. This is especially true of the Romance languages, Spanish, Italian, French, Romanian, and Portuguese. For instance, technical terms in Spanish for a description of an atom include: *atomo, molecula, electron, neutron.*

CHECKUP
---

1. What is involved in learning vocabulary in a content area?

Estimating Students' Vocabulary

The most important prerequisite for building vocabulary is having an estimate of the students' knowledge of words. With this understanding, the teacher can better select vocabulary as well as learning strategies. Teachers also need to evaluate the words students must learn and the degree of technical understanding students should have in a subject. Some words we know very well; others we know only vaguely. There also are some words about which we have everyday knowledge but lack a technical understanding. This is especially true of scientific terms. For instance, students understand *machine, power, motion, work,* and *weight* when used in everyday language, but may not know them when used in physical science.

Dale and O'Rourke (1971) described four stages of word knowledge:

1. I never saw it before.
2. I've heard of it, but I don't know what it means.
3. I recognize it in context—it has something to do with . . .
4. I know it. (p. 3)

Stahl (1986) describes three degrees of word knowledge: definitional, contextual, and generative. Definitional knowledge means that the student can tell what a word means. A *shelter* is "something that covers or protects us from the weather." Contextual knowledge, however, requires understanding the "core concept the word represents and how that concept is changed in different contexts" (p. 663). The student would understand the meanings of the word *shelter* in the expressions, "food and shelter," "sought shelter from the storm," and "a shelter for the homeless."

There are some words that are restricted to our receptive vocabularies. We grasp them when we hear them spoken or meet them in print, but we don't know them well enough to use them in our own speaking or writing. Generative knowledge is required before words become part of our expressive, or speaking and writing, vocabularies. Combining levels of knowledge and degrees of knowledge, Graves (1987) created six learning tasks for acquiring new words.

1. *Task 1: Learning to read known words.* This entails learning the printed forms of words that are in one's listening vocabulary. Novice readers face this task as they use phonics to sound out words. However, older students, especially those who are struggling readers or who are still learning English, also face this same task when they use phonics, syllabication, or a dictionary pronunciation guide to recognize words in print that they know when they hear them. Frequently, these are words such as *polymers, trough,* and *queue* whose pronunciations are difficult to predict from their spellings.
2. *Task 2: Learning new meanings for known words.* In science, there are a number of common terms that take on a specialized meaning. A student who knows *kingdom* and *family* would still need to learn the technical meanings of these words when they are used as part of a classification of animals.
3. *Task 3: Learning new words that represent known concepts.* Since the concept is already known, this simply entails learning a new label. A student learns that *humerus* is the technical name for the upper arm bone. This is a relatively easy task.
4. *Task 4: Learning new words that represent new concepts.* The difficulty of this task depends on the complexity of the concepts to be learned. Concepts such as *introvert, extravert, democracy, republic,* and *dictatorship* are abstract and complex.
5. *Task 5: Clarifying and enriching the meanings of known words.* Our understanding of recently acquired words may be general and vague until we have more experience with them. Words such as *focus, magnification, low-power, high-power, stage,* and *slide* take on more meaning for someone who has read and talked about a compound microscope and then uses it. Having partial knowledge of a word or tying it to one particular context limits students' understanding of the word; when they encounter it in their reading, they may misinterpret its meaning. For instance, one student thought that the word *ancestors* meant "relatives that he didn't see very often" (Curtis & Longo, 1999). This limited understanding of the word won't help him much when he encounters it in a history text. Students need to meet new words in many contexts.
6. *Task 6: Moving words from receptive to expressive vocabulary.* Because we have time to plan and revise what we say, our writing vocabularies should be richer and more varied than our speaking vocabularies. Writing is also a good place to start using new

Struggling Readers

Some very bright students are afflicted with a reading difficulty: they quickly grasp concepts presented orally but have difficulty when they have to get information from printed text because they are unable to read long or complex words even though they know their meanings and would recognize them if they heard them.

English Language Learners

When working with ELLs, determine whether an unknown word represents an unknown concept or is simply a new English label for a concept already known. A major vocabulary task for ELLs is learning the English equivalents for words they know in their native language.

Struggling Readers

If a text contains an overwhelming number of words that pose problems for students, it may be too difficult. See Chapter 9 for suggestions for handling difficult texts.

words, but students should also be encouraged to use newly learned words in their speaking. Planning opportunities to talk and write about newly learned concepts provides students with the opportunity and expertise needed to move words into their expressive vocabularies.

CHECKUP

1. What are the different levels on which words are known?
2. On what level should words be known in order for this knowledge to have an effect on students' comprehension?

Deciding What Students Need to Know

Before introducing vocabulary, decide what students need to know. Sometimes, this may be simply a matter of learning the graphic form of a word. For instance, from classroom discussions, students may be familiar with rocks called *gneiss*, dense rock occurring in layers, but may not recognize the word in print because of its *gn* spelling of /n/. With words of this type, simply teach students that the *gn* in *gneiss* is pronounced like the *gn* in *gnat* or *gnarled*. For many technical words, it will be necessary to develop conceptual knowledge. Words such as *symbiosis*, *anarchy*, and *latitude* and *longitude* require extensive teaching. Unfortunately, students are often familiar with labels but not the concepts behind them. This is especially true of abstract terms such as *republic* and *executive branch* and technical terms such as *digital* and *bytes*. Teaching vocabulary also involves clarifying and deepening students' understanding of known words and helping students use new words in their speaking and their writing. See Table 3.1 for a list of states of word knowledge and recommended instruction for each state.

TABLE 3.1 States of Word Knowledge

STATE	INSTRUCTION
1. Knows word when hears it but does not recognize printed form.	Teach printed form.
2. Knows word's oral and written form but does not use it.	Promote generative knowledge. Give examples of its use. Clarify word. Encourage its use in a "safe" environment.
3. Knows the concept but not the label.	Teach the label and relate it to the concept.
4. Has partial knowledge of the word. May have definitional but not contextual knowledge.	Develop fuller meaning of the word. Examine the word in several contexts.
5. Recognizes the label but has no real conceptual knowledge of the concept: *republic*. Or the word may have a familiar everyday meaning but an unknown technical meaning: *energy, motion*.	Develop the concept.
6. Both the concept and the label are unknown.	Develop the concept and the label.

Sources: Adapted from: "Vocabulary Knowledge and Comprehension: A Comprehension-Process View of Complex Literacy Relationships," by M. R. Ruddell. In R. B. Ruddell, M. R. Ruddell, & H. Singer (Eds.), *Theoretical Models and Processess of Reading* (4th ed.; pp. 414–417). Newark, DE: International Reading Association, 1994. From *Assessing and Correcting Reading and Writing Difficulties* by T. Gunning, 2010. Boston: Allyn & Bacon. Reprinted by permission.

In addition, there are some words for which a student has partial knowledge. Students know that a colonel is someone who is in the armed services, but may not realize that *colonel* designates a rank just below general. Or students may know a word but not use it because they are unsure of its meaning or pronunciation or both.

Selecting Words to Be Taught

A high school biology text lists more than 600 terms in its glossary. A middle school American history text lists nearly 300 terms. A two-page section in a text may contain more than a dozen potentially difficult terms. The number of new words in a content area can be overwhelming. Teachers need to select carefully words to be taught because our ability to learn new words is limited.

Students should be presented with only seven or eight new words. In order to decide which words to introduce, the teacher needs to ask, "What do I want my students to learn?" Two or three key concepts should be listed. The teacher should then go through the material to be learned and select the words necessary for an understanding of the key concepts. The teacher should also consider the overall importance of the words. Are these words that are important for a basic understanding of the content area? Are these words that the student will meet again and again? Also note whether the words are explained in context or in the margins. If so, these are words that students might learn on their own.

In addition to technical vocabulary, there may also be some general words that students may not know but that are essential to an understanding of the passage. This is especially true if you are working with ELL students or below-level readers. If there are a large number of general words that pose problems for students, you may want to seek an easier text or take other measures to make the text more accessible. (See Chapter 9 for suggestions for making difficult texts more accessible.)

The teacher selected the following key concepts and vocabulary as the most essential for understanding a selection on the Marshall Plan:

- The United States gave billions of dollars to countries in Western Europe to help them rebuild after World War II.
- Because of the aid given to them, countries in Western Europe became strong enough to stand up against communism.

| economies | starvation | resources | communism |
| poverty | prosperity | restored | |

To select words that your students should know, it is important to understand their level of vocabulary development. You do not want to over- or underestimate their knowledge of words. Observe the level of vocabulary students use in class discussions and in their writing. Conduct brainstorming sessions in which students can volunteer associations for terms written on the board. For instance, ask students to say words that come to mind when they hear the term *ecology*. Note the breadth and depth of responses.

Before teaching a unit, make a list of potentially difficult words and distribute it to the class. Have students place a check next to words that they know, or use the four-point scale described earlier in this chapter: (1) I never saw it before; (2) I've heard of it, but I don't know what it means; (3) I recognize it in context—it has something to do with . . . ; and (4) I know it. Dale and O'Rourke (1971) found this to be a useful way to assess students' vocabulary. Also, occasionally ask students to make a list of unfamiliar words encountered while reading a selection. If the list of unknown terms is very long, you may want to find an easier book.

In many instances, you may need to pare down the list of possible words to teach. You may decide to focus on just a few high-priority words and teach them to a conceptual level

English Language Learners

Self-Study Quizzes for ESL Students offers a variety of self-checking quizzes on common words, idioms, homonyms, and slang expressions. Also includes games and crossword puzzles. http://a4esl.org/a/h/vocabulary.html

(CCSS)

Acquire and use accurately a range of general academic and domain-specific words and phrases sufficient for reading, writing, speaking, and listening at the college and career readiness level; demonstrate independence in gathering vocabulary knowledge when considering a word or phrase important to comprehension or expression of knowledge. Other, less important or less frequently appearing words can be taught to a definitional level.

The good news about vocabulary development is that even minimal instruction helps. For example, after being given a definition of the word *biome*, a student later sees the word in her text and hears it used in a discussion. With each encounter, the student's knowledge of the word increases, and in time, her definitional knowledge may become contextual. Contextual knowledge is required before comprehension can be fostered. In addition to contextual knowledge, students must also have rapid access to word meanings and a network of meaningful connections (Beck & McKeown, 1983). Students reading the passage about the brain cited earlier in this chapter need to know the contextual meanings of the technical words. They also need to understand how these words are interrelated, and they should know the words well enough that they don't have to stop reading to try to remember what a key term means. If they have been given only a fleeting introduction to the key terms, they may have forgotten them or it may take a little time to recall the meanings; either situation interferes with comprehension of the reading.

To make your program of vocabulary development more effective, survey the text and make a tentative list of key words that should be introduced during an upcoming unit, semester, or school year. Note which words are most likely to pose problems, which words are most essential, and which are repeated. Focus instructional efforts on words that are essential and repeated. Also look for commonalties and relationships among words so that knowledge of one word reinforces understanding of others. For instance, when introducing the word *devaluation*, stress the prefix and suffix because they will help students with the words *deregulation* and *desegregation*, which they will encounter later in their U.S. history texts. Introduce words such as *conservative* and *liberal* at the same time because looking at opposites helps to clarify both words. Also stress these words because they will appear in a number of chapters and are in common use today.

English Language Learners

Although virtually all students struggle with the task of learning content vocabulary, the task is far more difficult for English language learners. Whereas estimates of the English word knowledge of native speakers of English range from 10,000 to 100,000 words, estimates of the English vocabulary of English language learners range from 5,000 to 7,000 words (Johnson & Steele, 1996).

CHECKUP

1. How should words be chosen for instruction in the content areas?
2. What steps can be taken if there are an overwhelming number of words that are unknown to students?

Paul Nation (2001), an authority on vocabulary, notes that the size of a student's vocabulary has an impact on his or her comprehension of text. Readers should know 97 to 98 percent of the words in a text in order to comprehend it well. Students who know the 2,000 most frequently appearing words in the English language would recognize approximately 80 percent of the words in school texts. Knowing the 570 word families on the Academic Word List (see Table 9.1) increases word recognition by about 8.5 to 10 percent. And acquiring the third most frequently occurring group of 1,000 words, for instance, would increase the percentage of words recognized by about 4.3 percent. Nation (2001) estimates that students should know between 15,000 and 20,000 word families. Otherwise, lack of word knowledge is likely to hinder ease of reading and comprehension.

Having an estimate of the number of words students know will help in the planning of vocabulary development for both English learners and the rest of the class. Scores on the vocabulary sections of tests can provide useful information. Informal observations of the words students use in speaking and writing can provide a rough estimate, but should be used with caution, as they can be deceptive. An easy-to-administer group measure of students' vocabulary knowledge, The Vocabulary Levels Test, is available at the School of Linguistics and Applied Language (University of Wellington) Web site www.victoria.ac.nz/lals/resources/vocrefs/default.aspx in the Vocabulary Resources Booklet under LALS 522. The Vocabulary Levels Test assesses students' knowledge of the 10,000 most frequently occurring words and the Academic Word List (AWL), a listing of words frequently used in academic settings. Five levels are assessed—the second 1000-word level, the third 1000-word level, the fifth 1000-word level, the academic word level, and the tenth 1000-word level. The upper levels of the test are challenging enough that even the most advanced native English-speaking students can be assessed. Results of the assessment can be used to determine the appropriate level for each student. Test results can also be used to select materials that gradually increase in difficulty. The 1000 and 2000 levels of the test are available in bilingual versions for Thai, Vietnamese, Mandarin (simplified and traditional), Korean, Japanese, Indonesian, and Tongan. Also available at the same site is the Vocabulary Sizes Test, which assesses knowledge of words at 14 levels from the first 1000 words to the fourteenth 1000 words.

The impact of a limited vocabulary can be quite dramatic. Hilcias, a high school junior, has been in the United States for five years. She had an excellent bilingual education, so she is able to function adequately in her classes, all of which are held in English. However, her English vocabulary is about 6,000 words. In addition to her lack of academic vocabulary knowledge, there are many everyday words that she doesn't know. Her scores on the SAT are understandably low. The Critical Reading section of the SAT includes Sentence Completions and Passage-Based Reading. Sentence Completion requires that students use comprehension ability and word knowledge to fill in the blanks with a pair of words or a single word. Passage-Based Reading includes vocabulary-in-context questions as well as a series of comprehension questions. The passages contain a high-proportion of advanced vocabulary words. The SAT requires that successful test takers have an extensive vocabulary. Thus, students with limited English vocabularies will be penalized. It is critically important that teachers do all they can to build their students' vocabulary skills.

A crucial factor in non-native English speakers' learning English vocabulary is the number of words students know in their first language. If a student's native language vocabulary is large, then learning vocabulary in English should be a somewhat easier task. In many instances, students will be learning English labels for concepts and words they already know in their native language. This is a far easier task than learning both new concepts and the English labels for those concepts.

While reading, many English language learners hesitate over nearly every word. This slows down their reading process so much that comprehension is nearly impossible. English language learners must be taught that they don't have to know every word; they should focus their efforts on crucial terms—those words that readers must know in order to be able to comprehend a passage. To help students learn to select crucial words, give them a copy of a text passage and ask them to underline unknown words that are essential to understanding the passage. In a textbook, these might be words that have been highlighted in some way. Discuss the words and use context, morphemic analysis, and glossary/dictionary skills to derive their meanings. Students might also seek out and identify cognates, words that are similar in both languages.

In one study, older English language learners found the dictionary to be a useful tool for deriving the meanings of unfamiliar words (Gonzales, 1999). Although a number of the words they looked up were content-specific words such as *ecological* and *demographic*, many were general terms, such as *deny* and *fierce*. A number of the words students looked up frequently appeared in formal prose, but were seldom heard in speech: *assertion, aftermath, cited*. Although they occasionally had difficulty deriving an understandable definition and they were sometimes hindered by inflected forms, the students saw the dictionary as an indispensable tool and were able to obtain appropriate definitions about 80 percent of the time. Fortunately, there are a number of techniques that can be employed to make word learning easier and more efficient for all learners, especially if the techniques are geared to the students' level of knowledge.

CHECKUP

1. What special challenge does vocabulary pose for English language learners?

Techniques for Teaching Words

One of the best ways to foster comprehension of complex content area reading is to make sure that students have a working knowledge of key words before they begin to read. Instruction should be conceptual so that students have a sufficient grasp of the key words

English Language Learners

Obtain dictionaries such as the *Longman Dictionary of American English* (Pearson), designed for English language learners. These contain more illustrations and simplified definitions.

CCSS

Acquire and use accurately a range of general academic and domain-specific words and phrases sufficient for reading, writing, speaking, and listening at the college and career readiness level; demonstrate independence in gathering vocabulary knowledge when considering a word or phrase important to comprehension or expression.

so that they don't have to pause and think about them as they are reading. A variety of techniques can be used to achieve this goal.

Brainstorming Techniques

One widely used approach that helps students organize new concepts and their labels and that also activates prior knowledge is brainstorming. In **brainstorming**, students are asked to say what comes to mind when they hear a certain term or phrase. Through their sharing, students learn from each other and build background knowledge for the whole class. Brainstorming techniques also provide the teacher with an opportunity to assess students' background knowledge. For example, if you are unsure about how much students know about Congress, you can have the class brainstorm about that topic. As a result of the brainstorming session, you can determine the depth and accuracy of students' topic and vocabulary knowledge and plan instruction accordingly. During or after brainstorming, you can fill in gaps in students' knowledge, clarify confusing issues, and correct misconceptions. Although they are highly effective, brainstorming techniques don't work very well unless students have at least some knowledge of the topic.

List–Group–Label

In one of its simplest forms, brainstorming can be presented through a **list-group-label** framework (Taba, 1965). The topic to be brainstormed is written on the board, and students are invited to tell what the topic makes them think about. Write the word *light* on the board, for example, and ask students to tell what comes to mind when they think of this word. List all responses, even those that don't seem to have any connection to the topic. After responses have been listed, the class—working together—categorizes the words into groups of three or more (a word may be placed in more than one group) and assigns each category a label. Words that don't seem to fit anywhere else might be placed in a separate group. As they group the words and label them, students explain why certain words should be placed together and why their category name is appropriate. Provide assistance with categorizing if it is needed. For younger students or students who are having difficulty, model the process of categorizing and labeling. As students supply responses, assess the depth and accuracy of students' knowledge of the topic.

As a member of the brainstorming group, you may volunteer words during the brainstorming portion of the procedure. For instance, if students didn't include *waves* or *spectrum*, you could add those to the list. Limit the number of brainstormed items to about twenty-five so the list doesn't become too cumbersome (Tierney & Readence, 2005).

Semantic Mapping

What is your concept of DNA? One way to find out is to list all the words that come to mind when you think about the word. Here are some responses compiled from three high school students.

Respondent A: cells, nucleus, protein, amino acids, double helix, life, code, traits

Respondent B: heredity, traits, eyes, hair, sex, nucleus, chromosomes, threads, chains

Respondent C: biology, body, genes, dominant, recessive, characteristics, hair, eyes, Watson, criminals, unique, fingerprints

If you analyze the responses, you can see that they vary from respondent to respondent. If you look closely at the responses, you can see that they are not discrete items, but are related in some way. As Lapp, Flood, and Hoffman (1996) note,

■ **Brainstorming** is a process in which members of a group attempt to accomplish a task by submitting ideas spontaneously.

■ **List–group–label** is a group brainstorming technique in which students tell what they know about a topic and organize that information.

Information and ideas seem to be connected with each other, even interdependent, in a web or network arrangement.

When we recall one thing, several associated ideas always seem to come along with it . . . (p. 292).

Because our ideas are webbed in networks, new ideas are linked to old ideas. In fact, new information cannot be added to our mental storehouse unless it can be linked to old information. Existing information serves as hooks on which to hang or associate new information. Prior knowledge provides a structure into which we can link new information. (p. 295)

Creating added links improves retention and broadens understanding. Part of helping students learn is enabling them to see relationships and forge links among ideas. Compartmentalized items of knowledge, such as isolated facts or lists of unrelated words, are harder to retrieve because there are fewer links to them.

Vocabulary words are best learned within a network of associations. One way of establishing relationships among concepts is through the creation of **semantic maps**, which is based on the list-group-label technique. In semantic mapping, after brainstorming, categorizing and labeling ideas, the class uses circles or rectangles and lines to show the relationships among the terms. More free flowing than outlines and easier to construct, semantic maps are popular with students. The steps in semantic mapping include announcing the topic, brainstorming, grouping and labeling, creating a map, discussing and revising the map, and extending the map. Semantic maps are also flexible. Items can be added to them during or after reading or even during subsequent lessons. The following lesson illustrates how a general science class created a map for the planets in preparation for reading the section in their science text on the planets.

In addition to being a prereading vocabulary development technique, semantic maps can also be used as a way of summarizing the content of a selection or as a prewriting activity. However, in order to be of optimum value, students should participate in the creation

> (CCSS)
> Demonstrate understanding of word relationships and nuances in word meanings.

> ■ A semantic map is a graphic organizer that uses lines and circles to organize information according to categories.

LESSON 3.1

Semantic Mapping

Step 1: Announcing the Topic and Inviting Brainstorming Responses
The teacher wrote the word *planets* on the board and asked the class to tell what came to mind when they thought of the word *planets*. Students responded with the following words: *the sun, far away, appear in sky, moving bodies, Earth, moons, Mars, Jupiter, Neptune, Mercury, Venus.* No one mentioned what the planets did, so the teacher asked what they did. One student volunteered that they orbited the sun. The words *orbit sun* were added. The teacher explained that there are eight planets, but they had listed only six. No one could think of the names of the other two, so the teacher added *Saturn* and *Uranus.*

Step 2: Grouping and Labeling Responses
Students discussed ways of grouping the words and possible titles for word groups. They constructed a preliminary map.

Step 3: Discussing and Revising the Map
The class discussed the map. One student stated that Earth turned on its axis and thought that the other planets did, too. The phrase *turn on its axis* was added.

Step 4: Extending the Map
The semantic map was displayed so that students could use it as a reference as they read. After students read and discussed the selection, the map was reviewed and students were invited to add additional elements. As students read, they learned that some planets were near and some were far and that the near planets were called *inner planets* and the far planets were called *outer planets.* They learned that the planets were made up of rock, liquid, and gas and have one or more moons. All of this information was added to their maps. A completed map is shown in Figure 3.1.

FIGURE 3.1   **Semantic Map for Planets**

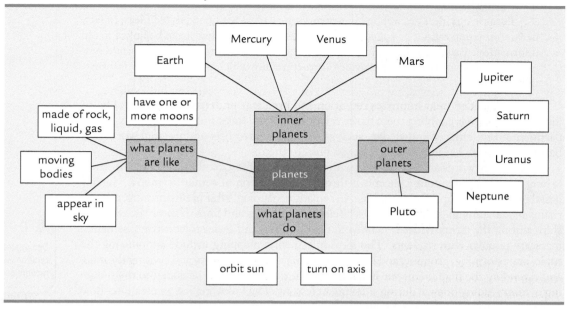

of maps so they will have the opportunity to sift through the information and organize and process the terms. According to research by Berkowitz (1986), students' performance doesn't show much improvement unless they have a hand in creating maps.

Conceptual Techniques

Concept Maps

Semantic maps are an excellent device for visually representing information and showing that concepts are related. However, they fail to say *how* the concepts are related. **Concept maps**, which are popular in the sciences, use brief phrases to link concepts and produce statements that show what the student understands about the concepts. For instance, a concept might include *energy, matter, food, living things, animals, plants, nonliving things.* A concept map shows how these items are related. The map is hierarchical, so the most general or superordinate concept is placed at the top of the page and subordinate or more specific items are placed lower. Coordinate concepts are placed on the same level. So how, you might ask, is a concept map different from an outline or notetaking? Concept maps are more visual so they show how ideas are related. In an outline, you can see how subtopic A is related to main topic I, but the outline won't show that subtopic A is also related to main topic II. Concept maps show crosslinkages as well as linear ones (Warner et al., 1991).

When created cooperatively, concept maps can be used to activate students' background knowledge and reassure them if they are intimidated by technical vocabulary—in a new science unit, for example. Working with classmates to create concept maps can demonstrate to students how much they already know and help them link this knowledge to the new information.

Concept maps can serve several functions. They can be used as an advanced organizer at the beginning of a unit, as a reference during the unit, and as a running summary that can be updated as the unit progresses. Concept maps are also excellent devices for reviewing a topic and for studying. In addition, they can be used as an assessment device to gauge the extent to which students are able to show interrelationships among the concept's key elements.

General steps for creating concept maps include:

Step 1: *Identify the most important ideas or key terms.* Write them in a list. Each concept should consist of a single word or brief phrase of no more than three words.

■ **A concept map** is a graphic device that uses lines and circles to organize information according to categories but also uses words and phrases to show interrelationships among concepts.

Step 2: *Place each concept on a separate piece of paper.* This way, they will be easier to manipulate.

Step 3: *On a table or desktop, arrange the concepts in order from the most general to the most specific.* Equal concepts are placed on the same line. Examples are highly specific and are positioned at the bottom.

Step 4: *Copy the concepts onto a piece of paper.* Put the concepts in boxes or circles. Write the most general ideas at the top of the page, and place the subordinate or supporting ideas underneath them. Continue until all the key ideas have been included.

Step 5: *Connect the ideas with lines.* Write a word or brief phrase on each line to describe the relationship between the two items joined by the line. Write only linking words, such as *is, are, can, be, has, such as, for example.*

Step 6: *Check your map.* Make sure that each concept (except the first and last) is linked to a concept above and below it, with only linking words (and not concept words) placed on the linkage lines.

Consider the map tentative. Make changes as necessary. And don't be concerned if your map is different from maps drawn by others. There are different ways of drawing concept maps. As long as you have included the most important ideas and their relationships, your concept map is correct (Miller & Levine, 2009).

Creating Concept Maps   Learning how to create a concept map takes time and guidance. Initially, teacher and students create concept maps together. As students gain more experience constructing maps, they begin to create their own. The following sample lesson shows how to teach students to use a concept map. The map in Figure 3.2 was created after students read a section on tissues in their tenth-grade biology text.

Frayer Model of Conceptual Development

Students may be surprised to learn that snails, giant clams, and octopuses belong to the same phylum because these creatures seem so different. A **graphic organizer** that will help them see how these creatures are related and also how they fit into the animal kingdom is

> **🌱 Struggling Readers**
>
> Struggling readers may have a limited understanding of the technical words in their vocabulary and so would benefit from additional activities that clarify and extend meaning and provide practice with the words (Kucan & Palincsar, 2011).

> ■ A **graphic organizer** is a diagram used to show the interrelationships among words or ideas.

FIGURE 3.2   Concept Map

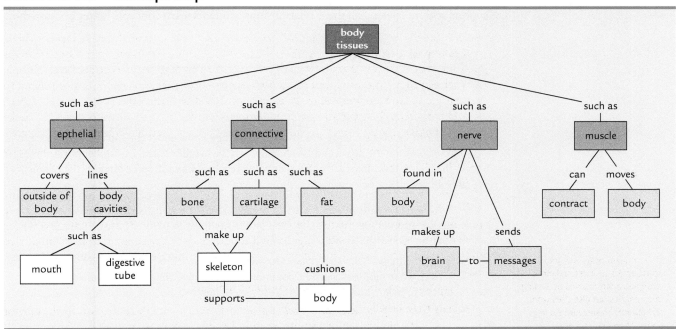

LESSON 3.2

Creating a Concept Map

Step 1: Introducing Concept Mapping
Explain what a concept map is and discuss its benefits. Show a concept map.

Step 2: Explaining the Construction of a Concept Map
Show how a concept map is created. Create a sample list of linkage words.

Step 3: Listing Concepts
After students have read a brief selection that lends itself to concept mapping, cooperatively list the key terms or concepts from the selection. For instance, after reading about body tissues, the class listed the following terms: *body tissues, muscle, can contract, nerve, messages, brain, epithelial, outside of body, body cavities, mouth, digestive tube, connective, bone, cartilage, fat, skeleton.*

Step 4: Arranging Concepts
Have the class cooperatively arrange concepts from most general to most specific.

Step 5: Adding Linkages
After key words have been put in place, have the class add linkages that show relationships among the concepts.

Step 6: Checking the Map
Have the class check the map to make sure that all the key concepts have been included and that linkages are correctly stated.

Step 7: Using the Map
Students can now use the concept map to review materials and to study for upcoming quizzes. As they acquire more information about tissues, they add it to the map.

---

the **Frayer model**. In this model, a concept is developed by having students discover relevant attributes, consider irrelevant attributes, and note examples and nonexamples (Peters, 1979). The concept is also organized into a hierarchy so students can see superordinate, coordinate, and subordinate categories; this allows them to view the overall conceptual scheme. Seeing all these relationships, students learn concepts better because they

■ The **Frayer model** is a graphic that organizes concepts hierarchically.

LESSON 3.3

Introducing the Frayer Model

Step 1: Brainstorming the Concept
In order to involve students and find out what they know about the topic, write the topic word *mollusks* on the board and ask students to tell what they know. List students' responses on the board. If students are unfamiliar with the term, mention some members of the phylum: snails, clams, octopuses.

Step 2: Discussing Examples of the Concept
From the information listed on the board, note examples of mollusks. If there are very few examples, list additional ones.

Step 3: Discussing Relevant Characteristics
Talk over what mollusks have in common; for instance, they have a similar body that includes a foot, gut, and mantle; they are invertebrates, soft-bodied, and cold-blooded; they usually have a shell.

Step 4: Arranging Concepts in a Hierarchy

Show where mollusks fall in the hierarchy. Show superordinate categories first, and then show coordinate categories. Mollusks belong in the same group as cnidarians, platyhelminthes (flatworms), nematodes (round worms), echinoderms, annelids (segmented worms) arthropods, and chordates. Discuss subordinate categories: bivalves, gastropods, and cephalopods.

Step 5: Discussing Common Characteristics

Help students decide what the relevant characteristics of a mollusk are: mantle, foot, soft body, and shell.

Step 6: Discussing Irrelevant Characteristics

Discuss irrelevant characteristics of mollusks: color, size, what they eat, climate in which they are found, whether they are found on land or in water.

Step 7: Discussing Nonexamples

Discuss why a fish, a whale, a worm, a toad, or a salamander is not a mollusk.

Step 8: Testing the Concept

Provide the students with examples and nonexamples of creatures and have them say whether or not they are mollusks, with explanations for their responses. An example of the Frayer model is shown in Figure 3.3.

have more semantic cues. The following lesson illustrates how the concept of *mollusks* might be taught.

The Frayer model works best when used with complex but well-structured concepts that have a hierarchical organization. As with other graphic organizers, it also works best when students are involved in providing examples and nonexamples, defining characteristics, and establishing the hierarchy (Tierney & Readence, 2005).

Concept of Definition

The **concept of definition** (CD) is also a highly effective graphic organizer for developing conceptual knowledge (Schwartz, 1988). The basic purpose of the concept of definition

■ **The concept of definition** is a graphic organizer used to define a word.

FIGURE 3.3 **Frayer Model**

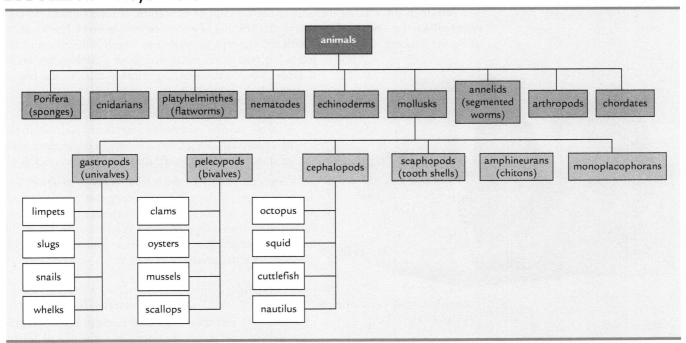

FIGURE 3.4
Concept of Definition Map

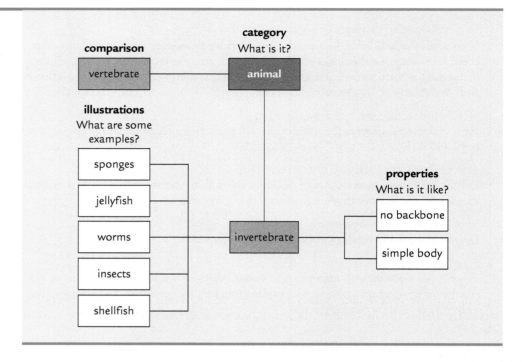

is to provide students with a strategy they can use to learn new words. When encountering a new word, students can decide on a category name, note the properties of the word or concept, provide examples of the word, and think of a word that contrasts with it. In doing so, students ask and answer questions such as What is it? What is it like? What are some examples of it? What does it compare with? In defining *desert*, for instance, students would note that it is a region and that it is characterized by very little rainfall. In supplying properties, it is important that students provide at least one feature that distinguishes the concept. For instance, a defining characteristic of a desert is that it receives no more than twenty-five centimeters of rain a year. Examples of deserts are the Sahara, the Gobi, and the Mojave. A desert could be compared to a rain forest.

Although the teacher introduces the concept of definition, students gradually take responsibility for applying it to derive the meaning of a concept from context. For instance, using the concept of definition with the concept *invertebrates*, which is discussed in the following paragraph excerpted from a biology textbook, students would create an organizer similar to the one in Figure 3.4.

> Invertebrates are animals that do not have backbones. They are much simpler creatures than vertebrates, animals that do have backbones. Some examples of invertebrates are sponges, jellyfish, worms, insects, and shellfish. (Bledsoe, 1994, p. 64)

Often only partial information is given in a text. For instance, a text might talk about energy but give no examples of energy. It is then up to the students to use their own background knowledge or other references to fill in the missing information or to complete as much of the map as possible, with the teacher's guidance.

Graphic Organizers

In addition to semantic maps and concept maps, graphic organizers include charts, diagrams, and other visual devices

Source: David Grossman/Alamy.

Students can use Inspiration and other software to create graphic organizers.

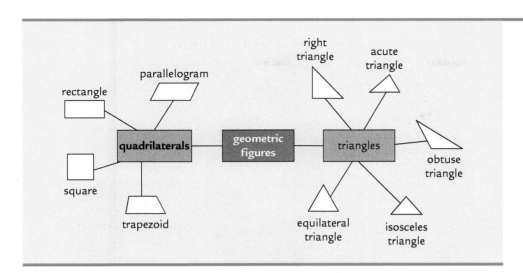

FIGURE 3.5
Pictorial Map

that help students establish and display relationships among words. Graphic organizers seem to work especially well with students who have difficulty seeing relationships that are expressed only verbally.

Pictorial Maps

As graphic displays, maps can include a combination of verbal and visual items. The words in semantic maps, for example, can be illustrated with drawings, or drawings can be used instead of words. This works especially well when working with concrete items. Figure 3.5 shows a pictorial map of two-dimensional and three-dimensional shapes.

Venn Diagram

The **Venn diagram**, which was originally used in math by John Venn to show logical relationships among sets, fosters the comparison and contrast of semantic features. In a Venn diagram, features shared by the concepts are placed within the overlapping circles. Characteristics belonging to only one concept are placed in the outer portion of the circle designated for that concept. A Venn diagram comparing and contrasting rabbits and hares is presented in Figure 3.6. Although they may be used before reading, Venn diagrams typically work better as postreading organizers of vocabulary and concepts.

Semantic Feature Analysis

In **semantic feature analysis (SFA)**, students compare items within a category to see which features they share (Johnson & Pearson, 1984). By highlighting similarities and differences among words, SFA activates prior knowledge and helps students see how words are related and note shades of meaning. SFA works best with words that have features that are either present (+) or absent (−). However, it can be adapted to include a graduated scale: A = always, S = sometimes, or N = Never, for instance. Lesson 3.4 illustrates the steps for teaching SFA.

Other Vocabulary-Building Devices

Possible Sentences

Possible sentences, one of the simplest vocabulary building techniques, may also be one of the most effective. This technique taps prior knowledge, arouses students' curiosity and interests, elicits predictions, fosters discussion,

■ **USING TECHNOLOGY**

Inspiration (Inspiration Software) or similar software can be used to create graphic organizers and add illustrations. A clip entitled "Visualizing Vocabulary" in iTunes U, shows a class of 9–12 students using drawings from Inspiration to illustrate newly learned vocabulary words. The clip is listed under K–12, Florida Department of Education, Graphic Organizer Tools.

■ **A Venn diagram** is a graphic organizer that uses overlapping circles to show relationships between words or other items.

■ **A semantic feature analysis (SFA)** is a graphic organizer that uses a grid to compare a series of words or other items on a number of characteristics.

FIGURE 3.6
Venn Diagram

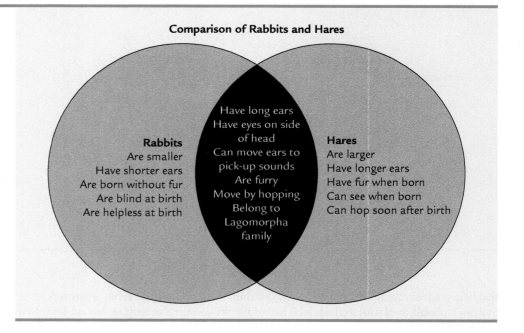

Comparison of Rabbits and Hares

Rabbits
Are smaller
Have shorter ears
Are born without fur
Are blind at birth
Are helpless at birth

Have long ears
Have eyes on side of head
Can move ears to pick-up sounds
Are furry
Move by hopping
Belong to Lagomorpha family

Hares
Are larger
Have longer ears
Have fur when born
Can see when born
Can hop soon after birth

LESSON 3.4

Semantic Feature Analysis

Step 1: Choosing a Category

Select a topic or category: for instance, *insects, government officials, trees, minerals.* Tell students what the category is and ask them to give examples. In preparation for reading a textbook section on energy, present the category *sources of energy.* Ask students to name sources of energy. Provide prompts if necessary.

Step 2: Creating a Grid

Place an outline of a grid on the board or on an overhead transparency. List *sources of energy* in a column on the left. Encourage students to suggest features or characteristics that at least one of the sources possesses. List these features in a row at the top of the grid. Not all features have to be identified at this point. Some may be added later.

Step 3: Determining Feature Possession

Put a plus (+) in the block if a particular source of energy possesses the feature being considered or a minus (−) if it doesn't. The plus need not signal that the source always possesses the feature; it can mean that it usually does. If the group is not sure whether the source of energy possesses a particular feature, put a question mark in the box.

Step 4: Discussion of the Grid

Discuss the grid with the class. If it is missing some words or features important to the overall concept, add them. After the grid has been completed, discuss its overall significance, noting that the SFA does not allow for making fine distinctions such as degrees of pollution and specific details about each category. Have the class note major similarities and differences among the sources of energy.

Step 5: Extension

After students have read the section on sources of energy, discuss it, and extend the grid to include sources of energy or features described in the text or to update or change responses. The class may also want to list additional features of energy sources. The completed SFA grid is displayed in Figure 3.7.

FIGURE 3.7
**Semantic Feature
Analysis**

Sources of Energy	renewable	nonpolluting	cheap	can be used anywhere	safe	widely used
biomass	+	−	+	+	+	−
coal	−	−	+	+	+	+
geothermal	+	+	?	−	+	−
natural gas	−	−	+	+	+	+
nuclear	−	−	−	+	−	?
oil	−	−	+	+	+	+
sun	+	+	−	−	+	−
water	+	+	−	−	+	−
wind	+	+	−	−	+	−

and helps students detect relationships among known and unknown words. Because it challenges students to predict how words will be used in a selection, the possible sentences technique is also highly motivating.

As with many of the other vocabulary techniques, the first step in possible sentences is to determine the major concepts that you want students to learn and then to list the key vocabulary needed to learn those concepts (Moore & Moore, 1986; Moore, Readence, & Richelman, 1989). Choose six to eight potentially difficult words (Stahl & Kapinus, 1991) and the same number of less difficult, familiar words that also are needed to understand the key concepts. Having familiar words available helps students make connections between the known and unknown. After recording the words on the board, ask students to read them and tell what the difficult ones mean, supplying help as needed. Briefly discuss the words. Explain that they have been taken from a selection that students will be reading. Invite students to think about the words and predict what the selection might be about. Then ask students to compose sentences using the words. Each sentence should contain at least two of the words from the list, and the words may be used in more than one sentence. Explain to students that the sentences should be like the ones that appear in the selection from which they were taken. Model the creation of one such sentence, explaining why you think it might be like one in the selection. Then invite students to create possible sentences, working individually, in pairs, or in small groups.

After students have composed their sentences, write them on the board and discuss them briefly before students read the selection. After students have completed their reading, discuss the accuracy of their sentences. Encourage them to use the text as a reference to clarify confusions, resolve controversies, provide proof for assertions, and revise inaccuracies. Students may expand sentences to include new information acquired from the selection or compose additional sentences using the words if their sentences did not incorporate the key concepts in the selection. Students may copy the revised and new sentences into their notebooks so that they have a record of key concepts contained in the selection. A possible sentences exercise completed by a group of sixth-grade students is presented below. The exercise was written in preparation for reading about the Ukrainian poet Taras Shevchenko.

KEY WORDS FOR SECTION ON TARAS SHEVCHENKO			
Ukraine	Russia	freedom	serf
hero	poet	arrested	Siberia
czar	ruled	criticized	estate

Students' Sentences

The Ukraine was one part of Russia.

Russia was ruled by a czar.

Taras Shevchenko was a serf.

Serfs worked on rich people's estates.

Serfs dreamed of freedom.

Serfs who ran away were arrested and sent to Siberia.

Poets wrote about the serfs who were heroes because they ran away.

Anyone who criticized the czar was sent to Siberia.

Struggling Readers

By exposing them to the thoughts of others and having their thinking clarified, think-pair-share helps students develop concepts and vocabulary.

Adaptations of Possible Sentences   In an adaptation of possible sentences, Jensen and Duffelmeyer (1996) incorporated think-pair-share into the activity. In think-pair-share, students think on their own about an issue or question raised in class, pair up with another student to discuss possible resolutions or answers, and then meet with another pair of students to share responses. After sharing in groups of four, one person from each group reports to the whole class. In this adaptation of think-pair-share, students were given two minutes to individually consider and match the key words, five minutes to share their responses with a partner, and five minutes to create possible sentences in groups of four. The class then met as a whole group and had ten minutes to share their possible sentences and write them on the board. According to Jensen and Duffelmeyer, the inclusion of think-pair-share resulted in richer discussions and improved sentences.

Predict-O-Grams

A technique that is similar to possible sentences but designed to be used with fiction, predict-o-gram challenges students to group words according to the likelihood that they will tell about characters, plot, setting, or other parts of a narrative (Blachowicz, 1986). Both known words and words likely to be unfamiliar are selected from the story and recorded on the board. Each major story category is represented: characters, setting, problem, action, and resolution. Students read the words and discuss their meanings and pronunciations if these are unknown. Then they classify the words according to how they believe they will be used in the story—describing the setting, characters, problem, action, or resolution. In addition to building vocabulary, this activity builds students' awareness of the structure of a narrative and fosters making predictions. After students have classified the words, they use them to predict the story's setting, characters, problem, action, and resolution. Students then read the story to assess their predictions. Words for a sample predict-o-gram from Langston Hughes's classic short story "Thank You, M'am" are listed below.

PREDICT-O-GRAM FOR "THANK YOU, M'AM"			
boy	large woman	pocketbook	suede shoes
street	furnished room	hungry	cake
ten dollars	thank you	kicked	

Word Sorts

A **word sort** is a categorization device that can be used to manipulate words. It can be especially useful for grouping technical terms (Tonjes, 1991). The words are placed on slips of paper or 3 × 5 cards, and the sort can be open or closed (papers with columns might be used instead of cards or slips of paper). In a closed sort, students are given the category name; in an open sort, they must compose one. An open sort forces students to discern relationships and state what those relationships are. An open sort taken from a health text is shown below. If you prefer a closed sort, provide the category labels: Diseases Caused by Viruses, Diseases Caused by Bacteria.

diabetes	scarlet fever	tuberculosis
rabies	measles	mumps
chickenpox	flu	cold

Vocabulary Self-Collection Strategy (VSS)

A versatile technique, vocabulary self-collection strategy (VSS) can be used to acquire general or content-specific vocabulary or a combination of the two (Ruddell, 1995; Shearer, 1999). The heart of the technique is self-selection of words. Each week students record five or more unfamiliar words that they encounter in or out of school. Each word and the context in which it was used are written on a note card. The student also writes down what she or he thinks the word means based on the word's context, but this is written on the back of the card. The student then checks the meaning of the word in a dictionary, compares it with his or her guess based on context, and writes down the dictionary definition on the front of the card. Containing the word, its use in context, and a dictionary definition, the front of the card can be used for studying the word.

At the end of the week students meet in small groups. Each student nominates one of his or her five words to be one that the whole class should learn. Reasons for the nomination are discussed. The group then selects one word. Each group presents its word to the whole class. The teacher may also choose a word.

Words are discussed including the context in which they appeared. Dictionaries and glossaries may be checked to make sure that the correct pronunciation and definition have been obtained. The discussion offers opportunities for clarifying the meanings of the words and modeling the use of context clues and the dictionary and refining students' use of these tools. The class reviews the entire list and enters them into their vocabulary notebooks and also engages in extension and application activities.

Although ultimately students should be using newly acquired words in their speaking and writing, using a newly learned complex word correctly often requires a depth of knowledge of the word. When students are in the initial stages of learning a word, instead of having them write sentences using new words, have them complete sentence stems that prompt them to use the word appropriately in a sentence, which shows that they know the meaning of the word: The leader facilitated the discussion by_____. To complete the sentence, students have to consider how a discussion might be facilitated (Beck, McKeon, & Kucan, 2002).

Students find the experience of choosing words very motivating. As one middle-school student explained, "I think that we should keep picking our own words because then we will want to study them more efficiently. If we get something handed or picked out by a teacher, we don't want to study something we don't like" (Shearer, 1999). Another student explained how the activity had changed his attitude toward learning new words:

> Now I often catch myself and when I listen to music or listen to someone talk, I listen to the words they say and I find myself asking what the words mean. I try to make sure

 Struggling Readers

Not having read much in the past, struggling readers often have a limited vocabulary. The vocabulary self-collection strategy is an excellent device for helping build their awareness of new words, which aids vocabulary acquisition.

■ **Word sort** is a categorization device used to help students discover common elements in words and make discoveries about words.

I understand what it means. I find that doing this helps me understand big words when I read them in a book or a textbook or even in a magazine. (Shearer, 1999)

VSS is a flexible technique. Students' selection of words to be learned can be focused on the content text or other texts that they are reading as part of their schoolwork. Unlike other vocabulary learning techniques, VSS is initiated after the text is read because it is believed that students won't know which words are important until that time.

Vocabulary Squares

Vocabulary learning is enhanced when students can construct a personal connection to a word they are learning. Applying this principle, Eeds and Cockrum (1985) devised an activity in which students used vocabulary squares to record personal experiences. In the first box of the four-box square, have students write the target word. Use the word in a sentence and then ask questions to help students relate the word to their personal experiences. For instance, for the word *irate*, ask, "Is there something that makes you angry?" After several students have responded with appropriate examples, note that these are examples of things that make people irate. In box two, have students briefly write about something that makes them irate. After a discussion, have students note, in box three, things that do not make them irate. In box four, have students write a definition of the word.

Adapting the technique, Hopkins (Hopkins & Bean, 1998–1999) had students create a visual association with the word. He further adapted the technique by using it with affixes and roots. In box one, students wrote the word element and its meaning; in box two, they wrote a word that used the element; in box three, they wrote a definition of the word containing the element; and in box four, they drew a picture of the item named. For the prefix *tri-*, students wrote "tri-three" in the first box. In the second box, they wrote "trilobite." In the third box they wrote, "An extinct three-lobed marine arthropod of the Paleozoic Era." In box four, they drew a picture of a trilobite.

Affective Words

William Funk, the famous lexicographer, listed the following as the ten most beautiful words: *chimes, dawn, golden, hush, lullaby, luminous, melody, mist, murmuring, tranquil* (Tonjes, 1991). Discuss with your students the affective side of words—the power of words to evoke strong feelings and images. They can compile a list of most beautiful words, favorite words, most frightening words, noisiest words, and so on.

Words can be ranked to show differences in power, size, or intensity (Nagy, 1988). For instance, the following words can be ranked in terms of intensity: *cold, chilly, freezing, cool, frigid, nippy, wintry*. Although judgments may be somewhat subjective, the process of ranking words introduces students to synonyms and provides an excellent opportunity to discuss specificity in word choice. To convey the concept of connotations of words, you can ask students whether they would rather be:

determined	or	stubborn
nosy	or	curious
clever	or	sly
cheap	or	frugal
carefree	or	irresponsible

Discuss students' choices. Consider the images and feelings that the words evoke and the importance of word choice. Talk over, too, how through our choice of words, we can make a person, place, or thing look favorable or unfavorable.

In one music class students were asked to create a new version of "Twinkle, Twinkle, Little Star" (Draper, 2008). Each group was given a word that they had to use to guide the sound of their song: *urgent, exuberant, forlorn, relaxed,* and *exasperated.* Discussing the meanings of these terms enriched students' knowledge of the words and also better prepared them to carry out the assignment.

Word Origins

Knowing the history, or **etymology**, of a word can foster an understanding of the word and also make the word more memorable. As a bonus, the etymologies of some words are miniature history lessons. For instance, knowing the origin of *boycott*, which is derived from the name of an English land manager in Ireland in 1880, helps to explain what the word means and also provides information about land ownership in Ireland.

Knowing the history of a scientific term can sometimes help students understand its importance. For instance, *radon* was named after radium because it is a radioactive gas produced when radium decays. It is found in areas having radium- and uranium-bearing rocks.

Studying the history or origin of words also can prevent confusion of terms. Math students often confuse the words *radius* and *diameter*: Math expert Rheta Rubenstein (2000) recalls hearing middle school students ask, "Is the diameter the short one or the long one?" (p. 493). Knowing the origins of these words would help students discriminate between the two. *Radius* comes from the same root as *ray*. If students picture the rays of the sun moving out from the sun, they can picture the radius of a circle starting at the center and radiating from there. *Diameter* comes from roots that mean "measure" and "through." The diameter of a circle is a measure through its center (Rubenstein, 2000). For a history of math words, see *The Words of Mathematics* (Schwartzmann, 1994). For general word histories, see the Reading List below.

To extend students' learning and to drive home the meaning of *radius*, you can talk about radio waves, radiant heat, or radial tires. If the approach is interdisciplinary, the biology teacher can talk about the radius, a bone in the forearm, and the chemistry teacher can talk about radium. The language arts teacher can have students create a **web**, similar to the one in Figure 3.8, that shows some of the uses of the root. In explaining *diameter*, a similar process can be initiated. Students can explore other words that contain *dia: diagonal, diabetes, diametric, diabolic,* and *diagnosis.*

Reading List: Word Histories

Almond, J. (2001). *Dictionary of word origins: A history of the words, expressions and clichés we use.* New York Kensington.

Ayto, J. (2009). *Oxford school dictionary of word origins.* New York: Oxford University Press.

Barnhart, D. K., & Metcalf, A. A. (1998). *America in so many words: Words that have shaped America.* Boston: Houghton Mifflin.

Chantrell, G. (2005). *Oxford book of word histories.* New York: Oxford University Press.

■ **Etymology** is the history of the origin and development of words.

■ **A web** is another name for a semantic map, especially a simplified one.

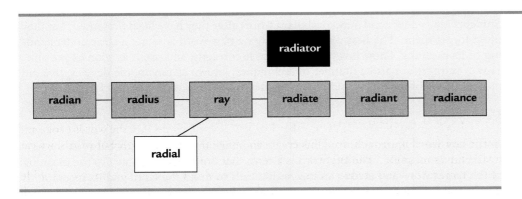

FIGURE 3.8
A Web

Exemplary
Teaching

Word Generation

Word Generation is an interdisciplinary program from the Strategic Education Research Partnership (SERP, 2009) that is designed to develop academic vocabulary. Words are drawn from the Academic Word List (see Table 9.1) and are embedded in content materials. The introductory articles discuss a high-interest but controversial topic such as cyberbullying or paying students to do well in school. Each content area teacher spends 15 minutes a week developing the words within his or her content area. On Monday, the English teacher introduces the words; on Tuesday, the math teacher presents the words in a word problem; on Wednesday, the science teacher presents the words in a science article; on Thursday, the social studies teacher has the students debate an article that contains the words; and on Friday, the English teacher leads the students to develop a persuasive essay using the words. The persuasive essay is based on the controversial isse that was introduced on Monday. In addition to improving their academic vocabulary, students learn to discuss and write about controversial issues.

Merriam-Webster. (2004). *Webster's new explorer dictionary of word origins*. Springfield, MA: Author.

Ehrlich, E. (2000). *What's in a name? How proper names became everyday words*. New York: Owl Books.

Feldman, D. (1989, 2001). *Who put the butter in butterfly? And other fearless investigations into our illogical language*. New York: HarperCollins.

Hendrickson, R. (2000). *The Facts on File encyclopedia of word and phrase origins*. New York: Facts on File.

Klausner, J. (1990). *Talk about English: How words travel and change*. New York: HarperCollins.

Websites

Fun-with-words.com
www.fun-with-words.com/

Wordorigins.org
www.wordorigins.org/

Take Our Word for It
www.takeourword.com/

Remembering Words

Students may understand new vocabulary words after they have been presented, but they often forget them. The best way to remember a new word is to get a clear understanding of its meaning, know how to pronounce it correctly, and use it as soon as possible. However, there are also a number of techniques, known as mnemonic devices, that aid memory. One of the most carefully researched techniques is the key word approach.

Key Word Approach

■ **The key word approach** is a strategy in which students create images to help them associate a meaning with a new word.

In the **key word approach**, students create an image that forges a link between the new word and its meaning. The key word is a term that both serves as a key to the meaning of the target word and evokes an image that calls to mind the word and its meaning. If possible, the key word should embody a portion of the target word. For instance, in one study, the key word for *angler* was *angel*. The mnemonic image showed an angel sitting on a cloud fishing. Two angels on a higher cloud have the following conversation:

> Angel 1: That ANGEL down there sure knows how to catch a lot of fish.
>
> Angel 2: That's because he's an expert ANGLER. (Levin et al., 1984, p. 8)

The key word method leads to better understanding if students create their own images by thinking about the target word and the kind of image that would appropriately depict it. The following lesson illustrates how the words *embargo, blockade, deserters,* and *impress* might be presented through the key word approach.

How effective is the key word strategy? In an experiment with 100 middle schoolers, students who used the key word approach learned almost twice as many words as students who used a contextual approach in which they composed sentences using new words (Jones, Levin, Levin, & Beitzel, 2000). When students worked in pairs, the technique was even more effective than when they studied alone. Although the students creating

LESSON 3.5

Key Word Approach

Step 1: Introducing the Approach

Discuss with students difficulties they may have had remembering the meanings of new words. Explain that you will be showing them a special way to learn new words that works well because they will be creating their own images to make links between the new words and their meanings.

Step 2: Explaining the Technique

Using a word that students are having difficulty with or need to learn, show how the technique works. Select the word *embargo*, for instance, explaining that you are going to create a key word and a picture to help you remember the word *embargo*. Tell students that you are going to create a picture in your mind that uses the word part *em* and shows the meaning of *embargo*. You picture a giant with an *m* on his shirt. He is pulling down a large bar in front of a ship's harbor and he is saying, "This is an em bar go. No ships go in. No ships go out!" A huge sign that says "Embargo" is nearby.

Step 3: Presenting New Words

Present the words *blockade, deserters,* and *impress*. Discuss the meanings of each and list some possible key words and interactive images: The king of England, putting up blocks around the coast of the United States, is saying, "I'll blockade these Americans." The captain of a ship is calling out to sailors fleeing the ships, "There will be no dessert for deserters." He is holding up a large cake. Two very muscular British sailors are grabbing an American sailor and saying, "I've got 'im. I've got 'im. 'Im's impressed!"

Step 4: Guided Practice

Provide practice in the use of the technique. For instance, say the word *blockade* and have the class tell what the key word is and describe the interactive image. Students then explain what the word means. Also say the key word *block* and have students supply the target word, the interactive image, and the target word's meaning. Continue until students have a firm grasp of the technique.

Step 5: Application

Encourage students to use the technique on their own, if they are able to create key words and interactive images without assistance. Periodically review the technique and give students opportunities to use it.

sentences were just as actively involved as the students using the key word technique, "they were not similarly engaged in producing essential retrieval links between the vocabulary items and the meanings to bolster subsequent memory and application" (p. 261).

CHECKUP

1. What techniques can be used to teach and reinforce vocabulary?
2. Which of these techniques would be most effective for your content area? Why?

Creating Independent Word Learners

Realistically, a systematic program of vocabulary development covers only about 400 words in a year's time. However, at the same time that students are learning these new words, they should also be learning strategies and acquiring habits that will foster independent word learning. Because you cannot possibly teach students all the words they need to know, you must help them use word recognition tools that will make them independent word learners. These tools include syllabic analysis, morphemic analysis, contextual analysis, and dictionary/glossary use.

Word knowledge and word recognition work together. I recall reading a war novel and mentally pronouncing *colonel* as "KahI-uh-nul." Context suggested that *colonel* was a term for a rank in the army, but since I did not know the correct pronunciation, I was unable to recognize the word when I heard it. Later in life I ran across the word *quiche*, which I pronounced "kwikch." Context indicated that it was some kind of food. Although I had heard the word *quiche*, I didn't connect it with the *quiche* I had seen in print. On the other side of the coin, having words in our listening vocabulary helps us to apply our decoding skills. While walking to my car after teaching a class at Central Connecticut State University, a visiting high school student asked if I knew where Koperneekus Hall was. Seeing my puzzled look, she showed me the printed invitation to attend an information session at Copernicus Hall. The student had done a relatively good job using syllabication skill to decode *Copernicus*. Had the word been in her listening vocabulary, chances are she would have been able to adjust her reconstruction of the word so that it matched the correct pronunciation. Learning to pronounce words also helps students to remember them (Rosenthal & Ehri, 2008). When presenting new words, write them on the board and say and underline the syllables. This will help all students, but will be especially beneficial to those who have difficulty with multisyllabic words.

Syllabic Analysis

Most students learn phonics and syllabic analysis in elementary school, but some continue to struggle with significant weaknesses in those areas in middle and high school. Shefelbine (1990) found that 15 to 20 percent of the students in the eighth-grade classes that he tested had difficulty with multisyllabic words. While it is not your responsibility as a content area teacher to provide basic instruction in analyzing multisyllabic words, you can help students with those terms that are common to your discipline and appear frequently in the texts you use. This need not be a time-consuming activity. As you discuss new vocabulary, write the words on the board and highlight the syllables. Have students read the words aloud so the vocabulary will be familiar when they encounter the words in print. For instance, when studying meteors, you might show the syllabication of the following words: *me-te-or, at-mos-phere, par-ti-cle, sil-i-cate, al-ti-tude,* and *lu-mi-nous.* Discuss the meanings of the words if the students do not know them.

For a student who had difficulty with the word *startle,* for example, McCabe led him or her through a series of *ar* words: *car, far, bar, jar, tar, star, starring, starred,* and finally, *startle.* Other *ar* words could also be presented: *stark* (stark poverty), *stardom, starfish, starch, starve, starvation, harbor, bargain, sparkle, target, jargon.* Much of his instruction focused on advanced patterns such as ci = /sh/ that have a high frequency but are not often taught.

Struggling Readers

McCabe demonstrates his technique for helping struggling students decode multisyllabic words in a lesson with a high school student at www .avko.org/free/free_video.htm

McCabe created an extensive list of spelling patterns that is available at nominal charge at his Web site www.avko.org, along with suggestions for implementing his "Sequential Spelling" approach. McCabe's approach is especially appropriate for older struggling readers because it teaches them step-by-step what they need to know and it builds on their prior knowledge. As McCabe demonstrates on his Web site, the approach is virtually failure-free: If students work through the successive spellings that are presented, they will be able to read and spell words like *malicious.*

CCSS

Determine or clarify the meaning of unknown and multiple-meaning words and phrases by using context clues, analyzing meaningful word parts, and consulting general and specialized reference materials, as appropriate.

Morphemic Analysis

Although not the longest word in the world, *pneumonoultramicroscopicsilicovolcanoconiosis* is the longest word in at least one unabridged dictionary (Flexner & Hauck, 1994). Even though it looks impenetrable, you may be able to derive its meaning if you break it down morpheme by morpheme. A **morpheme** is the smallest unit of meaning. The word *fear* has a single morpheme; however, *fearfulness* has three: *fear-ful-ness. Television* has three morphemes: *tele-vis-ion.*

> *pneumono* means "lung"
>
> *ultra* means "very"
>
> *microscopic* means "small"
>
> *silico* means "white powder"
>
> *volcano* means "volcano"
>
> *coni* means "cone shaped"
>
> *osis* means "disorder of"

How did you do? The *Random House Dictionary* (Flexner & Hauck, 1994) defines *pneumonoultramicroscopicsilicovolcanoconiosis* as "a lung disease caused by silica dust." If it serves no other purpose, *pneumonoultramicroscopicsilicovolcanoconiosis* demonstrates the power of **morphemic analysis**, the study of meaningful word parts, such as roots, prefixes, and suffixes. According to Nagy and Anderson (1984), about 60 percent of the new words a reader meets contain morphemic units that provide clear, usable clues to the word's meaning. Another 10 percent give helpful but incomplete clues. This is especially true of words in the sciences, many of which have been formed by combining two or more morphemes, for example, *carbohydrates, conductor, electromagnetic, hologram,* and *metalloids.*

Teaching Morphemic Elements

How might a knowledge of word parts help students better understand the following excerpt from a description of mollusks?

> The majority of mollusks are marine animals, but some live in fresh water, and a few live on dry land. They include

■ **A morpheme** is the smallest unit of meaning. The word *nervously* has three morphemes: *nerv(e)-ous-ly.*

■ **Morphemic analysis** is the examination of a word in order to locate and derive the meanings of the morphemes. Syllabic and morphemic analysis are sometimes referred to as "structural analysis."

clams, mussels, and oysters (bivalves), snails and slugs (gastropods), and cuttlefish, squids, and octopuses (cephalopods). (Brimblecombe, Gallannaugh, & Thompson, 1998, p. 495)

The *bi* should alert students that clams, mussels, and oysters have two valves. Knowing *gastro* and *pod* would help students realize that the locomotion of snails and slugs is close to their stomachs. Knowing *cephalo* and *pod* would help students realize that the means of locomotion for cuttlefish, squids, and octopuses is in the vicinity of their heads. Morphemic analysis can help students recognize hundreds of content area words.

Morphemic elements should be taught inductively and should build on what students know. For instance, students can use their knowledge of *thermometer* and *Thermos* to derive the meaning of *thermoplastic* and *thermal*. By noting the use of *therm* in all four words, the students should be able to derive a meaning for the morphemic form *therm*. Also using their knowledge of the words *geography* and *thermometer*, students may be able to derive the meaning of *geothermal*. Encountering the word *geothermal*, students can relate it to *geography* and *thermometer*. Morphemic analysis also aids memory. If students can't remember what *geothermal* means, they can use their knowledge of the combining forms *geo* and *thermal* to help them recall it. Morphemics is also generative: Knowing *geo* can help students learn and remember such words as *geology, geologic, geothermal, geophysical, geomagnetism, geophysics,* and *geopolitics*. Knowing *therm* will help students learn such words as *ectothermal, endothermal, endothermic, exothermic, hypothermia, isotherm, thermal, thermochemical,* and *thermodynamic*.

Making Connections   When introducing morphemic elements or new words, make connections whenever possible. For instance, suppose a textbook section on cells introduces the following words: *chromosomes, lysomes,* and *ribosomes*. If students are led to see the common element in the words (*somes* means "bodies"), they will understand them better, remember them longer, and be able to use morphemic units to decode them, even if they forget their meanings. Thus, *chromosomes, lysosomes,* and *ribosomes* are "small bodies that perform functions in a cell." You can then discuss the morphemic forms *chromo* (color), *lyso* (decomposition of), and *ribo* (sugary substance).

In addition to making connections between morphemic elements being taught, make connections between morphemic elements and students' current reading needs. In a geometry unit focusing on angles, introduce the morphemic forms that students will encounter: *polygon, heptagon, hexagon, octagon, pentagon, quadrilateral,* and *triangle*. Lead students to see the meanings of *gon* (angle) and the other morphemic elements. Have students do an illustrated web of the words. Then discuss some everyday uses of the morphemic forms. What would the building called the Pentagon look like? How many sides would it have? How many events are there in the pentathlon? As an extension, you might study other morphemic elements that indicate number (for instance, *mono-, uni-, bi-, di-,* and *dec-*) or spend additional time with *poly*, since this is a frequently occurring morphemic unit and easy to understand.

Before assigning students a selection, scan it to see if any of the potentially difficult words contain morphemic elements that could be taught ahead of time. Include an explanation of unfamiliar morphemic forms and help students note and build on morphemic forms that they already know. The key to teaching morphemic units is to build students' awareness of these elements in words so that when they encounter a difficult word, they can try to figure out its meaning by analyzing it morphemically.

Often, a variety of techniques can be used to help students comprehend and recall technical words. For example, students reading a section on cells in a middle-school science text must learn the following terms: *cell membrane, cell wall, chloroplasts, chromosomes, cytoplasm, mitochondria, nucleus,* and *vacuole*. One of the best ways to help students understand and remember these words is by using a diagram to show what each cell part looks like, along with its location and function. Morphemic analysis can also be used as an aid to understanding and remembering the terms. For instance, students learn that *cytoplasm* is formed from terms that mean cell (*cyto*) and the watery part of blood (*plasma*); *vacuole* is formed from the word *vacuum*, meaning "empty spaces," and the word part *ole*, meaning "small."

FYI

The Appendix contains an extensive listing of prefixes, suffixes, roots, and combining forms commonly used in secondary content area texts.

USING TECHNOLOGY

Word Central www.wordcentral.com/dailybuzzword.html Presents a new word each day, defines it, uses it in a sentence, and helps readers find its root.

LESSON 3.6

Morphemic Elements

Because they appear first in a word and generally have concrete meanings, prefixes are the easiest of the morphemic elements. The following lesson illustrates how the prefix *anti-* might be introduced.

Step 1: Construct the Meaning of the Prefix

Place the following words on the board: *antislavery, antiwar, anti-Lincoln, anti-constitution, antigun, antismoking, antifreeze.* Some of these words have been drawn from a chapter on the Civil War, which students are about to read. Discuss the words, noting how *anti-* changes the meaning of each word it precedes. Encourage students to construct a definition of *anti-*. Lead students to see that *anti-* is a prefix and explain how knowing the meanings of prefixes helps readers figure out unknown words. Demonstrate how you would syllabicate words that contain prefixes and how you would use knowledge of prefixes to sound out the words and determine their meanings.

Step 2: Guided Practice

Have students complete practice exercises similar to the following:
Fill in the blanks with these words containing prefixes: *antihighway, antiwar, antiunion, antifreeze, antismoking.*

- When winter comes, you will need to put _____ in your car's radiator.
- One town passed an _____ law that forbids smoking anywhere in the town.
- The _____ demonstrators gathered outside the White House when they heard that the United States planned to send soldiers into battle.
- The owner of the factory was _____ because he didn't want a union telling him how to treat his workers.
- Because they were against the new highway, the citizens set up an _____ group.

Step 3: Application

Have students read selection about the Civil War that includes the words containing the prefix *anti-*. Ask them to note words containing *anti-* in other reading that they do.

Step 4: Extension

Present the prefix *pro-* and have students contrast the meanings of the two prefixes. Using words containing the prefix *pro-*, have students make a list of things that they are in favor of: *procandy, proholidays, proallowance.* Using the prefix *anti-*, they can make a list of things that they are against: *antigangs, antidrugs, antigerms, antisuspension.* Students can also take note of these prefixes in science: *antibiotic, antibacterial.*

Step 5: Assessment and Reteaching

Fortunately, many textbook authors include morphemic clues to help students understand technical terms, as in this excerpt from a science text:

> *Sometimes scientists talk about nimbostratus clouds.* Nimbus *is a Latin word that means "rain." When you see* nimbus *or* nimbo- *in a cloud name, you know the cloud is a rain cloud.*
>
> *Clouds are also grouped by height above the ground. Some clouds are close to the ground, some are high in the sky, and some are in between. Clouds that form high in the sky have the prefix* cirro- *in front of their family name. Clouds that form at a medium height have the prefix* alto- *in front of their family name. (Badders et al., 1999, p. E 57)*

Highlight and discuss this feature so students take advantage of it. If the text fails to present useful morphemic clues, provide them to students.

Morphemic analysis can also be used to teach students how to predict the meaning of other unfamiliar words. For example, students might be asked, "If *cyt* means 'cell,' what do the following words mean?"

| cytology | cytochemistry | cytoanalyzer | cytotoxin |

Morphemic Analysis and Spanish-Speaking Students

One strategy that is effective for Spanish speakers is to seek out familiar morphemes. If students know prefixes, suffixes, and roots in Spanish, they can transfer this knowledge to English. A number of elements are identical in both languages or slightly different. For instance, the prefixes *ab, ante, anti, contra, inter, post, pro, re, sub,* and *super* are the same in both languages (Thonis, 1983). The suffixes *al, or, ar, able, ion* (except for the accent) are also the same. The suffix *tion* is slightly different in Spanish: It is spelled *cion*, but may also be spelled *sion* or *xion*. The suffix *ismo* is similar to the suffix *ism* in English. Hundreds of roots, such as *libro*, are also identical or similar.

Additional Reinforcement Activities

When a new word is presented, you might also introduce derived forms of the word. For instance, when introducing *confirm*, also introduce *confirmation*, and *confirmatory*. The following activities can be used to extend and reinforce use of morphemic elements.

Composing the Correct Form

Students rewrite words so that they incorporate the correct form:

> Not sure that she had been accepted into the program, Elena was relieved when she received a letter of (confirm).
>
> The coach warned the team that they would have to play with (intense) if they hoped to win.

Word Forms

Students fill out a from similar to the following, which shows the different grammatical forms that words can take (Nation, 2001):

Word Forms Chart

NOUN	VERB	ADJECTIVE	ADVERB
confirmation	confirm	confirmatory	
intensifier	intensify	intense	intensively
intensity		intensive	

CHECKUP

1. What are the key elements in the effective teaching of morphemic analysis strategies?

Contextual Analysis

■ Context clues are bits of information in the surrounding text that may help to derive the meaning of an unknown word. Context clues include appositives, restatement of the word's meaning, comparative or contrasting statements, and other items that might provide clues to the word's meaning.

Students have about a one in six chance of deriving the meaning of an unfamiliar word from context (Swanborn & de Glopper, 1999). The odds are more favorable if readers are trained in the use of context clues. Because content area reading is usually full of technical terms, writers often deliberately supply **context clues** for the reader. Note the technical terms in the following excerpt from a trade book on the oceans and the efforts the author takes to explain them. Even such nontechnical terms as *pierce, steep,* and *incline*, which may pose problems for some readers, are surrounded by contextual clues.

The ocean bed, or floor, is like a huge basin. In it there are channels, or trenches, that are deeper than the rest of the floor. Long lines of mountains and volcanoes rise from the ocean bottom, sometimes piercing the surface of the water to form islands. At the edges of the ocean, a steep incline called the continental slope separates the ocean bed from the more shallow seabed around the continents. The area nearest to the land is the continental shelf, where the water is not more than 650 feet deep. (Sauvain, 1996, p. 6)

Experienced writers want their readers to understand what they have to say and so they intuitively remove obstacles to comprehension, such as difficult words. Notice how science writer Seymour Simon (1998) explains in context the key words *optical* and *illusion*.

Now look at the figure below. Which line is longer, AB or BC? Measure each line with your ruler. Surprised? Both lines are exactly the same length.

You have been looking at two optical, or visual, illusions. An optical illusion is something you see that is not exactly what is really there. One line seems to be longer than another even though both are actually the same length. (p. 6)

Not only does Simon provide definitions in context of *optical* and *illusion*, he also gives an example.

Processing Context Clues

What context clues might students use to derive the meaning of the boldfaced word *turmoil* in the excerpt below?

To understand why these hundred or so people made that desperate voyage, we have to know something about the situation in England in their day. It was a country in **turmoil.** For one thing, after the long and stable reign of Elizabeth I, there came a time of much quarreling among factions in government. In particular, the Parliaments of the seventeenth century were attempting to take power away from the kings, and the kings of course resisted. In time there would be open warfare between king and Parliament.

For another, England, like much of Europe, was in the midst of the long-term, but profoundly important, switch from a farming economy to "capitalism"—the system of trade and manufacturing in which most Americans, Europeans, and others elsewhere today live and work. (Collier & Collier, 1998, p. 14)

Most use of context is automatic and cumulative, with readers acquiring more of the sense of a word's meaning with each encounter. Typically, readers don't make a conscious effort to derive the meaning of a word until they determine it is a necessity, usually because it is critical to understanding a passage. Readers use textual clues to activate background knowledge that will help them derive the meaning of a word. It generally takes five or six encounters with a word before the meaning of the word is grasped (Kibby, Rapaport, & Wieland, 2004).

Here is how the steps can be used to figure out the meaning of *turmoil*:

1. *Seeking clues.* What information in the sentence containing the unknown word will help me figure out what this word means? Is there any information in earlier sentences that will help? Is there any information in later sentences that will help?

   Helpful clues include information about quarreling between the king and Parliament and the switch from a farming economy to one of trade and manufacturing.

2. *Combining clues.* When I think about all the information given about this unknown word, what does the word seem to mean?

   When readers put all relevant clues together, they will see that *turmoil* seems to mean that there is great disturbance because so many changes are taking place.

3. *Using background knowledge.* What do I know that will help me figure out the meaning of this word? Readers think this would be like having Congress trying to get rid of the President and many people changing jobs. Life would not be calm.

4. *Trial substitution.* When I substitute "great disturbance" for turmoil, that fits.

LESSON 3.7

Steps for Using Context

Step 1: Seeking clues

Students read the entire sentence, saying "blank" for the unknown word. They then look for clues that might help them guess the meaning of the unknown word. If the clues in the sentence are inadequate, they look at earlier and later sentences.

Step 2: Combining clues

Students put all the clues together.

Step 3: Using background knowledge

Students activate their background knowledge prompted by the clues they have assembled and construct a tentative definition or meaning.

Step 4: Trial substitution

Students substitute the tentative word or phrase for the unknown word.

Step 5: Checking the substitute

Students check the context to see if the substitute word or phrase fits all the cues.

Step 6: Revision

If the substitute word or phrase does not fit, students revise the substitute and try another word or phrase.

Using past experience, readers may realize that if the king and Parliament were arguing and the way people made their living was changing, there was a great deal of disturbance. It would be like having Congress try to get rid of the president and at the same time having thousands of people change jobs. Life would not be calm or quiet.

Once readers have used context to construct a tentative meaning for the unknown word, they should try substituting that meaning for the word. If it does not fit the sense of the sentence, they should revise their substitution, use the dictionary, or get help.

Learning to use context clues is a complex process that requires instruction. Sternberg and Powell (1983) conducted an experiment in which one group was given instruction and practice in using context clues, a second group was given practice, and a third group was given neither instruction nor practice. Only the group given both instruction and practice improved, but its improvement was substantial.

Model the process, using a think-aloud to show how you used context recently to figure out the meaning of an unfamiliar word. For best results with the think-aloud, choose a word that is genuine puzzle. Provide guided practice with a passage containing potentially difficult words students will encounter in an upcoming lesson. Select essential words that have helpful context clues. During guided practice, ask such questions as: What are the context clues here? What are the clues in the sentence telling us? Are there any clues in the sentences before the hard-word sentence? Are there any clues in the sentences after the hard-word sentence? When you put all the clues together, what does the word seem to mean? Prompt the use of the steps listed above.

The payoff for using context clues is enormous. If students read a million words a year and 1 percent of the words are unknown, they will meet 10,000 unfamiliar words. Given a one in six chance in deriving the meaning of an unknown word, they will acquire 1,666 new words.

Types of Context Clues

There are eight main types of context clues. The following list is ordered by approximate level of difficulty. The examples have been drawn from a variety of content area materials.

Explicit explanation or definition. The easiest clue to use is a definition in context. For instance, the following passage gives an excellent definition of *resolution.*

> However, by the end of the 19th century, light microscopes had begun to hit resolution limits. *Resolution* is a measure of the clarity of an image; it is the minimum distance that two points can be separated by and still be distinguished as two separate points. Because light beams have a physical size, it is difficult to see an object that is about the same size as the wavelength of light. Objects smaller than about 0.2 micrometers appear fuzzy, and objects below that size just cannot be seen (Akre, Brainard, Gray-Wilson, & Wilkin, 2009).

Appositives. Definitions are sometimes supplied in the form of an appositive immediately following the difficult word.

> *Oxides*—the metal combined with oxygen—are important ore minerals (Dixon, 1992, p. 27).

Synonyms. Often, a synonym for a difficult word will appear shortly after the unfamiliar word. In the following sentence, *odor* provides a synonym for *aroma.*

> The sweet *aroma* of mince pies and pumpkin bread, floating from open bakery windows, contrasted sharply with the strong odors of oysters and cod hawked by fishmongers across the street (Litwin, 1999, pp. 9–10).

Function indicators. Context sometimes provides clues to meaning because it gives the purpose or function of the difficult word (Sternberg, 1987). In the sentence below, the reader gets a clue to the meaning of *foragers* in a sentence that tells what a forager does.

> We all have different jobs to do. Soldiers guard our nest, workers keep things neat and clean, and *foragers* look for food. (Parker, 1999, p. 12).

Examples. The examples—rain, snow, sleet, and hail—in the following passage give the reader a sense of the meaning of *precipitation.*

> Eventually the drops are too big to stay in the air, and they begin to fall as rain, snow, sleet, or hail. If you were to analyze the pH of this *precipitation*, you might discover readings as low as 2.0. (Badders et al., 1999, p. C. 84).

Comparison-contrast. By contrasting the unknown word *ascend* with the known word *descend* in the following passage, readers can gain an understanding of the unknown word. Understanding that *descend* means to "come down," the reader can reason that *ascend* means to "go up."

> The answer is that the sun and almost all heavenly objects—the moon, planets, and most stars—appear to *ascend* in the eastern half of the sky and *descend* in the western half of the sky (Schaaf, 1998, p. 52).

Classification. By noting similarities in items, some of which are known, readers can guess what an unknown word means. In the following sentence, they know from the word *town* and the earlier mention of Canada that places are being talked about; based on this conclusion, they can infer that *province,* the unknown word, is also a place. Because the sentence says that the town is in the province, they could infer that a province is larger than a town.

> Gordie was born on March 31, 1928, in the town of Floral, in the *province* of Saskatchewan. (Neff, 1990, p. 48).

Experience. A main clue to the meaning of an unfamiliar word is students' background experience. In the following passage, readers can use their own experience of being treated unfairly or being denied an opportunity to imagine how Abigail Adams feels; this will enable them to make an informed guess as to what the unfamiliar word *indignantly* means.

> Abigail had always regretted her lack of schooling and was embarrassed by her peculiar spelling and punctuation, which she called pointing. And Abigail resented how most families

neglected their daughters' education. "Every assistance and advantage . . . is afforded to the Sons," she commented *indignantly*. (St. George, 2001, p. 5).

A combination of clues can sometimes be used. In the following example, a republican form of government is contrasted with government by a king. The word *republic* is also defined in context.

Kings ruled Rome until 510 B.C. when the citizens expelled the last king, Tarquin the Proud. Rome then became a *republic* governed by officials who were elected by the people (Roberts, 1997, p. 10).

Context clues and morphemic analysis can often be integrated. For instance, students might use their knowledge of the root word *photo*, meaning "light," and context to derive the meaning of *photic* in the following sentence.

As we have already established, the part of the sea where sunlight penetrates is called the *photic* zone (Massa, 1998, p. 20).

Notice in the sentence below how the meaning of *di-* is suggested and how the meaning of *cotyledons* is provided.

The hibiscus is a *dicotyledon*. Its seedlings have two seed leaves, or cotyledons, and its leaves are broad with a central midrib and branched veins (Smith, 1996, p. 39).

Generating possible definitions from context requires some thought. Students may have to consider several possible meanings before arriving at one that seems suitable. Here is how Angela, a middle-school student, arrived at a tentative meaning for the word *qualms*, in a selection she was reading. First, the selection:

I had a few qualms at first about how Caroline and Julia would get along together. Julia was so different from all of our school friends that I felt sort of awkward with her myself (Duncan, 1977, p. 55).

Now Angela's reasoning:

Researcher: Talk to me. What do you think?

Angela: That maybe there are questions of how they are going to get together.

Researcher: What do you mean by questions?

Angela: Like are they going to get together or are they not. Like she's thinking in her head how is she like going to get along with her friend.

Researcher: So what does that tell you about the word *qualms?*

Angela: That she might be thinking in her head.

Researcher: What else can you tell me? (long pause before Angela responds)

Angela: Ideas.

Researcher: Keep talking.

Angela: Maybe like an uneasy feeling. (Harmon, 1998a, p. 586)

> **CCSS**
>
> Determine or clarify the meaning of unknown and multiple-meaning words and phrases by using context clues, analyzing meaningful word parts, and consulting general and specialized reference materials, as appropriate.

CHECKUP

1. What is involved in using context clues?
2. How might context clues be taught?

Dictionary Use

The dictionary or glossary is the word analysis strategy of last resort. Looking up a word interferes with the flow of reading and therefore can hinder comprehension. In most instances, students should use contextual or word analysis clues and, if they don't work, wait until after the section has been read to look up unknown words. However, if the word is central to the meaning of the section and context clues don't work, it should be looked up immediately.

Most content area textbooks and **trade books** contain glossaries. Glossaries are easier to use than dictionaries largely because they typically only present the definition of the word used in the context of the text. However, there may be some general words that the student doesn't know and some technical words may not be included in the glossary, so general-use dictionaries should be available. If your discipline has its own dictionary, it should be available too: These specialized dictionaries are the tools of the discipline.

Students sometimes need conceptual information about a term, information that goes beyond the dictionary or glossary's definition. It is helpful to have on hand either a general or discipline-specific encyclopedia. Fortunately, encyclopedias and dictionaries are relatively inexpensive and widely available, either on CD-ROM or online.

When introducing the textbook at the beginning of the year, spend some time talking about the glossary. In many texts, words defined in the glossary are boldfaced in the text the first time they are used. In some texts essential terms are glossed in the margins. Note, too, illustrations, sample sentences, phonetic respellings, and other aids provided in the glossary. Instruction in glossary and dictionary use should be functional. When students have difficulty with a word, have them look it up in the glossary or dictionary (Have the word looked up after the student has read the section, unless the word is essential for understanding the section.) Discuss the meaning they obtained and make sure it is appropriate for the context of the word they were looking up. Also make sure that the definition is understandable.

The key to turning students into skilled dictionary users is helping them discover the value of the dictionary. One way of doing this is by discussing the information that can be found in the dictionary. Students may be surprised to find out that in addition to providing definitions and spellings for words, dictionaries provide information on grammar and usage, weights and measurements, and spellings of geographical locations. In addition, some dictionaries provide a history of the language and common words found in other languages. A second way of turning students into dictionary users is by providing guided opportunities to use the dictionary in a functional fashion: to find the meaning of a difficult term in the text, to check the spelling of the name of a famous person, to check the pronunciation of a town or city. If students feel comfortable with the dictionary, chances are they will use it.

Because there are many general as well as technical terms that they may not know, English language learners will find the dictionary especially valuable. Dictionary usage is critical for ELLs. As they encounter unknown words in their reading, they have very little choice but to consult the dictionary. One problem is that the definitions often contain unfamiliar words. As one student put it, "I find word in dictionary. But meaning I do not understand. I have to find other meaning [in dictionary] to explain this word" (Gonzalez, 1999, p. 269). Despite the difficulty they experienced using the dictionary, ELLs in one study were able to determine correct definitions about 80 percent of the time (Gonzales, 1999). Fortunately, there are dictionaries that have been especially designed for students with limited English vocabulary. The *Longman Dictionary of American English* (Pearson Education Limited, 2008) defines words using only the 2,000 most commonly occurring words. In addition to clear definitions, the *Longman Dictionary of American English* also provides example sentences, which illustrate how the words are used. Special attention is paid to idioms and words that frequently occur together. Although designed for English learners, learner dictionaries might be used by all students.

USING TECHNOLOGY

Merriam-Webster www.merriam-webster.com/ game/index .html/ presents a number of vocabulary building exercises. The site also provides pronunciations for words.

English Language Learners

Students stymied by figures of speech may not realize that they can be found in the dictionary, usually under the key word in the phrase. For instance, the expressions "big heart," "take to heart," and "with all one's heart" would be found under *heart*.

Using a Thesaurus

The thesaurus can be an efficient tool for obtaining a number of synonyms for a word and also learning a number of new words with relatively little effort. For example, looking up the word *gaunt* in the *Longman Dictionary of American English* (Pearson, 2008), the student sees that the thesaurus entry, which is directly beneath the definition, lists the

■ **Trade books** are books written to be sold to the general public or collected in libraries, as opposed to textbooks, which are designed to be sold to schools.

synonyms: *thin, slim, slender, slight, skinny, lean, underweight, emaciated, anorexic, skeletal* (p. 424). A related activity might be to rank these words according to intensity and to discuss contexts in which they might be used.

Contextual Redefinition

Contextual redefinition is an excellent technique for reviewing and integrating dictionary usage with other word analysis strategies. This technique aids students in the use of context clues by contrasting definitions derived for words in isolation with definitions derived for words in context (Tierney & Readence, 2005). It also provides reinforcement for dictionary skills. An easy-to-implement but effective technique, contextual redefinition consists of four steps: (1) choosing hard words, (2) presenting words in isolation, (3) presenting words in context, and (4) checking derived meanings against those provided by a dictionary. Lesson 3.8 shows instructions for a sample contextual redefinition lesson.

Contextual redefinition provides practice in three interrelated word identification skills: morphemic analysis, contextual analysis, and dictionary usage. In deriving the meaning of *monarch*, students can use their knowledge of the combining form *mono* and the root *arch*, the context clue, and the dictionary definition to arrive at an understanding of *monarch*.

LESSON 3.8

Contextual Redefinition

Step 1: Selecting Hard Words

Choose words that are important to an understanding of the selection and that may be difficult for students.

Step 2: Presenting Words in Isolation

List potentially unfamiliar words on the board or on a transparency. Invite volunteers to pronounce them. Give help if it is needed and ask the volunteers to define the words. Because the words are presented in isolation, students rely on morphemic analysis clues to define them. Ask students to give reasons for their definitions. Because they lack context clues and the aid of the dictionary, their definitions may be off the mark. For instance, unless students spot the combining form *mon(o)* and the root *arch*, they might define *monarch* as "my bridge" or "one arch." Encourage students to agree on one meaning for each word.

Step 3: Presenting Words in Context

Next, present the words in context. Ideally, this would be the context in which the words are used in the selection to be read. However, if the context is not adequate, compose your own sentence.

Using the context, have students make their best guesses about the meaning of each word, working alone, in pairs, or in small groups. After they have attempted to derive the meaning of a word from context, ask them to explain why they composed a particular definition. This gives them an opportunity to learn from each other as they share their reasoning processes. Ask the group again to agree on the best guess as to the target word's meaning.

Step 4: Checking the Meaning in the Dictionary

Ask students to look up the word in the dictionary and discuss possible definitions with the group. The group chooses the most appropriate definition.

1. How might dictionary skills be taught?
2. What are the skills students need in order to become independent word learners?
3. How might you integrate the teaching of these skills with the teaching of your subject matter?

Integration of Skills

Although word analysis strategies have been presented separately, students should be encouraged to integrate their use. They may try context first, and if that doesn't work, they may try morphemic analysis, and, if all else fails, they may use the dictionary or glossary or seek help from a parent, a teacher, or a classmate. Alternatively, they may use partial clues from two or more sources of information. The strategies that students use depend on the nature of the word, the text, and students' ability and command of strategies. Struggling learners may use ineffective strategies. For instance, one struggling reader in middle school used primarily a phonic or pronunciation strategy, and if that didn't work, she would ask for help or skip the word (Harmon, 1998a). When prompted, she was partially successful with using context, but she did not use context on her own.

USING TECHNOLOGY

Provide access to electronic dictionaries for student use. Electronic dictionaries make it possible to locate words faster and are motivational. An electronic dictionary may also read aloud the word and its definition. This is a help for students whose reading skills are limited.

1. What instructional steps might be taken to integrate word analysis skills and strategies?

Exemplary Teaching

Building Vocabulary: An Effective Approach

Realizing that vocabulary is a key element in comprehension, tenth-grade English teacher Chris Sloan dutifully taught his students key vocabulary before they read a selection. However, students' comprehension failed to improve, and he wasn't even sure that the students' vocabularies were improving. After discussing his difficulty with two researchers, he devised a new approach to teaching vocabulary.

His revised approach embodied several facets. He taught students how to identify key vocabulary words—those that were especially important to an understanding of the selection—and he taught them strategies for learning unknown words. He also made sure that they learned the words in the context of the selection. As they read the selection, students underlined what they believed were the key words, used context to predict the words' meanings, and checked their predictions by looking the words up in the dictionary. The next day, students discussed the key words they had chosen as they discussed the selection they had read. Key words were related to the selection's characters, plot, or theme. For instance, they discussed the fact that Lemas, a character in the selection they were reading, was a *cynical* man who sought *vengeance*. His *cynicism* was related to his *profession* and his *motto,* "Trust no one." Through the discussion, the students deepened their knowledge of the selection and also developed their vocabulary (Dole, Sloan, & Trathen, 1995).

As with so many other areas, instruction in word analysis has to be affective to be effective. Instruction must include sessions in which the teacher assesses students' work in group or individual think-alouds to see what strategies students use and also to ascertain their attitudes. Feelings of inadequacy and an unwillingness to try must be addressed. "Listening to learners voice what they know and how they use what they know about word learning seems a necessary part of vocabulary instruction" (Harmon, 1998a, p. 592).

Summary

One of the chief barriers to learning in the content areas is posed by the technical vocabulary that each subject employs. An effective program of vocabulary development features in-depth understanding, multiple exposures, active involvement, seeing relationships among words, and acquiring strategies for developing new vocabulary. Techniques for teaching words include conceptual teaching of key words and brainstorming techniques, such as the list-group-label and semantic mapping approaches. Graphic techniques include the Frayer model, concept definition, semantic mapping, pictorial maps and webs, semantic feature analysis, and the Venn diagram. Other vocabulary teaching techniques are possible sentences, predict-o-grams, word sorts, vocabulary self-collection strategy, and contextual redefinition. Strategies for remembering words should focus on building understanding and the key word method. Vocabulary instruction should also include instruction in syllabic and morphemic analysis, contextual analysis, and dictionary use so that students can learn words on their own.

Reflection

Return to the Anticipation Guide at the beginning of this chapter. Respond once again to the items. Did your responses change? If so, how and why? How do you now feel about the number of words presented in content area texts in your field? As a content area teacher, what is your responsibility for helping students learn content words? What steps might you take to help students learn content words?

Extension and Application

1. Examine the technical terms in a text from your content area. Survey several chapters. How many new words are introduced per chapter? What kinds of strategies do the words lend themselves to? What kinds of morphemic elements might you introduce that would help students learn some of the new words? How helpful would contextual strategies be? What word learning aids do the chapters incorporate? Are words boldfaced and explained in context? Is there a glossary? Are illustrations used to help explain words?

2. Try out three of the graphic organizers described in this chapter. Use each one for at least a week with words that you are trying to help students learn. What are the strengths and weaknesses of each of the organizers? Which was easiest to use? Which seems most effective?

3. Use the key word technique to learn five new words. Test yourself a day later and then a week later. How did the technique work? Try out the technique with a group of students and assess its effectiveness.

Where the Classroom Comes to Life

Go to Topic 6: Vocabulary in the MyEducationLab (www.my educationlab.com) for your course, where you can:

- Find learning outcomes for Vocabulary along with the national standards that connect to these outcomes.
- Complete Assignments and Activities that can help you more deeply understand the chapter content.
- Apply and practice your understanding of the core teaching skills identified in the chapter with the Building Teaching Skills and Dispositions learning units.

Go to the Topic A+RISE in the MyEducationLab (www .myeducationlab.com) for your course. A+RISE® Standards2Strategy™ is an innovative and interactive online resource that offers new teachers in grades K–12 just-in-time, research-based instructional strategies that:

- Meet the linguistic needs of ELLs as they learn content.
- Differentiate instruction for all grades and abilities.
- Offer reading and writing techniques, cooperative learning, use of linguistic and nonlinguistic representations, scaffolding, teacher modeling, higher-order thinking, and alternative classroom ELL assessment.
- Provide support to help teachers be effective through the integration of listening, speaking, reading, and writing along with the content curriculum.
- Improve student achievement.
- Are aligned to Common Core Elementary Language Arts standards (for the literacy strategies) and to English language proficiency standards in WIDA, Texas, California, and Florida.

CHAPTER 4

Comprehension: Processes and Strategies

Anticipation Guide

For each of the following statements, put a check under "Agree" or "Disagree" to indicate your opinion. If possible, discuss your responses with classmates.

	Agree	Disagree
1. Reading comprehension is primarily a matter of grasping the author's message.	_____	_____
2. The key to comprehension is having solid knowledge about the topic being explained.	_____	_____
3. Comprehension is more difficult to teach than vocabulary.	_____	_____
4. Implementing effective reading strategies is the best way to improve comprehension.	_____	_____
5. If they are given proper instruction in the use of strategies, poor readers can do as well as average readers.	_____	_____
6. Comprehension strategies that are effective in learning history can be used in the sciences and vice versa.	_____	_____

Using What You Know

This chapter is the most important in the book. The essence of reading is comprehension—an active, constructive process that can be fostered by the effective use of **strategies**. What do you know about comprehension? What strategies do you use as you try to understand what you read? Do you use the same strategies in all content areas? Do you read a history text the same way you read a science or math text?

The Process of Comprehension

To gain some insight into the process of comprehension, read the following paragraph, which has been divided into a series of sentences. Stop after reading each sentence and ask yourself: What did the sentence say? How did I go about comprehending it? What does this paragraph seem to be about?

To scientists living 150 years ago, they looked like pieces of a giant jigsaw puzzle.

The edges in several of the pieces would fit neatly into the indentations of other pieces.

Could it all have been one giant piece?

If so, what caused it to break up?

From this and observations that rocks and fossils in South America were similar to those found in Africa, the theory of continental drift was born.

According to that theory, the Earth's crust was once one solid piece but broke apart into huge plates that move ever so slowly but have caused many changes in the Earth's surface. (Sattler, 1995)

At what point did you realize that the passage is about plate tectonics theory? If you are or were a geology major, you may have conjectured after reading the first sentence that this selection was talking about early inquiries concerning the shapes of the continents. Or perhaps you didn't catch on right away, but the third sentence, which talks about

■ **Strategies** are deliberate, planned activities or procedures designed to achieve a certain goal.

the unnamed object being one giant piece, provided a clue that led you to suspect what the passage was about. If your knowledge of geology is minimal, you may not have understood what the passage was about until the last sentence.

Schema Theory

Comprehending is a process of constructing meaning. What we take away from a text depends on what we bring to it. We bring our reasoning processes and our background of knowledge to our construction of meaning, so the more we know about a topic before we come to a text, the deeper and more complete our comprehension of that text will be. According to **schema** theory, our background knowledge is packaged in abstract units known as *schemata* (Rumelhart, 1984). A schema is the organized knowledge one has about people, places, things, and ideas. A schema might be broad—our schema for the chemical elements for instance—or it might be narrow—our schema for oxygen.

Mental Models Theory

Comprehension can also be thought of as the construction of a mental or situation model. Schema theory provides a good description of what happens when the students are reading about ideas, events, or processes for which they have some background knowledge. But what happens with new information, such as when readers who have never have heard of continental drift or even continents read about plate tectonics? The **mental models** theory is a more inclusive theory of comprehension because it can handle both schema-based and new ideas (McNamara, Miller, & Bransford, 1991).

Comprehension consists of three levels of understanding: surface structure, textbase, and mental model (Kintsch, 1994). The surface structure is composed of the exact words of the written piece. The **textbase** is the propositions or ideas conveyed by the surface structure. As students read, they transform text into propositions. **Propositions** are statements of information. Readers combine, delete, and integrate propositions to form a **macrostructure**. The macrostructure, which is a running summary of the text, may be composed of the statement of a cause and three or four effects or a main idea and three or four details. In addition to activating a schema, constructing a textbase requires four key processing abilities: understanding essential details at a literal level; integrating text across sentences and paragraphs; making low-level, text-based inferences; and monitoring for meaning.

The mental model is a deeper level of understanding. The mental model combines the reader's background knowledge with information from the text. For instance, when reading a section about exercise in a health text, a student operating on the surface structure level may answer the end-of-chapter question "What is aerobic exercise?" by copying the sentence from the text section that defines aerobic exercise. This student may not understand what the sentence says and probably would be unable to either explain his answer or put it in his own words. A student reading on the proposition level might find out that aerobic exercises build up muscle endurance and that resistance exercises build up strength and bulk. But without adequate background knowledge about the muscular system, the student would not be able to infer why this is so and is therefore would not be able to construct a mental model or representation. The student who lacks representational

---

■ A **schema** is a unit of organized knowledge. (The plural of *schema* is *schemata*.)

■ The **mental models** theory views comprehension as a "process of building and maintaining a model of situations and events described in text" (McNamara, Miller, & Bransford, 1991, p. 491). Schema theory describes how familiar situations are understood. Mental models theory describes how new situations are comprehended.

■ The **textbase** includes the statements or ideas conveyed by the surface structure.

■ **Propositions** are statements of information.

■ The **macrostructure** is a running summary of the text.

knowledge can recite the information that he has read, but cannot explain it or draw conclusions about causes, because he doesn't understand it well enough (Kintsch, 1994).

A student who has knowledge of the muscular system can create a representational model by combining information from the text with background information from biology class. She will be able to infer that aerobic exercises increase the efficiency of the flow of blood to the muscles so the muscles don't get tired as quickly and that resistance exercises cause the white fibers in the muscles to grow in size and add more contractile proteins. The student will then be able to apply this representational knowledge by planning a program of exercise designed to meet her personal goals of increased endurance or strength, or both.

Had the text reviewed the operation of the muscular system, the reader might have had sufficient background knowledge to infer why one type of exercise builds endurance and the other strength. Or the teacher could have built the necessary background. Because comprehension is a blending of reader, text, and context, the combination of a well-written, well-planned text and the teacher's building of essential background can fill in the gaps when students' background is inadequate.

Readers construct a **mental representation** when they integrate their prior knowledge, goal for reading, and other reader factors with the textbase. Students reading the same passage would construct a similar textbase, but their mental models would vary because their backgrounds, goals for reading, and perspectives vary. "Whereas the textbase is verbal—it consists of word meanings combined into propositions—the mental model can include imagery and even an emotional component" (Gunning, 2010, p. 4). As Hampton and Resnick (2009) explain,

> Readers move back and forth between the textbase and mental model. As they read, strong readers continually check their mental model against the textbase to make certain that the mental model accurately reflects what the text says and is consistent with their knowledge base. (p. 223)

In view of the mental models theory of comprehension, what might be done to make the following text more understandable and more memorable?

> Early in human development, a human embryo forms into a blastocyst. A blastocyst is a hollow ball of cells with a group of cells inside called the inner cell mass. The outer cells form tissues that attach the embryo to its mother. The inner cell mass become the embryo itself. (Miller & Levine, 2009)

The text provides information, and the information is clearly stated. However, there is not enough explanation provided to enable the reader to create a mental model of the text, to envision or create an image of what is being explained. The reader has nothing to hold on to but the facts, and chances are, since these are unconnected, they will soon fade away. The reader needs to be able to ask *how* and *why*. *How* do the cells keep the embryo attached to the mother and also *why* do they do this? Moreover, the text is not integrating new information with what the reader already knows. Even if the text is understood, it won't be integrated with the reader's background knowledge. Failure to integrate new information with prior knowledge is a recipe for forgetting.

CHECKUP

1. What are the two major, but related, theories of comprehension?
2. What implications do these theories have for instruction in the content areas?

Comprehension Strategies

Read the following excerpt from a review text designed to assist students with their science homework. Then complete the quiz that follows without looking back.

■ The mental representation (mental model) is the understanding that the reader creates. It combines the reader's background knowledge with information from the text.

The Speed of Sound

Sound travels about 1,100 feet (335 meters) per second or 740 miles per hour. It travels a little faster on hot days than cold days. Sound travels four times faster in water and even faster still through solids than through the air.

Sound doesn't travel nearly as fast as light. Take a close look at the marching bands the next time you see a parade. The marching band members closest to the drummers are slightly out of step from the band members farthest away from the drummers. This is because the faraway members hear the drumbeats a tiny bit later. (Zeman & Kelly, 1994, p. 118)

☐ How fast does sound travel?

☐ On which day would a call for help most likely be heard sooner? Why?

    a. December 1   b. July 1   c. October 1   d. March 1

☐ In a parade, which member of a marching band would most likely be out of step?

    A. The band leader.   B. The buglers up front.

    C. The trumpet players in the middle.   D. The bass drummer, who is last.

Please explain your choice.

After completing the quiz, check your answers. Then answer the following questions:

- Before reading the excerpt, what did you do? What were you thinking?
- As you read the excerpt, what thoughts were going through your mind? Did you do anything as you were reading?
- After you read the article, what did you do? What were you thinking?

The exercise of asking you to read the excerpt and answer the questions was designed to help you experience the use of strategies. The quiz was included because readers usually employ more strategies when they know they are going to be tested. Strategies are deliberate, planned procedures designed to achieve a goal. Adept readers don't become aware of their thinking process until they read difficult material and have to deliberately choose to use strategies. Otherwise, they use strategies automatically. Examples of comprehension strategies include previewing, predicting, summarizing, inferring, asking oneself questions, making images, and rereading.

How strategic a reader are you? Have you summarized main ideas? Have you questioned any of the statements made in this chapter? Have you made connections between an idea in the text and your personal experiences? Have you thought of times when you could recite from text but didn't really understand what you had read? Have you wondered what strategies you use? If you have done any of these things or involved yourself with the reading in any other way, these are signs that you are a strategic reader.

Building Metacognitive Awareness

To apply strategies, you must be aware of your thinking. Many teachers use a device called a **think-aloud** to model the processes they use when reading content area material so that students will gain insight into the strategies they employ. By showing students how they create visual images when reading, they reveal what is going on in their minds—what they see in their mind's eye—as they read the text. As they become more aware of their thought processes, students are better able to use cognitively based strategies to understand their content area texts more fully. Being aware of one's thinking is known as **metacognition** and is the foundation of comprehension instruction.

It takes time and effort to integrate think-alouds into a class routine. When researchers helped a secondary school put into practice a series of four interventions—two-column note-taking, think-alouds, extra reading, and writing

---

■ Strategies are deliberate, planned procedures designed to achieve a goal.

■ A think-aloud is a procedure in which a person describes her thought processes while engaged in reading, writing, or another cognitive activity.

■ Metacognition or metacognitive awareness means being conscious of one's mental processes.

to learn—think-alouds were the most difficult for the secondary school staff to implement (Fisher, Frey, & Lapp, 2009). The researchers reasoned that the other three interventions primarily involved changes in the way teachers used their time, whereas think-alouds required a change in behavior. One way of preparing yourself to engage in a genuine think-aloud is to become more aware of your thinking processes.

In order to understand metacognition and cognitive strategies, you must become aware of the strategies you use as you read and the thinking processes in which you engage. With practice, your use of strategies becomes relatively automatic. Stop your reading from time to time and think about the mental tools you are using to comprehend what you are reading. Do this especially when you are reading difficult material. Strategies tend to become more conscious when the material is difficult because you have to take deliberate steps to comprehend it. One technique that a group of highly successful staff developers and classroom teachers used was to try out each strategy on their own reading before teaching it. The result was that the staff developers and teachers improved their own comprehension:

> We test the strategies on our reading. We became more conscious of our own thinking processes as readers. We realized that we could concentrate simultaneously on the text and our ways of thinking about it. What seems most extraordinary, however, was that by thinking about our own thinking—by being metacognitive (literally, to think about one's thinking)—we could actually deepen and enhance our comprehension of the text. (Keene & Zimmermann, 1997, p. 21)

Careful metacognitive instruction is especially important for struggling learners because they are often the very students who lack insight into their thinking processes and who do not possess a repertoire of strategies; they must be taught the strategies, along with when and where to use them.

CHECKUP

1. What is metacognition?
2. Why is it an important element in comprehension?

Only a relatively small number of comprehension strategies have been found to be effective. These strategies are used in preparing, organizing, elaborating, and monitoring (metacognition) comprehension. There are also affective strategies (Weinstein & Mayer, 1986) in which motivation and interest play a role in the construction of meaning and rehearsal or study strategies, which are discussed in Chapter 7. Strategies are organized according to the thinking processes involved in their operation. Although strategies are presented in separate categories, there is some overlap. See Table 4.1 for a list of strategies.

Preparational Strategies

Students use preparational strategies to get ready to read a selection. Preparational strategies include previewing a piece before reading it, activating prior knowledge, predicting what a selection might be about, and setting a purpose for reading and goals. Did you have a purpose for reading? (A purpose is the question that the reader wants to have answered or information that the reader is seeking.) Did you set a goal? (The goal is the outcome that the reader is seeking.) Your goal may have been to do well on the quiz that followed.

TABLE 4.1 Comprehension Strategies

PREPARATIONAL	ORGANIZATIONAL	ELABORATION	METACOGNITIVE
Previewing	Organizational	Making inferences	Knowing oneself as a learner
Activating prior knowledge	Using text structure	Imaging	Regulating
Predicting	Determining essential information	Generating questions	Checking
Setting purpose and goals	Summarizing	Evaluating	Repairing

Previewing

Having a general idea of what they are about to read provides students with an overview of the selection and helps them organize their thoughts as they read. It also helps them activate prior knowledge. Students possess two kinds of knowledge: subject knowledge and personal knowledge. For instance, students who are preparing to read about a balanced diet may have studied this topic previously and may have some knowledge of the food pyramid or plate. They also possess personal knowledge that they have picked up from family, the media, or friends. Chances are they have been told that they should eat fruits and vegetables and that they shouldn't eat too much fast food. By bringing this knowledge to mind, students are preparing themselves to get more out of their reading.

A **preview** is a fast survey of a selection. Students read titles and headings, an introductory paragraph or blurb, if there is one, and the summary paragraph, if there is one. They might also glance at illustrations. As they preview, students infer or predict what the selection will be about. Previewing turns passive readers into active ones and is especially helpful when students encounter difficult text. Previewing should be brief and should take no more than three to five minutes. If a text is being read section by section, the readers can also briefly preview each section before reading it. This doesn't mean that the preview of the whole section or chapter should be skipped. It helps the student see how each of the sections is related to the whole and also how the sections are related to each other.

To introduce previewing, model the strategy using a think-aloud so students can gain some insight into the process. Conduct some group previews with the class. After students have caught on to the idea of previewing, have them practice with your guidance, and discuss their previews. Use naturally occurring opportunities such as getting a new textbook or beginning a new chapter to reinforce the concept of previewing. As part of the preparation for reading a section, pose questions that require students to preview, including asking them to make predictions about what the selection might be about. Give students a few minutes to preview. As you discuss their predictions, have them explain what they observed in the title, headings, illustrations, introduction, or summary that led to these predictions. Discuss when and where previews might be used, and provide other opportunities for them to preview independently.

Be sure to demonstrate the value of previews. Have students compare the results of reading a section after a preview and reading a section without a preview. You might give them a brief no-grade quiz so they can see that reading with a preview results in improved performance. A good preview can function as a framework for constructing a mental representation of the selection.

Activating Prior Knowledge

During the preview or during another step if there is not a preview, guide students in the activation of prior knowledge by inquiring what they know about a particular topic or asking a series of leading questions. Activating prior knowledge is a crucial step. Students comprehend by connecting new information with what they already know. However, if they don't realize that they have previously acquired information about a particular topic, they may not make the necessary connections. This is more likely to happen when topics are presented in formal, academic, or technical language. For instance, the concept *supply and demand* may seem totally new, but students may have paid scalpers' prices for tickets to concerts or sporting events that were sold out. They may have bought athletic shoes on sale and realized that the manufacturer made too many or that they are no longer popular so the price has been reduced. The concept will be more understandable if students can build on their knowledge base.

In some instances, students' prior knowledge is erroneous. Unless they are able to confront and modify their erroneous beliefs, students may not be able to construct an accurate representation of the material they are reading. (For more information about changing erroneous concepts, see Chapter 11.)

■ **A preview** is a quick survey of a selection in order to get an overview of its content.

By probing students' prior knowledge, you can clarify incomplete or erroneous concepts, judge how much instruction is necessary and which topics need the most emphasis, and select the most appropriate activities and materials. Part of tapping into students' prior knowledge is using activities and materials that are culturally relevant to students. For instance, when discussing nutrition, use as examples the foods that students are most familiar with.

English teacher Kelly Gallagher (2003) has students write everything they know about the Holocaust before they read *Night*, Elie Wiesel's (1955, 2006) first-person account of life in a concentration camp during World War II. Students then share what they have written. Writing activates each student's background knowledge. Sharing expands their knowledge as they learn from each other. Before reading Act 1, Scene 3 of *Romeo and Juliet* in which Juliet's parents decide whom she should marry, Gallagher's students do a **quickwrite** in response to the prompt: "Should your parents have any say in whom you date?" Responding to this prompt engenders interest in the play and helps students see its relevance to their lives. It also sparks a lively debate. Before reading the chapter in *1984* in which Orwell introduces the concept of thought crime, Gallagher's students respond to the following two-part prompt: "(1) Please brainstorm a list of all the methods the government of Oceania has used thus far to control the thoughts and actions of its citizens" and "(2) In this chapter Orwell will explain the concept of 'thought crime.' Before reading the chapter, predict what he means by thought crime." This brief writing task fosters a review of material read, prepares students for the upcoming reading, and makes reading more active by having students read to assess their predictions.

Predicting

Did you make predictions before you read the selection about the speed of sound? Predicting facilitates the activation of prior knowledge. Using a **prediction strategy**, a reader makes an educated guess about the course of events in a narrative or the kind of information that will be contained in an informational selection. Effective predictions are based on the thoughtful consideration of what we know. Predictions often determine purpose in reading. Students may read the selection to compare their predictions with the events or information contained in the selection.

Setting Purpose and Goals

All too often, students' **goal** for reading a text is to fulfill an assignment. They may reach their goal of reading the assigned section, but they come away knowing little more than they did when they started. They may even have as their goal answering the questions at the end of the chapter. This, too, can result in failure to derive any benefit from the reading. As noted earlier, one strategy that struggling readers use when reading difficult text is to match the words in the questions with the same words in the text and to simply copy the sentence in which these words appeared. Struggling readers may have picked up the idea that the object of reading is to pronounce the words, and they may not have the construction of meaning as their goal. The overall goal of all readers, whether struggling or adept, should be to construct meaning. Subsidiary goals might be to learn valuable or interesting information, prepare for an upcoming test, set up an experiment, or assemble a piece of equipment.

Students' **purpose** for reading consists of the specific question or questions that they are seeking to answer. Purposes are often set by the teacher, but they may be established by the students. For instance, students might create questions based on their

■ **A quickwrite** is a brief written response to a text passage, lecture, discussion, lesson, or prompt.

■ **A prediction strategy** is a deliberate attempt to foretell the content of a segment of text.

■ **The goal** for reading is the outcome the reader is seeking: to gain information, to prepare for a test, to upgrade a computer, to relax, etc.

■ **The purpose** for reading is the question that the reader wants to answer or the information the reader is seeking.

preview and read to answer those questions. The purpose for reading might grow out of activating prior knowledge. For example, students' activation of prior knowledge in preparation for reading an article about acid rain might cause them to realize that they know chemicals produced by pollution cause acid rain. Their purpose (question to be answered) in reading might then be to find out which chemicals cause acid rain and how they are formed.

Chances are, students have been taught to preview, predict, set goals, and activate prior knowledge in previous grades. However, students may not realize that these strategies can be applied to your content area, too; they also may not know how to apply them or understand their value. Provide guidance and encouragement in the use of these and other strategies so that students gain the confidence to use them on their own.

CHECKUP

1. What are the key preparational strategies?
2. How do they function together?

Selection/Organizational Strategies

Of all the strategies, those that help students organize information are the most crucial. Without some way of organizing information, students would be lost in a sea of details. Because concepts are stored in networks in our brains, we can understand and retain new information better if we relate it to already existing concepts. In fact, we probably won't comprehend new information or retain it if it is not connected to our existing framework of knowledge. In the content areas, one organizational strategy is to use the structure of the text as a framework for comprehending and storing information.

What makes the following excerpt from a U.S. history text easy to understand?

> Why were the Americans able, finally, to beat what had been considered the mightiest army in the world, supported by a great navy? For one, there was General Howe's slowness to take action at the beginning. Had he pushed hard at Washington in that first terrible winter, he might well have destroyed the American army and captured Washington. Instead, he let Washington drive him out of New Jersey at Trenton, and for the British a great opportunity was lost. For another, the general situation was ultimately favorable to the Americans.
>
> The British might beat the Americans as they did on Long Island, at Brandywine, and many other places; but Washington was always able somehow to find more men, more equipment, more courage. The British were always squeezing a balloon that would pop up at another place. Finally, the help of the French was critical. Loans of money, beginning even before the Battle of Saratoga in 1777, and materiel gave the Americans a chance. And French aid after Saratoga entirely changed the odds. Without de Grasse's fleet to bottle up the British at Yorktown, Cornwallis would have been eventually rescued by British ships, and gone on fighting. (Collier & Collier, 1998, p. 83)

The text is well organized. The main idea is clearly stated in the first sentence, so the reader has a good sense of the content of the passage. Better yet, the main idea is stated in the form of a question so that all the reader needs to do is read to answer the question. And the use of *why* signals to the reader that the author will be supplying reasons or causes. The causes of America's victory are clearly stated. And there is no extraneous information to distract the reader's attention. The causes are also highlighted by the use of signal words: *for one, for another,* and *finally.*

When reading, students need to activate two kinds of schema: prior knowledge and text structure. The content of a text cannot be separated from the way that content is expressed. Teachers are "well advised to model for students how to figure out what the author's general framework or structure is and allow students to practice finding it on their own" (Pearson & Camperell, 1994, p. 463). The better organized the text, the more apparent the structure of the piece will be and the higher the likelihood is that the reader will understand and learn from the text.

A key challenge when reading informational text lies in integrating the ideas presented. When reading narrative passages, students are aided by the familiar structures of a story. However, expository text has a logical, rather than a narrative structure. The reader must follow the author's reasoning and keep in mind main ideas and key details. In one study, proficient readers were able to answer questions after reading individual pages, but they had difficulty when asked to retell the entire expository selection However, when reading narrative passages, these students' local and global comprehension abilities were similar (Romero, Paris, & Brem, 2005). Making use of text structure can help students integrate ideas when they read informational text.

Effective readers make use of the structure of a text in three ways: It focuses attention on key ideas, it helps show how ideas are related, and it provides a framework to aid retention of information (Slater & Graves, 1989).

Types of Text Structure

There are two major types of text structure: hierarchical and coordinate (Simonsen, 1996). A hierarchical text structure features a main idea and subordinate details. The most commonly used hierarchical text structure, list structure, develops one idea at a time, allowing readers to focus on a single concept before proceeding to the next one; however, the list may fail to show how one main idea is related to another. In contrast, coordinate structures—which include comparison/contrast, cause/effect, problem/solution, time sequence, and steps in a process—show relationships among ideas (Armbruster & Anderson, 1981; Meyer & Rice, 1984; Simonsen, 1996).

Hierarchical Structures

List Structure   Most textbooks follow a list structure (Simonsen, 1996). The chapter title and introduction state the overall topic or theme. Each section of the chapter then announces its main idea in a heading or implies its main idea and develops it. Comprehending a list structure involves knowing what a main idea is, being able to recognize the main idea in a paragraph or section, and understanding how to connect the essential details to the main idea. Note the list structure in the following two paragraphs.

> The hydrogen atom is the simplest atom that can possibly exist. Its most common isotope is composed of a single proton and an electron. If you take away either of these parts, you no longer have an atom at all.
>
> The hydrogen atom is the most abundant in the cosmos. There is relatively little hydrogen gas in the earth's atmosphere, but there are plenty of hydrogen atoms showing up in hydrogen compounds—ordinary water, for instance. Then consider that every molecule of water in all the seas, lakes, and streams includes two hydrogen atoms. (Heiserman, 1992, p. 82)

Coordinate Text Structures

Coordinate text structures offer more guidance to the reader by highlighting relationships (Pearson & Camperell, 1994). Each type of coordinate text structure highlights a different type of relationship.

Comparison/Contrast   Comparison/contrast structures have two forms: block and alternating (Simonsen, 1996). In the block form, all of the characteristics of the first item are presented, followed by the comparative or contrasting characteristics of the second item. The advantage of the block structure is that the reader can focus on one item at a time. The disadvantage is that readers may fail to see similarities and differences. Here is an example of the block structure.

> Imagine that you are a typical student in Ontario, Canada. English is your first language at home and in school, and you study British history in your classes. Perhaps you come home to tea in the afternoon.

(**CCSS**)

Analyze the structure of texts, including how specific sentences, paragraphs, and larger portions of the text (e.g., a section, chapter, scene, or stanza) relate to each other and the whole.

USING TECHNOLOGY

Coh-Metrix Easibility
Easibility is a free text analysis system that measures cohesion and provides suggestions for improving student comprehension based on the analysis. Passages can be pasted in for analysis. Use search engine to locate URL (not available at time of printing).

In contrast, imagine that you live in Quebec, Canada's only predominantly French-speaking province. Your classes are probably taught in French. You might eat croissants for breakfast and toutiere, or pork pie, for lunch. Indeed as a Quebecois, your life might be quite different from that of a student living only a few hundred miles away in the province of Ontario. (Sager & Helgren, 1997, p. 178)

In the alternating format, the items are compared or contrasted by the first characteristic, the second characteristic, the third, and so forth. This is a more effective organization when there are a number of characteristics involved because the readers would have difficulty remembering those in the first block by the time they got to the second block. Here is an example of the alternating format.

Ulysses S. Grant was the exact opposite of Robert E. Lee. Where Lee was quiet and gentlemanly, Grant was rough and unpolished. Lee won several battles for the South by brilliant maneuvering. Grant won battles for the North by hammering away at his enemy without mercy. (King, 1996)

Signal words and terms for comparison/contrast structures include the following:

although	similar	on the one hand	however
but	different	on the other hand	different from

Cause/Effect   Either the cause or the effect is presented first, followed by the related effects or causes. Causes or effects may also be implied. Readers may have to reason that a cause or effect is being stated, as in the first two sentences in the selection that follows. Although the word *effect* is used in the selection, the word *cause* is not.

The working-class family underwent tremendous strain during hard times. Traditional roles of the father as provider and the mother as the homemaker became blurred as the entire family was forced to seek work to keep food on the table. The effect of a father's unemployment on the entire family was evident: "Bewilderment, hesitation, apathy, loss of self-confidence were the commonest marks of protracted unemployment. A man no longer cared how he looked. Unkempt hair and swarthy stubble, shoulders a-droop, and a dragging walk." In many instances the idle man just got in the way, hanging around home because there was no place else to go. Tempers grew short and tension between husband and wife resulted in quarreling. The family would lose touch with friends, especially those who were still working. (Nishi, 1998, pp. 30–31)

Signal words for cause/effect structures include the following:

because	therefore	thus
cause	since	for this reason
effect	as a result	consequently

Problem/Solution   In this structure, a problem is described and then a solution is explored.

The moment you step out of the house and are on the road you can actually see the air getting polluted; a cloud of smoke from the exhaust of a bus, car, or a scooter; smoke billowing from a factory chimney, fly-ash generated by thermal power plants, and speeding cars causing dust to rise from the roads. Natural phenomena such as the eruption of a volcano and even someone smoking a cigarette can also cause air pollution. . . .

The task of cleaning up air pollution, though difficult, is not believed to be impossible. The shift to less polluting forms of power generation, such as solar energy, wind energy, geothermal, tidal, and other forms of renewable energy in place of fossil fuel can be used for controlling pollution. (Edugreen, 2001)

Sequential   There are two types of sequential structures: time sequence and explanation/process. In the time sequence paragraph structure, the writer uses dates or other time-clue words to indicate the order in which events took place. In the explanation/process structure, one action leads to or causes the next action. Graphic organizers, such as time lines, work well with time sequence passages. Flowcharts or process diagrams work well with process structures.

Time Sequence   In a time sequence paragraph, the order of events is the key element.

> In 1928 Roosevelt was elected governor of New York in a very close election. When the stock market crashed the following year, the nation plunged into the Great Depression. FDR responded with a groundbreaking system of relief for the vast number of unemployed workers in New York. His popularity soared and he won reelection to the governorship in 1930. He began to be mentioned as a possible candidate for presidency. (Moss & Wilson, 1998, p. 11)

Signal words for time sequence text structures include the following:

after	first	and then
today	next	finally
afterward	second	earlier
tomorrow	then	later
before	third	dates

Explanation/Process   This structure explains a process, such as how sleet forms, cells divide, or a digital camera works. Notice that it, too, follows a sequence, but the sequence consists of the steps of a process, with one step leading to or causing the next, rather than a simple time order.

> Hurricanes always begin over warm water. Warm water heats the air just above it and supplies water vapor to it. Water vapor is water in the form of a gas. The warm, moist air is lighter and it rises. As it rises, the water vapor turns back into liquid water to form clouds. When the layer of warm air moves up, cooler air fills the space it has left. This movement causes winds.
>
> Over tropical waters that reach very high temperatures, the heat makes the air rise very quickly. As the winds and clouds rise, they move faster and faster. They also start to rotate in a spiral. When the winds in this spinning storm reach about 120 kilometers (74 miles) per hour, it is called a hurricane (Spilsbury & Spilsbury, 2010, p. 6)

Often, passages combine several organizational patterns, as in the following excerpt, which combines time sequence and list structure.

> Babylon began as a small town in central Mesopotamia, on the banks of the Euphrates. In 1894 B.C. it was captured by an Amorite chief called Sumuabum. Babylon became the capital of his kingdom, and he became the first king in a long line of rulers. One of the descendants of Sumuabum was a king called Hammurabi. Hammurabi became king of Babylon in 1792 B.C. He established Babylon as the greatest city in the Middle East. Hammurabi also conquered neighboring cities in north and south Mesopotamia, and Babylon became the capital of a new Mesopotamian empire. One of Hammurabi's most important acts was to draw up a set of laws that everyone in his empire had to follow. (Malam, 1999, p. 21)

Structure can be signaled in a number of ways. Titles and subheadings often indicate structure—for instance: Causes of the Great Depression, How Hail Is Formed, Solutions to the Acid Rain Problem. Introductions and summaries may also alert readers to the type of structure they will encounter. Graphic organizers also signal structure: A time line indicates sequence, a flowchart process, and a matrix comparison and contrast (Armbruster, 1996). Signal words or phrases, such as *first, then, because, however,* and *on the other hand,* are often found within running text and provide another way of detecting text structure.

Teaching Expository Text Structure

Instruction in use of text structures should be geared to the learners' level of development. Begin with simpler structures, which are easier to grasp and remember (Horowitz, 1985). For example, within coordinate structures, causal structures are more readily understood by less able readers or students whose knowledge of a topic is less advanced. Compare/contrast structures seem to be the most difficult and are more readily understood by students with advanced knowledge. Students with limited knowledge might need to pass through a stage in which they can establish simple causes and effects before they move into a more advanced stage where they are able to make comparisons and contrasts (Wylie & McGuinness, 2004).

Text patterns, along with their signal words, should be introduced one at a time. Start off with well-organized, single paragraphs that reflect the structure being taught. To provide practice in the recognition of signal words, use a cut-up paragraph or article and have students recreate the piece by using signal words and the sense of the piece as guides. For instance, students can use dates to help them rearrange a chronologically organized piece. Or they can use the signal words *first, second, next,* and *last* to arrange sentences or paragraphs explaining a step-by-step process. Gradually, work up to longer selections. Whole articles and chapters often use several text structures, and students should be aware of that. However, in many cases, a particular structure dominates. Most important of all, have students apply their knowledge of text structures to improve their reading of texts in your class.

Point out and discuss the usefulness of key text structures in your subject matter area. Before students read a chapter, have them examine the title and headings to help determine the structure of the chapter. Before preparing students to read a selection, analyze it for content and structure. Create questions and activities that reflect the structure of the text as well as the content. For example, a biographical sketch of Thomas Jefferson would use a time sequence structure. Instruct students to note key events and their dates to help keep them in order. As a postreading activity, have students create or complete graphic organizers that incorporate the structure of the text. For the biographical sketch of Jefferson, have them fill out a time line. After they read how rust forms or steel is made, have them create a process diagram. After they have read a section comparing and contrasting the Senate and the House of Representatives, have them create a Venn diagram.

Using Questions to Make Connections

Carefully planned questions can help readers establish relationships among ideas in a text. If the text has a cause/effect relationship, you can ask "why" questions that focus on that relationship. If students are reading a selection that uses a compare/contrast pattern to discuss how insects differ from arachnids, ask questions such as: How do insects and arachnids differ? How are they the same?

Not only can questions help students see relationships among ideas in text (internal relationships), but also they can help students relate ideas in the text to their own backgrounds (external relationships). Here are some questions (adapted from Muth, 1987) that might help students who have read a selection about air pollution make internal cause/effect connections:

What causes air pollution?

What are some effects of air pollution?

What are some of the most polluted areas? What are the main causes of pollution in those areas?

These questions focus on external connections:

How does air pollution affect you and your family?

How do you and your family contribute to air pollution?

What can be done to lessen air pollution? Why would these steps work?

English Language Learners

Students who are still learning English can transfer their ability to use text structure in their native language to English. However, students must be proficient readers in their native language and fairly proficient in reading English (Hague, 1987). A lack of proficiency in English "short circuits" the transfer process.

These questions require students to establish internal or external cause/effect relationships. Questions can also be created that foster relationships in comparison/contrast, problem/solution, or other kinds of patterns. Once students have grasped the concept, encourage them to create their own connection questions.

One way to help students, especially below-level readers, improve their comprehension is to use causal questioning. In causal questioning, students are asked *why* and *how* questions to help them make inferences. These questions can be asked during discussions or they can be added to the text at locations where comprehension is likely to falter, such as where important cause–effect relationships are being established, where a reference is being made to a fact or event covered earlier in the text (that may have been forgotten), or where the syntax is especially difficult (van den Broek & Kremer, 2000). Marginal notes known as *glosses*, which are covered in the next chapter, can be used for this purpose.

Also encourage students to use graphic organizers to make full use of text structure. Process diagrams can be used to show the key steps in scientific and historical processes. They can be as simple as one showing how sonar works or as complex as one showing photosynthesis. Note the process diagram for lightning in Figure 4.3 on p. 122. If students are artistically inclined, they might draw the actual objects involved in the process. Venn diagrams are excellent devices for comparing and contrasting technical concepts and terms. Note how the Venn diagram in Figure 3.6 on p. 68 highlights the similarities and differences between rabbits and hares.

Text patterns have a double value. They provide readers with a framework for organizing information as they read, which enhances comprehension and retention. Text patterns also can be used to help students organize and present their ideas as they write.

CHECKUP

1. How might text structure be used to help students better understand content area material?
2. What techniques can be used to foster the use of text structure to increase comprehension?

Determining Essential Information

Condensed because they are attempting to provide a survey of broad topics, such as American history, physical science, or biology, today's texts are crowded with information. Retaining all that information would be overwhelming, if not impossible. A key strategy for students is to determine the relative importance of information. By previewing the chapter, students can hypothesize what the main idea is. Generally, the key ideas in a text are signaled by the chapter title, headings, an introductory paragraph, and main idea sentences. When they have a sense of the overall main idea of the chapter, students can then structure the supporting details around it. For instance, in a trade book on the War for Independence, *The American Revolution: How We Fought the War of Independence* (Dolan, 1995), a chapter title is "The Roots of Revolution." Subheads include New Angers, a Massacre, A Tea Party, and Intolerable Acts. From these, students can correctly assume that the chapter will discuss the causes and events that led up to the Revolutionary War, and they will make note of these topics as they read. Observing that the chapter has a cause-and-effect structure, the students might take advantage of this as they read. Because this is a trade book and the author has more space to tell his story than a textbook author, he is able to explain each cause in a fair amount of detail. In order to make the reading manageable, the reader must focus on the important data, which means deciding which facts to stress and which to disregard.

Although trade books, newspapers, and magazines are often more interesting to read because they contain fascinating facts and more details, it may be more difficult to determine which details are essential. As Harvey (1998) notes, "The most important ideas in well-written nonfiction are often deeply embedded in rich detail" (p. 83). In addition, students may mistake interesting details for important ones. Fascinated by the fact that roaches can make themselves as thin as a dime, one middle schooler felt that this was an essential detail in an article about roaches. Although perhaps it was one of the most interesting facts

(CCSS)

Read closely to determine what the text says explicitly and to make logical inferences from it; cite specific textual evidence when writing or speaking to support conclusions drawn from the text.

about roaches, it was not one of the most essential (Harvey, 1998). To overcome this tendency, Harvey listed information about jellyfish that she had found interesting in one column and then discussed with students which of the interesting bits of information were
essential. After an extended discussion, students were able to narrow down their choices
to four key facts.

CHECKUP

1. Why is determining essential information an important strategy?
2. How might this strategy be taught?

Summarizing

Summarizing is a complex skill. Students often have difficulty deciding which information should be included in a summary. Although complex, summarizing is probably the
most valuable comprehension strategy. As Wade-Stein and Kintsch (n. d.) note, "A summary requires much more conscious thought, judgment and effort, whereas rereading is
generally a more passive activity. Ideally, the summary writer not only selects the important ideas from the text, but also reconstructs the meaning in a more succinct, general-
ized form" (n. d., p. 5). They recommend summarizing as a highly effective device for
improving comprehension of expository text, especially for students who are not adept at
actively constructing meaning. These students should have "intensive practice in working through many different examples of expository text at a deep level, for example, by
summarizing them. Lack of opportunities to practice actively comprehending text is a
major reason why students remain stuck in a passive reading mode" (p. 4). As they read,
students should summarize key ideas. At the end of each section, they should stop and
summarize or recite what they have learned from the section. This is the purpose of the
checkup questions in this text.

Summarizing serves several purposes. It lets the student know whether he has grasped
the information: If he can't summarize, then he must reread. It also gives him the opportunity to organize the information and fix it in his mind before he goes on to the next section. Summaries can be oral or written. Oral summaries are easier and faster to compose.
During class discussions, encourage students to summarize sections of a chapter or the
highlights of a discussion. To model oral summarizing, provide a summary of key content at the end of each class or ask students, "What are the main things we learned today?"
Also call attention to end-of-chapter summaries. Recognizing the value of summaries,
some authors also provide several interim summaries within a chapter. Prepare students
for creating written summaries by having them compose oral summaries.

Summaries can also provide valuable assessment information about students' understanding of text. As Wade-Stein and Kintsch (n.d.) explain:

> The answers to factual queries can be lifted right out of the text with minimal effort; infer-
> ence questions are easily misunderstood and often require background knowledge that stu-
> dents may not have. Simply having students summarize a chapter is more likely to uncover
> specific gaps in their understanding. It can help students formulate the right questions to
> ask, and can show teachers where more instruction is needed. (p. 6)

By examining students' written summaries, teachers can gain insight into the quality of students' comprehension and provided help if needed.

Written Summaries

Until about the time they enter middle school, students summarize by simply recording
what they have read word for word. They will need guidance in condensing information
and putting it in their own words. Model the process and provide practice with brief, well-
organized segments of text. Explain how you go about determining the main idea and how
you decide which details to include. Also show how you condense ideas and put them in
your own words. Remind students that when they put ideas in their own words, they own

USING TECHNOLOGY

Summary Street (Pearson) is a software
program that assesses students'
summaries and also provides feedback
that can be used to improve summaries.

the ideas. Have the whole class summarize some paragraphs from their texts and then provide guided individual practice. After students have learned to summarize brief selections, lead them into the construction of longer segments.

In addition, distinguish between writer-based and reader-based summaries. Writer-based summaries are composed as a study aid for the benefit of the student who is reading the selection and writing the summary. These may be somewhat longer and more informal. Reader-based summaries are more condensed and more polished because they are designed to be read by others. Because they require additional writing skills, reader-based summaries are more difficult to create. Research-based steps for creating summaries are listed below (Brown & Day, 1983; Rinehart, Stahl, & Erickson, 1986).

- Selecting or constructing the overall (main) idea
- Selecting important information that supports the main idea
- Deleting information that is not important or is repeated
- Combining and condensing information
- Polishing the summary

Instructions given to students might include the following:

1. Use the title, heading, and first sentence to get a sense of what the main idea and important details might be.
2. Read the selection and note which details explain or describe the main idea.
3. Write down the main ideas and key supporting details in your own words.
4. Shorten the summary. Get rid of unimportant details. Combine details if you can. Eliminate unnecessary words. (Show students how to paraphrase essential ideas, condensing as they do so. This involves explaining how to combine and collapse details into a more general statement. For instance, the sentences "Finally, the help of the French was critical. Loans of money, beginning even before the Battle of Saratoga in 1777, and materiel gave the Americans a chance" could be condensed to "The French helped with money and materiel.")
5. Read the summary. Confirm that it contains the main ideas and most important details. Make sure that it makes sense and is smoothly written. Polish it if it needs it.

 Struggling Readers

Frame summaries are especially helpful to struggling readers.

 English Language Learners

Because they rely less on language, graphic organizers are somewhat easier than traditional summaries for ELLs to compose.

To ease students into composing summaries, provide frame summaries that cover content in the text or in a class discussion. A sample frame summary is provided in Figure 4.1. In addition to preparing students to write their own summaries, frame summaries help them review content.

Graphic Organizers as Summaries   For some students and for certain topics, a visual summary such as an idea map (Berkowitz, 1986) may work better than a purely verbal one. To create an idea map, students write the title or heading of the chapter or section they are reading in the center of an 8½" × 11" sheet of paper, which has been placed horizontally. They use subheadings or skim the text to locate major topics, which are then numbered and placed in blocks arranged clockwise around the title. This gives them an overview of the section or chapter. After reading each section, students fill in the appropriate block with the most important details in condensed form, as shown in Figure 4.2.

The amount that you pay for a car is only part of the cost of owning and driving a car. Before you can drive the car, you must _____.

You will also need to pay for _____.

And you will need to pay for _____.

And you may have to buy _____.

Still another cost is depreciation. Owning a car can cost more than you think.

FIGURE 4.1
Frame Summary

FIGURE 4.2 **Idea Map**

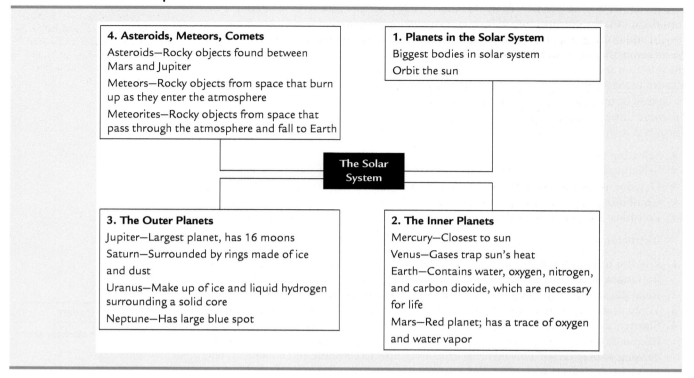

Graphic organizers are easier to compose than a written summary, but do an excellent job of highlighting important information and showing relationships among ideas. They can be created either as an end product or as a preparation for composing a written summary. In addition to idea maps, other graphic organizers such as semantic maps and Venn diagrams (introduced in Chapter 3) are easy to use and may be especially helpful for students who are struggling with summarizing.

Integrating the use of related strategies can result in more effective summaries, especially if practice is provided. Combining instruction in several strategies, Weisberg and Balajthy (1990) taught secondary students who were reading on a fifth-grade level to identify main ideas, construct graphic organizers, and write summaries. Students who were trained in the three procedures were compared with a control group and a third group of students who received both training and practice. Both the training and training-plus-practice groups demonstrated significantly better comprehension than the control group, but the training-plus-practice group did the best. Weisberg and Balajthy concluded that modeling, guided practice, and immediate feedback were key elements in the program.

Adapting Summarizing to Fit the Nature of the Discipline

Summaries should reflect the way that knowledge is structured. Summarizing in chemistry, for instance, might take the form of a chart that highlights the key concepts that a chemist would be concerned with: substances, properties, processes, and a summary of the atomic expression. "This strategy was not just about understanding text; it was also about understanding the essence of chemistry" (Shanahan & Shanahan, 2008, p. 54).

In history, students might create an events chart in which they summarize events that they are reading about by answering the questions: Who? What? Where? When? How? and Why? After doing this for each of the events that they have read about, students reflect on the events and compose a brief description of the relationships between them. And because the relationships between events are not always specified, students advance their understanding by inferring cause/effect or other relationships.

In a multiple gist strategy, which might be used when consulting several sources, students summarize information from one source and then incorporate information from other sources on the same topic. However, they keep the length of the summary the same; this requires synthesis of information and also use of academic terms such as *in contrast to* or *similarly* (Shanahan & Shanahan, 2008).

CHECKUP

1. Why is summarizing a difficult strategy to master?
2. What are specific methods for teaching summarizing?

Elaboration Strategies

With **elaboration** strategies, the reader adds to, transforms, judges, or applies information from text in some way. Through elaboration, the reader may draw an inference, create a mental image, or evaluate the material that was read. Think about your own reading. What elaborations do you construct as you read? Did you use elaboration strategies as you read the excerpt on the speed of sound? Did you visualize sound traveling through water or sound traveling on a hot day as opposed to a cold day? Did you make any inferences about why sound travels faster on a hot day? If you did any of these things, then your comprehension was enhanced. Elaboration typically improves comprehension by 50 percent because it involves a higher level of comprehension and a deeper level of processing, in addition to creating and strengthening bonds between brain networks (Linden & Wittrock, 1981). What elaboration might students use to comprehend the following paragraph?

> By the 1890s, Pullman stockholders were receiving an 8 percent annual dividend. Land that Pullman had paid $800,000 for was now worth $5 million. However, the return on his investment on that land, mostly rents from workers, only brought Pullman 4.5 percent. He was miffed over that, though his rents were 25 percent higher than comparable ones in Chicago. In 1893 he slashed wages 25 percent, and the company's dividends went up. (Rents stayed the same.) In the model town children went without shoes, homes without heat. (Hakim, 1994, p. 70)

You might infer that Pullman and the stockholders were greedy and uncaring. You might also infer that Pullman had made a huge profit on his investment. You might visualize Pullman at his desk with a very angry look on his face as he examines a balance sheet stating that he was receiving 4.5 percent on his rents. You might also visualize a dingy company town composed of poorly constructed workers' houses with children running about barefoot, even though it is a cold day. You might conclude that Pullman cared more about shareholders than workers. You might question why Pullman didn't treat his workers better. You might evaluate the passage by noting that the author has included only details that make Pullman look bad. You might wonder whether he had any good characteristics. Elaborations, especially visualizations, vary from reader to reader, because each of us brings a different background of experience to our reading.

Making Inferences

Read the following excerpt about Cambodia. What can you infer from the paragraph?

> During the dry season, an oxcart is piled high with harvested rice. A farmer steers the oxen to the village. Women prepare the rice. First, they pound it with a pole to loosen the husks. Then the rice is placed in a flat bamboo tray and shaken back and forth and tossed in the air to separate it from the straw and husks. (Kras, 2005 p. 11)

The paragraph suggests that rice is an important food in Cambodia. It also suggests that the people of Cambodia are poor and may not be technologically advanced because they use ox-drawn carts rather than trucks to take their goods to market and they prepare the rice without the help of machines. In addition, the paragraph suggests that the farms

■ **Elaboration** is the additional processing of text by the reader that may result in improved comprehension and recall. Elaboration involves building connections between one's background knowledge and the text or integrating these two sources through manipulating or transforming information.

are close to the villages. Otherwise, a trip by ox cart would take too long. The paragraph also suggests that the people might buy their food in village market places rather than in supermarkets. It is also possible to infer that Cambodia has two seasons: dry and rainy.

As you can see from these examples, much of the information that a reader derives from text is the result of constructing inferences. As you can also see, inferencing depends heavily on background knowledge. Some inferences are based primarily on the text. For instance, the rice is harvested during the dry season because that is when the wagon is being taken to the village and that the harvest was a good one because the wagon is piled high with rice. For many inferences, the reader uses background knowledge *and* information from the text to make inferences. For instance, our background knowledge tells us that oxen and carts are cheaper than cars or trucks, so when we read that ox-drawn carts are used, we infer that the people are too poor to buy cars or trucks.

Of all the elaboration strategies, making inferences is probably the most important. This strategy requires readers to go beyond the page and bring their own experiences and judgment to bear on the text. If they are struggling to get the literal meaning of a content area piece, students may not be able make inferences or draw conclusions. Some students may not realize that they can construct their own meanings, and they may even be confused when they are asked questions for which there is no definitively stated answer in the text. However, elaborated responses incorporate the kinds of higher-order thinking skills that content area standards are asking for and also the kinds of skills in which students do poorly on national assessments (National Center for Education Statistics, 2010). Thus it is essential that we teach our students this strategy.

Two essential elements in making inferences are being asked questions that require making inferences and having the kinds of discussions that involve higher-level thinking skills. Both of these are incorporated in the following sample lesson on making inferences.

Imaging

Which is larger, a rabbit or a squirrel? How did you decide? Chances are, you imagined a typical rabbit and a typical squirrel, mentally put the two side by side, and then decided on the basis of this visual comparison which one was larger (Moyer, 1973). In other words, you used a nonverbal process known as **imaging** to reason your way to the answer to the question. Imaging is a powerful cognitive tool for understanding, reasoning, and remembering. According to Paivio's **dual coding** hypothesis (1971), words that refer to concrete objects can be encoded in memory twice. The word *rabbit*, for instance, can be encoded verbally as a word or visually as a mental picture of a rabbit; thus, because it can be retrieved from memory either verbally or visually, theoretically it is twice as memorable. Indeed, in one research study, participants who encoded words visually remembered twice as many words as those who encoded the words just verbally (Schnorr & Atkinson, 1969).

Creating images has a host of benefits. It fosters increased comprehension and retention. Mental pictures provide a framework for organizing and remembering information and also lead students into deeper, more extensive processing (Gambrell, Kapinus, & Wilson, 1987). Creating images also serves as a metacognitive check on comprehension. As they attempt to create images, readers may find that they are unable to supply some details and realize that they need to go back to the selection. Imaging is an active, generative process.

Imaging is frequently used in the study of literature. Being able to create images of settings, main characters, and the characters' actions adds to our enjoyment of a selection as well as our understanding of it. However, imaging can also be used to picture historical scenes or scientific processes. For instance, a reader might use imaging to help him understand and recall the structure of an animal cell. Visualizing can assist in the comprehension of descriptions such as those found in the following

■ **Imaging** is creating sensory representations of items in text.

■ **Dual coding** is the concept that text can be processed verbally and nonverbally. Nonverbal coding focuses on imaging.

LESSON 4.1

Making Inferences

Step 1: Explaining the Strategy

Explain what is entailed in making inferences and give examples. Explain why making inferences is important, and when and how this strategy is used. Encourage students to give examples of times when they have made inferences. For instance, have them tell how they infer a person's mood.

Step 2: Modeling the Process

Model the process of making inferences with a brief piece of text drawn from students' content area text. Think out loud, and explain how and why you make inferences. For instance, after reading the segment presented below about the Pullman strike, explain that the text states that, although highly profitable, the Pullman Company cut wages for the fifth time.

> That summer, the highly profitable Pullman Company cut workers' wages for the fifth time. Pullman made railroad sleeping cars in a town near Chicago. When the company cut wages, it didn't cut the fees it charged workers for rent, heat, and lights, or to use the company church. The workers were angry; they went on strike. Soon the strike spread to 50,000 workers, throughout the railroad industry. The governor of Illinois said he could handle the situation. But Grover Cleveland's attorney general didn't agree. (The attorney general had been a railroad lawyer.) He insisted that the government take action against the workers and their union. Federal troops were sent to Illinois, which led to violence, deaths, and arrests. (Hakim, 1994, p. 70)

In your think-aloud, you might make statements similar to the following: "This makes me think that the company is greedy and doesn't care about its workers. And here the text states that even though the company cut wages, it didn't lower rents or other expenses that the workers had to pay. That adds proof to my inference that the company cared more about making money than it did about its workers. Here it says that the workers went on strike and the strike soon spread. That tells me the Pullman workers aren't the only ones who are fed up; other railroad workers are also unhappy. They are so unhappy that they are desperate. After all, these are poor people. By going on strike, they are giving up their pay and risking their jobs. You would have to be desperate to do such a thing." Model the process with several other sections, so students see that a variety of inferences can be drawn.

Step 3: Locating Evidence for an Inference

Ask students to take part in the inferencing process. Ask an inferential question about a brief paragraph or excerpt and then answer it. Have students supply supporting evidence for the inference from both the selection and their background knowledge. Discuss the reasoning processes involved in making the inference. Stress the need to substantiate inferences with details from the text. For instance, state that the attorney general favored business. Students should then locate evidence for this inference.

Step 4: Drawing an Inference

Ask students to read a segment of text and draw an inference. Provide the evidence. As an alternative, supply evidence and have the students draw an inference based on it. Either way, engage in a discussion of reasoning processes. For instance, based on their reading of the following excerpt, you might ask, "What kind of a person was Mother Jones?" Note that making inferences requires a command of background knowledge. The significance of Mother Jones's comment about Patrick Henry, Thomas Jefferson, and John Adams will be lost if the readers don't know how each of the men contributed to fundamental freedoms.

(continued)

The police said Mother Jones was a public nuisance. They arrested her. When the judge asked her who gave her a permit to speak on the streets, she said, "Patrick Henry, Thomas Jefferson, and John Adams!" Mother Jones was sent to jail—more than once. In jail she spoke of George Washington as a "gentleman agitator" who fought the powerful English establishment. Each time Mother Jones got out of jail she went straight back to speaking out for workers. (Hakim, 1994, pp. 105–106)

Step 5: Integrating the Process
Ask an inferential question. Have students make the inference and locate support for it. In time, turn total responsibility for making inferences over to students. Students create their own inferential questions and then supply the answers and evidence.

Step 6: Application
The students apply the process to texts and trade books.

Step 7: Assessment
Observe students as they make inferences in texts and trade books. Note how well they can do the following:

_____ Make an inference based on two or more pieces of information in the text.

_____ Make an inference based on information in the text and their own background of knowledge.

_____ Find support for an inference.

_____ Make increasingly sophisticated inferences.

Step 8: Reviewing the Strategy
In subsequent lessons, review and extend the strategy. To review the strategy, ask the following kinds of questions.

What strategy are we learning to use?

How does this strategy help us? (It helps us to read between the lines, to fill in details that the author has hinted at, but not directly stated.)

When do we use this strategy? (When we have to put together two or more pieces of information in a text and make an inference or conclusion. When the author has hinted at, but not directly stated information.)

How do we use this strategy?

As I read, I think, "What is the author suggesting here?"

I put together pieces of information from the text or pieces of information from the text with what I already know.

I make an inference or come to a conclusion. (Gunning, 2003; Scott, 1998)

paragraph. If the text is accompanied by illustrations, these should be used along with the text to create a visualization.

Cumulus clouds are puffy white clouds with a flat base. They look a little like pieces of cotton drifting along in the sky. They are sometimes called cauliflower clouds because of their shape. Cumulus clouds are formed by rising currents of warm air called thermals. (McKeever & Foote, 1998, p. 260)

Visualizing can also be used to help readers understand processes such as the one described in the following paragraph. To visualize this type of process, readers might want to create a series of mental images.

The human eye is a tough ball filled with fluid sitting in a bony socket. The cornea is the transparent protective surface of the eye. It also focuses light. The iris controls the amount

English Language Learners
Encourage students to draw pictures of concepts or topics along with using words to describe or talk about them. This provides ELLs who might have difficulty expressing their ideas through words alone with another medium for conveying their ideas.

of light passing through the pupil. It closes up the pupil in bright light and opens it wide in dim light. The lens helps focus light on the retina, which contains a layer of light-sensitive cells. These send signals via the optic nerve to the brain, where they are interpreted to build up our view of the world. (McKeever & Foote, 1998, p. 204)

Recitations or summaries can be visual as well as verbal. After reading a section in which she has visualized, the reader can see if she can recite what she has learned by picturing the whole image or a series of images or by making a quick sketch of the image(s). Or she might combine the visual and the verbal. In addition to taking verbal notes, the reader might include drawings of key elements. Translating verbal descriptions into pictorial ones is an excellent way to learn difficult material and retain it.

Because it relies more on mental pictures than on words, imaging can be an especially useful strategy for students who are still learning English because it allows them to show what they know without being hampered by their lack of facility with English. Many students, especially those who are not efficient learners, may fail to create images spontaneously as they read (Harris & Sipay, 1990). However, imaging is easy to use and has a powerful payoff (Gambrel & Bales, 1986; Sadowski & Paivio, 1994). Although imaging is seldom recommended as a strategy, it can be highly effective, and its use should be explained and encouraged. Provide students with passages that lend themselves to imagery and give them the opportunity to respond by making sketches or diagrams.

Source: Shutterstock.

The teacher provides assistance as a student applies a newly learned strategy.

As with other strategies, imaging should be taught formally, although you should also incorporate informal imagery instruction and application where feasible. If students are learning concrete terms such as *circuit, geyser, glacier,* or *meteorite,* have them learn verbal definitions and also images of the words. As students are reading, provide guide questions that ask them to create images of a process, person, or scene. After students have read a selection, ask them questions that require imaging: When the soldiers landed on the beaches of Normandy, what did they see? What did they hear? If you were near the epicenter of an earthquake, what would you see, what might you hear, and what would you feel?

Analogies

Encourage students to pay particular attention to analogies. Many analogies lend themselves to imaging and often clarify a concept in a way that literal descriptions cannot. For instance, the analogy of a dried sponge is used to provide a concrete explanation of the effect of drought on soil. The analogy helps students understand an unfamiliar concept by comparing it to a familiar experience. Chapter 5 contains additional information about the effectiveness of analogies.

Generating Questions

Students spend much of their time answering other people's questions. One of the most powerful comprehension strategies is to ask and answer your own questions. Question generation transforms the reader from passive observer to active participant. Through asking questions, students set their own purposes for reading, process the information they have just read, and begin to make it their own. They also can determine whether their comprehension is adequate. If they can't answer their own questions, they can then take steps to clarify confusions or relearn material that they couldn't recall. In fact, self-questioning is said to be the most effective way to monitor comprehension (Rosenshine, Meister, & Chapman, 1996).

Question generation also involves activating schema. When reading narratives, students can use their knowledge of story structure to ask such questions as: What is the setting? Who are the main characters? What is the story problem? (Singer & Donlan, 1989). For informational text, they ask such general questions as: What is the author trying to say?

USING TECHNOLOGY

Encourage students who are helped by imaging to use one of the many Web sites that do an especially good job of depicting events and processes, such as American Memory from the Library of Congress memory.loc.gov/ammem/amhome.html or the Franklin Institute www.fi.edu/learn/ educators.php

USING TECHNOLOGY

Many digital texts have film clips and audio recordings to add additional input. Many traditional texts have film clips and recordings on supplementary CDs or on publisher Web sites.

LESSON 4.2

Imaging Lesson

Step 1 Introducing Imaging

Explain what imaging is. Do a think-aloud as you read a passage and create an image. Tell what you see, hear, and feel. Explain, however, that imaging is individualized and that the students' images may differ from yours. Also explain the benefits of imaging, citing the experiment in which students learned twice as much when they created pictures of words in their minds. Tell them that when they create images, they process words twice, once as a word and the second time as a picture or other image.

Step 2: Focusing

Encourage students to relax and clear their minds of distractions. Have students close their eyes and listen to a brief, concrete passage, forming pictures in their minds as they do so. Invite students to draw pictures of their images. This fixes their original images in their minds so they don't get distracted by their classmates' descriptions of their images (Maria, 1990).

Step 3: Discussing

Discuss students' images, but remind them that images may vary. Also stress that the quality of the artwork is not important. It's the thought behind the drawing that counts. Prompt students to elaborate on their images.

Step 4: Guided Practice

Encourage students to create images of text as they read. Discuss the images students have created. If necessary, prompt students to elaborate on their images. Also discuss when and where the use of imaging is helpful.

Step 5: Review and Application

Review and reinforce imaging. Suggest where using imaging might be especially appropriate: picturing scenes, characters, or events in fiction; events or scenes in history; places in geography; and processes in science. Encourage students to use drawings, even if they consist mainly of stick figures. Also encourage the creation of charts, diagrams, geographical and semantic maps, and other visuals to display and organize information. Be sure to call attention to visuals included in their texts, especially those that foster a better understanding of the text.

What will I learn from this article? Or the student can ask more specific questions by using the title and heading to create questions. One way of getting students to ask their own questions is to ask them questions whose answers are questions. For instance, before students read an article, you might ask, "What questions does the title raise? What questions do you have about this topic? What questions would you like to have answered?" As students read, encourage them to ask questions about the subheads or to turn the subheads into questions.

Self-questions can be created on a variety of levels. Attempting to construct literal comprehension as she reads a selection about acids and bases, a reader might ask herself, "What is the author saying about bases and acids? What are the steps for determining acidity?" Or, operating on an elaborative level in which the reader draws inferences, makes judgments, makes comparisons, or thinks of examples or applications of the materials, she might ask, "What are some other examples of acids and bases? How might people use knowledge of acids and bases to test their swimming pools and add chemicals?" (Wood et al., 1999). Elaborative self-questioning is especially effective for comprehension because it builds connections between new knowledge and students' prior knowledge.

Asking good questions is a difficult skill to master. Many students lack the ability to ask higher-level questions (Van der Meij & Dillon, 1994). Students benefit greatly from specific instruction in question generation that includes the following elements (Davey & McBride, 1986).

Overview and Rationale   Discuss how and why creating questions improves comprehension and helps students check the effectiveness of their reading. Explain that if students can't answer questions that they have created, they must reread the passage. Explain, too, that creating questions helps students remember what they have read and may alert them to questions that may be asked on upcoming tests.

Creating Questions   Ask students to create questions about what they think are the most important ideas in a selection. After students become accustomed to creating questions, explore differences between explicit- and implicit-level questions. Explicit questions can be answered by citing a word or phrase from the text. More advanced explicit questions require the reader to put together two or more pieces of information from the text. Implicit questions require the reader to make inferences or draw conclusions based on information from the text. Some questions require readers only to make a judgment or to express an opinion. Known as "on my own" questions, they do not require using information from the selection. Show students how to write questions on both an explicit level and an implicit level. Provide students with some possible question words and some model questions.

Determining Essential Information   Show students ways to determine essential information in a selection and to compose questions that request that information. Require them to provide the answers to any questions that they compose.

Checking Questions   Supply students with four monitoring questions to respond to as they compose questions:

How well did I identify important information?

How well did I link information together?

How well can I answer my questions?

Do I use good signal words? (Davey & McBride, 1986, p. 258)

Practice and Application   Give students ample guided practice in identifying important information, generating questions, and responding to the monitoring questions. Students do best with question generation when given specific, concrete prompts to use. Being provided with *who, what, where,* and other words that signal questions is effective, as is being provided with generic questions, such as How are _____ and _____ alike? What conclusions can you draw about _____?

In pairs, small cooperative groups, or as part of whole-class activities, have students ask their questions. Each student can choose one question to ask. It is the responsibility of the student asking the question to judge whether the question has been answered fully. The inquiring student can ask for more details or for clarification and may call on more than one student to answer.

CHECKUP

1. What are the key elaboration strategies?
2. When and under what circumstances is each of these strategies most effective?

Categorizing Questions

Questions should be asked on a variety of cognitive levels. One way of categorizing questions is to examine the kinds of thinking processes involved in answering them. An arrangement of skills from least demanding to those that require the highest mental powers is known as a taxonomy. The following taxonomy of question levels is based on Weinstein and Mayer's (1986) system, which has also been used to classify the comprehension strategies presented in this text. However, the first level, remembering, is drawn from Anderson and Krathwohl's (2001) revision of Bloom's (1957) taxonomy.

Remembering   Students understand text on a literal level. They can tell when and where important events took place and who was involved. They can also list the effects of an event or cause. This level also includes having students put information in their own words. Comprehending (literal) questions often include the following question words: *who, what, where, when, how, how many, how much.*

Organizing   Students select important details from the text and construct relationships among them. This involves identifying or constructing main ideas, classifying, summarizing, and noting sequence and similarities and differences.

Organizing questions: How are _____ alike? How are _____ different? What is the main idea? How would you summarize the passage? In what order did the events occur? What happened first? What happened next?

Elaborating   Elaborating entails making connections between information from the text and prior knowledge, and includes a variety of activities: making inferences and predictions, creating images and analogies, and evaluating or judging.

Elaborating questions: What can you conclude? What picture does this bring to mind? What kind of a person is _____? How do you know? What do you predict will happen next?

Metacognitive (Monitoring)   Metacognitive questions involve reflecting on thought processes. Students pose questions about unfamiliar words, confusing passages, or elements that need clarifying. Asking questions of this type helps students become more aware of the quality of their comprehension as well as steps that they might take to repair comprehension.

Monitoring questions: Were there any confusing parts? Were there any unfamiliar words or expressions?

Listed below are examples of each type of question. They are drawn from *Profiles in American History: Civil Rights Movement to the Present* (Moss & Wilson, 1998).

Remembering

When was Nixon president? Why did he resign from office?

Organizing

Who were the important people in Nixon's growing-up years? In what ways did these people influence him? What were some of his accomplishments? How might you sum up his presidency? What personal characteristic did he and Robert Kennedy share?

Elaborating

What was Nixon's emotional life like when he was growing up? Why do you think he worked so hard to succeed? What kind of a campaigner was he? What kinds of techniques did he use to win elections? What are some examples of name calling that he used in his elections? Do you think the authors presented a fair description of Nixon and his presidency? Why or why not?

Were there any parts of the chapter that confused you? Did you run into any words whose meanings you didn't know? If so, what did you do? What does the word *impeach* mean? What did you do to try to get an understanding of the kind of person that Nixon was? What did you do to try to understand and remember the highlights of Nixon's presidency?

USING TECHNOLOGY

For an excellent explanation of Bloom's taxonomy and its revision, visit Wilson's Web site at www.uwsp.edu/education /lwilson/curric/newtaxonomy .htm

---

English Language Learners

Because it may be more difficult for them to formulate their responses in English, allow ELLs more time to respond and supply prompts as needed. Focus on the content of their responses rather than on the form.

One way to foster question generation among students is to invite them to submit questions for quizzes and tests and then use the best ones. Students might also create questions for review in preparation for a test. Anticipating the kinds of questions that a teacher might ask is a valuable study skill. Students can also make up questions and quiz each other.

Question–Answer Relationships   If they are only used to answering explicit questions, students may not realize that some types of questions require them to use their background knowledge and reasoning ability in order to respond adequately. They need to be taught Question-Answer-Relationships (QARs) activities, in which they learn to identify the sources of information needed to answer questions (Raphael, 1984, 1986). In one study, secondary students had the most difficulty with the implicit questions that entailed combining information from text with background knowledge or required the reader to make a judgment based primarily on background knowledge (Schoenbach et al., 1999). When students were taught QARs and given training and practice in finding the sources of answers, comprehension improved, especially for text-implicit questions.

 Struggling Readers

Ironically, struggling readers are often given less time than able readers to respond to questions. Provide added time and prompts.

CHECKUP

1. What are the main kinds of questions?
2. What are some techniques for helping students answer questions on a variety of levels?

Monitoring for Meaning (Metacognition)

Do you sometimes look up from your reading and realize that you just read a whole paragraph or page and you don't have the slightest idea what you read? Do you sometimes read a headline and realize that you misinterpreted it? You are using what is known as *metacognition*, or *monitoring*, which means that you are aware of your thinking processes, including your reading.

An essential element in our cognitive processing is the *executive controller* (Ashcraft, 1994), which is goal oriented. When we have comprehension as our goal and comprehension fails because we stopped paying attention or we misinterpreted a word, the executive controller makes us aware of that. Metacognitive awareness operates in terms of the goal we set. Thus, a key feature of metacognitive awareness for a student is knowing what she is expected to be able to do as a result of reading a selection. If her goal is to pronounce each word correctly in a passage and not worry about comprehension, she won't be notified if comprehension fails. Of course, awareness of misread passages is only a first step. The next step is to use strategies to repair a failed reading. This might include rereading the passage, looking up an unfamiliar word, using a map or diagram, or using a **lookback**. In a lookback the reader refers back to the text to retrieve a forgotten fact or clarify a misunderstanding or locate support for a conclusion.

Unfortunately, some students lack adequate metacognitive awareness or don't make use of it. Take the case of Benjamin, a tenth grader, who read the assigned section on DNA in his biology text. After twenty minutes, he had completed the reading and began filling in the answers on the study guide sheet that the teacher had provided. Benjamin hadn't fully understood the section, but he had a strategy for answering the questions. Searching through the text, he found a series of words that were the same as those contained in the question. These words were usually contained in the first part of a sentence. Benjamin then copied the words from the second part of the statement onto the blank space on the guide sheet. Benjamin was not aware that his comprehension was not adequate, so he took no steps to improve his comprehension. He didn't reread or use any of the illustrations or look up unfamiliar terms in the glossary. Benjamin is lacking metacognitive awareness.

As you can see from this example, metacognition is the key to comprehension in the content areas. It involves setting a goal of constructing meaning, assessing whether that goal is being met, and taking appropriate steps to remedy the situation if the goal is not being achieved. Metacognition is a conscious process, and it can be learned. Indeed, the

■ **Lookback** is a strategy that involves skimming back over a selection that has already been read in order to obtain information that was missed, forgotten, or misunderstood.

heart of any successful program of improved learning is metacognition. The four key areas in metacognition are: (1) knowing oneself as a learner, (2) regulating, (3) checking, and (4) repairing (Baker & Brown, 1984; Garner, 1994).

Knowing Oneself as a Learner

The student knows what her background is and has a realistic picture of herself as a learner. She may realize that she is a fast, global reader, but can slow down when she has to. She knows that she finds reading literature and history texts easier than reading science. Her background in science and math are poor, and she is less interested in these subjects than she is in history. She knows that she has to read the science and math texts very carefully. Concerned about her reading, she made an appointment with the school's reading consultant to get some help. The reading consultant suggested that she survey the text and read one section at a time, noting the many helpful visuals and diagrams that provide clarification for confusing passages. The consultant then demonstrated how she read difficult passages, using as an example one from a math text that she is reading as part of a graduate course in methods of teaching math.

> Math is not my best subject. I better slow down and read this carefully. Maybe I'll have to read this explanation twice.

Regulating

In **regulating**, the student assesses her performance in terms of her goals. She is aware of the structure of the text and how this might be used to aid comprehension. She also knows what she will be expected to do as a result of reading this selection: explain a process, discuss a selection in a small discussion group, set up an experiment, or write a response on an essay test. She surveys the material, gets a sense of organization, establishes a purpose for reading by creating questions to be answered, and selects from available strategies the ones that seem to be most appropriate.

> I really would like to be able to find out the height of trees and buildings. This article tells how to make a measuring instrument, but I can skip that part. The teacher has some that she'll let us use. I'll just read the part that tells how the instrument works.

Checking

The student assesses her performance. She is aware when comprehension falters because the text is dense or contains a complicated idea that she failed to grasp or an unknown term that is key to understanding the passage. At the sentence level, she is aware if the sentence she just read doesn't make sense. Or she may realize that she was daydreaming and was not paying attention to what she was reading and must reread. On a more global level, she may realize that although she just finished reading about a procedure, she does not really understand how it works and so rereads or looks at the diagram in the text. At the end of a section, she may test her understanding by summarizing what she has read or asking herself questions about the section. **Checking** also involves noting whether the focus is on important, relevant information and engaging in self-questioning, summarizing, or visualizing to determine whether goals are being achieved (Baker & Brown, 1984). Here is how the consultant demonstrates checking in her think-aloud.

> Let's see. This heading says, "Finding the Angle." I know how to measure angles. We measured them in class. So you must have to measure angles to find out how tall something is. I don't know how that works. But this will probably tell me.
>
> This tells me that you use an instrument called a theodolite to measure angles. I'm not sure how to say that word, but it doesn't matter. What does matter is that the article tells me how the theodolite works.

Inadequate monitoring for meaning may also be caused by poor comprehension strategies and material that has too many difficult words and concepts.

English Language Learners

Because they have had to examine and deliberately learn a second language, ELLs are more metacognitively aware than students who speak only English.

Struggling Readers

Struggling readers may set fairly low goals and be satisfied with a shallow understanding. Adept readers, on the other hand, tend to set more demanding goals. A key element in instruction is to help students set adequate goals.

■ **Regulating** is a metacognitive process in which the reader guides his reading processes.

■ **Checking** is a metacognitive process in which the reader assesses the adequacy of her performance.

When the reading material is too difficult, poor readers are unable to make full use of the strategies they do possess. If the text isn't making much sense because too many of the words are unknown, students may not comprehend the text well enough to see that there are inconsistencies.

Repairing

When checking reveals that comprehension is inadequate, students must take corrective measures. **Repairing** strategies include slowing reading rate, pausing, reading aloud, skipping portions of a text, looking back, rereading, paraphrasing, using graphic aids or references, and taking other actions when text is confusing (see Table 4.2). Pausing gives readers time to try to decipher the meaning of a word, think about what the author is saying, or

■ **Repairing** is taking steps to correct faulty comprehension.

TABLE 4.2 Repair Strategies

STRATEGY	DESCRIPTION	WHEN USED
Slowing reading rate	Reads at a pace that allows deeper concentration	With difficult, complex, and/or confusing text
Pausing	Stops momentarily and thinks	To decipher a word or expression or to figure out what might be done to resolve confusion
Reading aloud	Deliberately reads aloud (or in a whisper) a portion of the text to self	To achieve greater focus or overcome distraction
Skipping	Deliberately skips a word or phrase	Decides a word or phrase is unimportant or hopes that further reading will clarify meaning
Using background	Calls up relevant, explanatory background knowledge	Thinks about what he or she knows that will help him or her understand an idea
Looking back	Checks back to locate a forgotten or misunderstood piece of information	To obtain information lost from working memory or information overlooked on the first pass through text
Rereading	Reprocesses a portion of text	To obtain meaning not gotten on first reading
Paraphrasing	Puts text in own words	To translate a difficult passage into simpler language
Imaging	Pictures what text is describing	To translate a difficult passage into an image that shows what the words are describing.
Using text aids	Looks at illustrations, maps, charts, graphs, and other nontext elements	To resolve confusion or obtain added input
Using references	Consults a glossary, dictionary, encyclopedia, hypertext, or other reference work	To check an unknown word or concept or obtain needed information to resolve confusion
Reading an easier version	Uses an easier-to-read or less complex version	With target text that is too complex or confusing

Source: From *Creating Literacy Instruction for All Students in Grades 4–8* (3rd ed.) by T. Gunning 2012. Boston: Allyn & Bacon. Reprinted by permission of Allyn & Bacon.

figure out what has gone wrong and how to set it right (Walczyk & Griffith-Ross, 2007). The text may be difficult or may require closer reading, so students may have to adjust their rate of reading. Reading aloud can improve concentration and override distractions by providing auditory feedback; it can also foster monitoring of comprehension. Skipping is helpful when a word or detail is not understood but doesn't seem crucial to an understanding of the selection. Experienced readers know that spending too much time on unknown words or confusing details can interfere with comprehension (Walczyk & Griffith-Ross, 2007). Sometimes reading to the end of the paragraph or section provides needed clarification. Looking back enables readers to obtain information that was missed on the first reading (e.g., whom the pronoun *he* refers to). If students cannot remember needed details, they should skim back through the text to find them. Students might reread the preceding section to reprocess the text if they fail to grasp the gist of a section. Rereading can be disruptive, however, so experienced readers use it only when simpler repair strategies have failed. Rereading also can be used to compensate for poor reading skills or poorly written text (Pressley & Afflerbach, 1995). Rereading a sentence or paragraph may clear up a confusing point or provide context for a difficult word. Using background knowledge, translating a text by paraphrasing, or picturing it can be especially helpful with very difficult or dense text.

A second group of repair strategies involves the use of illustrations, maps, charts, graphs, or other graphic materials to provide clarification. A third group of repair strategies involves the use of a reference tool such as a glossary, dictionary, or encyclopedia to clarify a confusing concept or obtain needed background information. Some expert readers read a children's book or easy encyclopedia to get basic information about an unfamiliar concept before tackling a more advanced text on the subject. Following is an example of a student applying a repair strategy (Gunning, 2012).

> I'm not getting this explanation of how the theodolite works. It says you can calculate the height by finding out the angle to the top of the object and the distance to the object from where you are standing. Maybe the illustration will help. I see you line up the flat edge of the theodolite with the top of the tree and then the plumb line swings away from the center and marks the angle. The angle is 25 degrees. The distance is 1,000 feet. I think I'm getting it now.

Teaching Metacognition

In one highly successful program for underachieving ninth graders, metacognition was the centerpiece of instruction (Schoenbach et al., 1999). After being introduced to the concept of thinking about thinking, students were asked to respond to such questions as:

> How do you know when your understanding is breaking down? Can you point to certain places in text where you tend to "lose it"? How do you get back on track when you begin to notice that you are not "getting it"? (p. 58)

The students spent much of their time talking about how they learned. These conversations helped them to become more aware of reading processes in particular and learning processes in general. Once they were aware of the processes they used, they were in a better position to take control of them, shedding habits that hindered their learning and fostering strategies that enhanced their learning. In addition to discussion, students were required to read for twenty minutes each evening and to write a reflection on their reading and thinking processes in their learning logs. Instead of talking about plot or characters or ideas, students reflected on the ways in which they read their books. During discussions of their reading, students were encouraged to talk about the processes that they used when they read and to discuss how they dealt with puzzling passages and other obstacles to comprehension. In fact, they were given extra credit for being explicit about where and when they got lost in the text.

To build metacognitive awareness, make it a part of every strategy that you teach. Whenever a strategy is introduced, do a think-aloud so that students can observe your thinking. Also discuss how, when, and where strategies should be implemented and point out signs that indicate a strategy isn't working and another strategy should be tried. During discussions, include process as well as content questions: How did you happen to draw that conclusion? How did you figure out the meaning of that difficult word? What study strategies did you use? Encourage students to mark confusing passages with stick-on-it notes. This will give you insights into the kinds of difficulties they are having with a text and also provide opportunities to discuss repair strategies they might use.

After a new strategy has been introduced, have students discuss their experiences using it along with examples of occasions in which the strategy has been especially effective.

LESSON 4.3

Metacognitive Strategies

Step 1: Describing the Strategy

Explain the strategy in detail. Describe the strategy so that students know exactly how it works. For instance, in teaching a monitoring strategy, explain that after you have read a paragraph, you pause and ask yourself if you understood what you read. If not, you reread or take some other action.

Step 2: Explaining Why the Strategy Is Important

Explain and model why the strategy is a valuable one. Students may not realize that even you have difficulty with comprehension at times and need to monitor whether your reading makes sense. Also note that the advantage of checking your reading periodically is that it enables you to clear up puzzling sections and helps you to remember the material longer.

Step 3: Demonstrating the Strategy

Using modeling or another technique, demonstrate how you would use the strategy. Place a brief selection on the board or an overhead and show how you stop if the passage stops making sense. Choose a tricky paragraph that you misread the first time and show students how you stopped when you realized that you were not understanding the passage. Discuss the steps you took to repair the comprehension gap. Also explain to students that they might stop at the end of each section and ask, "Do I understand this section? What is the author saying here?"

Step 4: Explaining When and Where to Use the Strategy

When teaching a strategy, be sure to note when and where it is to be used. For instance, when teaching repair strategies, note when it's appropriate to reread the sentence or the paragraph and when it might be a good idea to read ahead because the next sentence or paragraph explains the word or idea with which you were having difficulty.

Step 5: Explaining How and Why to Evaluate a Strategy

Explain how to evaluate a strategy and why it is important to do so. For instance, you may need to see whether rereading a sentence works, because if it doesn't, you will need to use another strategy.

Steps 6 & 7: Guided Practice and Application

As part of instruction in metacognitive strategies, students need opportunities to try out strategies with guidance and feedback from you so they can clarify misunderstandings, make necessary adjustments, and get the feel of the strategy. Be sure to affirm students' successful efforts with specific praise: "I like the way you reread that sentence when you saw that it didn't make sense," or "I like the way you used the diagram to help you understand the paragraph." They also need ample opportunity to apply the strategy to a variety of texts in a variety of situations so that the strategies become automatic and they can determine which strategies work best in particular situations.

Struggling Readers

Provide struggling readers with extra instruction in metacognition. Struggling readers are less likely to detect lapses in comprehension and, when they do detect them, are less able to repair them. However, when instructed, struggling readers can and do learn to become effective monitors (Palincsar, Winn, David, Synder, & Stevens, 1993).

English Language Learners

One of the strengths that bilingual students bring to reading is a more fully developed sense of metacognition. Learning a second language often entails viewing language as an object of study. Being more metacognitively aware, they are quick to pick up difficulties with understanding text. Bilingual learners often use knowledge of their home language to help them comprehend text in English. For instance, they may use English and their native language to activate background knowledge or they may translate a difficult passage into their native language so they can understand it or explain it better (Jiménez, 1997).

CHECKUP

1. What are the key elements of metacognition?
2. How might metacognition be developed?

Applying Strategies: Step-by-Step Intensive Reading

It is important that students learn how to adjust the intensity of their reading to the nature of the text. When text is very difficult, as it so often is in content area reading, students may need to read in intensive, step-by-step fashion and integrate several strategies. One of the best ways to teach students how to read difficult text is to model the process. Here is how you might model the process of reading a section from a text on astronomy.

Explain to students that stories, biographies, and expository texts told in narrative form and text that deals with familiar ideas can be read with relative speed and ease. However, explanatory text that describes an unfamiliar and complex concept should be read very deliberately and, if it's difficult enough, step-by-step. Moreover, readers must fully grasp the first step before going to the second and must understand the second step and integrate it with the first before going on to the third.

Students who are used to reading fiction or simple expository text with relative ease may not realize that much of their texts in the content areas will require an intensive reading. This might mean reading a selection paragraph by paragraph or even sentence by sentence. Demonstrate this kind of reading by selecting a dense passage and telling students you are going to show how you might go about reading it. Explain not only what is going on in your mind but also why you adopt a particular strategy such as imaging, questioning, or relating a new idea to a known one.

Exemplary Teaching

Clarifying Confusing Concepts

Noting that her middle school class of English language learners was having difficulty reading Jane Yolen's (1992) *Encounter,* a fictionalized account of Columbus's arrival in the New World told from the native people's point of view, Carol put a key portion of the text on a transparency and gave students duplicated copies of the segments. As she read the segments, students raised their hands when an unknown word or confusing passage appeared (Harvey, 1998). When students asked about the word *landfall,* Carol asked if anyone knew what the word meant. One student believed that it might mean a place where the land falls off. But on rereading the text with that meaning in mind, he noted that it didn't make sense. A second student thought that it might mean a place where ships land. She explained that if one reread the sentence while keeping that meaning in mind, the text made sense. Pointing to the word on her transparency, Carol explained that the student had made very good use of context and that rereading a sentence containing an unknown word was an excellent way to try to find out what the word might mean. After arriving at a possible definition, it was a good idea to see whether that meaning fit the sense of the sentence and the selection.

As she read and students noted other problems, Carol discussed and demonstrated other strategies that might be used to repair comprehension. Later, students tried applying the strategies independently.

(Reading the heading, The Turning Earth)

This must be explaining how the Earth turns. I remember the teacher using a basketball to show us how the Earth turns on its axis. That must be what this section is about. I never really understood what he was telling us. This section will probably be tough. I better read it carefully.

(Teacher reads the first sentence.)

During a sunset, the Sun is essentially standing still while the Earth to the west of us is being turned upward, the land west of us rising up into a "hill" miles high (and soon miles higher) to block our view of the Sun. (Schaaf, 1998, p. 20)

I did not get all that. I better reread the sentence. This sentence has a couple of ideas in it. I'll focus on the beginning idea first. It says the sun is standing still during a sunset. I've heard that before but it never made any sense to me. When I look at the sunset, the sun seems to be setting in the west. But now it says that the sun is essentially standing still while the Earth to the west of us is being turned upward. Let's see if I get this. I know that the Earth rotates. I remember the teacher showing us a basketball and making it spin slowly around his finger to show how Earth rotates. So what's happening is that the Earth to the west of us—that's the direction in which the sun is setting—it is turning upward. I can picture that. The sun is basically still. But the Earth is moving and the part I'm on is moving away from the sun, so it will soon be dark.

Now I understand the second part of the sentence. If the Earth is moving upward and away from the sun, the land west of us will form a big hill and block our view of the sun. I think I'm getting it.

(Teacher reads the next sentence.)

Struggling Readers

Struggling readers may believe that achieving students read effortlessly. Teacher modeling of the process of intensive reading helps them to understand that reading difficult text is hard work and that even the best readers encounter passages that are puzzling and require careful application of a variety of strategies.

When we see what we call a sunset, what we are really watching is an earthrise—or at least part of the Earth heaving up to the west of us. (Schaff, 1998, p. 20)

This helps me understand the whole thing better. The sunset is not really a sunset. It's an earthrise. So that's what confused me. When people talked about sunsets and sunrises, I thought that the sun was moving. But the sun is just sort of sitting there. I'll remember this idea if I think of what's happening as an earthrise instead of as a sunset. Now I think I can picture this whole process in my mind.

As you think aloud, you should also explain why you use certain strategies. Tell students that when a sentence contains several ideas, as in the first sentence, you might read just a portion, especially if the second part of the sentence builds on the first part. Explain that visualizing the sun standing still as the Earth moves helps you to understand the process. Discuss the importance of activating schemata and deciding how a text is going to be read before beginning to read it. Emphasize the importance of monitoring for meaning. For instance, after reading the first sentence, you were aware that you didn't fully understand it, so you reread it.

Because students may not realize that certain types of text demand a great deal of effort from the reader, you should emphasize the active, effortful nature of intensive reading of dense text. Stress, too, that a number of strategies are used and the kinds of strategies employed depend on the nature of the text and the reader's background. Focus throughout on taking steps to make the reading as meaningful as possible. For instance, reading this passage at twilight and watching the sun as it sets would be an excellent way to make key concepts more understandable. As a way of retaining this information, the reader might also draw and label a diagram of the movement of the Earth and the setting of the sun.

Demonstrate how being an active reader fosters understanding and retention and, if the material is particularly technical, helps the reader to maintain interest and attention. Some other strategies that might help students construct meaning from difficult text are connecting new information with background knowledge, using graphic organizers, applying knowledge, reading out loud, and paraphrasing.

Connecting New Information with Background Knowledge

Encourage students to connect new information with their background knowledge. For instance, after reading the following passage, students might reflect on practical applications. They might note that tires are more likely to fail in very warm weather and after being driven for long periods of time. They might also explain why a basketball or football might be slightly larger on a warm day and slightly smaller on a cold day.

> When gases are heated, the gas molecules move faster and farther apart, causing the gas to expand. In a closed container the molecules strike the walls of their container with greater force. For this reason, tire manufactures recommend the tire pressure be checked only when the tires are cool. If you checked tire pressure in tires when they are hot, the pressure would appear too high and you would let out some air. Then when the tires cooled, they would be underinflated. (Cuevas & Lamb, 1994, p. 50)

Using Graphic Organizers

After modeling the strategy, encourage students to use a graphic organizer to help them comprehend and remember the steps in a complex explanation. In Figure 4.3, a process diagram is used to summarize the steps of the formation of lightning described in the following passage. Students should read the explanation once to get an overview and then go back and put the process into steps. By breaking the process down into more understandable chunks, they are also very carefully reviewing it and monitoring their understanding. If they have difficulty putting the process into steps, then they don't fully understand it and should take actions to repair their comprehension.

> The most familiar lightning strokes are the negative flashes from cloud to ground. They start near the base of a cloud as an invisible discharge called the stepped leader, which moves downward in discrete, microsecond steps about 50 m (165 ft) long. It is believed to be initiated by a small discharge near the cloud base, releasing free electrons that move toward the ground. When the negatively charged stepped leader approaches to within 100 m (330 ft) or less of the ground, a leader moves up from the ground—especially from objects such as buildings and trees—to meet it.
>
> Once the leaders have made contact, the visible lightning stroke, called the return stroke, propagates upward from the ground along the path of the stepped leader. Several subsequent strokes can occur along the original main channel in less than a second. These strokes continue until the charge center in the lower part of the cloud is eliminated. The explosive

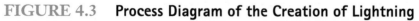

FIGURE 4.3   **Process Diagram of the Creation of Lightning**

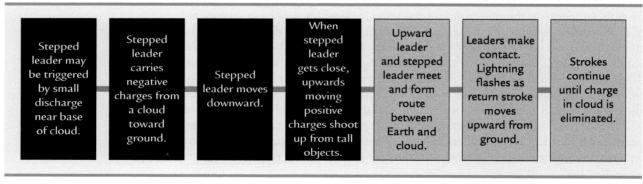

heating and expansion of air along the leader path produces a shock wave that is heard as thunder. (Grolier, 1997)

Using Manipulatives

When the text is especially dense as it is with the description of complex processes, you might have students use manipulatives. Instead of just reading about each step in a process or explanation, students carry out the step using replicas or illustrations. For instance, students might use a replica or illustration of the sun and one of the Earth to show what is happening. For the sentence "During a sunset, the Sun is essentially standing still while the Earth to the west of us is being turned upward, the land west of us rising up into a 'hill' miles high (and soon miles higher) to block our view of the Sun." the reader would move an illustration of Earth to show how it is moving in relation to the sun. For the article on lightning, the reader might show how the leaders move. Groups of students might make video clips of key processes.

The use of manipulatives has resulted in dramatic improvements in comprehension (Glenberg, Gutierrez, Levin, Japuntich, & Kaschak, 2004; Glenberg, Brown, & Levin, 2007). Observers as well as participants demonstrated improved comprehension. As students' comprehension improves, imaging can replace the use of manipulatives.

Reading Out Loud

When you read a difficult passage, chances are, you slow down considerably. You might even read the passage out loud or subvocally. The harder material gets, the more even the best of readers tend to subvocalize. Through vocalizing, we can "listen" to what we are reading, which can aid concentration. As one high schooler commented, "Reading out loud to myself helps me focus and remember important things. The reading seems more like a story that way. I also remember better if I reread the hard parts and then tell myself what I've read when I finish" (Harvey, 1998, p. 80).

Paraphrasing

When material is extremely dense and complex, one strategy students might use is to paraphrase it—carefully examining each phrase and translating it into language they understand. Notice how the reader paraphrased the following excerpt. The paraphrase need not be written. It can be oral, or the reader might just think of a paraphrase without saying it aloud.

> *Bernoulli's principle* law stating that the pressure of a fluid varies inversely with speed, an increase in speed producing a decrease in pressure and vice versa (such as a drop in hydraulic pressure as the fluid speeds up flowing through a constriction in a pipe) and vice versa. The principle also explains the pressure differences on each surface of an aerofoil, which gives lift to the wing of an aircraft. (Brimblecombe, Gallannaugh, & Thompson, 1998, p. 85)

Speed causes the pressure of a fluid to change. Increasing the speed of the flow makes the pressure decrease. Pressure increases when the speed of the flow is decreased. When fluid is pushed through a narrow pipe, the fluid speeds up and the pressure in the pipe drops. This principle explains what keeps planes up. Because air flows more swiftly over the top of a wing than the underside, there is less pressure and the airplane is given lift.

Struggling Readers

Of all the strategies explored in this text, the use of manipulatives proved to be the most powerful, especially when used with struggling readers.

CHECKUP

1. What are some strategies that students might use when the text is especially difficult to understand?

Summary

Comprehending is a process of constructing meaning. According to schema theory, our background knowledge is packaged in abstract units known as schemata. According to a mental models theory, comprehension requires that readers create a mental model of textual information (textbase). A mental model includes the reader's background knowledge and reading goal.

Comprehension strategies include preparational, organizational, elaboration, and monitoring (metacognition). Preparational strategies get students ready to read a selection and include: previewing, activating prior knowledge, predicting, and setting a purpose for reading and goals. Organizational strategies consist of selecting main ideas and relevant details and constructing relationships among them and include using the structure of a text, summarizing, and paraphrasing.

Elaboration strategies consist of constructing relationships between prior knowledge and knowledge obtained from print and include drawing inferences, visualizing, creating analogies, generating questions, and evaluating, or reading critically.

Although strategies have been presented one by one, they are applied in integrated fashion. In reading even a brief selection, students might use three or four strategies at a time. One of the best ways to teach students how to read difficult text is to model the process. When students are reading difficult text, it is important that they read it in step-by-step, intensive fashion. Some strategies that they can use to make dense text more understandable include connecting new information with background knowledge, using graphic organizers, applying knowledge, using manipulatives, reading out loud, and paraphrasing.

Reflection

Return to the Anticipation Guide at the beginning of this chapter. Respond once again to the items. Did your responses change? If so, how and why? What is your view of comprehension? What role might strategies play in the development of comprehension? What role might content knowledge play?

Extension and Application

1. The next time you are reading difficult text, stop and note the strategies that you use to make the text more comprehensible.

2. Try one or more of the strategies suggested in this chapter that you have not used before. Experiment with it over a period of several weeks. How did your use of the strategy change over that time? How effective was the strategy?

3. Which of the strategies discussed in this chapter would be most effective in the content area that you teach? Plan a direct instruction lesson for teaching one of these strategies. In your lesson, be sure to discuss what you are thinking about as you apply the strategy. If possible, teach it and evaluate its effectiveness.

Go to Topic 5: Comprehension in the MyEducationLab (www.myeducationlab.com) for your course, where you can:

- Find learning outcomes for Comprehension along with the national standards that connect to these outcomes.
- Complete Assignments and Activities that can help you more deeply understand the chapter content.
- Apply and practice your understanding of the core teaching skills identified in the chapter with the Building Teaching Skills and Dispositions learning units.
- Examine challenging situations and cases presented in the IRIS Center Resources.

Go to the Topic A+RISE in the MyEducationLab (www.myeducationlab.com) for your course. A+RISE® Standards2Strategy™ is an innovative and interactive online resource that offers new teachers in grades K–12 just-in-time, research-based instructional strategies that:

- Meet the linguistic needs of ELLs as they learn content.
- Differentiate instruction for all grades and abilities.
- Offer reading and writing techniques, cooperative learning, use of linguistic and nonlinguistic representations, scaffolding, teacher modeling, higher-order thinking, and alternative classroom ELL assessment.
- Provide support to help teachers be effective through the integration of listening, speaking, reading, and writing along with the content curriculum.
- Improve student achievement.
- Are aligned to Common Core Elementary Language Arts standards (for the literacy strategies) and to English language proficiency standards in WIDA, Texas, California, and Florida.

CHAPTER 5

Frameworks for Building Comprehension of Content

For each of the following statements, put a check under "Agree" or "Disagree" to indicate your opinion. If possible, discuss your responses with classmates.

	Agree	Disagree
1. Questions asked after a selection has been read help comprehension more than questions asked before the selection is read.		
2. Preparation before the reading of a difficult selection is more effective than explanation after the selection has been read.		
3. Most students depend more on memory of key concepts than on true understanding.		
4. The more direct instruction students are given, the more they learn.		
5. Using a few teaching techniques works best because this builds a sense of familiarity and continuity.	✓	

Using What You Know

hapter 4 focused on the cognitive processes and strategies involved in comprehension. This chapter builds on that information and presents a number of instructional frameworks. The lessons discussed will blend the teaching of content with strategies for learning. Think back on your secondary school experiences. What steps did your teachers take to foster your ability to use reading and writing skills and strategies to learn their subject material? What techniques seemed to be especially effective? What else could they have done to increase your learning?

Approaches to Teaching Comprehension

There are two main approaches to teaching comprehension: strategy and content analysis. As McKeown, Beck, and Blake (2009) explain, "A major distinction between the two approaches is that strategy instruction encourages students to think about their mental processes and, on that basis, to execute specific strategies with which to interact with text. In contrast, content instruction attempts to engage students in the process of attending to text ideas and building a mental representation of the ideas, with no direction to consider specific mental processes" (p. 219). As Wilkinson and Son (2011) comment, "The research on content-rich instruction is compelling in showing that it yields benefits for both students' reading comprehension and their content knowledge" (p. 376). Of course, the approaches can be combined so the reader attends to both strategies and content. This chapter explores approaches that take either a content approach or a combined content-strategy approach. The chapter will also examine approaches that are collaborative but that focus on content; that is, they focus on analyzing ideas rather than the strategies used to comprehend those ideas.

Building Conceptual Understanding

In their study of middle school students who were reading about events leading up to the Revolutionary War, McKeown, Beck, and Sanders (1996) found that many of the students didn't really engage with the text. They seemed to be reading the text in the same way that they might read a popular novel.

> Students took what they could get in one swift pass through the words on a page, and then formed them into a shallow representation of the text. This kind of cursory use of the text suggests that students resist digging in and grappling with unfamiliar or difficult content. (p. 101)

The students were failing to read for **conceptual understanding**. They put little investment into their reading, and they got little out of it. Just as conceptual understanding is an essential element in learning the technical vocabulary of content area subjects, it is also a key factor in the comprehension of content area text. Conceptual understanding doesn't happen automatically—it must be carefully built. Teachers help build conceptual understanding when they plan activities that lead students to construct a deeper understanding of the text.

The first step entails deciding which conceptual understandings are important for the student to acquire. The next step is to plan activities that will foster an understanding of these key concepts. Traditional activities, such as answering factual questions at the end of the chapter, lead students to locate and remember only the information requested. However, conceptual understanding requires students to integrate new information with their background knowledge and to construct generalizations about the information. Questions and activities must involve this integration, or conceptual understanding will not occur.

Developing conceptual understanding takes time. Through interacting with their text, the teacher, and peers, students find similarities and differences in ideas, note other viewpoints, and clarify their thinking, which leads to a deeper understanding of the material. A text that is simply read in order to answer questions at the end is undigested. The information might be retained in memory, but it has not been used to form new understandings. For instance, students who read about the Industrial Revolution may be able to cite its causes and effects, but they may not grasp the implications of what they have read or make connections with their own experiences or other texts they have read. As Roehler (1996) explains, "Students learn to provide answers to questions. They do not necessarily construct the larger conceptual understandings associated with the content and how these relate to their lives" (p. 145). If students have a discussion in class and compare the causes and effects of the Industrial Revolution with changes they have observed or read about in today's workplace, they can begin to relate what happened then to what is happening now. They can also construct charts, such as the one in Figure 5.1, in which they list causes and effects of the Industrial Revolution and compare them with causes and effects of today's Information Revolution. Your role as a teacher is to to ask the kinds of questions that help students compare these events; guide their thinking beyond factual understanding; allow them to make generalizations about changes in the workplace; and enable them to make predictions for the future. In this way, instruction becomes a

> process of intentionally orchestrating the classroom environment so that students are helped to construct the concepts specified by the curriculum. . . . [T]he teacher develops lessons that provide the support students need to learn and the challenge students need to internalize the knowledge. (Roehler, 1996, p. 144)

The way a teacher defines the learning task determines what students learn. Assigning end-of-the-chapter questions leads to low-level learning. Designing questions and activities that involve drawing conclusions from a reading, along with evaluating and

■ **Conceptual understanding** is a depth of understanding such that students are able to go beyond the surface structure and textbase to create a mental model of the text by which they grasp underlying principles and understand why an event happened or why a process works the way it does. Having conceptual knowledge means that they can apply this knowledge.

	Industrial Revolution	Information/Digital Revolution
Causes		
Positive Effects		
Negative Effects		

FIGURE 5.1
Comparison of Industrial and Information/Digital Revolutions

relating it to previously learned topics, leads to conceptual understanding. Once the learning task has been set, understanding is fostered by the nature and number of interactions. Classroom discussions that lead to generalizations and hypotheses result in conceptual understanding.

For the teacher, building conceptual understanding is purposeful. In light of the students' background knowledge and the key concepts of the topic, the teacher plans reading, discussion, and other activities that build necessary background and guide the students in a thoughtful processing of the text, integration of new and previously learned information, and the construction of conceptual understanding. The teacher emphasizes the understanding of information rather than the acquisition of information, gearing instruction to the students' current level of competence while guiding their thinking to higher levels of understanding.

The teacher also builds metacognitive awareness. As students become more aware of their learning processes, they can demand a deeper level of understanding. They also become aware of what it takes to achieve a depth of understanding. They realize that skimming through the text will generally result in a shallow grasp of key concepts. They come to know that thinking about what they have read; carrying on dialogue with the author; and talking with classmates, friends, or family about what they have read and similar activities lead to a fuller, deeper understanding.

Since the textbook is often the major source of information, the teacher should read the textbook in the way a student would and imagine what kinds of understandings the student might construct (Roehler, 1996). If reading the text would lead to a surface understanding, the teacher must supplement the text or provide activities that will lead to a conceptual understanding.

 Struggling Readers

Struggling readers may be satisfied with a lower level of understanding of the text and so may benefit from prompts that help them to analyze and compare. Discussions that help them relate new understandings to their own lives and to past learnings should prove especially helpful.

CHECKUP

1. What is conceptual understanding?
2. What steps might be taken to foster conceptual understanding?

There are numerous techniques that can be used to foster conceptual understanding. Before-reading techniques include the anticipation guide, PReP, survey technique, structured overview, and Frayer model. During-reading techniques feature frame questions and study guides, including glosses. After-reading techniques include reflecting, graphic post-organizers, applying, and extending. A technique that encompasses before, during, and after reading is KWL Plus. Teaching plans that foster comprehension before, during, and after reading include the instructional framework, the directed reading activity, and the directed reading-thinking activity. Collaborative techniques that incorporate several highly successful comprehension strategies are ReQuest, Reciprocal Teaching, Questioning the Author, and Cognitive Strategy Instruction. Collaborative techniques are explored in the next chapter.

Instructional Designs

How should content area reading lessons be structured to develop conceptual understanding? The structure of the lessons is determined by a number of factors, including learning objectives or standards, students' background knowledge and reading ability, the nature of the material to be learned, and students' motivation and ability to work independently. Formats range from being teacher directed to collaborative to student directed. Some offer heavy support; others provide gentle guidance. Regardless of the format used, the lesson should prepare students to read; offer guidance as they read; and help them summarize and organize what they have read, relate it to what they already know, and apply it. The instructional framework provides a flexible structure for designing lessons.

Instructional Framework

The **instructional framework** blends activities that foster the learning of content with activities that help students use content-related reading and writing processes (Herber & Herber, 1993). The instructional framework is composed of three main elements: preparation, guidance, and independence.

Preparation

Preparation includes all the activities designed to foster increased comprehension of the material to be read. This entails making connections between what is known and what is new; building vocabulary; establishing a conceptual context so that students can see how key ideas are organized; activating and building background; establishing a purpose for reading; and motivating the reading. As part of the preparation, you might review previous lessons and show how the upcoming topic is related to what the class has already studied. For instance, when embarking on a study of the Revolutionary War, the class could briefly review the French and Indian War and discuss how that conflict helped set the scene for the Revolutionary War.

Guidance

Preparation flows into guidance, in which you show students how to use reading, writing, and reasoning skills to learn content material. It includes direct instruction in strategies such as imaging, evaluating, summarizing, or drawing conclusions. As part of the preparation, you could discuss with students how to approach reading the text. For example, if the text has a strong bias, students might want to evaluate as they read. Or, if the author is describing Pickett's charge at the Battle of Gettysburg, students might want to create images in their minds as they read so they can visualize the horror of the battle and hear the sounds of war.

Modeling is an essential part of direct instruction. Guidance also involves providing clear directions, using cooperative grouping, monitoring students' efforts, and providing feedback.

Independence

Independence consists of applying both content knowledge and the processes used to acquire it. Initially, you will instruct and guide students in applying knowledge and skills. Over time, students gradually begin to apply content skills and knowledge independently.

Using the instructional framework, you can design your own instruction. Or you can use or adapt one of the many lesson structures that enjoy widespread use in content area instruction, such as the DRA (directed reading activity), the DR-TA (directed reading-thinking activity), and KWL Plus, which are described in this chapter, and ReQuest, Reciprocal Teaching, and Questioning the Author, which are highlighted in the next chapter.

■ **The instructional framework** is a structure used to teach reading. It is composed of three main elements: preparation, guidance, and independence.

Directed Reading Activity (Guided Reading)

A flexible procedure, the **directed reading activity** (DRA) has five steps: preparation for reading, silent reading, discussion, rereading, and follow-up.

Preparation

Through discussion, demonstration, use of a film clip or other audiovisual aid, and/or simulation, students are given guidance in the following areas.

Experiential Background/Concepts   Students often have some background in a subject, but may not realize it. Preparation includes activating students' background knowledge and building new background if necessary. If students have erroneous concepts, these must be confronted and clarified; sometimes this may be more difficult than simply building new concepts. If students are about to read a piece about solar cells, but have no experience with the subject, you might demonstrate the workings of a solar calculator. Concepts or ideas crucial to understanding the selection are also developed: basic concepts of electricity, the flow of electrons, and semiconductors. Chances are that students have some understanding of electricity, so you can activate that background and build on it.

Critical Vocabulary   Present vocabulary necessary for understanding the selection, along with explanations that show how the words relate to each other. Before reading an article about volcanoes, for example, students would be given the words *lava*, *magma*, *crater*, *crust*, and *plates*. A labeled diagram or graphic organizer might be used to show how the words relate to each other.

Reading Strategies   Students have to know how a selection should be read. Most selections call for a mix of preparational, organizational, and elaboration strategies, but for some materials, particular strategies are especially appropriate and effective. A primary source in history, for example, might require evaluation, and a science piece might require that students visualize a process. Because teaching a strategy is time-consuming, it would be best if the needed strategy were taught beforehand and then briefly reviewed during the preparatory discussion. At times, the format of a text might be unfamiliar. For example, before reading a weather map, students should be taught the symbols that the map uses.

Purpose for Reading   The purpose for reading usually embraces the overall significance of the selection and poses the question or questions to be answered by the text. Established by either the teacher or the class, the purpose also may grow out of the preparatory discussion. Students discussing hurricanes may want to know why they occur mostly in late summer and that would become the purpose for reading. You can also provide a strategy guide of thoughtful questions (see pages 146-150) or a graphic organizer to be completed.

Interest   Last but not least, build interest and engagement by helping students make connections between what they are about to read and their own lives (Neubert & Wilkins, 2004). To do this for an article about nutrition, you might bring up the idea that proper nutrition can improve school and athletic performance.

The key elements in the preparation step have been described separately here, but in actual practice they are merged. For instance, background concepts and the vocabulary used to label them are presented at the same time. The purpose for reading flows from the overall discussion, so an interest in the selection should be generated throughout the discussion. Reading strategies might become a part of the purpose. As part of preparation for reading a selection about dinosaurs, you might state, "As you read the selection, notice the possible causes for the disappearance of the dinosaurs (purpose). Think about the evidence given for each theory and judge on the basis of the evidence which theory makes most sense (strategy)."

 English Language Learners

Provide added preparation for English language learners. Review any figures of speech or idiomatic expressions that students still learning English may have difficulty with.

 Struggling Readers

If the text is especially complex, have students read and discuss it in short segments.

■ **The directed reading activity** is a traditional five-step lesson plan designed to assist students in the reading of a selection.

Silent Reading

The first reading is usually silent. Silent reading is faster than oral reading and promotes comprehension. Students are aware of their level of understanding and might stop to reread a confusing sentence when reading silently, but would not do so when reading orally. Oral reading places the focus on pronouncing the words correctly. Sometimes, teachers allow oral reading because the text is too difficult for students. A better solution would be to obtain a text on the appropriate level or use a technique such as Questioning the Author. During silent reading, students might take notes, complete a graphic organizer or strategy guide, use stick-on notes to flag puzzling passages, or write brief responses (Neubert & Wilkins, 2004). You might also break into the silent reading to remind students to use visualizing or another strategy that has been the focus of a recent lesson (Neubert & Wilkins, 2004). Students should monitor their comprehension to check whether they adequately understand what they are reading and, if necessary, take appropriate steps to correct the difficulties. You should note these monitoring and repair strategies. Be sure to display charts or diagrams created in preparation for reading the selection, along with vocabulary words. Also display the purpose for reading so that students are reminded of the key question they are attempting to answer as they read.

Reading might be done in class or for homework. If the text is difficult or contains a large number of concepts, students should read a segment and discuss it before going on to the next segment. This is especially helpful if the information is cumulative, with each section building on the previous one.

🌳 Struggling Readers

Believing that this will help struggling readers cope with a text that is difficult to read, teachers sometimes have students take turns reading the text out loud. This is a poor practice that embarrasses the struggling readers and bores the proficient ones. See Chapter 9 for suggestions for handling this problem.

Discussion

The discussion flows from the purpose for reading. Students read a selection for a specific purpose, and the discussion begins with the purpose question. If the students read about the effects of the Great Depression on farmers, the purpose question is: What effect did the Depression have on farm life? During the discussion, clarify and expand concepts; build background; and reinforce relationships between known and unknown, new and old. Evaluate students' performance, noting whether they were able to comprehend the main concepts in the chapter. Were they able to reconstruct the suffering that farmers endured? Although the discussion is partly evaluative, it should not be regarded as an oral quiz. Its main purpose is to build understanding, not test it (see Chapter 6). Use questioning techniques, such as probes, prompts, and wait time. Devote part of the discussion to asking students to describe their use of strategies, with a focus on the strategy being emphasized.

Before holding a whole-class discussion, you might have small groups discuss elements of the selection. If they have a strategy guide, they might discuss their responses to that. If they have read a short story, they might discuss their personal responses to the fate of the main character. Small-group discussions held prior to whole-class discussions give students an opportunity to clarify misunderstandings and solidify learning. These discussions provide good preparation for a whole-class discussion and a less threatening environment in which students can try out and modify their views before offering them to the whole group. They also give students additional experience with the material and thus promote learning and retention (Neubert & Wilkins, 2004). Another way of reinforcing learning is to have students compose a summary after taking part in the whole-class discussion.

Rereading

In most lessons, rereading blends in naturally with the discussion. As part of the discussion, students may reread to correct misinformation, obtain additional data, enhance appreciation, or deepen understanding. During the discussion, for example, students might indicate that they believe only the farmers in the Dust Bowl suffered (a mistaken notion). Students can then be directed to locate and read aloud passages that describe how farmers in other sections of the country also were affected by the Depression. In other situations, students might dramatize a literary piece that has a substantial amount of dialogue or reread a selection to gain a deeper appreciation of the author's style. A separate reading is generally undertaken for a new purpose, although it may be one that grows out of the discussion. Rereading is not a necessary step. Students may have grasped the essence adequatey in the first reading, and some selections simply do not merit a rereading.

In the rereading stage, oral reading should not be overemphasized. Unless a selection is being dramatized, it is generally a poor practice to have students reread an entire selection orally. Oral rereading should be for specific purposes: to clarify a misconception, substantiate a conclusion, or supply an answer to a question.

Follow-Up

Follow-up or extension activities offer opportunities to delve more deeply into a topic, apply knowledge, or, for controversial topics, consult another source. Students who have read a general article on recycling might want to read more about that topic, contact recycling groups, find out what their town is doing about recycling, or start a recycling project for the class. Every lesson need not have a follow-up.

Preparing a Directed Reading Activity

Creating a DRA starts with an analysis of the selection to be read. After reading the selection, decide what you want the students to learn from it. Content analysis of fiction may result in statements about plot, theme, character, setting, or author's style. For nonfiction, the statements concern the main principles, ideas, concepts, rules, or whatever the students are expected to learn. After analyzing the selection, choose three to five ideas or story elements that you feel are most important. The piece may be loaded with concepts; however, more than three to five cannot be handled in any depth at one time. Even if an accompanying teacher's guide lists important concepts or provides key story events, you should still complete a content analysis. That way, you, and not the textbook author, decide what is important for the class to learn. For example, for a section on the Civil War entitled "Gettysburg," you might compose the following list of major concepts to be learned. These will provide the focus for prereading and postreading activities and assist in the choice of strategies used for prereading, during reading, and postreading.

A series of bad decisions by Lee led to defeat at Gettysburg.

Gettysburg was a costly, deadly battle for both sides.

Gettysburg was the turning point of the Civil War.

After selecting these key ideas, make a list of vocabulary necessary to understand them. As a general rule, choose no more than seven or eight vocabulary words; five or six would probably be more effective. An excessive number of difficult words may be a sign that the selection is too demanding. From the list of difficult words, choose the ones that are most essential to understanding the selection and that students might find most difficult. For example, the following words were selected for the three learnings listed for the section on the Battle of Gettysburg: *overconfident, strategic value, frontal attack, direct assault, maneuver, concentrated his forces.* Selecting vocabulary also gives you a sense of what prior knowledge or schema the passage requires from your students.

Once you have chosen the major understandings and difficult vocabulary words, look over the selection to decide what major cognitive and reading strategies are necessary to understand it. For this selection, visualizing and using the map of the battlefield would be helpful strategies. Comprehension of the battle itself should be improved if students visualize the fighting that took place, as well as the number of soldiers involved and the number killed. However, students should also read to find the causes of the South's defeat and the effects.

Building background and vocabulary, activating schema, piquing interest, setting purposes, and giving guidance in reading and cognitive strategies are all done in the preparatory segment of the lesson. Generally, this takes the form of a discussion. Key vocabulary words are written on the board. When discussing each word, point to it on the board so that students become familiar with it in print. After introducing the new words, have students say them. The act of pronouncing words helps bond them in memory. Following is a simple DRA for a text segment on Gettysburg.

 Struggling Readers

Because it provides maximum guidance, the directed reading activity is especially effective with struggling readers.

LESSON 5.1

Directed Reading Activity

Step 1: Preparation

Have you ever played on a team that was overconfident? What happened? We have just read about Confederate victories at Second Bull Run and Chancellorsville. How do you think General Lee was feeling? Do you think he might have been overconfident? Lee decided to invade Gettysburg, but the North concluded that it had **strategic value** because so many roads led to Gettysburg. If you controlled Gettysburg, you could keep Southern soldiers from using those roads. Northern troops were sent to Gettysburg, and the two sides met almost by accident. No one had planned to have a battle there. But soon thousands of soldiers had gathered. Being **overconfident,** Lee decided on a **frontal attack.** What do you think a **frontal attack** might be? Instead of **maneuvering** around the enemy soldiers, you order a **direct assault.** You attack them directly. You try to go through the main parts of their lines. You try to hit a weak spot, but you may attack a place where an enemy commander has **concentrated his forces,** which means that he has gathered most of his soldiers at a certain place.

Read the section on the Battle of Gettysburg, from pages 63 to 69. Find out who won the battle and why and what effects this had on the war. As you read, try to picture the battles. Try to imagine what their battlefields looked like and what they sounded like. The map on page 67 shows the main places where the battle was fought.

Step 2: Silent Reading of Selection

Students read silently individually, or they may read in small cooperative groups.

Step 3: Discussion

The teacher begins the discussion with the purpose questions: Who won the battle? Why did the North win? What were the effects of the battle on the war? Why did Lee invade Pennsylvania? What mistakes did he make? What might have happened had he listened to Longstreet? How many men were lost at Gettysburg on both sides? (Figures are easily forgotten. This is a good point to model the strategy of looking back over a selection and skimming to find this fact.) How do you think Lee felt about the loss? As you read about the battles, what pictures came to mind? What sounds did you imagine?

Step 4: Rereading

Although rereading is listed as a separate step, it often occurs spontaneously during the discussion of the selection. For instance, during the discussion, students went back to the selection to obtain facts that they didn't recall and also to clarify and expand responses. Because the students' basic understanding of the selection was adequate, there was no need for a total rereading, only some lookbacks.

Step 5: Follow-Up

This step, too, is optional. Some possible follow-ups might include reading Crane's *The Red Badge of Courage* or viewing a video on the Battle of Gettysburg.

Directed Reading–Thinking Activity

The DRA is primarily a teacher-directed lesson. The DR-TA (**directed reading-thinking activity**) was designed to get students more involved in the learning process. In a DR-TA, the teacher leads students to establish purposes for reading and to decide when these purposes have been fulfilled. Because it involves making predictions based on what students know, the DR-TA works best when students have background knowledge to bring to the selection. If students are lacking in background, the DRA is a better choice.

By nature, we have a tendency to look ahead, to predict what will happen. Russell Stauffer (1969, 1970), the creator of the DR-TA, based the approach on our tendency to

■ The directed reading-thinking activity (DR-TA) is an adaptation of the directed reading activity in which readers use preview and prediction strategies to set their own purposes for reading.

Using an Adapted DRA

Using an adaptation of the DRA known as SRE (Scaffolded Reading Experience), Sally Rothenberg, a high school language arts teacher, helped her class of underachieving students read and appreciate *Macbeth* (Rothenberg & Watts, 1997). Prereading instruction focused on building a concept of literary tragedy and conveying a sense of the setting of *Macbeth:* Scotland in the eleventh century. To help students activate their prior knowledge, elements of *Macbeth* were compared to elements of contemporary works. There was also a minilesson on the structure of a play as literature. Students were shown how to use visualization, a strategy taught earlier in the year, to help them get a better sense of the play's action. Preparatory discussions and teacher-posed questions were used to guide each day's reading of the play. Students also dramatized the play. In addition, students kept a journal of their reactions to the play and their reflections.

As a follow-up activity, pairs of students responded to a statement in an account of Richard Nixon's death in which the former president was referred to as a "Shakespearean hero of tragic proportion." Students also viewed a film version of *Macbeth* and noted ways in which the movie version altered or affirmed their overall impression of the play.

Rothenberg successfully combined reading and literary instruction. With the careful scaffolding afforded by the structure of her instructional framework, she made the text accessible to these below-level readers so they could both understand and appreciate it. Building upon their enthusiasm, she encouraged students to create personal interpretations of the play. She also helped students relate the work to their lives and current events.

predict and hypothesize. Predicting and hypothesizing activate our background knowledge, and they also pique students' curiosity and cause them to become more active readers. As they discuss their predictions and listen to the predictions of others, students' background is built. The DR-TA enlists the same five steps as the DRA, but they are implemented differently.

Following is a lesson showing how a DR-TA might be used with the classic short story by James Thurber, "The Secret Life of Walter Mitty." The teacher provides the following prereading guidance: "Read the title. What do you think the phrase a 'secret life' means? What do you think this story might be about? What makes you think that? Does anyone have a different prediction? Read to the top of page 391. See how your predictions come out."

Students read to the top of the page 391 and discover that Walter Mitty has been dreaming that he was the courageous commander of a hydroplane. They discuss their predictions in light of what they have just read. The important point isn't whether the predictions are accurate; the goal is to determine whether students were able to make reasonable predictions and to ascertain whether this process helped to activate their background and make them more active and productive readers. As they discuss their predictions and Walter Mitty's actions, students will undoubtedly note that he is a dreamer. As they predict, read, and discuss additional sections, they will probably discover that he is downtrodden and browbeaten. During the discussion, they might note the influence of movies and reading on his daydreams and talk about times when they also have escaped into daydreams. This could be a possible writing topic.

The DR-TA is designed for use with both fiction and nonfiction, but probably works better with fiction. When the DR-TA is used with informational text, you can divide the piece into brief sections; in addition, students can think about what the selection is trying to explain to them. Following is a script recounting a segment of a DR-TA lesson with a seventh-grade class that is reading a segment of a trade book on plate tectonics, *Our Patchwork Planet* (Sattler, 1995). Note in the segment how the teacher is accepting of predictions, but prompts students to explain the reasoning behind their predictions. Although the discussions are student-centered, the teacher does step in to make sure that students

LESSON 5.2

Directed Reading-Thinking Activity

Step 1: Preparation

This step entails determining students' background, activating prior knowledge, and building background and vocabulary as necessary. Your task as a teacher is to lead students to predict what the selection will be about. Their predictions will be based on a survey of the selection. Direct students to examine the title of the selection to be read, headings and subheads, illustrations, and the introductory paragraph, if there is one. Based on this survey, which should take no longer than a few minutes, ask the class what they think the selection will tell or what information it will present. Also ask students to justify their predictions with what-makes-you-think-that questions. This leads students to think more deeply about the selection and to make better use of the survey. As predictions are being discussed and recorded on the board, you can assess students' background. If their background is very limited—if students have very little to say about the topic—you can build background and highlight key vocabulary and concepts. Not every student needs to offer a prediction; however, every student should either have her or his own prediction or endorse one that has been recorded. After all the student predictions have been recorded, ask if anyone has a prediction that was not recorded and list additional predictions, if any. Ask students to show by raising their hands which prediction they favor: How many favor the first prediction? The second? etc. Students now have a purpose for reading: to assess their predictions.

If the selection is lengthy or complex, it can be broken up into sections. For informational text, students can make a prediction based on the subhead and then read and discuss the section covered by the subhead before moving on. For a story or selection without a subhead, note logical stopping places where old predictions can be discussed and new ones can be made. Breaking a selection up in this way makes it easier to read. Students grasp one section completely before moving on to the next.

Step 2: Silent Reading

Students read silently until they are able to evaluate their predictions; this might mean a single page, several pages, or a whole chapter. Encourage students to modify their initial predictions if they find information that runs counter to them.

Step 3: Discussion

This stage is almost identical to Step 3 of the DRA, except that it begins with the consideration of the class's predictions. If students' predictions turned out to be accurate, they can discuss information from the passage that supports them. If there is a disagreement about the adequacy of a prediction, students can read passages to support their positions. If students' predictions turn out to be inaccurate and they changed them as they read, they can tell how and why they modified their predictions. During the discussion, place emphasis on the reasoning process involved and on students' willingness to alter predictions in the light of new information rather than on the rightness or wrongness of predictions.

Step 4: Rereading

This is the same as Step 4 of the DRA.

Step 5: Follow-Up

This is the same as Step 5 of the DRA.

grasp key concepts and vocabulary. The teacher wants to make sure that students know what a continent is and where the continents are located, since this is crucial to an understanding of the selection. The teacher prompts the students to use context to derive the meaning of *marine*. Through the discussion, the teacher also makes sure that the students have gotten the gist of the section and are ready to move on to the next section. Using a prediction strategy fosters comprehension because students will be unable to make reasonable predictions if they don't have a basic grasp of what they have read so far.

DR–TA Lesson

Teacher: Read the title. What do you think this section will be about? What do you think we will find out?

Student 1:   The title is "Unlocking Earth's Mysteries."

Teacher: What are some of Earth's mysteries?

Student 2:   How deserts were formed.

Teacher: Why do you think that?

Student 2:   The photograph on the page shows a desert.

(Teacher writes this and other predictions on the board.)

Teacher: Does anyone have a different prediction?

Student 3:   I think it might tell why Antarctica is covered with ice. The picture shows sheets of ice in Antarctica.

Student 4:   I think it will tell why some parts of the world are hot and some are cold.

Student 5:   I predict that the section will tell how the Earth has changed because one of the pictures shows a fossil.

Teacher: Excellent predictions. Read page 5 and see how your predictions play out.

(Students read page 5 silently.)

Teacher: How did your predictions play out? Which one of the predictions comes closest to stating what the text described?

Student 5:   The last prediction, the one about how the Earth has changed.

Teacher: How about the other predictions? Could they also be right?

Student 5:   Yes. The rest of the article will probably tell how mountains and deserts were formed, but I'm not so sure it will tell why part of Earth is cold and part hot.

Teacher: What made scientists believe that Earth had changed?

Student 6:   They found fossils of plants and plant-eating dinosaurs in Antarctica.

Student 3:   They found that a glacier had once been in the middle of the Sahara Desert.

Student 5:   They found animal fossils at the top of the Himalayan Mountains.

Teacher: That is something because the Himalayas are the tallest mountains in the world. But what was extra strange about finding animals at the top of the Himalayas? What kind of animals did they find?

Student 5:   It says they were marine animals.

Teacher: What kind of animals are marine animals? Read the second paragraph and see if you can figure from context what marine animals are.

Student 5:   (Reading from text) "Nor could marine animals swim to the top of the world's highest mountain—not if continents had always been where they are today." (p. 5)

Teacher: So what do you think marine animals are?

Student 5:   Sea animals. Like fish. Because they could swim.

Teacher: Very good. Marine animals are sea animals, so finding sea animals at the top of the world's tallest mountain would be a surprise. By the way, the sentence mentions continents. What are continents and how many are there?

Student 7: Continents are big chunks of land. I believe there are seven: North America, South America, Africa, Asia, Europe, Arctic, and Antarctica.

Teacher: There is one more. It's the smallest continent.

Student 7: Oh yeah. Australia.

Teacher: Good. The Arctic isn't really a continent and some geographers say that Europe and Asia form one big continent known as Eurasia. (The teacher points to continents on a world map.) What do you predict the next section will tell us?

(Students make predictions and read the next section. They continue in this fashion until they have read the entire text.)

CHECKUP

1. What are the steps in the instructional framework, DRA, and DR-TA?
2. What are the advantages and disadvantages of each technique?

KWL Plus: A Technique for Before, During, and After Reading

KWL Plus was created as researcher Donna Ogle and a number of classroom teachers sought a device to "build active personal reading of expository text" (Ogle, 1989, p. 206). KWL Plus (What I **K**now, What I **W**ant to Know, and What I **L**earned, **Plus** What I Still Want to Find Out) activates students' background knowledge, asks them to think about what they want to know or need to know, and, then, after reading, has them tell what they learned and what they would still like to find out. The before-reading stage of KWL is composed of four steps: brainstorming, categorizing, anticipating or predicting, and questioning. Brainstorming begins when you ask the class what they know about a topic. If students are about to read a selection about acid rain, for example, write the words *acid rain* on the board and ask students what they know about acid rain. Write responses on the board and discuss them. The group brainstorming activates prior knowledge so that students become more aware of what they already know and they also learn from others. If a disagreement occurs about a piece of information or if students seem unsure of a fact, these situations can be used to create what-we-want-to-know questions. After brainstorming, students record their personal knowledge of acid rain in the first column of a KWL worksheet. One of the advantages of having a group brainstorming session first and writing responses on the board is that it helps students with the spelling of technical terms. In tryouts, a number of students were reluctant to write down what they knew if they were unsure of the spellings of some of the content words.

In one version of KWL, students filled in two what-I-know columns on their KWL worksheets. The first column told what they knew about the topic before previewing; the second told what they knew after previewing (Richardson & Morgan, 1997).

After writing what they know about acid rain, students categorize their knowledge. Brainstormed items already written on the board are grouped into categories. Students then label the items already recorded in the what-we-know column with letters that name the categories, as shown in Figure 5.2: C = causes, E = effects, and M = measures taken to reduce acid rain. Students also predict what categories of information the author might provide. This helps them anticipate the content of the text and organize the information as they read it. Model the process of predicting categories by asking, "What kinds of information do you think this article will give us about acid rain?" and think aloud as you try to figure out possible categories of information. Students then volunteer their predictions. Possible categories of information are recorded at the bottom of the KWL worksheet. (The KWL approach can be simplified by omitting the categorization phase.)

After deciding on possible categories of information, the students discuss what they want to know about acid rain and compose questions that are written on the board. The class also records these questions in the second column of the worksheet. Each student

■ KWL Plus (Know, Want to Know, and Learn) is a technique designed to help readers build and organize background and seek out and reflect on key elements in a reading selection.

FIGURE 5.2 **KWL Plus Chart**

Name: _____ Date: _____

Topic: _____

What We Know	What We Want to Know	What We Learned	What We Still Want to Know
C Acid rain is caused by dirty air. C Cars, trucks, and buses are the main causes of dirty air. C Factories also cause dirty air. E Acid rain harms forests. E Acid rain harms streams and lakes. E Acid rain kills fish. M Using tall smoke stacks helps cut down on acid rain.	How does acid rain form?	Burning coal, oil, and gasoline create sulfur dioxide and oxides of nitrogen. Acid rain forms when sulfur dioxide and oxides of nitrogen combine with water, oxygen, and oxides. Power plants that make electricity give off 70% of the sulfur dioxide and 30% of the oxides of nitrogen. Cars also give off these pollutants.	Is acid rain getting better or worse? Where is acid rain the worst? Do other countries have an acid rain problem? If so, what are they doing about it?
	Is acid rain getting better or worse? Does acid rain do damage besides harming forests and streams and lakes? Does acid rain harm people?	Acid rain damages buildings and statues. Acid rain causes tiny particles of dirt to float in the air. These particles worsen lung diseases such as asthma and bronchitis.	
	Where is acid rain the worst? What is being done to lessen acid rain?	Tall smoke stacks carry particles higher into the air. The particles are carried by the winds to distant places. Cars and power plants are reducing their emissions.	

might also compose and record his or her personal questions. The questions might be the same as or different from those created by the group or a combination of group and personal questions.

Using their questions as a guide, the class reads the text. After reading, students record their responses and then discuss what they learned. Information is organized, misconceptions are clarified, and emerging concepts are developed more fully. After the discussion, students write in the third column what they learned both as a group and personally. Based on this information, they cross out any misconceptions that they entered in the first column. If students still have unanswered questions or if new questions have cropped up, they can create a fourth column entitled What We Still Want to Find Out and enter their unanswered questions (Sippola, 1995). Discuss with the class how they might go about finding the answers to the questions they still have. If the information that students have

Struggling Readers

KWL was specifically designed for secondary students who were having difficulty understanding their textbooks. KWL builds on what students know and makes them active participants.

is important and if they need to retain it for a test or future units of study, you might also have them create a semantic map incorporating the information they have learned and also compose a summary based on the map (Ogle, 1996). The ultimate purpose of KWL is to lead students to ask KWL questions automatically as they read. A completed KWL worksheet is presented in Figure 5.2.

Adaptations of KWL

In one version of KWL known as the Six-Step Topical Guide, students divide what they know into two categories: What I Know Definitely and What I Think I Know. They then read to verify their knowledge. After reading and discussing their reading, they note which of the items they listed are accurate, which are inaccurate, and which they are unsure of. They then record questions that they still have, along with possible sources for answers to these questions (Egan, 1999).

One problem with KWL is that students might neglect to pose questions about vital areas. In one adaptation of KWL, the teacher adds focus questions. These might be key questions that grow out of the objectives for the unit being studied, or they may be modifications of questions posed at the end of the chapter (Huffman, 1998). For each question, students tell what they know, what they want to know, and what they learned.

A flexible technique, KWL has been used in surprising ways. One teacher used KWL as an introduction to the reading of a Shakespeare play. Students were asked two questions: What do you know about Shakespeare, *Macbeth*, and literary tragedy? And what do you want to know? Students' responses were used to assess their background knowledge and also to determine techniques and activities that might be used to help them read *Macbeth* with understanding and appreciation (Rothenberg & Watts, 1997).

Don't shortchange this technique. Be sure to discuss fully what students learned. Also consider any questions that were unanswered or that came up as they were reading. Provide opportunities and materials for students to seek answers to these questions the at the school library or on the Internet.

CHECKUP

1. What are the steps in KWL Plus and its adaptation?
2. What are the main benefits of using KWL?

Before–Reading Techniques

Before-reading teaching techniques provide an overview of the selection to be read, activate prior knowledge, build background and vocabulary, set goals, and construct strategies for reading and reasoning. Before-reading techniques feature the anticipation guide, PReP, the structured overview, and drawing and writing before reading.

Anticipation Guide

At this point, you are in a position to judge the effectiveness of the anticipation guide because one appears at the beginning of each chapter of this text. An **anticipation guide** consists of a list of three to six carefully worded controversial or debatable statements designed to challenge students to think over what they know and also to arouse their curiosity and interest. Students respond to the statements by indicating whether they agree with them. An anticipation guide gets students involved in thinking about a topic before they read about it. In addition to activating their prior knowledge, it may also highlight erroneous concepts that they may have about a topic so these can be addressed prior to reading. Note, however, that anticipation guides only work if students have some knowledge of the topic. Steps for creating and using an anticipation guide are outlined below (Head & Readence, 1986).

■ An anticipation guide is an instructional technique designed to activate and have students reflect on background knowledge.

LESSON 5.3

Anticipation Guide

Step 1: Identifying Major Concepts
List two or three major ideas that you want students to learn.

Step 2: Determining Students' Background
Considering students' general knowledge and beliefs about the content of the selection to be read, what misunderstandings might they have about the topic? List them. Also consider the attitudes and values of the community. Students who live in an area that has coal mines or oil wells might have different opinions about using fossil fuels than students who live in a community that is attempting to use alternative sources of energy.

Step 3: Creating the Guide
Compose three to six statements that incorporate the major concepts you listed in Step 1, keeping in mind ideas or events about which students may have misconceptions or doubts. Do not compose statements on subjects about which students have no knowledge because they won't be able to say whether they agree or disagree. The most effective statements are those for which the students have enough information that they can respond but not so much that they won't be gaining new knowledge as they read. Avoid writing statements that are really true-false items and thus don't require students to evaluate their knowledge, beliefs, and opinions (Head & Readence, 1986; Readence, Moore, & Rickelman, 2000). Opinion statements work better than factual statements. Settle on the statements that best fit the nature of the material to be read and students' goals for reading. Statements can be listed in order of coverage in the text, in an order that is most conducive to discussion, or from least to most important.

Step 4: Introducing the Guide
Explain the guide. Then place it or project it on the board or duplicate and distribute it to students. Read the directions and the statements orally and ask students to respond to each statement by checking "Agree" or "Disagree." Students may work independently, in pairs, or in small groups. Small groups may be most effective in getting students to reflect on the topic and confront misconceptions.

Step 5: Discussing Responses
Discuss each statement. Students raise their hands to indicate whether they agree or disagree and provide reasons for their choices. Elicit at least one "agree" and one "disagree" statement for each item so students consider both sides of an issue. The discussion should help students open their minds as they assess their beliefs in relation to the beliefs of others. The discussion should also motivate students to want to read the selection so they can better evaluate their beliefs.

Step 6: Reading of Text
Summarize students' responses, highlighting areas of controversy or doubt. Then have students read the selection. As they read, they should consider their responses and those of others in light of the information presented in the text.

Step 7: Discussion of Text
Students again respond to the statements. Based on what they have read, they can change their responses. Discuss the responses once more, emphasizing changes students may have made and their reasons for making them.

Instead of using Agree and Disagree categories, you can have columns labeled "Author" and "Me" in which the student checks statements with which he agrees and statements with which the author agrees. Another possibility is to have an "Anticipation" column, in which the student checks statements with which he agrees before reading the text, and a "Reaction" column, in which he checks statements with which he agrees as a result of reading the text.

Extended Anticipation Guide

The extended anticipation guide adds a second part in which readers indicate whether they have found support for their responses in the text (Duffelmeyer, Baum, & Merkley, 1987). If, on the other hand, they have found information that conflicts with their beliefs, they rewrite, in their own words, this information This can be an effective way of motivating students to revise erroneous notions.

PReP

When presenting a new topic, it is important to have a sense of what students already know about it. They may have limited or erroneous knowledge about the Spanish-American War, Reconstruction, the French Revolution, DNA, or cell division. A technique that combines assessment with the development of background knowledge and that also helps students activate prior knowledge is the **Pre-Reading Plan (PReP)**. PReP is a three-step assessment-instructional procedure that helps the teacher determine what students know about a particular topic, how that information might be organized, and what kind of language the students use to describe or explain that knowledge. The teacher can then assess how much background and vocabulary might need to be developed before the students will be able to understand the text (Langer, 1981). For students who know a great deal about a topic, PReP can be used to help them organize and clarify their knowledge. For students who didn't realize how much they knew, PReP can help them access their background knowledge. PReP can also help build knowledge for those whose background is limited or who have erroneous perceptions about a topic (Tierney & Readence, 2000). Following are the three steps in applying PReP.

During the PReP discussion, build concepts. Talk about why the United Nations was started and what it has done to promote peace. You might also lead students to see that the United Nations performs a number of humanitarian, research, and regulatory or advisory functions in addition to keeping the peace. Depending on the types of responses given, you may find that students need no instruction, a little, or extensive background building. By building on what students know and using their concepts and language, you will be better able to give them the kind of preparation they need for reading a selection.

Structured Overview

In order to study how students read content materials, Barron (1969) took on the role of a student in a high school biology class, a subject in which he had little background. Overwhelmed by a long list of unfamiliar technical terms, he wondered how he would cope with all the new words. The solution was not long in coming:

> Later that evening, as I attempted to read the chapters associated with the unit, a simple fact began to dawn on me. *All the vocabulary words were related in some way.* I started to arrange the words in a diagram to depict relationships, occasionally adding terms from the two preceding units. Gradually, much of the content with which I had been struggling became clear. (pp. 172–173)

Out of this experience was born the structured overview. A **structured overview** builds on what students

■ The Pre-Reading Plan (PReP) is an instructional technique designed to help the teacher build background knowledge.

■ A structured overview is a graphic organizer in which the key concepts and vocabulary of a topic or unit of study are displayed. The structured overview is designed to help students relate new words and concepts to known words and concepts.

LESSON 5.4

PReP

Step 1: Initial Associations with the Concept

Using a key word, phrase, or illustration from the text to be read as a prompt, say, "Tell me anything that comes to mind when you hear the words *United Nations*." List students' responses on the board.

Step 2: Reflections on Initial Associations

In order to assess students' associations with the key word or phrase, point to each student's response and ask a question about it. If one of the responses is the word *peace*, for instance, ask, "What makes you think of *peace*?" Students become aware of their network of associations and their own thinking as well as the associations and reasoning of the other students. They can consider, alter, accept, or reject ideas and associations as they become aware of their changing conceptions.

Step 3: Reformulation of Knowledge

To give students a chance to express associations that have been modified by the discussion, you might ask, "Based on what we have talked about, do you have any new ideas about the United Nations? Have you changed any of your ideas as a result of our discussion?" Since students have had a chance to think about their ideas, their responses usually are more refined at this point. To determine the extent and quality of the students' prior knowledge, analyze their responses, using the criteria supplied by Langer, outlined below.

Much knowledge

Responses include superordinate concepts, definitions, analogies, or linking of the concept with another concept. *The United Nations is like a world congress. Police force for the world. Organization devoted to peace of the world.*

Some knowledge

Responses include examples, attributes, or defining characteristics. *Gives food to hungry people. Place where countries talk over problems. Works for peace.*

Little knowledge

Responses include low-level associations, such as words that sound like the stimulus word, or associations that aren't quite relevant. *United. All together. Nations. Countries. Lots of people. It's in New York. Our class went there once.*

Struggling Readers

Because it provides an assessment of students' prior knowledge and a means for building background, PReP is an excellent device to use with students whose background is weak.

already know, showing how new words in a selection or unit that students are about to study are related to words that are familiar to them. For instance, students can better understand the word *mollusks* when they realize that the category includes *clams, snails, scallops, oysters,* and *octopuses*. The original structured overview was very much teacher directed and followed a series of six steps, as outlined in Lesson 5.5.

Revised Structured Overview

The original structured overview is teacher directed and works well with students who have little background to bring to a topic. In the revised structured overview, students are more actively involved. Barron (1979) found that when students played a role in constructing an overview, they learned more. He also found that the structured overview worked well when it was used to organize information after the students had read the target sections.

The revised overview begins with brainstorming (Estes & Vaughn, 1985). Place the key concept on the board and discuss it. A concept such as *diet* would probably not work well for a prereading structured overview because students may have little background to bring to the concept. However, you might use a more familiar concept, such as *food*. As

LESSON 5.5

Teaching a Structured Overview

Step 1: Selecting Key Concepts

Read over the selection or unit to be studied and select two to four concepts or ideas that you wish to emphasize. In introducing a unit on diet, for example, you might choose to stress the following ideas:

Macronutrients, micronutrients, water, and fiber are needed to keep our bodies healthy.

Macronutrients include carbohydrates, proteins, and fats.

Micronutrients include vitamins and minerals.

Step 2: Selecting Related Vocabulary

Analyze the vocabulary in the selection and choose words that you feel would be needed to understand the key ideas.

Step 3: Arranging Words

Arrange the words so that you show relationships. You can place words on cards so that they are easier to organize or you can use software, such as *Inspiration* (Inspiration Software), to create graphic organizers.

Step 4: Inserting Known Words

Add words that the students already know so that they can relate the new words to known words.

Step 5: Checking the Overview

Look over the overview. Are relationships clearly shown? Is the overview easy to understand? A completed overview is shown in Figure 5.3.

Step 6: Introducing the Overview

Place the overview on chart paper or the board or project it. Point to the word *diet* and tell students that they will be reading about foods and other substances that we need to stay healthy. Ask them what they can tell about diet by examining the overview. Talk about the fact that in addition to food, the body needs water and fiber. Discuss the three main kinds of macronutrients and two main kinds of micronutrients, and provide examples of each. Also discuss fibers. Clarify any concepts that seem confusing. Make changes to the overview as needed.

Keep the overview in a prominent place so that as students read about foods, they can refer to it. As students learn more about diet, encourage them to add to the overview. You may want to add sections that contain key words that give specific examples of sources of macronutrients and micronutrients.

the students respond, supply prompts, asking such questions as: What are the main kinds of foods that you need? What are some examples of fats? Proteins? What do you need besides food to stay healthy?

After listing on the board what students know, add some of your own items, especially if key concepts were omitted. Have students help you group items and devise titles or category names for the groups. Then arrange the items in a structured overview. Again, at this point, feel free to add important concepts or vocabulary that have not been mentioned. Also review the overview and tie it in with the students' purpose for reading the selection. The students can use the overview to predict what the selection will be about; after reading, they can add to the overview.

FIGURE 5.3 Structured Overview

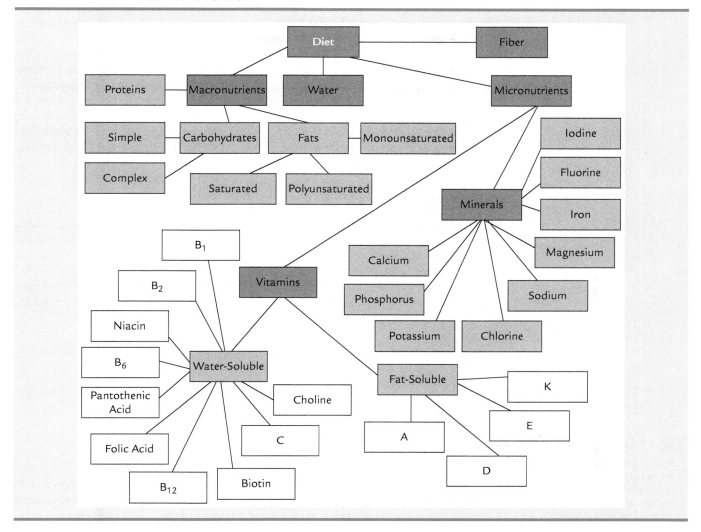

Drawing before Reading

Most prereading activities involve some sort of verbal interchange. One way of having students activate prior knowledge is to ask them to draw what they know about a topic. This works especially well with English language learners. Working first with an adult class and then with younger pupils, McConnell (1992–1993) used drawing as a way of having students convey and refine their concepts of a rain forest and the greenhouse effect. When students seemed unable to convey in words their concepts of a rain forest, McConnell asked them to draw their impressions of it. Other students were asked to sketch their concepts of the greenhouse effect. The results were startling. Students' concepts varied widely, as did their perspectives. Some focused on the causes of the greenhouse effect; others on the effects; still others depicted what the greenhouse effect meant to them personally. The students shared their drawings in a small group and noted similarities and differences. Later, the class as a whole discussed the drawings.

After the class discussed the features of the drawings and the teacher listed them on the board, she and the class created a semantic map of the topic. Students then read an article about rain forests. After discussing the article, students revised their drawings in light of what they had learned. Because they had learned so much, some students created entirely new drawings.

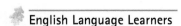

English Language Learners

Drawing is a good way for ELLs to show what they know.

As a final step, students discussed changes in their drawings and the differences between their before and after depictions. Students frequently justified or clarified their changes by reading pertinent passages from the text. They also sought out other books on rain forests for additional information about the topic to help them with their drawings.

Using drawings as a springboard and integrating them with discussion and reading of the text, the students activated schemata, set a purpose for reading, and created a framework for organizing new knowledge. As McConnell (1992–1993) noted, drawings provide "a visible and explicit record of learning which can be reflected upon, altered, and developed" (p. 269). In addition to helping students explore prior knowledge and develop purposes for reading, drawings also fostered comprehension and language use and helped clarify concepts that are easily misunderstood. And they did all this in a novel, interesting way.

Writing before Reading

Instead of being asked to tell what they know about a topic, students can be asked to write what comes to mind when they think of it. Free writing is a kind of written brainstorm. For a period of about three to five minutes, students are asked to write whatever they want about Canada, solar power, or a similar topic. One advantage of free writing is that it is nonthreatening. It also gives students a little "think time" because they have a few minutes to respond, as opposed to the immediate response usually required in a prereading discussion. And it allows everyone to participate.

CHECKUP

1. What are some effective before-reading techniques?
2. How might each technique be taught?

CCSS

Read closely to determine what the text says explicitly and to make logical inferences from it; cite specific textual evidence when writing or speaking to support conclusions drawn from the text.

During-Reading Techniques

During reading, strategic readers construct meaning. Using chapter organization and the structure of the text as a framework, they seek out main ideas or themes and supporting details. Distinguishing between relevant and irrelevant details, they seek essential information. As they read, they integrate information from text with prior knowledge, make inferences, and make judgments about what they read. They may create images of processes or events described in the text. Strategic readers also regulate their rate of reading and monitor their understanding of the passage. They may reread or seek clarification if their comprehension breaks down. During-reading instructional techniques include strategy guides and glosses, teacher-created devices designed to foster comprehension; frame matrices; information maps; and adjunct or embedded questions.

Strategy Guides

Strategy guides, which are sometimes known as *study* or *reading guides*, are learning aids that help students comprehend and organize information during as well as after reading, listening, and/or viewing (Wood, Lapp, Flood, & Taylor, 2008). Strategy guides range in complexity from very simple guides designed to help students master basic facts to guides that require higher levels of thinking and application. They can include fill-in-the-blank, true-false, or matching items. Or they can feature graphic organizers

Strategy guides help students focus on important information.

Source: David Grossman/Alamy.

or questions designed to help students reflect on what they have learned. The most effective guides foster conceptual understanding and reflection. It is important to note that all guides should be complemented by discussions that help students construct and reconstruct their understandings.

Procedures for creating a study guide are as follows:

1. Analyze the selection to be read, listened to, or viewed. Note the major concepts or principles that you think students should learn. Make a note of the sections that students must read to grasp these concepts.
2. Consider elements of the text that may pose problems for students, such as complex concepts, technical vocabulary, figurative language, confusing explanations, or poor organization.
3. Determine the dominant organizational patterns of the chapter, such as comparison/contrast, sequential, process/explanation, or other (see Chapter 4 for a description of patterns). Note that more than one pattern may be used.
4. Determine strategies that students can use to grasp key concepts.
5. Construct a guide that leads students to essential content, helps them overcome possible obstacles to comprehension, and guides them in the use of effective strategies. Also make the study guide as interesting as you can. Pose intriguing questions, include items that challenge the reader, and, where appropriate, include gamelike activities, such as crossword puzzles.

Pattern Guides

Determining the dominant pattern in a section of text promotes both comprehension and retention (Herber, 1970). For example, if readers realize that the author is using a comparison/contrast pattern to describe the status of the North and the South during the Civil War, they can mentally sort the information into the proper categories. If readers know that a piece has a process/sequential organization, they can mentally keep track of the main steps.

Pattern guides come in varied formats. A pattern guide may include a partially completed outline in which just the main ideas are included and the reader is asked to supply supporting details. Or it may involve matching causes and effects or a compare/contrast pattern (Estes & Vaughn, 1985). The sample cause/effect pattern guide in Figure 5.4 helps students not only obtain essential information from the section but also organize that information so they can note both positive and negative effects.

> **CCSS**
>
> Analyze the structure of texts, including how specific sentences, paragraphs, and larger portions of the text (e.g., a section, chapter, scene, or stanza) relate to each other and the whole.
>
> Analyze how and why individuals, events, and ideas develop and interact over the course of a text.

Concept Guides

Concept guides focus on one or more key concepts. Through questions or other activities, they help students see how the concepts were formed. A sample concept guide is presented in Figure 5.5.

Levels of Thinking Guide

Levels of thinking guides are designed to foster comprehension at three levels: literal (comprehending, organizing), interpretive (elaborating), and applied (elaborating); (Herber & Herber, 1993). To construct a levels of thinking guide, create questions or activities that incorporate understanding and organizing essential information, drawing conclusions, evaluating, and/or applying.

After students complete the guides, have them meet in groups of four or five and discuss their responses. Be sure they explain and support their responses.

Where possible, students should be prepared to refer to the text to support their responses. After small groups have completed their discussions, have the class meet as a whole. A representative from each group summarizes his or her group's discussion. After you have summarized the groups' responses, you can answer any questions students may have and clarify confusing points.

FIGURE 5.4
Pattern Guide

> **Chapter 18: Prosperity and Change**
>
> In this section of the text, the authors use a cause/effect pattern to explain that automobiles had both positive and negative effects on life in the United States. Read "A Changing Way of Life," page 420. List some of the positive effects:
>
> 1. _____
>
> 2. _____
>
> 3. _____
>
> 4. _____
>
> Read "Automobiles Brought Problems," page 421. List some of the negative effects.
>
> 1. _____
>
> 2. _____
>
> 3. _____
>
> 4. _____
>
> **For Discussion**
>
> Based on a consideration of positive and negative effects, what would you conclude about the overall effect of the automobile on the way people lived?

FIGURE 5.5
Concept Strategy Guide

> *Our Patchwork Planet* by Helen Roney Sattler
>
> Read "Unlocking Earth's Mysteries."
>
> **Creating and testing hypotheses.** Through observations and careful thought, scientists create hypotheses. They then use experiments or observations to test their hypotheses.
>
> 1. What observations led scientists to believe that the Earth had changed?
>
>   a. _____
>
>   b. _____
>
>   c. _____
>
> 2. What observation led scientists to believe that Africa and South America had once been part of the same continent?
>
>   _____
>
>   Look at a map that shows the continents of Africa and South America. Do you agree with this observation? Why or why not?
>
>   _____
>
> 3. How did scientists test the hypothesis that South America and Africa had once been part of the same continent?
>
>   a. _____
>
>   b. _____
>
> 4. What conclusion did scientists draw about the cause of the changes in the Earth?
>
>   _____

FIGURE 5.6 **Three-Level Guide**

Read "Oscar de la Renta," pages 208-213 of *Latino Biographies*.

A. Literal: Using the dates below, make a time line of the key events in Oscar de la Renta's life. Most of the key events are given a definite date. However, you sometimes have to put two pieces of information together to get a date. For instance, the story does not tell what year Oscar de la Renta left the Dominican Republic, but it does say that he was 18 when he left, and it gives the year of his birth, so you can put the two pieces of information together and this tells you about when he left.

B. Interpretive: The answers to the following questions are not directly stated, but they are implied. Use information from the story and think about what you have read to answer the questions.

1. What do you think would have happened to Oscar if his mother hadn't arranged for him to leave home?

   _____

2. Why did Oscar de la Renta give up painting?

   _____

3. What makes you think that Oscar de la Renta is a kind man?

   _____

4. What makes you think that Oscar de la Renta is very rich?

   _____

C. Applied: Read the following statements. Think about the events in Oscar de la Renta's life and the kind of person he was. Put this information together with what you know and believe from your own experience. Then, based on what you read and your own experience, put a check mark next to each statement you agree with. Be prepared to discuss with members in your group the statements that you checked.

_____1. Money can't buy happiness.

_____2. Helping others is more important than making money or becoming famous.

_____3. Enjoying your work is more important than making a lot of money.

_____4. People need people.

_____5. By helping others we help ourselves.

Three-level guides can be composed of statements rather than questions. Students check statements with which they agree or that seem accurate. These guides are more thought provoking than traditional guides because students must think about and reject statements with which they disagree or that seem inaccurate and provide support for statements that are correct or with which they agree. Responding becomes a more active process.

Three-level guides apply the processes of QAR (Question-Answer Relationships). Literal statements are constructed so that justification can be found in a single place. Although also literal, integration statements involve using information from two or more places in the text. Interpretative statements require that the student connect information from the text with information from her own background of experience. Application statements require students to apply the information in some way. A sample three-level thinking guide is shown in Figure 5.6.

Selective and Process Reading Guides

An indispensable skill for students is knowing how to distinguish between valuable information and inessential material. Some students believe that everything they read is important and may become overwhelmed when they try to learn every detail. A selective reading guide can be used to highlight the most essential information in a chapter.

FIGURE 5.7 **Process Guide**

Chapter 4: Private Sector Decisions: Consumers and Businesses

Putting ideas into your own words and thinking how they apply to your life make them easier to understand. This also helps you to remember important ideas. Read the following sections. After reading each section, answer the questions **in your own words.** Read a section and answer the questions before going on to the next section. The ideas build on each other. Understanding the first section will make the second section that much easier to understand. And unless you understand the first two sections, you will have difficulty understanding the third section.

Private Ownership—Private Benefit, pages 52–53

1. What are private goods?

   _____

2. What are some private goods that you own?

   _____

3. What are public goods? What are some public goods that you use?

   _____

4. How do private goods differ from public goods?

   _____

5. Are most goods in the U.S. public or private? Explain.

   _____

Private Sector—Private Choice, pages 53–54

The key idea in this section is the economic principle that "Individuals will choose the alternative that produces the maximum benefit or the minimum private cost to them."

6. How would you put this in your own words?

   _____

7. Give three examples of ways in which you have used this principle.

   _____
   _____
   _____

Efficiency and Individual Choice, pages 54–55

8. This section applies the principle that we make choices based on maximum benefit or minimum cost. Describe a time when you made a choice based on maximum benefit or minimum cost.

   _____

9. What is efficiency? How does efficiency fit in with the principle of making choices based on maximum benefit or maximum cost?

   _____

10. What happens to businesses that are not efficient? Describe a business that failed because it was not efficient.

   _____
   _____

 Struggling Readers

Glosses are an especially useful device for providing struggling readers with added guidance as they read. In the gloss, you might call attention to maps, graphs, tables, and visual information. Students who don't fully understand the verbal part of the text may be able to use graphic information to aid comprehension.

■ **A gloss** is a study guide in which the teacher writes explanatory notes to students to provide them with added guidance as they read.

Process guides focus on strategies that students can use to understand and retain content. A process guide tells students how a selection should be processed and provides suggestions for strategy use. Process guides are especially helpful to students who lack strategies or aren't sure which strategies to use. These guides can tell students when they can skim material and when they need to read carefully, when questioning is a helpful strategy, and when summarizing can foster learning. A sample processing guide is shown in Figure 5.7.

Glosses

Glosses are strategy guides in which the teacher writes explanatory notes to students (Singer & Donlan, 1989).

The glosses, which are written in the margins, may define hard words, explain a key concept, paraphrase a difficult passage, tap prior knowledge, point out a key point, suggest a strategy for reading the passage, or note a helpful visual. Various kinds of questions might be included, such as those that help a student relate new information to old, use a key comprehension strategy, or set a purpose for reading (Richgels & Hansen, 1984). Use no more than two or three glosses per page; otherwise, they become burdensome and overwhelming to students (Stewart & Cross, 1993).

Illustrations as well as text can be glossed. You can use glosses to direct students to maps, charts, and illustrations so that they can make some use of the text. Your gloss might also contain a summary of the most essential information written in easy-to-understand language. These glosses are especially helpful for students for whom the text is simply so overwhelming that they cannot comprehend it, no matter how much assistance you provide.

To create a gloss, first examine the text and decide what you want the students to get out of reading the text. List two or three key concepts. Then note any elements in the text that might hinder students' understanding of the key concepts. Create a gloss that helps students work with these difficult elements. The gloss may be written in the margin of the text and then photocopied and distributed to students. Or you can line up a sheet of paper next to the text and write your gloss notes next to the target text. Make copies and distribute them to students.

Frame Matrix

Each discipline has its own way of looking at reality as well as its own tools of investigation. Each discipline also has its own questions. Science asks such questions as: What is it? How might it be classified? What are its parts or systems? How do its parts or systems operate? What laws or regularities does it follow? The social studies ask such questions as: What happened? When did it happen? What were its causes? What were its effects? What conclusions can be drawn? Math is concerned with questions of measurement and quantifiable relationships.

Learning the content of a subject is easier if students know the kinds of questions to ask. Questions help determine what information is most important and how that information is organized. Knowing the questions that a discipline asks helps us to determine the categories of information that it provides. By determining categories of information, we are organizing the information presented. Texts that answer implied or explicit content area questions are known as **frames** (Armbruster & Anderson, 1981). One device designed to take advantage of frame organization is the frame matrix.

A simple but effective device, the **frame matrix** helps students organize information and see similarities and differences. It facilitates comparing and contrasting because the categories being analyzed are lined up side by side. Frame matrices are most effective when the text focuses on major categories of information. A frame matrix has two intersecting parts: a frame, which highlights essential categories of information, and the matrix, which allows the comparison of two or more elements in terms of the frames or categories (see Figure 5.8). For example, a frame for countries might include *location, area, population, natural resources, economy,* and *government.* The matrix would be the countries being compared: United States, Canada, India, China, Russia. A history frame, reflecting the content area's concern with causes and effects, might detail the major causes of the Revolutionary War. A student who knows what questions are important in history would know to ask: "What were the causes of the Revolutionary War? What were the effects?" The student could also take advantage of the cause/effect pattern in the writing to better understand the material, see cause/effect relationships, and organize the material for study purposes.

To construct a frame matrix, create the essential categories of information for a topic. Then note how each category might be subdivided. If you are familiar with a topic, you might set up a tentative frame and then verify it by checking the text that students are about to read (Armbruster, 1996). You might also check the topic in an encyclopedia, as encyclopedias often organize articles around major categories or frame types of questions.

Information Map

An adaptation of the frame matrix known as the **information map** restates categories as questions and is useful for studying and self-testing. In an information map, categories on the left (the frame items) are translated

■ **Frames** are categories of information that answer implied or stated questions.

■ A **frame matrix** has two intersecting parts: a frame, which provides essential categories of information, and the matrix, which allows the comparison of two or more elements in terms of the frames or categories.

■ An **information map** is an adaptation of a frame matrix that restates categories in question form.

FIGURE 5.8
Frame Matrix

Oceans of the World	Arctic	Atlantic	Indian	Pacific
Location	top of world	touches Europe, Africa, North America, and South America	touches Africa, Australia, East Indies, and Asia	touches North America, South America, Africa, and Asia
Size	5,440,000 square miles	31,530,000 square miles	28,356,000 square miles	63,000,380 square miles
Average Depth	5,010 feet	14,000 feet	13,000 feet	14,000 feet

into questions, which makes them easier for students to respond to. Students can self-test themselves by covering the answers in the matrix cells and asking the questions on the left. After reciting the answers to themselves, they can verify their responses and review items that posed problems. Information maps can be constructed for a limited topic, such as comparing types of fog, or they can be created for topics studied over a full unit or semester (Heiman & Slomianko, 1986). An information map could be constructed that compares all fifty states, chemical elements, or the major systems in the body. An extended information map might be constructed over several months or even an entire semester and cover a portion of a wall.

Questions in an information map should seek essential information and should not be able to be answered with a "yes" or a "no" (Heiman & Slomianko, 1986). The questions should also apply to all of the categories in the matrix. A sample information map is presented in Figure 5.9.

Embedded Questions

One relatively easy way to provide guidance during reading is to use **embedded questions**. Most text questions appear at the end of a chapter. These questions help the student summarize what was read, but don't help with ongoing processing. Embedded questions are posed at key points in the text and help students process information while reading the text. Many students are passive readers who simply run their eyes over the text, hoping that they "get it." Embedded questions can provide guidance to help them "get it," to let them know when they have gotten it and when they haven't, and to help them know what to do if they haven't gotten it (Weir, 1998).

The boldfaced checkup questions in this text are examples of embedded questions. Have you used them? Have you found them to be helpful? Why or why not?

When creating embedded questions, focus on the most essential information, provide guidance with elements that are most likely to cause difficulty, and prompt the kind of strategies that skilled readers would use. Create questions that will lead readers to predict; summarize; question; create images; evaluate; and apply or use context, glossary, or other word-analysis clues. After students have completed passages containing embedded questions, discuss their responses. As Salomon, Globerson, and Guterman (1989) note, talking about the responses to embedded questions may have as strong an impact as answering the embedded questions.

Some content area texts provide embedded questions. For instance, *Biology, the Living Science* (Miller & Levine, 2009) provides checkpoints that ask the reader to answer a question about the key information in a section that has just been read.

Checkpoint questions for the section on DNA include: How does DNA replicate? How does RNA differ from DNA? What does RNA polymerase do? What are the three main forms of RNA? The text is difficult and complex. With subsequent sections building on previous ones, students will soon be overwhelmed if they don't grasp the key points.

■ Embedded questions are questions that are placed within the text rather than before or after it. The checkup questions in this text are embedded.

FIGURE 5.9 **Information Map**

Mesoamerican Civilizations

	Olmec	Maya	Toltec	Aztec
Where was this civilization?	Mexico's Gulf Coast	southern Mexico, Belize, Guatemala, Honduras, western El Salvador	central Mexican highlands	central and southern Mexico
When did it exist?	1200–400 B.C.	250–900 A.D.	900–1200 A.D.	1200–1600 A.D.
How was it ruled?	priests	no central government; ruler for each city and surrounding region	priest-king	emperor, nobles ruled cities
How did the people make a living?	farming	farming, trading	farming	farming, trading
What happened to it?	No one knows.	No one knows; could have been drought or disease.	No one knows.	defeated by Spanish
What were its main contributions?	first calendar; counting system; art: huge stone heads	calendar; paper; writing system; math with zero; astronomy; temples & pyramids	built greatest city of its time	roads & buildings

The embedded questions in the form of checkpoints give students the opportunity to see whether they have understood the section's key points so that they can go back over the material if they need to. Perhaps more important, it helps students review what they have learned before going on to a new topic.

CHECKUP

1. What are some techniques that can be used to foster comprehension during reading?
2. How might these techniques be presented?

After-Reading Techniques

After completing reading, strategic readers may mentally summarize what they have read or ask themselves questions about the material. They may critically evaluate the new information and see how it fits in with what they already know. They may apply the information in some way, and they may seek clarifying information on confusing points or additional information on the topic. Techniques that can be used to foster after-reading activities include constructing analogies, creating graphic organizers, writing after reading, and extending and applying.

Constructing Analogies

Analogies can foster comprehension and are frequently used in the content areas, especially in science. Because electricity can't be seen, students better understand an explanation of the flow of electricity when it is compared to the flow of water in a pipe. However, when teaching with analogies, it is important to point out where the two items being

■ **Analogies** are full or partial comparisons between a concept to be learned and a familiar concept: for example, memory and file cabinet.

compared differ. For instance, unlike water, electricity is not limited to flowing down-hill (Baker & Piburn, 1997).

Recognizing and constructing analogies is one way of helping students bridge the gap between the new and the old. Point out analogies when they appear. Traditional analo-gies include the eye and a camera, the heart and a pump, the brain and a computer, cells and a factory, and memory and a file cabinet. The best analogies are those in which the items being compared share a number of features, which is why the analogy between the eye and a camera is especially effective. However, it is important that the item that is the basis for comparison (the camera) be familiar. If students don't know how a camera works, the analogy won't be very helpful (Glynn, 1994). Help students create their own analogies by comparing old information and new concepts. You might ask, for instance, "How is the eye like a camera? How is memory like a file cabinet?" Self-created analo-gies are generally more effective than those made up by others.

For best results in using analogies, discuss the analogy thoroughly. After introduc-ing the target concept, explain the analogy and identify both similarities and differences between the target concept and the analog. Clarify any confusions that students might have (Glynn, 1994).

Graphic Organizers

Graphic organizers are one of the most effective devices for promoting understanding and retention of the kinds of complex concepts presented in content area material. Because they involve encoding verbal material visually, graphic organizers provide another route for storing and retrieving information and so aid recall (Robinson, 1998).

The content and structure of material and the teaching-learning purpose dictate the type of organizer used: structured overview, time line, or an organizer that highlights the steps in a process, contrasts elements, or identifies causes. Whatever form it takes, the visual display should focus on the most essential information and do so vividly. Key con-cepts should "jump out at the students as soon as their eyes meet the page" (Robinson, 1998, p. 100).

Systematic Use of Organizers

The organization of the material and the processing skills required to understand and retain the information dictate the kind of organizer used. Hyerle (2001) matched each of eight kinds of thinking with a graphic organizer that fosters that specific kind of cogni-tive processing (see Table 5.1). The table displays only the basic form of each kind of map. Each map can be expanded or altered to display increased complexity. The Key Graphic Organizers are an adaptation of Hyerle's Thinking Maps® and are arranged according to the complexity of thinking they represent. Hyerle recommends that schools, or at least departments, adopt a common set of organizers and systematically introduce them so that students not only are able to construct all eight organizers and their adaptations, but also have a deep enough understanding of the organizers that they can decide which one is most appropriate to use and why. Most important of all, students should develop the think-ing skills—categorizing, comparing and contrasting, inferring—that the Key Graphic Organizers incorporate.

Simple Relationships

The simplest of the graphic organizers is the web or descriptive map, which is used to show a main idea and supporting details. The main idea is written in a circle or box, which is centered, and supporting details are written in circles or boxes surrounding the main cir-cle or box. Lines are used to show that the surrounding circles or boxes are linked to the main circle or box, as in Figure 5.10. The second organizer in Table 5.1, a classification or semantic map, requires that items be categorized and so involves a higher level of thinking

For some information, such as showing the parts of the brain (see Figure 5.11), the best graphic organizer is a diagram. Although a blank diagram might be drawn or traced

TABLE 5.1 **Key Graphic Organizers**

ORGANIZER	THINKING SKILL	EXAMPLE
Descriptive Map (Web)	Locate and assemble main idea and details	
Classification Map (Semantic Map)	Categorize and classify	
Sequence Map	Arrange in chronological order	
Process Map (Chain or Flow Map)	Arrange in step-by-step fashion	
Cyclical Map	Arrange in circular fashion to show a process	
Tree Diagram	Categorize and classify in hierarchical fashion	
Frame Matrix (or Venn Diagram)	Compare and contrast	
Cause-Effect Map	Locate or infer causes and/or effects	

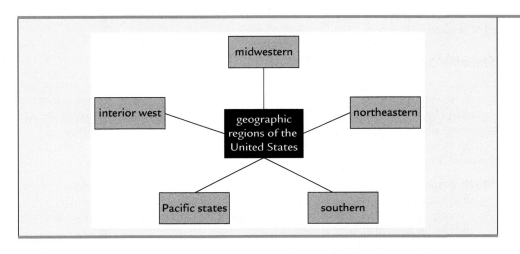

FIGURE 5.10
Simple Web

by the teacher and distributed to students, involving students in creating their own diagrams or drawings makes learning a more active process. When they draw an object, students have to note its parts. A variety of diagrams (including the drawing of the brain in Figure 5.11), are available from clip art collections.

FIGURE 5.11
The Four Lobes of the Cerebral Cortex

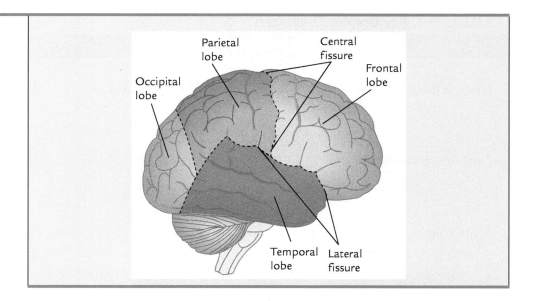

Comparison/Contrast Relationships

To show similarities and differences, you can use Venn diagrams (explained in Chapter 3), information maps, or frame matrices. Venn diagrams can be expanded to include three items and are useful because they prominently display similarities and differences. However, because they can be expanded to an almost unlimited number of items and generally do a better job of showing comparisons across a number of categories, frame matrices and information maps are generally preferable to Venn diagrams.

Hierarchical Relationships

Tree maps, which show hierarchical relationships, include the structured overview, Frayer's model, and concept maps. Frayer's model and concept maps were explained in Chapter 3. The structured overview and Frayer's model are frequently used as preparation for reading. However, they can also be used to review and extend concepts. For instance, if students are using the structured overview on diet shown in Figure 5.3, they can add specific examples of fats after reading the section on fats and carbohydrates after reading that section. Once students have experience with structured overviews, they can create their own after reading a selection.

Showing Sequence and Processes

Flowcharts are especially useful for showing processes. A circular or cyclical flow chart can be used to show processes that are continuous and never-ending, such as the water cycle, as shown in Figure 5.12. Linear flowcharts can be used to show processes that have a definite beginning and end point, as in the operation of a digital camera, shown in Figure 5.13.

An excellent teaching and learning tool, graphic organizers are used widely. To get the most out of graphic organizers, Egan (1999) recommends the following:

- Be prepared. Try out the graphic organizer before asking the class to use it. You may discover unexpected difficulties or needed adjustments.
- Promote interaction among students. Graphic organizers lend themselves to group discussion and construction.
- Use graphic organizers with discrimination. If overused, graphic organizers can become tiresome. Graphic organizers should be used selectively, when they are the device that best fosters learning in a particular situation. The organizer selected should fit in with the learning objective and the nature of the material. Thus, a Venn diagram would be more appropriate than a semantic web when two ideas are being compared and contrasted.

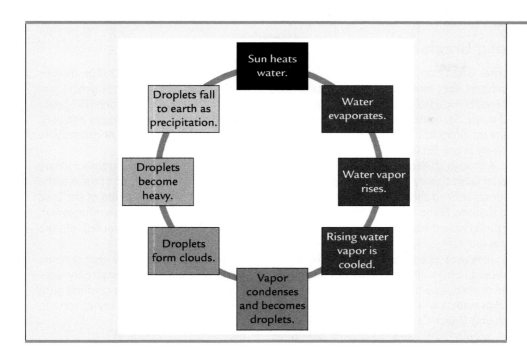

FIGURE 5.12
Cyclical Flow Chart

- Expand the use of graphic organizers. Graphic organizers can be used with nonprint material to organize information presented in lectures, simulations, experiments, or discussions.

Writing after Reading

After reading, students can summarize what they have learned in a quick write, or they can complete an entry in a learning log. In a quick write, students are given three minutes to tell what they have learned about a topic, raise questions, request additional explanations, or voice concerns. The quick writes can be discussed at that point in pairs, small groups, or the whole class. A more extensive reading-writing discussion activity is Save the Last Word for Me (Buehl, 2001). In Save the Last Word for Me, students are given five index cards and invited to record from their reading five statements that they found interesting or controversial or that they would just like to write about. The statements are marked with a check or sticky note. After they finish reading, students copy the statements onto their index cards. On the reverse side of the card, they write a reaction or comment that they would like to share with their group. For instance, Juan records the statement, "Historically, consumers purchasing used goods have had to follow the doctrine of caveat emptor, which is a Latin phrase that means 'buyer beware.'" Later, Juan writes his reaction to the statement. "*Caveat emptor* is unfair. Sellers should tell buyers if there is something wrong with the used car or furniture they are buying." After students have written their statements and comments, they meet in groups of four or five. Students take turns reading their statements. After the first student reads his statement, each member of the group comments on it. After all the other students have commented on the statement, the student who read the statement first reads his comment. A second group member then shares her statement and the process begins all over again.

Extending and Applying

After reading, students should reflect on what they have learned. They might ask themselves such questions as: How does this fit in with what I already know? Is there anything confusing about this information? Is there anything else about this topic that I would like to know? How can I use this information? This reflection can be informal, or students can keep learning logs, as explained in Chapter 8. Students can also have a discussion about what they have learned and their reactions to their reading. Discussions can be whole class, in pairs, or in small groups.

Using Graphic Organizers

Teacher Gwen Hurt's tenth-grade class used graphic organizers to study the 1960s. In their organizers, they made comparisons between key elements in the 1960s and their generation. Categories included politics, entertainment, fashion, civil rights legislation, leaders, TV shows, and music. Students worked in small cooperative groups. They brainstormed topics and used many resources to obtain information, including interviews with relatives and neighbors who grew up in the 1960s.

Although students did much of their work in English class, the unit was interdisciplinary and included twenty-five of the high school teachers. To investigate the music of the era, the students learned the songs and dances popular at that time. Their investigation of the tone and customs of the times were conducted in social studies classes. To obtain this information, they interviewed teachers. To learn more about the science of the times, they looked into the space program.

They used an enlarged frame matrix to summarize information gathered. A Venn diagram was used to highlight commonalties and differences between the two eras. Despite the passage of time, a number of commonalties were found. In both eras, there were conflicts with foreign leaders and troops were sent to foreign lands. Civil rights was also a key concern in both eras (North Central Regional Educational Laboratory, 1995).

If students have unanswered questions or if their interest has been piqued, they might extend their knowledge by reading one of the books in the text's bibliography or by visiting a Web site on the topic or even creating one of their own. The additional reading could take the form of reading a book of historical fiction, a biography of a scientist, or a book of math puzzles. After reading about diet, students may want to take note of what they eat. After reading about recycling, they may want to plan a recycling program.

Need for Adaptation and Persistence

As you will discover when you attempt to use the techniques advocated in this and other chapters, the lesson might not always go as planned. However, it is important not to drop a technique because it doesn't work well the first couple of times you try it. It takes time to learn to implement a technique effectively. You also need to select those techniques that fit in with your teaching style. And you need to adapt techniques so that they are a good fit for your students.

CHECKUP

1. What are some effective after-reading techniques?
2. What are the key elements in each technique?

Summary

Conceptual understanding is a key factor in the comprehension of content area text. To develop conceptual understanding, content area reading lessons should specify content objectives and take into consideration students' abilities, interests, and background knowledge. Lessons should prepare students to read; offer guidance as they read;

and help students summarize and organize what they have read, relate it to what they already know, and apply it. Approaches that incorporate these elements include the instructional framework, the directed reading activity, and the directed reading-thinking activity. Along with these broad approaches, there are a number of specific techniques that can be used to foster conceptual understanding. Techniques designed to be used primarily before reading include the anticipation guide, PReP, structured overview, and drawing and writing before reading. During-reading techniques include strategy guides, glosses, frame matrices, information maps, and embedded questions. After-reading techniques include constructing analogies, creating graphic organizers, writing, and extending and applying. A technique that encompasses before, during, and after reading is KWL Plus.

Reflection

Return to the Anticipation Guide at the beginning of this chapter. Respond once again to the items. Did your responses change? If so, how and why? Which teaching techniques discussed in this chapter do you think would be most effective in helping students better comprehend the texts in your content area?

Extension and Application

Create an advanced organizer for a topic in your content area. If possible, try it out with students and evaluate its effectiveness.

Create a strategy guide for a topic in your content area. Select a topic that is important, but that students find difficult to understand. If possible, try it out with students and evaluate its effectiveness. Note whether the guide helped students grasp key points. Note, too, what might be done to make the guide more effective.

Try out a DRA or DR-TA with a group of students. What were the strengths of the technique? The weaknesses? New techniques take a while to learn. If possible, teach a series of lessons.

Go to Topic 8: Study Skills and Strategies and Topic 5: Comprehension in the MyEducationLab (www.myeducationlab.com) for your course, where you can:

- Find learning outcomes for Study Skills and Strategies and Comprehension along with the national standards that connect to these outcomes.
- Complete Assignments and Activities that can help you more deeply understand the chapter content.
- Apply and practice your understanding of the core teaching skills identified in the chapter with the Building Teaching Skills and Dispositions learning units.
- Examine challenging situations and cases presented in the IRIS Center Resources.

Go to the Topic A+RISE in the MyEducationLab (www.myeducationlab.com) for your course. A+RISE® Standards2Strategy™ is an innovative and interactive online resource that offers new teachers in grades K–12 just-in-time, research-based instructional strategies that:

- Meet the linguistic needs of ELLs as they learn content.
- Differentiate instruction for all grades and abilities.
- Offer reading and writing techniques, cooperative learning, use of linguistic and nonlinguistic representations, scaffolding, teacher modeling, higher-order thinking, and alternative classroom ELL assessment.
- Provide support to help teachers be effective through the integration of listening, speaking, reading, and writing along with the content curriculum.
- Improve student achievement.
- Are aligned to Common Core Elementary Language Arts standards (for the literacy strategies) and to English language proficiency standards in WIDA, Texas, California, and Florida.

CHAPTER 6

Collaborative and Cooperative Approaches for Learning

For each of the following statements, put a check under "Agree" or "Disagree" to indicate your opinion. If possible, discuss your responses with classmates.

	Agree	Disagree
1. Learning through group discussions in superior to learning by lecture.	_____	_____
2. Student-led discussion groups are more effective than teacher-led groups.	_____	_____
3. In small-group learning, the least able students are usually left out.	_____	_____
4. The main problem with student discussion groups is that they are difficult to manage.	_____	_____
5. Struggling learners do better with teacher-led instruction than they do with student-led groups.	_____	_____

Using What you Know

Have you ever been a member of a cooperative learning group or studied with a friend? When you were in high school or middle school, did your parents try to help you with your homework or a project, and even though they weren't quite sure what to do, you worked on the problem together? Did you ever work with a classmate who knew more about the subject than you did, but you were able to make a limited contribution? If so, you have experienced collaborative/cooperative learning, which is what this chapter is about. As you reflect on your experiences, think how collaborative/cooperative learning might be used to foster learning in the content area that you teach.

Collaborative Learning

Collaborative learning is an approach that views students as active participants in the construction of meaning rather than as passive recipients of knowledge. In collaborative learning, teacher and student(s) work as collaborators in order to build meaning. Conceptual learning is emphasized as students reflect on their learning, test out ideas, and learn to listen to other viewpoints through small-group and whole-class discussions. The atmosphere is cooperative rather than competitive. Students feel free to express ideas without being criticized and also learn to tolerate diverse perspectives.

In some forms of collaborative learning, the teacher is very much a part of the group as an active participant or even discussion leader. In other forms, commonly referred to as *cooperative learning* or *cooperative grouping*, students complete tasks as members of a student-directed group.

There are two main approaches to teaching reading comprehension strategies: the direct instruction/explanation approach and the collaborative approach, also known as the transactional approach. In the direct instruction/explanation approach, teachers introduce, explain, and provide guided and independent practice (National Reading Panel, 2000). Strategies presented in Chapter 4 represent a direct instruction/explanation approach. In a collaborative approach (the topic of this chapter), students are taught strategies, but the role of the teacher is different: The teacher facilitates discussions in which students "collaborate to form joint interpretations of text" and "discuss the mental processes and cognitive strategies that are involved in comprehension" (National Reading Panel, 2000,

■ **Collaborative learning** is a form of learning in which students are active participants in the learning process and work with the teacher to construct meaning or solve problems.

4-122). Although strategies are explicitly taught, the emphasis is on the "interactive exchange among learners in the classroom" (National Reading Panel, 2000, 4-123). As Wilkinson and Son (2011) note, dialogic or discussion approaches "probably provide a natural vehicle for students' use of strategies" (p. 376). Because of adolescents' strong attachment to peer groups, collaborative learning can be especially effective for middle and high school students.

Reading a dense textbook may be an overwhelming experience for some students. Collaborative approaches such as ReQuest, Reciprocal Teaching, Questioning the Author, or Collaborative Strategic Reading provide support from both teacher and peers and may be an excellent way to introduce students to effective content area reading. When students reflect on and discuss a reading, they have the opportunity to think about and reorganize the information they have derived from the reading. It also gives them the opportunity to get the viewpoints of others and to assimilate information they may have missed while reading.

ReQuest

An easy-to-implement but highly effective collaborative technique for fostering comprehension and student participation is ReQuest (Manzo, 1969; Manzo & Manzo, 1993; Manzo, Manzo, & Albee, 2004). **ReQuest** may be used with individual students, small groups of students, or whole classes. Using ReQuest, the teacher and student(s) alternate asking questions about the text until the students have built enough background to predict what the rest of the text might be about and then read the text on their own. ReQuest can be implemented by following the steps outlined in the following sample lesson.

Unless they have had experience creating questions, students may initially ask lower-level questions; but with coaching and modeling, they should soon begin asking higher-level ones. Whenever possible, call attention to especially effective student questions so that these become models for other students to follow. Students should feel free to ask questions about words or ideas that are puzzling to them. For example, a student might ask, "How do you say the second word in the first sentence and what does it mean?" Presented below is an excerpt from a ReQuest lesson.

The Living Earth

Struggling Readers

ReQuest was originally devised as a technique for helping struggling readers improve their comprehension. It works well with all students, but is also effective with students who have very serious comprehension difficulties.

Living things play a part in soil creation from the beginning. Lichens and mosses can colonize bare rock surfaces. They produce acids that eat into the rock surface, releasing the minerals that plants need to grow. The mosses and lichens also help to trap wind-blown particles in cracks and depressions in the rock surface. Over long periods, soil begins to form. (Snedden, 1999, p. 36)

Student: What plays a part in soil creation?

Teacher: Living things.

Student: When do the living things start playing a part in the creation of soil?

Teacher: From the very beginning.

Teacher: Do you have any more questions for me? Okay. It's my turn. My question is what does the sentence mean when it says "living things"?

Student: The sentence doesn't say. From the picture I would guess that *living things* means plants. But maybe it means earth creatures, too.

Teacher: Good thinking. That's my only question.

Student: What is the correct pronunciation for *l-i-c-h-e-n-s?*

Teacher: The *ch* has a *k* sound, so the word is pronounced "Ligh-kenz."

Student: What are lichens?

Teacher: Lichens are plants.

Teacher: Where do lichens grow?

■ **ReQuest** is a procedure in which the teacher and student(s) take turns asking and answering questions.

LESSON 6.1

ReQuest

Step 1: Explaining the ReQuest Procedure to Students
Tell students that they will be using a technique in which they get a chance to ask questions. Explain that you and they will take turns asking and answering questions about the first part of the selection. Explain that asking and answering questions will help build comprehension and will also help prepare them for reading the rest of the selection on their own.

Step 2: Surveying the Text with the Students
Have them read the title, examine any illustrations that are part of the introduction, and discuss what the selection might be about.

Step 3: Asking Students to Read the First Significant Segment of Text
This could be the first sentence if the text is very dense. Or it could be the first paragraph. Explain that as they read, they are to think up questions to ask you—the kinds that a teacher might ask (Manzo & Manzo, 1993). Students can make up as many questions as they wish. Read the segment silently with the students.

Step 4: Giving Students the Opportunity to Ask Their Questions
Place your book facedown. Students keep their books open and may refer to their texts. If necessary, questions can be restated or clarified and answers can be checked by referring back to the text.

Step 5: Switching Roles with Students
After students have asked their questions, reverse roles and ask your questions about the same segment of the test. Beginning with the third or fourth sentence or paragraph, model higher-level questioning by asking for responses that require integrating several details in the text. Some of the questions might also focus on difficult concepts or vocabulary in such a way that these are clarified for students. At the end of your questioning, read the next segment and have students ask questions again. When students ask especially appropriate or insightful questions, affirm their efforts with comments such as, "That's a good question," or, "That's the kind of question that really makes me think about what I've read."

Step 6: Alternating Questioning with the Students
The questioning proceeds in alternating fashion until the students know all the key words in the first section or paragraph and have acquired enough background information to set a purpose. That purpose could be to predict what the remainder of the text is about: "Now that we have read about the importance of oxygen, what do you think the rest of the article will tell us?" If the selection is complex, you can have students proceed through several paragraphs before turning it over to them. Manzo and Manzo (1993) recommended that the questioning be concluded as soon as a logical purpose or prediction can be established, but no longer than ten minutes after beginning. Otherwise, students may begin to lose their focus.

Step 7: Discussing Predictions and Other Questions
After the rest of the selection has been read silently, discuss the predictions and any related questions.

Step 8: Following Up
Any one of a number of activities can be used to extend the learning. Students might summarize the selection in a graphic organizer, write a reflection in a learning log, continue reading, or read a related text.

Student: It says that lichens colonize bare rocks, so I suppose that means that they grow on bare rocks.

Teacher: Good answer. Lichens are made up of lots of tiny plants known as algae and fungi. Because there are many of them growing together, they are said to colonize or set up colonies.

Student: What do lichens produce?

Teacher: Acids.

Student: What do the acids do?

Teacher: The acids eat into the rocks, and this begins to break them down.

Student: What is released?

Teacher: Minerals.

The discussion continues until concepts and vocabulary are clarified and a purpose for reading the rest of the article is set.

ReQuest can be made more effective if students are taught why asking questions is an effective strategy and are given instruction in how to formulate questions (Conley, 2008). To show students the cognitive processes involved in creating questions, do a think-aloud as you create questions.

Reciprocal Teaching

A second collaborative technique that relies heavily on student questioning is **Reciprocal Teaching**, which was created for use with small groups (Palincsar & Brown, 1986). Under the teacher's guidance, students take turns leading a discussion about segments of expository text. In a sense, students become cognitive apprentices as they use the teacher as a model, but gradually take over increased responsibility for their learning and implementing of Reciprocal Teaching's strategies. More complex than ReQuest, Reciprocal Teaching fosters four highly effective strategies: predicting, questioning, clarifying, and summarizing. Clarifying is a metacognitive strategy in which the reader recognizes that there is a problem and asks that a word, expression, or concept blocking comprehension be cleared up (Palincsar & Brown, 1986). Because Reciprocal Teaching is more complex than ReQuest, it will take longer to introduce. Steps for introducing a Reciprocal Teaching lesson are presented below as a guide.

In the beginning stages, you will play a major role in the implementation of Reciprocal Teaching. During the early sessions, you will provide prompts and probes and model strategies as necessary. Because creating questions is difficult for many students, model how you compose questions, use prompts to help students reword confusing questions, and supply model questions and possible question words. Over time, students will take on added responsibility for leading discussions answering questions, and implementing strategies.

The following is a sample Reciprocal Teaching lesson conducted with eighth graders and is based on the reading of the first part of a chapter about Eleanor Roosevelt in the book *Profiles in American History, Volume* 7 (Moss & Wilson, 1998).

(Lead-in question)

Adam (student discussion leader):	My question is, what was Eleanor Roosevelt's childhood like?
Carmen:	She was rich. And her family was famous.

(Clarification request)

Reginald:	The book says that her family was one of the original "400" aristocratic families in the United States. That needs to be clarified. I don't know who these 400 people were. And I'm not sure what *aristocratic* means.
Charles:	*Aristocratic* means high class. I think maybe 400 is referring to the top 400 people in the United States. Maybe the richest 400.
Teacher:	You are on the right track. I'm not sure myself how the 400 were chosen. That's something for us to research.
Adam:	Eleanor Roosevelt did come from a wealthy family, but she had some problems. What were they?
Janine:	Her mother was cold. She wasn't a very warm person. I mean she probably never hugged Eleanor.

LESSON 6.2

Reciprocal Teaching

Step 1: Introduction

Tell students that they will be using a technique in which they take over the role of the teacher. Explain the purpose of the technique: to increase comprehension by using four of the best comprehension strategies and discussing a selection. Inform students that they will be taking turns leading the discussions.

Step 2: Teaching Key Strategies

Introduce and explain each of the four strategies: predicting, questioning, clarifying, and summarizing. If students are already familiar with these strategies, review them. Instruction is most effective if the strategies are taught or reviewed shortly before they are used (Hattie, 2009).

▶ *Predicting.* Explain to students that predicting helps them think about the key ideas in a selection and gives them a purpose for reading. Modeling the process, show students how you would use the title or heading, illustrations, and introductory paragraph, if there is one, to make predictions about the upcoming content. If the prediction is about a segment in the middle of the selection, use your knowledge of what has happened or the information and headings provided previously to make a prediction. Provide opportunities for guided practice.

▶ *Questioning.* Show students how you create questions as you read. Also explain that you ask questions about the most important ideas in a selection. Provide sample questions and guided practice.

▶ *Clarifying.* Explain the need for clarifying and show what you do when you encounter a word, phrase, or passage that you find puzzling. Encourage students to locate words, expressions, or concepts in a sample selection that need clarifying. Discuss what might be done to provide clarification: rereading, using context or glossary to derive the meaning of a difficult word, using illustrations, etc.

▶ *Summarizing.* Explain to students that summarizing may be the most important reading strategy of all because it helps them concentrate on important points while reading. It also helps them review the main points and check on their understanding. Remind students that if they can't summarize a passage, this is a sign that they may not have understood it and should go back and reread it. Provide guided practice.

Alicia:	And she criticized her. Her mother told her she was awkward and too serious. She called her "Granny."
Charles:	And her father was almost never home.
Carmen:	Not even on Christmas.
Teacher:	Good observation. What problem did Eleanor's father have?
Paula:	He drank. He was an alcoholic. What a family. It just goes to show that money isn't everything.
Adam:	But the family wasn't all bad. What good things did they teach Eleanor?
Carmen:	They taught her to be kind. The father gave money to crippled kids. And Eleanor was sent to soup kitchens to help out.
Teacher:	Good answers. Can you summarize this section of the chapter, Adam?

(Summary)

Adam:	This section says that Eleanor Roosevelt's family was rich and famous, but they had problems. The mother was cold and critical, and the father drank too much and was hardly ever around. Still, he taught Eleanor to help others.
Teacher:	That's an excellent summary, Adam. You've given us the highlights of this section.

English Language Learners

English language learners do especially well in cooperative learning situations because they are more willing to use their developing language skills in a small-group situation and they are more willing to ask for help.

(Prediction)

What do you predict will happen next?

Adam: I think the next section will tell us how Eleanor Roosevelt overcame some of the difficulties of her childhood and how she happened to meet and marry Franklin Roosevelt.

Teacher: Does anyone have a different prediction? Okay. Let's read the next section to see how our prediction works out. Who would like to be the leader for this section?

Although designed for use with small groups, Reciprocal Teaching can be adapted for use with the whole class. First, students use the headings to make two predictions about the content of the text they are about to read. Second, after reading a segment, they write two questions and a summary and note any items that require clarification. The predictions, summaries, and clarification requests are discussed after the selection has been read. However, like other effective techniques, Reciprocal Teaching takes a commitment of time. High school students who received twelve to sixteen training sessions evidenced gains; those who participated in only six to eight sessions did not. In another study, junior high students' comprehension did not begin to improve until after seven lessons (Alfassi, 1998). Maximum gains weren't reached until after the fourteenth session. Then they began to stabilize. However, gains can be substantial. Average gain for students who took part in reciprocal teaching was 27 percentile points (Hattie, 2009).

Students should read fairly easy passages until they have a good grasp of Reciprocal Teaching strategies. It's difficult to learn to implement the strategies when the text is so difficult that it requires maximum effort to comprehend it (Mosenthal, 1990).

Using Reciprocal Teaching with English Learners

Presenting reciprocal teaching in both English and Spanish resulted in better comprehension than just presenting reciprocal teaching in English. The four reciprocal teaching strategies were introduced in the student's native language to foster internalization of the strategies and then reviewed the next day in English (Fung, Wilkinson, & Moore 2003). Because the strategies were introduced in the students' native language, they were able to use their full mental energies to learn them. During reciprocal teaching lessons in English, students were encouraged to make generous use of the clarifying strategy to help them with unfamiliar English words, and they spent about half of each English session working with unfamiliar vocabulary.

Although the students did better using reciprocal teaching when they used their native language, using the strategy in English led them, with the teacher's help, to formulate questions and responses. In addition to building comprehension, the students were developing their ability to use English. As the intervention progressed, students' ability to ask and answer questions in English improved.

The amount of student-to-student talk increases when Questioning the Author is implemented.

Source: Shutterstock.

CHECKUP

1. What are the key elements in ReQuest and Reciprocal Teaching?
2. Why would using ReQuest be good preparation for using Reciprocal Teaching?

Questioning the Author

Concerned that students weren't learning very much from their American history texts, Beck, McKeown, Sinatra, and Loxterman (1991) revised the texts to make them more

Exemplary Teaching

Reciprocal Teaching in Action

How effective is reciprocal teaching when applied in a classroom setting? Brady (1990) provided an in-depth look at the effect of using of reciprocal teaching on the reading performance of 18 Native Alaskan students in grades 5 through 8. Students were provided a form to help them keep procedures in mind. The form included the following:

Questioning: Ask questions about the most important information. Use the questions words: *who, what, where, when, where, why, how.*

Summarizing: In one sentence, tell what the paragraph's most important information is. This paragraph tells us that _____. ("This paragraph tell us that _____" turned out to be a better prompt than "What is the paragraph about?" The latter prompt results in the students stating a topic, but not really summarizing: "This paragraph is about global warming.")

Clarifying: Tell which parts of the passage were especially difficult. I had trouble understanding _____.

Students also completed a postreading semantic map. They created personal maps as well as group maps. In their maps students noted the overall topic, the main ideas, and supporting details. Students practiced the procedures with single sentences first and then paragraphs drawn from reading skills texts. Practice materials were also drawn from science and social studies materials and articles from periodicals.

Students were given daily tests. Daily comprehension readings were 400 to 475 words long and assessed ability to answer three different levels of questions. Average scores increased from 40 percent to 74 percent. Scores did not begin to improve until students transitioned from reading brief, isolated workbook selections to reading science and social studies texts. Instruction was assessment based and included substantial modeling and guided practice. "Because these students were engaged in overt actions, I could listen to what they were saying and provide immediate information about their performance" (Brady, 1990, p. 100). The approach also made use of peer relationships. Students tried harder because they wanted to show the other students that they "could be the 'teacher' and do a good job" (p. 101). After five weeks, the group was able to function on its own. For some students the semantic maps became a visual aid. "It was as if students could close their eyes, recall the shape of the map, and thereby remember the information contained in the map" (p. 102). About half the students used semantic maps on their own after the five-week experiment was concluded, and many also continued employing the reciprocal teaching strategies that they had learned. Brady found that questioning and summarizing resulted in the most processing. However, the clarifying strategy had limited payoff. Clarifying most often consisted of seeking a definition for a word. Using context and the glossary only produced correct responses some of the time. Predicting also had limited usefulness. Brady found that it was difficult both for the students and for him as a teacher to make predictions based on the social studies and science texts.

understandable. Students' comprehension increased by 25 percent. As they revised the texts, the researchers realized the strategies they were using would also help students do a better job of constructing meaning. They planned a program called Questioning the Author (QTA) in which students would read with a "reviser's eye," making the text more understandable to themselves. In this program, students read brief segments of text and then responded to teacher queries so that they were cooperatively constructing meaning as they processed the text instead of reading through the entire text and then answering questions.

The researchers told the students that sometimes the author's meaning wasn't clear, so they would have to ask themselves such questions as: "What is the author trying to say here?" Having students ask the author questions made reading a more active process. Rather than simply extracting information from text, readers would have to build a genuine understanding of the text. Beck, McKeown, Hamilton, and Kucan (1997) compared it to the difference between building a model ship and being given one. The student who

CCSS

Read closely to determine what the text says explicitly and to make logical inferences from it; cite specific textual evidence when writing or speaking to support conclusions drawn from the text.

has assembled a model ship knows a great deal more about its parts than the one who has simply looked at the finished model.

The program used queries instead of questions. Questions assess students' comprehension after reading and promote teacher–student interaction. Queries assist students in their attempts to construct meaning and promote student-to-student interaction. Students construct meaning "on line" rather than after the entire section or chapter has been read. Reading a chapter segment by segment rather than all at once is a key element in QTA. The purpose of segment-by-segment reading is to limit the amount of text read so that students aren't overwhelmed by complex ideas. In the words of the creators of QTA, "Readers should 'take on' a text little by little, idea by idea, and try to understand, while they are reading, what ideas are there and how they might relate those ideas to one another" (Beck & McKeown, 2006, p. 31).

The first segment to be read and discussed provides a foundation for the comprehension of the next segment. Because the text is discussed segment by segment, instead of just at the end, students are better able to discuss complex ideas, resolve confusions, and integrate information. To initiate the discussion and to keep it moving, use queries such as: "What is the author trying to say here? What is the author's message? What is the author trying to tell us?" Follow-up queries help students construct meaning. If a passage is puzzling, ask, "What did the author mean here? Did the author explain this clearly?" Queries that help students make connections include: "Does this make sense with what the author told us before? How does this connect to what the author has told us here?" Other follow-up queries prompt students to seek reasons: "Does the author tell us why? Why do you think the author tells us this now?" Queries might also prompt students to see how the information they are learning relates to their prior knowledge: "How does this fit in with what you know?" The purpose of discussion is to "ensure that students are indeed comprehending what they read" (Beck & McKeown, 2006, p. 29). The teacher's role is to make sure all students grasp key ideas. Collaborative construction of meaning is emphasized. Instead of evaluating responses, as often happens in after-reading discussions, the teacher encourages students "to consider an author's ideas and to respond to one another's interpretations of those ideas" (p. 36).

To create discussions that foster the construction of meaning, there are six Question-the-Author moves: marking, turning back, revoicing, modeling, annotating, and recapping.

Marking. The teacher calls attention to a student's comment that is important to the meaning being built. The teacher might remark, "You are saying that the creation of highways was a good thing. It meant that people could get around more easily and could live farther from their jobs."

Turning Back. The teacher turns students' attention back to the text so that they can get more information, fix up a misreading, or clarify their thinking: "Yes, I agree that highways helped the country to develop and changed the way that we live. But what does the author tell us about the effect of highways on cities?"

Revoicing. The teacher helps students express what they were attempting to say: "So what you're telling us is that although people found cleaner air, less noise, and more room when they moved to the suburbs, they lost a sense of neighborhood and community."

Modeling. The teacher demonstrates how she might go about creating meaning from text. She might show how she rereads a confusing passage, refers to a map or illustration to get additional information, visualizes a complex process, or uses the glossary to get the meaning of a key word. The teacher might say, "Here's what was going through my mind as I read that section," or, "Here's why I had to read that sentence twice," or, "Here are the kinds of questions I ask myself when I read about a controversial issue."

Annotating. The teacher fills in information that is missing from a discussion but that is important for understanding key ideas. It might be information that the author failed to include: "The author tells us that highways help people get to their jobs and see sights that they never would have seen and help companies transport goods. What the author doesn't say is that highways are becoming more and more crowded and that each year drivers are wasting more time sitting in traffic jams."

Recapping. The teacher highlights key points and summarizes: "Now that we understand how highways have changed the country in some ways that are beneficial and some ways that are negative, do you think it was the best thing to spend all that money on roads, or should some have been spent on the railroads and other means of transportation?"

Steps in a Questioning the Author lesson are listed in Lesson 6.3.

Implementing Questioning the Author

To implement Questioning the Author, arrange seating so that it is conducive to discussion, such as in a U-shaped or circular arrangement. Explain to students that they will be reading and discussing what they read in a new way that is known as Questioning the Author. Explain that authors are real people who try hard to present information clearly, but who may leave out important facts, use unknown words, or write sentences that might be hard to understand. It is therefore the reader's job to try to figure out what the author meant and also to fill in details that the author might not have included. "The important message is that students hear the teacher say specifically why texts might be confusing and difficult. Such an explanation can reduce student defensiveness about not understanding" (Beck et al., 1997, p. 193).

To show students what you mean, read a text and think aloud as you do so. Note potentially confusing segments and demonstrate how you deal with them. Discuss with students portions that the author made clear and segments that were puzzling or misleading. From this discussion, students will realize that reading is a kind of conversation with an author in which the reader must ask questions in order to make meaning.

Struggling Readers and Writers

Questioning the Author works with all students, but has been especially successful with struggling readers.

LESSON 6.3

Questioning the Author

Step 1: Analyze the text and decide what you want students to know or understand as a result of reading the text. List two or three major understandings.

Step 2: Note any potential difficulties in the text that might hinder students' comprehension. These could include difficult vocabulary or concepts, density of facts, lack of needed background knowledge, or explanations that are difficult to understand.

Step 3: Segment the text into readable blocks. The segments depend on the major understandings that you believe students should acquire. A stopping point might coincide with the end of the presentation of a key understanding. A segment could be a single paragraph, if that incorporates a major idea, or a whole section.

Step 4: Plan queries based on the understandings you wish students to acquire and the possible difficulties the text poses. If a segment seems especially complex, you might plan a query such as "What is the author trying to say here?" that will help you assess what students got out of that segment and then use added queries to build on what they learned. Create queries for each segment.

Step 5: Introduce the selection. Discuss difficult vocabulary and build background necessary to understand a particular segment before that segment is read.

Step 6: Ask students to read the first segment silently.

Step 7: Discuss the first segment with students.

Step 8: Have students go on to the next segment.

Step 9: At the conclusion, the class, with your help, sums up what they have read.

In addition to improving comprehension, Questioning the Author has changed the nature of classroom discussions. Teachers' Questioning the Author questions emphasize extending understanding rather than simply retrieving information. Students, in turn, spend more time integrating ideas rather than retrieving text information. The amount of student talk, student-to-student interactions, and student-initiated questions also increases (Beck et al., 1997). A sample Questioning the Author dialog follows.

The class just read a text segment about the presidency of James Buchanan, which stated that many people believed that he liked the South better than the North because he said that owning slaves should be a personal choice. The teacher began the discussion by posing a general query. After a student responded, the teacher asked a follow-up question.

Teacher: This paragraph that Tracy just read is really full of important information. What has the author told us in this important paragraph?

Laura: They think that Buchanan liked the South better because he said that it is a person's choice if they want to have slaves or not, so they thought that he liked the South better than the North.

Teacher: Okay. And what kind of problem then did this cause Buchanan when they thought that he liked the South? What kind of problem did that cause?

Janet: Well, maybe less people would vote for him because like in Pennsylvania we were against slavery and might have voted for him because he was from Pennsylvania. But now since we knew that he was for the South, we might not vote for him again.

Jamie: I have something to add on to Janet's 'cause I completely agree with her. We might have thought that since he was from Pennsylvania and Pennsylvania was an antislavery state, that he was against slavery. But it turns out he wasn't.

Teacher: Just like someone whom you think is your best friend, and then all of a sudden you find out, oh, they're not. (McKeown, Beck, & Sandora, 1996, pp. 112–113)

CHECKUP

1. What are the main steps in Questioning the Author?
2. How would you go about implementing Questioning the Author?

The Power of Talk

CCSS

Read closely to determine what the text says explicitly and to make logical inferences from it; cite specific textual evidence when writing or speaking to support conclusions drawn from the text.

Prepare for and participate effectively in a range of conversations and collaborations with diverse partners, building on others' ideas and expressing their own clearly and persuasively.

Classroom talk can be a powerful tool for learning. In fact, the right kind of talk might be the most powerful learning tool. Providing opportunities for extended discussion of text meaning and interpretation was one of five recommendations for improving adolescent literacy made by a distinguished group of literacy scholars (Kamil, Borman, Dole, Kral, Salinger, & Torgesen, 2008). As Applebee and colleagues concluded, "Results converge to suggest that comprehension of difficult text can be significantly enhanced by replacing traditional I-R-E [Initiation-Response-Evaluation] patterns of instruction with discussion-based activities" (2003, p. 693). Initiation-Response-Evaluation is a typical verbal exchange in the classroom. The teacher initiates a question, a student responds, the teacher evaluates the student's response. I-R-E is more a verbal quiz than a discussion. Although they are effective at checking students' comprehension, I-R-Es don't do a very good job of fostering comprehension. One approach designed to foster deeper comprehension is Quality Talk.

Quality Talk

Quality talk is an approach based on the view that talk is a tool for thinking. Extensively researched, quality talk draws from nine high-quality discussion approaches, including Questioning the Author and Junior Great Books (Wilkinson, 2009). Quality talk is a shared approach in which both teacher and students play essential roles. The teacher selects the text and the topic and provides an authentic question to begin the discussion. An authentic question is one for which there is no definite answer or for which there are several possible answers, such as: "What other decision might the main character have made? Should everyone be required to provide a DNA sample? Should everyone be required to have health insurance?" The teacher models higher-level tasks and scaffolds students' responses. However, students are encouraged to respond freely and to ask their own questions, which fosters uptake. Uptake occurs when students build on each other's responses. Teacher modeling and scaffolding are especially important in the earlier stages to raise the level of discussion above an exploratory level (Wilkinson, 2009).

The foundation of quality talk is an interesting and challenging selection that students are motivated to discuss in detail, along with questions that stimulate students' thinking. Questions should be both analytical and affective. Discussions work best if there is an emotional component, if students feel deeply about their positions or views. However, students should be respectful of each other and should support their views with text-based details and reasons. As the creators of quality talk explain:

> Another important feature is fostering a moderate to high degree of emphasis on the expressive and efferent stances toward the text. We have found that a moderate degree of affective and knowledge-driven engagement is necessary, though not sufficient, for students to interrogate or query text in search of its underlying arguments, assumptions, or beliefs. Students need to be encouraged to make spontaneous, emotive connections to the textual experience (i.e., a personal, expressive response) while reading to acquire and retrieve information (i.e., an efferent stance). Through such a connection with the text coupled with a general understanding of it, students are then well positioned to adopt a critical-analytic stance toward the text. (Wilkinson, Soter, & Murphy, 2009)

Quality talk also requires an atmosphere of trust and curiosity. Quality discussions don't happen automatically. Ground rules need to be established and practiced. Junior Great Books uses the following guidelines, which can be adapted to fit your situation.

1. Read the selection before participating in the discussion.
2. Support your ideas with evidence from the text.
3. Discuss the ideas in the selection and try to understand them fully before exploring issues that go beyond the selection.
4. Listen to others and respond to them directly.
5. Expect the leader to ask questions, rather than answer them. (Carr, Coulson, Gendler, & Levine, 2001, p 4.)

Just as in Questioning the Author and other discussion techniques, there are a number of moves to foster a discussion. These include summarizing, modeling, prompting, marking, and challenging.

Summarizing: Let's stop here and summarize the challenges that Jonathan has met.

Modeling: When I hear something that I disagree with, I want to shout out, "That's not right." But then I tell myself that everyone has the right to his own opinion. I make myself listen carefully so that I fully understand what the person is saying. And if I still disagree, I say, "I understand what you are saying, but here is the way I see the situation."

Prompting: What makes you think that? What does that mean that Victor was an angel?

Marking: Did you notice what Mary did? She went back to the text to find evidence.

Challenging: Some people might say, "Does what you're talking about happen to everyone? Do you think that makes sense?" (Wilkinson, 2009)

Quality discussions are beneficial for all students, but can be especially helpful for struggling learners. In her observations of low-achieving students engaged in quality-talk

USING TECHNOLOGY

Great Books Foundation Assessment Tools www.greatbooks.org/fileadmin/pdf/JGB_7-9_IGB_1-3.pdf Provides rubrics for assessing discussions.

types of discussions, Reninger (2007) found that discussions improved the low achievers' comprehension of a complex text. Comments and questions posed by their higher-achieving peers led to this improved comprehension. After these discussions, low achievers succeeded in engaging in high-level talk and used the same features of higher-level talk that the high-achieving students did. Discussions also had an impact on low-achievers' writing, as they incorporated both the content and the reasoning processes of the discussion into their writing.

Shared Inquiry Discussion

Of the nine discussion approaches examined, Junior Great Books and its Shared Inquiry Discussion approach resulted in the greatest gains (Wilkinson, 2009). Shared Inquiry is the foundation of Junior Great Books (Great Books Foundation, 1999). In Shared Inquiry Discussion, students respond to interpretive questions posed by the leader. The expectation is that each student will develop his or her personal interpretation based on a careful analysis of the text. Three kinds of questions are posed: factual, interpretative, and evaluative. A factual question has only one correct answer, which can be found directly stated in the text or can be easily inferred. An interpretive question has more than one answer. Although not explicitly stated in the text, the answer can be supported with evidence from the text. In Langston Hughes's "Let America Be America Again," the question "What will be necessary, according to the speaker, to redeem the land?" has no definite answer but is subject to a variety of interpretations that might be supported by the text (Great Books Foundation, 1999). An evaluative question asks the reader to make a judgment based on his or her experiences and values. It also requires an understanding of the text. After reading "Let America Be America Again," students are asked, "How can the products of injustice be redeemed?"

After the discussion, students revise their responses in light of what they learned during the discussion. As a closing activity, students reflect on the discussion and its impact on them. They discuss such questions as: "Did you change your answer? Did you hear an idea you especially liked?" They also talk about what went well during the discussion.

On the secondary level, Junior Great Books provides materials for literature, science, and history. Discussions vary somewhat according to content area. In discussions of scientific texts, for instance, content questions are included to help readers grasp the scientific information in the selection. Application questions require going beyond the information expressed in the text (Great Books Foundation, 1999). In literature units, questions geared to a close reading of the text are featured.

Great Books recommends the following moves to make discussions more effective:

- **Ask Questions When Something Is Unclear.** Simply asking someone to explain what he or she means by a particular word or to repeat a comment can give everyone time to think about the idea in depth.
- **Ask for Evidence.** Asking "What in the text gave you that idea?" helps everyone better understand the reasoning behind an answer, and it allows the group to consider which ideas have the best support.
- **Ask for Agreement and Disagreement.** "Does your idea agree with hers, or is it different?" Questions of this type help the group understand how ideas are related or distinct.
- **Reflect on Discussion Afterward.** Sharing comments about how the discussion went and providing ideas for improvement can make each discussion better than the last. (Carr et al., p. 5)

CHECKUP

1. What are the key components of Quality Talk?
2. What is Shared Inquiry? How might Shared Inquiry be implemented?

Creating an Environment Conducive to Talk

Karen Waters (2010) is an experienced educator with a depth of knowledge about teaching in an urban setting. She was surprised when a lesson in which she had students share with each other to enrich their understanding of a text was met with silence. The students simply had nothing to say. As she recounts the experience, "When asked to turn and talk during natural breaks in the story, the students just sat silently, not even looking at one another, generally slumped over the desk with one arm outstretched, the other dangling over the side. To my complete surprise, in a classroom where students seemingly had no difficulty discussing the latest hip-hop artists, urban fashion, or their attitudes about homework, they simply did not utter a sound" (pp. 231–232).

Afterwards, in an analysis of the lesson with her co-teacher, Waters learned that the students were not accustomed to talking about what they were learning. Waters and her co-teacher began modeling the process of discussion. They also developed comprehension strategies so that students would better understand what they were reading and have more to talk about. And they built an atmosphere in which students felt free to talk. Waters purchased a classroom subscription to *Time for Kids* so that her students would have relevant topics to read about and discuss: the roles of women in India, the historical significance of having a woman candidate and an African American candidate for president, and other topics of interest. As students' trust was built and they began to form a community of learners and catch on to the processes required for class discussions, they discussed the characters in the graphic novel version of the *Prince and the Pauper*, debated themes of courage and cowardice in *The Red Badge of Courage*, the Holocaust in *The Boy in the Striped Pajamas*, and racial prejudice in *Maniac McGee*. As Waters observed, "Gradually, students began to recognize the critical elements of bias, perspective, and unanchored opinion as they readily connected with the themes of their culture unleashed through stories and music about turbulent times in a world fraught with injustice, social inequality, oppression, and death" (p. 237).

Other Techniques for Fostering Discussions

Using prompts to scaffold students' responses, showing cognitive empathy, and using wait time can be used with any approach to build better comprehension.

Scaffolding Prompts

Be aware of students' difficulties and pose questions that guide their thinking. Cognitive empathy and responsive elaboration incorporate scaffolding in order to guide students' thinking.

Cognitive Empathy

As you help guide students' thought processes, show **cognitive empathy**, an approach through which teachers work with students to help them use strategies to comprehend a puzzling passage or derive the meaning of a difficult word (Anderson & Roit, 1993). Students are encouraged to view reading as a problem-solving activity and to be open about any difficulties they are having so they can work collaboratively with the teacher to solve them. Teachers should look for signs that students are attempting to straighten out a confusing passage or to solve a similar literacy puzzle. Students indicate difficulty with comments, but also with

> ... furrowed brows, pauses, puzzled looks, and even short intakes of breath. Teachers use cognitive empathy to pick up on these reactions—to catch the moment when strategic

■ **Cognitive empathy** is a collaborative approach through which teachers use reading problems faced by students to help students resolve difficulties in their reading.

thinking occurs—and to encourage students to make thoughts public by asking such questions as, "What's on your mind? You seem to thinking about something. How are you going about it? How can we help?" (Anderson & Roit, 1993, p. 2)

Teachers capitalize upon these teachable moments to show empathy and to encourage students to reveal their thinking, as in the following exchange with a group of students who were having difficulty with the term *human aging:*

Teacher:	I see a confused look here. Which part is confusing you?
Student 1:	The part that says "human again."
Teacher:	I guess it isn't really "again." Does anyone have a strategy to figure that one out? You usually have very good ones.
Student 2:	"Agging."
Teacher:	Do you know what "agging" means?
Student 2:	To bother?
Teacher:	I think that if I relate this word to the title, "Growing Old," that would help me to get an idea.
Student 1:	Aging.
Teacher:	Aging. What helped you get that?
Student 1:	After you said growing old, I looked at the title and I just remembered that someone growing old is aging. (Anderson & Roit, 1993, p. 6)

Imitating the teacher's behavior, the students soon began to show cognitive empathy toward each other. Students gave suggestions to each other and discussed strategies that they used. Cognitive empathy is especially important when working with students who have a history of failure. "Having endured criticism from self and others, older low-achieving readers are naturally reluctant to talk about or even admit that they have problems with reading" (Anderson & Roit, 1993, p. 2).

Responsive Elaboration

Responsive elaboration also focuses on students' thought processes but tends to be more teacher directed than cognitive empathy. Teachers listen to answers to determine how students arrived at those responses. Instead of asking, "Is this answer right or wrong?" they ask, "What thought processes led the student to this response?" And, if the answer is wrong, "How can those thought processes be redirected?" Instead of calling on another student, telling where the answer might be found, or giving obvious hints, teachers ask questions or make statements that help put students' thinking back on the right track. The key to using responsive elaboration is asking yourself two questions: "What has gone wrong with the student's thinking?" and "What can I ask or state that would guide the student's thinking to the right thought processes and correct answer?" (Gunning, 2010). The following is an example of how a teacher might use responsive elaboration with a student who has been asked to give the main idea of a paragraph but has inferred a main idea that is too narrow in scope:

Student (giving incorrect main idea):	Getting new words from Indians.
Teacher:	Well, let's test it. Is the first sentence talking about new words from the Indians?
Student:	Yes.
Teacher:	Is the next?
Student:	Yes.
Teacher:	How about the next?
Student:	No.

Struggling Readers

Cognitive empathy was highly successful with older struggling readers because it built on strategies that they were using and used peer as well as teacher collaboration so that students shared their thinking with each other as well as with the teacher.

Teacher: No. It says that Indians also learned new words from the settlers, right? Can you fit that into your main idea?

Student: The Indians taught the settlers words and the settlers taught the Indians words.

Teacher: Good. You see, you have to think about all the ideas in the paragraph to decide on the main idea. (Duffy & Roehler, 1987, p. 517)

Wait Time

Perhaps the simplest way to improve students' responses is to use **wait time**, which simply means that after calling on a student, you wait for a response. Teachers often expect an immediate answer and, when none is forthcoming, call on another student. Because it gives students time to think, waiting five seconds results in longer, more elaborate, higher-level responses. There are also fewer no-responses and I-don't-knows. Teachers who use wait time actually grow in their ability to help students clarify and expand their responses (Dillon, 1983; Gambrell, 1980). Wait time after a response has been given also helps. Teachers tend to call on another pupil the second the respondent stops talking. Often, however, students have more to say if given a few seconds to collect their thoughts. The postresponse wait time must be a genuine grace period (Gunning, 2010). Maintain eye contact for five seconds after the student has responded to provide him or her the opportunity for elaboration or explanation. Failing to maintain eye contact and turning away are cues that your attention is being diverted and will shut down any additional response that the student is about to make (Christenbury & Kelly, 1983).

Wait time is actually part of a larger approach. Instead of using questioning as an oral quiz, you employ it as a device to build students' understanding. Wait time can increase student confidence, especially in those who struggle. Using wait time also has the power to alter the teacher's perceptions of struggling students. When struggling students are provided with wait time, chances are, their responses will improve, becoming more elaborated and more accurate. This, in turn, signals to the teacher that the students are more capable than he or she may have judged. "Seeing that the students are more capable, the teacher expends more teaching resources on them and thus an upward spiral is created" (Gunning, 2006, 72). Wait time works best when it is combined with authentic, thought-provoking questions along with cognitive empathy and appropriate prompts.

 Struggling Readers

Because teachers may feel that struggling readers don't have much to contribute, these students are typically given less wait time and fewer prompts when called on.

Think-Pair-Share

Think-Pair-Share is an easy-to-apply discussion technique that can be used by students in virtually every content area (Lyman, 1981). In the "think" part of the technique, the teacher poses a question or idea and the students reflect on it for a minute or so. As an option, they can write a brief response. The purpose is to give them some time to gather their thoughts. In the "pair" segment, students share their thinking with a partner. By talking about their thoughts and listening to a partner share, students are provided with an opportunity to organize their thoughts and also to hear another perspective. As an option, two pairs can then share with each other, which further expands the students' thinking. In the "share" portion, the pairs or groups share with the whole class. The person speaking must share not only his own thoughts but also those of his partner or group. Being asked to share the thoughts of others provides students with the opportunity to practice their listening skills. Think-pair-share is an excellent device for having students talk over ideas. Whole-class sharing is usually enriched when students have had some think time and also the opportunity to share with a partner and another pair.

To begin using think-pair-share, model the technique. Show students what the speaker does and what the listener does, so they have an understanding of both roles. You might give them specific direction, such as, "If you are the first one to share, tell your partner what you think the government's role is in providing health care for young people who

■ **Wait time** is waiting five seconds or so after asking a question or after getting the student's initial response in order to give the student time to think and compose a fuller or more thoughtful response.

are healthy and don't believe they need health care insurance. Briefly explain or support your position. If you are the listener, listen carefully to your partner. You can agree or disagree, but be polite. Then tell what you think the government's role is and why." You might use a simplified version of think-pair-share known as *turn and talk*. Students simply turn to their partner and respond and discuss a topic or question that the teacher has provided (Calkins & Mermelstein, 2003). Think-pair-share is an excellent device for enlivening discussions and increasing participation. It's an effective device to use with English language learners, struggling readers, and shy students because they are more likely to participate in a paired or small-group discussion. Listening in on students' sharing is also an excellent way to check for understanding.

In an adaptation of think-pair-share, math teacher Miim Kwak (2002) asked pairs of students to take notes as they reflected upon and shared their thoughts on the difference between inverse and direct relationships and to provide an example of each. During the share portion, students listed points of agreement on one side of a sheet of paper and differences on the other side. Kwak noted that think-pair-share was an effective device for clarifying confusions and summarizing students' work. A flexible technique, think-pair-share also can be used with images. Geology teacher Heather McDonald (2011) showed students an image of a rock formation and asked such questions as: "Are these igneous, metamorphic, or sedimentary rocks? Can you identify any unit that is present on both sides of the image?" Each student filled out a four-column form, with the first column containing the prompt; the second, the student's thoughts; the third, the partner's thoughts; and the fourth, what the partners would share.

Think-pair-share and similar discussion techniques can be used to plan instruction. For example, physics teacher Eric Mazur posed a question in which students had to apply the physics principle being taught, such as how much water an object would displace. Students worked in pairs and discussed their responses. Then they responded to the question again. At that point, Mazur polled the class to judge the accuracy of the responses and used this information to adjust his lesson (Trees & Jackson, 2003).

USING TECHNOLOGY

Increasingly "clickers," which are electronic response systems that allow an immediate analysis of responses to questions or problems posed are being used in secondary classrooms. See Toolbox at lt.osu.edu/resources-clickers for more information.

CHECKUP

1. What is think-pair-share?
2. What are some of the ways in which think-pair-share might be used?

Cooperative Learning

CCSS

Prepare for and participate effectively in a range of conversations and collaborations with diverse partners, building on others' ideas and expressing their own clearly and persuasively.

Although much of our learning is solitary, talking over concepts helps deepen our understanding of them. One of the best ways to foster understanding of a complex idea is to explain it to someone. Before we can explain it, we have to sort it out ourselves and translate it into understandable terms. Discussion as a way of learning is the basis of cooperative learning. **Cooperative learning** comes in many forms. It can be as simple as having a pair of students study or complete a project together. It can be as complex as having an entire class divided into four or five groups, with each group assigned a different segment of an overall task and each member of each group fulfilling a specific role to help complete the group's segment. It can be informal and temporary or highly structured and longstanding.

Cooperative learning has a dual payoff. Not only do students improve in their subject matter areas (Slavin, 1987), but they also feel better about themselves and have the added satisfaction of working with and helping others (Johnson & Johnson, 1994). For secondary school students, positive peer relationships have a powerful influence on learning (Roseth, Fang, Johnson, & Johnson, 2006). As Roseth et al. commented, "If you want to increase student academic achievement, give each student a friend (2006, p. 7). Although all students benefit from cooperative learning, struggling learners, members of minority groups, and English language learners benefit the most.

■ **Cooperative learning** is a format in which students work together to complete a learning task.

> **United States History**
>
> Topic: *After the Great War*
>
> Subtopic: *Wilson loses the peace*
>
> Read Chapter 2, Fourteen Points, pages 16–20, in the *Oxford History of US*, by Joy Hakim.
>
> 1. What was the purpose of Wilson's Fourteen Points?
> 2. What was the League of Nations?
> 3. Why did Wilson want the United States to join the League of Nations?
> 4. Why were many Americans opposed to the League of Nations?
> 5. What happened as a result of Wilson's stroke?
>
> Discussion: If you had been living in the time just after World War I, would you have been for or against the League of Nations? Why? Would you have voted for Wilson? Why or why not?

FIGURE 6.1
Jigsaw Expert Sheet

Jigsaw

Cooperative learning activities can take a variety of forms and serve a number of educational purposes. However, the major purpose of cooperative learning is to develop a deeper understanding of course content. Two of the most widely used types are jigsaw and study group. As its name suggests, **jigsaw** divides a project into four or five subtasks, with each member of the group assigned a separate portion of an overall topic (Aronson, 1978; Slavin, 1996). For a class studying ancient Egypt, the teacher might divide the overall topic into five parts: the nature of the Nile, trade and commerce, everyday life, major rulers, and accomplishments. Each member of a group is assigned one subtopic and is given a series of questions to guide his or her reading. The goal is that each student will become an "expert" on the assigned subtopic. After getting their assignments, students do their reading and join an expert group. A sample expert sheet is presented in Figure 6.1. Each member of the expert group has the same assignment. For instance, all the students investigating Egypt's contributions join together in an expert group. Expert group members help each other with confusing concepts, difficult terms, and misunderstood details. If students are unable to resolve an issue or question, they may seek help from the teacher. The teacher, of course, actively monitors each group's progress. After students have mastered their subtopics, they meet with their teams. Each team member instructs the others in his or her subtopic. The members of the team make sure that everyone has a good grasp of all the subtopics. The goal is to have each team member pass a quiz prepared by the teacher.

Team members are assessed on their individual performances. Teams may also be assessed as a group on total score, number of members receiving a passing score, and/or degree of improvement. Based on the students' performance, the teacher reteaches content if necessary. The teacher also evaluates group processes to see how well the members worked together.

Study Groups

In a study group, students help each other learn information on a specific topic or from a particular section of the text (Hotchkiss, 1990). The teacher presents the information to be learned, provides practice, and then assigns students to heterogeneous groups to study or engage in additional practice. Team members work as a whole group or in pairs to complete the exercises. The goal is to help each student become knowledgeable in the topic being studied so that all can pass a test on the material.

Managing Cooperative Learning

One problem with cooperative learning is that students may spend time talking about nonacademic matters such as favorite TV shows or the latest fashions. However, if students find the tasks and discussions in which they are engaged interesting and valuable

USING TECHNOLOGY

Cooperative Learning Rubric www .readwritethink.org/.../lesson95/ coop_rubric.pdf Presents a useful rubric for assessing individual and group performance

■ A jigsaw cooperative group is one in which students divide up a task and then share what they have learned with the other members of their group.

and if self-regulating behaviors have been emphasized, chances are they will stay on task (Herber & Herber, 1993). Based on extensive experience with cooperative learning, a group of content area teachers identified four key roles that teachers fulfill: directing, monitoring, probing, and supporting.

Directing

Directing means making sure that students understand and can carry out the cooperative learning tasks that have been assigned to them. Directing includes explaining, modeling, reviewing, and coaching.

Monitoring

Monitoring involves observing students and taking steps to improve performance as required. However, teachers must be careful not to disrupt or take over discussions. Students are given the opportunity to discover and work on areas needing improvement for themselves.

Probing

Probing consists of using prompts and other devices to help students better understand content. Probes can be used to help students clarify confusions, evaluate responses, draw conclusions, perceive fallacies, obtain more information, or even apply what they have learned. Probes include prompts such as, "Can you clarify that statement? Can you tell me more? How might this be applied? Can you give me examples?" However, think-alouds in which teachers show how they might analyze a problem or draw a conclusion also can function as probes. Questioning whether other solutions might be posed or other conclusions drawn or whether all the evidence has been considered are other ways teachers can foster students' thinking (Herber & Herber, 1993).

Supporting

Supporting consists of using praise, affirming statements, and, in some instances, direct assistance. To be effective, praise must be genuine and specific. "You did a great job!" is too general. "You did a good job supporting your conclusions" is more effective. Specific support lets students know what they did right so they know what to do again. Otherwise, students, especially those who have a shaky sense of self-efficacy, may believe that you are just being nice to them. Statements that affirm students' efforts can also be helpful: "Keep at it. You're on the right track." Where possible, you want the students to find their own solutions and reach their own conclusions. However, when they are genuinely stuck, provide assistance that is needed. This is especially important when students need information in order to continue their efforts (Herber & Herber, 1993).

> **USING TECHNOLOGY**
>
> The Cooperative Learning Center at the University of Minnesota www.clcrc.com/index.html has valuable additional information about cooperative learning.

CHECKUP

1. What is cooperative learning?
2. How might cooperative learning using jigsaw groups be implemented?

Collaborative Strategic Reading

> ■ **Collaborative Strategic Reading** is an approach to cooperative learning that incorporates effective learning strategies. It is designed for mainstreamed students.

One form of cooperative learning has been specifically designed to help students with learning disabilities learn in regular classrooms. With increasing diversity in the classroom, content area teachers are faced with the question: How can I provide for the needs of all the students in each of my classes? One possible answer is **Collaborative Strategic Reading** (Vaughn, Klinger, & Schumm, n.d.), which combines cooperative learning with the use of high-payoff strategies and helps both regular education students and students with special needs become more effective learners. These high-payoff strategies include previewing, developing key vocabulary thorough the use of click and clunk, getting the gist or main idea, wrapping up by stating the most important information learned that day, and composing questions that they think could be on a test. Collaborative Strategic Reading has been specially designed to help struggling learners, but may be used with all learners. Here's how it works.

Before assembling in cooperative groups, students are introduced to the topic they will be reading about. The teacher discusses the new topic and, if appropriate, ties it in with what was covered the previous day. The teacher introduces words that students might not be able to figure out on their own. The teacher also tells the class how much of the text is to be read. Students read the text section by section. Younger students might read a paragraph at a time, and older students might read longer portions.

Previewing

After the introduction, students begin working in cooperative groups, using previewing as their first strategy. Previewing has two steps: brainstorming what is known about a topic and using the title and headings to predict what they will learn in this section. As they read the section, they can make new predictions. Students then read the text silently section by section.

Click and Clunk

A unique feature of Collaborative Strategic Reading, which is a favorite of students, is **click and clunk**. Clicks and clunks are compared with driving a car. When everything is going smoothly, the car is clicking along. When the car hits a pothole, there is a clunk. Clicks are portions of the text that are easy to understand. Clunks are problem portions. When students hit clunks, which are generally hard words or confusing sentences, they attempt to clarify them. If the clunk is a hard word, students might look for a familiar word part or use context, syllabic or morphemic analysis, or the glossary or dictionary. If unable to resolve a clunk, a student may request help from other members of the group. If no one in the group can help, students seek help from the teacher, who also instructs them in repair strategies, including those needed for removing comprehension clunks. A student who is especially adept at fixing clunks might be appointed the group's clunk expert.

Getting the Gist

Getting the **gist** entails understanding the main idea of the section. After reading a section, students ask themselves, "What is this section mostly about (topic)?" and "What is the most important idea about the topic?"

Wrap-Up

Wrap-up is a review of the day's reading. Students wrap up in two ways. They review or summarize the most important information they have learned—for example, by creating a graphic organizer to highlight essential information. As part of the review, students also create potential test questions about the most important information in the selection. Students select their best questions and pose them to other members of the group.

At the end of the lesson, the class meets as a whole, and students discuss what they have learned. The teacher has groups talk about the most important things they have learned, ask their best questions, or share their toughest clunk. The teacher makes sure that students understand key concepts and clarifies any misunderstandings.

Before students work on their own, the teacher models strategies and has students try them out. Content area periodicals and brief news articles provide good materials for try-outs. Once students have grasped both the reading strategies and the procedures for working in groups, they begin working in groups on their own, with the teacher monitoring their work and providing assistance as needed.

Struggling Readers

Because it features teacher guidance and structured ways in which students can work together and help each other, Collaborative Strategic Reading is especially effective for helping struggling learners.

■ **Click and clunk** is a procedure for monitoring and clarifying meaning and repairing comprehension.

■ **The gist** is the main idea of a selection or what the selection is all about.

Each student fulfills a specific role. The teacher may assign these roles, or the students decide among themselves who will fulfill which role. Roles should be changed periodically. Cue sheets provide guidance to students as they fulfill their roles. Possible roles include the following:

- *Leader*—gets the group started and leads discussions.
- *Clunk expert*—provides assistance with clunks. Has a series of printed clunk cards that contain prompts that might be used to resolve clunks.
- *Timekeeper*—times each section. For example, allows three minutes for preview, six minutes for reading a section and getting the gist. (Time may vary depending on length of selection.) Allows five minutes for wrap-up.
- *Recorder*—records review, best questions, and unresolved clunks.
- *Supervisor*—makes sure the group stays on task and encourages everyone to participate.

CHECKUP

1. What are the main elements in Collaborative Strategic Reading?
2. How might this approach to collaborative learning be implemented?

Discussion Groups

Another popular form of cooperative learning is the discussion group. In a discussion group, all members explore the same topic, but they have different roles. One popular type of discussion group is the **literature circle**, which is composed of four to six students who are reading the same book, either by choice or by assignment. Groups are formed in much the same way as other cooperative learning groups. The teacher assigns roles, or the group decides who will fulfill each role. Key roles are the discussion leader, summarizer, literary reporter, illustrator, word chief, and connector (Bjorklund, Handler, Mitten, & Stockwell, 1998; Daniels, 1994, 2002).

All of the group members read the book. However, the discussion leader creates questions for the group and leads the discussion. The summarizer summarizes the selection. The literary reporter locates passages that contain key incidents, feature imaginative language, or create vivid pictures. The reporter might read the passages out loud, ask the group to read them silently and discuss them, or involve other members of the group in dramatizing them. An illustrator depicts a key part of the selection with a drawing or graphic organizer. The word chief identifies potentially difficult words or expressions in the selection, checks their meanings in the dictionary, and records their definitions. At the circle meeting, the word chief discusses the words with the group. The connector creates links between the book and other books the group has read or with events, problems, or situations in real life; explains the connection; and discusses it with the group. Although each student has a specific role, any member of the group may bring up a question for discussion, call attention to a passage that is memorable, ask about a confusing word, or note a personal or literary connection.

The roles reflect the kinds of strategies that expert readers apply as they read a text. They raise questions in their minds, make connections, create images, summarize, note key passages, decode difficult words and confusing passages, and appreciate expressive language and literary techniques. Students switch roles periodically so that each member of the circle has the opportunity to experience each of the roles.

Students are provided with job sheets that give them directions for fulfilling their roles. A sample job sheet for a discussion leader is shown in Figure 6.2 Although the job sheets are fairly specific, the teacher discusses and models key tasks, such as creating questions, identifying imaginative language, deriving definitions of difficult words, and making connections. It is also helpful if the groups practice their jobs with a relatively easy selection first.

■ **Literature circles** are cooperative learning groups set up for the purpose of reading and discussing a work of literature. They may be adapted to discuss content area trade books.

The discussion leader's job is to create and ask questions about the selection that the students in your group read. The questions should help readers better understand the selection and relate what happened in the selection to their own lives. Some kinds of questions that you might ask are:

- Were you surprised by anything that happened in this part of the selection?
- Was there anything in the selection that puzzled you?
- Who is your favorite character so far? Why?
- If the author were here, what would you say to her or him?
- What do you think will happen next?

Write your questions on the lines.

1. _____
2. _____
3. _____
4. _____

FIGURE 6.2
Discussion Leader Job Sheet

Role sheets provide structure and scaffolding for students' efforts. Like all scaffolds, they should be gradually reduced or eliminated so that students can take control of the circles. Otherwise, they tend to limit students' performance and engagement (Daniels, 2008). However, on the other side of the coin, if literature circles are flagging, introducing or reintroducing roles might shore them up.

After a literature circle has been formed, the group meets and sets up a reading schedule. They might also decide on roles, unless the teacher has made that decision. After reading, students complete their job sheets and write in a response journal, if assigned. As the teacher visits each group, she might model asking questions or responding to a selection, or simply be another participant. Whole-class sessions are held so that groups can share with each other.

After the books have been read and discussed, students meet in groups according to the roles they fulfilled, just as students met in expert jigsaw groups. All the discussion leaders meet, as do all the summarizers, connectors, illustrators, word chiefs, and literary reporters. Students discuss the book they read from the point of view of their roles. Through this regrouping, the students get to know the books read in other groups. Literature circles can also be organized in a less formal way so that members meet to talk over their reading, but don't have specific roles.

The type of organization used in literature circles can also be adapted to form discussion groups about reading undertaken in social studies, science, and other content areas. These readings are drawn from trade books on key topics assigned by the teacher or selected by the students.

Using blogs and in-class discussions, content area teachers in one research study (Thompson, 2008) adapted literature circles to explore ways in which they might use discussion groups to foster learning in their content areas. Language arts, math, social studies, and science teachers adapted the traditional roles of story mapper, discussion director, and illustrator so that they fit in with the demands of reading in their disciplines. Students were encouraged to make the roles multimodal. In science, for instance, some students brought in real-life examples, including newspaper or magazine articles, blogs, and video clips. Others were responsible for experiments that illustrated the concept. In math, students used diverse approaches and modalities to solve problems, and brought in real-life examples of math being used to solve everyday problems.

 Struggling Readers

Discussion groups might be set up in such a way that students are reading and discussing texts that are on their level. For instance, if students are having difficulty with the core text because it is above their reading level, they might read and discuss trade books that cover the same topics but are easier to read.

Inquiry Circles

Inquiry circles are a variation of literature circles (Daniels, 2008). Instead of focusing on a particular book or set of books, participants focus on an inquiry—a question that is answered by seeking out and reading research materials and discussing, writing, and reflecting on the question. Possible topics include prejudice, cell phones, presidential debates, civil rights, and even exponential functions. Teachers use students' curiosity and background to help them formulate interesting but significant questions.

Ivey and Broaddus (2007) showed that students remember the curriculum much better when their teachers figure out which aspects of it are interesting to them. If students can't think of questions or lack the background to do so, the teacher poses questions: Why do we bother exploring Mars? Will people ever live in space? What will it take to live in space? Should there be a bank of everyone's DNA? Should people have their DNA tested for possible future diseases? Should we worry about endangered animals? Do you know who made the clothes you wear? Do you know what their working conditions were? Barron and Hammond (2008) advise, "Education must help students learn how to learn in powerful ways so they can manage the demands of changing information, technologies, jobs and social conditions" (p. 12). The best framework for this kind of adaptive thinking, the authors continue, is complex, meaningful projects that "require sustained engagement, collaboration, research, management of resources, and the development of an ambitious performance or product" (p. 12).

Inquiry learning can start with a question. Then, books that explore that question are selected. Or inquiry learning can start with using a book to determine which inquiry questions might be asked (Wolk, 2009).

CHECKUP

1. What are discussion groups?
2. What are some possible roles in a discussion group?

Discussion Web

One problem that arises with discussion groups is the tendency for one or two individuals to dominate. A technique known as the Discussion Web alleviates this problem (Alvermann, 1991). In this technique, based in part on think-pair-share (McTighe & Lyman, 1988), each student thinks about the ideas that he wants to contribute. Students then pair up with a partner and share their ideas. This gives them a chance to clarify and extend their thinking. The partners then meet with another pair of partners. The four students discuss their conclusions and reasons, come to a consensus, and decide on reasons that best support their conclusion. Discussion Webs are incorporated within the framework of a lesson and are part of a six-step procedure.

The Discussion Web can be reworded to accommodate questions that do not lend themselves to a yes-no responses. In science, students might create two or more hypotheses for a phenomenon and provide possible reasons for supporting each one. In social studies, the categories might be positions taken by key figures on important issues. Students might, for instance, write reasons to support Hamilton's or Jefferson's views on democracy.

CHECKUP

1. What is a Discussion Web?
2. What are the steps in implementing a Discussion Web?

LESSON 6.4

Steps in Discussion Web

Step 1: Preparation

Introduce the selection in a similar way to a guided or directed reading activity. Activate background, introduce new concepts and vocabulary, build interest, and set a purpose for reading.

Step 2: Reading

Ask students to read the story silently.

Step 3: Initial Discussion

Discuss the selection. Ask students, working in pairs, to create a Discussion Web in response to a key question that has supporting reasons for and against it: Should the United States have dropped the atomic bomb in World War II? Should the United States have joined the League of Nations after World War I? Should coal-burning energy plants in the Midwest be required to eliminate pollution so that the air in the Northeast will be cleaner? Have students jot down brief telegraphic phrases as reasons, with an equal number of reasons in the "yes" and "no" columns.

Step 4: Second Discussion

Ask each pair to meet with another pair to form a group of four. Members of the group compare and discuss their reasons and attempt to reach a consensus.

Step 5: Report of Conclusions

After the groups have reached their conclusions, have each group select a spokesperson and also discuss and choose the reason that they feel best supports their conclusion. Also note dissenting opinions. The spokesperson for each group reports the group's conclusion, best reason, and dissenting opinions. Having groups choose a best reason reduces the possibility of duplication as the groups give their reports.

Step 6: Follow-Up

Ask students to write individual essays in which they state and support their conclusions. Encourage students to use both the reasons that they composed on their own and the reasons that the group suggested.

Although the effective approaches explored in this chapter and also the previous chapters vary, they have a number of key elements in common. They include all or most of the following elements, which are research-based principles that apply to virtually all learning (Marzano, 2007):

- Fostering active engagement by students.
- Providing preparation for reading through surveying, predicting, activating background knowledge, making connections, or some other means.
- Using purpose questions or student questions to foster directed reading.
- Promoting strategies or other activities that stimulate interaction with the material.
- Featuring after-reading activities such as discussions or extensions that provide opportunities for deepening an understanding of the material that was read.
- Emphasizing the power of working together to construct an understanding of the material.
- Breaking the material into chunks so that it can be better understood and assimilated.

Summary

Collaborative learning is an approach that views students as active participants in the construction of learning rather than as passive recipients of information. In ReQuest, Reciprocal Teaching, Questioning the Author, and Collaborative Strategic Reading, teacher and students work together to construct meaning. These are examples of collaborative learning in which the teacher plays a very active role. All of these approaches can be used with both whole classes and small groups.

The simplest of the techniques is ReQuest, which consists of having teacher and students ask each other questions about text. Reciprocal Teaching stresses four highly effective strategies: predicting, questioning, clarifying, and summarizing. Using open-ended queries instead of questions, Questioning the Author is designed to help students, under the teacher's guidance, construct meaning from a text by carefully examining brief segments of text and asking and discussing the question: What is the author trying to say here? Quality talk is an approach based on the concept that talk is a tool for thinking. It uses five moves: summarizing, modeling, prompting, marking, and challenging. Junior Great Books, which uses Shared Inquiry, makes use of similar moves. Think-pair-share, in which students gather their thoughts, talk to a partner, and share with the larger group, also builds thoughtful discussions.

The term *cooperative learning* is typically used to refer to small groups of students working and learning together. Although cooperative learning can take many forms, two of the most widely used are jigsaw groups and study groups. In jigsaw groups, each student is responsible for completing a section of the report or project and teaching other group members. In study groups, students reflect on and discuss material in preparation for a test. They might subdivide the topic or have everyone contribute on the whole topic. In Collaborative Strategic Reading, which was designed to help struggling learners in regular classes and in discussion groups, students help each other construct meaning from text. Although they all read the same text, each has a separate role in the group. In discussion groups, students also read the same material and have different roles. Discussion Webs incorporate think-pair-share.

Cooperative learning requires careful management. In fostering cooperative learning, the teacher fulfills four roles: directing, monitoring, probing, and supporting.

Reflection

Return to the Anticipation Guide at the beginning of this chapter. Respond once again to the items. Did your responses change? If so, how and why? What are some key features that collaborative approaches have in common? How might cooperative or collaborative learning be used in content area classrooms? How might cooperative and collaborative learning be used to help struggling learners?

Extension and Application

Find out more about Questioning the Author by reading Beck and McKeown (2006).

Try out ReQuest or one of the other approaches described in the chapter. Assess its effectiveness. What seems to be its advantages and disadvantages?

With three or four other members of the class, set up a cooperative group for a particular learning task. It may be the reading of an article or a chapter in this text. Decide on the form your group will take and the role that each member will fulfill. Also evaluate the effectiveness of your group.

Go to Topic 7: Planning for Instruction in the MyEducationLab (www.myeducationlab.com) for your course, where you can:

- Find learning outcomes for Planning for Instruction along with the national standards that connect to these outcomes.
- Complete Assignments and Activities that can help you more deeply understand the chapter content.
- Apply and practice your understanding of the core teaching skills identified in the chapter with the Building Teaching Skills and Dispositions learning units.
- Examine challenging situations and cases presented in the IRIS Center Resources.

Go to the Topic A+RISE in the MyEducationLab (www.myeducationlab.com) for your course. A+RISE® Standards2Strategy™ is an innovative and interactive online resource that offers new teachers in grades K–12 just-in-time, research-based instructional strategies that:

- Meet the linguistic needs of ELLs as they learn content.
- Differentiate instruction for all grades and abilities.
- Offer reading and writing techniques, cooperative learning, use of linguistic and nonlinguistic representations, scaffolding, teacher modeling, higher-order thinking, and alternative classroom ELL assessment.
- Provide support to help teachers be effective through the integration of listening, speaking, reading, and writing along with the content curriculum.
- Improve student achievement.
- Are aligned to Common Core Elementary Language Arts standards (for the literacy strategies) and to English language proficiency standards in WIDA, Texas, California, and Florida.

CHAPTER 7

Study Skills and Strategies

For each of the following statements, put a check under "Agree" or "Disagree" to indicate your opinion. If possible, discuss your responses with classmates.

	Agree	Disagree
1. Content area teachers should be responsible for teaching the study skills necessary to learn their subject matter.	_____	_____
2. One of the most effective study strategies is to reread material carefully.	_____	_____
3. Memory techniques such as making up rhymes are generally ineffective.	_____	_____
4. Poor study habits and poor self-discipline, rather than a lack of study strategies, is the main cause of poor preparation for content area tests.	_____	_____
5. Most students learn effective study techniques without any formal instruction.	_____	_____
6. Studying with a group is better than studying alone.	_____	_____

Previous chapters have presented a variety of suggestions for improving reading in the content areas. This chapter goes beyond reading to learn and explores strategies for reading to remember. Before reading this chapter, think about the way you study. What special techniques do you use? Do you employ different techniques for different subjects? How effective do these techniques seem to be? What is your attitude toward studying? How would you rate your study habits? How might you help students improve their studying?

Using What You Know

Reading to Remember

Frank is discouraged. Although he had given up watching his favorite TV shows to read the chapter on plant life in his general science text, he had failed the quiz. Frank was determined to do better. In preparation for the next quiz, he read the chapter twice, even though it took up just about all his evening. However, he still failed the quiz. One question asked about the parts of a plant. He remembered reading about the parts of a plant, but except for petals, he couldn't remember what they were. "I guess I'm just stupid," Frank thought to himself.

The nature of Frank's reading assignments has changed now that he is in secondary school, but Frank's strategies haven't. Even when reading expository text, Frank uses a narrative style. He plunges into the text without any preparation or purpose, except that of getting to the end of the chapter. He reads the concept-laden material as though it were a story. As he reads, he does nothing to organize the information or check his comprehension of it. And when he's finished reading, he closes his book. He does nothing to promote retention of the material.

Although he already knows how to read, Frank must now learn how to learn through reading. He must acquire study strategies. In addition to learning how to comprehend complex materials, he must become skilled at organizing and retaining that material. As learning experts Pashler, Bain, Bottge, Graesser, Koedinger, McDaniel, and Metcalfe (2007) concluded, "students' ability to manage their own studying is one of the more important skills that students need to learn, with consequences that will be felt throughout their lives" (p. 1).

Frank is not alone. Many students lack suitable study strategies. When searching for students for an investigation of study techniques, researchers looked for individuals who had adequate decoding skills but poor study strategies (Madden, 2000). They had no difficulty finding participants. Two-thirds of the students they screened met the criteria. High school students report using the following strategies: reading more slowly, rereading the text, and underlining the text (Schallert & Tierney, 1980). None of these strategies is particularly effective. They may work when the material is relatively easy and students have to remember it for only a short period of time. However, for heavy-duty studying, more effective strategies such as outlining, taking notes, or using a study system work better. The good news is that students do improve their studying when provided with instruction, practice, and guidance (Hattie, 2009). Study approaches include three main aspects: task-related cognitive skills, such as summarizing or reciting; metacognitive skills, such as selecting study strategies and monitoring whether material has been learned; and affective dispositions, such as motivation, confidence, and discipline (Hattie, Biggs, & Purdie, 1996).

CHECKUP

1. How effective are most students' study skills?
2. What are the three essential components of successful studying?

The Importance of Study Skills and Role of the Content Area Teacher

Even students who have adequate comprehension may have difficulty preparing for tests or completing assignments. Students may read for understanding, but fail to read to learn and remember. Students may lack study strategies, motivation, or confidence in themselves as learners. An effective program of study skills instruction will help them get to know themselves as learners and use this knowledge to set goals, plan study sessions, make use of a variety of study strategies, and monitor their studying.

However, the role of the content area teacher is critical. Study skills instruction is most effective when students are learning specific content. As Hattie, Biggs, and Purdie (1996) concluded, based on their analyses of 51 studies, "The best results came when strategy training was used meta-cognitively with appropriate motivational and contextual support" (p. 129). The most effective programs were embedded in the content to be learned. Embedded programs were especially effective when deeper understanding rather than surface knowledge was the goal (Hattie, 2009).

How We Remember

We are in a better position to foster retention if we understand how memory works. Memory is composed of three essential processes: **encoding, storage,** and **retrieval**. Outside data are translated into a code (encoded) that is placed into working memory and then long-term memory, from which they can later be retrieved through recall or recognition. The memory process begins when raw data enter the sensory register. The data are held there for only about a second. During that time, attentional processes select from the data

■ **Encoding** is the process through which sensory information is changed into a form, such as a phonological or visual form, that can be stored in the brain.

■ **Storage** is the process of placing and keeping information in memory.

■ **Retrieval** is the process of locating and using information stored in memory.

entering the sensory register those stimuli that we wish to process further. Sensory data that have been chosen enter *working memory*, the system that temporarily stores information during the performance of such cognitive tasks as reading a sentence or working out a math problem in one's head (Hulme & MacKenzie, 1992).

Working memory makes use of information stored in long-term memory as well as information that enters from the sensory register. When you read words at the end of a sentence, you relate them to words at the beginning of the sentence (which are stored in working memory). However, you also relate the unfolding meaning of the gist of sentences and previously read paragraphs now stored in long-term memory to experiences you have had, which is also information stored in long-term memory (Gunning, 2010). Because the words at the beginning of a sentence are stored in working memory while the rest of the sentence is being processed, an efficient working memory is crucial to comprehension. Otherwise, by the time the reader reaches the end of the sentence, she may have forgotten the content of the beginning of the sentence (McCormick, 1987).

Classical research suggests that the average person can retain about seven pieces of information (Miller, 1956). Other, more recent research indicates that the number might be five bits of information (Huitt, 2003). More information can be retrieved if it is chunked into meaningful units. For instance, S C B comprises three bits of information, but CBS has been chunked into one piece of information. Working memory is variable and develops with age. Some students might only be able to keep three units of information in mind at one time because working memory operates as a bottleneck. If students have to think about new terms such as *corpus callosum* and *hemispheres* as they are reading about the brain, then their cognitive capacity for thinking about what they're reading is reduced and comprehension is likely to suffer. If they are thinking about how to punctuate a sentence or spell a word while writing, then they have less cognitive capacity to apply to their writing. That's why it is important that processes be automated though practice so that maximum capacity can be applied to higher-level tasks.

Clear Encoding

Generally, information is remembered better if it is clearly encoded. In order to remember a fact or idea, we need to have an accurate representation of it. We can't possibly remember a person's name if we didn't hear it clearly. We are more likely to remember the name if we listen attentively to it and also if we intend to remember it: By forming an intention to remember someone's name, we will take steps to remember it. We may rehearse the name—that is, we may say it over and over again. This process, known as a *maintenance rehearsal*, keeps the name from slipping out of our minds. It keeps it in working memory, but may not place it in long-term memory. To make sure the name gets placed in long-term memory, we may use a more meaningful strategy, such as making an association. After meeting Joseph Snow, we may visualize him as a snowman. Or we may think that his name really fits because he seems to be a cold person, a kind of an emotional snowman. The more distinctive we can make our memory clues, the better. Distinctive clues are more memorable.

What holds true for remembering names is also true for ideas. Fuzzy or confusing ideas are soon lost. We have nothing to hold on to. When getting a set of directions, it's a good idea to have them repeated to make sure that you understand each part of the direction sequence. It's also a good idea to repeat the directions in your own words. That way, the person giving the directions can make sure that you got them right. And you can check your understanding. If you can't put an idea or directions into your own words, chances are that you don't really understand them and won't remember them.

Encoding Specificity

The way we encode information determines how we remember it. This is known as *encoding specificity*. For instance, name the days of the week as fast as you can. Now name the days of the week in alphabetical order. Naming the days of the week in alphabetical order is more difficult because when we encoded the names of the week into memory, we organized them chronologically (Ashcraft, 1994). We tend to retrieve information in the same way that it was encoded or stored into memory. The lesson in all of this is that the way we study should match the way we will be tested. The best way to prepare for an oral exam is to practice responding orally to possible questions. The best way to prepare for a practical exam—recognizing slides under a microscope, for instance—is to practice looking at slides under a microscope.

Information is not encoded into memory as isolated bits of data; rather, it is encoded into a "richer memory representation, one that includes any extra information about the item that was present during encoding" (Ashcraft, 1994, p. 228). The context in which you learn something serves a retrieval cue or memory prompt. For instance, if you studied the foods that make up a balanced diet by visualizing key foods in a food pyramid, then visualizing the pyramid will help you recall the names of the foods. If you paid particular attention to category names, such as grains, vegetables, fruits, milk, meat, and beans, the category names should serve as retrieval cues.

Rehearsal

Rehearsal is the process of committing information to memory. There are two kinds of rehearsal: maintenance and elaborative (Craik & Lockhart, 1972). **Maintenance rehearsal** is relatively simple. It's what you do when you look up a phone number and then punch the number in your phone's keypad. To keep the number in memory, you might repeat it two or three times. Once you stop rehearsing the number, it fades away. This simple rehearsal was enough to keep the number in working, or short-term, memory, but not strong enough to move it into long-term memory. In addition, there is the question of intentionality. Because you had no intention of retaining the number, you didn't rehearse it sufficiently or take steps to place it in long-term memory. **Elaborative rehearsal**, on the other hand, involves meaningful processes in which learners create connections between new information and information that is already known. When information is rehearsed in elaborative fashion, it is stored more deeply in the memory system.

If you are learning a list of terms such as *circumference, diameter, radius, sector, arc,* and *chord* that are used to define the parts of a circle, you might organize the words to show how they are related to each other. You might also relate the words to experiences that you have had or create a visual image in which the words are placed as labels on the key parts of the image. You might also use roots and affixes to help you better understand the meaning of each term and relate these new words to known words—relating *circumference* to *circle*, for instance. This elaborative processing creates connections with other concepts in memory and so results in more thorough storage.

Information can be processed in shallow or deep fashion. Shallow processing is similar to maintenance rehearsal. Deep processing corresponds to elaborative rehearsal. It means making meaningful connections so that the information is stored more deeply in the memory system and so is more readily retrieved. Although we sometimes remember pieces of information that were processed in shallow fashion, we are much more likely to remember information that is deeply processed (Ashcraft, 1994).

CHECKUP

1. What are the main components of memory?
2. How does memory work?

■ **Rehearsal** is the process of committing information to memory.

■ **Maintenance rehearsal** is the process of keeping information in memory by saying it over and over again or using some other low-level process.

■ **Elaborative rehearsal** is the use of meaningful processes, such as making meaningful associations or reflecting on the information, in order to keep information in memory.

Conditions That Foster Remembering

Based on what is known about the workings of memory, we can say that the following conditions foster remembering: meaningfulness, organization, imagery, associations, and metamemory.

Meaningfulness

It is part of our human nature to strive to make sense of our world. For decades, psychologists used meaningless wordlike syllables to explore the workings of memory. They employed nonsense words so that the participants would not be able to use the meaningfulness of materials as a memory aid. However, the psychologists discovered that cognition, including memory, is an active constructive process because the participants invested the nonsense syllables with meaning. For instance, they might associate the nonsense syllable *yeg* with the name *Meg*.

The more our students can build meaningfulness into their studying, the better they will be able to retain the material. For instance, a student may memorize the fact that water is denser than oil because although the oil molecules are larger, they are spread farther apart. From TV news stories about oil spills, the student knows that oil floats on water. Now she can apply that knowledge to better understand and remember that oil is not as dense as water. She can hypothesize that the oil does not sink into the water because the denser molecules of the water hold it up. By integrating new knowledge with old knowledge, she achieves a better understanding and retention of both. Later, when she reads about methods of cleaning up oil spills, she is better able to understand and remember why it is possible to scoop up the oil for a period of time after a spill. The efficiency with which we learn new information depends not just on how much we have to learn, but on how easily the new information fits in with what we already know (Carlson & Buskist, 1997).

Organization

In addition to being meaning-makers, we are also organizers. Try this: Write down the names of as many birds as you can think of within a two-minute period. Now look at your list. Chances are, it is organized in some way. You may, for instance, have placed all the song birds together and all the hunting birds together. When a researcher asked participants to learn a list of sixty items, the participants grouped the items into categories (Bousfield, 1953). The participants recalled the words in the way they had organized them. For instance, they recalled the animal names as a group and then the vegetable names as a group.

How effective is categorizing or clustering information? When information is presented in an organized fashion, students retain almost twice as much (Bower, Clark, Lesgold, & Winzenz, 1969). In one study, when 112 relatively unfamiliar terms were presented in an organized display, students learned all of them after just four presentations. When the same terms were presented in an unorganized display, the students learned just 70 percent of the words. The organized display, by the way, was presented in much the same way as semantic maps are drawn (see Figure 3.1). If there is no logical organization presented, people tend to impose a subjective organization (Tulving, 1962).

Why is organization so important? Our concepts are stored in networks. We can understand and retain new information better if we relate it to already existing concepts. For instance, if students have a well-developed schema for the French and Indian War, they are better able to understand the events that led up to the start of the Revolutionary War. By creating connections between the two wars, they can better understand why the British raised taxes on the colonies, and why some tribes sided with the British and others sided with the colonists. Comprehension is also fostered if students use the organization of the text to help them better understand and retain key ideas.

Making connections not only makes text more understandable, it also reduces the load on memory because the ideas are remembered as part of a network rather than as isolated bits of information.

Imagery

Imagery has a unique, but apparently underused, potential to foster storage of information (National Reading Panel, 2000). Imagery can add encoding power to a word. According to Paivio's dual encoding hypothesis (1971), words that refer to concrete objects can be encoded in memory twice. The word *camel*, for instance, can be retrieved from memory in two ways: It can be encoded verbally just like other word, and it can also be encoded visually as a mental picture of a camel. A word such as *truth*, however, would typically be encoded only verbally since it lacks a visual counterpart. It could be encoded visually, but it would take time to create an image.

CHECKUP

1. How do meaningfulness, organization, and imagery foster remembering?

Associations

Associational devices are used to facilitate learning when there are no basic principles underlying the information that would enable meaningful connections to be made. This occurs when relationships are arbitrary—for instance, when learning the names of presidents, formulas, or a similar type of material. Associational memory devices include rhymes, acronyms, acrostics, the keyword approach, and other mnemonic methods. They make use of information already stored in memory to help us remember new information.

Mnemonics are devices used to create artificial connections between the known and the unknown. Mnemonic devices foster memory by adding elaborations such as a visualization, a rhyme, or a series of known words. Because more information is stored, it has more retrieval hooks and so is easier to remember. Mnemonic devices are structured in such a way that remembering a part leads to retrieval of the whole; for instance, the rhyme that tells how many days there are in each month of the year is a mnemonic device—the rhythm and rhymes it contains provoke memory. Mnemonic devices follow three principles of memory: (1) the material to be learned is practiced repeatedly, (2) the material is integrated into an existing memory framework, and (3) the practice provides an excellent means of retrieving information.

Naomi James (1979), the first woman to sail around the world alone, made her voyage both longer and more dangerous when she confused the words *latitude* and *longitude*. One runs north and south, the other east and west. Can you say for sure which is which? If students know the word *lateral*, they could relate *lateral* and *latitude*. Both refer to directions that are sideways, rather than up and down. In addition, a simple mnemonic to distinguish the two words would have saved Naomi James a lot of stress: The word *longitude* has an *n* (for *north*) in it, but *latitude* does not (Pauk, 1989).

Other associational devices include reconstructive elaborations, acronyms, rhymes, acrostics, first-letter mnemonics, and narrative stories.

Reconstructive Elaborations

The key word strategy, which was introduced in Chapter 3 as a way to remember the meanings of new words, has been adapted for use with content area information in a device known as **reconstructive elaborations**. The process is reconstructive because it involves modifying a word or other information so it will be more familiar or meaningful. It is elaborative because it involves linking or elaborating pieces of information.

■ **Mnemonics** is a process to aid memory that makes use of artificial associations, such as rhymes. Mnemonics represents a deeper level of processing than simply saying an item over and over.

■ **A reconstructive elaboration** is a memory device that involves modifying and elaborating a concept to be learned in order to make it more memorable.

Thus, elaborative reconstruction fosters better recall because it improves encoding by making it more meaningful and more familiar (Mastropieri & Scruggs, 1989).

To learn the fact that deciduous trees shed their leaves in the fall, students are taught a reconstructed key word for *deciduous*. The word chosen is *decided* because it is familiar, looks like *deciduous*, and partially sounds like *deciduous*. Then, either the students or the teacher create an interactive illustration—for example, a picture of a tree that is clearly labeled as deciduous, with a statement saying, "It's fall and I'm cold, so I have decided to let my leaves fall" (Mastropieri & Scruggs, 1989, p. 342). The statement becomes the elaboration that links the word *deciduous* with the concept that leaves are dropped in the fall. Discussing the illustration helps students make the connection between the words *decided* and *deciduous* and the concept that deciduous trees drop their leaves in the fall.

In a unit on the history of highways, for instance, key terms are listed and transformed into reconstructive elaborations. For the word *eroded*, the key word *road* is chosen. The interactive illustration shows a road and a hillside that are obviously eroded. A sign in the hillside warns, "Danger: Erosion," and a person nearby says, "The road has eroded" (Mastropieri & Scruggs, 1989, p. 394). Other important terms are presented in this same way. The authors of this adaptation report that through reconstructive elaboration, students have doubled their learning and retention.

Acronyms

An **acronym** is a word composed of the first letters of a series of words to be memorized. *HOMES* is an acronym for the names of the Great Lakes: Huron, Ontario, Michigan, Erie, and Superior. In recalling the names of the Great Lakes, the student uses *HOMES* as a mnemonic aid because each letter of the acronym represents the beginning letter of one of the Great Lakes. Students are not restricted to real words; they may use made-up words or even several made-up words. For instance, *ROY G. BIV* is a mnemonic for the colors of the spectrum: Red, Orange, Yellow, Green, Blue, Indigo, and Violet.

Rhymes

Rhymes are also used to assist memory.

> Use *i* before *e* except after *c*.
> Or when sounded as *a*
> As in *neighbor* and *weigh*.

Acrostics

An **acrostic** is a sentence or rhyme in which the first letter of each word stands for the first letter in a series of words to be memorized. The sentence My Very Exceptional Mother Just Served Us Noodles is a mnemonic to assist in the retrieval of the names of the planets: Mercury, Venus, Earth, Mars, Jupiter, Saturn, Uranus, and Neptune. The acrostic Please Excuse My Dear Aunt Sally helps in remembering the order of operations in algebra problems: Parentheses, Exponents, Multiplication, Division, Addition, and Subtraction. This can be combined with a mental image of your aunt arriving late in an operating room to further aid retention (Applegate, 2001).

First-Letter Mnemonics

First-letter mnemonics uses both acronyms and acrostics to form mnemonic devices. *FIRST* is an acronym for the steps that students use to compose these devices (Bulgren, Hock, Schumaker, and Deshler, 1995):

Form a word
Insert a letter(s)
Rearrange the letters
Shape a sentence
Try combinations

Struggling Readers

Reconstructive elaboration and other memory devices have been used successfully with struggling readers and students with learning disabilities who may need more teacher guidance than achieving readers.

■ **An acronym** is a word made up of the first letter of each of a series of words.

■ **An acrostic** is a device in which the first letters in a series of words spell out a word or phrase or correspond to the first letters in another series of words to be memorized.

To form a word, the student writes down the first letter of each word to be remembered. From these letters, the student forms a word. For instance, if the student is trying to learn the three forms of matter, she might form the word *slag* for solid, liquid, and gas.

Because the list of words may not yield the letters necessary to form a word, the student can insert a letter to help. For instance, in learning the names of the main kinds of rocks—metamorphic, igneous, and sedimentary—the student might create *mis* and add an *s* to it. If, even after adding a letter, the student is still unable to form a word, he can rearrange the letters if the order of the items is not important. If nothing else works, the student can use each of the letters as the first letters of words in a mnemonic sentence. For instance, the mnemonic sentence Every Good Boy Does Fine was created as a memory aid for the notes on a musical staff: E, G, B, D, F.

If students are still unable to form a mnemonic, they can rearrange and insert letters to make up a word or sentence. For instance, for the Romance languages, which include Italian, Spanish, French, Romanian, and Portuguese, you might make up the acrostic I See Five Red Porsches.

Creating mnemonics is an excellent group activity. Because it involves a lot of planning and discussion, students report that the activity of creating mnemonics fosters retention of the material to be learned.

Creating a list of important information only works if the student knows which items are important enough that they need to be memorized. The teacher sometimes supplies a list, but often students must be able to determine a list on their own from information provided in a lesson or from the text.

How well did first-letter mnemonics work? According to Bulgren and colleagues (1995), students using first-letter mnemonics improved their test averages by 30 percentage points.

Students should be encouraged to be flexible and creative in their use of mnemonics. In some situations, mnemonics can be combined. For example the previously mentioned mnemonic device for the Great Lakes, *HOMES*, can be combined with the key word method so that students picture large homes on the Great Lakes. This adds visualization, a powerful mnemonic to verbal clues (Scruggs & Mastropieri, 1990). In another example, the acronym *TAG* can be used for the Central Powers in World War I: Turkey, Austria-Hungary, and Germany. Using key word visualization, students can imagine Turkey, Austria-Hungary, and Germany playing tag in Central Park (Mastropieri & Scruggs, 1991).

Narrative Stories

Another way to learn a list of unrelated terms is to create a story using the words. Use the first item as a story starter. Then construct a narrative that includes the other items in the order in which they are to be memorized. Putting words to be memorized in a narrative results in a significant increase in recall (Bower, Clark, Lesgold, & Winzenz, 1969).

Mnemonic devices aid memory in three main ways: (1) They supply a structure for learning, such as familiar events or a rhyme; (2) they create a durable memory by using visual images, rhyming words, or another device; and (3) they create guidance through retrieval by providing cues for recall. This characteristic is especially important because much of our forgetting is really a failure of recall. How many times have you had a fact or a person's name on the tip of your tongue while taking a test but couldn't retrieve it from memory until after the test (Ashcraft, 1994)? Although using already created mnemonic devices aids memory, creating your own can be even more beneficial. To be most effective, use of mnemonic devices must be metacognitive: The student must know when and where to use them.

CHECKUP

1. What are some associational techniques that can be used to aid memory?
2. How do associational techniques work?

Metamemory

Metamemory is our awareness of our memory processes. It is knowing how to remember. As we develop cognitively, we not only acquire information; we also learn *how* to acquire information and how to retain the information we have acquired. For instance, young children must be shown how to rehearse a series of numbers such as a phone number so as to memorize it. Lacking in metamemory, they don't see the need to rehearse. Even older students may have a limited metamemory. Researchers found that the middle school students they observed had to be shown that an association method was more effective than a repetition strategy for learning new words (Pressley, Ross, Levin, & Ghatala, 1984). An essential component of studying is having enough metacognitive awareness or metamemory to know when you have learned something and when you haven't, and, of course, knowing what steps to take if your learning has not been successful. Strategic learners realize that special effort must be made to encode information into memory and keep it there.

What is the state of your metamemory and other metacognitive skills? On a conscious level, what do you do when you realize that you are facing a difficult studying task? Do you assess the task and think of steps you might take to better understand and retain the materials for your test? Do you consciously try to make the material more understandable? Do you use visualization or create a mnemonic device? If you were to name the planets in order, would you use a mnemonic device (Ashcraft, 1994)?

CHECKUP

1. What is metamemory?
2. What role does it play in remembering?

Questions to Aid Retention

When attempting to commit information to memory, students should ask themselves the following questions, which attempt to help them form relationships between new and old learning and incorporate a variety of memory-fostering strategies:

1. How does this relate to what I already know?
2. What does it remind me of?
3. What can I associate it with?
4. Can I picture it in my mind?
5. What can I link this picture to?
6. How does it relate to the topic as a whole?
7. What crazy things pop up into my mind when I think of it?
8. How can I use crazy associations to help me remember?
9. How does this relate to what I learned before?
10. How does it relate to my life outside this class? (Devine, 1987, p. 302)

Using Quizzes to Foster Retention

Although primarily used for evaluation, quizzes can be a device for fostering retention of material (Pashler et al., 2007). Quizzes should contain items such as filling in the blanks or constructed responses that require retrieval of information. Taking a test can be more effective than spending extra time studying because the act of recalling information to answer a question helps to establish it in memory. The quiz can be in a game-like format and it can be an informal quiz—it doesn't have to count toward a grade. Corrective feedback should be provided; otherwise, incorrect information will be retained.

CHECKUP

1. How do questions and quizzes aid retention?

■ Metamemory is our awareness of our memory processes. It is knowing how to remember.

SQ3R: A Research-Based Study System

A five-step technique known as **SQ3R**—Survey, Question, Read, Recite, and Review—implements many of the principles presented in the previous section (Robinson, 1970). In use for more than half a century, it is the most thoroughly researched study technique in the English language (Caverly & Orlando, 1991; Caverly, Orlando, & Mullen, 2000). SQ3R is based on the following principles:

- Surveying headings and summaries increases speed of reading, helps students remember the text, and provides an overview of the text.
- Asking a question before reading each section improves comprehension.
- Reciting from memory immediately after reading fosters retention. When students in one study were asked questions after they had read a selection, they were able to answer only about half of them (Robinson, 1970). After just one day, 50 percent of what they had learned was forgotten. Students were then able to answer just 25 percent of questions asked about a text. However, those who recited after reading the material had a retention rate of more than 80 percent one day later. In another study, students who spent 20 percent of their time reading and 80 percent reciting were able to answer twice as many questions as those who simply read the material (Gates, 1917). The 20-80 rule works best with fact-laden material. For biographies and similar materials, 60-40 would be sufficient. The denser the materials are, the shorter the segment of text that should be read before reciting.

Recitation is probably the most important step in SQ3R, and it fulfills a number of functions. First of all, recitation is metacognitive. It lets you know how well you have understood the material. The more you can recite, the better your understanding of the material. It also leads you to repair comprehension problems on the spot. If you can't recite, you know that you have to reread. Recitation is also motivational. You will read each section a little more purposively because you know that you will be reciting at the end of the section. Being able to recite is a reward (Pauk, 1989).

- Comprehending major ideas and noting relationships among ideas aids comprehension and retention.
- Engaging in brief review sessions and relating information to personal needs and interests foster comprehension and retention.

SQ3R prepares students to read and helps them organize, elaborate, and rehearse information from text. In addition, SQ3R is metacognitive. It leads students to establish goals for studying, directs them to assess whether those goals are being met, and leads them to modify their processing if they haven't learned the material they set out to learn (Caverly, Orlando, & Mullen, 2000).

Applying SQ3R

1. *Survey.* Survey the chapter that you are about to read to get an overall picture of what it is about. Glance over the title and headings. Quickly read the overview and summary. Note the main ideas. (You might also want to predict what you think the chapter or section will be about.) This quick survey will give you a framework for organizing the information in the chapter as you read it.
2. *Question.* Turn each heading into a question. The heading "Events Leading Up to World War I" would become "What events led up to World War I?" Answering the question you created gives you a purpose for reading. (Textbook headings do not always lend themselves to questions or may even be misleading about the content that follows. If you find this to be so, change your question.)
3. *Read.* Read to answer the question that you posed: What events led up to World War I? If the question doesn't work out, change it to one that does.

■ SQ3R is a five-step study technique: Survey, Question, Read, Recite, Review.

4. *Recite.* When you come to the end of the section, stop and test yourself. Try to answer your question. If you cannot, go back over the section and then try once again to answer the question. The answer may be oral or written. However, a written answer is preferable because it is more active, it forces you to summarize what you have learned, and the response can be used for review later on. Use a two-column note system, with the question in the left column and the answer in the right column. The answer should also be brief; otherwise, SQ3R takes up too much time. Do not take notes until you have completed the entire section because it will interrupt your reading and could interfere with your understanding. Repeat steps 2, 3, and 4 until the entire selection has been read.

5. *Review.* When you have finished the assignment, spend a few minutes reviewing what you read. If you took notes, cover them up. Then, asking yourself the questions you created from the headings, try to recall the major points that support the headings. Check your responses by looking at your notes. The review helps you put information together and remember it longer.

In general, special elements should be treated in the same way as text. For graphs, tables, and maps, turn the title into a question and use the information to answer the question (Robinson, 1970). A diagram may be as important as the text and merits special effort. After examining the diagram carefully, students should try to draw it from memory and then compare their drawings with the diagram in the book (Robinson, 1970). Drawing becomes a form of recitation.

Adaptations of SQ3R

Over the years, numerous adaptations have been made to SQ3R. A step that several practitioners advocate adding is *reflecting* (Pauk, 1989; Thomas & Robinson, 1972; Vacca & Vacca, 1986). After reading, students are encouraged to think about the material and how they might use it. Vacca and Vacca (1986) also recommend that before reading, students reflect on what they already know about the topic.

Teaching SQ3R

To use SQ3R fully, students should be able to generate main ideas. It also helps if they have some knowledge of text structures (Caverly, Orlando, & Mullen, 2000; Walker, 1995). Teaching SQ3R requires a commitment of time and effort. Each step must be taught carefully, with ample opportunity provided for practice and application. Early and Sawyer (1984) recommended spending at least a semester when presenting it to older students. Even high school students may need ten hours of instruction or more (Caverly, Orlando, & Mullen, 2000). SQ3R requires periodic review and reteaching even after it has been taught carefully and practiced conscientiously.

When teaching SQ3R, build on what students already know about reading and studying. Chances are, they have already been taught to survey and generate questions and to read to answer those questions. Begin with easy, well-structured content selections. Although you can teach SQ3R in a few sessions, learning to apply the technique might take months.

Have conferences with students periodically to discuss their application of SQ3R. At that time, go over their SQ3R notes. Since studying is idiosyncratic, allow individual adaptations of SQ3R.

A key factor in the success of any study technique is attitude. Using SQ3R or another study system requires hard work and active involvement on the part of the students. Passively reading and even rereading material is much easier. Students need to see how the extra effort is paying off in their learning more material and earning higher grades. You also need to help students streamline the technique so there is no wasted effort.

Another key element is the attitude of the teacher. If the teacher believes that SQ3R will help students learn more from the text and conveys that message, students are more likely to use the strategy. For instance, Landy, a high school chemistry teacher, felt that SQ3R was an excellent aid for helping her students read their highly technical chemistry

 Struggling Readers

Although all students can benefit from learning a study strategy such as SQ3R, struggling readers stand to benefit the most because they often do not have effective study strategies.

text (Moje, 1996). She carefully introduced SQ3R and also made its use a part of students' homework assignments. They took SQ3R notes as they read and discussed them in class the next day. Since they were keeping three-column notes, they used the extra column to take class notes. Students used SQ3R regularly and believed that it helped them read a difficult text with understanding. Describing her use of SQ3R, one student commented:

> I think it reinforces what I know. . . . I think it's the actual steps that help, because what I do is I make up questions. . . . And I just make sure I answer the questions I made. That makes sure that I know what I read. (Moje, 1996, p. 184)

A second student commented:

> I use the SQ3R because it helps when I write things down. . . . The process helps because then I know exactly what I'm supposed to know or write down. It's the way you're supposed to do it for this class. I know this is the best way for this material. I trust Ms. Landy. (Moje, 1996, p. 187)

Note that part of the second student's motivation for using the strategy was that she trusted her teacher. She also implied that SQ3R worked for subjects like chemistry. A heavy-duty study system, SQ3R is probably most effective when students are reading very difficult, fact-packed texts. Students who used SQ3R for chemistry did not use it when reading for English class. Students will not automatically transfer the use of a study strategy. Each content area teacher must show how a strategy can be used in a particular domain and must encourage its use.

If you are a content area teacher, you might want to team up with the reading teacher. Perhaps the reading teacher will introduce the technique and you can show students how to apply the technique to your content area text.

CHECKUP

1. What are the steps in SQ3R?
2. How might SQ3R be taught?

Providing Judicious Review

Teachers can enhance the impact of students' studying through judicious review. For initial learning, Nuthall's (1999) research indicates that three of four varied presentations or experiences are necessary. Presentations should be within two days of each other. Otherwise, the concepts being developed are likely to fade away. After being developed, these concepts should be reviewed. The reviews should be spaced according to how long the information is to be retained. The longer the information is to be retained, the greater the spacing of the reviews. Rohrer and Pashler (2010) recommend that the interval between initial learning presentations and review should be approximately 5 to 10 percent of the time that the information has to be retained. (However, the spacing should not be so long that the information is forgotten.) If the information has to be retained for 60 days, then the reviews should not be scheduled for at least three to six days (5% × 60 days or 10% × 60 days).

Does the delay make much difference? In a study of eighth-grade history classes in which students were charged with memorizing a series of facts on which they were tested nine months later, the group that reviewed the facts after 16 weeks did twice as well as the group that reviewed the facts after just one week (Carpenter, Pashler, Cepeda, & Alvarez, 2007). Materials should be reviewed several weeks and also several months after their initial learning. This can be done in a variety of ways: schedule periodic review sessions; use homework to review material; and schedule cumulative quizzes, midterms, and finals as a way of reviewing materials. By making these assessments cumulative, review is fostered.

CHECKUP

1. How does timing affect estimating how much one knows and the scheduling of reviews?
2. How should reviews be scheduled?

Notetaking

Pretend that you are back in high school or middle school. Picture this: An experienced notetaker comes into your class and takes careful, well-organized notes and posts them on the Web, where they can be downloaded for free. The notes are neat and well organized. Sound like a fantasy? At some universities, students can obtain on the Web notes compiled by professional notetakers (Steinberg, 1999). Although the notes supplied might be somewhat better organized and neater than those taken by the average student, there is a problem. Notetaking serves two functions. First, it supplies students with a record of essential ideas that would otherwise be forgotten. The professional notes do quite well in this regard. However, notetaking leads students to select the most important information and organize it, which fosters comprehension and retention of material. Notetaking also makes students more active learners. Students who buy or download notes are cheating themselves of a learning opportunity. Not surprisingly, students who took their own notes did better than those who used the notes of others.

Notetaking promotes selective attention. Through taking notes, students are more likely to focus on main ideas. Notetaking also fosters the integration of new information with old information, especially if students are taking notes from oral or written text in their own words and not simply copying (Cook & Mayer, 1988). Like any other learning strategy, the more students put into notetaking, the more they get out of it. The most basic and least beneficial form of notetaking is simply copying from the text. More elaborated forms include putting the text ideas into one's own words, showing hierarchical and other relationships, and including one's own ideas. "The farther students move along the continuum from verbatim to elaborated notes, the greater the benefit they receive" (Smith & Tompkins, 1988, p. 46).

CHECKUP

1. What are the characteristics of effective notetaking?
2. What are the benefits of effective notetaking?

The Four Main Notetaking Skills

Taking notes involves four skill areas: selectivity, organization, consolidation, and fluency. *Selectivity* means choosing the most important information. Students generally record only 50 percent to 70 percent of the main ideas given in a lecture, with most students being closer to the 50 percent mark (Anderson & Armbruster, 1984). You can increase this percentage by signaling important details in your lectures.

Organization involves showing how ideas are related so supporting details and examples fall under the main idea. One method of improving organization is to encourage students to take two-column notes. Questions or cue words in the column on the left organize the details in the column on the right and can even be used to show cause-effect, opinion-proof, and other relationships.

Consolidation entails selecting the most important information and putting it in a telegraphic style so that only the most important and most necessary words are included. In general, when taking lecture notes, students should not attempt to put information in their own words because this will detract from their attempts to record the most important information (Pauk, 1989). Modeling notetaking and discussing finished products are effective ways to improve consolidation.

Fluency in taking notes is enhanced by all of the above, especially consolidation, along with use of symbols and abbreviations. Students should be encouraged to use some of the same abbreviations and symbols that they use when texting. Some frequently used notetaking symbols and abbreviations include:

w = *with*   & = *and*   b = *but*

Notetaking Tips

Here are some tips that students can use to improve their notetaking.

- Write a dash and leave room for information that they didn't have time to write. This can be filled in later.
- Write question marks for anything they don't understand. Refer to the text or get help from the teacher to clear up any confusion.
- Use an asterisk to signal information that is especially important—for instance, an item that the teacher announces will appear on the upcoming test.
- Use two columns for vocabulary. Put the new word in the left column and the definition in the right.
- Make sure to include sample problems, charts, diagrams, or other visuals.
- Make sure all notes have dates and headings.

Despite the importance and universality of taking notes, even the best students vary greatly in the quantity and quality of their notes. An analysis of notes taken by tenth-graders in an advanced placement history class revealed that notes ranged from extensive near-verbatim notes to restatements of main ideas to sketchy telegraphic notes (Armbruster, 1996). If students are having difficulty taking notes, ask to see samples and analyze their performance. Figure out where they are having difficulty and provide help accordingly (Heiman & Slomianko, 1986).

CHECKUP

1. What are the four main notetaking skills?
2. What are some tips for effective notetaking?

Taking Notes from Text

Taking notes from text is easier than taking lecture notes. Today's content area texts often have an overview and headings and subheadings that help students organize information. And, of course, printed materials are easier to deal with because they don't disappear the way spoken words do. Following is a sample lesson for teaching students to take notes from text.

LESSON 7.1

Notetaking

Step 1: Explain the purpose and value of notes. Draw from experiences students have had taking notes and discuss ways in which taking notes has helped them. Also discuss some difficulties they have had taking notes. If students have just started taking notes for academic purposes, talk about everyday experiences that they may have had, such as jotting down phone messages. Using a well-designed segment from a text that contains headings and subheadings and that students are required to study, demonstrate how you would take notes.

Step 2: Show students how you survey the whole chapter to get an overview, make predictions based on the overview, and activate prior knowledge. Also demonstrate how you establish a goal and set a purpose. (The goal is the reason for reading—for example, to prepare for a test or class discussion on the Constitution. The purpose is to find specific information or to answer a question: What led up to the creation of the Constitution?) Self-prompts that might be used include:

What is this all about? (survey)

What do I know about this? (prior knowledge)

Why am I reading this? (goal)

What do I want to find out? (overall purpose)

Step 3: Explain that headings announce main topics. Turn each heading into a question just as was done with SQ3R. Explain how you read to answer that question. (As noted in the section on SQ3R, remind students that headings are sometimes misleading. The section following the heading might not develop the topic announced by the heading, or it may contain additional information. The reader must be flexible and create questions that are answered by the text. This means they might have to read the section first and then compose a question about the text content. For initial demonstrations, however, seek out text that has appropriate headings.)

Step 4: Think aloud so students can see that as you read the section, you keep your question in mind, but read flexibly. Show that you are prepared to change the question if necessary. Emphasize that you do not take any notes until you have finished reading the section. Taking notes while reading interrupts the process and results in including too many details in the notes.

Step 5: Still thinking aloud, show students how you record your notes. Explain that at first you try to answer the question without looking back at the text, just as you did with SQ3R. After jotting down your notes, which is a form of recitation, reread them to see if you have included all the important information. If not, go back to the text to locate and record missing details. Stress the need to be selective. Only essential information should be recorded. Otherwise, you will be overwhelmed with details. Notes should be written in abbreviated form to save time—but not be so abbreviated that they don't make any sense when you return to study them. Take notes on illustrations as well as text, especially if important information is presented only visually. Include key illustrations, such as the parts of a cell, in the notes.

Step 6: Review. Show students how you go over all the notes once you have finished so that you get a complete picture of the information. Explain that writing a brief summary of your notes for a section of text will help fix all of the most important information in your mind; it is also excellent preparation for an essay test. Demonstrate how you might quickly compose a summary.

Explain to students that it is best for them to master one section at a time because then they will be better prepared to understand the next section. Follow up with opportunities for the class to take notes on some sample sections of content area text, under your guidance.

CHECKUP

1. What are the steps in teaching students to take notes from text?

Structured Notetaking

One way to ease into notetaking is to provide structure for students. For instance, if they are taking notes on a text assignment, you might set up the questions or topics in the left column and perhaps some of the details in the second column, as shown in Figure 7.1. As they become more proficient, you can gradually withdraw the support. Students might also use graphic organizers, such as webs, frames, or Venn diagrams, to take notes.

Lecture Notes

Because of the transitory nature of speech, taking notes from lectures is more difficult than taking notes from text. In addition, the organization of the information in a lecture

FIGURE 7.1
Structured Notetaking

Requirements for National Office

President	1. Must be 35
	2.
	3.
	4.
Senate	1. Must be 30
	2.
	3.
	4.
House of Rep.	1. Must be 25
	2.
	3.
	4.

is not as apparent as it would be in an informational text containing heads and subheads. Students are in a better position to take notes if they have read the chapter for the day's topic the night before and therefore have some knowledge to bring to the class. This will help them organize their notes and determine which information is essential enough to be recorded. If students paraphrase or elaborate on the notes, this will aid comprehension and retention, as will the use of visuals and graphics to illustrate notes. Students should pay particular attention to any items that the instructor highlights on the board or shows on the overhead such as technical vocabulary, formulas, and figures.

Assisted Notetaking

If students are novice notetakers or have difficulty taking notes, provide practice. Present short, well-structured lectures and provide students with a partial sketch of the lecture notes. You might provide the major topics of the lecture and two of the three subtopics for each and have students add the missing elements. Two-column notes, as explained below, are recommended. Topics would be written in the left column and supporting details in the right.

Using cueing techniques is also helpful. Tell students what the main idea of the lecture is, or write it on the board. Also, use signal words to indicate the number of details: "There are three main kinds of rocks." "There are six kinds of nutrients." "Here are the four main effects of that law." Arrange lecture notes into categories so students can make use of the organization and write important terminology or information on the board or in a PowerPoint. Also, summarize your lectures and pause occasionally to give students time to catch up.

If students are in the early stages of learning to take notes, stop after a brief interval and discuss the notes they have taken. Periodically collect notes and provide feedback as needed so their notetaking becomes more effective and efficient. Also, have students compare their notes with those of a partner to make sure that main points have been recorded (Boyle, 2007). They can read their notes to each other so there is no embarrassment because of bad handwriting or poor spelling. Based on any differences in the content of their notes, the partners can decide to make changes. Scheduling a review of notes at the end of the lecture also gives students a chance to make sure they have recorded essential information. Over time, have students take increased responsibility for taking notes if you are certain they have the ability to distinguish important from unimportant information. Independent notetaking should not be undertaken by students who are unable to identify main ideas (Santa, Abrams, & Santa, 1979) because "they will tend to take verbatim notes of irrelevant concepts" (Caverly & Orlando, 1991, p. 121).

Source: Shutterstock.

Successful studying combines positive attitudes, good work habits, and effective strategies.

1. What are some techniques that might be used to help students learn to take lecture notes?

The Cornell Notetaking System

There are a number of systems for taking notes. In a typical system, students use indentations or an outline format to show the relative importance of ideas. Other systems use two or three columns to record notes, with the extra columns being used to write names of topics or key words, comments, questions, or notes on the same topic from other sources. One of the best known of the multicolumn notetaking procedures is the Cornell system. Widely used for nearly half a century, the **Cornell notetaking system** is more than just a way of arranging notes in two or three columns (Pauk, 1989). It is a series of well-thought-out strategies for learning comprising six steps.

Step 1: Record

On a sheet of paper turned to a landscape orientation, divide the paper into two columns, the first 2-1/2 inches wide and the second 6 inches wide. The student records telegraphic style notes in the second column, using indentations to show the relative importance of information.

Step 2: Reduce or Question

As soon as possible after taking notes, the student should add missing information, clarify confused information, and rewrite portions that might be unclear. Then, she should reread her notes, run through the lecture in her mind, and reduce each major idea to key words or phrases, which are written in the left column. These key words or phrases become cues to ideas and details written in the right column. As an alternative to recording key words, the student may elect to create questions that encompass major ideas in the notes.

Step 3: Recite

Using a blank sheet of paper, the student covers up the notes in the right column and uses the key words or questions to quiz herself on the material. She should state the questions and the answers out loud. Items that she has difficulty answering should be checked. She should also recite in her own words. Translating information into one's own words requires deeper processing and understanding and increases retention. Reciting increases retention of material fourfold (Pauk, 1989).

Step 4: Reflect

The student thinks about the information in her notes, tries to relate it to what she already knows about the topic and considers ways in which she might apply the information. She asks such questions as: What are the main ideas and most important facts? How does this information fit in with what I already know? How might I use this information? Through reflection, she integrates new information with old and personalizes it.

Step 5: Recapitulation

The student writes a brief summary of her notes. In addition to providing a review, this helps her highlight essential information.

Step 6: Review

The student periodically reviews her notes.

A third column of notes might be used when students are combining lecture and text notes (Pauk, 1989). The notetaking page is set up with a 2-1/2-inch column and two 3-inch columns. Lecture notes are recorded in the center. Questions or cue words are written in the left-hand column. Notes from the text are written in the right-hand column. The notes from the lecture and the text are aligned with the question or cue words in the first column, as shown in Figure 7.2. Summarizing three-column notes is especially important because it provides an opportunity for students to integrate information from the text with information from lectures. Instead of being used as a way of combining lecture and text notes, the third column can be used to record key vocabulary words, raise questions, or make comments.

 Struggling Readers

If students are having difficulty taking notes, ask to see samples and analyze their performance. Note where they are having difficulty and provide help as needed.

■ In the Cornell notetaking system, students record notes in one column and comments, questions, or key vocabulary in a second column.

Exemplary Teaching

Taking Notes

Learning specialist Carol Josel (1997) was not surprised when her eight-grade students at Arcola Intermediate School in Norristown, Pennsylvania, asked her to repeat her lecture on Bunker Hill because they weren't able to get it all down, even though she had spoken at a slower-than-usual pace. Never having been taught how to take notes, the students had attempted to write down and spell out every word of the lecture—an impossible task. Josel's first step was to teach them how to use abbreviations. (Used to texting, most of today's students should have no difficulty with this aspect of notetaking.) She gave another brief lecture and then showed them her notes, which contained only the essentials and had lots of abbreviations. With Josel's modeling and some practice, her students became confident, proficient notetakers.

Adapting Notetaking to Fit the Discipline

Generic systems of notetaking should be adapted to fit the nature of the discipline being studied. In math, for instance, students might use an adapted version of three-column notes. In the first column students write the big idea being studied; in the second column, they explain the idea; and in the third column, they place a formula, diagram, or graph. Definitions should be precise (Shanahan & Shanahan, 2008).

CHECKUP

1. What is the Cornell notetaking system, and what are its advantages?
2. What are the steps in the Cornell notetaking system?

FIGURE 7.2 Three-Column Notes

U.S. History, Panama Canal, Oct 23	Lecture Notes	Text Notes

How did US get rights to build Pan Canal?	Polit Backgd.
	  Pan. Part of Colum.
	  Pan. wanted indep.
	  T. Roos, helped Pan.
	  Made deal with Pan.
		Treaty with Pan favored US
		Gave US control of canal
		Canal returned to Pan. 12-14-99

What were the problems encountered in building the canal?	Build. of Canal
	  1880s French group tried.
	  Gave up.
		Had heat, disease, & engine problems
		Lost more than 20,000 men
		
		US wiped out yel. fev. & red. malaria

What was the cost of building the canal?	US start can. in 1904 Fin. 1914 Lost 5,000 men Cost 380 mil.	
What were the benefits of the canal?	US ships no longer had to sail around S. Amer. to get from east part of US to west & vice versa. Made trip from coast to coast shorter.	Before can., ship going from NY to SF had to go 18,000 + miles After can, 5,200 miles
	Trip from east US to Hawaii, China, & Japan shorter.	14,000 + ships use can. each yr.
	Navy ships could go from Atl to Pacif or Pacif to Atl more easily	Too small for v lrg ships like sup carriers

Other Forms of Notetaking

Graphic organizers and techniques such as KWL Plus, frame matrices, and information maps, which were covered in Chapter 5, can also be used to record notes.

Technology and Notetaking

Many digital programs and electronic devices have notetaking features. Even without these features, students can electronically copy text from online references and Web sites unless it is in a form that prohibits copying. This makes taking notes easier. However, students must be careful to put copied material in quotes and to copy the source of the material. One disadvantage of electronic notetaking is that if students put less of the material in their own words, they won't process it as deeply. Encourage students to paraphrase and summarize along with cutting and pasting. Also discuss when it is best to paraphrase and summarize and when it is best to cut and paste. If students paraphrase or elaborate on the notes, this will aid comprehension and retention.

USING TECHNOLOGY

NoteStar http://notestar.4teachers.org
NoteStar assists in taking notes from online sources. Source information (title, URL, etc.) is automatically recorded in order to assist in work citation. Less writing is involved because students may cut and paste from text. The teacher can use NoteStar to view students' work and e-mail comments.

Outlining

Outlining is a highly effective aid to comprehension, studying, and planning because it requires that students note the relative importance and interrelationship of major and supporting details. However, outlining is also a difficult skill to learn. As Anderson and Armbruster (1984) observed, "A potential problem with outlining as a study aid is that it is very time consuming to think through the logical relationships in text and represent the meaning in outline form" (p. 673).

As with other study skills, find out what students already know about outlining. To assess their knowledge, you might ask them to outline a brief, well-organized selection. After analyzing the results, build on what they know. Emphasize the importance of determining the relative importance of ideas rather than the formatting of an outline. You might also take advantage of the outlining capacity of word processing programs. In Microsoft Word, students' text can be displayed in correctly formatted outline form, and they can rearrange their headings and subheadings.

To introduce or review outlining, explain the value of this technique and show examples of various kinds of outlines. Discuss how the table of contents in a book is a kind of outline of main topics that encompasses up to three levels. Note that the headings in a book can be used to construct an outline. Demonstrate how you might create an outline for a brief, highly organized selection. Start with a three-level outline and gradually move to one that has more subdivisions. Guide the class as they construct group outlines for text that they have read.

After constructing group outlines, have students complete partially finished outlines, as in Figure 7.3. You might start with a three-level outline in which all the main ideas and most of the supporting details have been recorded. All the students need to do is record the missing details. In future practice outlines, students should be responsible for adding a greater proportion of details, until they reach a point where they are adding all the details. Then have them complete outlines in which details are provided but some of the main ideas are missing.

As an alternative to full outlining, have students create simple outlines in which they are given a proposition and asked to list supporting details, or are given some pros and cons and asked to list additional pros and cons, or are given a cause and requested to list effects, as is shown in Figure 7.4.

CHECKUP

1. What are the advantages and disadvantages of outlining?
2. How might outlining be presented?

FIGURE 7.3
Incomplete Outline

Parts of Plants Eaten as Vegetables

I. Roots	IV. Flowers	VII.
A. Carrots	A. Broccoli	A. Corn
B. Beets	B.	B. Peas
II. Stems	V. Fruits	C. Beans
A.	A. Tomatoes	VIII. Tubers
B. Rhubarb	B. Cucumbers	A. Potatoes
III. Leaves	C. Eggplants	B. Turnips
A. Spinach	VI. Bulbs	
B. Kale	A.	
C.	B. Garlic	

Power Thinking

Another alternative to the use of formal outlines is **power thinking**, which is a way of showing the relationship among central and important details (Santa, Havens, & Maycumber, 1996). All main ideas are preceded by a 1; second-level or supporting ideas by a 2; third-level details, which are those that support the second-level ideas, by a 3; and so on. For most texts, three levels will encompass all the essential information. Power thinking is outlining without the emphasis on formatting.

By eliminating the concern about whether the subhead should be preceded by an uppercase or lowercase *a*, the focus is placed on showing the hierarchy of ideas and the organization of the piece. It also provides a way of signaling the relative importance of ideas. A power 1 is a main idea. A power 2 supports the main idea. A power 3 supports a

■ Power thinking is a way of outlining that doesn't require knowledge of outlining format.

FIGURE 7.4
Informal Outline

Convenience Foods

Pros	Save time
	Save work
	Need less work space and equipment to prepare
Cons	Cost more
	May not be as nutritious
	May have additives
	May not taste as good as homemade foods

The Mexican War

Causes of Mexican War	Mexico was against Texas becoming a part of US.
	After Texas was annexed, there was a boundary dispute.
	Mexico owed US citizens money.
	People in US were eager to expand.
	US cavalry was defeated by Mexican forces in disputed land. Polk used this as a reason to ask Congress to declare war.
Effects of Mexican War	Rio Grande became southern boundary of Texas.
	US paid 15 million for Calif, Utah, Nevada, & parts of Arizona, Colorado, & New Mexico.

power 2 and so forth. If you tell students that you are talking about a power 1 idea, they know you are talking about a main idea. If you say that certain ideas are power 2 ideas, students know those ideas are supporting details. Recommended in CRISS, an exemplary program for teaching content area reading (Santa et al., 1996), power thinking has been used successfully by thousands of students. Power thinking has two major rules. The structure must be parallel; all 1s must be equal in power, as must all 2s and 3s and so forth. The powers must be arranged hierarchically in terms of their inclusiveness such that power 1s include power 2s and power 2s include power 3s.

To demonstrate power thinking, start with readily definable categories from your subject matter area, such as transportation, types of food, or parts of the nervous system. Here is how the category of cats might be arranged. Note that, as in traditional outlining, subpowers are indented so that indentations are indicators of the relative importance of ideas.

1 Cats
   2 Wild
      3 Big cats
         4 Lions
         4 Tigers
         4 Cheetahs
         4 Leopards
      3 Small cats
         4 Bobcat
         4 Lynx
         4 Ocelot
         4 Wildcat
   2 Domestic
      3 Calico
      3 Tabby
      3 Manx
      3 Siamese
         4 Blue point
         4 Seal point

To introduce the concept of power thinking, place the power thinking analysis of cats on the board, but don't include all the 3s and 4s. Explain to students that power thinking is a way of organizing ideas that will help them better understand how main ideas and supporting details are related. Describe power 1s, power 2s, and so on. If students are familiar with outlining, explain that this is a form of outlining. To involve them in the exercise, ask them to help fill in some 3s and 4s. Stress the need to maintain parallel structure. After the power outline has been completed, do several outlines cooperatively until students have mastered the concept and format of power thinking.

Provide students with blueprints of increasingly complex power outlines. Easy exercises will contain a two-level power thinking outline. Provide lines indicating where the 1s and 2s should be placed, and fill in the 1s. Have students fill in the 2s from a list provided. Gradually work into more complex pieces in which students have to list 2s, 3s, and 4s, or, if they are given 2s, 3s, and 4s, they have to list the 1s.

Apply power thinking to text. Drawing well-constructed examples from materials students are reading, show how the 1s, 2s, and 3s might be used to show relationships among ideas. Using duplicated copies of the selection, have students put a 1 next to power 1 ideas, 2 next to power 2 ideas, and so on. Or have students complete a power thinking outline, either individually or as a group. Cut up well-structured paragraphs and ask students to arrange the cut-up details into power thinking outline form.

 Struggling Readers

Power thinking helps students focus on relationships among ideas, especially main ideas and supporting details.

💻 **USING TECHNOLOGY**

If students are using mobile electronic devices or a computer, they might download an app such as Swipe Study www.swipestudy.com that has electronic cards of key terms or other items already prepared or that can be used to create study cards.

Use naturally occurring opportunities to reinforce the concept of the hierarchical organization of details. After students have read a passage, ask them what the power 1 idea is and what the power 2 ideas that support it are. When students are writing a paragraph, ask them what power 2 ideas they will use to support their power 1 idea.

CHECKUP
---

1. What is power thinking?
2. Why might it be more effective than traditional outlining?

Study Cards

One way of committing technical terms, dates, formulas, and other important information to memory is to use study cards. Students put the item to be learned—the word *monarch*, for instance—on one side and information about the item on the other (Moore, Moore, Cunningham, & Cunningham, 1992). The information could be a definition or the word used in a sentence or both. Or it could be a reconstructed, interactive image: Queen Elizabeth riding on a monorail, with a caption stating, "The monarch rode the monorail." The student might also note that *mono* means "one" and *arch* means "ruler," so that *monarch* means "one ruler."

Cards can be color coded to show similarities in information to be learned. For instance, in chemistry, the molecular formulas of ions are organized by charge: Ions with one negative charge are recorded on a particular color card, ions with two negative charges are recorded on another color, and so on. So that students don't forget which color refers to which group of ions, they might use the color whose name comes first alphabetically (blue) to indicate one ion, the next color (green) two ions, the next color (orange) three ions and so on. By calling attention to the ion variable, color coding helps in encoding and retention of the information (Hurst, 2001).

Some biology tests require students to identify slides of cells, cell structures, or parts of the anatomy. The diagram or figure from the lab book or textbook can be photocopied in reduced form so that it fits on a flash card. Students can make two copies, one with the terms that identify the structures intact and one in which they have been omitted. One copy is pasted on one side of the card; the other copy is pasted on the reverse side. To test themselves, students try to identify the structures whose labels have been omitted. They check their responses by turning the card over to the side that contains the labels (Landsberger, 2001). Study cards for other kinds of diagrams can be created this same way.

Putting lists of words to be memorized in alphabetical order can be helpful. For instance, the major systems of the human body are: the circulatory, musculoskeletal, endocrine, reproductive, digestive, lymphatic, respiratory, excretory, and nervous systems. When put in alphabetical order, the list contains two series of consecutive letter combinations, *c-d-e* and *l-m-n*, plus *r* (Landsberger, 2001).

When presenting study cards, model and discuss how you would choose items to include and how you might decide what kinds of information to write on the other side of the card. Also model how you would study the cards. You might, for instance, attempt to identify the word on the card. Then check your response. If correct, put it on the pile on the right. If incorrect, see why it's wrong and put it on the pile on the left for further study. Stress the need for review.

It's a good idea, too, to have sessions of guided practice with students studying with partners so you can help them make the most of their efforts. You can post prompts on a poster to remind students of this and other study procedures. Moore, Moore, Cunningham, and Cunningham (1992) posted the following suggestions for using study cards:

1. Identify important terms.
2. Record one term on one side of a card and memory aids on the other.
3. Review the cards regularly. (p. 94)

In research on paired associates learning conducted by the Center on Research for Learning (Lenz, Deshler, & Kissam, 2004), struggling learners created and used study cards on which a test question was written on one side and the paired associate with its mnemonic device was written on the other. Before using the strategy, students got an average of 13 percent of the items on a quiz correct. After students mastered the strategy, their average score was 85 percent.

Items to be learned can be put on a single sheet of paper instead of on cards. That way, lists of related items can be assembled. For instance, the student might put on one list all the words that pertain to maps. The paper might be folded in two, with the words to be learned in the left column and definitions or other identifying information on the right. The student could self-test by folding the paper and attempting to recite the definitions while looking just at the words and then unfolding the paper to check responses.

CHECKUP

1. How might study cards or sheets be used?

Importance of Practice

Practice is essential for a number of reasons. First, practice enables students to reach a certain level of competence. With practice, a student can learn to write a simple essay that contains a beginning, a middle, and an end. Practice also fosters extended development of a skill. With extensive practice, a student can learn to write a fully developed essay that has an interesting beginning and memorable conclusion (Willingham, 2009).

Practice also makes skills automatic. Once we have learned a skill or strategy, we need to keep on practicing it until it becomes automatic. Working memory only has so much capacity. If, as we read, we are focused on using a newly learned strategy such as making predictions, the strategy takes up a portion of our working memory and so less capacity is available for comprehending the passage. If, however, we have practiced the strategy of predicting so that it is automatic, then all of our working memory is available for comprehending.

Periodic practice also aids retention. If reviews are spaced, the skills or information learned are retained longer. Because it deepens understanding and awareness, practice also fosters transfer to new situations. If students work a number of varied problems with a similar structure, they will be more likely to be able to work a new problem with a different surface structure but the same underlying structure as the earlier problems (Willingham, 2009).

To be effective, practice must meet certain requirements (Willingham, 2009). Effective practice requires both intentionality and feedback. Intentionality means that you want to improve and are taking steps to do so. Practice also requires feedback from a knowledgeable source who can let you know when you need to make adjustments or move on to a higher level. I engaged in effective practice when I served as a staff writer on an educational periodicala number of years ago. I decided to learn how to write in a journalistic style and wrote several articles each week. I received frequent expert feedback from editors and co-workers. As I implemented their corrective feedback, my writing gradually improved.

Distributed Versus Massed Practice

In general, short, spaced study sessions are more effective than long ones, especially when students are memorizing information. Periodic reviews also lessen forgetting. Spacing studying over a number of sessions is known as **distributed practice** and works better than massed practice when the students are engaged in such rote learning tasks as learning chemical formulas or memorizing the names of the bones in the leg. It is easier to

■ **Distributed practice** is studying or doing practice exercises at intervals.

focus and concentrate for brief periods of time. **Massed practice**, or studying for extended periods of time, is more effective when the task has a wholeness, such as reading an essay or writing a report, in which the train of thought would be lost if it were segmented into several separate sessions. Massed practice is also known as *cramming*.

Overlearning

Students may not be aware of how much studying is required in order to learn a list of new words or several concepts thoroughly. They may lack a criterion for success. They may simply rehearse a series of words for ten minutes and stop. Instead, they should continue to study until they know the words. If they are aware of the principle of overlearning, they will continue to study even after they know the words. **Overlearning** entails continuing to study even after information can be recited. The purpose of overlearning is to reduce forgetting. In one experiment, participants had to repeat a list thirty-two times before they could recite it perfectly. However, when the group recited the list thirty-two more times for a total of sixty-four recitations, they remembered it twice as well (Ashcraft, 1994). In another experiment, participants who simply studied a list of words until they could say them perfectly remembered less than 25 percent of the list one day later and had forgotten almost all the words four days after that. In contrast, participants who overlearned the material remembered a significant proportion of the list two weeks later (Krueger, 1929).

CHECKUP

1. What are the principles of overlearning and distributed versus massed practice?
2. What implications do the principles of overlearning and distributed versus massed practice have for studying?

Dyadic Learning

One way of improving students' studying is by arranging for them to help each other. Dyadic learning is a way of studying in which pairs of students check and bolster each other's learning (Larson & Dansereau, 1986). Steps in the process are listed below.

Step 1: Both students read the passage.

Step 2: One student acts as recaller and the second is a listener/facilitator. The recaller summarizes the passage orally without referring back to it. The recaller is encouraged to draw diagrams, if that is helpful. The listener may interrupt to make essential corrections.

Step 3: After the recaller has summarized the selection, the listener makes corrections and supplies missing details. The listener is encouraged to expand on the summary, relate important details to previously learned material, or evaluate the material. To make the text more understandable and more memorable, the listener is also encouraged to create mental images or drawings of the material. The listener may look back at the text.

Step 4: The recaller assists the listener in correcting or elaborating on the summary, relating it to known information, or evaluating it. At this point, the recaller may look back at the text.

Step 5: Students discuss what they learned from each other. Although originally used as a study technique, this method can

■ **Massed practice** is studying or doing practice exercises all at one time.

■ **Overlearning** is the practice of continuing to study after the material has been learned in order to foster increased retention.

be adapted for use in a variety of reading/writing situations. However, students need to be taught how to fulfill their roles, and their performance should be monitored. You also need to make sure that the students who work together are compatible and somewhat similar in achievement. Pairing a very low achiever with a very high achiever may create a difficult situation for both students. One advantage of dyadic learning is that as students are working together, you can visit pairs and diagnose difficulties and provide assistance as needed.

Metacognition

As noted throughout this chapter, instruction should include a metacognitive component that helps students decide which strategies are most appropriate for their particular study conditions. In fact, metacognition is the foundation of effective study strategies: It enables students to decide what to study, how to study, and how long they should study. As Eggen and Kauchak (2001) note, "The effectiveness of study strategies depends on the thought involved in making decisions about what is important enough to highlight, include in notes, or use in organizing ideas" (p. 339).

Estimating How Much Is Known and How Well

A key metacognitive skill is knowing when material being studied is known. Most students overestimate how well they know material or how well prepared they are for a test (Pashler et al., 2007). One problem is that students make judgments based on what they recall right after studying, when the material is freshest in their minds. A technique for better estimating how well one knows material is to use a delayed judgment. Students should assess their knowledge after a delay, which could be as short as an hour, but could be a day or two. Students should respond based on a question or other cue, but they should not have access to the answers. To help students incorporate this technique into their studying, demonstrate its use in class. Hold a study session. Then, after about an hour's delay, provide students with questions one at a time and have them judge how likely it is on a scale of 1 to 100 that they would be able to answer the question. Direct students to review questions for which they did not receive a score of 100.

Students might use a delayed keyword technique to determine how much they recall from reading a section that they have completed (Pashler et al. 2007). After a delay, students attempt to summarize what they have read by using keywords or sentences to convey major concepts. Students who used this technique did a better job of studying their textbooks.

CHECKUP

1. What role does metacognition play in effective studying?

Motivation

In addition to teaching students how and when and how long to study, it is important to motivate them. The best motivator, of course, is success. Some students undoubtedly have put time into preparing for tests in the past but still did poorly because they used ineffective study methods. Discouraged or attributing their failure to lack of ability, they may not adequately prepare for tests because they don't think that studying will help them. Results are more convincing than the most impassioned exhortations, especially when we are asking students to make significant changes in their behavior. By the time they reach high school or even middle school, most students have firmly established study habits, which all too often are ineffective. One way of helping students adopt more effective techniques is to help them discover for themselves which techniques actually work best. High school teacher Jenny Watson Pearson (Pearson & Santa, 1995) involved students in a series of experiments in which they read several articles, studied each one in a different way, and then wrote down all the facts they could recall from each article. Students then graphed the results, analyzed them, and reflected on them. It became clear that some approaches were better than others, but that these results could vary from student to student. However, most of the students concluded that they learned more when they organized the information in some way and when they talked over what they had learned with others. The experiments clearly demonstrated to the students the value of effective study techniques. As Watson commented (Pearson & Santa, 1995):

> As a high school teacher, I often thought about what is really important for my students to learn. I now think that it is most important to enable my students to make that decision for themselves. Through the investigation of their own learning styles and discovery of suitable study strategies, my students can become responsible and discriminating purveyors of their own knowledge. (p. 469)

Study Habits

Study involves will as well as skill, although the two are related. The best study strategies are of little benefit if they are not applied. Students are most likely to study if the following conditions are met:

- They know how to study. This knowledge could be subject specific. If students are not studying for a particular subject, it may be because they do not know how to study for that subject. Students may know how to study history, but not geometry.
- They are interested in the subject. If students are interested in a subject, they are motivated to learn and put forth more effort. However, engagement is a more important factor. Even if the material is lacking in appeal, if students engage themselves in the study process, learning and retention will be promoted (Hattie, 2009).
- They have a sense of their own self-efficacy. That is, they believe that studying will result in learning the material and obtaining a higher grade. High-achieving students attribute their success to hard work. Low-achieving students may attribute their failure to a lack of ability. If students believe they aren't succeeding because they simply don't have the ability to learn the material, they have no motivation to study. Attributing success to hard work means that students believe that they will be successful if they study.

Some students may come to your class with a long history of failure and a diminished sense of self-efficacy. To build students' sense of self-efficacy, help them see the connection between hard work and achievement. Give some in-class assignments that are challenging, but within the grasp of these students. Provide sufficient guidance so that students are virtually guaranteed a measure of success. Praise their effort so that they can see the connection between work and achievement. However, also praise their ability to learn. If you praise only their effort, they may believe that they are lacking in ability and therefore have to work harder than everyone else. This kind of thinking can weaken their sense of self-efficacy. Promote the idea that learning your subject area material is largely a matter of working hard and using one's abilities. Make sure that quizzes, tests, and assignments are structured in such a way that students who put forth effort will be at least partly successful. Success is fostered when:

- Students know what type of test they will be given and how to prepare for it. This follows the principle of task specificity. If you are giving an essay test, let students know. Demonstrate the kinds of preparation that might go into studying for an essay test.

- Students set goals for a course. The goals should be written and should state what students hope to learn or how they hope to change as a result of taking the course. Students should also note what steps they will take to reach their goals. Setting goals and creating a plan to attain them provide motivation for studying.
- Students build study routines. If possible, students should have a place to study that is quiet and free from distractions and contains the necessary equipment and supplies. Equipment and supplies should be organized so that they are readily accessible. Each subject's materials could be color coded, with history folders or notebooks being blue and science materials red, for instance. Students might also find it helpful to study at the same time each day. Studying should precede recreation. In fact, recreation such as watching a favorite show might be used as a reward for studying. To help students get in the habit of studying, encourage them to keep a study log—a record of the date, the study task, the amount of time spent studying, the study techniques used, comments and questions, and results of studying. Encourage students to reflect in their logs and have periodic conferences on them so that they can assess their progress and plan any needed changes in their study habits or techniques. A sample study log is presented in Figure 7.5.

English Language Learners

Because they may be slower at processing English, English language learners should allocate more time for studying.

Time Management

With sports, clubs, recreation, media, social networking, and part-time jobs competing for students' attention, time management is a crucial factor in an effective study program. One way of gaining more time is to manage it better. It is easy for students to dawdle away countless minutes and hours of time. To assess your own use of time, keep track of how you spend your time for a week or so. Discuss your findings with students and have them do the same. Discuss ways in which time might be used more efficiently. Also encourage students to set schedules. Students might set up both a master schedule for the week, which shows their class time, work time, activities time, and time for eating and sleeping. They can then decide, based on the time available, when they will study and for how long. A semester schedule that includes major long-term assignments should also be drawn up. Most important of all, students should make the commitment to keep to the study portions of their schedules; however, they should be flexible and realistic about this commitment.

Discipline

The hardest thing that students will have to master is themselves. Studying takes discipline and is especially challenging for underachieving students, because they don't have a history of success to encourage them and, in fact, might never have been rewarded for their efforts. Just as with a physical exercise regimen, a nonstudier should begin slowly, studying for just thirty minutes a day and gradually work up to an hour or two or whatever is required. Study assignments should be crystal clear, interesting, and doable.

FIGURE 7.5 Study Log

Date	Study Task	Time Spent Studying	Study Method Used	Questions, Difficulties, Comments	Results (Test or Quiz Grades, Class Discussions)
3-5	Read Chapter 6 in chemistry book.	7-7:45	SQ3R Mnemonic for kinds of reactions.	Not sure how to balance equations.	Named 5 kinds of reactions on quiz but was not able to balance equation.
	Read Chapter 4 in history book.	8-8:50	SQ3R & information map.		

Successful completion should be affirmed with praise and encouragement. Students might also be encouraged to create a chart to track their progress.

Self-talk can be helpful in maintaining discipline. Students might use self-talk to help themselves get started. They might pretend to be cheerleaders: "Let's go, team. Let's hit those books." When energy and motivation begin to flag and they are tempted to quit, they might give themselves another cheer: "Defense! Defense!" They might call time out. Or they might tell themselves, "When the going gets tough, the tough get going." After a successful study session, they might give themselves a victory cheer.

Even disciplined students may find that they have a difficult time studying for subjects that aren't interesting to them or that are especially difficult. If the subject is boring, students should be encouraged to find some way to make it interesting. If this doesn't work, perhaps they can reward themselves for studying the subject by having a treat or watching a favorite TV show.

Social factors also can be a powerful motivator for studying. Students who have difficulty studying alone might work with a friend or join a small study group. Talking with others helps to clarify confusing points and also provides a more congenial way to study. Observing a disciplined peer study might also inspire students who find studying to be a struggle. However, the decision of whether to study alone or in a group is a matter of personal preference.

Students might find it easier to study if they attain an awareness of how and when they study best. Some students study best under conditions of absolute quiet; others prefer a little background noise. Some like to lie down when they study; others prefer a straightback chair. And some may study best while pacing back and forth. Discuss your own study strategies and habits, and encourage students to do the same. Stress the strategies and habits that seem most effective. Also talk with students about factors that promote studying as well as obstacles to studying. As you discuss the obstacles, try to figure out some ways to overcome them. Note factors, such as a textbook that is too difficult, that might require intervention. Or students might be so hopelessly behind in a cumulative subject such as math or chemistry that they need help catching up.

CHECKUP

1. What are the essential study habits?
2. What are some techniques that might be used to foster essential study habits, including discipline and time management?

Assessing Students' Study Strategies and Habits

To assess students' use of study strategies and their study habits, conduct an interview such as the one in Figure 7.6. Have a discussion with students about how, when, and where they

FIGURE 7.6
Study Strategies and Habits Interview

1. How often do you study?
2. When do you study?
3. About how much time do you spend studying?
4. Do you take breaks during your study sessions? If so, how many and for how long?
5. Where do you study?
6. What special things do you do to learn and remember information?
7. Which subject is easiest to study for? Why?
8. Which subject is most difficult to study for? Why? Pretend that you are studying for a quiz in that subject. Show me how you would go about studying for it. [Note whether the text is on the appropriate level of difficulty. Note study strategies that the student uses. Also ask the student to describe the strategies he is using.]
9. What kinds of tests do your teachers give? How do you know what to study for those tests?
10. How do you go about studying for short-answer tests? For multiple-choice tests? For essay tests?

study. A good way to get some insight into their study skills and habits is to set aside some time during class and observe them as they study. To make it realistic, assign a section of the text and explain that you are going to give them some time to study and then have a quiz. Note how rapidly students get down to business, how well they are able to concentrate, and what techniques they seem to be using. As part of the quiz, you might ask them to write a brief paragraph explaining how they studied the material. The study logs described earlier might also shed some light on students' studying. They might, for instance, be asking a lot of questions that indicate they are confused by their assignments.

CHECKUP

1. How might students' study strategies and habits be assessed?

Providing Continuous Support

Learning a new habit, such as studying on a regular basis when one hasn't done so in the past, takes about three months or more (Prochaska, Norcross, & DiClemente, 1994). But change is difficult. As they go through the following stages of change, students need continued support and encouragement.

Precontemplation. Students often don't see a need for change. They may blame their low grades on outside forces: poor teaching, a dull subject, or a difficult textbook. Or they may feel that they are in a hopeless situation. Having gotten poor marks all through their schooling, they may have given up. Students at this stage need to become aware of their problem. This might be done in general class discussions, through attending lectures about the importance of studying on a regular basis, or in informal one-on-one talks or counseling sessions.

Contemplation. Students note that their marks are low and that this is related to a lack of effective study. They are thinking about changing, but haven't made any attempts to do so. They may feel that they will fail if they try, so they put off trying. They focus on the problem rather than the solution. A sign that they are ready to change is that they shift their attention to possible solutions. They also begin to contemplate the future rather than regretting the past (Prochaska, Norcross, & DiClemente, 1994). To help students in this stage, continue to build their awareness, but also help them become aware of the benefits of changing. Discuss and have them visualize what will happen if they begin studying. Have them picture the excitement of learning new information, the praise they will get from their teachers and family, and how school will be much more pleasant because they won't dread being called on or failing tests. Help them to create an image of themselves as good students. Actual change is often preceded by visualized change.

Preparation. Students are getting ready to change but haven't started, or they have made a few minor changes, such as recording homework assignments and setting aside a quiet place to study. Students need encouragement to help them move into the action stage. They specifically need to see that the benefits of change will outweigh the negative aspects, such as having less free time or giving up some favorite activities or having nonstudying friends become jealous because they are getting good marks. They also need to believe that they can change. Out of these beliefs is born commitment.

Action. Students have started to make changes. This is a critical, fragile period. They need intensive guidance and encouragement. Action, however, is not the same as change. Although students may have studied each night for a week or two, they haven't fully implemented the change and need support to help them to stabilize the change.

Maintenance. Students stabilize the changes so that they become a part of their lives. This step is also critical. Unfortunately, at this point, the teacher may have felt that she has expended enough effort to get students to change and now they should be on their own. Students don't need the kind of intensive guidance and encouragement required in earlier stages, but they do need continuous support. This stage may take two or three months or more.

Termination. This applies to changes such as giving up smoking. Changes such as adopting more effective learning habits probably never reach the termination stage. In addition, the learning tasks that students encounter change and grow more complex over the years. Booster sessions and continuous support are highly recommended.

It's important to know what stage students are in and to gear instruction and support accordingly. For instance, students in the precontemplation stage really don't see a need for change and probably would not respond to exhortations. They need to be moved to the contemplation stage, where they see a need for change. On the other side of the coin, students who are in the action stage should not be held back from implementing their changes. They don't need encouraging messages telling them why they should change. They already know that. They need the kind of support that will help them to continue to change.

Although the stages have been presented in a list form, they are not linear. Students may move back and forth between stages and even relapse. They need to know that we all slip, but we can pick ourselves up and start anew. In fact, most people who have changed successfully had to make several attempts. Even failed attempts moved them farther along the road to change, if they were able to learn from these failures and try again.

CHECKUP

1. What are the stages of change?
2. How might the teacher use knowledge of these stages to help students adopt more effective study habits?

Rate of Reading

An often overlooked factor in effective studying is rate of reading or fluency. Excessively slow reading will hurt the student in two ways: When the reading speed falls significantly below thinking speed, the mind tends to wander, and comprehension suffers. Slow reading is also time consuming. A student reading 100 words a minute will take twice as long to finish an assignment as one who reads 200 words a minute. As assignments grow heavier, the slow reader may simply not have enough time to complete them.

Flexibility in Reading

Slow reading is not necessarily bad reading. Contracts, math problems, and difficult, concept-laden material should be read slowly. Slow reading is only a problem when everything is read in low gear. Some students may be slow readers because they don't automatically recognize words. Their reading rate can be boosted by having them read many easy books so that their reading rate equals their thinking rate. On the other end of the continuum are students who are always in high gear. Often, they are superior readers who read everything in sight. Having honed their skills on narrative materials, which are designed to be read quickly, they race through chapters on rock formation or the founding of the thirteen colonies, and wonder why they do poorly in class discussions or on science and history quizzes.

Average reading rates are presented in Table 7.1. However, there is a considerable range in reading rate. For instance, the average reading rate in grade 7 is 191 wpm, but rates may range from 96 to 282 words a minute (Carver, 1992). In high school the range is even greater, with one study noting rates ranging from 65 to 334 words a minute (Leslie & Caldwell, 2001).

According to Carver (1990, 1992), each of us has a rate of normal reading known as rauding. The word *rauding* was formed by combining the words auding, which means to

TABLE 7.1 Average Silent Reading Rates

GRADE	WORDS PER MINUTE
1	55
2	85
3	130
4	150
5	165
6	175
7	190
8	205
High School	250

listen for meaning, and *reading*. Rauding refers to the rate at which we comprehend material that we are reading or listening to. Our reading and listening rates are apparently the same and are governed by our thinking speed or cognitive rate. Some students might be slow readers because they think in a slow, deliberative way. Rauding entails recognizing each word, encoding the meaning of each word, and integrating words and sentences into meaningful units. The rates provided in Table 7.1 are rauding rates. However, depending on our purpose for reading, we have a number of reading rates. From fastest to slowest, these are scanning, skimming, rauding, learning, and memorizing (see Table 7.2). In scanning, we search printed materials to find a target word. If you were reading a section in a history text about the post–World War II era and you couldn't remember which countries belonged to NATO, you might quickly search the section for the acronym NATO. Skimming is a quick reading to get an overview of a passage. Rauding is the kind of reading we usually do. Learning is a slower form of reading in which we check to make sure the information is understood and remembered. The slowest form of reading is memorizing. The key to effective reading is to select an appropriate rate.

Flexibility is the key word. Rate of reading should match the nature of the material and the purpose for which it is being read. A light novel being read for entertainment could be read rapidly. A complex novel being read in preparation for a discussion or a test should be read more slowly. Degree of familiarity with material will also help determine rate. The amateur herpetologist who is reading a selection on snakes can move through it much more quickly than someone who has only a passing familiarity with serpents. As part of preparation for reading, discuss the rate at which the material should be read. Ultimately, of course, students should be led to choose their own rates.

Struggling Readers

An excessively slow rate of reading could be a symptom of an underlying difficulty. The material could be too hard, the student might be lacking in strategies, he might be overly concerned about understanding all the information in the text, or he might not have much experience reading difficult text.

TABLE 7.2 Major Rates of Reading

READING PROCESS	PURPOSE	RATE FOR AVERAGE HIGH SCHOOL STUDENT (WORDS PER MINUTE)
Scanning	Recognizes target word	550
Skimming	Gets quick overview of meaning of passage	400
Rauding	Understands both main ideas of passage and details	250
Learning	Checks to make sure material is remembered	175
Memorizing	Says material over and over to bolster memory	100

Source: Extrapolated from *Reading Rate: A Review of Research and Theory* by R. O. Carver, San Diego, CA: Academic Press, 1990.

SQ3R and other study techniques act as a natural check for those who speed through content area material. Knowing that they have to recite at the end of a section tends to slow down students who are inclined to read too rapidly. Conversely, the survey step tends to speed up reading for the slow or average reader since it gives an overview. This overview can also provide students with some clues as to how fast they can read the material. If it suggests the subject is familiar, the students may elect to read the materials fairly quickly (Bush & Huebner, 1979).

Often, reading rate improves without being worked on directly. Students may be reading slowly because the material is too hard, their vocabularies are limited, they don't know why they are reading, or they are easily distracted and so must reread. Building background and vocabulary, making sure that students have materials on appropriate levels, setting purposes for reading, emphasizing comprehension, and playing down oral reading often result in increased reading rate.

CHECKUP

1. What are the major rates of reading?
2. What are some ways in which flexibility and appropriate rate of reading might be fostered?

Test-Taking Strategies

In addition to teaching students how to study, show them how to take a test. The best way to prepare for a test is to study consistently and strategically day in and day out. A well-organized way of teaching test-taking strategies is to implement **PLAE: P**replanning, **L**isting, **A**ctivity, and **E**valuating (Nist & Simpson, 1989).

Preplanning. Students describe the study task, asking questions such as: What will the test cover? What kind of questions will be asked? What will the format of the questions be? Model the process of preplanning for a test. Under your guidance, have the whole class create a plan for studying for a test in either your class or another class. Later, have students gather in small groups to create study plans and finally, have students create individual plans for themselves. A sample preplan might be:

- The test will cover Chapter 3, Acceleration, Force, and Motion.
- I will need to know three laws of motion, key terms, and formulas.
- The questions will be short answer and essay.

Listing. Based on preplanning information, students list the steps they will take to prepare for the test by answering the following questions: How will I get ready for the test? When will I study? How long will I study? Which study strategies will I use? A sample list might be:

- To get ready for the test, I will review the chapter, the notes that I have taken on it, and my class notes.
- I will put the three laws of motion, formulas, and key words on note cards.
- I will study half an hour each night for three nights and one hour the night before the test. I will study note cards on the bus and at odd times.

Activity. Students activate their plans and monitor them. They ask themselves, "Am I following my plan? If not, why not? Is my plan working? Am I learning what I need to learn? If not, what changes do I need to make in my plan? Am I using the best study strategies?"

Evaluating. Based on their performance on the test, students evaluate the effectiveness of their study plans. They might ask, "Which questions did I miss? Why? Did I study all the material that the questions were based on? Did I remember the material? How could I have studied to get more questions right?" After evaluating their

■ **PLAE** is a procedure for studying that includes preplanning the nature and content of a test, listing steps to get ready for the test, activating a plan, and evaluating its effectiveness.

study plan, students should make any necessary changes to improve it for the next test. They may decide to start a study group or to work sample problems using the formulas covered in the chapter.

For tests in your subject area, provide students with the type of information that will allow them to show what they know. Let them know what the test will include. Will it cover just the book, or will it include information in both the book and notes? Will it be essay, short answer, or multiple choice? Also show students how to study for the test. If students are going to take a national standardized test or a standardized test in the content area that you teach, provide some preparation and practice sessions to familiarize them with the format of the test and improve their test-taking skills.

To help students establish effective study strategies, arrange for practice study sessions and practice tests. Create a test that is similar in content and format to tests that you usually give in your subject matter area. Discuss the nature of the test and ways in which students might prepare for the test. After administering the test, discuss the results. Help students determine how effective their studying was and what they might do to improve. If students are preparing for essay tests, they might adapt a strategy such as PORPE.

PORPE Strategy

Searching over a period of four years for a writing strategy that students could use for planning, monitoring, and evaluating their learning in the content areas, Simpson (1986) devised a technique known as **PORPE: P**redict, **O**rganize, **R**ehearse, **P**ractice, and **E**valuate. While assisting students with their learning, PORPE also develops their ability to write more effective essay exams. PORPE is modeled on the expert readers' ability to use strategies to identify key ideas, monitor for meaning, and take corrective action if comprehension is lacking. Following is how a PORPE lesson might be introduced.

L E S S O N   7 . 2

PORPE

Step 1: Predict

After explaining that PORPE is a strategy designed to help students prepare for essay tests, tell students that the first step is to predict what kinds of essay questions the teacher might ask. This step is subdivided into three phases.

Phase A. Introduction of Essay Terms. Introduce terms commonly used to compose essay questions: *describe, discuss, explain, compare, criticize, contrast, defend, support.* (Add the kinds of question words that you use if they aren't already included.) Discuss what each of the question words is asking students to do. For instance, explain that *discuss* means to give reasons and explanations in some detail; *criticize* means to judge but to give reasons for each judgment.

Phase B. Prediction of Possible Questions. Model and discuss with students what clues they might use to predict essay questions: points emphasized by the teacher, major points in texts, hints given by the teacher, past tests, notes, and ideas that were repeated. Tell students that the teacher may even give hints from time to time by noting that a certain topic or issue would make a good test question or that a certain idea is very important.

Phase C. Completion of Predicted Questions. Provide students with key words (*explain, compare, discuss*) and have them create sample essay items. They might do this in pairs or cooperative groups. Discuss whether their questions have covered all the most important topics. Also determine which questions seem to be most likely to appear on the test.

(continued)

■ **PORPE** is a procedure for preparing for essay tests that includes predicting the content of the test, organizing information for possible answers, rehearsing (studying) the material, taking a practice test, and evaluating the results.

English Language Learners

Essay tests are especially difficult for English language learners because their English language development typically lags behind that of native speakers of English. Spend some time instructing students in some of the kinds of expressions that are commonly used to respond to essay questions in your subject matter. Also consider letting students respond in the language or combinations of language that will enable them to display their knowledge best.

Step 2: Organize

Using outlines, information maps, or other graphic organizers, have students chart answers for the predicted questions. In the initial stages, you might model your own organizer, but students should eventually create their own. Display and discuss especially effective organizers. Guide students as they improve organizers that are not adequate. For instance, help them see the importance of including examples and reasons to support their positions.

Step 3: Rehearse

After reviewing steps for effective studying and modeling how you might study for a test, have students study their organizers. Emphasize the need to self-test oneself through reciting. Stress the need to restudy the material if the recitation isn't adequate. Also explain the value of overlearning and distributed practice. For an extended answer, students might do one section at a time, just as in SQ3R, but ultimately put the whole answer together. Rehearsal should also be continued over a period of several sessions.

Step 4: Practice

Students write a practice essay. Supply suggestions for students to follow: creating a semantic map or outline before starting, writing an opening sentence that clearly incorporates the essay question, or using a deliberate organizational pattern, such as "The Great Depression had five major causes." Then note the causes, using *first*, *second*, and so forth. Students supply examples, if appropriate, and end with a concluding sentence that restates the gist of the question or sums up the answer. Students also check the answer, asking, "Did I really answer the question as asked? Did I include all the main points? Is the answer as clear as I can make it in the time allowed?"

Step 5: Evaluate

Using a checklist or rubric that the teacher and the class compose, the students evaluate their responses and refine them as necessary. After three weeks of intensive training, PORPE students were able to use the technique on their own.

Other Suggestions for Taking Essay Tests

Students should be aware of how much time they have and allot it proportionately. They should not make the mistake of spending so much time on the first question that they have to rush through the second question and have no time for the last one. Should students misjudge their time, they should jot down a quick outline of the answer and a note saying they ran out of time.

Students, especially those who are struggling, should be encouraged to use mnemonic devices such as acronyms, rhymes, or reconstructive elaborations to help them retrieve essential information.

Students who have difficulty expressing themselves on an essay test may do better if they resist the temptation to dive right in and start answering the question. Instead, they might take a few minutes to organize their thoughts, construct a brief outline, and then begin answering the question.

CHECKUP

1. What are some techniques that might be used to help students prepare for tests?

Test Anxiety

Taking tests is an affective as well as an academic activity. Being a little nervous before taking a test is natural. A little anxiety heightens performance. However, about one student out of every five becomes so anxious that his performance is harmed (Gaudrey & Spielberger, 1971). Test anxiety is a state of intense apprehension that may include physical

Exemplary Teaching

Test Preparation

As part of preparation for the PSAT, Laflamme (1997) had his tenth-graders compose testlike selections and multiple-choice questions. Writing fostered a deeper understanding of both the structure of the selections and the nature of the questions. Composing the selections was preceded by a careful analysis of the kinds of selections contained on the PSAT, the types of questions asked, and recommended steps for answering those questions. Students were provided with a flowchart that summarized the basic structure of questions on the PSAT and also sample stems for the different types of questions asked. Students who wrote sample test selections and engaged in intensive vocabulary study outperformed those who took part in a traditional PSAT preparation course.

symptoms, such as an upset stomach or a headache, and that are so severe that they interfere with students' functioning. Test anxiety is linked to fears of negative evaluation, a dislike of tests, and inadequate study skills. Students with high test anxiety have lowered self-esteem and feel less in control of outside events. They have more difficulty understanding and organizing material initially and have more difficulty concentrating.

Test anxiety requires a two-pronged approach: Students need to have a good grasp of study strategies, and they need to have their confidence built so that they can overcome their unreasonable anxiety. School counselors might be called on to help with the confidence building, but content area teachers can help, too. Some steps that can be taken to lessen test anxiety include:

- Instruction in comprehension and study skills. This might need to be subject specific. Some students may become anxious only before math or science tests.
- Instruction in test-taking skills.
- Instruction and counseling that builds self-efficacy and helps students learn to handle stress. This might include instruction in cognitive self-talk. Students are taught to overcome negative thoughts with positive self-assertions that provide them with specific actions that they can implement to reduce anxiety, such as taking a deep breath and relaxing and using specific test-taking strategies, such as doing the easy items first and then working on the difficult ones (Wark & Flippo, 1991).

Test Preparation for High-Stakes Tests

The teacher watched in amazement as his ninth-grade class worked on the first section of a standardized reading test. Although the directions had clearly stated that there was a ten-minute time limit, most of the students were poking through the section. This vocabulary section of the test required that from the five alternatives provided, they choose the one that gave the best definition of the target word. There was no dense reading to be done. Test-wise students would have quickly answered all the items they were relatively sure of and then gone back to take a look at the more difficult, unanswered items. But these students plodded through. Many attempted only half the items. They did no better on the comprehension subtest. The teacher was not surprised that the scores were low, but he realized that the scores were probably lower than they should have been because the students obviously lacked test-taking skills.

After a semester of intensive instruction in reading and writing strategies, the students' scores shot up. In just five months, some students were showing a gain of three or even four years. Wise to the ways of group assessment, the teacher realized that he couldn't take full credit for the students' improvement. Although some of their gains were most likely due to genuine improvement in reading vocabulary and comprehension, some of the gains were due to increased skill in taking tests. After receiving some instruction in test-taking skills that included pacing; active, focused reading; answering the easiest items first; informed guessing; and checking responses, the students were better able to handle group standardized tests. Their scores now provided a more realistic estimate of their abilities.

Taking tests is a life skill. Students take tests to get into special programs, to get admitted to certain high schools, and for admission to college. In some school systems, passing standardized tests is a prerequisite for being passed on to the next grade or receiving a high school diploma. In addition to these high-stakes tests, there are the numerous quizzes, tests, and exams that students are given in each of the subjects that they study.

Modeling the Process of Taking a Test

Discussing and modeling test-taking strategies is also helpful. Share some of the experiences you have had taking tests. Also show how you would go about taking a test of the type that your students are given. Explain your thinking processes as you read and follow directions. Think aloud as you eliminate distractors when you are not sure of an answer to a multiple-choice question. Show, too, how you check answers and pace yourself. Encourage students who typically do well on tests to discuss their test-taking strategies. Provide extra help for those who work too rapidly and fail to check answers as well as those who work too slowly and are overly concerned with making a mistake. If the test has a number of challenging passages, provide students with strategies for reading difficult passages and answering tough questions. Also discuss the correction factor. On some tests, students lose a quarter of a point for wrong responses, and so they are better off leaving an answer blank if they have no idea which of the options is correct. However, if they eliminate more than one of the options, the odds of getting the right answer are in their favor. Of course, if the test does not have a correction factor and there is no penalty for guessing, students should make a careful guess.

SAT and ACT Preparation

More than half of today's secondary students will take either the SAT or the ACT or both. Both tests are demanding and place heavy emphasis on reading comprehension. The Critical Reading section of the SAT consists of sentence completion exercises in which students fill in one or two blanks such as the following:

Hoping to _____ the dispute, negotiators proposed a compromise that they felt would be _____ to both labor and management.
(A) enforce . . useful (B) end . . divisive (C) overcome . . unattractive (D) extend . . satisfactory (E) resolve . . acceptable

The section also contains comprehension passages that contain both fictional and informational pieces followed by a series of questions that demand careful reasoning. In one section, test takers are required to read two brief passages and respond to comparison/contrast questions. Students are given approximately one minute per question.

The ACT Reading Test has 40 questions asked about four lengthy passages drawn from Prose Fiction, Humanities, Social Studies, and Natural Sciences. The ACT emphasizes questions that require going back to the passage. Both the SAT and the ACT have one item that requires selecting the definition of a word according to the way it is used in context. On their Web sites, both the SAT and the ACT provide thorough explanations of the tests, tips for taking the tests, and practice tests. If carefully analyzed, the practice tests could provide information on areas for needed study. Both tests are written for high levels of reading ability. Students reading below grade level should practice with material on their reading level. However, the level of difficulty should be gradually increased so that students reach or, at least approach the reading level of the tests. English learners are at a distinct disadvantage with these tests. First of all, even English learners who are accomplished readers read at a slower rate because they are dealing with a second language. In addition, their vocabulary and hence their familiarity with the words on advanced reading passages will typically be more limited. (In one study, the average scores of English learners was 45 points below that of native speakers [Pearson, 1993]. However, the English learners' college GPAs were similar to that of native speakers who had higher scores.) Wide reading in all subject matter areas, extensive voluntary reading, and a systematic program of vocabulary enrichment are the best preparation for English learners and all students. Test prep courses are also helpful as long as they do not substitute for regular classroom instruction. Test prep is most effective when a pretest is given in order to spot the kinds of items that pose problems and instruction is geared to teaching students how to respond to those or similar items (Hattie, 2009; Witt, 1993).

Probing Processes with a Think-Aloud

To find out whether students are applying effective test-taking strategies, use a think-aloud. While students are taking a practice test, have them tell you what's going on in their minds. Ask them what they are thinking about both as they read the passage and as they answer questions. Record their responses or take careful notes. You might also interview students after they have taken a test. First, have them read the test passage orally. Assess their performance to gauge whether the test is on their level of ability. They may be getting items wrong because the passage is too difficult. Or maybe they give up because the passage is a very challenging one. Scruggs, Bennion, and Lifson (1985a, 1985b) found that students who were able to describe specific strategies had higher scores. Two effective strategies were text referring ("I thought I had seen that in the story, so I checked back") and inferring strategies ("I figured this must be the correct answer because of what the story said"). Struggling students were far less strategic. A strategy, such as QAR (as mentioned in Chapter 4) adapted to test taking, should prove to be effective in helping students decide whether the answer is right there, so that if they don't recall it, they can go back over the passage and find it, or whether it's implied, so that students know they have to make an inference based on information contained in the passage.

Probe low-scoring students carefully to find out how they handle difficult passages, which they are certain to encounter. Do they give up? Do they take random guesses? Or do they try to make as much sense out of the passages as they can and, if all else fails, match up unknown words in the answer options with the same words in the selection? Students need to know that they can sometimes answer questions correctly even when they don't know every word in the passage. Also question students as to how sure they are of the correctness of their answers. Higher-scoring students are better able to predict their performance. This is an advantage because then they know which items to recheck (Scruggs & Mastropieri, 1992).

CHECKUP

1. What are high-stakes tests?
2. What steps might be taken to prepare students for them?

The Ethics of Test Preparation

Test preparation must be ethical. There is no question that providing students with examples from the actual test is wrong. It is also unethical to raise students' scores without also increasing their underlying knowledge and skill. As one testing expert cautioned, "No test preparation practice should increase students' test scores without simultaneously increasing students' mastery of the assessment domain tested" (Popham, 2000, p. 82). The purpose of test preparation is to provide students with the test-taking skills that enable them to show with accuracy what they have learned. In fact, teachers would be negligent if they did not help students attain test-taking skills that make it possible for them to demonstrate what they truly know.

Keep test preparation to a minimum. The best preparation is a carefully taught course complemented by conscientious student participation and studying. In her study of high-performing versus low-performing secondary schools, Langer (1999) found that students in schools in which teachers incorporated skills assessed on high-stakes tests into the curriculum did better than schools in which teachers focused on test preparation.

Incorporating test preparation into the curriculum can be accomplished in a number of ways. You can ask the kinds of questions that demand the same type of cognitive processes as those posed on the high-stakes tests. For instance, many high-stakes tests ask students to back up responses with facts and reasons. You can do the same. In history, you might ask students to tell whether they think the Spanish-American War was justified and to give reasons for their opinions. In science, you might ask students to explain what scientists have learned about asteroids and what questions they still have. They might use their texts and a recent article on asteroids. If a rubric is used to assess students' work, you can use the same type of rubric to judge students' assignments. The rubric should be thoroughly discussed so that students understand what they are being required to do. In at least some of your quizzes and tests, use the same format, if applicable, that the high-stakes tests use.

CHECKUP

1. How much and what kind of test preparation should students be given?

Summary

Studying requires remembering in addition to understanding material. Retention of material depends on clear, active encoding, encoding material in the same way as it is to be tested, and adequate rehearsal or studying. Material that is meaningful and well organized aids memory storage. Retrieval is also improved by imagery and other forms of elaboration. Having an intention to learn and overlearning enhance retention. Associational or mnemonic devices are recommended for learning materials that lack meaningful connections. Quizzes that require retrieval foster retention, as does properly spacing review. Development of study skills is most effective when it is embedded in specific content. Therefore, content teachers are responsible for teaching study skills required to understand and retain information in their content areas.

A study strategy that has been effective with a variety of students is SQ3R (Study, Question, Read, Recite, Review), which is based on a number of learning strategies that involve preparing, organizing, and elaborating, as well as metacognition.

Notetaking is a key technique and includes four skills: selectivity, organization, consolidation, and fluency. Two-column or three-column notes as implemented in the Cornell system are recommended. Formal outlining or informal systems such as power thinking are useful study strategies.

Studying has cognitive skill, metacognitive, and affective or motivational components. Because studying is affective as well as cognitive and metacognitive, students need to establish effective study habits. If students suffer from test anxiety, they may need confidence building and counseling along with instruction in studying and test-taking techniques.

Practice fosters extended skills development and also makes skills automatic. Distributed practice generally produces better results. Massed practices work well with extended tasks, such as reading an essay. Overlearning, which is continuing to study after knowing facts or steps in a procedure, fosters retention.

If students read too slowly, comprehension suffers and they have a difficult time keeping up with their reading assignments. There are five rates of reading: scanning, skimming, rauding, learning, and memorizing. Flexible readers choose the rate that matches the task.

An effective technique for taking tests is PLAE (Preplanning, Listing, Activity, and Evaluating). PORPE is an effective strategy for taking essay tests. The best prepara-tion for high-stakes tests is to incorporate the content and skills being assessed into the regular curriculum. Test prepa-ration that raises students' scores without also increasing their knowledge and skill is unethical.

Reflection

Return to the Anticipation Guide at the beginning of this chapter. Respond once again to the items. Did your responses change? If so, how and why? What is the role of the content area teacher in teaching study skills? How might effective study skills and habits be fostered in your content area?

Extension and Application

1. Assess your study strategies and study habits. How effective are they? What might you do to improve them?
2. Create a mnemonic device for learning some important facts in your content area. Using the device, memorize the facts. Then assess yourself a week later. How well did the mnemonic work?

3. Try out one of the study strategies described in this chapter for at least two weeks. How effective does it seem to be? What are its advantages and disadvantages?

Go to Topic 8: Study Skills and Strategies in the MyEducation-Lab (www.myeducationlab.com) for your course, where you can:

- Find learning outcomes for Study Skills and Strategies along with the national standards that connect to these outcomes.
- Complete Assignments and Activities that can help you more deeply understand the chapter content.
- Apply and practice your understanding of the core teaching skills identified in the chapter with the Building Teaching Skills and Dispositions learning units.

Go to the Topic A+RISE in the MyEducationLab (www.myeducationlab.com) for your course. A+RISE® Standards2Strategy™ is an innovative and interactive online resource that offers new teachers in grades K–12 just-in-time, research-based instructional strategies that:

- Meet the linguistic needs of ELLs as they learn content.
- Differentiate instruction for all grades and abilities.
- Offer reading and writing techniques, cooperative learning, use of linguistic and nonlinguistic representations, scaffolding, teacher modeling, higher-order thinking, and alternative classroom ELL assessment.
- Provide support to help teachers be effective through the integration of listening, speaking, reading, and writing along with the content curriculum.
- Improve student achievement.
- Are aligned to Common Core Elementary Language Arts standards (for the literacy strategies) and to English language proficiency standards in WIDA, Texas, California, and Florida.

CHAPTER 8

Writing to Learn

For each of the following statements, put a check under "Agree" or "Disagree" to indicate your opinion. If possible, discuss your responses with classmates.

	Agree	Disagree
1. Writing is an excellent way to learn content area material.	_____	_____
2. The responsibility for teaching writing skills belongs primarily to language arts teachers.	_____	_____
3. Content area teachers have a right to expect that students will have sufficient writing skills such that they will not need to instruct students in writing.	_____	_____
4. Content area teachers are responsible for teaching those writing skills that are specific to their content area.	_____	_____
5. The more direction students are given, the better they write.	_____	_____

When you were a middle or high school student, what kinds of writing did you do in your content area classes? What were your favorite writing assignments? What kinds of writing did you find particularly difficult? What techniques did the teachers use to help you with your writing? Which of these techniques was most effective? Over the years, writing instruction has changed dramatically and is believed to be more effective. This chapter provides an overview of the ways in which writing is taught today and has some suggestions for ways content area teachers might use writing to foster learning.

Using What You Know

Importance of Writing

Proficiency in writing is more essential than ever. A number of states have exit exams and other high-stakes tests that include writing on demand. The SAT test requires a writing sample, as do most Advanced Placement exams. A writing sample is optional on the ACT. According to research by ACT (2005), approximately one-third of college-bound students are not adequately prepared for college-level writing. Nor are students prepared for the type of writing required in the workplace. Eighty percent or more of the companies in the service and finance, insurance, and real estate (FIRE) sectors assess writing during hiring (National Commission on Writing, 2006). For some, this sample might be the letter of application or resume. In other situations, the sample could be an on-demand writing task. Most employers cite writing skills as critical and growing in importance for successful job performance. However, many students are not living up to the demand for increased writing proficiency. In the latest NAEP writing assessment for which results are available, 15 percent of eighth-graders scored below basic, 54 percent were at basic, and 31 percent were at the proficient level or above (Salahu-Din, Persky, & Miller, 2008). Performance for twelfth graders was 18 percent below basic, 58 percent at basic, and 24 percent at proficient or above.

Writing to learn is most valuable when it uses the language and discourse of the discipline and also furthers students' understanding of key concepts or procedures. For instance, a typical writing assignment in math is to have students reflect on how they solved

Exemplary Teaching

Writing to Learn

Math teacher Dan Siebert gives his students the following instructions to guide their writing: Characteristics of a Good Explanation

- Good explanations are based on images or models rather than symbols.
- Every number is carefully linked to some quantity or relationship between quantities in the image or model.
- Every operation is described in terms of actions performed on the image or model (Draper, 2008, p. 76)

Siebert explained that statements "don't focus on '*How* did I get the answer?'" Rather, they "focused on justifying *why* each step works and what it means" (p. 76). After a discussion of what makes a good explanation, Siebert divided the students into pairs and had them use the following guidelines for discussing their work:

1. Everyone read [an addition] and [subtraction] explanation from the homework for everyone in the group.
2. [Discuss] good things (name two and be specific).
3. Restate their ideas.
4. Give suggestions (be kind and be honest). (p. 76)

Commenting on Dan Siebert's lesson, Draper stated

> *He was not satisfied that his students were simply writing; he also insisted that they write explanations that articulated accurate representations of the mathematics by requiring them to base their explanations on images of quantities and operations. Furthermore, Dan insisted that the explanations fit the conventions of mathematical writing—in this case, mathematical proof. Dan was not satisfied when his students' explanations simply described the algorithm they used to compute the correct answer.... writing that does not focus on making sense of the mathematics or merely requires students to put words to their algorithms should not be recommended for mathematics classrooms just so mathematics teachers can fulfill the "writing-to-learn" mandate. (pp. 76–77)*

the problem. While this assignment has value, a more effective writing to learn task would be to explain what each step means and why it works (Draper, 2008).

Writing to Learn

USING TECHNOLOGY

The National Writing Project
www.writingproject.org/Research/NWP/
nwp.html provides information about
writing research and instruction.

Although we may write to inform others or to meet school or job requirements, writing is also a way to explore, discover, and synthesize information.

> Writing organizes and clarifies our thoughts. Writing is how we think our way into a subject and make it our own. Writing enables us to find out what we know—and what we don't know—about what we're trying to learn. Putting an idea into written words is like defrosting the windshield: The idea so vague out there in the murk, slowly begins to gather itself into a sensible shape. (Zinsser, 1988, p. 16)

Langer and Applebee (1987) concluded that writing supports the learning of content in three different ways. First, writing can be used as a preparation so that students write to access what they already know about a subject. Students might also write about related personal experiences so that they become motivated to study a topic. Second, writing can be used to review and consolidate what has been learned. And third, writing can be used to help students reformulate and extend ideas.

The Michigan Department of Education (Blakeslee, 1997) also concluded that writing in the content areas supports learning in a number of ways:

> Writing gives students a chance to think carefully about what they have observed and how they account for their observations. When held to high expectations for clarity in writing, students have to think deeply about the terms they choose to express their thoughts, as well as the logic of their arguments. Writing gives all students a chance to think about questions posed in class, rather than just listening to others' descriptions and explanations, providing a valuable forum for expression for those students who are reluctant to join into class discussions. . . .

CHECKUP

1. How does writing support learning?

Responsibility for Teaching Writing

When students reach secondary school, they are typically given demanding writing assignments. However, along with the assignments, teachers should provide the instruction necessary to complete them. It is safe to say that students below the basic level will need considerable instruction and scaffolding. Students at the basic level will also need guidance, but it will not need to be as extensive. Even students writing beyond the basic level will benefit from instruction. Just as content area teachers assume responsibility for teaching students the vocabulary and reading skills specific to their subjects, they should also teach students how to write lab reports, field notes, summaries of experiments and observations, syntheses of the information contained in primary sources, and other kinds of writing that a scientist, geographer, or historian might be expected to do. Part of teaching a content area subject is instructing students in the skills needed to learn and communicate more effectively in that content area. Writing in the content areas also expands students' overall writing skills, because it gives them the opportunity to use a range of forms and to write for a variety of purposes.

Although English teachers are often given the responsibility of developing writing skills, much of the writing that students do is assigned by content area teachers. Part of being literate in subject matter areas is having the ability to write about what has been learned or observed. In order to learn your subject matter and communicate what has been learned, what kinds of writing do your students need to be able to do? The answer to this question will depend on the content area that you are teaching. You may also be guided, in part, by considering the kinds of writing that students will be required to do once they have completed their schooling.

CHECKUP

1. What is the content area teacher's responsibility for the teaching of writing?

Instructing Students In Writing: The Process Approach

> **CCSS**
>
> Develop and strengthen writing as needed by planning, revising, editing, rewriting, or trying a new approach.

Instruction using the **process approach**, which is based on the way successful students and professionals write, has resulted in improved writing (Ballator, Farnum, & Kaplan, 1999). In a landmark study, Emig (1971) found that twelfth-graders generally wrote in one of two modes: extensive and reflexive. **Extensive writing** is the kind of

> ■ **The writing process approach** is an approach to teaching writing that is based on the way students and professionals write.

> ■ **Extensive writing** is the kind of writing typically composed for school assignments.

writing typically composed for school assignments. The teacher is the ultimate audience. Little time is devoted to preparing for the writing or revising the piece. **Reflexive writing**, on the other hand, has a genuine audience, perhaps a friend or a group of peers. There is more planning and revising. In this and other studies, writing is viewed as a process that has five major parts: prewriting, composing or drafting, revising, editing, and publishing.

Prewriting

Prewriting includes the steps that a writer takes in preparation for writing. Depending on the nature of the writing and the age and experience of the writer, it may involve many hours of research or just a few minutes of contemplation before beginning to write. Included in prewriting are topic selection and revision, gathering material, and brainstorming or outlining one's topic or engaging in some other prewriting activity in preparation for writing.

Prewriting should take into consideration the nature of the writing task. When the writing task requires a summary of information or the explanation or elaboration of a single topic, activities designed to activate knowledge, such as brainstorming, work best. However, if the task requires analyzing or comparing and contrasting ideas, prewriting activities that help the student organize information, such as outlining or webbing, would be more effective. When students lack a solid grasp of information, they are more likely to write a summary piece even if an analytical piece is called for. Unable to analyze the information, they simply recite what they know. In this instance, teaching students how to write an analytical piece will not suffice. They need to explore the topic until they have a sufficient understanding to analyze it. Writers also need sufficient information so that they can use details to elaborate on a topic and make it interesting (Langer, 1984).

Teacher guidance during the prewriting stage can be especially effective. Secondary English teacher Jack Graves didn't want his students who were writing an essay on *Romeo and Juliet* to feel lost (Langer & Applebee, 1987), so he had them meet in small groups to discuss alternative courses of action that Juliet might have taken when she learned that her parents had arranged a marriage for her. Using their notes from the discussion, the class debated possible alternatives. Graves then talked about ways in which this information might be used in an essay. Included in the discussion were some possible topic sentences and some examples that might be used to support the topic sentences. The results of the preparation were well-developed essays and a better understanding of the play. Graves found that in providing guidance for students, he had to walk a fine line. Without guidance, the students might founder. With too much guidance, they would be parroting his thoughts rather than making discoveries on their own.

Adolescents thrive on choices. Whenever possible, offer students choices in topics and types of writing. Give them lots of writing activities that build confidence and get them interested in writing. Help students discover areas of expertise and support their writing about topics in those areas. Also encourage students to keep a writer's notebook in which they record topics of interest. Periodically have students share interesting topics.

 Struggling Readers

Struggling learners can create illustrations or graphic organizers to prepare for their writing. Illustrations sometimes act as a prompt to remind writers of details that they might not otherwise include in their writing.

Drafting

The core step in the writing process is composing, or **drafting**. Emphasize the concept of drafting and getting thoughts down on paper so that students don't feel they have to produce a finished product in one sitting. With many students, the more planning they do, the more productive the drafting will be. There are two schools of thought on the relationship between planning and drafting. Some writers like to have a fairly well formed idea of what they want to say before

■ **Reflexive writing** is writing that has been composed for a genuine audience, perhaps a friend or a group of peers.

■ **Prewriting** is part of the writing process that includes all the things a writer does before composing, including selecting a topic and planning.

■ **Drafting** is that part of the writing process in which the writer composes a message. Drafting implies that the product is not finished and that the writer will engage in a revision process.

they begin writing. Others view writing as a discovery process. Some fiction writers, for instance, say they can't wait to write each day so they can see what their characters are going to do. Many writers plan their writing in a general way so that there is plenty of room for discovery. Rehearsal can be an important part of the process. During rehearsal, writers compose stories, letters, or even informational pieces in their heads so that when they sit down to write, their ideas flow.

Talking can be a way of rehearsing and may help some students prepare to write. Some students can dictate a piece in their heads. Others do better if they have someone to whom they can dictate their thoughts. Model the process. Talk through an incident or process and take notes as you do so. Have students pair up, with one talking about an incident, event, or process while the other student takes notes; then have them switch roles. Students who are more visually oriented might use drawings or graphic organizers to rehearse the piece they are about to write (Gallagher, 2006).

Students may approach writing from a top-down or a bottom-up approach. Students who take a top-down approach and see the big picture right from the start may jot down the theme or main idea and then generate supporting details. Students who take a bottom-up approach may generate details and then build a main idea or theme from those details (Meltzer, Roditi, Haynes, & Biddle, 1996).

Audience also has a major impact on students' writing. Often, the audience is the teacher as examiner. In this case, students focus on teacher expectations and stress surface features that are likely to result in a good grade. "When students had to shape their message constantly to fit the expectations of an examining audience, then whatever interest they had in the message eventually gave way to the details of its presentation" (Marshall, 1984b, p. 110). Students' writing has the potential to become more expressive when they have a genuine audience.

Revising

Revising extends beyond having a concern for capitalization, spelling, and punctuation. It literally means to re-envision the piece and take a close look at the content and ranges from adding a few details to completely rewriting the piece. Revising is aided by two factors. The first is the ability of the writer to step back and take a look at the writing from the audience's point of view and ask such questions as: Is the piece understandable? Is it complete? Is it well written? **Distancing** also helps. Writers should let their pieces sit for a day or so. This puts a little distance between the labors of the writing and the written piece and helps the writer review the piece more objectively. Feedback from others is also invaluable, especially if it's constructive. To foster constructive criticism, discuss with students positive ways to respond to classmates' work. Model how you go about pointing out positive aspects of a piece and providing suggestions in an affirming fashion. Discuss and demonstrate how peer editors or the teacher might point out elements that they particularly liked and ask questions about parts that were not clear or that might be expanded: "Your beginning really grabbed me. I never realized how many lives seat belts save. I'm not sure though how the three-point seat belts work. You said that there are many other safety features that could be added to cars. Could you give some examples?" A constructive climate leads to constructive criticism.

Respond to writing as a reader not a grader. Uses phrases such as:

- As a reader, I wonder about ____.
- I am confused by ____.
- Could you explain? ____
- What do you want the readers to do as a result of reading this? (Gallagher, 2006) ____

Revising can be especially effective when needed guidance is supplied. In one example, chemistry teacher Kathryn Moss was concerned that her students were having difficulty drawing

CCSS

Produce clear and coherent writing in which the development, organization, and style are appropriate to task, purpose, and audience.

■ **Revising** is that part of the writing process in which the author reconsiders and alters what she has written.

■ **Distancing** is the process of allowing time to pass between the writing of a piece and looking at it to assess its merit or need for revision. Distancing fosters increased objectivity.

Peer editing helps students with their writing.

Source: Shutterstock.

conclusions about the experiments they conducted (Langer & Applebee, 1987). Instead of interpreting the data, they simply told what happened. In practice exercises, she showed them how drawing a conclusion was telling what one can believe as a result of conducting an experiment. As a group writing activity, students composed and revised statements about rates of chemical reactions and then wrote conclusions. In the coming weeks, the class composed additional practice conclusions and received feedback. Moss's focus was on helping students draw carefully considered, clearly expressed conclusions—an important goal in science.

It is sometimes easier to see the shortcomings in others' writings than it is to find problems in one's own work. Have students revise published pieces or anonymous pieces from past years. Select papers that can benefit from revision but are not so poorly written that students are overwhelmed. Do some pieces as a whole class and then have students work in small groups or pairs. Be sure students discuss their reasons for revising (Spandel, 2008).

Have students read their drafts out loud. When reading silently, students tend to read what they expect should be there. Reading orally, they are more likely to note confusing passages, missing words, and other problems. Reading aloud is an effective technique for peer editing. One student reads the other's draft out loud to detect needed changes. As Collins states, "Listening to your own writing and listening to others read your writing is the best single editing technique" (2004, p. 3).

Students are also more likely to revise when the piece they are writing is intended for a wider audience than just the teacher. That wider audience might include classmates, peers, readers of the school or town newspaper, or visitors to the class's Web site. The more complex the writing task is, the more extensive the revising is likely to be. In one study, papers that involved analysis or theorizing were much more likely to be revised than papers that required only summarizing (Butler-Nalin, 1984). Thus, papers written for language arts were more likely to be revised than social studies or science pieces. The extent and type of revisions were determined in part by the expertise of the writer. Struggling writers made more revisions, but often these were at the word or sentence level. The more accomplished writers made a greater number of higher-level changes and revisions that affected more than one sentence (Butler-Nalin, 1984).

More accomplished writers are also more likely to produce multiple drafts, which provide students with the opportunity to obtain different views of their writing. Issues may pop up in a third draft that were not noticed in a second draft. Struggling writers may not realize how much they have to say, so they need more guidance in considering the overall impact of their piece as they revise. Their past education may have placed too much focus on spelling and punctuation mechanics and not enough on content. Conferences designed to draw out their knowledge of a topic should help them see the potential for revision.

English Language Learners

To help convey their ideas, English language learners might be encouraged to use illustrations along with their writing.

USING TECHNOLOGY

Talking software can help students edit their writing. Hearing their pieces read on a talking word processor, students are better able to note dropped *ings* and *eds,* omitted words, and awkward expressions.

■ **Editing** is that part of the writing process in which the author searches for spelling, typographical, and other mechanical errors.

Editing

Editing involves correcting spelling and mechanical errors and may also include rewriting awkward sentences or confusing expressions. You might prepare a style sheet for your particular subject matter that provides the capitalization and spelling of key technical terms and writing conventions specific to your content area. In chemistry, this will include the writing of abbreviations and formulas. In math, it might include such matters as when to write numbers as words or numerals and how to separate numerals with commas.

Publishing

Most school-type writing, such as assigned reports and critical essays, is composed for the teacher. Because the teacher already has expert knowledge of the subject, students do not have the experience of explaining a process or idea to someone who has little or no knowledge of their topic. **Publishing**, which entails writing assignments designed for real audiences, has the potential to enrich students' creations. Publishing includes writing a children's book to describe an historical event or a scientific process, creating a video, writing an article for the school or local newspaper, establishing a Web site, posting a blog, adding to a wiki, or creating a profile for Facebook.

Sites such as Youth Voices http://youthvoices.net offer genuine publishing possibilities. Youth Voices is a Web site on which students and their teachers share, distribute, and discuss their inquiries and digital work. Students are encouraged to post photos, video clips, audio clips, or written pieces and also to comment on the submissions of others. The purpose of the site is to have students interact with each other. The site has a mechanism for creating MP3 files from telephone calls so that spoken comments can be posted. The site also has a *What's Up?* feature that encourages students to miniblog by telling what they are thinking about or reading, with guides that show how to share thoughts on books.

Publishing digitally can be motivational. As Stephens and Ballast comment, "For digital natives, posting work to a wiki is deemed far more valuable, more important than completing traditional pen and paper work" (2011, p. 73)

The downside of online writing is that it might provide experience but not practice. As cognitive psychologist Willingham explains, "Experience means that you simply engaged in an activity. Practice means you tried to improve your performance" (2009, p. 149). An examination of a large number of teen postings revealed that many were inadequately developed and poorly expressed. In many instances, the postings had not even had the benefit of a spell check. While the experience of posting has positive benefits for self-expression, it will not result in improved writing unless there is instructional input, a genuine attempt to improve, and feedback.

Benefits of the Writing Process

Although it is presented in step-by-step fashion, the writing process is recursive. The writer might plan and revise and even edit as he composes. As writers grow in expertise, the way they write changes, as does the relative amounts of time devoted to the processes they use. Less experienced writers use a knowledge-telling mode. They tell what they know about a topic and don't spend much time planning; this is similar to providing an oral explanation. It requires "no greater amount of planning or goal setting than

CCSS

Use technology, including the Internet, to produce and publish writing and to interact and collaborate with others.

USING TECHNOLOGY

Teen Lit http://www.teenlit.com/ provides a forum for teens to publish and discuss their writing.

USING TECHNOLOGY

Students might also use some of the Web 2.0 tools explained in Chapter 14 to gather information, collaborate with others, and publish their creations. When the Internet is used, steps need to be taken to ensure students' safety.

■ **Publishing** is that part of the writing process in which the author makes her writing public.

Exemplary Teaching

Technology and Process Writing

Penny Kittle (2008), a teacher at Kennett High School in Conway, New Hampshire, had students post drafts and encouraged them to comment on each other's drafts. The assignment was motivational. Students wrote about events and issues that were of immediate concern to them. One of the things that Kittle noticed was that posting drafts within the school's site or on Google docs helped students build a sense of audience, even within the school. They were more careful with their writing and put more effort into it because others would be reading it and responding. They also were able to get helpful suggestions from their readers. Students had been taught to be respectful of each other's writing, and they often used the same language to evaluate their peers' writing that the teacher had used to talk about their writing.

ordinary conversation" (Bereiter & Scardamalia, 1987, p. 9). In **knowledge telling**, the writer simply records information without reflecting or putting much of himself into the process; students engaged in knowledge telling probably do not learn very much through their writing. In contrast, in **knowledge transformation**, students alter their ideas as they write. As they compose, their writing affects their thinking, and their thinking affects their writing. Instead of merely summarizing thoughts, they reconsider and draw conclusions, which are reflected in their writing. Knowledge transformation should lead to a deeper understanding of the topic being written about. "Thus it is that writing can play a role in the development of their knowledge" (Bereiter & Scardamalia, 1987, p. 11).

Langer and Applebee's (1987) research supports Bereiter and Scardamalia's conclusions. Working with twenty-three secondary science, home economics, English, and social studies teachers, they found that writing in the content areas has the following benefits: Students gain new knowledge, review, reflect on, elaborate, and extend ideas. As might be expected, the benefits derived depended on the type of writing involved. Short-answer study questions in which students located answers and copied them resulted in recall of literal information and involved little reflection. Writing tasks that required comparing, contrasting, concluding, and evaluating and other processes in which students manipulated information led to deeper understandings.

The more reflective and analytical the writing, the more it fostered a deeper understanding. Students' writing also was more effective when the following conditions were met.

1. *Ownership.* Students knew why they were engaged in a particular writing task. They understood how completing the task would help them to better understand the content material. Students should go beyond simply summarizing information or following a rigid outline. "Effective instructional tasks must allow room for students to have something of their own to say in writing" (Langer & Applebee, 1987, p. 141).
2. *Appropriateness.* Students knew how to complete the tasks they were given. They had both the required knowledge and the necessary skills.
3. *Instructional support.* The teacher provided direct instruction, including modeling and feedback, in the types of writing that students were expected to do.
4. *Internalization.* Students internalized effective writing strategies.

As students move through the grades, they are called upon to write pieces that are more interpretive and analytical and that require higher levels of thinking and organization. They must move from writing pieces that summarize information and have a narrative or chronological organization to producing pieces that are interpretive and organized according to a variety of patterns of argumentation, such as the theses/support in English and social studies classes and the lab report in science classes. Both require students to construct a formal argument (Durst, 1984). In studies, students learned the new formats, but were sometimes overly constrained by them, especially the five-paragraph essay. In the five-paragraph essay, students write an opening paragraph that gives the essay's thesis, write three paragraphs that develop the thesis, and write a concluding paragraph. Although students need to learn how to structure their writing, they should be taught a variety of approaches. While expository pieces all have a beginning, middle, and end that consist of an introduction, development, and conclusion, these elements can be structured in different ways. If students are taught formulaic approaches, they might come to see writing as "rote and unengaging" (Alliance for Excellent Education, 2007). The five-paragraph essay might be taught as a structure that is helpful to writers who are just learning to compose more extended expository or persuasive pieces. However, students should be encouraged to move beyond this structure and to try other, more creative approaches. It would be helpful to look at the kinds of approaches that accomplished writers have taken and use them as models. There is nothing wrong with the five-paragraph essay. However, it should be regarded as a starting point, not a stopping point.

■ **Knowledge telling** is a process in which writers simply write down what they know without reflecting on it.

■ **Knowledge transformation** is a writing process in which writers reflect as they compose so that their thinking affects their writing and their writing affects their thinking.

CHECKUP

1. What is the process approach to writing?
2. What are the major parts of the process approach?

Teaching the Writing Process

Modeling the writing process is a highly effective way to teach it. You might model the entire process from topic selection through revising and editing. You might also have students who are accomplished writers discuss and/or model ways in which they write. As you model the process, it is important that you not only show students what you do but also make your thought processes known by thinking out loud so they get a deeper understanding of how topics are selected and pieces are revised.

Writing is learned, in part, through imitation. Provide students with mentor texts. Mentor texts are written pieces that provide clear examples of effective writing techniques. You might locate and use texts that illustrate engaging beginnings, vivid descriptions, amusing anecdotes, or convincing reason, for instance. However, one problem with using models from published writers is that the level of writing is beyond that of most students. More realistic models can be obtained by saving samples of students' work from past years so that your current students can see what an excellent term paper or lab report looks like. You might also create models of the kinds of writing that you are asking students to do. Students might abstract the techniques that they feel are especially effective—starting a paper with an anecdote or a question, for instance. Group compositions also help students understand how a piece is put together. As a group, and under your guidance, the class might compose a critical essay or a journal entry. However, you should encourage students to find their own voices eventually

LESSON 8.1

Writing: Learning from a Model

Step 1: Introducing the Model Passage
Students examine a passage about Kublai Khan to see how the author developed the piece. They find the topic sentence: "Kublai Khan ran his empire well." They locate the details that explain the main idea. They note that the supporting details are frequently expanded or explained. The supporting detail "He saw to it that roads were good and trips were pleasant" is further developed by the explanation "There were stones to mark the way. And trees were planted to give shade to travelers." The class concludes that the piece follows a main idea/supporting details structure. Make note of some areas in which the piece could be improved; for instance, it doesn't end with a strong concluding sentence.

Step 2: Modeling the Writing Process
After analyzing and discussing the text, model how you might compose a similar piece. As you model the composition, include the steps of the writing process: prewriting, drafting, revising, editing, publishing. Model how you go about selecting a topic, discussing, for instance, why you would choose Marco Polo to write about. Discuss how you would obtain information, organize the information, and draft your piece. Also go through the revising and editing processes.

Step 3: Introducing Guide Sheets
Guide sheets, which are modeled on the think sheets created by Raphael and Englert (1990), provide a series of prompts designed to help students plan, organize, draft, revise, and edit their writing. There are separate sheets for the planning/organizing phase, the revising phase, and the editing phase. The planning sheets focus on main idea/detail organization,

(continued)

USING TECHNOLOGY

The Value of Modeling
www.phwritingcoach.com/demo/
writingcoachdemo.html Click on Main Menu > Videos and select Modeling video. High school teacher Kelly Gallagher explains the importance of modeling.

Struggling Readers

Guide sheets are especially helpful to struggling readers and writers. They might be omitted or modified for accomplished writers.

as in Figure 8.1. Planning sheets might also be created for other organizational patterns: compare/contrast; explanation/process; and problem/solution. (See Chapter 4 for a discussion of organizational patterns.)

A revision plan sheet (see Figure 8.2) poses a series of prompts designed to help students take a careful look at their papers and determine how they might strengthen them.

An editing guide sheet might be created that would alert students to check the mechanics: sentence structure, usage, spelling, capitalization, punctuation, and any special format requirements. As students gain in skill, the guide sheets can be phased out.

Step 4: Providing Modeling, Guided Practice, and Application

Go through the guide sheets one by one. Discuss the planning guide sheet first. Model how you might fill out a planning guide. Next, fill out a sample sheet as a whole-class activity. Then have students complete their own sheets. Discuss with students how they can use their planning sheets to compose a first draft, and then have them create their first drafts. Model the use of the revision sheet and fill one in cooperatively with the class. Have students complete their revision sheets and use them to revise their pieces. Discuss their revisions and introduce editing guide sheets.

Step 5: Publishing

After students have written, revised, and edited their pieces, share them in some way. Students' finished pieces might be posted, read aloud to classmates, placed on the class's Web site, collected in a class booklet, or put on display in some way.

FIGURE 8.1
Planning Sheet

Author's name _____ Date _____
Topic _____
Audience: Who am I writing for? _____
Details: What are some details that I need to include in my piece so that my audience will be convinced? What explanations of these details might I include?

_____
Detail 1: _____ Explanation _____
Detail 2: _____ Explanation _____
Detail 3: _____ Explanation _____
Organization: How might I organize my details? _____
In order of interest to the reader _____
In order of importance _____
In the order in which they happened _____
Ending: How might I end my piece so I sum up or conclude my piece in an interesting way?
_____

FIGURE 8.2
Revision Plan Sheet

Author's name _____ Date _____
Title _____
What do I like best about the paper? _____
Do I have a clear topic sentence? Is my topic sentence interesting? _____
Have I included all the important details? _____
Have I explained all or most of the details? _____
Do I have a strong closing? _____
Are there any parts that need changing? _____
How might I make the paper more informative, more interesting, or easier to understand?
_____

Strategy Instruction

CCSS

Write informative/explanatory texts to examine and convey complex ideas and information clearly and accurately through the effective selection, organization, and analysis of content.

Strategy instruction in writing follows the same basic steps that have been established for strategy instruction in reading. The strategy is explained, demonstrated, and modeled. Guided and independent practice are provided, as are review sessions.

Step 1: *Introducing strategies and setting goals.* Help students set individual or group goals. A goal might be to use examples to make writing more convincing and more interesting. Once goals have been decided, explain that almost any operation that improves writing can be taught as a strategy. Discuss with students the strategies you use when you write. In collaboration with students, decide which strategy should be introduced to help them reach their goals. For instance, if students have difficulty generating content and their goal is to write more elaborated pieces, you might choose brainstorming as the strategy to be presented.

Step 2: *Developing preskills.* Students are taught any skills needed to understand and apply the strategy about to be taught. For instance, if students were going to learn how to use varied patterns to organize their writing, they would first need to be taught how basic paragraphs are organized.

Step 3: *Discussing the strategy.* Explain the strategy, its steps, its value, and when and where it might be used. A very basic strategy to begin with is how to develop a topic using examples. Have students examine pieces of writing in which examples are used to develop a topic. Talk about the paragraphs and the value of using examples to write convincing pieces. Discuss when and where examples might be used. Have students tell how they might use the strategy in their writing.

Step 4: *Modeling the strategy.* Model the strategy using any prompts, charts, mnemonics, or other aids that students might find helpful. For instance, you might write a piece telling why John F. Kennedy was one of our greatest presidents. Model the process of writing the piece, noting the steps you used:

State the topic.

Write examples to prove the topic sentence.

Explain each example.

Add an interesting ending.

Take a look at the piece to see if you have used convincing examples.

Step 5: *Providing scaffolding.* Use think sheets, mnemonics, visual displays, and other devices to prompt students to follow all the steps. As incorporated into Step 4, the mnemonic prompt for using examples is SWEAT. "With a little SWEAT, you can write an interesting piece." Using the mnemonic, students memorize the steps in the strategy.

Step 6: *Planning for collaborative practice.* Have students try out the strategy. During conferences, emphasize the strategy that has just been taught. Provide feedback and guidance. Feedback should be specific: "I like the way you used SWEAT to help you put three convincing examples in your piece."

Step 7: *Applying the strategy.* Students apply the strategy on their own or with some guidance. However, review sessions are held to refine strategy use and to foster improved use of the strategy (Gunning, 2010).

For students who are having serious difficulties with their writing, you might try Self-Regulated Strategy Development (SRSD; Santangelo, Harris, & Graham, 2008). Writing is a complex, demanding activity. It requires will as well as skill. Discipline and persistence are foundational attributes of effective writers. To address the discipline aspect of writing, SRSD features strategies for self-regulation. Self-regulation components include goal-setting, self-assessment, self-instruction, and the writing environment. As

Santangelo and colleagues warn, students with learning difficulties are often beset by "self-doubts, learned helplessness, low self-efficacy, maladaptive attributions, unrealistic pre-task expectancies, and low motivation and engagement in academic areas" (p. 81).

Using Rubrics

A rubric is a written description of what is expected in order to meet a certain level of performance. Writing projects assigned at the secondary level are often complex and include a number of elements. Although often used primarily as a way of assessing writing, rubrics can be useful in all phases of the writing process. Rubrics help clarify the writing task and provide direction for developing, revising, and editing the writing piece.

A writing rubric translates a writing task into a series of criteria so that the quality of the finished product might be judged. A well-researched, extensively used set of criteria for judging writing is Six Traits or Six Traits Plus. Six Traits consists of Ideas, the heart of the message; Organization, the internal structure of the piece; Voice, the personal tone and flavor of the author's message; Word Choice, the vocabulary a writer chooses to convey meaning; Sentence Fluency, the rhythm and flow of the language; Conventions, the mechanical correctness of the writing; and Presentation, how the writing actually looks on the page (Spandel, 2008). Although generic rubrics can be used, it is more effective to gear rubrics to the specific type of writing being judged. For an explanatory piece, criteria focus on how clearly and completely the piece explains the topic. For a persuasive piece, the focus is on how convincing the piece is.

Criteria should be created in such a way that they can be translated into instruction. A criterion that specifies that the piece "should contain three examples" can be used by students who are revising their papers and can note how many examples they have. Or it can be used by the teacher to indicate that an insufficient number of examples has been provided. To check to see if their essays meet the criteria, students might use highlighters to mark examples in their essays to show that their writing meets each criterion in the rubric (Saddler & Andrade, 2004).

A sample writing rubric for a persuasive piece is presented in Figure 8.3. The teacher should also use anchor pieces along with the rubric to assess compositions. Anchor pieces provide examples of excellent, skillful, sufficient, developing, and needs support pieces. The teacher decides which of the anchor pieces a student's composition most closely resembles.

Constructing a Rubric

To construct a rubric, first analyze the standard or objective to be met. Then ask yourself: How will I be able to tell when this standard has been accomplished? What criteria might I use to judge it? The next step is to decide how many levels of competence should be included and to write descriptors for each level. Ideally, these descriptions should be grounded in students' performance. If possible, use papers from last year's class, and divide them into as many groups as you have levels. Note the characteristics of the top group and each of the other groups. Number each category, or choose names such as accomplished, adequate, apprentice, novice. Construct a frame that includes the descriptions you have chosen. For each description or criterion, include possible indicators that the criterion has been met. The criterion is the general description of what the student needs to do; for example, "The paragraph persuades the reader to take an action." The indicator is a specific example of how the criterion might be met: "The paragraph recommends a specific course of action that is supported by at least three reasons." Discuss the rubric with students, or, better yet, involve them in the construction process. Try out the rubric with a set of papers and revise as necessary.

To help students understand and use a rubric, involve them in trying out the rubric with some sample pieces of writing (Gallagher, 2006). (These might be anonymous pieces written by past years' students, samples provided by the state department of education for its writing prompt, or examples that you have composed.) For instance, in looking at a sample piece of writing, students may decide that it has a good introduction because it

FIGURE 8.3   Rubric for Assessing Writing to Persuade

	Excellent	Skillful	Sufficient	Developing	Needs Support
Development of Position	Formulates a clear position that recognizes multiple significant aspects of the issue and insightfully addresses the complexities of the issue. The response fully addresses other perspectives, by thoroughly evaluating implications of the writer's position, and/or by using affective arguments that are consistently persuasive.	Formulates a position that usually acknowledges multiple significant aspects of the issue, but may not fully address some of the complexities of the issue. The response partially addresses other perspectives, by evaluating some implications of the writer's position, and/or by using affective arguments that are usually persuasive.	Takes a position and may acknowledge significant aspects of the issue. The response demonstrates some understanding of other perspectives and may evaluate some implications of the writer's position. If affective arguments or examples are used, they are persuasive.	States a position, but addresses only some of the aspects of the issue. The response shows little understanding of other perspectives, although most ideas are relevant to the persuasive purpose.	States a position and provides a few reasons to support the writer's position.
Reasons & Evidence	Provides strong persuasive reasons and evidence to support the writer's position. Approaches to the development of ideas (e.g., summarizing, narrating) are used skillfully to support the persuasive purpose.	Usually provides persuasive reasons and evidence to support the writer's position. Approaches to the development of ideas are usually used skillfully to support the persuasive purpose.	Provides adequate evidence to support the writer's position, but their development may be uneven. Approaches to the development of ideas are adequate, but their relevance to the persuasive purpose may not always be clear.	Some relevant reasons and evidence for the writer's position, but they are not developed enough to be convincing, or may be unevenly developed. Approaches to development of ideas are evident, but they may not be clearly relevant to the persuasive purpose.	A few reasons may be given, but are not developed enough to be convincing. If details and examples are present, they are brief, general, or inadequately developed, and may not be clearly relevant to the persuasive purpose.
Organization	Ideas are clearly focused on the topic throughout the response. Organization demonstrates a logical, well-executed progression of ideas that effectively supports the persuasive purpose and is relevant to the writer's approaches to organization (e.g., analyzing, evaluating, narrating). Transitions effectively convey relationships among ideas.	Ideas are usually focused on the topic. Organization is clear and may demonstrate a logical progression of ideas that supports the persuasive purpose and is relevant to the writer's approaches to organization. Transitions clearly convey relationships among ideas.	Ideas are usually focused on the topic, and an organizational structure is evident. Ideas are logically grouped and adequately reflect the writer's use of relevant approaches to organization. Relationships among ideas are mostly clear.	Most ideas are focused on the topic. The response uses a simple organizational structure, and, for the most part, ideas are logically grouped. There is some evidence of the writer's use of approaches to organization, but they may not be clearly relevant, or they may be confusing. Relationships among ideas are sometimes unclear.	Some ideas may not be clearly focused on the topic. The response shows an attempt to organize thoughts by grouping ideas, and there may be minimal evidence of relevant approaches to organization. However, relationships among ideas are often illogical or unclear.

(Continued)

FIGURE 8.3 **(Continued)**

	Excellent	Skillful	Sufficient	Developing	Needs Support
Sentence Structure	Sentence structure is well controlled and varied to communicate relationships among ideas. Word choice is precise and evaluative and supports the persuasive purpose. Voice and tone are well controlled and effective for the writer's purpose and audience response.	Sentence structure is well controlled to communicate relationships among ideas and varied as appropriate for the writer's purpose. Word choice is usually precise and evaluative and usually supports the persuasive purpose. Voice and tone are usually controlled and effective for the writer's purpose and audience.	Sentence structure is adequately controlled and somewhat varied to communicate relationships among ideas. Word choice is clear, often evaluative, and adequately supports the persuasive purpose. Voice and tone are mostly controlled and usually effective for the writer's purpose and audience.	Sentence structure is usually correct, and there may be a little sentence variety to communicate relationships among ideas. Word choice is usually clear and sometimes evaluative, but at times may not be appropriate for the writer's purpose. Voice and tone show some understanding of what is appropriate for the writer's purpose and audience.	Sentence structure is sometimes correct, but there is little, if any, sentence variety. Word choice is rarely specific and does little to support the persuasive purpose. Voice and tone show little understanding of what is appropriate for the writer's purpose and audience.
Conventions	Though there may be a few minor errors in grammar, usage, and mechanics, meaning is clear throughout the response.	Grammar, usage, and mechanics are usually correct with a few distracting errors, but meaning is clear.	Grammar, usage, and mechanics are mostly correct with some distracting errors, but meaning is clear.	Grammar, usage, and mechanics are mostly correct, but with some distracting errors that may occasionally impede understanding.	Grammar, usage, and mechanics are usually correct, but with many distracting errors that impede understanding.

Adapted from: National Assessment Governing Board. (2010). *Writing Framework for the 2011 National Assessment of Educational Progress.* Washington, DC: Author.

has a thesis statement and it grabs the reader. They decide that another piece of writing exceeds the standard because it has an original introduction, which they define as not being like everyone else's. In this way students determine the key standards for an effective essay. As they do so, they discuss what each standard means and what specifically needs to be included to meet or exceed it. They also have models of pieces that meet, exceed, or fail to meet standards. Rubrics can be personalized by having students select two standards that reflect their personal writing goals or needs. For instance, one student might need to meet an editing standard for punctuation and a revising standard for including explanatory details. These areas are determined by a quick reading of the first draft, and noting one revision is needed and one edit is needed.

CHECKUP

1. How might the process approach be taught?

Applying Process Writing to the Content Areas

Realizing the importance of facilitating students' ability to communicate, one chemistry teacher incorporated imaginative chemistry-based problems into her course (Zinsser, 1988). Students not only had to solve a chemistry problem, but also had to explain, discuss, or apply the results. Although students complained that they shouldn't be given such an assignment because this was chemistry class, not English, they soon entered into the spirit of the task, and some became quite creative. After studying acids and bases, one student created an imaginary product that would keep the pH levels of a fish pond safe for the fish that lived there. She wrote a letter to a customer explaining how to use the product. Not wanting to take time away from chemistry, the teacher did not instruct the students in the mechanics of writing, but did advise them that help was available at the school's writing center. The teacher found that incorporating writing into chemistry was a valuable activity for reasons that went beyond the learning of chemistry.

> I believe that writing is an effective means of improving thinking skills because a person must mentally process ideas in order to write an explanation. Writing also improves self-esteem because mentally processed ideas then belong to the writer and not just to the teacher or textbook author. (Zinsser, 1988, p. 208)

Writing can be used to help students rid themselves of misconceptions about a content area and gain new insights into its possibilities. As Countryman (1992), who has made extensive use of writing to teach math, states:

> Writing mathematics can free students of the assumption that math is just a collection of right answers to questions posed by someone else. Writing—and this includes writing notes, lists, observations, feelings, in addition to term papers, lab reports, and essay questions—will expand the narrow view of mathematics that many children carry around in their heads. (p. 11)

One of the benefits of writing is that it actively engages students. Instead of having just one student summarize a lesson or explain a procedure, you can have all students explain it in writing. "Once students are writing they are automatically taking an active role in the classroom. Instead of waiting for the teacher, or another student, to do, explain, discuss, summarize, or evaluate, each student is engaged in the learning process" (Countryman, 1992, p. 13).

The following writing activities can help clarify complex topics and deepen students' understanding of them.

- Comparing, contrasting, or evaluating key points in a chapter
- Writing critical reports on famous people or events, taking on the role of the famous person, or describing the key event as though one were there
- Interpreting the results of a science experiment conducted in class
- Writing an essay on a social studies or science topic: What does the Bill of Rights mean to me? What can we do to clean up our home, the earth?

As much as possible, help students relate what they are studying to their personal lives. For example, make the Bill of Rights provisions more concrete by having students write about how they exercise their rights every day or about an incident that made them appreciate their freedom to use their rights.

Students' writing in the content areas often consists of simply retelling information. One solution is to have them make firsthand investigations and report the results. They might undertake activities such as the following:

- Writing observations about a natural phenomenon (for example, changes in plants that are being grown from seeds)
- Summarizing and interpreting the results of a classroom or school poll
- Interviewing older family members about life when they were growing up

A writing activity that can be used in any content area class is to ask students to explain a process to someone who has no knowledge of that process. Processes include describing procedures for setting up a scientific experiment, how a seismograph works, and how to find a particular location on a Google map. Students can also use graphics to help explain a process. Other kinds of writing-to-learn activities include the following (Noyce & Christie, 1989):

- Writing letters to convey personal reactions or request information on a topic
- Writing scripts to dramatize key events in history

USING TECHNOLOGY

Links to Educational Resources
www.writeenvironment.com/linksto.html
Provides links to dozens of sites related to writing.

(CCSS)

Write informative/explanatory texts to examine and convey complex ideas and information clearly and accurately through the effective selection, organization, and analysis of content.

- Writing historical fiction
- Writing a children's book on an interesting social studies or science topic
- Writing an editorial or commentary about a social issue
- Writing an illustrated glossary of key terms
- Creating captions for photos of a scientific experiment
- Creating a puzzle for key terms

Journals and Learning Logs

Journals and learning logs can foster students' understanding of content concepts and writing skills. **Journals** are a record of daily events and reflections. They vary in content and purpose from highly private musings to travelogues to observations of nature or scientific experiments. Journals are often used for personal self-discovery, but they can also be a powerful learning tool (Roe & Stallman, 1995).

Writers' Journals

Writers have long used journals to record observations, personal reflections, and story ideas, and to try out new styles of writing. Journals provide students with the opportunity to record memorable passages from their reading, collect possible writing topics and techniques, and try out new techniques and styles. They also can be used to help novice writers expand and hone their writing skills and to experiment. In their journals, novice writers might

- Record interesting dialogue they have heard and use it as the basis for creating a story of their own.
- Record favorite passages from their reading and note why they like the passage.
- Imitate the style of an admired writer or piece of writing.
- Create interesting settings.
- Write from different points of view.
- Reflect on how an event might look from someone else's point of view.
- Note interesting words and expressions and then use them.
- Note fascinating facts or interesting events and reflect on them.
- Raise questions about intriguing, puzzling, or disturbing information.
- Reflect on issues and topics.

Journals can be private or academic. Establish a set of ground rules with students. If you will be reading their journals, inform students so that they don't include information or thoughts they wish to keep private. Including journals as part of the writing program encourages students to make entries. It also gives you insight into the students' writing and provides the opportunity for you to offer guidance and encouragement through your responses. Although students might be given credit for keeping a journal, journals are not graded or corrected. Otherwise, the flow of ideas will be hindered. However, knowing that you will read and respond to their journals with comments will motivate students to put time and thought into their journal entries.

One of the disadvantages of journals is that they can become routine and lifeless. Provide thought-provoking prompts from time to time, and, as you respond to students' journals, encourage them to explore topics more deeply. You might also read from your own journal or have volunteers read from theirs so that students see some of the many kinds of topics or formats that might be included in a journal entry. Another way to enliven journal writing is to have students share their entries with a partner or small group. Students can exchange journals or simply read aloud excerpts from their journals. By reading excerpts aloud, students may omit details that they would rather not share with classmates.

To get students started with journal writing, you may want to use a prompt. Following are some generic prompts.

- What was the highlight of the day?
- If I close my eyes and think about the day, what scene comes to mind?

■ **A journal** is a daily record of events, thoughts, ideas, or feelings.

- If I could change anything that happened today, what might it be?
- What did I learn today?
- If I were to text a friend about the day, what would I say?
- What are my plans for tomorrow?

If students can't think of a particular topic to explore, they can try freewriting, in which they write whatever comes to mind, keeping their pens moving for about ten minutes. If they can't think of anything to write, they may simply state that they can't think of anything to write about and perhaps reflect on why this might be so.

Writers' journals tend to be private and personal. Whereas writers' journals focus on helping students expand topic ideas and develop writing skills and strategies, dialogue and double-entry journals and learning logs concentrate on helping students learn and reflect on content area topics. These more subject-oriented formats are discussed in the following pages.

Dialogue Journals

After she initiated a program in which students chose their own reading, Nancy Atwell soon realized that students needed opportunities to reflect on and discuss their reading. Because each of her classes had twenty-five students, individual conferences were impractical, so she asked her students to write **dialogue journals**. She believed that "writing would give them time to consider their thinking and thoughts captured would spark new insights" (Atwell, 1987, p. 165). She also believed that an exchange between students and a knowledgeable adult would deepen their understanding. Note the following exchange in which Jennifer reflects on her reading of the *Diary of Anne Frank* and compares it to the play by Hackett and Goodrich. Note, too, how Nancy Atwell's comment to Jennifer builds on and extends Jennifer's understanding.

Ms. A.,

Just to see what Anne Frank was going through was miserable. Her "growing up" with the same people every day. I think she got to know them a lot better than she would have if they weren't in hiding, her mother especially. That sudden change, going into hiding, must have been hard.

It amazed me how much more they went downstairs in the book. It also told a lot more of her feelings, right up until the end. It must have come suddenly—to see police come in and arrest them.

J.J.

P.S. I think she could have been a writer.

Dear J.J.,

I don't have any doubt—if she'd survived, she would have been a writer all her life. Her prose style is so lively, and her insights are so deep. And she loved to write.

We've talked about how movies alter (often for the worse) the books on which they're based. Plays can't help but do the same thing. All that inner stuff—reflections, dreams, thoughts, and feelings—doesn't easily translate into stage action, although Hackett and Goodrich tried with Anne's between-act voice-overs.

If you're hungry for more information on Anne, please borrow my copy of Ernst Schnabels's *Anne Frank: Portrait in Courage* when Tom Apollonio returns it to me.

Ms. A. (Atwell, 1987, pp. 165–166)

Dialogue journals are kept in spiral-bound notebooks. At the beginning of the school year, explain the purpose of the dialogue journals, which are written in the form of letters.

In your letters talk . . . about what you've read. Tell what you noticed. Tell what you thought and felt and why. Tell what you liked and didn't and why. Tell how you read and why. Tell what these books said and meant to you. Ask questions or for help. And write back about your ideas, feelings, experiences, and questions. (Atwell, 1987, p. 193)

■ **Dialogue journals** are written exchanges in which students share thoughts with teachers or peers and are frequently used as a way of responding to and discussing literature.

Students can submit their dialogue journals as often as they wish. However, they should be required to turn them in at least once every two weeks.

Dialogue journals should be just that—a two-way conversation—between student and teacher. It is important that the teacher resist the temptation to evaluate and correct. "The teacher's role is to help expand and modify topics, not to direct or correct, although he or she may occasionally need to take the initiative in preventing or resolving communication breakdowns" (Dolly, 1990, p. 361). Because the focus is on expanding the meaning of the text, dialogue journals lead to a more active reading in which the dialoging readers construct meaning. Readers are encouraged to voice their opinions, so they are more likely to interact with the author. "Rather than passing over an author's comment with a vague sense of approval or disagreement, they will be motivated to think about why they agree or object" (Dolly, 1990, p. 362). Dolly found dialogue journals to be especially helpful when working with English language learners. Their dialogues often went beyond the reading to issues about language and culture that puzzled them.

In a study comparing students' views about dialogue versus reflection journals, students felt that dialogue journals were more valuable (Roe & Stallman, 1995). Although students agreed that both kinds of journals improved their writing, helped them to think critically, and provided a tool for them to reflect on what they were learning, they felt that the dialogue journal added an extra dimension. As one student explained, "To me the response journal was just part of my classwork, whereas in the dialogue journal somebody was answering and paying attention to what you said" (p. 9).

Double-entry Journals

In a DEJ (**double-entry journal**), the left-hand page contains a stimulus for reflection or explanation, such as a science experiment, a math problem, a lab drawing, a drawing of a plant, notes, or a prompt. In a sense, the left-hand page is the data. The right-hand page is an explanation of the data or a reflection on it. For instance, in one DEJ entry, students drew diagrams of an experiment with batteries on the left-hand page. On the right-hand page, they explained what was happening in the experiment and its implications. The left-hand side might contain a new vocabulary word or concept. The right-hand side could then be used to explain the word or concept or give examples of its use or application. A description of the pH scale on the left might be complemented by a reflection on its use in swimming pool testing kits and soil testing kits. A math problem might be solved on one side and an explanation of the solution provided on the other side.

Learning Logs

Another type of journal that fosters active involvement in the learning process is the **learning log**. In these journals, which are usually in spiral notebook form, students, on their own or in response to a teacher's prompts, "observe, speculate, list, chart, web, brainstorm, role play, ask questions, activate prior knowledge, collaborate, correspond, summarize, predict, or shift to a new perspective" (Atwell, 1990, p. xvii).

Learning log entries may be completed at home or in school. Entries should be brief and written in five or ten minutes. Although students should feel free to reflect on any aspect of their learning, prompts should be used in the beginning until students become familiar with the activity. Prompts can be generic. Some postreading or postlesson prompts include: What did I learn today? How does this fit in with what I already know? How might I use this knowledge now or in the future? What questions do I have about the topic? What else would I like to learn about the topic?

Prompts might be used to integrate affective and cognitive reactions: How did I feel after I read about the Holocaust? How did I feel when I read about the Great Famine in Ireland? How did I feel when I read about the slave ship?

■ **Double-entry journals** are journals in which the student makes an observation or other entry in one column or page and in the next column or page composes a reflection or other comment on the original entry.

■ **A learning log** is a student's written account of his or her learning.

Possible prompts for a unit on viruses and bacteria, only one of which would be provided for any one session, might include:

- What do I know about viruses and bacteria? What are some things that I don't know?
- What are some diseases caused by bacteria and viruses?
- Which of the diseases caused by bacteria have I had? Which sicknesses caused by viruses have I had? Which of these sicknesses was the worst?
- How are diseases caused by viruses treated?
- How are diseases caused by bacteria treated?
- What false ideas, if any, did I have about bacteria and viruses?

Prompts that promote reflection, manipulation of information, evaluation, and relating information to one's personal life lead to deeper understanding and longer retention of information. Learning logs also help a teacher keep in touch with her class. As she went over her students' logs, Countryman (1992) noted sources of confusion and frustration and used this information to help her students.

Some log entries may be composed before students read a selection or at the beginning of a lesson or experiment. Before reading about Ancient Egypt, students might jot down what they know about the topic. Afterwards, they might note what they learned. Prelearning and postlearning entries help students activate prior knowledge and become more aware of what they already know and what they are learning (Santa, 1994).

Some log prompts might be used to elicit students' thoughts and feelings about key instructional activities: Which classroom activities do you find most helpful? Least helpful? Which classroom activities are easy for you? Which are difficult? What questions do you have about Ancient Egypt [or whatever the topic is] that we haven't covered? The best prompts are open-ended and personally involve writers by asking them "to discover their own opinions, draw on their prior experiences" (Atwell, 1990, p. 167).

One tenth-grade biology teacher had her students use learning logs to summarize concepts they had recently learned. In their learning logs, they also interacted with text by recording a running commentary on their reading. They could summarize, raise issues, ask questions, or express opinions about what they had read. The purpose of these assignments was to provide students with the opportunity to relate new information to their background knowledge. The teacher checked the log entries, but did not grade them so that students could write more freely. This informal writing was preparation for the later writing of essays (Marshall, 1984a).

Learning logs can be handled in a variety of ways. The class members can discuss their learning logs, or the teacher can collect them and respond to them in writing. The main purpose of logs is to have students think about their learning and ask questions about any elements that might not be clear (Atwell, 1990). Logs can also be used to record questions. Before reading a selection, students might record the questions they have about that topic. Later, they can evaluate how well their questions were answered. Whether students pose a question, jot down a reaction, or create a semantic map, the activity should help them reflect on their learning.

How effective are learning logs? According to a tenth-grade biology student, learning logs helped her to learn and forced her to think:

> If you write about it, you learn without wanting to. You don't have to sit there and study it. Phillips [the student's biology teacher] has you write down everything you know about a subject and that way you learn what you don't know . . . so you learn without trying. On multiple choice tests, you could guess. When you have to write, you have to think. (Marshall, 1984b, p. 168)

Science Notebooks

Science notebooks are sometimes used along with or instead of journals or logs. Science notebooks are designed to mimic the kinds of notes and observations that a working scientist might make as they engage in investigations. In their notebooks, students

USING TECHNOLOGY

Science Notebooks in K-12 Classrooms East Bay Educational Collaborative Scientist's Notebook toolkit http:// ebecri.org/content/toolkit Provide information and resources for using science notebooks.

record inquiry or focus questions, predictions or hypotheses, planning of investigations, conclusions and reflections. They may also include notes on general classroom lectures and demonstrations, readings, and other related science activities. In a sense the notebook becomes a record of students' thinking and can be used to monitor students progress (East Bay Educational Collaborative, 2010).

As noted earlier, personal journals such as the writer's journal should probably not be graded because that would tend to stifle creativity. However, logs and journals and academic notebooks in which students record and reflect on their learning may be assessed using a rubric created with your students. An informal survey of journal rubrics used by teachers revealed varied criteria. Some criteria judged journals on the basis of whether students made connections between class discussions and their reading, others counted neatness, whether students wrote in complete sentences, whether students drew illustrations for observation, or whether students spelled their entries correctly.

💻 **USING TECHNOLOGY**

Science Writer http://sciencewriter.
cast.org/welcome Provides a report structure broken down into manageable segments, possible sentence starters for major parts of the report, checklists for revising, dictionary, translator, and text-to-speech so that students can hear what they have written.

Discipline Specific Writing

Students need to be able to write in the style and manner specific to each of the content areas they study. A lab report demands skills that are different from those required to compose a book report. "There are distinct ways of reading and writing and communicating among different groups. Writers choose particular sorts of words, arrange them in particular sorts of ways, imagine a particular sort of audience, and bend their language to suit the particular purposes and values of the discipline" (Deshler & Ehren, 2008). Discuss the kinds of writing undertaken in your content area. Give specific directions and instruction for lab reports, analytical essays, research reports, or opinion pieces. Introduce the writing activity according to the steps of the writing process. Provide time for introducing the assignment and prewriting. Although drafting can be done at home, provide time and instruction for revision and editing in class. Also encourage peer editing. You might team up with the English or writing teacher to help work with the class on content-specific writing.

Content Area Autobiographies

Students who have weak backgrounds or who have negative experiences with a subject will be hindered in their quest to learn that subject. To find out what kinds of experiences students have had with your content area and also to provide them the opportunity to voice their feelings about the subject, have them write a content area autobiography (Countryman, 1992). In a content area autobiography, students describe their experiences with a subject from their earliest exposure to the present time. They are encouraged to describe failures as well as successes and to discuss how they feel about the subject. They should not, however, use the autobiography to criticize others. Autobiographies, such as the following, provide the teacher with valuable insight into students' attitudes and background in math and help her take steps to remove barriers to learning.

> Up to about fifth grade I enjoyed and was quite good at math. After that, I often became confused, and, most of all, frustrated by it. A main problem that I have in math is that I will understand some of the material very well, but when I don't catch something right away or in a short amount of time, I have a problem ever understanding it. Sometimes I get so frustrated I think I hold myself back from learning it. This is strange because sometimes I find things which other people have trouble with quite easy, and vice versa. Either way, I always end up doing badly in math, and that's probably why I dislike it. (Countryman, 1992, p. 25)

CHECKUP

1. What are some ways the process approach to writing can be applied to the content areas?

Writing Workshop

One of the best ways to develop writing skills is through a **writing workshop**. In a workshop approach, both group and individual instruction are provided. A writing workshop consists of minilessons, strategic writing, writing time, conferences, and sharing. Workshops are most effective if they are held on a regular basis. Language arts and writing teachers may be able to hold writing workshops every day or every other day; other content area teachers may be able to hold writing workshops on only a once-a-week basis. Even if you can't schedule writing workshops on a regular basis, you may still be able to implement some of the following principles and techniques used in writing workshop.

Minilesson

In the **minilesson**, which lasts for only about ten minutes, a needed writing skill is taught. Possible subjects are a review of the correct form for writing chemical formulas, selecting topics, proper e-mail format, or any one of a dozen fairly easy-to-teach skills. The minilesson is taught to the whole class or a small group.

Strategic Writing

A **strategic writing** lesson is similar to a minilesson except that it embraces a more complex skill or strategy and takes more time to develop. Developing a topic, summarizing, and other more complex skills and strategies are taught during strategic writing. A strategic writing lesson may take ten to twenty minutes or more and may be taught along with or instead of a minilesson. Strategic writing lessons might be geared to small groups of students who have specific needs. For example, you might assemble a group of students who are having difficulty supplying interesting examples to illustrate a point and present them with a lesson on composing examples. Discuss the strategy and how it will help their writing. During the lesson, provide examples of the strategy as it appears in selections that students are reading and also in pieces written by students or you. Model the use of the strategy, showing how you might include interesting examples in a piece that you are writing. Provide guided practice and have students apply the skill by using it in their own writing. Revision and evaluation should focus on providing interesting examples. The skill should be reviewed and reintroduced in conferences and follow-up lessons until it becomes part of the students' repertoire of writing strategies.

Writing Time

Writing time may vary, but typically it lasts for thirty minutes or longer. Students work on their individual pieces, have peer or teacher conferences, or meet in small groups to discuss their writing. Students also can meet in strategic writing groups for lessons geared to each group's specific needs. During writing time, hold one or two small-group strategic writing sessions if you have grouped students according to common needs. After meeting with groups, and as time permits, move about the room and provide on-the-spot help and encouragement. You might explain to one student when a source needs to be quoted, help another narrow a topic, and encourage a third who is having trouble getting started. During this time you might hold individual **conferences** with several students, hold a

USING TECHNOLOGY

Open Directory Project Kids and Teens/School Time/English/Writing
http://dmoz.org/Kids_and_Teens/ School_Time/English/Writing Lists a number of sites that assist students with their writing.

CCSS

Write routinely over extended time frames (time for research, reflection, and revision) and shorter time frames (a single sitting or a day or two) for a range of tasks, purposes, and audiences.

■ A **writing workshop** is a way of organizing writing instruction that includes a minilesson, strategic writing, time for students to write, individual and group conferences, and whole-class sharing.

■ The **minilesson** is a brief lesson on a needed writing or reading skill. The skill is usually applied in the following writing or reading workshop.

■ **Strategic writing** is an approach to writing in which students are given direct instruction in writing strategies for which they have demonstrated a need.

■ A **conference** is a conversation between teacher and student(s) or among students designed to foster the development of one or more aspects of the writing process.

conference with a group of students who are writing about a similar topic or who have similar concerns, or sit in on a peer conference that students have arranged.

In peer conferences, students may meet in pairs or in small groups of four or five. During these conferences, one or more students may read from their papers and seek suggestions for improvement or reactions from the other members of the group. Because they provide individual focused assistance, conferences are probably the most valuable part of writing workshop.

Group Sharing

At the end of the workshop, students gather and volunteers read their pieces. The atmosphere is positive and constructive. After a volunteer has read his piece, other students affirm the author by first telling what they liked about the piece. They also ask questions about any parts that might be unclear or about which they have a special interest. They also make constructive suggestions. By getting audience reaction, student writers get a sense of what's working and what's not and how to add clarification and elaboration. Other class members get a sense of what their peers are writing about and learn about techniques that others are using that they might adapt.

Management of the Writing Workshop

Writing workshop works best when it is well organized. Before initiating the workshop, explain the setup of the room and note where supplies and materials are located. Involve the students in developing a series of routines. To prepare students for peer conferences or small sharing groups, discuss and model these activities.

Make sure, too, that students have specific plans for the workshop; for example, to revise a piece, confer with the teacher, or seek additional information about a topic. You may find it helpful to keep a record of students' activities in a workshop log.

As you move about the room, note students' progress and specific needs. If everyone seems to be having difficulty with the format of a report, discuss this in a minilesson. If a few students are writing pieces that have very little elaboration, schedule these students for a group conference or strategic writing lesson. Note the social dynamics of groups that are meeting, particularly whether some students are dominating and others are being left out and whether the group is staying on task.

> **CCSS**
>
> Write narratives to develop real or imagined experiences or events using effective techniques, well-chosen details, and well-structured event sequences.

CHECKUP

1. What is writing workshop?
2. How might writing workshop be conducted in my content area?

Composing Narratives

Narrative writing includes nonfiction as well as fiction. Often, narratives are used to introduce or enliven argumentative or explanatory writing. "A narrative is a moving picture. Like description, narratives need to have a rich texture of details so that the reader is seeing, hearing, smelling, and touching" (Writing Across the Curriculum, 2010). A narrative paints a picture of what happened. It introduces the character(s) and describes the setting or scene and events in vivid detail so that the reader can experience what happened. However, the narrative is selective. It does not include every possible detail. Since a narrative typically includes a series of events, writers use transitional phrases to maintain the flow and coherence of the piece. As students acquire advanced skills, they consider the pacing of the piece. At times the piece moves forward rapidly, but at critical moments the pacing is slowed down so that suspense can be built or critical events detailed. For example, an account by John Updike of Ted Williams's last time at bat builds suspense by describing each pitch, but speeds up when describing that hit so that the reader can picture the ball in flight.

Skills involved in writing a narrative include:

- Organizing and presenting a series of events
- Using transitional phrases
- Using concrete phrases and vivid descriptions
- Using dialogue and action to develop the narrative
- Using pacing to slow down the piece and speed it up

Composing the Research Report

One of the most complex tasks students face is writing a research report, especially when they are asked to synthesize multiple sources (Many, Fyfe, Lewis, & Mitchell, 1996). Writing a report involves setting a goal, planning the content, locating sources, selecting information, understanding and synthesizing information, recording information, composing the report, and revising. Although this writing task is expressed in linear fashion, in fact, these processes are recursive. For instance, students may revise their overall plan in light of unexpected information that they have located.

Obtaining Information for a Report

Students vary in their ability to obtain information for a report. As one secondary history teacher commented,

> Even older kids have a difficult time reading scholarly books and determining what's significant and what's not. Some of my eighth and ninth graders are adept at locating information. Those at the other end of the spectrum prefer to use the textbook. Their skills of accessing information are not that great, so they rely on one source. (Palmer and Stewart, 1997, p. 637)

In their study, Palmer and Stewart (1997) found some students who could not locate appropriate references, some who could locate appropriate references but were unable to find the information they needed, and some who could find the information but had difficulty interpreting or synthesizing it. Of course, there were a number of students who were able to complete their reports successfully.

Students vary in their understanding of what research involves. In a study of eleven- and twelve-year-olds given the assignment of researching and writing on a topic related to World War II, the students were found to view research in one of three ways: accumulating information, transferring information, or transforming information (Many et al., 1996). The way they viewed research directly affected the processes they used. Those who saw research as a matter of accumulating information or transferring information were most concerned with task completion. Their goal was to fill up the twelve-page booklets they had been given. There was little concern for audience or sticking to the topic.

The information accumulators paid little attention to the planning webs they had constructed at the beginning of the project. They included any information that was interesting, even though it did not support their specific topic, and they selected references because they were available, even if they weren't appropriate, instead of seeking out sources that addressed their topics. Information was recorded through a paraphrasing process.

Students who viewed research as a transferring process sought out relevant materials, but did not go beyond recording information in their own words. Although they may have used multiple sources, they did not synthesize information. Instead, they used one source for one subtopic and another source for a second subtopic, and so forth.

Those who viewed report writing as transforming information saw their task as providing information for a specific audience, in this case, students their own age. They engaged in careful planning, reviewed and revised their work in light of their planning, and considered their audience. They also were more likely to synthesize information from multiple sources and to reflect on the information they presented. Instead of focusing on filling up the pages, these students were concerned with conveying accurate information in an interesting way.

A key element in the research process was the availability of appropriate resources. When the references were difficult to read, even the most capable writers resorted to sentence-by-sentence paraphrasing or word-for-word copying.

The following steps can be implemented to turn information accumulators and information transferrers to information transformers.

Step 1: Discuss the nature and purpose of the assignment. With the class's help, draw up a rubric so that students know exactly what is expected of them. (For more information about rubrics, see Chapter 13 and the sample rubric in Figure 8.3.) Rubrics are especially effective when students work in pairs or small groups and use the rubrics to make suggestions for improving both their own work and that of their peers.

Step 2: Select or assign topics. If possible, students should be given a choice of topics so that they have a sense of ownership over the project and are willing to invest the time and energy needed to compose an effective report. Students who have little knowledge of an area would have difficulty choosing an appropriate topic. Before students select a topic, encourage them to do some preliminary investigation so that they are better able to pick an interesting topic and have some idea about how to develop it. Also, help them pick a topic that is neither too broad nor too general. As part of their initial investigation, they can get some sense of whether there is adequate information at a suitable level of difficulty available on the topic.

Step 3: Have students complete a preliminary planning guide once they have chosen a topic. The planning guide can be an oral discussion or a written guide such as the one shown in Figure 8.4. The guide might include a brief description of the audience, the topic, key supporting subtopics, and a list of sources of information. The planning guide should be flexible so that as students make discoveries about their topic, they can revise the plan.

Step 4: Have students select sources of information. Discuss possible sources. Also discuss ways in which students can determine whether the sources contain relevant information.

Keeping their topic in mind, students should examine the index and table of contents of the source, if it is a book, in addition to looking at the title, to see whether it has relevant information (Dreher & Guthrie, 1990). Finding relevant information is deceptively difficult (Gans, 1940). Modeling, discussion, and guided practice can help. For guided practice, pose questions or topics and have students search through indices and tables of contents to locate what seem to be relevant passages. For print or Internet articles, have students note subheads and skim the articles. Then have the class read the passages and decide

⟨ CCSS ⟩

Gather relevant information from multiple print and digital sources, assess the credibility and accuracy of each source, and integrate the information while avoiding plagiarism.

FIGURE 8.4
Planning Guide

Name _____ Class _____ Date _____
Audience _____
Topic _____
Key Supporting Subtopics
_____
_____
Sources of Information
_____
_____

whether they really are relevant. You might also distribute copies of selected passages and have the class decide whether they are relevant to a particular topic (Singer & Donlan, 1989). Students are asked to decide whether the passage helps answer their questions. If it does, students take notes from it. When passages fail to answer their questions, students sometimes mentally modify the question so that the passage seems relevant (Gans, 1940). Suggest that students write down the target questions so there is less chance that they will be modified. Also discuss and monitor students' research results to make sure that they are selecting relevant information.

Step 5: Have students extract relevant information from the text once students have located it. Because less expert writers have a tendency to copy, they need to be taught how to take notes and cite sources. You can teach students a paraphrasing strategy in which they read a relevant passage, recall what they have read, and summarize what they have read in their own words. Once students have gathered the information, they can begin to organize their cards. Note cards, real or electronic, containing information on the same subtopic are grouped together. Groups of cards are arranged in either sequential or another kind of logical order, and the report is ready to be written.

Step 6: Have students compose their reports using information they have extracted and paraphrased. When using multiple sources, students may employ a cut-and-paste synthesis or a **discourse** synthesis. In a cut-and-paste synthesis, students first jot down information from one source and then information from a second source. In discourse synthesis, students integrate the information from two or more sources. Teach students the importance of citing sources as well as methods for doing so.

Step 7: Ask students to review their reports to make sure they are accurate and contain sufficient information (Many et al., 1996). They may check facts or decide that there are unanswered questions. They also check to see that sources have been cited.

Step 8: Ask students to revise/edit. Although there is some overlap between this step and the previous one, the focus here is more on presentation. Students consider whether their reports are clear and interesting, and they also check the mechanics.

■ **Discourse** is a form of speaking or writing that extends beyond a sentence.

Exemplary Teaching

Impact of Writing on Achievement

Reeves (2000) studied a number of 90/90/90 schools. These are schools where 90 percent of the students are members of a minority group and 90 percent live in poverty, but 90 percent achieve at or above grade level. One of the characteristics of 90/90/90 schools is a focus on informational writing (Parker, 2002). Students are required to produce an acceptable piece of writing on a periodic basis. After being provided with thorough guidance and instruction, students write an informative piece and then are required to revise and edit as much as necessary in order to produce an acceptable product. For elementary schools, this is once a month. For secondary schools, it is once a quarter. Writing is a whole-school activity and is assessed using a common rubric. The rubric highlights key characteristics of effective writing. The principal and teachers regularly discuss and share students' writing to maintain their focus on key characteristics of students' writing.

In their informational pieces students must include information that they do not already know so that the project becomes a genuine quest for new knowledge. The format can vary and might include a report, a persuasive editorial, a biography, or an explanation of a process in science. In writing their pieces, students not only increase their content knowledge, but also they develop thinking and writing skills.

Instruction is both whole group and small group. The whole class is instructed in procedures or skills that all need to learn. Small-group instruction is used to teach groups of students who have common needs.

Modeling the Process

One of the best ways to show students how to create a research report is to model the process. Show how you might go through the process of selecting and narrowing a topic, locating sources, extracting information, composing, reviewing, revising, and editing. Do a think-aloud in which you make known the cognitive processes involved in each of these steps. Also conduct lessons for key elements. For instance, provide direct instruction, guided practice, and application in the extraction and recording of information. Conduct these activities with material from your content area so that students are learning content as they learn writing skills.

Provide models of research reports, perhaps exemplary reports written by students from a previous year. If possible, do a cooperative report with the class. In a cooperative report, the class selects a topic, narrows it, researches it, and goes through all the necessary steps as a group to gain a better understanding of the process. Students might also do reports as part of a cooperative group before attempting to create reports on their own.

Because report writing is a complex, long-term undertaking, have the students complete it in parts. For instance, part one is topic selection and completion of a planning guide. Part two is the first draft. Part three is revising and editing. And part four is the finished report.

Reports can be creative. Tenth-grade biology teacher Judith Stenroos asked her students to pretend they were Gregor Mendel's lab assistant and that they were writing to apply for a grant to further their research. In their applications, they had to write a clear explanation of their findings (Alvermann & Phelps, 2002). They were given a list of terms to include, such as *recessive*, *dominant*, *hybrid*, and *genes* and were reminded to explain the outcomes of the following gene combinations: two dominant genes, two recessive genes, and one dominant and one recessive gene. An eighth-grade teacher, Janyce Hepp, asked students to pretend that they were new immigrants. They were to write a letter to a relative back home telling about their experiences in this new country. Students were supplied with a list of possible topics that they might develop as part of the letter.

Research in the Age of Wikipedia

With well over three million articles, Wikipedia is a massive source of information. For many secondary school students, Wikipedia is their first and sometimes only stop as they seek information for reports and research projects. Since Wikipedia is an open project and just about anyone can be a contributor or editor, the accuracy, reliability, and trustworthiness of the articles are sometimes called into question. In some schools students aren't allowed to cite Wikipedia. However, one study found that Wikipedia was almost as accurate as *Encyclopedia Britannica* (Giles, 2005). Despite this vetting, readers should carefully consider the credibility of information obtained from Wikipedia.

One advantage of Wikipedia is that, since it is in digital format, it can be read by a text-to-speech device. Wikipedia is also available in eight languages: English, Spanish, French, German, Italian, Turkish, Polish, and Romanian.

Wikipedia editors admit that some articles may lack neutrality, and they supply lists of entries that may not be neutral. Students in an eleventh-grade class were asked to read short articles from the lists and note probable bias (Harouni, 2009). From the list students selected articles and edited them so that they would be unbiased. Instead of just being asked to detect bias, students were being invited to correct bias.

Building critical analysis had entailed quite a bit of extra work on the part of the students. As Harouni concluded, personal engagement was an essential part of the process. "In teaching critical literacy for research, I have had to separate research from its dry, academic context and consider it an everyday practice of becoming informed about issues that have an impact on students' lives" (p. 490).

CHECKUP

1. How can students be taught to write reports?
2. How might students be taught to critically evaluate the sources they use for writing reports?

Exemplary Teaching

Developing Critical Reading

In his work with eleventh graders, Harouni (2009) found that students liked analyzing films, photographs, and music, but they displayed little interest in analyzing other sources of information and they were also less critical of information from print sources. When he listened to their first research reports, he noted that they were accurate and factual, but shallow and unquestioning. Realizing that he had focused on the end product, he began to emphasize the process. His first step was to observe students as they worked on their reports in the computer lab. It was an awakening. Every student was using Wikipedia. Instead of banning Wikipedia or simply warning students of potential problems of reliability, Harouni had students carefully investigate Wikipedia. Students examined a site that had been obviously vandalized. This led to a discussion of the process used to create articles and both the benefits and dangers of such an open process. Guidelines for assessing the credibility of sources were discussed. The following guideline questions were used:

1. Does the document contain facts that are verified?

2. Are the opinions unbiased?

3. Does the work extensively or marginally cover your topic?

4. Does the document clearly cite reliable third-party sources for its facts? Is the author associated with a reputable organization?

5. Is there a process by which the accuracy, timeliness, and thoroughness of the sources in question are verified?

Harouni realized that judging the credibility of a source is difficult unless you are familiar with the topic. Otherwise, how can you tell that the information is erroneous or that critical information has been omitted? Pairs of students examined the entry on a topic with which they were familiar to see if they thought the information was credible. They were instructed to "Read for any statements that you strongly doubt." In follow-up homework assignments students used the guide questions to reflect on and write about additional articles on familiar topics. Students' papers showed that the process was working. Some students went beyond the guidelines to note that some information was missing and even that some perspectives were absent.

Writing Guides

Students may be unfamiliar with the kinds of writing required in the content areas. Just as strategy or study guides help students to understand content material better, guides can be used to help students write about content area topics. In a **writing guide**, the task is structured so that students are provided with prompts and suggestions that will help them write more effectively. Although somewhat similar to the guide sheets discussed earlier in the chapter, writing guides are more specific and topic oriented. Initially, writing guides can be tightly structured so as to provide maximum help. As students become more confident, the guides can be less structured and more flexible. Writing assignments can be straightforward or creative, such as writing an editorial about the effects of the Industrial Revolution (Figure 8.5), or writing a diary of a young worker during the Industrial Revolution (Figure 8.6).

RAFT

One way to provide guidance for students is to use **RAFT**, a structured technique that helps students step out of

■ **Writing guides** are sets of questions, suggestions, and directions designed to assist students in the completion of a writing task.

■ **RAFT** is a structured approach to writing that helps students focus on four key elements: Role of the writer, Audience, Format, and Topic.

FIGURE 8.5
Writing Guide: Industrial Revolution

Read the section on the Industrial Revolution (pp. 287–290). Notice how the Industrial Revolution changed the way people lived. Then take the role of an editorial writer. Write an editorial in which you are either for or against the Industrial Revolution. Write a topic sentence in which you give your opinion of the Industrial Revolution. Then give three to five reasons or examples to back up your opinion.

_____

_____

_____

FIGURE 8.6
Creative Writing Guide: Industrial Revolution

The year is 1790. You are a young person working in a textile mill in England during the Industrial Revolution. Although most workers can't read or write, you can. Write a diary entry telling what a day in the life of a young worker might have been like. In your diary, you might:

- Describe your home
- Tell where you work
- Tell what your job is
- Describe the long hours that you work there
- Talk about other young people who worked there
- Tell about your boss
- Remember what life was like before you moved from the family farm to the city

themselves, focus on their audience, use their imaginations, explore a varied format, and write with conviction (Santa et al., 1996). RAFT is an acronym for the following elements: **R**ole of the writer, **A**udience, **F**ormat, and **T**opic.

Role of the Writer

The writer can be a famous author, a scientist, a governor, a newspaper reporter, a detective, a creature from outer space, or even an animal or inanimate object.

Audience

The audience can be a judge of a writing contest, a district attorney, an ancestor, a legislative body, a favorite author, a talk show host, or whomever else the writer might want to address.

Format

The piece could be a children's book, an editorial, a news story, a movie script, a journal entry, a speech, a memo, an infomercial, a play, a Web page, or whatever format seems to fit best.

Topic

The statement of the topic is accompanied by a strong verb so that it is an expression of the writer's purpose; for example, *urge* everyone to block the new chemical plant, *demand* a refund for a faulty product, *persuade* a radio station to let the town's teens have an hour-long show each week, *convince* an investor to back your new invention.

To introduce RAFT, explain its purpose and components and model writing a RAFT piece. Brainstorm possible topics. The topics might fall under a general theme. For instance, if you are studying the colonial period, have students suggest possible RAFT pieces, such as a teen writing a letter to his cousin in England, a merchant writing a letter of protest about the new taxes, or an editorial writer urging independence. A plan for a RAFT piece is shown in Figure 8.7.

FIGURE 8.7
RAFT Planning Sheet

Role	Audience	Format	Topic
thirsty plant	*rain clouds*	*letter*	*drought*

Summarizing

After Columbus and other Europeans began exploring America, there was a two-way exchange of food. From the Americas foods such as _____.

From Europe, Asia, and Africa foods such as _____.

Because of the exchange, _____.

Explaining a Process

The process of _____ has _____ steps. In the first step, _____.

In the second step, _____.

In the next step, _____.

For the fourth and final step, _____.

If all the steps have been followed, _____.

Providing Support for a Judgment

_____ has my vote for being the best _____ for a number of reasons.

First, _____   Second, _____.

Most important of all, _____.

You won't find a better _____ than _____.

FIGURE 8.8
Framed Paragraphs

Framed Paragraphs

Of all the techniques for supporting writing, **framed paragraphs** are the most structured. They are particularly useful when introducing new types of writing and when working with struggling writers. In a framed paragraph, the main idea of the piece is supplied. The frame indicates how many supporting details the piece might contain and it may also supply transition words and a conclusion. The amount of support and structure supplied can be varied. You might start out supplying maximum support and gradually fade the support until students are writing without the assistance of the frames. See Figure 8.8 for a sample frame.

CHECKUP

1. What are writing guides?
2. How might writing guides and framed paragraphs be used in the content area that I teach?

Writing for English Learners

Still learning the nuances of the language, even advanced English learners tend to make more surface errors and different kinds of mistakes than native speakers (Harklau & Pinnow, 2009). Cultural factors also enter into students' writing. For instance, Chinese students place the main idea at the end of a piece because they feel that providing the main idea at the beginning is too direct (O'Byrne, 2001). Chinese students might also use prepositional phrases at the beginning of sentences to indicate time because Chinese verbs do not have a well-defined way of indicating tense.

Talking and reading should be essential elements in a program to develop ELLs' writing skills. Swain and Lapkin (1998) put forth a socio-cognitive theory in which dialogue with other students plays a key role in the writing development of English learners, and Krashen (1985) advocates a comprehensible input hypothesis in which reading fosters writing. Actually, forming a written response might be easier for English learners because they have more time to construct a response and might use a dictionary or other reference sources.

English learners may not receive high-quality writing instruction, especially if they are placed in low-level classes. Teachers may view them from a deficit perspective and interpret their limited English as indicating limited academic ability. However, students who are proficient writers in their native language tend to be better writers in the second

■ **Framed paragraphs** provide support for students who are having difficulty organizing their thoughts. The frames can also prompt students to add needed details.

language. To find out if students are proficient writers in their native langue, ask them to bring in a piece they have written and read it to you and translate it.

If they are in the early stages of second language acquisition, English learners may write in their first language and translate. As they become proficient, they will make more use of the second language. Gear instruction to students' level of writing development. They might need instruction in writing paragraphs or even sentences. As appropriate, use frames and guided writing assignments, mentor texts, starter sentences, lists of needed words, and lots of modeling. Show them how dictionaries and handbooks could aid them. A reference such as the "Learner's Handbook," which is part of the *Longman Dictionary of American English, Fourth Edition* (Pearson Education Limited, 2007), would be especially useful. Texts or programs such as *The Longman Academic Writing Series* (Butler, 2007), which systematically develop the writing skills of English learners, might also be used. If possible, plan a program with the ESL or bilingual teacher.

Putting It All Together: The Collins Program

The foundation of the Collins (2004, 2010) program is the concept of *focus correction areas* and the creation of writing assignments that are clear and that focus on the essentials. As Chadwell (2002) notes, an "everything counts" approach to assessing writing can be overwhelming for students. He recommends focusing on one to three areas. These focus correction areas, or FCAs, can range from using commas correctly to utilizing examples to develop a topic. Collins (2004) recommends including at least one FCA devoted to improving content. Others might deal with organization, style, or mechanics. FCAs are stressed in prewriting discussions and instruction, in conferences, in revision, and in assessment. Papers are written, revised, and assessed with the FCAs in mind. Focus correction areas can be provided for individuals, groups, or the whole class. FCAs are included in writing assignments and are noted at the tops of students' papers. Focus correction areas are not applied to informal writing such as quickwrites and journals. However, when students write a paper that is to be formally published, FCAs might be applied in the early drafts, but the final copy is subject to complete editing. Although students write on a regular basis, only four or five of their papers are published each year.

Providing clear assignments is also an essential element in the Collins program. Assignments are centered on the four components of RAFT plus the focus correction areas, a description of the steps that will be taken to complete the assignment, and a summary of the assignment. The summary states the rationale for the assignment and a description of the end product. The summary is designed to clarify the project for both teacher and students. Note the summary presented in the following section.

Project Summary

As a student in a career and technology program, you must master many tasks to prepare for the workplace. Each task requires that you be aware of the circumstances associated with the task, have all the materials and equipment that you need, and perform the necessary actions. Choose a procedure or task that is important in your technical area. You must use precise language, include all steps in the procedure, and get the steps in the correct order.

For this assignment, the key focus correction areas are having all steps in order and avoiding a particular pitfall, along with one to be determined by the teacher. The procedures include

- Reviewing the task and clarifying any steps that you are unsure of
- Identifying needed terms and procedures
- Using a Focus Sheet entitled "Describing a Procedure or Task" to list steps, materials, and circumstances involved in completing the task
- Completing the first draft
- Reading the draft to yourself and making needed changes
- Working with a peer editor get feedback and check FCAs
- Writing a second draft (Chadwell, 2009)

All key writing tasks in the program were accompanied by similar detailed assignments. From research cited by Collins Education Associates (2009) and interviews from teachers who implemented the program, students' writing showed significant improvement.

Composing Biographies

Biographies put a human face on inventions, scientific discoveries, and important historical events. Until I read a biography of Mendel, to me he was just an obscure monk who grew a lot of peas. A biography made him and his ideas come alive. Each content area has its key people. Composing a biography about a famous inventor, leading scientist, president, or explorer is an excellent complement to material in the textbook. Written as they are for a general audience, biographies typically take special pains to explain their subjects' contributions clearly and to put these contributions in context.

Because every person's life has interesting aspects, biographies are an engaging kind of writing, if the biographer goes beyond the bare details of the subject's life and seeks out key incidents that define him or her. Patricia and Fredrick McKissack (2001a, 2001b), who have collaborated on more than fifty biographies, offer the following suggestions for student biographers.

1. Choose a person that you care about. This doesn't mean that you have to like the person. You just have to be interested in her or him.
2. Read an encyclopedia entry or other articles about your subject. This will give you an overview of the person's life.
3. Research your subject thoroughly. Check books, newspaper and magazine articles, and Internet sources.
4. Be objective about your subject. Don't leave out the person's failures or bad points because you like the person. And don't emphasize bad points because you dislike the person. Let the person's life speak for itself.
5. Be accurate. Check all your facts.
6. Tell a good story. Highlight interesting incidents in the person's life. Emphasize events that show what kind of a person your subject is. If you were writing a biographical sketch of Franklin D. Roosevelt, you might start off your biography with an account of his battle with polio. In a biography of Frederick Douglass, the McKissacks highlighted Douglass's use of a sailor's protection papers to escape to New York.

USING TECHNOLOGY

Biography Maker www.bham
.wednet.edu/bio/biomak2.htm
Provides step-by-step directions for
composing biographies.

Persuasive Writing

Tests or assignments often call on students to compose persuasive pieces. However, persuasive pieces may well be the most difficult writing assignment (Gleason, 1999). The heart of writing persuasive pieces is understanding how to back up claims with logical, carefully reasoned arguments that contain convincing evidence (see Figure 8.3 Rubric for Assessing Writing to Persuade). All too often, students' persuasive pieces contain more heat than light and engage in circular reasoning and unsupported statements such as "The space program should be supported because it's good for the country."

A study showed that curriculum designed to foster improved persuasion skills resulted in dramatically improved persuasive writing (Gleason, 1999). The curriculum included the following features.

- Discussion of a model of persuasive pieces.
- Direct instruction in writing an opinion statement, offering supporting reasons/facts, and elaborating on these supporting reasons/facts.

CCSS

Write arguments to support claims in an analysis of substantive topics or texts using valid reasoning and relevant and sufficient evidence.

USING TECHNOLOGY

iCivics www.icivics.org Has an outstanding program for developing students' ability to compose a persuasive piece (argument) in a series of eight thorough, carefully crafted but engaging lessons beginning with "Lesson 1: So You Think You Can Argue."

- Direct instruction in writing a conclusion.
- Planning sheets that guided students through the process.
- Checklists that helped students note whether key elements had been included.
- Direct instruction on how to locate support for an argument in periodicals, textbooks, or other sources. In addition to being taught the process of composing a persuasive piece, students were directly instructed in how to locate supporting information and take notes on it so they could use it in their pieces.

The teacher's role was an active one. The teacher modeled the process, broke the task down into manageable chunks, and provided feedback. In addition, students engaged in small-group discussions and reviewed each other's work. Students also engaged in mini-debates so that they could apply the reasoning skills they were learning.

Logical argumentation is a high-level cognitive skill. Students' ability to write persuasive pieces depends in large measure on their ability to argue in logical, convincing fashion. Their writing reflects their thinking. Learning how to debate orally prepared students to write persuasive essays.

Fostering Higher-Level Thinking Through Writing

Struggling Readers

When teaching students to use varied text structures, you might use selected passages in their textbooks or content area periodicals as models. This fosters growth in both reading and writing, because the use of text structures is a way of organizing information that we read and write.

In addition to being taught to read like an historian, students need to be taught how to write like one. Along with composing reports that summarize events, issues, or the lives of key historical figures, students need to be able to write opinion pieces in which they take a stand on issues and, most important of all, offer support for their stand. In their study of tenth-graders in advanced placement history classes, Stahl and colleagues (1996) found that when students were asked to form an opinion based on their reading of multiple texts on a controversial issue, they tended to make unsupported statements even though their notes contained details that would have buttressed their opinions. They apparently didn't realize they were supposed to support their opinions.

In science classes, a typical writing assignment consists of completing lab reports. The report may have a highly structured format and offer little opportunity for students to reflect on their observations or explore their thoughts. To foster reflection and exploration, the science writing heuristic is designed to help students conduct experiments and write in such a way that they are engaging in knowledge transformation (Keys, 2000).

The intent of the science writing heuristic is threefold: (1) to show students that writing is generated through the experimental process and is not just a summary of the experiment; (2) to stress the collaborative nature of science as students discuss experiments in small groups; and (3) to help students make connections among their observations, claims, and evidence. Students are asked to describe a pattern, make a generalization, state a relationship, or construct an explanation. They are then asked to support their claim, compare their claim with other sources of information, and reflect on what they have learned. This is designed to help students "bridge the gap between raw data and scientific meaning" (Keys, 2000, p. 680).

When given instruction in the writing of a thoughtful report, most students draw inferences, create and support hypotheses, and explain observations. For instance, after completing an experiment on erosion, one student produced the following segment, which contains thoughtful observations, several inferences, and explanations and hypotheses about the causes and effects of erosion.

The grass is worn down where people have walked, water has run down the hill, where gravity and wind have moved soil. The erosion is bad enough that rocks once under the surface have been exposed and gullies have formed. I measured the gullies. They seem to vary in their depth due to their width. The more narrow gullies were deeper and had more rocks exposed.

This is probably because of the concentration of the water and how hard it must have been raining at the time. The wider gullies seem to be more shallow because the water spread out over a larger area. (Keys, 2000, p. 687)

Once students have a clear sense of the purpose of their lab experiments, they are better able to write reports. As secondary science teacher Christina Hart reports, "Having a clear purpose for writing . . . greatly enhanced the quality of their descriptions of the experimental procedure" (Hart, Mulhall, Berry, Loughran, & Gunstone, 2000, p. 664).

Techniques for Improving Students' Writing

What is the most powerful technique for improving students' writing? Recent research provides an answer to that question. Research by Graham and Perin (2007) analyzed the research on techniques and teaching practices designed to improve the writing of adolescents. Each technique and practice was assigned an effect size. An effect size of .2 is small, .5 is moderate, and .8 is large. For an average student, an effect size of .8 would move the student from the 50th to the 75th percentile and is equivalent to almost a year's growth. The techniques and the effect sizes are listed in Table 8.1. As you can see, the top techniques are teaching students writing strategies and teaching students to summarize. Each has an effect size of .82.

USING TECHNOLOGY

Online Writing Labs (OWLs) are extensions of campus writing labs set up by colleges to help their students. But many, such as Purdue's http://owl.english.purdue.edu/ have an open-door policy. Purdue's OWL has a special section for grade 7–12 students.

TABLE 8.1 Technique/Teaching Practice Effect Size

Strategy Instruction—strategies for planning, revising, and editing	.82
Summarization—learning to summarize reading material	.82
Peer Assistance—work together to draft, revise, and edit	.75
Setting Clear, Specific Product Goals—set purpose and characteristics of a piece	.70
Word Processing—use readily available word processing	.55
Sentence Combining—combining simple sentences into a more complex one	.50
Training Teachers in the Process Approach—extended writing opportunities	.46
Inquiry Approach—analyzing and comparing data and evaluating evidence	.32
Prewriting—gathering and organizing information	.32
Use of Models—analyzing and imitating models of good writing	.25
Writing to Learn Content—includes summarizing, reflecting, evaluating, extending, applying	.23

Adapted from Graham, S., & Perin, D. (2007). *Writing next: Effective strategies to improve writing of adolescents in middle and high schools — A report to Carnegie Corporation of New York*. Washington, DC: Alliance for Excellent Education.

1. How can students be helped to write effective biographies? Persuasive pieces?
2. How might writing be used to foster higher-level thinking skills?

CCSS

Write narratives to develop real or imagined experiences or events using effective technique, well-chosen details and well-structured event sequences.

Digital Storytelling

Adapted from traditional storytelling, digital storytelling typically has a personal point of view and uses digital technology along with words to tell a story or advance a cause. Possible topics of stories are virtually infinite and may include personal accounts, personal adventures, descriptions of people in our lives, discoveries we have made, places we have visited, our homes, lessons learned, memorable moments, times of wonder, an outstanding accomplishment, mysteries, a favorite book, an historical event, a scientific discovery, a wonder of nature. Faculty and students at the University of Houston (2010) list ten elements of educational digital storytelling. These include

1. *The Overall Purpose of the Story:* What is the point of the story? Why am I telling this to you? Is it to inform or inspire?
2. *The Narrator's Point of View:* What is the narrator's perspective? Is it a personal retelling? Is it told from a third-person point of view?
3. *A Dramatic Question or Questions:* What key question(s) does the story attempt to answer? What made me the way I am today? What does it mean to be a friend? Who are the heroes in my life? Is the story personalized to make it more understandable or reliable?
4. *The Choice of Content:* Does the content come alive? Does it connect with the audience?
5. *Clarity of Voice:* Is the voiceover loud enough, clear enough, and expressive? Voiceovers should match the video. The voiceover can be shorter than the video, but not longer. Still images should appear for 3 to 5 seconds. Rate of speech is about 2–3 words per second so voiceovers for still pictures should be about 9 to 14 words.
6. *Pacing of the Narrative:* Does the narrative flow? Does the pacing fit in with the story's theme? Fast pacing suggests action. Slow pacing signals contemplation.
7. *Use of a Meaningful Audio Soundtrack:* Does the soundtrack fit in with the nature of the story?
8. *Quality of the Images, Video, and other Multimedia Elements:* Are the digital images of high quality? Do they enhance the story?
9. *Economy of the Story Detail:* Is just enough content used to tell the story? You might limit the number of words and images that can be used. Digital stories tend to run between 150 and 400 words.
10. *Good Grammar and Language Usage:* Are good grammar and correct usage used throughout?

Although digital stories draw on the traditions of oral storytelling, the concept of combining digital media with words can be adapted to the creation of a wide variety of multimedia presentations, ranging from PowerPoint reports to a video clip explanation of science or math concepts or video ads for books. These projects can be completed individually or by a group. The group discusses possible ideas, selects one, and composes a treatment. The treatment is a condensed version of the presentation. The treatment includes an overview of the story or idea, a description of characters, location, background music, images, and special effects. It could be written in a paragraph or two.

Because images, voices, and sounds are being combined, digital stories require a storyboard, which is a graphic display of the treatment, to show where the elements go. A storyboard consists of a sequence of rough sketches that detail the production. The storyboard shows the placement of images, voiceovers, soundtrack, and transitions and

FIGURE 8.9
Sample Storyboard

Chanda is throwing juice box into an overflowing trash can.	Herman is putting glass bottles and cans into recycling bins at the town's recycling center. As he places cans and bottles into the bins where they belong, he explains what he is doing.	Stephen is gathering old newspapers and cardboard boxes.
Voiceover: What did you throw away today? Every year each of us makes hundreds of pounds of trash. Some of that trash can be reused.	Herman: Aluminum cans and glass bottles can be reused and made into new cans and bottles. Some recycling centers have separate bins for brown, green, and clear glass and another bin for aluminum cans.	Stephen: Newspapers, writing paper, and cardboard boxes can be reused up to five times
Alicia is putting a plastic milk jug in curbside recycling bin.	Alicia is sitting on a plastic outdoor chair.	Maria is holding up a notebook that is marked made of recycled paper.
Alicia: The plastic soft drink bottles and milk jugs that you recycle today could end up being the lining in the coat that you wear on a cold winter's day. Or they could be the lawn chair that you sit on on a warm summer day.	Alicia: Plastic containers can be cut up, melted, and made into hundreds of products. The chair that I am sitting on is made entirely of plastic. It took more than 200 milk jugs to make this plastic chair.	Maria: Another way to cut down on trash is to buy recycled products. If we each do our part, we'll cut down on the trash that we make, and we'll save our natural resources.

Adapted from Gunning, T. (2005). *Creating Literacy Instruction for All Students* (5th ed.). Boston: Allyn & Bacon.

special effects. In Figure 8.9, the top box shows the scene and might be illustrated with stick figures or digital photos. The storyboard becomes a set of directions for creating the production. Use large sheets of poster board and sticky notes to manipulate the elements.

CHECKUP

1. What is digital storytelling?
2. What are the steps in creating a digital story?

The Affective Component of Writing

Writing is affective as well as cognitive. Just as students who have had bad experiences with numbers may develop math anxiety, students who have had negative experiences with writing may develop writing apprehension. Students have writing apprehension when their anxiety about writing is so intense that they resist writing or avoid it (Singer & Donlan, 1989). Instructional situations that contribute to writing apprehension include unclear or vague assignments; writing tasks that are new and complex, such as writing a research report or term paper for the first time; having work assessed, especially if the assessment is a stringent one; and, of course, having had papers or exams assessed as unsatisfactory (Daly & Hailey, 1984). To combat writing apprehension, provide needed guidance; establish a constructive, positive atmosphere; and give students choice whenever possible. You can also plan some kinds of writing in which success is virtually guaranteed. Students can free write, compose group stories, or write cooperative pieces—pieces for which students suggest ideas and you write them on an overhead transparency or on the chalkboard. A discussion of past experiences with writing might alert you to negative attitudes.

Responding to High-Stakes Writing Tests

For responding to timed writing prompts, Gallagher (2003) recommends using the ABCD approach:

Attack the prompt

Brainstorm possible answers

Choose the order of your response

Detect errors before turning the draft in

Writing prompts can contain multiple steps. All too often, students confuse and/or skip a step, particularly the one that tells them to support their response (Gunning, 2006). By *attacking the prompt*, they simplify it and list exactly what they are supposed to do. Students circle the action words that tell them to *discuss, list, support, explain*, etc. Then they draw an arrow to the object of each verb, which tells them what they are supposed to discuss, list, support, or explain. They then list these steps. Then, students *brainstorm possible topics* and choose one. After they have brainstormed their topic, students *choose the order* in which they will provide main points and begin writing. Finally, students take a minute or two to read over their essays to *detect and correct errors*. In addition to correcting errors, they can add or delete details at this time. Before students write their essays, have them do a number of practice runs in which they complete the ABCD portions. Have students write in response to a prompt every three weeks.

Essay Test-Taking Strategy

In this research-based strategy students are taught to analyze the question, organize the information they know, write their answer using a specific structure, and revise and edit so as to produce a polished piece of writing. After instruction, students' scores for essay test-taking behaviors improved from 5 percent to 85 percent, and their essays earned higher ratings (Center for Research on Learning, 2009).

Implementing a Content Area Writing Program

Based on extensive studies of students' writing, Langer and Applebee (1987) suggest using the following questions as guidelines for writing-to-learn programs. Although written over two decades ago, the guidelines are just as valid now as they were then.

1. Does the task permit students to develop their own meanings rather than simply follow the dictates of the teacher or text? Do they have room to take ownership of what they are doing?
2. Is the task sufficiently difficult to permit new learnings to occur, but not so difficult as to preclude new learnings? Students being given their first research or library paper may feel overwhelmed unless provided with lots of guidance and support.
3. Is the instructional support structured in a manner that models appropriate approaches to the task and leads to a natural sequence of thought and language?
4. Is the teacher's role collaborative rather than evaluative? In collaborative writing, "the teacher's role is one of helping students toward new learning rather than of testing the adequacy of new learning" (p. 143).
5. Is the external scaffolding removed as the student internalizes the patterns and approaches needed? (pp. 180–181).

> **CCSS**
>
> Write routinely over extended time frames (time for research, reflection, and revision) and shorter time frames (a single sitting or a day or two) for a range of tasks, purposes, and audiences.

A key component of an effective writing program is providing opportunities for students to write on a regular basis. Students who wrote long answers related to reading on a frequent basis scored significantly higher than students who seldom engaged in such writing (National Center for Educational Statistics, 2010). Frequent writing builds fluency and confidence and provides opportunities for students to try out and practice new techniques. However, students also need instruction. Instruction before writing enables students to try new techniques. Instruction during the revision process encourages students to make changes. Without guidance that indicates the kinds of changes that should be made and a desire to make those changes (as well as monitoring to ensure that the changes have been made), it is doubtful that students' writing will show much improvement. Guidance can be obtained from a teacher or another experienced writer or by seeking out models to see what kinds of techniques other writers used. Think back to a time when you learned a specific writing technique or approach to writing. What helped you? What hindered you?

A number of years ago I took a sojourn from teaching in order to accept a position as a staff writer for *Know Your World Extra*, an educational periodical for struggling readers. I was hired on the basis of my experience teaching in an urban setting rather than on my experience writing, which had consisted of writing term papers for undergraduate and graduate courses. The challenge was two-fold. I had to learn how to write in a journalistic style, and I also had to write on a third-grade level. The publisher provided formal instruction, but I also sought help from experienced writers on the staff as well as models of writing. I analyzed how the writers at *Time* and *Newsweek* composed their pieces and examined the techniques used by writers who staffed other educational periodicals. Since this was a weekly publication, I received suggestions from my editor each week. Monthly meetings were also held to look at ways to make the periodical better. Guidance and instruction were intense but effective. I was able to switch from my formal term-paper-style writing aimed at impressing professors to a lively, down-to-earth style designed to explain complex events to struggling readers. I became convinced from personal experience that people can be taught to make significant changes in their writing—but it takes a substantial, ongoing effort. Looking back at that period, it is clear that in addition to intense instruction and lots of practice, goal setting and motivation were key elements. At the core of the change was a firm commitment to learn a new style of writing.

CHECKUP

1. What are the characteristics of an effective writing program?
2. Why is frequent writing important?
3. Why should frequent writing be accompanied by instruction and feedback?

Summary

Writing is a powerful way to foster learning in the content areas. Students who use a process approach outperform those who don't. The five elements in the writing process are prewriting, drafting, revising, editing, and publishing. Although the English teacher may play a major role in teaching general writing skills, content area teachers are responsible for teaching those skills that are specific to their content area. Current nationwide standards include a call for writing proficiency in the content areas. Techniques for teaching writing include modeling and direct and guided instruction.

Types of writing in content area programs include writers' journals, dialogue journals, double-entry journals, learning logs, science notebooks, content area autobiographies, biographies, reports, persuasive writing, structured types of writing, and the types of writing normally demanded in the content areas. The benefit students obtain from writing depends on the type of writing they do. Completing short-answer questions helped students learn details. Taking notes led to a concentration on information, but little integration of that information. Writing essays resulted in generating, evaluating, and integrating information. Although teachers should offer students support as they write, there should be a balance so that students receive the guidance they need, but maintain a sense of ownership of their writing.

Reflection

Return to the Anticipation Guide at the beginning of this chapter. Respond once again to the items. Did your responses change? If so, how and why? What are your current views on teaching writing in your content area?

Extension and Application

1. To experience the benefits of a journal or learning log, keep one for this course or another course that you are taking.
2. Plan and try out, if possible, a guided writing lesson in your content area.
3. Write a content area autobiography for the content area you teach and also for writing. Reflect on the positive and negative experiences you have had, and how these might have shaped your learning.
4. Examine the lessons on writing a persuasive piece (argument) at iCivics www.icivics.org. Begin with "Lesson 1: So You Think You Can Argue." Note the elements of effective instruction incorporated in the lessons. If possible teach the lessons and reflect on their effectiveness.

Go to Topic 4: Writing in the MyEducationLab (www .myeducationlab.com) for your course, where you can:

- Find learning outcomes for Writing along with the national standards that connect to these outcomes.
- Complete Assignments and Activities that can help you more deeply understand the chapter content.
- Apply and practice your understanding of the core teaching skills identified in the chapter with the Building Teaching Skills and Dispositions learning units.
- Examine challenging situations and cases presented in the IRIS Center Resources.

Go to the Topic A+RISE in the MyEducationLab (www .myeducationlab.com) for your course. A+RISE® Standards2Strategy™ is an innovative and interactive online resource that offers new teachers in grades K–12 just-in-time, research-based instructional strategies that:

- Meet the linguistic needs of ELLs as they learn content.
- Differentiate instruction for all grades and abilities.
- Offer reading and writing techniques, cooperative learning, use of linguistic and nonlinguistic representations, scaffolding, teacher modeling, higher-order thinking, and alternative classroom ELL assessment.
- Provide support to help teachers be effective through the integration of listening, speaking, reading, and writing along with the content curriculum.
- Improve student achievement.
- Are aligned to Common Core Elementary Language Arts standards (for the literacy strategies) and to English language proficiency standards in WIDA, Texas, California, and Florida.

CHAPTER 9

Teaching Content Area Literacy to Diverse Learners

Using What You Know

Most of us have struggled with one or more content areas. Maybe it was advanced algebra, physics, or history. Or maybe it was learning a skill such as using a complicated computer program or playing a new sport. How did you feel when you were struggling to learn? How did you cope with the situation? What help were you given? How effective was it? What else might the teacher have done to help you? Thinking back on your school days, can you recall any teachers who were especially effective at helping struggling learners? What did they do? What steps can you take to help struggling learners who are studying your discipline?

Teaching Diverse Learners

Secondary schools are becoming more challenging and more diverse. As a result of mandates to prepare every student to be college- and career-ready (U.S. Department of Education, 2010), the response to intervention (RTI) initiative highlighted in the Individuals with Disabilities Education Improvement Act (IDEIA) (2004), and Common Core Standards (National Governors Association Center for Best Practices and Council of Chief State School Officers, 2010), there is a movement to provide high-level content for all students, not just those who plan to attend college. Secondary school courses are becoming more demanding than in prior decades. More topics are presented and, in many instances, the information students are required to know is more complex. For instance, in the past, biology students only needed to know the definition of DNA. Now they are required to know the chemistry of DNA, the function of DNA in genetics, and some of the ways that knowledge of DNA is being used (Deschler, Schumaker, Bui, & Vernon, 2006). In addition, secondary school classes now include students with physical and learning disabilities as well as students who are still learning English. Large percentages of students are economically disadvantaged as well.

Not all students who come from diverse backgrounds have difficulty learning in the content areas. Many do exceptionally well. However, a fairly large proportion of diverse learners experience some difficulty learning and are said to be at risk.

Economically Disadvantaged Students

The percentage of children living below the poverty level has risen recently. Some 18.2 percent of the nation's children aged seventeen and under live below the official poverty level (U.S. Bureau of the Census, 2010). Poverty is usually associated with lowered achievement. Part of the problem is that **economically disadvantaged** students are often provided with an inferior education, with some lagging up to four years behind their more affluent peers (Achievement First, 2011). As compared with practices in high-performing countries, "education systems in the United States tend to give disadvantaged and low-achieving students a watered down curriculum in larger classes taught by less qualified teachers—*exactly the opposite of what high-performing countries do*" (National Governors Association, Council of Chief State School Officers, & Achieve, 2008, p. 34). Even so, many students achieve success despite poverty, especially if their homes are achievement oriented and they are given effective instruction (Achieve, 2011; Snow et al., 1998).

Students with Disabilities

Some 6.6 million, or 13 percent, of school-age students receive services through the Individuals with Disabilities Act (IDEA) (Aud et al., 2010). Of the students served by IDEA, 39 percent have been classified as having a learning disability. About 80 percent of students judged to have a **learning disability** (LD) receive their classification because of a reading disability. Although most learning disabilities are discovered in elementary school, some may not develop or be detected until secondary school. Until the reauthorization of the Individuals with Disabilities Education Act in 2004 (IDEA 2004, PL 108-447), a discrepancy definition was used to identify students with learning disabilities; that is, students were said to have a learning disability if there was a significant difference between their measured disability and their achievement. Because the difference needed to be a large one for classification purposes, identification of a learning disability was often delayed. In addition, there were controversies surrounding how to measure ability. Now school districts may use an approach known as *response to intervention (RTI)* along with or instead of a discrepancy definition; alternative methods may be used as well.

RTI is typically a three-tier process but may have four or more tiers. In Tier I, subject matter teachers provide the student with additional help. Tier I is designed to improve the overall instructional program so that everyone benefits; for instance, in secondary schools teachers provide enhanced differentiated instruction so that all students will have the opportunity to learn. If a student continues to lag behind, despite being provided with differentiated instruction, he or she is given supplementary instruction (Tier II). This assistance is usually provided in a small group for a period of 12 to 20 weeks. If the student still fails to make adequate progress, a more intensive intervention program is provided (Tier III), which may consist of one-on-one instruction. If progress is still inadequate, placement in special education is considered. However, most of the students who enter secondary school reading significantly below grade level do not have a learning disability. If a student learns at a satisfactory pace after being taught needed skills, this is an indication that he or she does not have processing or memory problems. A satisfactory pace means that the student learns at about the same rate as other students. If a student is placed at the appropriate instructional level, but fails to learn unless provided extraordinary amounts of instruction and review or if he or she requires specialized techniques, such as tracing words, then this suggests a learning disability.

■ **Economically disadvantaged** individuals are those whose lives and opportunities are limited or put at risk by having insufficient economic resources.

■ **Learning disability** is a general term used to refer to a group of disorders that are evidenced by difficulty learning to read, write, speak, listen, or do math. Speaking and listening difficulties are not caused by articulation disorders or impaired hearing.

As a literacy teacher in a junior high, I once taught 10 seventh graders who were reading on a beginning level. When students are that far behind, a learning disability is suspected. However, after being provided with systematic instruction on their level, 9 of the students made adequate progress. One of the students experienced extraordinary difficulty. An assessment revealed that he had a learning disability, which was manifested in a severe difficulty learning to associate letters with sounds and printed words with their spoken equivalents. Up to 15 percent of a school's special education funds may be spent on improving the regular education program and providing extra assistance to students in need, even though they haven't been given a special education placement. Under RTI, the learning disabilities specialist or another professional could have provided the 10 students with an intervention program without their being labeled. The tenth student would have been evaluated for a possible learning disability because he failed to respond to increasingly intensive intervention.

RTI may include screening all students as they enter middle or high school to identify those who are at risk and also periodic screening to identify students who are falling behind. A number of secondary schools provide literacy improvement classes for entering students who fail to reach a certain benchmark. RTI also usually includes monitoring of students' progress. In some programs, all students are monitored three times a year. Students being provided interventions or extra help may be given monthly or even biweekly assessments to see if they are making adequate progress, and if they are not, the intervention is intensified or expanded.

RTI is more than just a method for identifying students with learning disabilities. It is a whole-school improvement program that enlists all staff members, the community, and parents to ensure that the literacy potential of every student is fully developed. The idea behind RTI is that all staff members will work together to provide each student with effective instruction. Under an RTI approach, there is a shared responsibility. Content teachers, the reading specialist, special education personnel, the school psychologist, the speech teacher, ESL teachers, administration, and other staff members work together for the benefit of all students. As Duffy (2007) explains, "RTI is a schoolwide effort to refocus attention from identifying deficiencies in students to identifying scientifically based instructional practices that support the learning of all students" (p. 7.).

Although the principles and premises of RTI are just as valid for secondary school as they are for elementary school, they are more difficult to implement because of the complexities of high school. Here is how one high school set up its RTI program. At the 1,800-student Palmer High School in Colorado, a committee examined the school's resources and set interventions of increasing intensity (Samuels, 2009). Where possible, the school built on interventions that were already in place. A tutoring center was also set up to provide assistance in all subjects to any student who was struggling. Since even achieving students struggle from time to time, there was no stigma attached to seeking help in the center. Special attention was paid to incoming ninth graders, especially those who were reading below grade level. To provide personalized monitoring and guidance, individual teachers took responsibility for 10 struggling students. The mentor teachers monitored the progress of the 10 students and provided guidance and encouragement, along with program adjustments as needed. One advantage of RTI at Palmer was that the line between special education and regular education was being blurred and students received extra help without being labeled.

English Language Learners

Of the 55.2 million children who are school age, more than 21 percent or 10.9 million speak a language other than English in their home (Aud et al., 2010). Of the total number, 5 percent or 2.76 million speak English with difficulty. Seventy-five percent or 2 million of those who speak English with difficulty have Spanish as their primary language. The number of students who speak a language other than English is increasing, with most classrooms having at least one student who is an English language learner.

Bilingual instruction is now being de-emphasized in some areas in favor of programs that specify English-only instruction. **English language learners (ELLs)** in grades 3 through 8 are required to take tests in English reading and language arts after

Struggling Readers

Recently introduced to help struggling students, RTI is both a method for identifying students with learning disabilities and a whole-school improvement program that enlists all staff members, the community, and parents to ensure that all students' literacy potential is fully developed.

USING TECHNOLOGY

National Clearinghouse for English Language Acquisition and Language Instruction www.ncela.gwu.edu/ Provides information and resources for teaching English language learners.

■ **English language learners (ELLs)** are students whose native language is not English but who are in various stages of learning English.

A Model RTI Program

At Rolling Meadows High School, RTI is one component of a five-part Model for Student Achievement: Professional Learning Teams (PLT) and Professional Learning Communities (PLC), Response to Intervention, Social-Emotional Learning, Teacher Leadership, and Program Improvement (Rolling Meadows High School, 2010). The foundations of Program Improvement are the professional learning teams (PLTs) within each discipline. The teams meet with each other in Professional Learning Communities (PLCs). PLC representatives from all disciplines work on broad-based skills. For instance, the high school has a PLC that includes English, Biology, Social Studies, and Information Processing PLTs who work on the freshman reading program. The PLTs and PLCs are charged with the general goal of improving the school program. Step 1 of the process is to create or adopt measurable standards and use formative and summative assessments to evaluate whether students are meeting standards. The standards and summative assessments are drawn from ACT. Step 2 of the process is to use assessment data to increase the number of students who meet standards. A goal is set that states the percentage of students expected to master the standard. For example, the PLT goal might be that 80 percent of the students will meet all four standards and half the remaining 20 percent will be just one benchmark below the standard.

Using a three-tier RTI model, the PLT determines whether 80 percent of students are meeting standards. If not, steps are taken to improve the regular program. Scores of students who fail to meet standards of the Tier I program are analyzed to see what they have in common and to provide an appropriate intervention. Students who have common needs are grouped so the system won't be overwhelmed. It is expected that about 15 percent of students will quality for Tier II interventions. Students who still do not make adequate progress are provided with Tier III intervention. Progress is monitored by the PLT, and changes and improvements are made as needed.

In implementing the program, major needs were taken care of first (Johns, 2009). For instance, classroom teachers were frequently spending a great deal of time with one or two students. When these students were provided with intervention, this relieved some of the burden from the classroom teacher. The PLT also dug deeply into the data to get at root causes. Some students who were failing to complete assignments initially were identified as being resistant to doing work. But in many instances these students didn't turn in their assignments because they did not want anyone to know that they lacked the necessary reading or writing skills. Cajoling them to turn in assignments didn't work. What did work was teaching them the skills they needed to complete the assignments.

English Language Learners

When working with ELLs, focus on their understanding of what they read. Because of limited English, second-language readers may have difficulty fully explaining what they know about a selection they have read. They may mispronounce words whose meanings they know. The key element is whether students are getting meaning from these words, not whether they are pronouncing them correctly.

completing just 10 months of instruction. According to bilingual experts, oral proficiency in conversational English may take two or more years to develop. However, it may take five or more years for students to reach the same level of proficiency in academic English obtained by their English-speaking peers. Catching up is difficult because while ELLs are acquiring more advanced English language skills, so are the native speakers of English (Cummins, 2001). Proficiency with conversational English may hide ELLs' deficiencies in the kinds of higher-level language skills needed to learn content area material (Sutton, 1989). Although ELLs may be able to exchange ideas with friends, they may have difficulty with the abstract, formal language used to convey content area concepts. As a content area teacher, you may find that you need to assist some of your students with learning both the language of instruction in general and the language of your content area.

CHECKUP

1. Who are the diverse learners?
2. What factors hinder the progress of many of the diverse learners?
3. What role is RTI playing in the identification and instruction of students who struggle?

Assisting Struggling Learners

USING TECHNOLOGY

For more information on learning disabilities contact: Learning Disabilities Association of America: www .Ldanatl.org International Dyslexia Association: www.interdys.org Council for Exceptional Children: www .cec.sped.org

The first step in helping struggling learners is to find out who they are and what their difficulties might be. Bulgren and Lenz (1996) note that "many teachers lack information about which students in a class have learning disabilities and which instructional techniques, activities, and materials have proven effective with these students" (p. 418). In addition to students who have been labeled as having a learning disability or reading problem, there may be a number of other students who are struggling to learn but have not been identified. Plan a conference with both the learning disabilities specialist and the reading specialist. Seek out information on the students' difficulties as well as ways to help them learn the material in your content area. The specialists may provide demonstrations or even work with the students in your classroom. However, simply observing one or two high-achieving students and one or two low-achieving students and their responses to instruction has helped teachers revise their planning to accommodate students at both ends of the spectrum (Bulgren & Lenz, 1996).

Teaching SMARTER

One approach that content area teachers can take in order to cope with both the over-stuffed curriculum and the increased academic variability of today's classes is to teach SMARTER (Bulgren & Lenz, 1996; Lenz et al., 2004). SMARTER is an acronym for a guide for planning for classes that include struggling learners. However, SMARTER is designed to benefit all students. The seven steps are Select, Map, Analyze, Reach, Teach, Evaluate, Reevaluate.

1. **Select** the key content that you want students to learn. State the content in terms of questions that students will be expected to answer: What has Roman civilization contributed to our way of life? What has Greek civilization contributed to our way of life? How does understanding how people lived in early times help us to understand ourselves? Students can use these questions to assess their grasp of key concepts. Creating questions is a concrete way of restating course objectives or standards that can help you link planning, instruction, and assessment. As Bulgren and Lenz (1996) note, "Questions require the teacher to think about how he or she would like the student to think about or talk through the content or task" (p. 46). Students can ask themselves key questions and see if they can answer them.
2. **Map** the organization of the content to show how key concepts are related to each other and to students' current knowledge. Maps can be created for the whole course, a unit, or individual lessons. For units and lessons, it is recommended that the map include no more than seven elements.
3. **Analyze** why the content may be difficult to master. Consider such factors as density and complexity of concepts and student background and interest.
4. **Reach** decisions about how to teach the content. Consider especially what might be done to enhance learning. Instructional enhancements include advanced organizers such as structured overviews, graphic organizers, charts, graphs, tables, and demonstrations. Many of the techniques covered in previous chapters qualify as enhancements.
5. **Teach** the content and also teach the enhancements. Students may not realize that you are using special devices or techniques to foster learning. Students make better use of enhancements when they are pointed out and their purpose and application is explained. You might explain, for example, that the enhancement known as the structured overview will help the class understand what kinds of animals are reptiles and how reptiles are grouped in comparison to other animals.
6. **Evaluate** students' learning. Evaluation can take many forms. It may be observation of students' discussions, lab work, or assignments, or it may take the form of quizzes and tests.

Building on Students' Interests

Struggling readers are often reluctant readers. Because they are not proficient readers, they read less. Reading less, they fall further and further behind. To break the cycle, it is essential that they read, read, read. Cris Tovani broke that cycle with her ninth-grade reluctant readers by bringing to class newspaper articles that touched students' lives (Harvey, 1998).

One editorial blasted her high school for allowing smoking on campus even though smoking was prohibited in virtually every other place and it was illegal for students under eighteen to purchase cigarettes. Students became highly defensive. One student claimed that smoking was no big deal and that 95 percent of adults smoked. Tovani suggested that the class research the issue. For the next week, using the Internet and other sources, students intensively researched the topic. One student found from an authoritative source that only 28 percent of adults smoked. Another learned that smoking was indeed a big deal: She had located a long list of smoking-related health risks.

Having learned the truth about smoking, students felt a sense of accomplishment and self-efficacy. They were also in a better position to make an informed decision about smoking. And they had learned the value of sustained expository reading. As the year progressed, they investigated other topics of interest.

7. **Reevaluate** the effectiveness of the instruction and revise as necessary. Review concepts and skills that students had difficulty with, especially if they form the foundation of future learning.

Helping Students Become Self-Regulated Learners

Although students at the Benchmark School, a school for struggling readers, responded well to carefully programmed instruction—99 percent returned to a mainstream class reading at or above grade level—the staff realized that the students needed more than a command of academic strategies (Gaskins, 2005; Gaskins & Elliot, 1991). Many of the students had to overcome maladaptive learning habits and styles that either caused or were a result of their earlier struggles with school. All too often, their performance was marred by impulsivity, rigidity, and lack of persistence or follow-through.

A first step in working with struggling learners is to help them set goals. Goals should be challenging but realistic. Three sets of goals should be drawn up: long-term goals, mid-term or in-between goals, and short-term goals (Eisenberger, Conti-D'Antonio, & Bertrando, 2000). Long-term goals provide focus but lack immediacy. Mid-term goals provide a convenient place for pausing to see how things are going and making some needed adjustments before it is too late. Short-term goals help students to focus on daily tasks.

The beginning of a school year or semester or the beginning of a unit or project is a good time to set goals. Students should be involved in the goal-setting process so that they have a sense of ownership. A long-term goal might be to create a PowerPoint presentation of the life of Teddy Roosevelt for American history class. Short-term goals might be to gather material on Roosevelt, write up the material, revise the material, learn how to use PowerPoint, set up a presentation, try out the presentation, and give the presentation. Part of goal setting might be having students assess their academic strengths and weaknesses: What do they do that helps them learn history? What could they do to improve their work in history class? Responses could be used to set learning goals: reading the text, taking notes in class, or handing in assignments on time, for instance.

Once they have set their goals, students should draw up a plan for achieving them. They might list all the steps they will take and deadlines for finishing each step. To help in both their goal setting and their planning, students might visualize the finished product and each of the steps. For instance, they might imagine themselves gathering the material, putting the material together, writing their report, revising their write-up, and transferring their write-up to PowerPoint.

After drawing up a plan, students put it into action, constantly assessing their progress and making adaptations when necessary. Reflection helps students judge the effectiveness of their actions and grow in independence as they take responsibility for their learning. Teachers should model the process of reflecting on their learning so that students see that this is something that even experts need to do. Frequent reflection also keeps students on task. Some students find it helpful to complete a written reflection and discuss it with their teachers. Possible areas for reflection and discussion include progress made toward reaching the goal, aids to reaching the goal, obstacles, plans for overcoming obstacles, and next steps.

Self-talk can be used to overcome fears and worries and sudden attacks of negativity. Students might tell themselves that they can take the test and do well on it. Or, yes, they can stand in front of the class and give an oral report. To help them overcome negative thoughts, students might write a series of "I can't" statements, such as "I can't spell. I can't do math"; they then list the negative associations that they have with each statement. They might then think of ways in which they can turn the "I can't" situations into "I can" ones (Eisenberger et al., 2000).

CHECKUP

1. What are some steps that might be taken to assist struggling learners?

Working with English Language Learners

Based on their research and observation, Gersten and Baker (2000) identified five specific instructional components in a program for English language learners:

1. vocabulary as a curricular anchor, 2. visuals to reinforce concepts and vocabulary, 3. cooperative learning and peer tutoring strategies, 4. strategic use of the native language, and 5. modulation of cognitive and language demands.

Vocabulary as a Curricular Anchor. A major barrier for English language learners is having a limited English vocabulary. Vocabulary instruction should be intensive and should focus on key words—those most needed to grasp major concepts in a discipline. Typical high school students can recognize up to an estimated 50,000 to 100,000 words when they meet them in print (Nagy & Herman, 1987). However, second language learners may recognize only 5,000 to 7,000 English words. Students need not know all the words in a selection in order to grasp it. However, ELLs often have a tendency to read each word slowly and deliberately (Johnson & Steele, 1996). Instruction for ELLs should include guidance on those key terms essential for an understanding of the selection's major points.

Visuals to Reinforce Concepts and Vocabulary. Visuals, dramatizations, and gestures should be freely used. In fact, visuals including illustrations and graphic organizers should be used whenever possible when instructing English language learners.

Cooperative Learning and Peer Tutoring Strategies. Working with peers provides excellent opportunities for English language learners to apply language skills. In a small group, ELLs are less reluctant to speak. In addition, they are better able to make themselves understood and better able to understand others.

Strategic Use of the Native Language. Teachers should use the level of English that students are familiar with. However, for developing complex concepts, they should use the students' native language, if possible, or ask another student to provide a

CCSS

Initiate and participate effectively in a range of collaborative discussions (one-on-one, in groups, and teacher-led) with diverse partners on grade-level topics, texts, and issues, building on others' ideas and expressing their own clearly and persuasively.

■ **Self-talk** is the recitation of self-positive beliefs such as "I can do it" in order to overcome negative feelings and attitudes or self-defeating behaviors.

USING TECHNOLOGY

Dr. Mora's Website is an excellent source of information about bilingual education: http://coe.sdsu.edu /people/jmora

translation. That way, the student doesn't have the burden of trying to understand difficult content expressed in terms that may be hard to understand.

Modulation of Cognitive and Language Demands. When cognitive demands are high, language expectations should be simplified. Teachers may accept brief or partial responses in English. When cognitive demands are low, the teacher might demand more extensive use of English. For instance, for the literal-level question from a U.S. history text, "What contributions did Eads and the Roeblings make to bridge construction?" (Boorstin & Kelley, 2002, p. 453), ELLs might be able to respond primarily in English. Words needed to respond are directly stated in the text. However, for a related question, "How did bridge building contribute to the growth of cities?" (p. 453), which requires constructing a generalization, students might need to be allowed to make use of their first language.

It used to be said that every teacher is a teacher of reading because reading is such an essential skill. Now, with so many ELL students in schools, this adage has changed to every teacher is a teacher of English. This doesn't mean teaching English skills from the ground up. Rather, it entails teaching those language skills that students are lacking, but need in order to learn key concepts in the content area you teach. As Echevarria, Vogt, and Short (2000) note:

> Because of the large numbers of English language learners in schools today, all teachers are teachers of English, even if their content specialization is science, math, or social studies. For students learning English, teachers must create ample opportunities to practice using academic language, not simply social uses of language. (p. 92)

CHECKUP

1. What are five key components in a program for ELL?
2. How might these components be implemented?

Building Language

Because it takes English learners a considerable amount of time to achieve the same level of language proficiency as native speakers of English, it is imperative that every teacher factor in language acquisition as part of his or her teaching approach. As a distinguished panel of experts on English learners recommended:

> One major theme in our recommendations is the importance of intensive, interactive English language development instruction for all English learners. This instruction needs to focus on developing academic language (the decontextualized language of the schools, the language of academic discourse, of texts, and of formal argument). . . . Daily academic English instruction should be integrated into the core curriculum. Consider asking teachers to devote a specific block (or blocks) of time each day to building English learners' academic English. . . . Provide high quality vocabulary instruction throughout the day. Teach essential content words in depth. In addition, use instructional time to address the meanings of common words, phrases, and expressions not yet learned. (Gersten et al., 2007, p. 2)

Stages of Second-Language Acquisition

Acquisition of a second language develops in approximately five stages (see Table 9.1): preproduction, early production, speech emergence, intermediate, and advanced. (Stages are adapted from Díaz-Rico, 2004; Guzman-Johannessen, 2006; and Northwest Regional Educational Laboratory, 2003.) Teach in terms of students' proficiencies. Gear questions and other activities to students' language levels (Lalas, Solomon, & Johannessen, 2006). For the lowest levels, for instance, ask *what, who,* and *where* questions because they can

Exemplary Teaching

Preparing English Learners for College

Secondary students, including English learners, are expected to pass demanding, high-stakes tests in at least 20 states. The Pathway Project was initiated to help English learners achieve at the high levels demanded by high-stakes tests and the world of work and post-secondary education. The basic premise of the project was that "if ELLs are treated from the early grades as if they are college bound, if they receive exemplary curriculum and explicit strategies instruction, and if there are consistent, coherent, and progressively rigorous expectations among the learners from grades 6 through 12, students will attain the necessary literacy skills to succeed in college" (Olson, 2007).

Over an eight-year period, fifty-five secondary English teachers taught thousands of English learners an approach that features the development of reading and writing strategies. For seven consecutive years, students who were instructed through the strategy approach outperformed students taught through a traditional approach. The project demonstrated that when they are carefully taught effective strategies, English learners can acquire challenging content at a high level. As a result of the research, the project directors concluded that English learners do best when they are given a challenging curriculum and taught the skills and strategies necessary to learn that curriculum. They noted that teachers of English learners are most successful when they use a variety of techniques, teach a range of genres, scaffold students' learning, and provide opportunities for extensive interaction.

be answered with single words. As students acquire more English, move up to *when* questions, which might require a phrase, and then move on to *how* and *why* questions, which demand more elaborated language. In preparation for teaching ELLs, take note of the students' level of knowledge and language. Also consider the kinds of difficulties that students still acquiring English might experience. Ask, "What am I doing to make the content of the lesson comprehensible? How will I differentiate for ELLs at different levels of proficiency? How will I build language?" Survey the text you plan to use and note features, such as illustrations, that will help make the text comprehensible to ELLs. Note

TABLE 9.1

LEVEL OF LANGUAGE	CHARACTERISTICS OF LEARNER	TEACHING SUGGESTIONS	BUILDING LITERACY
Preproduction	Students know a few English words, but mainly use gestures and pointing to communicate. This stage is known as the *silent period*, because students speak only a few words of English or none at all. This stage may last up to six months or a year. Students may acquire an understanding of up to 500 words.	Use concrete objects, gestures, and pointing; repeat and paraphrase; speak slowly; ask *what, who, where,* and *yes/no* questions.	Students can use very simple books that label illustrations and are designed for ESL students. Encourage drawing and writing of labels and captions.
Early production	Students can understand and use some common words and expressions such as "OK," "Good morning," "What time is it?" This stage may last up to six months. Students may acquire a combined listening-speaking vocabulary of 1,000 words.	Use concrete objects, gestures, and pointing; speak slowly; simplify language; build English vocabulary; ask *what, who, where,* and *either/or* questions and questions that elicit a simple list of words.	Students can understand easy books that have a patterned text. These might be beginning readers from intervention programs for secondary students. Encourage writing of brief pieces that use basic sentence patterns.

(Continued)

TABLE 9.1 *(Continued)*

LEVEL OF LANGUAGE	CHARACTERISTICS OF LEARNER	TEACHING SUGGESTIONS	BUILDING LITERACY
Speech emergence	Students can use brief, everyday expressions and have greater receptive than expressive command of English. Students begin to participate in class discussions. This stage may last for up to a year. Most students acquire about 3,000 words by the end of this stage.	Use heavy visual support and gestures; develop English vocabulary; ask *what, who, where,* and *when* questions and questions that can be answered with a phrase or brief sentence.	Students can read heavily illustrated easy text. They can gradually expand basic sentence patterns.
Intermediate	Students have a fairly good command of everyday English and begin to grasp and use academic English. They can work in groups. This stage may last up to a year. Most students acquire about 6,000 words by the end of this stage.	Use visual supports, including graphic organizers, and gestures; use prompts to foster elaboration; ask *what, who, where, when,* and *why* questions and questions that require explanation or elaboration. Some students can benefit from sheltered English (see pp. 288–289).	Students may need easier texts and/or assistance with texts. Scaffold writing by introducing needed vocabulary and forms; use frame paragraphs (see p. 255).
Advanced	Language is comparable to that of a native speaker. Students may take up to five years or more to reach this stage. Continue to provide visual support and build vocabulary.	Students can read grade-level texts but may need extra help with vocabulary. Develop higher-level thinking skills; develop a full range of writing skills.	

Adapted from Gunning (2010).

Struggling Readers

Both English learners and struggling students benefit from instruction designed to develop academic language. Academic language includes the discourse used in classrooms and the thinking skills of analyzing, explaining, inferring, and organizing.

words, syntactic structures, concepts, and text features that might pose barriers to understanding. Make plans for overcoming these barriers. After each lesson, ask yourself, "Have I fostered language development? Was I able to make the text accessible?" (Lalas, Solomon, & Johannessen, 2006).

Building Academic Language

In reality, English learners have to learn two additional languages (Zwiers, n.d.). They first learn the heavily contextualized social language used to communicate with English-speaking friends, understand the media, and conduct the business of everyday living. By pointing and generous use of gestures and using their ever-increasing store of everyday English words and expressions, they are able to communicate. After about two years, their social communication is fairly well developed. However, English learners must also acquire academic language. Academic language is "the set of words and phrases that (1) describe content-area knowledge and procedures, (2) express complex thinking processes and abstract concepts, and (3) create cohesion and clarity in written and oral discourse" (Zwiers, n.d.). Academic language includes the thinking skills of analyzing, explaining, inferring, and organizing as well as language skills. It requires the ability to think and talk about language as well as use language. And it requires acquisition of background knowledge on a wide range of topics and ideas (Gunning, 2010). Teachers can foster the acquisition of academic English by "analyzing the conceptual and critical thinking of grade-level curriculum and taking the time to ensure that all students are explicitly taught such requirements" (Díaz-Rico, 2004, p. 305).

Academic Vocabulary

Academic vocabulary can be compared to bricks and mortar (Dutro & Moran, 2003). Bricks are the technical words such as *radius, circumference,* and *pi.* Mortar consists of the words and expressions used to describe and explain the concepts represented by the technical words: *distance, center, around,* and *across.* Academic language also includes common phrases, which use figurative language: *going forward, in the long run, be that as it may, all other things being equal* (Zwiers, 2008).

Academic Word List

A listing of academic word families from the Academic Word List (AWL) is presented in Table 9.2 (Coxhead, 2000). A word family consists of a base word, its inflected forms, and closely related derived forms. The word *benefit* would include *benefits, benefited, benefiting, beneficial, beneficiary,* and *beneficiaries.* Because it was created from college texts, the AWL

CCSS

Acquire and use accurately general academic and domain-specific words and phrases, sufficient for reading, writing, speaking, and listening at the college and career readiness level; demonstrate independence in gathering vocabulary knowledge when considering a word or phrase important to comprehension or expression.

TABLE 9.2 Adapted Academic Word List

ACADEMIC WORD LIST: BASIC A1 AND A2				
A1	cycle	locate	somewhat	cooperate
accurate	design	major	task	detect
achieve	device	medical	team	displace
adult	encounter	normal	topic	display
aid	energy	obvious	transfer	dispose
approach	enormous	occur	uniform	draft
area	environment	paragraph		drama
assume	estimate	period	*A2*	edit
attach	expand	portion	adjust	eliminate
available	expert	positive	appreciate	emerge
aware	final	previous	appropriate	error
challenge	function	primary	assign	export
chapter	goal	principal	assist	foundation
chart	grade	publish	author	furthermore
chemical	grant	purchase	capable	globe
code	image	remove	channel	guarantee
communicate	indicate	research	clarify	identical
community	individual	respond	conduct	index
compound	involve	reveal	construct	initial
contact	issue	route	consume	injure
couple	label	series	contribute	insert
create	legal	shift	convert	inspect
culture	link	similar	convince	instruct

(Continued)

TABLE 9.2 (*Continued*)

ACADEMIC WORD LIST: BASIC A1 AND A2				
investigate	precise	resolve	substitute	transmit
lecture	predict	restrain	sufficient	transport
likewise	proceed	restrict	sum	vehicle
notion	recover	retain	summary	violate
overlap	register	reverse	suspend	visible
overseas	reject	schedule	target	vision
participate	relax	secure	text	
plus	rely	structure	tradition	

ACADEMIC WORD LIST: INTERMEDIATE B1 AND B2				
B1	credit	journal	project	technique
abandon	data	labor	range	technology
accompany	decade	layer	react	temporary
adapt	define	maintain	region	theory
alter	definite	mental	release	unique
alternative	demonstrate	method	require	vary
apparent	depress	military	resource	volume
approximate	despite	minimum	role	
aspect	economy	minor	section	*B2*
assure	element	nevertheless	seek	access
attitude	establish	nuclear	select	accommodate
benefit	expose	obtain	sex	assemble
bond	feature	odd	site	attain
brief	federal	partner	source	collapse
capacity	file	percent	specific	commence
category	focus	phase	stable	comment
complex	fundamental	physical	stress	comprise
conclude	generation	policy	style	confer
conflict	identify	potential	survey	confirm
considerable	illustrate	principle	survive	consequent
consist	impact	process	symbol	consult
constant	item	professional	tape	contrary

ACADEMIC WORD LIST: INTERMEDIATE B1 AND B2

converse	exhibit	license	phenomenon	sphere
core	exploit	manipulate	philosophy	strategy
correspond	extract	manual	pose	submit
debate	fee	margin	preliminary	sustain
derive	flexible	mechanism	prime	tense
dimension	formula	media	priority	theme
distribute	fund	medium	prohibit	trace
document	generate	migrate	promote	transit
domain	ignorance	minimize	publication	trend
dominate	imply	monitor	random	undertake
duration	inevitable	network	reside	version
ensure	insight	option	restore	visual
equip	institute	outcome	revise	voluntary
equivalent	intense	overall	scheme	welfare
exceed	interval	parallel	sole	widespread
exclude	liberal	perspective	specify	

ACADEMIC WORD LIST: ADVANCED C

C1	component	enable	income	output
accumulate	concentrate	enforce	input	panel
acquire	concept	estate	instance	perceive
adequate	consent	evaluate	intelligence	precede
affect	constitute	eventual	internal	prior
ambiguous	contemporary	evident	interpret	proportion
analyze	context	evolve	invest	prospect
annual	contract	explicit	isolate	psychology
authority	contrast	external	justify	pursue
bulk	decline	factor	logic	radical
cease	deny	finance	mature	ratio
circumstance	devote	framework	modify	regulate
civil	distinct	hence	neutral	revenue
clause	domestic	hypothesis	objective	revolution
commission	emphasis	impose	occupy	rigid

(Continued)

TABLE 9.2   *(Continued)*

ACADEMIC WORD LIST: ADVANCED C				
sequence	arbitrary	coordinate	incorporate	regime
significant	assess	corporate	induce	reinforce
statistic	attribute	crucial	initiate	reluctance
status	bias	currency	integrate	scope
subsequent	cite	denote	integrity	straightforward
technical	classic	diminish	intermediate	subordinate
thereby	coherent	discriminate	intervene	successor
transform	colleague	distort	levy	supplement
trigger	commit	diverse	mode	terminate
ultimate	commodity	dynamic	motive	thesis
whereas	compensate	enhance	mutual	undergo
	compile	erode	nonetheless	underlie
C2	complement	ethic	offset	unify
abstract	comprehensive	ethnic	passive	utilize
academy	compute	format	persist	valid
acknowledge	conceive	hierarchy	practitioner	via
adjacent	confine	highlight	predominant	whereby
advocate	conform	implement	quote	
amend	condradict	incentive	rational	
anticipate	controversy	incline	refine	

Gunning, Thomas G., *Creating Literacy for All Students in Grades 4–8*, 3rd, ©2012. Printed and electronically reproduced by permission of Pearson Education, Inc., Upper Saddle River, New Jersy.

English Learners

The *Longman Dictionary of American English* (Pearson Education Limited, 2008) is especially designed for English language learners and provides easy-to-understand definitions and examples.

has been adapted here, and words not typically found in secondary texts have been eliminated. In the 510-word adapted AWL in Table 9.2, words are listed according to three levels of tested difficulty: basic, intermediate, and advanced. Each level is split in two, with the first half comprising the higher-frequency words and the second half comprising the lower-frequency words in that level.

You can use the following techniques to develop both general English and academic language.

Using a Hierarchy of Questions

Match the difficulty level of questions with the students' level of English. At the lowest level, students might nod or shake their heads or answer *yes* or *no*. Either/or questions can be used once students are speaking: "Is this line the diameter or the circumference?" *Wh* questions come next, with *why* questions being posed last (Díaz-Rico & Weed, 2002).

Using Cued Elicitation Questions

Cued elicitation questions incorporate a portion of the response: "Diamonds are used in drills because _____." "The theme in this story is similar to the theme in _____." Use restatements and other devices to encourage students to use more specific or more abstract language (Zwiers, 2008).

Collaboration and Negotiation of Meaning

Teacher and student can work together to construct meaning, as illustrated in the following interchange that took place in a science lab.

> *Student:* I put it here (points to microscope slide on mounting platform).
>
> *Teacher:* You mounted the slide.
>
> *Student:* Yes, it has it—it has plant.
>
> *Teacher:* You mounted a leaf on the slide?
>
> *Student:* No, not a leaf. The plant, um, ground (gestures to indicate under the ground).
>
> *Teacher:* Oh. You mounted a plant root on the slide.
>
> *Student:* Yes. Root.
>
> *Teacher:* Can you draw what you see (she makes drawing movements on an imaginary paper)? Make a drawing.
>
> *Student:* Make a drawing for the root. (Díaz-Rico, 2004, pp. 104-105)

Notice how the teacher interacts with the student to derive a meaning. The learner uses gestures and the teacher uses rephrasing ("You mounted the slide") to co-establish meaning and to foster the use of academic language.

Word Walls and Sentence Starters

As you teach new procedures, routines, and concepts, post a list of key words or expressions needed to talk and write about them and to carry them out. Put the words or expressions on strips so they can be moved and manipulated. You and the students also might analyze a text before it is read and make a list of the key academic words; then create an academic word bank or word wall (Zwiers, n.d.). Also suggest opening sentences that students might use to take part in a discussion:

> "I think the setting supports the theme, and this is why I think so. The setting _____."
>
> If students are making a comparison, discuss the meaning of the word *compare* and some words that you might use in a comparison: *similar, alike, also* (Zwiers, n.d.). You might provide a frame and show how you would complete the frame in making a comparison.

In the Pathway Project, the English learners were provided stems, such as the following, that would enable them to talk about and apply strategies (Olson & Land, 2007).

- I got lost here because . . .
- I need to reread the part where . . .
- To understand better, I need to know more about . . .
- Something that is still not clear is . . .
- This reminds me of . . .
- In my mind I see. . .
- The key information is . . .
- The character I most identify with is . . .
- Something that I would like to know is . . .
- The most important message is . . .

USING TECHNOLOGY

If available, electronic clickers are ideal for checking for understanding. On a more personal basis, have individual after-class conversations with students who don't seem to be understanding.

Checking for Understanding

Checking for understanding is a hallmark of effective teaching and is a valuable practice for all students, especially ELLs. Look for signs of understanding. Periodically ask students to give a thumbs up if they understand or a thumbs down if they don't. Ask students to demonstrate understanding by showing what they are expected to do, explaining the concept being discussed, or answering a question about it, completing a quickwrite or exit slip, or taking part in think-pair-share. Monitor students' understanding during think-pair-share sessions and also any other classroom activities in which they are engaged. Students should be shown how to seek help when they don't understand (Díaz-Rico & Weed, 2002).

Empowering Students

Help students develop strategies for getting their meaning across: asking for help from listeners when necessary, slowing down, carefully enunciating words, repeating or using other words if listeners don't seem to understand, pointing, and using gestures. Students might compile a dictionary of useful academic terms and expressions.

Recasting

In recasting, you ask students to rephrase what they are saying. How could you say that using the new words we learned: *setting*, *time*, and *place?* What might you add to what you just explained so that someone who wasn't here would understand it? (Zwiers, 2008)

Co-shaping

In co-shaping, you provide prompts that help the student shape responses that make use of scientific language. Notice how a teacher co-shapes the following interchange:

Student: It happened in some kind of jungle place in olden times.

Teacher: Do you remember where the rain forest was?

Student: South America.

Teacher: Do you recall what part of South America?

Student: It was in the edge.

Teacher: Yes, the setting is the rain forest at the tip of South America. Do you remember when the story took place?

Student: Olden times. About a hundred years ago.

Teacher: Yes, the setting is the rain forest at the tip of South America in the beginning of the 20th century. (Gunning, 2010)

Correcting Errors

Learning a language is a complex undertaking. As might be expected, English learners make many mistakes on their way to developing proficiency in English. The question arises: Should their mistakes be corrected? This decision requires professional judgment. Correcting every mistake would destroy the English learner's confidence and would almost certainly cut off the flow of language; it would also interrupt the flow of the lesson. In deciding whether to correct a student, consider the following:

- Based on the student's level of English language development, is this element one the student should be using correctly?
- Is the mistake a crucial one? Does it impact the student's understanding of the lesson?
- What is the nature of the error? Is it one that would be easy to correct?
- What impact would the correction have on the student? Would it embarrass her or him?

Also consider how the error might be corrected. When one student referred to the "Day of Thanksgiving," in a questioning tone, it was clear that he was asking whether he had used the correct form. The error was quickly corrected by saying, "You mean, 'Thanksgiving Day.'" Focus on meaning rather than on correcting errors. Correcting errors could embarrass the student and lead to a reluctance to take risks with language. You might provide a rephrasing, as long as you believe it will not demean or discourage the student.

> *Student:* There are too much fact. They are crooked in my mind.
>
> *Teacher:* Yes, there are too many facts. No wonder you have trouble keeping them straight.

Be proactive. Anticipate students' errors. Provide students with a list of errors frequently made by speakers of their language. For Spanish, the list might include items such as the mispronunciation of short *i* by giving it a long *e* sound: saying *beet* for *bit* or *heat* for *hit* or, using *of* for possessives when *'s* should be used: *Books of the students* for *the students' books.* If students are easily embarrassed or highly sensitive, or the mistakes are complex, hold private conferences to discuss corrections (Teachscape, 2006).

Using the Student's Language

On occasion, depending on their language proficiency and the nature of the material being learned, English language learners can benefit from having concepts explained in their native language. Clarification can be provided by the teacher, a bilingual aid, or another bilingual student. It can occur on a one-to-one basis. If there are no other resources available, the teacher can turn to content area texts written in the students' native language (Echevarria et al., 2000). In addition, an electronic translator such as the one found on Altavista *Babel Fish* (http://babelfish.altavista.com/) that translates text up to 150 words long and even Web site content, can be used. You can type in key words or phrases or summaries of key concepts and get the equivalent in the students' language. Students can also use these tools to translate difficult English passages into their native language. The guiding principle in whether to use English or the students' native language is to do whatever it takes to foster understanding.

USING TECHNOLOGY

More than 3,000 books in Spanish, ranging from beginning reading to secondary reading can be found at Renaissance Learning (www .renlearn.com/store/quiz_home.asp). Click on Advanced Search and search by Spanish language. Readability levels are supplied.

Teaching Discourse Patterns

School language has a linear discourse pattern. Explanations follow a definite sequence. Events are explained in the order in which they occurred. The speaker sticks with the topic and does not include information that is not directly related to the topic. However, there is some evidence that many Spanish speakers, Native Americans, and African Americans use a nonlinear discourse pattern (Escamilla & Cody, 2001). When writing about an event, students from these cultures may include a number of details that happened at the time of the event but were not directly related to the event. Their discourse style may be more associative: They include details that they associate with the main idea but that do not directly support it. Their descriptions and explanations might be quite accurate, but they seem more roundabout because they include what seem to be extraneous or nonessential details. Teachers may give them lower grades for their responses, even though the information they are supplying is accurate.

These students need to be exposed to academic discourse, both spoken and written. They need to be shown how to think and write in linear fashion and how to exclude extraneous details. Escamilla & Cody (2001) note

> When Spanish-speaking students are learning to write in English they must be explicitly taught English linear logic and the rhetorical and discourse patterns used in English writing. It is not enough to simply learn the mechanics of writing in English as a second language. Students must also learn how to "think" in English. (p. 55)

Fostering Output

Output has three functions: noticing/triggering, hypothesis testing, and reflecting (Anthony, 2008). When trying to express an idea, a student might realize that she lacks the appropriate words and so takes steps to acquire the needed words. Then, she composes her message, which leads to the second function of output: hypothesis testing. In hypothesis testing, the student delivers the message and uses feedback to revise it if necessary. The third function of output is assessing the message and altering it if necessary. Concluding that what she said didn't clearly convey her idea, the speaker can then take steps to correct her statement (Swain, 2008). Attempting to communicate, even if imperfectly, makes students more active learners and can be a confidence builder if they are able to convey their meaning (Gunning, 2010).

Developing Academic Language through Reading

Reading is an exceptionally effective way to foster the development of academic language. "Reading texts helps students see the organizational structure of sentences and paragraphs in both narrative and expository form. In contrast to listening, reading allows students to revisit confusing parts and fix up comprehension glitches. Reading gives students time to see and process many new words and expressions that are not commonly used in conversation" (Zwiers, n.d.).

If the text is too difficult for students to read on their own, scaffold the reading by implementing a kind of advanced shared reading. Read the text to students, going over unfamiliar words and phrases as you read. Stress academic language that is especially useful. Do a think-aloud as you demonstrate the strategies you use to construct meaning as you read. Invite students to read portions of the text that would be easy for them. Call attention to text features such as illustrations and glossary entries that enhance access to the text. Once you have read the text with students, invite them to read it on their own. However, provide a new purpose for reading and also a guide sheet or gloss that might assist them as they read. Have available talking dictionaries so the students can have unfamiliar words pronounced and defined. A second rereading provides practice engaging with academic text.

If the text is almost accessible, do an advanced text walk in which you go through the text page by page and provide an overview of the content. Call attention to and explain any words, phrases, or other elements that might be difficult for students. At the conclusion of the text walk, have students read to answer the purpose question(s) established by you or the class. These same techniques can be used with native speakers of English who are struggling readers.

Article of the Week http://
kellygallagher.org/resources/articles.html
To build students' background, high
school English teacher Kelly Gallagher
assigns students an article about a
current topic each week. Procedures
and a list of articles is presented on
his Web site.

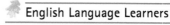

English Language Learners

Before students read a piece, activate
their prior knowledge. Because of
cultural and linguistic differences,
students might not realize that they
have background to bring to a story or
article. Also, emphasize comprehension
over pronunciation (Chamot &
O'Malley, 1994).

C H E C K U P

1. What are the stages of language development? Why should instruction be geared to the stages?
2. What instructional techniques might be used to develop English learners' academic language?

Building Background

Because of gaps in their schooling, in which they may have missed topics because of transferring to a new school or moving to another country, ELLs may lack background for key content area concepts. One solution is to teach lower-level concepts. However, if possible, grade-appropriate content should be taught. The better solution is to build students' background so that they will be prepared to learn the concepts being taught. If the whole class needs the background, this can be done as a whole-class activity, but if just one or two students need help, this can be accomplished in a small-group session. If tutors are available, they might do the background building. Vogt (Echevarria et al., 2000) uses a jumpstart technique in which she previews material for underprepared ELLs before it is introduced in the regular class. These jumpstart minilessons include reviewing key concepts, introducing new vocabulary, going through the chapter or section to be read and providing an overview of it, conducting or observing experiments, and taking part in simulations and role playing.

Considering Cultural Factors

ELL students are faced with more than just learning English. They must also learn the customs and culture of the classroom. Students from some countries may see their role as memorizing what they have been taught; in their culture, thinking for themselves is

Exemplary Teaching

Planning for English Learners

Noting that despite having several years of ESL classes, ELLs were failing their tenth-grade English class at a high rate, teachers at a Toronto high school initiated a transition class and met with the school's ESL teachers to plan a program (O'Byrne, 2001). Using samples of students' work, the ESL teachers helped the English teachers look beyond surface errors to see how English language learners developed—over time—the ability to compose written responses. The ESL teachers explained the importance of finding out where students were in their development and discussed ways in which the English teachers might build on the ELLs' competencies and advance their proficiency. The ESL teachers explained the importance of modeling, especially in view of the fact that many of the students had come from educational systems that emphasized memorizing.

The English teachers adopted a competency model of instruction. With the help of ESL teachers, they were able to compose a list of language competencies that the ELLs would need to acquire. The English teachers identified specific areas in which English language learners needed instruction and ways in which that instruction might be provided. They came to realize that language acquisition was a long-term process and that, although the ELLs had been provided a good start by the ESL teachers, they still needed additional instruction. Instead of setting as their goal the understanding of core texts, the English teachers began to think in terms of the acquisition of key reading and writing proficiencies. They placed additional emphasis on oral proficiency.

One thing the English teachers learned about language acquisition was that grammatical errors persist for many years. Although grammar had been a key element in the evaluation of students' work, the teachers learned to place less emphasis on its role. With their new understanding of second language acquisition, the teachers were better able to develop their students' literacy and help them to make a successful transition to regular classes.

---

not encouraged. In addition, questioning the teacher might be interpreted as a sign of disrespect. Students need to be guided to see that it is not only okay to think for oneself, it is desirable. However, this is a gradual process, especially for older students who may have spent years in a school culture that discouraged independent thought.

An example is Deng, a native of Laos and Hmong speaker, who found both the language and the culture of his U.S. school confusing (Brock, 2000). In his language arts classroom, the teacher wanted to contrast the words *home* and *homelessness*. Deng was not aware of the meaning of *contrast*. He confused it with the word *contest*. He wondered if it referred to some sort of race. But Deng did not ask the teacher to clarify the meaning of the word. And he never responded to questions by the teacher. In Laos, students were not expected to ask questions and were punished if they gave wrong answers.

As a result of language confusions and cultural constraints, Deng did not do well in whole-group lessons. However, he performed much better in small groups. Other students helped him with difficult words and confusing procedures. They also provided prompts so that Deng was able to take part in their discussions.

Using Group-Guided Language Experience

Use **language experience** with English language learners. A language experience selection is one in which students dictate the content of a written piece and the teacher functions as a facilitator and scribe. Because students dictate the story, the language is theirs. This works well with students who are less proficient in English and also in situations in which the textbook is too difficult. As students gain in proficiency, use a collaborative approach, in which you and students work together to create a selection. As an active participant, you can scaffold the language to a higher level. Here is how one teacher helped his secondary students create a story. They first read Maupassant's

■ **Language experience** is a teaching technique in which the teacher writes down an experience or ideas dictated by students; then students, with the teacher's guidance, read the dictated piece.

classic tale, "The Necklace," in which a poor but socially ambitious woman borrows what she thinks is an expensive necklace from a wealthy friend so that she can make an impression at a party (Schifini, 1999). After she loses the necklace and is too embarrassed to admit it, she slaves at menial jobs for years in order to replace it. Later, prematurely aged by her efforts, she encounters the owner of the necklace and learns that the necklace was just an inexpensive piece of costume jewelry. She had sacrificed her youth and beauty in vain. After reading and discussing the selection, the students discussed times when they had borrowed items. Then they decided to write their own story involving borrowing as a general theme. Cooperative groups were set up. Each group created an element of the story, with one group creating characters, another the setting, a third, the plot. The groups then met as a whole class and, through discussion and negotiation, created their story.

As the class, with the teacher's help, created their story, the teacher emphasized one or two teaching points. For this selection, he suggested that students incorporate dialogue and review ways of writing dialogue. After creating the story, reading it, and revising it, the students used a word processing program to create a book, complete with illustrations. They then read the book to younger students.

Reading Aloud to Students

English Language Learners

Teachers may wonder when—or even whether they should—correct students' English. One guideline is to offer some sort of correction if the student fails to communicate. The teacher simply provides the correct pronunciation or form without comment or explanation.

One way to build background and language is to read aloud to students. Reading to students helps to familiarize them with the more formal language of print. Choose books that are heavily illustrated, have a straightforward style, and don't use figurative language or idioms, which pose special problems for English language learners.

For older students who are more proficient in English, select books that are more detailed and complex, but also focused and well illustrated. Choose books that have a favorable print-to-illustration ratio and illustrations that do an especially effective job at depicting key concepts.

Preparation for the oral reading should take into account students' language ability, proficiency, and needs. Before reading the text, provide an overview so that students have a sense of the plot or the main ideas. This will help them get ready for a higher level of language comprehension. As you read the selection, make use of illustrations to help convey its meaning. Also demonstrate and act out key words. After reading a section of the selection, discuss it with students so they can reflect on and use the information they have learned.

Building on What Students Know

Cognitive and academic skills learned in one language transfer to a second language (Cummins, 1994). If I know the water cycle or understand the functioning of a cell in Spanish, I will know it in English once I acquire the proper labels. If I learn to read and write Spanish, I can transfer these skills and strategies into English once I learn the language.

Several English language learners taking a state mastery test in English were puzzled by the selection presented about ostriches, because the word *ostrich* was unfamiliar to them. They knew what ostriches were, but they didn't know the English label. Comprehension was hampered, not by a lack of background knowledge, but because they didn't have the English label for the creatures. Another group of students had difficulty reading a selection about a farm because, although some of them had been raised on farms, they didn't know the English label *farm*.

English language learners can be stymied by words such as *farm* and *ostrich*, which you might assume they know. If the unknown words are key words, they may lose the whole sense of the selection. Before students read a selection or listen to a lecture, go over the key terms with them. If they speak one of the romance languages, such as French, Spanish, Italian, Portuguese, or Romanian, have them seek out cognates, words that are descended from the same language or form. The word for *electricity* in Spanish is *electricidad*. Seeing the word *electricity*, the Spanish-speaking reader often realizes that it means the same thing as *electricidad*. Native speakers of Spanish may not realize how many Spanish words have English cognates.

Spanish–English Cognates

Although pronunciation may differ, many words are spelled the same in Spanish and English: *abdomen, base, capital, canal, film, larva, superior, usual, variable*. In hundreds of others there are slight changes in spelling as in the following:

> added *a: artista, dentista, forma, secreta*
>
> Added *o: acto, barbero, globo, infinito, objecto*
>
> Added *e: abundante, accidente, heroe, importante, residente*
>
> Omitted *e: aptitud, gratitud, latitud*
>
> Presence of *cia* instead of *ce: abundancia, distancia, competencia*
>
> Suffix *cion* instead of *tion: conversacion, educacion, nacion*

In some cognates there are several changes in spelling, so students might need to examine them carefully before recognizing them as familiar elements—for example, *hidrosfera* for *hydrosphere* or *actitud* for *attitude*. Students also need to be cautioned that there are false cognates. The word *exito* looks like the English *exit*, but it means "success." Likewise *largura* does not mean "large"; it is the Spanish word for *length*. Students need to be taught to use context to check to see if the word that seems to be a cognate makes sense in the sentence (Thonis, 1983). Model the process of using cognates by demonstrating how you use cognates to read Spanish words.

Unit or thematic organization also works particularly well for English language learners. By viewing the overall topic being explored or question being asked, students are better able to make sense of instruction. Since concepts are developed in more detail in thematic units and vocabulary is naturally repeated, thematic organization is more meaningful to English language learners (Freeman & Freeman, 2002).

CCSS

Identify and correctly use patterns of word changes that indicate different meanings or parts of speech (e.g., *analyze, analysis, analytical; advocate, advocacy*).

CCSS

Use context (e.g., the overall meaning of a sentence, paragraph, or text; a word's position or function in a sentence) as a clue to the meaning of a word or phrase.

CHECKUP

1. What are some techniques that might be used to help English language learners master content material?
2. Which of these techniques would be most effective in the content area that you teach?

Role of the Classroom Teacher in Instructing English Language Learners

Classroom teachers have a twofold responsibility in teaching English language learners: They must make content accessible and they must build their students' ability to understand the language of the subject they teach. The first step is to teach as effectively as possible. Good teaching is good teaching. All students benefit from having clear goals, high expectations, direct instruction, challenging content, engagement, in-depth class discussions, checking for understanding, adequately paced review, and a caring, well-prepared teacher. Direct instruction is helpful for all students, but is especially helpful for ELLs. In addition to implementing effective instructional approaches, teachers can employ several strategies to make the content more accessible. An overview of the content might be presented in the students' native language before it is presented in English. A second approach is to have students read about the content in materials that grow progressively more difficult. Students might begin by reading easy books or articles in which they know almost all of the words and then continue to read material that increases in difficulty until they reach the desired level (Goldenberg, 2008). With the wealth of informational trade books available today, it is possible to locate materials on a variety of levels. Another approach is to use simplified language when discussing or explaining new concepts. Topics discussed might then be highlighted in a summary dictated by students and composed on a smart board or computer with a projector so that it can be readily printed for students. In that way they have clearly presented material to study.

Another possibility is to use a preview-review approach in which you or a translator previews a topic and key terms in the students' native language before presenting it in English (Goldenberg, 2008). Then, when the lesson is previewed in English, students already will have some sense of the content to be delivered. At the end of the lesson, the material can then be reviewed in the students' native language. In research, preview-review proved to be more effective than just reading the material in English or just translating the material from English into Spanish as it was being read. In order to provide systematic instruction both in content and language, content teachers can use an approach known as sheltered English.

Using Sheltered English

In **sheltered English**, teachers make a special effort to make content instruction understandable to all students, including those who are still acquiring academic English. This is something that conscientious teachers have always done. However, sheltered instruction has a second component. While presenting content, the teacher also takes steps to foster language development. Colburn and Echevarria (1999) comment that sheltered classes are "distinguished by careful attention to students' needs related to learning another language" (p. 36). In a sense, content and language objectives are combined.

A good place to begin sheltered instruction is building on what has worked in the past and adapting these techniques to ELLs. Schifini (1994) suggests that you ask yourself, "How does any youngster come to comprehend and glean new information from text? What has worked well for students I have taught in the past?" (p. 162). Make a list of the effective techniques. Then ask yourself a third question, "How can I adapt or modify these techniques so that they will help ELLs learn?" Some adaptations that may help include the following:

- Make your presentation as understandable as possible. Speak slowly and distinctly. Use simple, direct language. Avoid jargon, figurative language, idioms, and cultural references that may be unfamiliar to students.
- Use the visual to support the verbal. Use audiovisual aids, gestures, facial expressions, demonstrations, and skits to make the language as meaningful as possible.
- Make directions as clear as possible. Show students what to do in addition to telling them. If possible, model the process for them. Have students attempt to carry out directions or apply a concept under your guidance. Provide feedback as needed.
- Emphasize hands-on activities, drawings, webs, and maps so that students can use techniques that are less language dependent to deepen and express their knowledge.
- Use brainstorming, quick write, and similar techniques to tap prior knowledge. In a quick write, students are given two or three minutes to sum up what they know.
- Modify the use of text. You might use Questioning the Author to help students collaboratively construct meaning.
- Obtain texts that use a simpler language.
- Encourage students to discuss content in their native language as well as in English.
- Provide prompts that encourage students to clarify or expand responses: "That's interesting. I'd like to hear more about that. Can you explain that? Can you tell us more? So what happened next?"
- Scaffold instruction. Provide prompts and other assistance as needed.
- Provide opportunities for students to talk over ideas in whole-class discussions, pairs, or small groups. This gives English language learners the opportunity to use academic language as they engage in activities and discuss procedures and findings.
- Pantomime actions and demonstrate processes.
- Use time lines, graphs, videos, and videoclips. Use manipulatives such as globes and models.
- Use realia such as recycling and nutrition labels, menus, job applications, and bank deposit slips.
- Provide generous amounts of wait time. Instead of expecting students to answer as soon as you ask a question, wait a few seconds. This benefits all students (Lake, 1973;

■ **Sheltered English** is the practice of teaching subject matter content in English to English language learners who have learned conversational English but not academic language. The purpose of sheltered instruction is to build both language skills and content knowledge.

Rowe, 1969) but is especially helpful to ELLs because they may need extra time to formulate their responses.

■ When assessing, allow students to demonstrate their knowledge in multiple ways. Where possible, include ways that don't rely so heavily on language. They might conduct an experiment, draw a diagram, or complete a project.

Here is how one secondary teacher sheltered the content in her social studies class (Schifini, 1999). As part of a unit on indigenous cultures, the class was studying the Mayan culture. To introduce the lesson, the teacher provided each group with an artifact from the culture and asked them to discuss the nature of the artifact and how the Mayan people may have used it. After discussing the artifacts, students then read about them in the easy-to-read, heavily illustrated *New True Book about the Maya* (McKissack & McKissack, 1986).

As part of this discussion of the Maya, students wrote one thing that they liked about the Maya. Students also looked at pictures of the Mayans and wrote things that they knew or thought they knew based on the illustrations. Students then participated in a KWL activity, as explained in Chapter 5, and read a portion of the book. Generally, brainstorming is the first step of a KWL activity and there is no prior preparation. The discussion of the artifacts had built a solid foundation for the KWL activity. As a result of the preparation, students were able to read the text with enhanced comprehension. They had little difficulty filling out their KWL charts and noting what they had learned. Because of their well-prepared reading, they engaged in a lively discussion of the topic.

Summarized below is a well-planned science lesson designed to introduce students to the concepts of density and buoyancy (Colburn & Echevarria, 1999). How might this lesson be adapted to meet the needs of ELLs?

Into a tank of water, the teacher placed two oranges, one that had been peeled and one that hadn't. The class discussed why the peeled orange sank. Students then created boats and charted in graph form how much they could load onto their boats before they sank. As the students worked, the teacher circulated around the room and asked students, "Tell me what you're thinking," to get insight into their thought processes. The teacher also discussed the relationship between density and buoyancy. Then, the teacher assigned the section of the textbook that explains density and buoyancy.

With its hands-on activities, demonstration, and emphasis on inquiry, the lesson was highly effective and helped the students to experience the concepts of density and buoyancy, not just talk or read about them. However, there are several steps that could be taken to shelter this same content.

■ In addition to giving students oral directions, the teacher could demonstrate what she wants them to do. Instead of just telling them to make boats, she could make one as an example and load it up until it sinks. This helps ensure that students who miss a word here or there know exactly what to do because they have seen a demonstration.

■ To foster language development, the teacher could highlight key vocabulary words and discuss them and, if possible, show illustrations of them or demonstrate them. This way, there would be an increased probability that students will have used them in their discussions.

■ The teacher in this case walked around the room as the students worked and asked what they were thinking. In addition, it would be helpful to observe the graphs the students were working on. If a student's academic language is limited, her graph may reveal an aspect of her thinking that she can't put into words.

■ The teacher could provide more preparation for reading the textbook assignment. She could give the students an overview of the content or read portions of it to them. In addition, she could prepare a gloss or strategy guide.

English Language Learners

Subjects such as math, science, and social studies provide a built-in context that can help students acquire language more easily.

Cooperative learning works well with ELLs because there is more opportunity for feedback and clarification.

C H E C K U P

1. What is sheltered instruction?
2. How is it implemented?
3. What is the role of the content area teacher in instructing ELL?

Helping Students Who Have Serious Reading Problems

Many content area classes contain students who have serious reading difficulties. This is not a new phenomenon. There have always been older students who are not able to read despite being in a school system for nine years or more. With increased accountability occasioned by the standards movement and high-stakes testing, this shortcoming has become more visible. If students have serious reading problems, they should be provided the opportunity to receive expert assistance from well-trained professionals. This textbook has made a number of suggestions for making information accessible to students who can't read it for themselves.

However, you may find that you are the only source of help for a student, or perhaps you want to offer assistance to students who have serious reading problems or like to help out in your school's tutoring program. Or maybe you simply want to gain a better understanding of how older struggling readers can be instructed. Following are several suggestions for working with older students who have serious reading problems.

- *Find out the student's reading level.* One way to do this is to have the student read a series of passages that gradually increase in difficulty. You can use the benchmark passages in Chapter 2 for this purpose. Have the student read the passages orally. On a copy of the passages, note errors that the student makes while reading orally. Errors include misreading words, inserting words, or omitting words. A student's instructional level is the point at which he or she can read 95 percent to 98 percent of the words. The frustration level is 90 percent word recognition or below. In other words, at the frustration level, students are misreading 10 or more words out of 100. To assess students' comprehension, ask questions about the passages or ask students to tell you what they read. The instructional level for comprehension is found at 70 percent to 75 percent correct answers.
- *If students are reading on a first- or second-grade level, they will need instruction in basic phonics and syllabication skills.* The Phonics Inventory, a quick test of phonics, can be found on the Building Literacy Web site, at http://wordbuilding.org. The Inventory will indicate students' level of phonics knowledge and which patterns they need to be taught. Also analyze the results of the benchmark passages. Note the kinds of errors the student made. The Building Literacy Web site has suggestions for teaching phonics. You may also choose to use a commercial program. Some commercial programs are listed in Table 9.3.
- *If students are reading on a third grade level or above, they have mastered basic phonics but may need some additional help with multisyllabic words or morphemic elements.*
- *Students may do well reading the words, but have difficulty understanding or remembering what they have read.* Techniques such as ReQuest and Reciprocal Teaching, which were discussed in Chapter 6, should work well with these students.

Commercially Produced Intervention Programs

Three of the most widely used commercial intervention programs for secondary students are Scholastic's *Read 180*, *Wilson Language*, and *AMP*. *Read 180* combines computer technology with a workshop approach to teaching reading. *Read 180* features monitoring software that analyzes, monitors, tracks, and reports on student accuracy, and instructional software that adapts to students' responses and provides oral and visual feedback.

The *Wilson Reading System*, which is designed for students who have severe reading difficulties, is one of many based on the Orton-Gillingham (OG) approach, which presents the isolated sounds of letters and then builds these individual sounds into words. The program is highly structured and designed specifically as a remedial program for students

HELPING STUDENTS WHO HAVE SERIOUS READING PROBLEMS

Exemplary Teaching

Matching Instruction to Students' Needs

In an urban high school, students' reading levels will vary, with most being significantly below grade level. In Hartford, Connecticut, for instance, the average reading level for ninth graders in the system's three high schools is 6.9, with nearly one of every four students reading at a fourth-grade level or below. Concerned by its high dropout rate, the school system created a "school within a school" for its ninth graders. The ninth-grade academies were given their own administrators, teachers, and counselors. Emphasis was placed on matching instruction to the students' individual needs. Both the reading and the content area programs were transformed. In the reading program, students were placed according to their level of achievement and provided with a carefully monitored, structured program designed for older students. Many of the students skipped several levels. In science class, a hands-on program was adopted that emphasized inquiry-oriented instruction so that the students would also be minds-on. As their reading skills improved, students began feeling good about themselves and their attitude toward school began to change. Instead of nodding off during science lectures, they became deeply involved as they constructed DNA models and built robots. Two ninth graders who had just been suspended even asked if they could come back for science class. As a result of a changed attitude toward school, the dropout rate decreased by 10 percent (Gottlieb, 2001).

who have decoding problems. Like other programs that use highly controlled vocabulary, the reading materials tend to be contrived: "Tim sat in the shop. A mom and a tot came in. The mom got gum for the tot" (Gunning, 2010).

The *AMP Reading System* is a reading intervention program for striving middle and high school students reading at a third- to sixth-grade level. The program has an online library that provides three levels of scaffolding. Students can read the article as is, they can get help from an animated coach that provides strategy tips, and they can have the article read out loud. The animated coach might make a suggestion, model a strategy, or demonstrate use of a strategy. The program also has a dictionary so that students can click on words and obtain the pronunciation of the word and its definition. At periodic stopping points students answer multiple-choice or open-ended questions that include making connections or constructing personal responses. A listing of major intervention programs for struggling readers can be found in Table 9.3. It is designed to be relatively comprehensive, but note that just because a program is listed, that should not be interpreted as a recommendation to use it. All of the programs listed adhere to basic standards of instruction. However, some of the programs are better designed and more effective than others. Programs also embody varying philosophies and approaches. For instance, *Corrective Reading* is a scripted behavioral approach that emphasizes decoding. *Read 180* is a more holistic program that stresses extensive reading, but relies heavily on technology and is very expensive.

Using the Language Experience Approach

It is sometimes not possible to obtain texts that are on the students' reading level. One way to provide even the poorest readers with content area selections that they can read is to compose an experience text. Language experience text can be used to create a readable content area information text for struggling readers. An experience text is a selection that has been dictated by a single student or a group and recorded by the teacher. Once the text has been recorded, the students who dictated it then read it. Because the students dictated it, the language is familiar to them. If the selection is brief and simply written, it can be used as the students' reading material. This technique is a tried-and-true method for working with illiterate adults as well as school-age students who have serious reading problems. However, it can also be highly effective in a content area class. Lesson 9.1 shows how it works.

TABLE 9.3 **Programs for Older Struggling Readers**

TITLE	PUBLISHER	INTEREST LEVEL	GRADE LEVEL	OVERVIEW
AMP	Pearson	6–12	3–6	Has three levels. Focus is on developing vocabulary and on key comprehension strategies.
Corrective Reading	SRA	3–12	1–5+	Scripted direct instruction in decoding and comprehension.
Edge	Hampton-Brown	9–12	1–9	A four-book series builds decoding, vocabulary, comprehension, and writing skills. Features high-quality reading selections. Has an online coach that assists with vocabulary, figurative language, and comprehension and will read text to students. Has a recording feature that notes misread words so students can practice them.
Fast Track	McGraw-Hill	4–8	1–5+	High-interest selections. Has word work, comprehension, and fluency strands. Has phonics program for students who need it.
High Noon	High Noon	3–12	1–4+	Features systematic instruction in decoding and comprehension. Good bet for students reading on a beginning level.
High Point	Hampton-Brown	4–12	1–6	Develops decoding, comprehension, writing, oral language. Emphasis is on ELLs.
InZone Books	Hampton-Brown	9–12	1–9	Provides voluntary or guided reading.
Language!	Sopris West	1–12	1–9	A comprehensive six-level systematic, highly structured program that develops decoding, comprehension, spelling, and writing with an emphasis on oral language. Is designed for readers with severe disabilities.
Ramp Up to Literacy	America's Choice	6–12		A comprehensive program that develops phonics, comprehension, vocabulary, fluency, and writing explicitly and includes cross-age tutoring and independent self-selected reading.
Read Naturally	Read Naturally	1–8	1–8	Students read along to a recording of a selection and then practice reading the story on their own, timing themselves until they can read it at a predetermined goal rate. Exercises also reinforce phonics, syllabic analysis, vocabulary, and comprehension.

TITLE	PUBLISHER	INTEREST LEVEL	GRADE LEVEL	OVERVIEW
Read 180	Scholastic	4–12	3–9	Combines computer technology with a workshop approach to teaching reading. Features adaptive software that analyzes, monitors, tracks, and reports on student progress. Also includes high-interest reading material. Writing and vocabulary are also an integral part of the program. Uses film clips to build background.
Rewards	Sopris West	6–12	2–4+	Designed for students who have mastered the basic decoding skills associated with K–2 grade reading, but they have not mastered multisyllabic words and they read slowly (60–120 words/minute). Focus is on reading multisyllabic words, but reinforces fluency, vocabulary, and content-area reading.
Sipps Challenge	Developmental Studies Center	4–12	1–4+	Challenge program focuses on reading multisyllabic words. Has optional library for reinforcing skills taught.
Soar to Success	Houghton Mifflin-Harcourt	K–8	K–8	Features cooperative groups and teaching of comprehension and decoding strategies. Uses high-interest trade books.
S.P.I.R.E.	EPS	1–8	1–5+	Based on the principles of Orton-Gillingham, develops decoding, spelling, fluency, vocabulary, and comprehension for students who have mastered initial consonant correspondences. Is designed for readers with severe disabilities.
Success for All	Success for All Foundation	K–8	K–8	Whole-school reform program. Builds decoding, comprehension, and writing.
System 44	SRA	3–12	1–2	Adaptive software delivers direct, explicit, research-based phonics instruction. Provides instruction and practice in the use of a variety of decoding strategies, including morphemic analysis. Apply skills by reading high-interest selections. Also builds vocabulary.
Voyager Passport	Voyager Learning	3–12	1–2	Combines dramatic videos, online technology, high-interest reading passages, and intensive instruction in 15-day units to build syllabic and morphemic analysis, fluency, vocabulary, and comprehension.

(Continued)

TABLE 9.3 (*Continued*)

TITLE	PUBLISHER	INTEREST LEVEL	GRADE LEVEL	OVERVIEW
Wilson	Wilson	3–12	1–4+	Based on the principles of Orton-Gillingham, provides extensive instruction in phonemic awareness, phonics, and fluency. Also reinforces vocabulary and comprehension. Designed for readers with severe disabilities.
Word Detectives Introductory	Benchmark School	5–8	2–3+	Builds decoding skills, use of strategies, spelling, and summarizing. Useful for students who have some knowledge of phonics but are not applying their skills or who are poor spellers.

LESSON 9.1

Composing Experience Text

Step 1: Obtaining Information
Information for the experience can be obtained in a number of ways. The text might be written about an actual experience. For instance, students may have taken a trip to a historical site, they may have observed or conducted an experiment, they may have had a discussion about a segment in a text, they may have viewed a video on eating disorders, or a segment of a textbook may have been read to them.

Step 2: Discussing the Information
Discuss and summarize the field trip, experiment, video, or other source of information.

Step 3: Recording of Experience Text
Record the information on the board, overhead transparency, or computer projector. Prior to recording the information, help students organize it. They can put events in sequential order, describe a process step by step, or note the main points in a history chapter. Record the information in the students' own words. If this is a selection to be read by a group, you can do some light editing. However, don't rewrite the selection because students will lose their sense of ownership. An experience story is presented in Figure 9.1.

Step 4: Reading of Experience Text
Read the text to students. Discuss with them whether the text says what they want it to say. Ask if there are any details that they would like to add, take out, or change. After changes have been made, read it a second time. Ask students if they are satisfied with the changes. These multiple readings will familiarize students with the text so that they will be better able to read it on their own. Through these multiple readings you are also reviewing the key points covered.

Step 5: Student Reading of Experience Text
The experience text is duplicated, and it becomes the students' text. If the experience text has been composed on a transparency, the transparency can be copied, as long as the writing is readable. If it has been composed on a computer that projects on a screen large enough for everyone to see, copies can be printed for everyone. After being given printed copies, students read the selection for any of the same reasons they may read a textbook. They may read it that night to review information covered in class or to prepare for a quiz. They can also provide illustrations, such as a map or diagram, to go along with written information. Experience text selections can be saved and put into a folder or binder. They also can serve as a source of review so students can study the selections in preparation for a test.

Struggling Readers

Hands-on experiences help make abstract concepts more understandable and more concrete. For instance, students achieve a deeper understanding of kinetic energy when they calculate the kinetic energy of a cart running down a ramp.

> **Antarctica**
>
> Antarctica is at the bottom of the world. It is where the South Pole is. Antarctica is the coldest place on earth. One time the temperature hit 100 degrees below zero. It is the only place on Earth where no people live all the time. Scientists come there and stay for a few months, but no one lives there all year round.
>
> People think that Antarctica has lots of snow and ice. There is plenty of ice there. In some places the ice is 5,000 feet thick. But it hardly ever snows there. Antarctica only gets about two inches of snow a year. The reason is that air gets drier as it gets colder. The air is so cold that it is very dry.
>
> Antarctica is very large. It is larger than the United States and Canada put together. There is also one very surprising thing about Antarctica. It has a volcano. Most people don't know that. It is hard to believe that the coldest place on earth has a volcano.

FIGURE 9.1
Experience Story

Providing students with printed copies of key topics gives them materials that they can study. It also builds content area literacy, so that in time students may be able to read content area texts on their own. This technique can also be used with literary selections that students may not be able to read on their own. One way of structuring an experience text is to read a literary selection to students and then have them retell it. Their retelling is recorded for future reading (Crawford, 1993).

The experience text approach can be used with all students, but is especially valuable for English language learners because it uses their language. If the group is composed entirely of English language learners who speak the same native language, students may include in the recorded text words and expressions from that language.

Interactive whiteboards—large, touch-controlled screens that work with a projector and a computer—can be used to compose experience accounts. The projector displays the computer's desktop image on the whiteboard. Users can write on the interactive whiteboard (with a finger or dry-erase marker) and also display screens from computer applications; whatever appears on a computer screen can be displayed on an interactive whiteboard. Thus, a language experience story could be written on the whiteboard, illustrated with clip art or digital photos, and sent to classroom computers or printed out. Using the computer's voice technology, students could have the story read to them. Since the story is saved on the computer, it can be reviewed as often as students want and edited if desired (Gunning, 2010). With some systems, the whole lesson can be recorded on video and replayed.

CHECKUP

1. What are some techniques and approaches that can be used to help struggling readers?
2. How might the language experience approach be used in your content area?

Using Technology

Technology can be used in a number of ways to make material accessible to struggling readers. Universal Design for Learning is an instructional approach that uses technology to help meet the needs of all learners. "Universal Design for Learning (UDL) is a framework for designing curricula that enable all individuals to gain knowledge, skills, and enthusiasm for learning. UDL provides rich supports for learning and reduces barriers to the curriculum while maintaining high achievement standards for all" (CAST, 2009). For students who have serious reading problems, text-to-speech systems such as the *Kurzweil 3000* (www.kurzweiledu.com), *Read and Write Gold* (www.readwritegold.com), and *Wynn Wizard* (www.freedomscientific.com) are available. These consist of a scanner, optical character recognition (OCR) software, a word-processing program, and a speech synthesizer. The text that the student wishes to read is scanned into the word-processing program and analyzed by the OCR software. Then it is read aloud by the computer's voice synthesizer at the same time it is highlighted on the screen so that the student can follow along.

Students who have difficulty reading can read along with the text-to-speech version of a Web site.

Source: Shutterstock.

In addition, the systems have a number of useful study tools including an audible spell checker, a note-taking feature, and access to a dictionary and other reference materials.

If the materials are in a digital format, they need not be scanned. For instance, Pearson HTML books are digital versions of the company's course materials designed for students with learning, print, speech, and language disabilities. Because they are digital versions, they can be used with a **screen reader** so that the text can be read aloud. They can be read with the computer's built-in screen reader or enhanced screen readers, such as *Kurzweil 3000, Read & Write Gold, Read Out Loud* www.donjohnston.com, and *gh Player* (www.gh-accessibility.com/products/ghplayer). *Blio*, a free software e-reader program, has text-to-speech ability, a number of study skill features, a translation feature, and the ability to play audio and video clips. It can be read on PC laptops as well as most smart phones and electronic pads. *Blio* also has a library of more than a million books. Many e-readers, such as Kindle, have a text-to-speech feature along with a dictionary.

Some text-to-speech programs are multilingual, so students can find the equivalent of an English word in their native tongue. Or the student can use translation software such as Yahoo's *Babel Fish* (http://babelfish.altavista.com) to have passages translated from English into their native language or vice versa.

If the text is in digital format and text-to-speech software is not available, students can use the text-to-speech feature available on most computers. To activate this feature on the Mac choose Apple menu > System Preferences, click "Speech" and then click "Text to Speech" and follow the directions.

Many texts have audio versions. *Holt's World Geography Today* (Sager, & Helgren, 2008), for instance, has a direct reading of the chapters in MP3 format. A Spanish version of the chapters is also available.

Using E-books

Because they are in a digital format, e-books have a number of advantages. For one thing, they can be read by a screen reader or a talking word-processing program. This makes them accessible to struggling readers. To make them even more accessible, e-books can be linked to a dictionary so that students can get help with difficult words. A third advantage for many e-texts is that the text can be added to or altered. You might add explanatory notes or illustrations or even rewrite difficult portions. E-books are readily available on the Internet from a number of sources including Project Gutenberg (www.promo.net/pg) and the University of Virginia (http://etext.virginia.edu/subjects/Young-Readers.html), which has a Young Readers collection of public domain texts, and commercial sites such as Amazon and Google Books (http://books.google.com/). The Awesome Talking Library (www.awesomelibrary.org/Awesome_Talking_Library.html) has links to a number of e-book sites.

The Center for Applied Special Technology's *UDL Book Builder*, which is an easy-to-use program for creating e-books, offers a variety of e-books, many on the secondary level. *Book Builder* features a number of devices, including tools for creating a glossary and linking the definitions to the text, virtual coaches that provide prompts or explanations as students read the text, a library of illustrations, the ability to add spoken commentary or even read the selection, and a library of illustrations and clips.

Additional information about assistive technology and software is available from national, regional, and local sources. Two of the best overall sources are Center for Applied Special Technology (CAST) (www.cast.org) and Alliance for Technology Access (ATA) (www.ataccess.org). Using the concept of Universal Design, CAST has extensive

■ **A screen reader** is a program that will read aloud whatever appears on a computer screen.

information on numerous ways of making materials accessible and a wide range of high-quality links. ATA, which also provides links to a large number of sites, is a national network of community-based resource centers, product developers, vendors, service providers, and individuals.

Online Texts

Online texts have a number of helpful features. *Holt's World Geography Today* (Sager, & Helgren, 2008) is accompanied by video clips, interactive maps, graphic organizers that can be completed online, a grapher, current events, a researcher that allows students to consult other social studies sources, and content updates. Online texts may be cheaper than print textbooks and they could be used to solve the problem of outdated texts. Students who are reluctant to take a physical text home might be willing to read and respond to an online text.

CHECKUP

1. How might technology be used to help struggling readers?

Obtaining Texts on the Appropriate Level

In an average class, the textbook is too difficult for nearly one student in every three. One solution is to eliminate the text and conduct learning through hands-on activities, lectures, and discussions. The problem with this approach is that students are denied the opportunity to learn to read content area material. Another solution is to obtain texts that are easy to read. A list of easy-to-read texts is presented in Table 9.4. Presented below is

TABLE 9.4 Easy-to-Read Content Texts

TEXT	PUBLISHER	GRADE LEVEL	READING LEVEL	LEXILE LEVEL
Language Arts				-
AGS American Literature -	AGS	8–12	3–4	820
Revised				430–1550**
AGS Basic English	AGS	6–12	3–4	650
AGS Basic English Composition	AGS	6–12	3–4	580
AGS Basic English Grammar	AGS	6–12	3–4	580
AGS British Literature	AGS	8–12	3–4	850
				640–1630**
AGS Discover Life Skills Handbook	AGS	7–12	3–4	730
AGS English for the World of Work	AGS	6–12	3–4	870
AGS English to Use	AGS	6–12	3–4	630
AGS Life Skills English	AGS	6–12	3–4	800
AGS Exploring Literature-	AGS	8–12	3–4	880
Revised				540–1500**

(*Continued*)

TABLE 9.4 (*Continued*)

TEXT	PUBLISHER	GRADE LEVEL	READING LEVEL	LEXILE LEVEL
AGS Language Arts and Literature Courses 1–3	AGS	6–8	4–5	720–760
				480–1530**
AGS World Literature-	AGS	8–12	3–4	710
Revised				740–1620
Guidebook to Better English	Phoenix	7–12+	4–7	
Pacemaker American Literature	AGS	6–12	3–4	710
Pacemaker Basic English Revised	AGS	6–12	3–4	650
Pacemaker Basic English Composition	AGS	6–12	3–4	590
Pacemaker World Literature, 2nd Ed	AGS	6–12	3–4	870
History & Social Studies				
AGS Career Planning	AGS	6–12	3–4	880
AGS Economics	AGS	6–12	3–4	840
AGS History of Our Nation:	AGS	6–12	3–4	870
1865 to the Present				
AGS History of Our Nation:	AGS	6–12	3–4	930
Beginnings to 1920				
AGS United States Government	AGS	6–12	3–4	870
- Revised				
AGS United States History –	AGS	6–12	3–4	880
Revised				
AGS World Geography and	AGS	6–12	4–5	770
Cultures - Revised				
AGS World History - Revised	AGS	6–12	4–5	760
*America's History: Land of Liberty**	Steck-Vaughn	8–12	5–6	
*America's Story**	Steck-Vaughn	7–12	2–3	
English Explorers: Social Studies	Benchmark	4–8	2–4	
Pacemaker Careers	AGS	6–12	3–4	890
Pacemaker United States History	AGS	6–12	3–4	760
Pacemaker World History	AGS	6–12	3–4	760
*World Geography and You**	Steck-Vaughn	6–12	3–4	
*World History and You**	Steck-Vaughn	6–12	4	
Science				
AGS Biology - Revised	AGS	6–12	3–4	840
AGS Biology: Cycles of Life	AGS	6–12	3–4	850
AGS Chemistry	AGS	6–12	3–4	880

TEXT	PUBLISHER	GRADE LEVEL	READING LEVEL	LEXILE LEVEL
AGS Earth Science - Revised	AGS	6–12	3–4	840
AGS Environmental Science	AGS	6–12	3–4	870
AGS General Science - Revised	AGS	6–12	3–4	840
AGS Life Skills: Health - Revised	AGS	6–12	3–4	840
AGS Physical Science - Revised	AGS	6–12	3–4	840
English Explorers: Science	Benchmark	4–8+	1–3	100–460
Pacemaker Computer Literacy	AGS	6–12	3–4	720
Pacemaker Health	AGS	6–12	3–4	800
Wonders of Science*	Steck-Vaughn	7–12	2–3	
Math				
AGS Algebra - Revised	AGS	6–12	3–4	760
AGS Algebra 2	AGS	6–12	3–4	790
AGS Basic Math Skills - Revised	AGS	6–12	3–4	770
AGS Geometry - Revised	AGS	7–12	3–4	820
AGS Mathematics: Concepts	AGS	6–12	3–4	720
AGS Mathematics: Pathways	AGS	6–12	3–4	870
AGS Pre-Algebra - Revised	AGS	6–12	3–4	750
AGS Life Skills Math	AGS	6–12	3–4	810
AGS Math for the World of Work	AGS	6–12	3–4	860
Earning Money	Phoenix	7–12	5–6	
Essential Math Skills	Phoenix	7–12	5–6	
Using Money	Phoenix	7–12	5–6	

*Designed for adult education
**Indicates range of Lexile scores for individual selections within the anthology

a passage from an easy-to-read world history text. Although designed for use by high school students, the text is written on a fourth-grade level. The text presents difficult vocabulary at the beginning of each chapter and has a summary and chapter checkup at the end of each chapter. Also listed below is a passage on the same topic from an on-grade text. What are the differences between the two texts? What are the advantages and disadvantages of using easy-to-read texts?

Passage from Easy-to-Read Text

Sometimes the rivers flooded and washed rich bottom-soil up on the land. This made the land good for farming. People settled on this rich land. They grew their crops and raised animals. In the south, in a land called Sumer, a great civilization grew.

The people of Sumer are called Sumerians. Although the land they settled was fertile, it was not a perfect place to live. (Suter, 1994, p. 29)

Passage from Grade-Level Text

In Sumer, as in Egypt, the fertile land of a river valley attracted Stone Age farmers from neighboring regions. In time their descendants produced the surplus food needed to support growing populations.

Just as control of the Nile was vital to Egypt, control of the Tigris and Euphrates was key to developments in Mesopotamia. The rivers rose in terrifying floods that washed away topsoil and destroyed mud-brick villages. (Ellis & Esler, 2001)

The obvious problem with easy-to-read texts is that the characteristics that make them accessible may limit what students learn. They may be exposed to fewer vocabulary words and less information. If you do use easy texts, make sure that you present through discussion, experiments, simulations, audiovisual aids, or other means important information that was omitted.

Making the Text Accessible

Sometimes, it is not possible to obtain easy-to-read texts for students who need them. There are a number of steps that can be taken to make a text more accessible.

- *Record summaries of chapters (Vogt, 2001) or obtain recorded versions of texts.* Recorded versions of texts are available from some publishers and also from Recordings for the Blind and Dyslexic.
- *Mark key text to be learned with highlighter.* A few copies of a text or even a whole set might be highlighted to reduce the demands of reading the text. Highlight key segments and sections that you think the students will be able to handle on their own. Most texts have extraneous material that can readily be deleted.
- *Provide written summaries.* One way to provide students with ongoing readable text is to use a language experience approach to summarize key concepts. After a discussion or demonstration, have students orally summarize key points. As they dictate their summaries, write them on the board or on chart paper. Students can copy these summaries and then read them over as an assignment and use them as a basis for studying.
- *Accumulate a library of easy-to-read explanations of key concepts.* These could be excerpts from easy-to-read texts, easy-to-read trade books, magazine articles, materials from the Internet, or materials that you have constructed. The library could also include recorded books, e-books, and videos. See Table 9.5 for a list of easy-to-read trade books that cover key concepts.
- *Read aloud.* Read portions of the text out loud to students. The most difficult vocabulary and concepts often come at the beginning of the chapter. You might read an initial section to provide an overview and build background so students can read the rest of the chapter on their own.
- *Adapt the text.* Rewrite portions of the text to make it more readable. Rewriting a whole text would be a monumental task, so rewrite segments that present key ideas. If you rewrite one segment a week or even every two weeks, you will soon have a substantial amount of rewritten material. The major goal of rewriting is to make the text more accessible to students. Rewriting should result in easier vocabulary and simpler syntax. However, it should go beyond merely substituting easier words and simpler sentences. Before rewriting, take a look at the main concepts being explained. Perhaps they demand background that hasn't been supplied. In your rewrite, fill in the needed background. Also look at the presentation of the material. Is it clear? If not, clarify it. Also, relate key concepts to students' background. Authors sometimes include interesting details that actually interrupt the flow of information. If so, delete these. On the other hand, the authors may be trying to cover too much material. Decide which are the essential ideas and develop these fully. To rewrite a text, do the following:

USING TECHNOLOGY

Some e-texts can be altered so that text could be adapted to make it easier and helpful explanations and learning aids could be added.

TABLE 9.5 **Easy Content Books for Older Readers**

TITLE	PUBLISHER	READING LEVEL	INTEREST LEVEL
Fearon's Freedom Fighters Includes eighty-page biographies of Martin Luther King, Nelson Mandela, Cesar Chavez, Fannie Hammer, and Malcolm X.	Pearson School	3–4	7–12
Hidden Worlds Series of four books about the inner workings of malls, stadiums, hospitals, and police stations.	Capstone	3	3–9+
Incredible Space Series of six books about traveling and living in space.	Capstone	3 600–700 Lexile	3–9+
Illustrated Classics Features seventy-two classics in illustrated format.	Pearson School	3–4	6–12
Killer Animals Series of sixteen books about fierce predators.	Capstone	3	3–9+
Reading Essentials in Science Series of twenty-four books covering key topics in science.	Perfection Learning	710–1110	3–8+
Reading Essentials in Social Studies Features a range of books covering key topics in U.S. and world history, geography, and government.	Perfection Learning	520–1200	3–8+
Start-to-Finish: Step into History Features biographies of Rosa Parks, Frederick Douglass, Harriet Tubman, and Cesar Chavez.	Don Johnson	4	7–12
24/7 Goes to War Dramatizes key battles: Gettysburg, Pearl Harbor, D-Day, and Hamburger Hill.	Scholastic	700–800	7–12

- Decide what is important for the learners to know. Add essential information if it is missing.
- Delete unnecessary details. Eliminate details that are interesting, but off the topic.
- Explicitly explain essential information or supporting details that are only implied.
- Explicitly state the main idea or topic.
- Make clear the relationship between the main idea and supporting details.
- Make sure that antecedents and their referents are clearly marked. If there is some distance or the possibility of confusion between a pronoun and its antecedent, repeat the antecedent.
- Define words in context. Use simpler terms when possible. Limit the number of technical terms.
- Break up or rewrite lengthy confusing sentences, especially those that have embedded clauses. However, don't break up sentences that are lengthy because they are showing relationships. Breaking up the sentence "The colonists were angry because they were being taxed but had no say in the government" into the sentences "The colonists were angry. They were being taxed. But they had no say in the government" forces the reader to establish relationships. The three short sentences are harder than the one long sentence in this instance.
- Provide background or an orientation to the topic if necessary. Explain how this topic ties in with a previously studied topic.
- Use concrete examples and analogies.

Special Services for Students with Reading Disabilities

Make use of special services for students with reading disabilities. For students who have severe reading difficulties, obtain recorded versions of their texts and review ways of studying information from an oral source. Recordings for the Blind and Dyslexic www .rfbd.org provides recorded versions of school textbooks for students with reading problems. The National Library Service for the Blind and Physically Handicapped (NLS) www .loc.gov/nls/ offers a variety of books and periodicals in Braille and recorded form for persons who are blind or who have an organically based reading disability. Also available are playback devices that play at variable speeds so the listener can pick a reading rate that is comfortable. Bookshare™ http://bookshare.org is an online library of digital books for people with print disabilities. Bookshare members download books, textbooks, and newspapers in a compressed, encrypted file. They then read the material using adaptive technology, typically software that reads the book aloud (text-to-speech) and/or displays the text of the book on a computer screen or Braille access devices. Bookshare offers free memberships to U.S. schools and qualifying U.S. students.

CHECKUP

1. Why is it important to provide students with materials on their level?
2. What are some of the advantages and disadvantages of using easy-to-read texts?
3. What are some approaches that can be used to make difficult text accessible?

Helping Students Who Have Comprehension Problems

Nothing is more frustrating to students than to read a chapter and then realize they do not know what they have read. Most students have the necessary decoding skills to read content area texts but, for one reason or another, they fail to comprehend what they have read. Possible reasons for having comprehension difficulties despite possessing adequate decoding skills include the following:

- *Lack of adequate background.* Students without some knowledge of algebra and some general background in science, for instance, will have difficulty with a physics text.
- *Lack of comprehension strategies.* Students who are passive readers, who don't know how to read for main ideas, make inferences, summarize as they read, or monitor as they read will have difficulty comprehending challenging text.
- *Lack of purpose or goal in reading.* Students who simply read to fulfill the assignment, but do not have any particular questions in mind that they are seeking to answer and do not have a specific reason for reading will gain little from their reading.

For some students, the problem may be a combination of all three reasons: poor background and lack of strategies, purpose, and goals. To help students become better comprehenders, it is not necessary for you to become an expert in teaching reading. You are an expert in reading in your subject matter area. You are better at reading your content area than the school's reading specialist. In a sense, you are the person best qualified to help your students. All you need to do is share with your students the strategies you use to comprehend written materials in your subject area. As an expert in your area, you probably do not think much about the process you use to understand text. To get a feel for your approach as a reader, slow down your reading and try to become deliberately conscious of the strategies that you use. You might try reading a text that is particularly challenging and note what you do to construct meaning. Once you become familiar with your processes, demonstrate them to students. Model the process of reading the textbook. Note how you survey the text, activate background, make predictions, and read for specific purposes or questions to be answered. Also show how you reread when you have not fully understood a passage.

Because struggling readers lack metacognitive awareness, help them to become aware of their thought processes as they read so they can take steps to control them better. To foster metacognitive awareness, encourage students to place a sticky note next to any sentence or passage that is confusing to them. Students should also take steps to resolve their confusions. In class, discuss confusing passages and delineate the steps that were taken to resolve them. Through discussing confusions and how they were resolved, students learn strategies from each other.

Provide help with unresolved confusions. Also note whether there is a pattern present—whether students have problems making inferences or imaging scenes, for instance. These can form the basis for future modeling. Also build background if necessary.

High school English teacher/reading specialist Cris Tovani (2000), who at one time had been a noncomprehender, recommends the following steps for implementing a demonstration think-aloud:

1. *Select a short piece of text.* It could be an especially difficult section from your class's text. It should contain material that would lend itself to the demonstration of the particular strategy you have chosen to demonstrate. If you are demonstrating imaging, for instance, select a high-imagery passage. Place the text on a transparency and/or give students a copy.
2. *Foresee difficulty.* Analyze the passage and note elements that might pose problems for your students—figurative language or long, involved explanations, for instance. Do not overwhelm students with a passage that contains too many difficulties. If you want to demonstrate how you use your background knowledge to comprehend text, tell what you know about the topic and explain how this relates to the topic and helps you to understand it. For instance, when reading about limbs atrophying because of disuse, you might relate how you know from personal experience about this because your arm lost almost all of its strength when it was in a cast after you broke it. Explain also how relating what you are reading to a personal experience or something that you have read or heard about helps you make connections and improves your understanding of what you are reading.
3. *Read the text out loud and stop often to share your thinking.* When you are reading the text, point to the sentence you are reading. When you are sharing your thinking, look at the students so they know you are talking about your thoughts.
4. *Point out the words in the text that trigger your thinking.* "When I read the words *oil spill cleanup*, I picture people cleaning seabirds who are coated in gooey oil. I picture people shoveling up chunks of tar on sandy beaches. And I picture ships putting large floats around oil spills to keep them from spreading. This helps me to understand some ways in which oil spills are cleaned up. It also helps me to understand how difficult it is to clean up an oil spill."

Focus on Key Strategies

High-payoff strategies include the following:

- Surveying
- Activating background knowledge and predicting
- Setting a purpose for reading
- Asking questions as one reads
- Distinguishing important information
- Summarizing
- Making inferences
- Imaging
- Monitoring for meaning and using fix-up strategies

Providing Help during Reading

To give assistance as students read, provide a gloss or strategy guide that highlights both essential information and strategies that might be used to comprehend that information (see Chapter 5). In the beginning, focus on brief segments of text. As students build background and learn to apply strategies, increase the amount of reading.

Helping Students Who Have Decoding Problems

Although students may have mastered single-syllable phonics, they frequently experience difficulty with multisyllabic words. Unfortunately, many programs for older struggling readers focus on building comprehension, but neglect this vital skill. In a program that included ten minutes a day working with multisyllabic words in combination with instruction in vocabulary development, comprehension, and daily independent reading, struggling seventh and eighth graders gained an average of four years of growth in both word identification and comprehension (Shearer, Ruddell, & Vogt, 2001). To help students who have difficulty with multisyllabic words, review key multisyllabic words from the text that students are about to read. Write the words on the board so students form a visual image. Pronounce each syllable in the words and say the syllables as you underline them. Also have students pronounce the words. Pronouncing words helps bond them in memory.

CHECKUP

1. What are some steps that might be taken to help students who have difficulty with comprehension?
2. How might students who have decoding problems be helped?

Holding Students Accountable

Because they realize that their students are not getting much out of their reading, many content teachers discuss the reading assignment the next day or provide the information in lecture form. Students quickly catch on that it is not necessary to read the material. All they need to do is listen in class. Students should be held responsible for reading the text; otherwise, the process is short-circuited. When the time comes that students run into a situation where the teacher does not explain the text, they are lost. They find that the skills they need never developed because they never had to read challenging text.

If reading a chapter is an overwhelming burden because students are underprepared, have them read brief segments and provide a great deal of preparation and encouragement so that they can read the text with a measure of success. Make sure that they are held accountable for the reading, however. Have them respond in logs or journals, in strategy guides, or in small or large discussion groups. Students may need sustained support in the beginning, but gradually lead them to the point where they are becoming increasingly independent.

Collaborating with Other Professionals

Although you can implement a program of assistance on your own, enlist the help of specialists. They may be able to provide help with students who have more serious reading problems and may render technical assistance. If at all possible, get the entire school staff, or as much of the staff as possible, involved. Although each content area has its own special demands, there are basic strategies that are common to all disciplines. If all the teachers are saying basically the same thing about reading and writing in the content areas, and they all emphasize surveying, summarizing, and monitoring for meaning in each class, students are far more likely to learn these skills faster and better. Just as you may enlist help with students who have reading problems, you might also seek assistance with English language learners.

In one example of successful collaboration, Dan, a dedicated teacher, was concerned about his inability to reach the second language learners who were appearing in increasing numbers in his language arts classes (Coppola, 2002). He was also frustrated because the ELL students missed many of his classes to attend pull-out ESL sessions. Meanwhile, Leah, the ESL teacher, was feeling somewhat overwhelmed by the demands of colleagues. Often colleagues would give her an overview of a unit and ask her to help students learn the major concepts of that unit.

Fortunately, Leah and Dan decided to collaborate. All of Dan's ELL students were placed in one class. Instead of attending pull-out ESL sessions, students stayed in Dan's class, but were assisted by Leah, who began co-teaching with Dan. Leah taught the reader response part of the lesson in which students discussed the selections they had read, while Dan took responsibility for comprehension skills and correlated reading.

Leah was able to demonstrate effective techniques for supporting ELL students and engaging them in reading and discussion. Dan became better acquainted with effective techniques that a classroom teacher might adopt for helping ELL students. Leah learned more about the curriculum and some of the obstacles to working with ELL students in a regular classroom. Over time, the English language learners became integrated into the regular classroom. For the first time, they became active participants in discussion groups and had access to grade-level curriculum. They were also able to read related materials on their instructional levels. These materials had been housed in Leah's office, but she had never had time to use them. Both Dan and Leah felt more satisfied with their roles in working with ELL students, especially since the students were making excellent progress.

Although programs work best when the administration supports them, Dan and Leah constructed their collaboration on their own. They met before and after school. They demonstrated that lack of administrative support is no excuse for a lack of professional collaboration.

In a more extensive collaboration, one that might become a model for other school districts, curriculum leaders and teachers in language arts, special education, and bilingual/English as a second language classes in Arlington, Virginia, began collaborating (Zolman & Wagner, 2002). The members of the three departments found that they were facing the same issues: struggling readers, struggling teachers, and high frustration. When creating curriculum, representatives from all three areas met. Thus, when the language arts teachers designed programs, the special education and ESL specialists made suggestions for ways in which their students might be served, including making modifications in approaches and acquiring easier-to-read materials. The new materials and approaches were modeled by the special education and ESL teachers, who then reported back to the other special education and ESL teachers. The curriculum was differentiated in such a way that provisions were made for all students.

For a unit on Mark Twain, regular education teachers, special education teachers, and ESL teachers met and discussed the need for the unit, the skills incorporated in the unit, and possible activities. Later, a small collaborative group selected materials, including adaptations, and created activities and lesson plans. These were introduced to the entire staff. In a related project, book lists were created that included titles on a variety of difficulty levels.

Collaboration is a highly effective approach for working with at-risk learners. Although your school or district might not have the same type of carefully planned collaboration that is implemented in Arlington, Virginia, you can seek out other professionals in your school and plan ways in which you can work together to provide better instruction for at-risk learners.

Providing for All Students

Proficiencies and abilities vary greatly in the secondary school. The Content Learning Continuum provides a model of the kinds of instruction needed to cover a full spectrum of learning needs. Developed over a period of more than three decades at the University of Kansas Center for Research on Learning, the Content Literacy Continuum is a whole-school approach to improving literacy for all students in secondary schools, enabling them to meet higher standards. It has five levels of assistance that increase in intensity (Center for Research on Learning, 2009a, 2009b).

Content Literacy Continuum (CLC)

Level I: Content mastery—instructional approaches that build proficiency in critical content for all students, regardless of literacy levels, that equip them with competitive, high-end skills that ensure successful post-graduate options

Level II: Embedded strategy instruction—instructional strategies within and across classes for all students using large-group instructional methods that allow optimal access to rigorous college-ready curriculum

Level III: Explicit strategy instruction—instructional approaches that build mastery of specific strategies for students needing short-term instruction on strategies embedded throughout classroom instruction

Level IV: Intensive skill development—instructional approaches that build mastery of entry-level literacy skills for students needing intensive, accelerated literacy intervention

Level V: Intensive clinical intervention—instructional approaches that build mastery of language underpinnings related to the curriculum content and learning strategies occurring throughout classroom instruction for language-disabled students

Closing the Literacy Gap

Secondary school is the last chance for most students with reading disabilities to acquire the literacy skills necessary to function in today's society. Under a mandate to provide all students with adequate academic preparation, middle schools and high schools have an

---

Exemplary Teaching

Providing for Underserved Students

Mastery Charter School has an approach to intervention that stands out because it recognizes that significant difficulties with reading require a significant effort and a substantial amount of time. Even sessions held every day aren't enough to close the gap for students who are three or four or more years below grade level in reading. Mastery offers during-school, after-school and Saturday sessions and a generous amount of homework so that students can apply their skills. Mastery also provides encouragement and personal support, which are key components of effective intervention programs.

Mastery Charter Schools were designed to prepare underserved students for college and the world of work. Median test scores for entering Mastery students are approximately two-to-three grades behind in reading, with more than 10 percent of incoming ninth graders scoring at or below the third-grade level. To provide appropriate instruction at the students' incoming skill levels, Mastery created multiple course options at the seventh, eighth, and ninth grades, which are the grades in which most students enter Mastery. Students reading below grade level are provided courses designed to accelerate reading skills. The aim is to have students gain two years in one. Accelerated classes are smaller; they have only 20 students. At the high school level, struggling readers are given an extra period of reading instruction. By sophomore year, all students take the same English course, but struggling students take an additional reading course. The goal is to have all eleventh-grade students taking rigorous pre-college course work. How effective is Mastery's program? In the last academic year for which results are available, 100 percent of Mastery Charter graduates were accepted by a college or university (Mastery Charter Schools, 2010).

obligation to provide effective sustained literacy instruction for those who need it. The effort must be a whole-school effort that involves the total staff. This doesn't mean that content area teachers need to become reading and writing specialists, but they should work with specialists and support their efforts. Support can be as simple and as natural as recognizing that some students have difficulty pronouncing technical content vocabulary and taking steps such as writing difficult words on the board, pronouncing them, and underling the syllables. However, it also means providing students with access to the curriculum. This could take the form of finding and using materials on their reading level or employing devices that will "read" the materials to them. (See pp. 300–301 for additional suggestions.)

Secondary students who are reading significantly below grade level need extensive practice reading material on their level in order to catch up. For each year that students are behind, they might need between 100 and 200 hours of reading on their reading level (Guthrie, 2004). This degree of extensive reading can only be achieved if students are reading content area materials on their level. Reading in connection with reading support classes is an essential factor, but would not provide sufficient practice.

CHECKUP

1. What is the Content Literacy Continuum? How might this be implemented in the typical secondary school?
2. What is the content teacher's role in working with struggling readers?

Summary

In the past, content area teachers typically geared their instruction to average students and expected that students would arrive with the prerequisite background knowledge. Given the greater diversity in today's content area classes and the inclusion of students who were previously taught in special education settings, today's content area teachers benefit, more than ever, from finding ways to teach struggling learners. The weaker the student's preparation, the greater the need for using techniques and devices that help the student learn.

About 25 to 35 percent of the nation's students are at risk for failing for a variety of academic and nonacademic reasons. It is also estimated that 25 to 40 percent of American students do not read well enough to cope with the texts in their content courses in middle and secondary schools. Students at risk include economically disadvantaged students, students with learning and other disabilities, and English language learners. Identifying struggling learners, adjusting content to fit the needs of diverse learners, and teaching SMARTER are some of the approaches that can be taken to help at-risk students. Recently introduced to help struggling students, RTI is both a method for identifying students with learning disabilities and a whole-school improvement program that enlists all staff members, the community, and parents to ensure that all students' literacy potential is fully developed.

Both English learners and struggling students benefit from instruction designed to develop academic language. Academic language includes the discourse used in classrooms and the thinking skills of analyzing, explaining, inferring, and organizing.

Instructional components for an effective program for English language learners feature (1) focus on vocabulary, (2) use of visuals, (3) cooperative learning and peer tutoring, (4) strategic use of the native language, and (5) adjustment of cognitive and language demands. Programs should also build content area background and consider cultural factors. Sheltered instruction is recommended. In sheltered instruction, teachers make a special effort to make content instruction understandable to all students, including those who are still acquiring academic English. The language experience approach in which the teacher scribes key content area concepts dictated by students can be an effective learning tool for both ELL students and disabled readers.

Struggling learners benefit when they are helped to become self-regulated learners. With increased accountability occasioned by standards and high-stakes testing, students with serious reading disabilities have become more visible. It is important to provide these students with materials on their level. Materials can be made more accessible through the use of talking software, screen readers, rewritten texts, and added preparation for reading.

Students who have decoding problems may need specialized assistance but would benefit by being provided with help for reading complex technical terms. Students who have adequate decoding skills but are poor comprehenders can be taught a series of strategies for becoming active, metacognitively aware, meaning-seeking readers. A program for helping at-risk learners will be more effective if professionals collaborate.

Reflection

Return to the Anticipation Guide at the beginning of this chapter. Respond once again to the items. Did your responses change? If so, how and why? What would be your approach to working with at-risk learners in your classroom?

Extension and Application

1. Read the following account of a secondary teacher who works with adolescents who had difficulty reading their texts: Tovani, C. (2000). *I read it, but I don't get it.* Portland, ME: Stenhouse. If available, view the DVDs: *Thoughtful Reading* and *Comprehending Content* (Stenhouse, 2006). How might you use the techniques advocated by the author?

2. Investigate the availability of easy-to-read textbooks in your discipline. Evaluate the coverage provided. Is it adequate, or will it need to be supplemented?

3. If possible, observe a sheltered English class. Even though you are not a trained bilingual or ESL teacher, how might you adapt the techniques used in sheltered English? Also examine e-books. What aids do they provide for struggling readers? How might these aids be used to make the text more accessible?

4. Try using a language experience approach for one or more lessons with struggling readers or English language learners. What are its advantages? Disadvantages? How might you adapt it to make it more effective?

5. Rewrite a segment of a textbook so that it is easier to read. If possible, try it out with students with reading disabilities. You might rewrite a segment of an e-book from the C-K Foundation (www.ck12.org/flexr) or another source that can be modified or create your own text, perhaps as a class project. What difference do you notice between students' ability to handle rewritten text and their ability to handle regular text?

6. Explore talking software or screen readers. How might you use these with struggling learners?

Go to Topic 1: Diversity, Culture, and Literacy, and Topic 10: Struggling Readers in the MyEducationLab (www.myeducationlab.com) for your course, where you can:

- Find learning outcomes for Diversity, Culture, and Literacy and for Struggling Readers along with the national standards that connect to these outcomes.
- Complete Assignments and Activities that can help you more deeply understand the chapter content.
- Apply and practice your understanding of the core teaching skills identified in the chapter with the Building Teaching Skills and Dispositions learning units.
- Examine challenging situations and cases presented in the IRIS Center Resources.

Go to the Topic A+RISE in the MyEducationLab (www.myeducationlab.com) for your course. A+RISE® Standards2Strategy™ is an innovative and interactive online resource that offers new teachers in grades K–12 just-in-time, research-based instructional strategies that:

- Meet the linguistic needs of ELLs as they learn content.
- Differentiate instruction for all grades and abilities.
- Offer reading and writing techniques, cooperative learning, use of linguistic and nonlinguistic representations, scaffolding, teacher modeling, higher order thinking, and alternative classroom ELL assessment.
- Provide support to help teachers be effective through the integration of listening, speaking, reading, and writing along with the content curriculum.
- Improve student achievement.
- Are aligned to Common Core Elementary Language Arts standards (for the literacy strategies) and to English language proficiency standards in WIDA, Texas, California, and Florida.

CHAPTER 10

Reading and Writing in Language Arts, Social Studies, Art, Music, and World Languages

Anticipation Guide

For each of the following statements, put a check under "Agree" or "Disagree" to indicate your opinion. Discuss your responses with classmates.

	Agree	Disagree
1. The key to developing an understanding of literature is being aware of the historical context in which the piece was written.	____	____
2. Students need to be taught the correct interpretation of difficult pieces of literature.	____	____
3. Most primary documents are too difficult for students to read.	____	____
4. Students need to be taught to read history texts critically because history texts are subjective.	____	____
5. Subjects such as art and music make minimal use of literacy skills.	____	____
6. The vocabulary and comprehension skills used in general reading can be readily applied to using textbooks designed to teach a foreign language.	____	____

Using What you Know

What kinds of reading do you do in your spare time? How does your approach to reading a piece of literature differ from the way you read a popular novel? How do you go about reading a history or geography text? How is reading a history or geography book different from reading a work of literature or a popular novel? How do you go about reading foreign language, art, and music books? Although there are some common processes used when students read a work of literature, a popular novel, a history text, a foreign language, an art, or music book, each genre makes different demands on the reader. Reading literature requires a deeper level of involvement than a popular novel. Reading history or geography text generally places greater demands on organizational skills and memory. Reading a foreign language book places demands on memory and translating skills. Art and music books have their own technical vocabulary and may involve following complex directions and being able to use imaging to construct the sights and sounds described in the text.

Reading Literature

The study of literature has a number of jumping-off points. Literature may be seen as a product of the times and thus is viewed in an historical context. Or, literature may be seen as autobiographical and interpreted in terms of the author's life. Literature may also be seen in humanistic terms as a source of inspiration and guidance. To Langer (2011), literature is a way of thinking. "Through literature, students learn to explore possibilities and consider options; they gain connectedness and seek vision" (p. 2). However else it may be viewed, literature is regarded as a work of art that blends elements of style and substance in an original way. Given its originality and creativity, literature has the power to evoke a deep emotional and aesthetic response.

Literature makes demands that go beyond those made by science or social studies texts or popular fiction. Social studies and science texts may inform, and popular fiction may entertain, but only literature has the power to evoke the feeling of wholeness or wonder

USING TECHNOLOGY

National Council of Teachers of English www.ncte.org/standards Common Core State Standards for English Language Arts www.corestandards.org/assets/CCSSI_ELA%20Standards.pdf Provide standards for literature and the other language arts.

at being lifted out of oneself that is the hallmark of the aesthetic response. As Rosenblatt (1978) notes, in **aesthetic reading** the reader is carried away by feelings evoked by the text: "In aesthetic reading, the reader's attention is centered directly on what he is living through during his relationship with that particular text" (p. 25). In contrast, **efferent reading** involves reading for information; the reader's attention is directed to "concepts to be refined, ideas to be tested, actions to be performed after the reading" (Rosenblatt, 1978, p. 24). In efferent reading, the reader "carries away" meaning. In aesthetic reading, the reader is "carried away" by feelings evoked by the text. The same text can be read efferently or aesthetically. For example, we could read an essay efferently for ideas, but if we respond to its irony or the author's graceful style and humor, our stance becomes aesthetic. As Rosenblatt (1991) explains, "We read for information, but we are conscious of emotions about it and feel pleasure when the words we call up arouse vivid images and are rhythmic to the inner ear" (p. 445). Growing out of the aesthetic view of literature is **reader response theory**, which perceives reading as a transaction between reader and writer. In this transaction, the reader is changed by the text and the text is changed by the reader. Because the transaction grows in part out of the reader's experience and consciousness, the response is personal. The poem that stirs deep emotion in one reader may leave another reader unmoved. Teaching literature is largely a matter of creating an environment in which students can respond to a selection in terms of their personal experiences and sensibilities and then clarify the meaning and impact of the selection. Although students' initial responses may be personal and concrete and expressed primarily on a gut level, over time, through discussion and guidance, their responses become more refined and more evaluative. Personal response becomes the basis for "growth toward more and more balanced, self-critical, knowledgeable interpretation" (Rosenblatt, 1990, p. 100).

Choosing literary works that touch students' lives and to which they can readily respond is a first step in eliciting an aesthetic response. However, Rosenblatt cautioned that it is important to have a clear sense of purpose when asking students to read a particular piece. The purpose should fit in with the nature of the piece and the objective for presenting it. By its nature, for instance, poetry generally demands an aesthetic reading. But if the focus of the reading is on literal comprehension, then the experience will be efferent. The reading is aesthetic if the focus is on experiencing the poem or story and savoring the sounds, sights, and emotions that the words conjure up (Gunning, 2010). Rosenblatt (1991) comments:

> Textbooks and teachers' questions too often hurry students away from the lived-through experience. After the reading, the experience should be recaptured, reflected on. It can be the subject of further aesthetic activities—drawing, dancing, miming, talking, writing, role-playing, or oral interpretation. It can be discussed and analyzed efferently. Or it can yield information. But first, if it is indeed to be literature for these students, it must be experienced. (p. 447)

All too often, students have the sense that a poem or other work of literature has a single interpretation. Failing to engage with the work, they wait for the teacher to tell them what the work means. In a way, works of literature have as many interpretations as there are readers. Although there is no one correct interpretation, interpretations should be based on a careful reading of the text. Students should be prepared to discuss and clarify their responses; a response that is based on a misreading of the text should be revised. Students who have misread the text should be encouraged to go back over the text, get the correct information from the text, and modify their response accordingly.

■ **Aesthetic reading** is the experience of emotions evoked by a piece of writing.

■ **Efferent reading** is reading to comprehend the information conveyed by a piece of writing.

■ **Reader response theory** is a view of reading in which the reader plays a central role in constructing the meaning of a text. The meaning is not found in the text or in the reader but rather in the relationship or transaction between the two.

C H E C K U P

1. What are the aesthetic and efferent stances?
2. Which of these is more appropriate for the reading of literature? Why?

Developing Envisionments

Langer (1990, 1995, 2011) calls the development of responses to literature *envisionments*. An **envisionment** is "the understanding a reader has about a text—what the reader understands at a particular point in time, the questions she has, as well as her hunches about how the piece will unfold" (1995, p. 812). Envisionment changes as new ideas come to mind. As students create an envisionment, they go through a series of stances, or changing relationships with the text. However, they are not linear. The reader can move back and forth between stances.

1. Being outside and stepping into an envisionment
2. Being inside and moving through an envisionment
3. Stepping out and rethinking what you know
4. Stepping out and objectifying the experience
5. Leaving an envisionment and going beyond

USING TECHNOLOGY

Making Meaning in Literature: A Video Library, Grades 6-8 www.learner.org/ libraries/makingmeaning/making meaning Series of high-quality videos demonstrate the implementation of the envisionment process.

Stance 1: Being Outside and Stepping into an Envisionment

Students use their background knowledge and comprehension of the unfolding story to make "initial ideas and supposition about the characters, plot, setting, situation—and how they interrelate" (Langer, 2011, p. 17). In a sense, students are beginning a conversation with themselves about the world that they have entered (Langer, 1995). They are trying to "step into" the world of the story.

Stance 2: Being Inside and Moving Through an Envisionment

Having entered the text world, students are building a more elaborated meaning. "We take new information and immediately use it to go beyond what we already understand, asking questions about motives, feelings, causes, interrelationships, and implications. We make connections among our thoughts, move our understandings along, and fill out our shifting sense of what the piece is about" (Langer, 1995, p. 17).

Stance 3: Stepping Out and Rethinking What You Know

Readers step away from the story and think about their own lives in terms of the story. "They use what they read in the text to reflect on their own lives, on the lives of others, or on the human condition in general" (Langer, 1990, p. 813). This stance does not occur as often as the others because every piece we read does not personally affect us, and it also may take a cumulative experience with literature before we begin to experience its effect (Langer, 1995).

Stance 4: Stepping Out and Objectifying the Experience

"We distance ourselves from the envisionment we have developed and reflect back on it" (Langer, 2011, p. 20). We analyze and judge the piece and compare it to other works that we have read.

Stance 5: Leaving an Envisionment and Going Beyond

In this stance, which does not always occur, readers use the envisionment in a new situation or they move beyond the envisionment. "We step away from our envisionsments, often moving into an entirely new envisionment" (Langer, 2011, p. 21). In a sense, they are applying or building on what they have experienced.

The concept of envisionments provides a basis for instruction. Because responses depend on students' background knowledge, experience, and predictions, students need to feel free to offer responses and have them accepted. Discussions are patterned on the kinds of conversations that a group of adults might have about a book they have all read or a movie

■ **Envisionment** is the understanding that a reader has of a text. The understanding may change with reflection, additional reading, or discussion.

Struggling Readers

For struggling readers, read aloud portions of a novel that they are required to read to help them form an overall picture of the text and to introduce characters, the setting, and some difficult terms that might occur throughout the book.

(CCSS)

Read closely to determine what the text says explicitly and to make logical inferences from it; cite specific textual evidence when writing or speaking to support conclusions drawn from the text.

Determine central ideas or themes of a text and analyze their development; summarize the key supporting details and ideas.

(CCSS)

Analyze the structure of texts, including how specific sentences, paragraphs, and larger portions of the text (e.g., a section, chapter, scene, or stanza) relate to each other and the whole.

Assess how point of view or purpose shapes the content and style of a text.

(CCSS)

Interpret words and phrases as they are used in a text, including determining technical, connotative, and figurative meanings, and analyze how specific word choices shape meaning or tone.

Struggling Readers

Consider using easy classics with struggling readers. Hemingway's short stories are written in relatively easy-to-read language.

---

they have seen. The students have "a real conversation in which they interact with and build from one another's ideas" (Langer, 1995, p. 44). In such an environment, the teacher assumes that each student can and does make sense of literature. The assumption is also made that any "misreadings, misinterpretations, or weakly founded views can and will be noticed and rethought by the individual, using ideas from the group to stimulate but not direct thinking" (Langer, 1995, p. 75). To foster a developing response to literature, the teacher listens intently to understand the student's growing envisionment and works to help the student more fully develop that envisionment. Students are encouraged to pursue their own ideas while accepting and considering the viewpoints of others. This helps students to enrich their own interpretations as they reflect on ideas that they had not considered and also assess their own interpretations. Langer suggests that teachers engage in four types of questions.

1. *Initial understandings.* Ask open-ended questions that invite students to share their reactions to the piece. What comes to mind as you think about the piece? Which part of the work stands out in your mind? Was there anything in the work that bothered you, surprised you, or that didn't seem to fit? Do you have any questions about the work? One teacher asks her students to jot down "questions that you think we need to talk about" (Langer, 1995, p. 64).
2. *Developing interpretations.* Pose questions that encourage students to explore their envisionments. These questions can help students think more deeply about motivations, character development, theme, or setting: Why were the main character's actions surprising? What do you think made the man give all his money away? Could this story have taken place today? What is the author trying to say here? Students might also be encouraged to look at the events in the selection from the perspective of other characters or from a classmate's viewpoint.
3. *Reflecting on personal experience.* Ask questions that help students relate what they have read to personal knowledge or experience—people they know, experiences they have had, or events they have witnessed. Does the main character remind you of anyone you know? Have you ever been in a situation similar to the one she was in? How would you have handled it? Does this story make you think of anything that has happened in your life?
4. *Taking a critical stance.* Once students have responded personally to the piece and have developed their interpretations more fully, encourage them to step out of the piece and critically consider issues that have been raised. What do you think the author is trying to say in this piece? Do you agree with the author's interpretations? What are some other interpretations that might be just as valid? Does the author reveal any biases? Whose side does the author seem to be on? How does the author describe the good guys? The bad guys? Also ask students to view the work from an aesthetic point of view in which they take a careful look at the author's craft. They might compare it with other pieces they have read and critique its character development, originality, development of plot and theme, and overall impact: What was the best part of the piece? Did the characters seem real? What made them seem real? What special techniques did the author use? How did the author keep you guessing up until the very end? What original expressions or figurative language did the author use? Which of these did you like best? If you were the author's editor, what would you say to the author? What changes might you suggest that the author make? Why? How would you compare this piece to other similar pieces that you have read? One teacher has his students read critical reviews after they have critiqued a piece and compare their views with those of the critic (Langer, 1995).
5. *Stocktaking.* At the end of a lesson, the teacher acknowledges students' differing interpretations and sums up key issues, agreements, and disagreements. The teacher also points out concerns not fully addressed but leaves "room for further envisionment building" (Langer, 2011, p. 105).

An integral part of the process of building envisionments is learning the concepts and language needed to discuss literature, such as *metaphor, theme, symbolism,* and *omniscient point of view.* Noting that her students lacked the concept of *characterization,* one teacher had the students assume the roles of the characters in the short story "Charles," by Shirley

Jackson, at various points in the story. They discussed the way they believed the characters might think and behave and then role-played the characters (Langer 1995).

Role of Small-Group Discussions

Small-group discussion is an excellent way to foster the building of envisionments. In small groups, each student has a better opportunity to express his or her response to the piece and compare it with that of others. Discussion is essential because it leads to deeper exploration of a piece. For a short piece, students might read and jot down their responses. Writing offers students the opportunity for thoughtful personal reflection and provides a foundation for discussion. In order to evoke a personal, aesthetic response, Rosenblatt (1982) suggests asking questions similar to the following: "Did anything especially interest (annoy, puzzle, frighten, please) you? Did anything seem familiar (weird)?" (p. 276).

Probst (1992) recommends similar questions: "What feelings did this text evoke in you as you read? Did this text awaken any memories, recall for you any memories, recall for you any people, or places, or experiences?" (p. 64). "What memory does the text call to mind—of people, places, events, smells, or even of something more ambiguous, perhaps feelings or attitudes?" (Probst, 2004, p. 83).

After the small groups have discussed the piece for about ten minutes, invite the whole class to discuss it. Each group might summarize the responses of its members. The group might then discuss commonalities and differences in the responses and any especially evocative or puzzling issues that arose. No attempt should be made to come to a consensus interpretation or response. However, the teacher should help students see commonalities in responses or viewpoints despite varied interpretations. Students may agree that the ending was powerful even though they disagree on its suitability. With longer selections, students might compose their responses as reflections in journals.

> **CCSS**
>
> Initiate and participate effectively in a range of collaborative discussions (one-on-one, in groups, and teacher-led) with diverse partners on grade level topics, texts, and issues, building on others' ideas and expressing their own clearly and persuasively.

CHECKUP

1. What are envisionments?
2. How might they be implemented?

Using Journals to Elicit Responses

Response journals, or literary logs, provide an excellent opportunity for students to reflect on their reading. In their response journals, students might pose questions about puzzling passages, point out particularly powerful language, identify symbols, note the theme, identify conflicts, comment on characters, note feelings evoked, comment on the plot, predict forthcoming events, warn or scold characters, note similarities between this and other works, or point out weaknesses in the plot. Responses need not be strictly verbal. Students might also illustrate a scene, draw a character, create a character web, design a storyboard, compose a plot outline, map a journey, create a time line, or compose a family tree.

Not all response formats are equal. Some yield higher-level and deeper responses than others. Ollmann (1996) tried out seven different response formats. Vague invitations to respond often resulted in plot summaries. One of the most successful prompts asked the readers to record specific quotes from the text in their double-entry journals and then analyze them. This required them to think about aspects of the story such as key plot events and character development and motivation. In double-entry journals, students tell what is happening in one column and reflect on it in a second column (Probst, 1992).

Another format that worked well was the character journal, in which students take on the role of the main character and respond in the journal in the way they think the character would respond. This practice was especially effective in helping students better understand the main character. Students' responses tended to be formal and stilted when they were directed to the teacher; however, when they wrote to each other in book buddy journals, their tone was much livelier and more natural. In book buddy journals, pairs of students discuss their responses. Students gather in pairs, small groups, or as a whole class to

> ■ **Response journals** are notebooks in which students write their responses to literary selections, compose observations, or pose questions.

Students sometimes share their response journal reflections with other students.

Source: Thinkstock.

discuss the work and their envisionment. The discussion is based on their journal entries. The teacher might initiate the discussion with the following comments:

> Now that you've read the chapter (novel, essay, play) and recorded what happened as you read, read back over your notes and think back over the experience. What is your own sense of the text or of the experience it offered you— does it have any significance for you; does it recall memories, associations; does it affirm or contradict any of your own attitudes or perceptions? (Probst, 1992, p. 65)

Once students have personally responded to a piece, they are better able and more willing to look at the construction and literary significance of it. They can then better understand how the author's choice of words, original images, symbolism, or development of plot or theme evoked the response that it did.

Modeling the Reading of Literature

Although they have the power to evoke deep feelings, works of literature can be difficult to read. Model how you go about reading a difficult piece of literature. Read a challenging poem and discuss the thoughts and feelings that come to mind. Note language that is particularly appealing to you. Discuss how you respond to the author's allusions, create an interpretation of figurative language, or deal with a theme that is only hinted at. Stress, however, that response is very personal. Your favorite poem might be one that someone else dislikes.

🍁 English Language Learners

Response journals help ELLs learn how to respond. Because responses are written, students have time to compose their thoughts and might use drawings and graphic organizers. They might be encouraged to respond in their native language when they are unable to express their thoughts or feelings in English.

CHECKUP

1. How might journals and modeling be used to foster response to literature?

Writing in Language Arts Classes

According to a study of highly effective English classes, one of the components contributing to success was the emphasis on writing (ACT & Education Trust, 2005). Most teachers assigned brief writing projects weekly and longer projects monthly. Writing logs were encouraged. Almost all the teachers used essay tests to assess their students. Instruction was through, systematic, and rigorous.

Fostering Voluntary Reading

The amount of reading that students do on their own has a powerful impact on their literacy development. It also impacts their cognitive development. Based on their research, Cunningham and Stanovitch (1998) concluded that reading "will build vocabulary and cognitive structures" (p. 7). They commented that reading was especially important for students "whose verbal skills are most in need of bolstering, for it is the very act of reading that can build those capacities" (pp. 6–7). Krashen (1993) concluded that frequent reading was a necessary condition for adequate literacy development. Based on his research, he stated that students who read frequently:

Scaffolding Instruction for English Language Learners

Composing a thoughtful analysis of a piece of literature is a demanding task for all students. However, it is doubly difficult for English language learners. In her class, Ms. Ramirez provides a number of scaffolds for her English language learners as they prepare to analyze portions of *Lord of the Flies* (Golding, 1954) (Teachscape, 2006). At the start of the period, students correct grammar mistakes in verb usage in a practice paragraph that also summarizes the chapter of *Lord of the Flies* that they will be working with. Ms. Ramirez explains the purpose of analytical paragraphs and displays a sample paragraph on the overhead projector. Parts of an analytical paragraph are reviewed, along with the academic language needed to talk about them: *topic sentence, transitions, lead-ins, quotations, sentences of commentary,* and *concluding sentence.* Ms. Ramirez reads the paragraph out loud and labels each of the elements of an analytical paragraph. She also points out that difficult vocabulary words and idioms have been glossed, with explanations placed in brackets: "The rest were shock-headed [with thick, messy hair]." Each element is carefully discussed. Ms. Ramirez then distributes a handout that contains passages from the text, with each passage followed by a series of commentaries. Students are directed to grade each commentary and justify the grade they assigned. They are aided by the following symbols and descriptions:

+ = good, strong commentary

R = retells the quotation

DNS = does NOT support the topic sentence

Not S = commentary needs to be more specific

Ms Ramirez reads the passage and commentaries, and students then grade them independently. After grading the passages independently, students engage in a think-pair-share activity and discuss the grades they assigned. They complete a frame that indicates the result of their discussion: "My partner and I agreed because _____ " or "My partner and I did not agree because _____ ." The whole class discusses students' responses and decides on a grade. The process is repeated with a second set of commentaries. For a third passage, students create a partially composed commentary. The class decides on the best commentary and best concluding sentence. The parts of an analytical paragraph are reviewed, and students compose an analytical paragraph independently.

With its careful progression from teacher demonstration to scaffolded guided practice to independent application and its use of frames and glosses, the lesson provided a wealth of assistance for English language learners. However, this same lesson would also be of benefit to all students (Teachscape, 2006).

will become adequate readers, acquire a larger vocabulary, develop the ability to understand and use complex grammatical constructions, develop a good writing style, and become good (but not necessarily perfect) spellers. Although free voluntary reading alone will not ensure attainment of the highest levels of literacy, it will at least ensure an acceptable level. (p. 84)

Unfortunately, the older students are, the less they read (Knoester, 2009; Strommen & Mates, 2004). In his study of young adolescents, Knoester found that students who enjoyed reading talked about their reading frequently with parents and peers. Knoester also raised the question about identity. Adolescents may reject an identity that includes enjoying reading or they may not feel accepted as part of a community of readers. In their study of sixth and ninth graders, Strommen and Mates identified students who were readers and not-readers. Readers clearly enjoyed reading, and pleasure reading was an integral part of their lives. Not-readers preferred other activities to reading and did not engage in reading for enjoyment. Readers came from families who enjoyed reading and talking about books, and they also enjoyed talking about books with their peers. As in the Knoester study, reading for enjoyment had a social aspect and was personally rewarding. Readers read for the fun of it; reading had intrinsic value. Not-readers readily admitted that reading was a valuable activity, but they did not view it as an enjoyable one. Not-readers claimed that they had no time for leisure reading. Readers, who had similar schedules, always found time for reading.

Becoming a reader is more than acquiring the prerequisite skills. Many of the not-readers were highly skilled readers. Some were in honors classes. Readers trace their love of reading to family members who were readers and who encouraged them to read, made books accessible to them, and discussed books with them. Teachers can incorporate these same elements in their classes. They can make books accessible, encourage reading, and provide students with opportunities to talk about their reading. Pitcher and colleagues (2007) recommend the following:

- **R**ecognize the multiple literacies in which students are engaging outside of the classroom and find ways to incorporate them into classroom instruction;
- **M**odel their own reading enjoyment;
- **E**mbrace engaging activities, such as literature circles and book clubs, into regular instruction in secondary schools;
- **I**nclude reading materials of varied formats, levels, and topics in the classroom; and
- **I**ncorporate elements of choice in readings and projects. (pp. 394–395)

Do these suggestions work? Lapp and Fisher (2009) structured a course in which at-risk eleventh graders were given a wide variety of materials from which to choose. Students were able to select the books they read; they had the opportunity to discuss their books with peers; and they were encouraged to use a wide variety of print and digital literacies. Lapp and Fisher added one more element—one that should be at the top of the list. They provided interesting reading. Not only did students read the books chosen for the course, but they requested the opportunity to read additional books. They were so captivated by a Sharon Draper novel, *Romiette and Julio*, that they expressed the desire to read all her novels. As Lapp and Fisher observed, "We are convinced that the impetus for this level of engagement was that we followed the lead of our students when they asked if they could partner with us to choose the texts, the topics, and the assignments for their English class" (p. 557).

Motivating Voluntary Reading

For Kelly Gallagher, a high school English teacher, the most important factor in motivating his students to read was establishing a classroom library of 2,500 books. As Gallagher (2003) comments, "I surrounded them with a variety of high-interest reading materials. . . . It's true that some of these books are also available in the school library, but something powerful happens when books are brought to the students, when teachers take time to talk the books up, when students are immersed daily in print" (p. 5). To keep his library current, Gallagher asked graduating seniors to donate their favorite book to his classroom library.

To demonstrate that reading was an important part of his course, Gallagher directed students to maintain a reading log for independent reading. In addition to listing titles read, they kept track of their reading time each week. The reading log was not graded, but students were required to read for 120 hours a semester and must have read 12 major works in order to obtain an A. Gallagher had students note passages that were unclear and share their confusions in small group discussions. He also explained how he had experienced difficulty understanding a text and talked about how he overcame that difficulty. He stressed the satisfaction of meeting the challenge. Gallagher shared exciting passages and invited students to do the same. Students also shared new facts that they learned along with their favorite first lines of books.

Building on Students' Interests

Based on their survey of 266 secondary school students, Nilsen and Donalsen (2009) found that having a choice in what they read is a key factor in motivating students' voluntary reading. Students like reading books by familiar authors, and they are motivated to read a book after seeing the movie version. A large number of students like reading nonfiction for information. However, students' reading tastes are extremely varied. When asked to list their favorite authors, 144 different names were listed. No one author dominated. Students listed friends, family, teachers, and librarians in that order as people most likely to give them ideas for leisure reading. Key sources for books were stores, libraries, and the Internet.

Students are engaged in a variety of digital literacy activities outside of school. Number one was using Google to find information. A close second was sending text messages to friends, followed by using a cell phone to take a photo, sending e-mail, visiting a social network, finding information on Wikipedia, putting writing online, and reading about a book online. In fact, the Internet was the top source of reading material in the home, followed by books, newspapers, and magazines. The researchers' advice for fostering increased recreational reading was to give students' a choice and obtain books that are fun and interesting.

Capitalizing on adolescents' interests is the key to motivating them to read. Observing students and talking to them are excellent informal ways to get a sense of the kinds of things that they might be interested in. However, administering a survey questionnaire might better enable you to get a fuller look at their interests. In addition to providing valuable information about the kinds of literacy materials and activities that students prefer and that might motivate reading, questionnaires and interviews lead to conversations about reading that can lead to steps taken to foster increased free reading (Nilsen & Donelsen, 2009).

Adapt the Survey of Interests in Table 10.1 to fit your situation. You might also administer the Adolescent Motivation to Read Profile (Pitcher et al., 2007). The Adolescent MRP includes two parts. The first is a written questionnaire, which can be administered to groups. The second is a follow-up interview that is given individually. The questionnaire portion is designed to reveal students' attitudes about reading and common classroom literacy practices. The conversational interview probes the kinds of books the student likes to read, how reading material is chosen, the kinds of literacy activities in which the student engages, and the kinds of activities that might motivate the student to read.

A Study of the Voluntary Reading and Writing of Adolescents Living in a High-Poverty Area

In a study of 716 adolescents living in a high-poverty area, 92 percent reported reading outside of school three to four times a week and 82 percent reported writing outside of school at least once a week (Moje, Overby, Tysvaer, & Morris, 2008). However, only 30 percent reported reading novels at least once week. Only the reading of novels correlates with high achievement in school. In order of frequency, students read websites, letters, notes, music lyrics, e-mail, magazines, and novels, short stories, and plays. Students' out-of-school writing consisted of e-mails, chats, shout outs, blogs, letters, notes, music lyrics, graffiti, and creative writing (stories and poems). Often school-based materials were noted as being favorites. School, it seems, can be a source of the texts students read.

Students read and wrote for a variety of reasons. Reading helped students maintain social relationships and establish identities. It also was a means of self-improvement. Students read and wrote "for self-expression, to work through problems, or seek information or models to help them live in their homes, schools, and communities" (Moje et al., 2008, p. 131). Peers were typically a source of reading materials. Some students belonged to informal reading and writing networks. Sometimes students were motivated to read by a specific interest, such as cars, games, or popular culture. Often they shared information with friends and relatives. Graphic novels and books based on movies were also a popular draw. Graphic novels have illustrated panels just as traditional comic books do, but are, in general, of higher quality. One graphic novel, *Maus: A Survivor's Tale* (Spiegelman, 1990), an

TABLE 10.1 **Sample Student Interest Survey**

NAME _____	DATE _____

Survey of Interests

Answer each of the following. Be honest. Answers will not be graded.

1. What is your favorite movie?
2. What is your favorite TV show?
3. What is your favorite musical group?
4. What are your three favorite out-of-school activities?
5. What are your hobbies?
6. What is your favorite book?
7. Who is your favorite author?
8. What school clubs or activities do you belong to or take part in?
9. What out-of-school groups or activities do you belong to or take part in?
10. Do you work? If so, where?
11. Do you speak a language other than English?
12. If so, what other language(s) do you speak?
13. What special skills or talents do you have? (singing, playing a musical instrument, playing a sport, fixing things, designing Web sites)
14. Do you play any video/computer games? If so, which ones do you play?
15. Do you have a computer at home? If so, how do you use it? (play games, surf the Net)
16. About how many minutes did you spend reading outside of school last week?
17. Do you read any newspapers or magazines? If so, which ones?
18. What is your favorite part of the newspaper?
19. Do you read information from the Net? If so, what kinds of information do you read?
20. Do you read books for fun? If so, what are the titles of books that you are now reading or have read in the last month?
21. About how many minutes did you spend reading for fun last week?
22. Do you visit any sites regularly? If so, which ones?
23. Do you use any electronic devices besides the computer? If so, which ones? Briefly explain what you use these devices for.
24. What makes a good reader?
25. If someone asked you what he or she could do to become a better reader, what would you tell him or her to do?
26. What are your career goals?
27. It is your 50th high school reunion. A classmate who hasn't seen you since graduation asks what you have been doing over the past half-century. What kind of answer would you like to be able to give to your classmate?
28. What kinds of reading do you like? Circle as many as apply.

sports	mystery	historical fiction	animals
science	supernatural	biography	science fiction
adventure	music	rock stars	romance
humor	information	growing up	teen problems
fantasy true-life adventure			
books based on a movie or TV show			
other (Please list.)			

autobiographical account of the Holocaust, won a Pulitzer Prize in 1992. Graphic novels include a range of subjects, including classic works. As with any materials used in schools, graphic novels should be selected with discretion.

Reading helped students explore and construct their identities. Some ELL students described reading in their native language so they could maintain their engagement. Sammie enjoyed reading *Always Running* (Rodriguez, 1993) because the main character was Mexican and the book was about immigration. Students also read to seek information, such as to find out about college, to follow news stories of interest, or to comparison shop.

One way of fostering increased reading and writing is by creating the kinds of social networks that engage students outside of school and that occasion much of the reading and writing students do outside of school. For example, because a number of students mentioned that a book they read in school was a favorite, the school could foster reading by introducing and making available high-interest books and periodicals. Schools might also set up discussion groups devoted to areas of interest, such as cars, fashion, video gaming, popular culture, and college. Students would then be able to share their reading and make recommendations to each other for additional reading.

CHECKUP

1. How might voluntary reading be fostered?
2. What were the ingredients in Gallagher's and Lapp and Fisher's approaches to motivate student reading?

Reading and Writing in the Social Studies

Drawing from a variety of disciplines, social studies includes the study of history, geography, political science, anthropology, sociology, and psychology. Complex vocabulary, unfamiliar writing styles and organization, topics with which students have had little experience, and abstract concepts can make social studies challenging to read, especially for students who have little experience with expository text. For instance, a student may have little difficulty reading a narrative about a teenager living during the Revolutionary War. Students are aided by an interesting story line, familiar story structures, and familiar words. However, students may have difficulty with a section in their textbook that discusses the topic "democracy, not monarchy." This is a complex, abstract idea. Moreover, the section may include terms such as *separation of powers, civil rights, limited government,* and *representative government.* The student has little experience that obviously relates to these concepts. However, the overall concept is one of the most important in social studies (Parker, 2001).

History

History is, above all, a story, and that is how it is learned and understood by students. Students weave together a chain of temporal-causal events in order to create a reconstruction of what happened. The initial understanding is rapid (Perfetti, Britt, & Georgi, 1995). Students read in order to find out what happened in much the same way that they might read a piece of fiction. However, history is more than a story. It also involves reasoning and interpretation; understanding the story seems to be a prerequisite for reasoning about events and issues. Students' ability to reason about history improves as their knowledge increases. As students learn more, their understanding becomes more complex.

Learning history, however, is a gradual process. Although the story may be reconstructed fairly rapidly, learning essential details takes somewhat longer. Details are most readily learned if they are connected to the story. In their study of students' comprehension of historical topics, Perfetti and colleagues (1995) found that rereading multiple texts added to students' knowledge of details and led to increased reasoning about events. What students learn is also determined in part by their learning styles. Some readers depend more on the text; others rely more heavily on personal knowledge. Some read for the big picture; others take in details such as dates and names. And some do both.

CHECKUP

1. What is involved in understanding history?

Comprehending History Texts

History texts often combine narrative and expository writing. Because narrative text tells a story, it is concrete and, generally speaking, easier to follow and understand than expository text. Expository text is more analytical and requires more cognitive effort. The reader is called on to compare and contrast, note causes and effects, draw conclusions, interpret, and evaluate. At the lowest levels, history texts are primarily narrative but may be a mixture of

USING TECHNOLOGY

National Council for the Social Studies www.socialstudies.org/standards **Provides an overview of the revised social studies standards and the ten themes espoused by the standards.**

CCSS

Reading Standards for Literacy in History/Social Studies www .corestandards.org/assets/CCSSI_EL A%20Standards.pdf **Provides literacy studies for history and social studies.**

USING TECHNOLOGY

National Center for History in the Schools www.nchs.ucla.edu/ Standards/ **Presents history standards.**

USING TECHNOLOGY

History/Social Studies Web Site www.execpc.com/~dboals/boals.html **Provides help for using the Web as a resource for teaching history and geography.**

CCSS

Determine central ideas or themes of a text and analyze their development; summarize the key supporting details and ideas.

Analyze how and why individuals, events, and ideas develop and interact over the course of a text.

narrative and expository writing. At the higher levels, history texts become more abstract and require greater depth of reasoning. Technical vocabulary also increases and can become quite extensive (Chall, Bissex, Conard, & Harris-Sharples, 1996).

A history book's chapter on the Industrial Revolution tells the story of the switch from goods made in homes to goods made in factories. However, it also discusses the causes and effects of the Industrial Revolution and introduces abstract concepts such as *imperialism, investors, raw materials, natural resources*, and, of course, *Industrial Revolution*. The chapter has two major structures: a time sequence structure and cause and effect. Creating a time line of key events would help the reader comprehend and remember key events leading up to and extending through the Industrial Revolution. A graphic organizer, such as a web, would help readers organize the causes and effects of the Industrial Revolution. Reflecting on ways the Industrial Revolution formed the foundation of modern life would help students achieve a deeper understanding of the period. Students might relate the Industrial Revolution to other sweeping changes that have taken place, in particular the technology revolution and the changes it is producing. By comparing and contrasting the two movements, students will achieve a deeper level of understanding of the causes and effects of broad changes on society.

Understanding history requires having a grasp of the basic facts and events. But it also means understanding the causes and effects of events and theories, such as mercantilism and imperialism, that motivated key movements. Understanding key theories and movements puts events within a conceptual framework and makes them more memorable.

At times, texts attempt to cover too many theories in too few pages. One eighth grade text introduces imperialism, mercantilism, and balance of trade in just two columns of text. Balance of trade is explained in just two lines. In situations of this type, the text needs to be supplemented with discussions, explanations, and/or additional readings. At other times, extraneous material is introduced. For instance, the text that devoted just two lines to explaining balance of trade presents a three-page description of the Great Exhibition of 1851. If time is a deciding factor, this segment could be condensed or omitted.

CHECKUP

1. What are some factors that make history texts difficult to understand?

Making History Come Alive

Although it tells the story of our past, history is one of the least-liked subjects. It is often seen as a series of events, dates, and people's names and accomplishments to be memorized. Students fail to see that history has relevance to their lives and has the potential to offer discovery and insight. As professional historian Tom Holt (1990) observes, "We are all historians. . . . Moreover in the process of doing history, one can be changed, transformed by what one learns. Stories have power. The power to change things" (p. 11).

One way to make history come alive is to make the work of history visible and open to students. History texts chronicle events and facts. They tell who did what. However, they also interpret and draw conclusions. Students get caught up in the facts and view history as something to be memorized. They don't realize that although the facts are valid, the interpretation is open to question. By reading and analyzing primary documents, students can draw their own conclusions. Primary materials are "'live' that is, they allow the students direct access to see and hear for themselves and thus to formulate their own questions and answers" (Holt, 1990, p. 23). However, interpretations are not always objective. "The act of interpretation cannot be value neutral or entirely objective. The discipline we aspire to brings the values and subjective influences out into the open. In other words, we must ask questions of ourselves as well as of the documents" (Holt, 1990, p. 360).

American Memory

In order to achieve a fair and balanced understanding of the past, students need to learn to understand how history is constructed. Using primary sources helps them to achieve this understanding. In reading primary sources, students must not only ask what the

CCSS

Integrate and evaluate content presented in diverse formats and media, including visually and quantitatively, as well as in words.

USING TECHNOLOGY

Docs Teach http://docsteach.org Contains more than 3,000 primary sources. Has lessons and tools for creating lessons that help students evaluate issues and events.

USING TECHNOLOGY

http://memory.loc.gov/ammem/index.html Features a vast collection of primary materials.

Generalization	Support

FIGURE 10.1
Generalization/Support Organizer

documents have to tell them; they must also ask whether the documents can be trusted. Context is also needed. Interpretation requires knowledge of the times and the circumstances under which the document was produced and also information about the person or group who created the document. One of the goals of using primary documents is to help students become more analytical readers of history. Realizing how history is created, they will be better able to read with a critical eye.

History becomes more understandable if students learn to see similarities in events and draw conclusions about these similarities. In order to learn to form generalizations about historical events, students should ask such questions as these:

- What was the long-term significance of these events?
- What impact did these events have on people living then? Living today?
- What can we who are living today learn from the past?
- And taken together—as a whole—what do these events tell us about the way the world of people works? (Hennings, 1993, p. 368)

Students might create organizers that show how generalizations they have formed are supported, as in the sample organizer shown in Figure 10.1.

Comprehending history also requires understanding historical figures in the context of the times in which they lived. When reading about famous people, students should ask themselves the following questions in order to develop their own hypotheses about historical cause-and-effect relationships.

Exemplary Teaching

Reading Primary Sources

Zev was a typical high school history student. When asked to read and discuss an actual letter in which ex-slaves pleaded to be allowed to retain land that had been given to them but was about to be taken back, Zev expressed reluctance. He saw history as facts carved in stone, not something that could be imagined or thought about or interpreted: "You can't just read into a document like it's some kind of story that ends any way you want it to" (Holt, 1995, p. 41). Because Zev's teacher was complementing the course textbook with primary sources, Zev read the letter and other primary sources. The letter was an eye-opener. Zev had believed that the slaves were illiterate—yet the letter was an eloquent plea. It caused Zev to shift his thinking about the freed people and the problem facing them. Illiteracy was not their problem; rather, their problem was getting the people in power to listen to them. Zev imagined the three signers of the letter sitting around a table drafting and redrafting the letter until it said exactly what they wanted it to say.

Zev then made a connection between the letter writers and more current figures in the Civil Rights Movement. He related their breaking of the literacy barrier to barriers broken by Malcolm X, Martin Luther King, and others. Thinking of the letter writers, Zev was also better able to reflect on one of the overall messages of the unit, which was the concept of *freedom:* Is freedom just freedom from slavery, or is it also the freedom to develop one's abilities and quality of life to the fullest? Zev had learned that to "do" history is to "pursue an idea, to fit it out with facts, to test it, and to ask what it means" (Holt, 1995, p. 48).

- What were the influences on this person that made him or her do what he or she did?
- What were the influences that made him or her become the kind of person he or she was?
- What effect did this person have on people and events of that time and of today? (Hennings, 1993, p. 366)

For instance, in older, traditional history texts, Columbus is portrayed as a courageous explorer. In revisionist texts, Columbus is described as being greedy and the chief cause of the downfall of a peaceful people. In a postrevisionist text, Columbus is portrayed as a product of the times and as neither better nor worse than other explorers (Hynd, 1999).

Providing a Personal Perspective

USING TECHNOLOGY

NAEP U. S History Assessment http://nces.ed.gov/nationsreportcard/ushistory/ Check this site for results of the 2010 U. S. History Assessement.

One way to activate students' schemata and to help them understand themes and key concepts in history is by having them relate historical events to happenings in their lives. For instance, in preparation for reading about the Pilgrims' voyage to America, students might gather in small groups and discuss moves that they have made: how far they moved, why they moved, how they moved, the adjustments they had to make to their new home, and how they felt about the whole experience. Students who have never moved might tell where they would like to move to and why. As they read, students can compare their experiences to those of the Pilgrims.

The Impact of Increased Literacy on Learning History

According to the NAEP U.S. History Assessment, students' knowledge of history was significantly better when assessed in 2006 than it was in 1994 and 2001 (Lee & Weiss, 2007). Ironically, the improvement came at a time when students are spending less time studying history in elementary school. With the emphasis on reading, writing, and math occasioned by NCLB legislation, many school districts have added time to the study of these test areas by taking time from the study of history and other content areas. So why did performance on the history assessments improve? According to Lee and Weiss, one possible reason for improvement is that students are reading better and thus are able to get

---

Exemplary Teaching

Taking Civic Action

At the Metropolitan Arts and Technology High School in San Francisco, students play an active role in statewide elections. California typically has a number of propositions on its ballots. Students choose a proposition that they are interested in, pick a position on the proposition, and then join a group whose purpose is to create a TV ad persuading voters to vote for or against the proposition. Each group of five students carefully reads the proposition and then researches its ramifications, listing the pros and cons of the proposition and some ideas for an ad. The groups take turns making presentations to the class explaining their proposition and their ideas for a possible ad. The class provides constructive criticism.

Through the project, students are presented with a problem and then work to solve it. Motivated by the problem, students become invested in their work, researching the issue, writing about it, discussing it, and using technology to create their ads. The digital media teacher also works with the students. As part of their research, students discuss the proposition they are working on with a focus group composed of voters. This helps them to gain insight into the concerns that voters have about the proposition.

Students present a rough form of their ads and use the feedback to improve their ads Parents are invited to view the finished ads. Voters view the ads and are also urged to vote on the proposition.

To create their ads, students need to develop a deep knowledge of their issue. As their teacher, Justin Wells, commented, "You show that you know something deeply when you are able to use that in the process of creation" (21st Century Skills, 2009a).

more information from their history text and are more prepared to read and respond to questions on the History Assessment. This suggests that fostering literacy in the content areas pays off in students learning more content. Ideally, of course, content areas such as history would not have instructional time stolen from them. Actually, reading and writing in the content areas is one of the best ways to foster literacy development.

Although there have been improvements in the historical knowledge of students, there is much room for improvement. At grade 8, just 65 percent of students are at the basic level or higher. That percentage falls to 47 percent at grade 12.

CHECKUP

1. What might be done to make history more interesting and more understandable?

Geography

Learning geography requires the ability to use a variety of specialized tools and resources. Major tools in geography are maps and atlases. Charts, graphs, tables, and time lines are also widely used. Most students have a basic understanding of how to use these tools as long as they are fairly simple. However, many students have difficulty with the graphs, charts, and tables that have a degree of complexity. Students have an especially difficult time explaining graphically displayed data in terms of outside factors. They can tell what happened, but they cannot explain why. For instance, twelfth-grade students using a bar graph could correctly determine during what years hydrocarbon production increased and decreased, but had difficulty using background knowledge to explain how environmental, economic, or other factors might account for a rise and fall in pollution levels. In fact, only one student in a hundred successfully completed the task by providing two possible reasons for a rise and fall in hydrocarbon levels (Hawkins et al., 1998). Students at all grade levels had difficulty using higher-order thinking skills and formulating written responses.

USING TECHNOLOGY

www.ncge.org/i4a/pages/index
.cfm?pageid=3314 **Presents geography standards.**

Survey Technique

Relying heavily on maps, charts, graphs, tables, and photos, geography makes special demands on students' ability and willingness to make use of visual information. In many

---

LESSON 10.1

Using the Survey Technique

Step 1: Modeling the Process

Discuss the importance of visuals in geography. To show students how important visuals are, select a chart or map and put the information conveyed by the visual into words. Note that the information is detailed and also harder to understand when it is in a verbal rather than a visual form. Using a think-aloud procedure, model how you use both visual and verbal means to survey a chapter or section before reading it.

Step 2: Guiding the Process

Guide students as they survey a chapter in their geography books. In a chapter on natural resources, guide students as they read the title, read a brief chapter preview, read the headings, and look at the visuals and read the captions. After the survey, discuss what they believe the chapter will cover. If students fail to use the visuals, guide them through a survey in which they use just the visuals and see how much information they can garner.

Step 3: Practice and Application

Guide students through additional practice sessions. Once they have caught on to the idea of surveying, encourage them to use it on their own. However, review the process from time to time and ask questions that require students to analyze the visuals in a selection.

disciplines, visuals are helpful adjuncts. In geography, visuals convey critical information. One technique that helps students make effective use of visuals is the **survey technique.**

CHECKUP

1. What are the steps in the survey technique?
2. How does the survey technique help make geography more understandable?

Art

USING TECHNOLOGY

The Nation's Report Card: Arts 2008 Music & Visual Arts http://nces.ed .gov/nationsreportcard/arts Provides information about eighth graders' knowledge of music and art and their ability to create art.

USING TECHNOLOGY

National Standards for Arts Education www.menc.org/resources/view/ the-national-standards-for-arts- education-introduction Presents standards for dance, music, theatre, and the visual arts.

Even though it is a highly visual and hands-on discipline, art also requires a specific set of literacy skills. Key concepts, such as *perspective, line, theme,* and *mood* take on a new meaning in art that is different from their everyday usage or their use in literature. Like other disciplines, art has is it own vocabulary. It also has its own mode of writing. Writing in art is highly descriptive. It also makes generous use of comparisons as works of art are compared with each other.

As Light (2004) explains, comprehension is just as important in art as it is in reading.

> If we are to teach young artists to create art that expresses ideas or feelings articulately, we must also teach them to comprehend the meaning to be found in works of art made by others. The critical process (describing, analyzing and interpreting works of art) is itself a form of reading. (p. 116)

Light recommends building on what students know and also developing critical vocabulary so that students have the words to see how works of art relate to their projects and also to enable them to voice their appreciation of the work of others. She recommends the use of the Frayer model, concept maps, semantic webs, and word walls.

From the student's perspective, art allows another way of understanding the world. "Visual art can be a means for students to learn to communicate ideas and to learn new ways to think about problems and text" (Zoss, 2008, p. 183). As Wilhelm (1997) comments, "The creation of artwork provides students with concrete tools and experiences to think with, talk about, and share" (p. 141).

Whiteboards in Art

Perhaps more than most content areas, art lends itself to digital displays. At first, secondary art teacher Joy Mane refused to accept an interactive whiteboard when she was offered one. When she finally agreed to have one, she asked that it be put in the back of the room where it would be out of the way. She was persuaded to put the board in the front of the room and was provided with ample instruction in the board's use; now she has become an enthusiastic proponent of interactive whiteboards. As Mane says, "I can take kids through a lesson step by step and it's visual. You can see the textures in a Monet painting, even from the back of the classroom." In addition to displaying works of art, she uses the board to explain techniques that students use in their creations, "If I have a drawing lesson, I can walk students through a technique step by step" (Powers, 2010).

Music

USING TECHNOLOGY

National Standards for Music Education www.ncge.org/i4a/pages/index.cfm? pageid=3314 Lists standards for music education.

Acknowledging that many music teachers are overwhelmed by performance demands, Gerrity (2004) nonetheless states, "The integration of reading and music will augment the learning process and do much to produce musicians who have a greater appreciation and understanding of their work" (p. 161). Music has its own code. Just as in reading, students need to learn the code. Music teachers can adapt a technique such as a concept map to help develop musical concepts. For instance, in developing an understanding of staccato, students can draw the notations that indicate staccato, give the meaning of the term, and provide examples of musical works that contain staccato as well as the opposite notation legato. The explanation of staccato would, of course, include an aural example of staccato. Students might be directed to Wikipedia to hear an example of notes played with and without staccato. If possible, students might copy this non-copyrighted file into their concept map.

As Gerrity (2004) notes, students' musical performance can be enhanced if they have a full understanding of the piece they are playing or singing, for instance, if they know the origin and purpose of the spirituals they are singing. Students can also be encouraged to discuss the nature of a piece and how its theme might best be expressed. As Gerrity comments, "As with Literature Circles or other discussion approaches, students actively engage in conversation and construct their own knowledge about a piece instead of being passive recipients of information transmitted by the teacher" (p. 164).

Art, music, and literature have much in common. All are designed to elicit an aesthetic response and they often reinforce each other, with literary pieces being illustrated by art and films being enhanced by background music. They use a common language: *theme*, *mood*, and *tone*, and often classify their works in similar ways: realistic, romantic, modern. Art, music, and literature also have a close relationship with history. The arts often reflect the time in which they were produced and have the potential to add emotional understanding to past events. History fosters understanding of the arts, and the arts foster understanding of history.

World Languages

Many of the techniques advocated for teaching English literacy can be applied or adapted to teaching world languages. A major task in learning a foreign language is acquiring vocabulary. The key word technique described in Chapter 4 was originally used to help students remember foreign language vocabulary words. In many instances, students learning a foreign language are learning new labels for familiar words, so teaching techniques stress associative rather than conceptual learning. If students are learning one of the Romance languages (French, Italian, Spanish, Portuguese, Romanian), then seeking cognates is a useful strategy. Morphemic analysis also comes into play in Romance languages. Many of the prefixes and suffixes used in English are similar to those found in the Romance languages. Syllabication is also a useful strategy for reading and pronouncing words in another language. Languages such as Spanish and Russian have more multisyllabic words, so syllabic analysis becomes an essential skill. However, students need to know the generalizations and patterns that govern the language being studied. Just as in English, contextual analysis is an essential skill to acquire, as students will be encountering a large number of unknown words. Dictionary skills are also an essential component of learning another language.

As in English reading, comprehension is the ultimate goal. Because students will often be reading about an unfamiliar culture or country, building and activating prior knowledge becomes even more important. Vocabulary, figurative language, and unfamiliar syntax also need special attention. As they grapple with learning a new language, students will also need to use effective comprehension strategies, such as predicting, inferring, summarizing, and monitoring for meaning. Because students may have limited fluency with the language being learned, their reading will be slower and more cognitively demanding. Reading brief segments with questions in mind and summarizing at the end of each segment should foster reading for meaning. Discussing selections read in pairs and small groups should also promote comprehension as well as listening and speaking skills.

USING TECHNOLOGY

National Standards for Foreign Language Education www.actfl.org/i4a/pages/index.cfm?pageid=3392 Presents standards for world languages.

Just as when reading in English, there should be a match between the difficulty level of materials and students' foreign language reading ability. Students will do best when they are familiar with at least 95 percent of the words in a text.

Standards for world language learning are summarized as Communication, Cultures, Connections, Comparisons, and Communities (American Council on the Teaching of Foreign Language, 2010). As explained in the standards, the study of foreign language, in addition to developing communication in that language, typically includes a study of the people who use the language and descriptions of their cultures. A study of a foreign language develops additional understanding of world history and world literature and provides possible connections to other content areas. Studying another language also deepens an understanding of one's first language as comparisons are made between the two. As a result of studying a second language, students acquire a deeper metacognitive understanding of language.

Summary

Literature has the power to evoke the feeling of wholeness or wonder at being lifted out of oneself that is the hallmark of the aesthetic response. In aesthetic reading, the reader is carried away by feelings evoked by the text. In contrast, efferent reading involves reading for information. Growing out of the aesthetic view of literature is reader response theory. In reader response theory, reading is viewed as a transaction between reader and writer. Personal response is viewed as a basis for growth in understanding and appreciating literature.

The development of responses to literature can be thought of as *envisionments*. An envisionment is the understanding a reader has about a text. Envisionments change as new ideas come to mind. Large- and small-group discussions and writing in journals and logs can be used to develop responses to literature. Key elements include accepting students' responses and using responses to build deeper, more critical responses and aesthetic appreciation.

Voluntary reading builds background knowledge, language skills, and cognitive ability. Choice and ready availability of interesting materials are key components in motivating voluntary reading.

Complex vocabulary, abstract concepts, unfamiliar writing styles and organization, and topics with which students have had little experience can make social studies challenging to read. Students are better at identifying facts than they are at interpreting them. History texts often combine narrative and expository writing. Because it is telling a story, narrative text is concrete and easier to follow and understand than expository text. Expository text is more analytical and requires more cognitive effort.

Students often fail to see that history has relevance to their lives. Reading and analyzing primary documents can make history come alive and help students learn to understand how history is constructed. Because of difficult vocabulary, complexity of concepts, and archaic language, the documents can be hard to read. The reading is more manageable if preparation is provided.

As they read history, students need to grasp the basic facts and also go beyond the facts to interpret their significance. History becomes more understandable if students learn to see similarities in events and draw conclusions about these similarities. Comprehending history also requires understanding historical figures in the context of the times in which they lived. One way to activate students' schemata and help them understand themes and key concepts is by having them relate historical events to happenings in their lives.

Learning geography requires the ability to use maps, atlases, charts, graphs, tables, and time lines. Most students have a basic understanding of how to use these tools, but have difficulty interpreting graphically displayed data. The survey technique helps students make effective use of visual and verbal information.

Art and music, which require their own sets of literacy skills, provide students with another way of viewing the world and expressing themselves. Art, music, and literature are designed to elicit an aesthetic response and often reinforce each other.

Many of the techniques advocated for teaching English literacy can be applied or adapted to teaching world languages. Techniques used to foster vocabulary acquisition and comprehension in English can be adapted for use in learning a second language,

Reflection

Return to the Anticipation Guide at the beginning of this chapter. Respond once again to the items. Did your responses change? If so, how and why? Which content areas seem more difficult to read? Why? Why might a student with good general reading skills still have difficulty reading in the social studies?

Extension and Application

1. Examine a social studies text. What reading skills does the text require? Does the text have any suggestions for reading it effectively? If so, what are they?
2. From the Library of Congress (http://lcweb.loc.gov) or another source, locate some primary source material. How might you use this material with students who are reading social studies or language arts?
3. With a small group of students, select a piece of literature to read. Try the reader response approach in your discussion. What are the strengths of the approach? Its weaknesses?
4. Analyze a foreign language text. How might general vocabulary and comprehension skills and strategies be adapted so as to foster increased understanding of the text?
5. Analyze an art history and music performance or music appreciation text. Discuss with classmates or fellow teachers the question: What are the key reading skills and strategies needed to effectively read these texts?

Go to Topic 4: Writing, Topic 5: Comprehension, and Topic 6: Vocabulary in the MyEducationLab (www.myeducationlab.com) for your course, where you can:

- Find learning outcomes for Writing, Comprehension, and Vocabulary along with the national standards that connect to these outcomes.
- Complete Assignments and Activities that can help you more deeply understand the chapter content.
- Apply and practice your understanding of the core teaching skills identified in the chapter with the Building Teaching Skills and Dispositions learning units.
- Examine challenging situations and cases presented in the IRIS Center Resources.

Go to the Topic A+RISE in the MyEducationLab (www .myeducationlab.com) for your course. A+RISE® Standards2Strategy™ is an innovative and interactive online resource that offers new teachers in grades K–12 just-in-time, research-based instructional strategies that:

- Meet the linguistic needs of ELLs as they learn content.
- Differentiate instruction for all grades and abilities.
- Offer reading and writing techniques, cooperative learning, use of linguistic and nonlinguistic representations, scaffolding, teacher modeling, higher order thinking, and alternative classroom ELL assessment.
- Provide support to help teachers be effective through the integration of listening, speaking, reading, and writing along with the content curriculum.
- Improve student achievement.
- Are aligned to Common Core Elementary Language Arts standards (for the literacy strategies) and to English language proficiency standards in WIDA, Texas, California, and Florida.

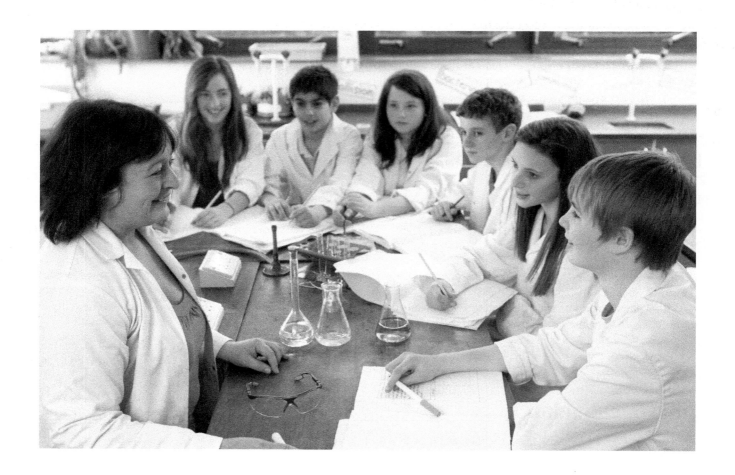

CHAPTER 11

Reading and Writing in Science, Career and Technical Education, and Math

Anticipation Guide

For each of the following statements, put a check under "Agree" or "Disagree" to indicate your opinion. Discuss your responses with classmates.

	Agree	Disagree
1. Reading in the sciences is easier than reading in the social studies because the sciences are less abstract and better organized.	____	____
2. Students who have adequate general reading skills should have little difficulty reading math and science texts.	____	____
3. The biggest obstacle to understanding reading in science is the large number of technical terms that students encounter.	____	____
4. Of all the content areas, physics is the most difficult to read.	____	____
5. Struggling readers do well in math because they are dealing mostly with numbers rather than words.	____	____

Using What You Know

Which of the sciences did you find most difficult? How would you compare the difficulty of reading a biology text with that of reading a general science or chemistry text? What were the main obstacles to reading each type? How did you overcome these obstacles? What special strategies did you use? What steps did your science teachers take to help you read the texts more effectively? How would you compare reading in math with reading in the sciences? What makes reading math problems difficult? Did your math teachers suggest strategies for reading problems? If so, what were they and how well did they work?

USING TECHNOLOGY

The Nation's Report Card: Science 2009 http://nces.ed.gov/nationsreportcard/pdf/main2009/2011451.pdf provides information on fourth, eighth, and tenth graders knowledge of science

Building Literacy in the Sciences

The Nature of Learning Science

Just as in reading comprehension, scientific knowledge is constructed (Baker & Piburn, 1997). It is built on students' personal knowledge, or schemata using an **inquiry approach** in which students ask questions, plan and conduct experiments, observe and quantify, reflect and reason, draw conclusions, and solve problems. Students don't replace old knowledge with new knowledge; rather, they develop new understandings of a scientific idea by reconstructing their existing knowledge of that idea. "Prior knowledge and experience are crucial resources that the individuals use to make sense of new information and construct new understandings" (pp. 404-405). For instance, students may understand that the moon is a heavenly body, but they may believe that the moon is stationary. Through observation and discussion, students can be led to understand that the moon rises and sets and moves across the sky.

Many schools overemphasize textbooks, which tend to stress facts and vocabulary. Feeling pressured to cover the text, teachers accept a low level of understanding. Students read about science instead of doing science. When students read about concepts such as *work* and *energy*, which are abstract, they gain little meaning from the text; they need real experiences. Today's students, in contrast to farm children of a few generations ago, have few direct experiences with nature. They have plenty of

> ■ In the inquiry approach, a question is posed and students gather information through reading, experimentation, observation, or other means and compose an answer or come to a conclusion based on the information gathered. In a scientific inquiry, students ask questions, plan, and conduct experiments, observe and quantify, reflect and reason, draw conclusions, and solve problems.

images from TV and computers, but they need the experience of growing plants, raising classroom animals, examining rock collections, building robots, and experimenting with sound waves and carbon compounds. By doing science, students acquire a store of experiences that they can reflect on and use to build concepts. In inquiry science, students are actively engaged with the real world. Teamwork and collaboration are promoted, and different learning styles are accommodated.

CHECKUP

1. How is science learned?

The Nature of Science Texts

One reason science is difficult is the number of new concepts introduced. In fact, according to one study, secondary school texts introduce more new vocabulary words per page than foreign language texts do (Carey, 1986). Of all the major content areas, science texts have the highest lexical density or proportion of technical words (Shanahan & Shanahan, 2008).

An examination of a current chemistry and a current physics text reveals that each contains more than 400 technical terms. Moreover, it isn't enough just to know the meanings of words in science. For measurement terms, students must go beyond defining *gram* or *kilogram* and be able to manipulate these measurements. Words such as *density* and *velocity* require knowing and being able to apply a formula. Symbols in chemistry must be understood on two levels: The student needs to recognize that H_2O is water and also that there are two atoms of hydrogen for every atom of oxygen.

Science texts are written in complex, precise language. However, the difficulty of science texts differs from discipline to discipline. When researchers Chall, Bissex, Conard, and Harris-Sharples (1996) set out to create a scale for measuring the difficulty of science texts, they soon found that they needed two scales because the patterns of writing and reasoning processes involved in comprehending the life sciences and physical sciences are so different. The **life sciences** are primarily descriptive/technical and are more concrete. They describe creatures that can be directly observed, sometimes with the help of a microscope, or depicted in a visual. Texts are devoted to describing the makeup and characteristics of various species. At the easiest levels, life science texts are concrete and devoted primarily to describing familiar creatures and phenomena. As the texts increase in difficulty, they become more technical and detailed and deal with more abstract concepts.

The **physical sciences** are more conceptual and theoretical. At the easiest levels they, too, are concrete and deal mainly with familiar topics. But more advanced texts are more abstract and deal with concepts such as *space* and *relativity* that cannot be seen and may require an understanding of math in order to be comprehended. There is, of course, overlap between the two kinds of science reading. The life sciences also deal with abstractions and theories, and understanding the physical sciences frequently requires a grasp of technical details. However, in general, reading in the life sciences places a heavy burden on memory, whereas reading in the physical sciences places a greater demand on reasoning, especially as students move into higher levels. (The earth and space sciences include characteristics of both the life and physical sciences).

Both the life and physical sciences demand a precise kind of reading in which students construct an exact rather than an interpretive meaning, identify and organize key ideas, note cause and effect and other relationships, use graphic information, and understand scientific formulas and symbols. The ability to read and follow directions in order to carry out lab experiments is also a key skill.

■ **The life sciences** include biology and ecology.

■ **The physical sciences** include physics, astronomy, geology, chemistry, and space science.

Demands on the Reader in the Life Sciences

Because of the distinctions between life and physical sciences, texts in these subjects differ in their presentations of ideas and require specific kinds of reading and study strategies. The life sciences frequently follow a list structure in which a main idea is stated and supporting details follow. Often there are a number of details that must be understood and remembered. Most details are concrete and may be depicted by illustrations in the text. The difficult part is remembering all of them. For instance, a chapter in a tenth-grade biology text explains what a cell is and then describes in words and illustrations the parts of the cell. (Miller & Levine, 2009). The following terms are introduced and carefully explained: *cell membrane, cytoplasm, nucleus, nuclear envelope, cell organelles, mitochondria, ribosomes, endoplasmic reticulum, golgi bodies*, and *vacuoles*. To learn all of these details, readers need some way of organizing them as well as some solid study strategies to remember them.

The best way to foster retention is to build understanding. In other words, students will remember the parts of the cell better if they understand why the cell needs each of its parts to sustain life: The nucleus can be seen as the control center; the nuclear envelope its covering; the vacuoles are storage containers for food and water; and so on. Knowing the morphemic structures of the terms will also aid understanding. For instance, the term *cytoplasm* is easier to remember if one knows the *cyto* means "cell" and *plasm* means "living substance." Knowing that *endo* means "within" and *reticulum* means "little net" will help the student understand that the *endoplasmic reticulum* is a netlike structure within the cell's plasma.

Other strategies that may help are visualizing the cell and its parts, constructing and labeling a diagram of the cell, and, of course, viewing a cell under a microscope. Creating an analogy also helps students understand and remember the parts of the cell and their functions. In one text, the operation of a cell was compared to the operation of a factory. Diffusion was compared to having a group of people pass through a crowded room. In the sciences, knowledge is often cumulative. Future chapters in the text build on the students' knowledge of the cell. In fact, the next section in the text describes plant cells and contrasts them with animal cells. When layer after layer of information is presented in this way, plan activities in which students demonstrate their understanding of one topic (such as by writing a summary or completing a diagram) before moving on to the next one. Students need to monitor for meaning so they become aware of when they fail to understand a concept. Be sure to have effective strategies, such as rereading, paraphrasing, using visuals, or consulting other sources to help them achieve understanding. Because of its technical nature, science requires continuous review of previously learned concepts (International Reading Association et al., 2006).

Although the chapter on cells follows a basic list structure, it also requires comparing and contrasting as students are asked to note how plant cells are similar to but different from animal cells. The chapter also gets into higher reasoning skills as it concludes with an explanation of cell theory and how this developed.

As students' knowledge becomes more advanced, the explanations of processes become more detailed. Students will have a difficult time remembering these explanations if they don't understand why Step A leads to Step B and Step B leads to Step C. Cause-and-effect reasoning is involved. Creating process diagrams should help students better understand and retain explanations of these processes.

Demands on the Reader in the Physical Sciences

A chapter in a high school physics text discusses waves. The chapter begins with a general description of waves. Following a list structure, the text discusses types of waves and properties of waves. Technical vocabulary is introduced, such as *crest, trough, transverse, longitudinal, compressions, refraction, amplitude, wavelength, frequency*, and *speed*. The speed of a wave is expressed in mathematical terms with a formula: $v = f \times \lambda$ (Greek letter lambda) where wave speed (v) = frequency (f) × wavelength (λ). Within the chapter, cause/effect and comparison/contrast structures are used to show what causes waves and to compare different types of waves. Both the language and the concepts are abstract. The basic idea being conveyed—that a wave is a disturbance that travels through matter or space—is difficult to picture. The concept that the transfer of energy causes a wave is also abstract. It is also counterintuitive. Watching an ocean wave, one might think water moving toward the shore causes it, and might be surprised to learn that energy causes waves.

As in the life sciences, the material is cumulative. Concepts build on each other. Reading in small doses and checking one's comprehension through summarizing and self-questioning are recommended. It is essential that students understand key concepts before moving on. Using graphics and visualizing facilitate comprehension. Making a chart of the characteristics of different types of waves helps make the information more concrete and more memorable.

The vocabulary load is heavy and abstract. Common words take on exact, specific meanings. *Speed* and *velocity* are used interchangeably in ordinary conversation, but have different meanings in physics. Morphemic analysis should help. It also helps if students try out the mathematical formulas used to define terms. Calculating the velocity and wavelength of a wave will help students better understand all three terms involved: *velocity*, *wavelength*, and *wave*. Students might also discuss technical terms, such as *hertz* and *high frequency*, that are used in everyday life so they can relate what they know to what they are learning.

CHECKUP

1. What are the key characteristics of science texts?
2. How do the demands made by physical science texts differ from the demands made by life science texts?

Understanding Key Ideas

To understand science, students must get the "big picture" or the main ideas that the science explores. For instance, a key idea in chemistry is that all matter consists of very tiny, characteristic particles called atoms (Dickson, 1995). This key idea helps students to understand such key concepts as the states of matter, elements and compounds, the periodic table, the structure of atoms, and the formation of compounds. Keeping this key idea in mind will help students organize and better understand other key concepts. In the most effective science classes, fundamental ideas are presented and expanded and understanding is fostered. In a biology course, for instance, the nature of lipids—their insolubility in water and solubility in other lipids—is used to help students understand the advantages of having a lipid membrane surrounding cells and of having a transport vesicle encased in lipids. Teachers also build on students' background knowledge. In a physics class, students use their knowledge of refraction and concave mirrors to figure out why a flashlight's beam narrows when the head of the flashlight is rotated (ACT & Education Trust, 2005).

Understanding Science Concepts

Students cannot simply memorize concepts. They must construct their own understandings. "They must be guided to actively construct their own mental models of the basic concepts. Passive acceptance of the teacher's own mental model will not suffice" (LeMay, Beall, Robblee, & Brower, 2000, p. T7).

Science concepts are learned in spiral fashion. Most concepts are not learned once and for all and forever. Many concepts are changed or refined as we gain new knowledge or have additional experiences. As we encounter and reencounter a concept over the years, our understanding becomes deeper and richer.

The Learning Cycle

In keeping with the way knowledge is constructed, concepts are presented through a learning cycle. Emphasizing the importance of experience, the **learning cycle** has three phases: student exploration or discovery, teacher explanation, and student application. This cycle reverses the typical sequence of presenting a new concept. Traditionally, the concept was explained and was followed by a demonstration or experiment. In the learning cycle approach, instruction begins with the experiment or demonstration and progresses to explanation and application.

Exploration

The exploratory phase is designed to create new understandings or refine old ones. It is also designed to spark students' interest. Students are provided with a set of materials to explore. They may be given a series of objects with various buoyancies and a container of water. They work with the materials and make predictions about them. After conducting experiments with the materials, they discuss their findings in small groups.

Explanation or Concept Development

In the explanation phase, the teacher helps students discover target concepts as they focus on the findings of their experiments. This might be done through a discussion of the experiments—why some objects sank and others floated, for instance. The teacher can introduce scientific terminology such as *buoyancy* and *density* at this point. Concepts are also developed through reading, lectures, and demonstrations.

The use of analogy can be an aid to understanding because it uses familiar objects or situations as a way of explaining unfamiliar concepts. For instance, in one high school chemistry text, atoms were compared to letters in the alphabet to explain how 100 atoms can be combined in a variety of ways to form hundreds of substances:

> There are about 100 elements, which means that there are about 100 different kinds of atoms. These atoms combine to form each of the vast number of substances that make up the world around us. In a sense, atoms are like the 26 letters of the alphabet, which in different combinations form the immense number of words in the English language. And just as the rules of spelling and phonics define how letters can combine to form a word, so do certain scientific laws govern how atoms combine to form matter. (LeMay et al., 2000, p. 93)

Application

Students apply their newly learned concept or expand it. For instance, they can investigate methods of measuring buoyancy (Marian, Sexton, & Gerlovich, 2001). They can also apply newly learned concepts through lab work, problem solving, or discussion of environmental, consumer, or other issues.

Some of the best applications are those that can be applied to everyday life. In a chapter in a chemistry text in which the authors have introduced the concept of atoms, the authors explain that the phrase "100 percent natural" that is often used by advertisers is a bit misleading from a chemical point of view. Because all atoms in each molecule of a given chemical compound are identical to the atoms in every other molecule, the combination of atoms found in that compound in nature will be identical to those found in that same compound assembled in a lab. "A compound's properties come from the identity and arrangement of its atoms, not the place where those atoms were assembled" (LeMay et al., 2000, p. 93).

To foster full development of concepts, use the learning cycle and the following techniques.

1. Focus on fewer concepts, but in greater depth.
2. Use a variety of teaching strategies.
3. Present concepts from several different viewpoints.
4. Elicit students' misconceptions and directly address them in class.
5. Encourage students to discuss concepts with one another.
6. Include concept mastery questions on tests. (LeMay et al., 2000, p. T7)

Struggling Readers

Holding demonstrations before students read in their textbooks about the principles they illustrate provides preparation for reading. Students acquire the vocabulary and background knowledge needed to read the text and get more out of it.

■ The learning cycle is a student-centered approach to learning concepts and has three phases: student exploration or discovery, teacher explanation, and student application.

Exemplary Teaching

Building Deep Conceptual Learning

In order to teach students problem solving and to develop deep conceptual learning, tenth-grade biology teacher Annie Chien explains the difference between *e. coli* that glow and those that don't and then has students map out how they would remove the DNA from glowing *e. coli* and transfer it into nonglowing *e. coli*. Students gather in small groups, discuss the steps they would need to take in order to make the transformation work, and create a written plan. Annie Chien discusses their plan, and, building on what the students have mapped out, provides them with a series of procedures to be followed. After students have completed their experiments, they discuss the results and compose a written reflection explaining them. Through pre-experimental planning and reflecting on results, they achieve a deeper understanding of what gene therapy looks like on a very basic level. They also develop an understanding of the scientific method. Perhaps most important of all, they begin to think of themselves as scientists (21st Century Skills, 2009b).

Using Imagery

Imagery is an excellent aid to fostering science understanding. For instance, to help students understand the chemical molecular theory, have them visualize molecules bouncing off each other the way pool balls do, except that they keep on moving. Chlorine gas might be envisioned as greenish particles in constant motion. We can imagine the gas particles being heated within a balloon. Heat causes the particles to move faster. Moving faster, they push against the surface of the balloon and so expand it (Dickson, 1995).

CHECKUP

1. What is the learning cycle?
2. How does this foster the learning of science concepts?
3. What are other ways to foster an understanding of science concepts?

Using Think–Alouds

One way to help students understand their text is to show how you, an expert reader, go about constructing the meaning of a science text. Think-alouds provide students with insight into the thinking processes and strategies that readers use to comprehend text. Here is a sample think-aloud for an excerpt from a text on astronomy.

> The **meridian** is the line that bisects the sky by running from the due north point on the horizon up to the zenith and then down to the due south point on the horizon. (Schaaf, 1998, p. 7)

> > *Meridian is* boldfaced, *so it must be important. This word* bisects, *I've never seen it before. But* bi *means two, as in* bicycle *for two wheels and* binomial *for two numbers. So I think it means divides something in two. And that's what the drawing shows, the sky divided into an eastern part and a western part.*

> If you don't know where due north and due south are at the place where you're now standing, just look back toward the setting sun. And once you know which way west is, you can figure where north and south are and where the meridian runs. (Schaff, 1998, p. 7)

> > *Let's see. The sentence says, "And once you know which way west is, you can figure where north and south are and where the meridian runs." But I can't. I'll look at the illustration. It shows a man looking west toward where the sun is setting. Well, I do know that the sun rises in the east and sets in the west. But how does that help me figure out which way north is? Let's see; the drawing shows that north is to the right of the man as he stands facing west. Now I get it. But how will I remember that north is to the right and south is to the left when you are facing west? Hey, they call lefthanders southpaws, so I'll just remember it that way. South is to your left when you're facing west.*

But why is the meridian, dividing the sky into eastern and western halves, more important than a line dividing the sky into northern and southern halves? (Schaff, 1998, p. 7)

That's a good question. I wonder why.

The answer is that the sun and almost all heavenly objects—the moon, planets, and most of the stars—appear to ascend in the eastern half of the sky and descend in the western half of the sky. (Schaff, 1998, p. 7)

Ah ha! Now I get it.

Discuss with the class strategies that you used as you read. Talk over, for instance, how you monitored for meaning as you read, how you used an illustration to help you, and how you responded to the author in an interactive way. When the author asked questions, you attempted to answer them.

After modeling the process of thinking your way through a difficult segment of text, provide students with opportunities to do the same. They can work in pairs and take turns thinking aloud as they read to a partner. Discuss any difficulties that they may have encountered as they read and ask them to describe strategies they used. In their journals, they can reflect on their reading strategies as well as the content that they read. As their reading requires the use of specialized strategies, demonstrate with think-alouds and provide guided practice. For instance, you might demonstrate imaging and summarizing as effective strategies to use when reading about processes involving a number of steps.

Building Background

When examining a text, note in particular the background required to read the text. For instance, many upper-level science texts assume the ability to apply algebraic formulas. Some biology texts may assume knowledge of chemistry or physics. Also note the depth of coverage and the rate at which new concepts are introduced. Texts vary greatly in the number and depth of concepts they contain and the amount of technical vocabulary they introduce. It is better that students learn the basic concepts well than be overwhelmed by trying to master more concepts than they can handle.

Using Questioning to Build Background

Although it is a challenging subject, science begins on the most concrete of levels: observation. Students begin to learn science as they observe plants grow, the sun rise and set, the tides move in and out, the body respond to medicines, steam rise from boiling water, and other phenomena. By observing several events, students form concepts as they abstract commonalties of these events. Abstracting relationships among concepts leads to generalizations. And abstracting relationships among generalizations leads to laws and theories. Because science begins on a concrete level, it is accessible to all students (Singer & Donlan, 1989).

By using a technique for teaching known as **Quest (Question Sequence for Teaching Thinking)** (Taba, 1965), students can be led from an observational level to a generalization level (Singer & Donlan, 1989). Quest begins with stating the lesson objective—for example, to develop the generalization that sound passes faster through media in which molecules are closer together. The teacher then decides what kind of observations students would need to make in order to come to this conclusion. What experiences, either direct or indirect, might be set up in order to provide the foundation for this conclusion? The teacher decides to drop a felt blackboard eraser and a pen on a long table and have a student tell how the sound waves traveled to her ears (Cuevas & Lamb, 1994). The student would note that she didn't hear the eraser hit the table, but she heard the sound waves from the pen as they traveled through the air. Then the teacher repeats the experiment, but the student puts one ear to the table and covers the other one with her hand. The student notes that this time she heard the waves from both the felt eraser and the pen traveling through the table. The teacher discusses the experiment and other related experiences that students

■ Quest (Question Sequence for Teaching Thinking) uses observations and carefully planned questions to lead students to construct generalizations.

TABLE 11.1 FELS Questioning During a Quest Science Lesson

TYPE OF FELS QUESTION	PURPOSE	QUESTION
Focusing	Focus on topic.	How did the student hear the sound waves before she put her ear to the table? How did she hear the waves after she put her ear to the table?
Extending	Gather more information on the same level.	How do whales communicate with each other? How does the sound travel? What did we learn about sound on the moon?
Lifting	Raises level of students' responses.	What can we say about sound? What kinds of things carry sound?
Substantiating	Requires students to provide support for their responses.	How do we know that sound travels faster along solid objects? Why did Native Americans put their ears to the ground when they were searching for buffalo? In what two ways was the sound traveling? Which was the faster way?
Lifting		Do you think sound travels faster on a hot day or on a cold one? What did we learn in the last unit about the molecules in the air on cold and hot days? How might the closeness of the molecules affect the speed of sound? What can we say about the relationship between the speed of sound and the closeness of the molecules in the medium through which sound is traveling?

have had using a series of questions known as FELS, for Focusing, Extending, Lifting, and Substantiating as shown in Table 11.1.

Although many texts first explain scientific principles or generalizations and then have students conduct experiments or observations, the reverse is a more effective procedure for building a foundation of knowledge and understanding upon which to base the generalization (Baker & Piburn, 1997). After students have experience with the Quest procedure, they can be given Quest guides to use in a cooperative learning group or in an individual effort to formulate generalizations.

CHECKUP

1. How might think-alouds and background-building techniques be used to develop an understanding of science texts?

Correcting Misconceptions

Science is sometimes made more difficult because of the way our minds work. We are constantly trying to make sense of the world around us. We create theories about why the sun rises and sets and why it is warmer in summer than in winter. According to our observations, we would probably attribute summer warmth to the theory that the sun is closer to the Earth during the summer months. Once we have constructed theories, they become part of our schemata. Changing a **misconception** may mean reorganizing a whole network of ideas. Even when we understand the new idea, we may not want to let go of our misconception. Students find it difficult to accept the idea that the sun is actually closer

■ **Misconceptions** are erroneous ideas that people have about scientific and other phenomena. These misconceptions may be formed through observation, reasoning, erroneous information from others, or misinterpretation of correct information. Some science educators refer to misconceptions as preconcepts (Baker & Piburn, 1997).

to Earth in the wintertime and it isn't the distance of the sun from the Earth that causes seasons to change, but the angle of the sun's rays (they are less direct in the wintertime).

Students' misconceptions may not be addressed because teachers are unaware that students have them. Whenever a new concept is introduced in any subject, the teacher should first assess students' understanding of that concept. For instance, the teacher might ask, "Why is it hot in the summer and cold in the winter?" Responses will reveal students' conceptions and thinking. The teacher can then confront misconceptions and also build on accurate ideas students may have.

Beliefs that are deeply entrenched are especially hard to change (Chinn & Brewer, 1993). An entrenched belief is one for which the believer has a significant amount of evidence, especially if that evidence comes from several sources. The young child's flat earth belief is deeply entrenched because it is supported by frequent observations. Some beliefs are firmly held because they reflect the believer's concept about the fundamental characteristics of matter. For instance, students may believe that force, heat, light, and current are material substances and may continue to believe that the electrical current making a circuit is weaker at the end of its circuit than it is at the beginning (Dupin & Joshua, 1987).

Students are more likely to change beliefs when the source of new information is credible. For instance, students are more likely to believe that plants make their food through photosynthesis when they see that plants placed in a closet wither. They are also more likely to replace erroneous concepts when all possible explanations for them are shown to be false. For instance, if students believe that plants placed in a closet don't grow because of lack of fresh air and not because of lack of sunlight, it would be necessary to place the plants in a room in which there was fresh air but no sunlight. Care must be taken to find out what the students' objections are and to answer each of them. Students should also be encouraged to think carefully about the information that contradicts an erroneous concept. They are more likely to alter concepts if they engage in deep processing. For instance, if students are asked to explain a concept to others, they are more likely to confront and rethink their erroneous information. It also helps if they have a personal involvement in the issue (Chinn & Brewer, 1993). For instance, students are more likely to change their misconception that plants get their food from the soil if they are asked to explain photosynthesis to their cooperative group or if they are placed in charge of the class's plants.

CHECKUP

1. What are some steps that might be undertaken to correct misconceptions in science?
2. Why are some science misconceptions difficult to correct?

Evaluating Scientific Information

One of the marks of scientific literacy is the ability to interpret scientific information that appears in the media, which is a key source of ongoing scientific information, especially after students have completed their formal schooling. Indeed, scientific information is pervasive and can be found in most newspapers and magazines. Many of our personal decisions, such as seeking medical recommendations and caring for the environment, as well as civic decisions, such as deciding on where to place landfills and how to deal with toxic wastes and pollution, are influenced by these sources of information (Phillips, Norris, & Korpan, 2000). Unfortunately, even students who have a fairly rich scientific background are not very good at interpreting scientific information. They tend to overestimate the validity of information and frequently accept tentative conclusions as proven. In one study of older students who had a relatively rich background in science, only one student in three was able to interpret cause–effect statements correctly (Phillips, Norris, & Korpan, 2000). They also had difficulty making predictions based on scientific information and interpreting explanations. Even scientifically literate students need to learn to apply critical reading/thinking skills to scientific information.

Scientific Writing

Scientific writing is different from the narrative, expressive writing with which students are probably more familiar. It is marked by clear, often detailed descriptions and explanations expressed in precise terms. Emphasis is placed on providing neutral descriptions rather than imaginative expressions. Writing is factual rather than expressive. Conclusions are carefully drawn and supported with data. Students are also expected to present their data in the format (tables, line graphs, scatterplots) that expresses it most clearly. Many science courses require lab reports. In the most effective classes, students are provided with a specific format for completing their lab reports, as in the following example drawn from an exemplary teacher:

> Each lab performed in class must be written in a lab report that conforms to the following guidelines.
>
> The first page should have the names of the lab group members at the top, along with the date. The following sections must be included:
>
> - Title of the lab
> - Purpose—Briefly describe, in one or two sentences, why and how you did this lab.
> - Procedures—Describe what you did (using outline form is preferred). You may borrow from any pre-lab handouts. Include precautions, safety issues, and sketches of lab apparatus.
> - Observations—Use sensory observations only. For example, appearance of reactants, motion of objects. Do not interpret what you observed.
> - Data—Include all data collected during the lab. The data should be organized in a chart, table, or graph. Include any experimental error determinations, if appropriate. Use the correct number of significant figures.
> - Calculations—Show all work and results of any calculations made using the collected data.
> - Questions—Answer the questions given in the lab handout in one or two sentences.
> - Conclusions—Write a short paragraph including the effectiveness of the results or procedure, any error and the sources of the error, conclusions based on the observations, and knowledge gained or concepts learned. (ACT & Education Trust, 2005, p. 69)

Explicit step-by-step instruction in scientific writing is helpful to students, as are modeling by the teacher, providing example lab reports, having the class cooperatively compose some sample labs, and holding conferences to discuss the content and format of the labs. Composing learning logs or journals and writing critiques of journal articles are also useful writing experiences. A popular activity is to have students create picture books of key scientific concepts and present them to elementary school children. Students might also write letters to the editor about pollution, clean water, carbon footprint, or other topics of concern that are related to areas of study in their science classes.

Solving Problems

Science texts frequently present activities that require students to apply principles or concepts that they have learned by solving problems. Before being asked to solve problems, students should have achieved a conceptual understanding of the topic. The process of solving problems should be modeled. Students should also be encouraged to think of the method for solving a problem rather than jumping in and mechanically applying a formula. Students should also be taught to be flexible, so that if one method of solving a problem fails to work, they can try another. Encourage students to use think-alouds and discuss how they go about solving problems. Understanding students' thinking can help you provide needed guidance.

Working sample problems in the textbook will also foster problem-solving ability. Each problem usually has some feature that is not present in previous questions, so students gradually build up the ability to solve a wider range of problem types (Krause, 2001). It is also helpful if problems to be completed by students are interspersed by example problems that have already been worked out so that students can apply procedures demonstrated in the interspersed example problems (Pashler et al., 2007). To aid students in solving problems, Singer and Donlan (1989) suggest demonstrating the solution of similar problems, using the following steps.

Step 1: List the formula.

$$\text{Density} = \text{mass/volume or } d = m/v$$

Step 2: Show how the formula may be manipulated so that given any two variables, the third can be calculated.

A. Given mass and volume, find density: $d = m/v$

B. Given density and volume, find mass: $m = dv$

C. Given density and mass, find volume: $v = m/d$

Step 3: Show how a problem that is stated in various ways can be reworded so that the student knows which formula to apply.

Aluminum has a density of 2.7 g/cm^3. Gold has a density of 19.32 g/cm^3. Which object contains more matter, a block of aluminum that has a volume of 500 cm^3 or a block of gold that has a volume of 50 cm^3?

Step 4: Apply the scientific principle that is necessary for solving the problem.

You are given two small metal bars. Both have the same mass: 1500 g. But Bar A needs a box that is 133 cm^3 to contain it, while Bar B fits in a box that is 142 cm^3. Which one is lead? Which one is silver? The student would apply the following principle. The more dense a substance is, the less space it takes up. Matter varies in its density. Density is often used to determine the composition of an object.

Step 5: Assess the solutions or answers to see whether they make sense. Because you can see on a density chart that lead has a higher density than silver, you know that an equal volume of it would take up less space.

English Language Learners

ELLs benefit from working with other students. They feel free to ask questions of their peers, and their peers are more likely to use the kind of language that will clearly explain puzzling concepts.

English Language Learners

ELLs often do better in hands-on situations such as completing labs because they are less hampered by their lack of familiarity with English. When discussing lab procedures and activities, hold up or point to the piece of equipment or element to aid students who are still acquiring English.

CHECKUP

1. What can be done in science labs to foster improved problem-solving ability and increased literacy?

Applied Science: Physical Education

As taught in today's secondary schools, physical education has as its goal helping students form lifelong habits that promote physical well being. Fitness, healthy habits, and knowledge of exercise science are developed. Students are exposed to a variety of physical activities and sports so they can choose those that appeal to them. Physical education includes both scientific and mathematical concepts that are applied in practical ways. At Naperville Central High School, for instance, students learn about cardiovascular endurance and aerobic conditioning and use the Karvonen formula to determine their target range for heart rate while exercising. They also learn the names, locations, and functions of the body's muscle systems and how to build both muscle strength and muscle endurance. In addition, they study principles of strength training. Students access a variety of information sources, including Tone Teen (www.toneteen.com), an exercise site designed for teens; Kidnetic (www.kidnetic.com), a site that promotes healthy eating; and a variety of other sites. Videos accompanied by response sheets and a variety of checklists, templates, and instructional or informative handouts are also provided. As PE teacher Paul Zientarski states, "Exercise in itself is not fun. It's work. So if you can make them [students] understand it, show them the benefit—that's radical transformation." (Ratney & Hagerman, 2008, p. 23). Literacy is very much a part of physical education at Naperville Central, but perhaps the most unusual feature of the school's physical education program is its Learning Readiness Physical Education component.

Learning Readiness and Physical Education

According to research by Harvard professor, John Ratney (Ratney & Hagerman, 2008), exercise promotes brain growth in the hippocampus, which is involved in learning and remembering. According to Ratney's research and that of others, exercise can make you smarter. In an experimental program designed to see if physical exercise would translate into improved achievement, a group of struggling readers volunteered to take an early morning physical education class just before they took their reading improvement class. The exercise group outperformed another group who took the same class but didn't precede it with an exercise class. Experiments with other classes confirmed the results. Students who exercised before class outperformed those who didn't. A number of large-scale studies support the results found at Naperville Central (Ratney & Haqgerman, 2008).

Career and Technical Education

Career and technical education encompasses information technology, automotive, communication, construction, manufacturing, energy, business, environmental, health, and other career and technical fields. Although they are generally hands on, most career and technical courses require the reading of complex manuals and writing of technical reports. Key skills include acquisition of the area's technical vocabulary, the ability to follow complex directions, and the ability to use detailed graphics. In electronics, for instance, much of the information is conveyed through complex schematics. Because technology changes so rapidly, another essential skill is the ability to keep up with changes through reading the field's print or online publications.

Technical manuals and textbooks can be quite complex. Students should be provided with strategies, such as previewing, surveying, paraphrasing, questioning, visualizing, summarizing, and monitoring and should read the text in brief segments. Provide whatever scaffolding is needed including rewriting segments of the text. However, insofar as possible, develop students' text reading skills, so that ultimately they will be able to read the materials on their own.

Building Literacy in Mathematics

With its density of ideas expressed in precise terms, math requires a slow, focused style of reading, and careful monitoring. Even function words have a meaning: *The* has a different meaning from *a*. Rereading and close reading are key skills (Shanahan & Shanahan, 2008). Students need to stop when they do not understand an idea. A key strategy for students is to put the idea in their own words.

Math is cumulative, with concepts building on each other. If students find they are having trouble comprehending the segment they are currently reading, they might have to go back to an earlier part of the chapter or text to build the understanding they need (International Reading Association et al., 2006). Perhaps, because of its complexity, students frequently fail to read their math texts. They go directly to the problems that have been assigned, using sample problems when they need to. They rely on teacher demonstrations, rather than textbook explanations. Unfortunately, this limits their ability to read math and expand their knowledge (Mower, 2003). As in the other content areas, you should preview text, activate schema, go over unfamiliar vocabulary and concepts beforehand, and provide a purpose for reading. Make suggestions for strategies to be used while reading; after reading, discuss the text and go over the problems to foster proficiency in math reading. During the preview, it is especially helpful to review any background needed to understand the text (Mower, 2003). Modeling how a math text might be read is also helpful to students.

When asked how math texts should be read, mathematicians stressed the need for students to understand and memorize exact definitions: "prime refers to a positive integer not divisible by another primary integer (without a remainder) except by itself and by 1" (Shanahan & Shananhan, 2008, p. 52). They also stressed the importance of knowing symbols. Since variables change their meanings, they pose special problems. One mathematician memorized the variables before reading so that he would not have to look back to find the definitions and thus have his reading and thinking interrupted.

The Importance of Mastering Technical Vocabulary

Although we may conjure up images of numbers when we think of math, this content area also introduces a number of technical terms. In a unit on geometry, for instance, students need to know such words as *angle, protractor, polygon, quadrilateral, pentagon, hexagon, octagon, perimeter, area, parallelogram, circumference, radius, volume, space,* and *figure.* Learning and being able to automatically apply key technical terms is an essential skill in math. For instance, to understand what a ray is, students need to know how it differs from a line and a line segment. They also need to have had enough exposure to the terms so that when they hear them or see them they will immediately know how to apply them. If students have to stop and think about the meanings of key terms, this hesitation may hinder their understanding of a new concept or problem that uses the terms. Unless students have a firm grasp of the meaning of the term *ray,* they will have difficulty with the following definition: "An angle is formed by two rays with the same endpoint. The endpoint is called the vertex of the angle" (Globe Fearon, 2000, p. 340). Without automatic knowledge of the term *ray,* students will be hindered as they follow directions for using a protractor: "Read the number of degrees where the second ray crosses the protractor. Use the scale that reads 0 degrees" (Globe Fearon, 2000, p. 342).

CHECKUP

1. What can be done to foster the development of technical vocabulary in math?

Reading Word Problems

Word problems pose special difficulties for students. In addition to requiring careful reading and the ability to translate a series of written directions into mathematical operations, math problems also require knowledge of specialized symbols and technical vocabulary. In one study, about one third of the errors made by low-achieving math students were, in fact, reading problems. Students were simply unable to decode or understand critical words or phrases (O'Mara, 1981).

Solving Problems

What literacy skills are involved in reading the following explanation for solving equations with more than one operation?

USING TECHNOLOGY

NCTM Standards nctm.org /standards Lists NCTM math standards.

CCSS

Common Core State Standards for Mathematics www .corestandards.org/assets/CCSSI_M ath%20Standards.pdf Lists Common Core math standards

CCSS

Interpret words and phrases as they are used in a text, including determining technical, connotative, and figurative meanings, and analyze how specific word choices shape meaning or tone.

USING TECHNOLOGY

National Council of Teachers of Mathematics www.NCTM.org Provides a wealth of material about the teaching of math, including a downloadable copy of math standards, a variety of sample lesson plans, and video clips of exemplary lessons that demonstrate how standards may be implemented.

English Language Learners

Because of the universality of math symbols, ELLs may do well with computations, but, because of their unfamiliarity with some English terms, have difficulty with math problems and explanations given in their math texts. You might post key math terms in both English and the students' native language.

To solve equations involving more than one operation, do the following steps:

1. First undo any addition and subtraction.
2. Then undo any multiplication or division.

Solve for x. $2x + 5 = 15$

Step 1: First undo the addition with subtraction. $\qquad$ $2x + 5 - 5 = 15 - 5$

Subtract 5 from both sides. $\qquad$ $2x = 10$

Step 2: Then undo the multiplication with division. $\qquad$ $2x/2 = 10/2$

Divide both sides by 2. $\qquad$ $x = 5$

Step 3: To check, replace the variable in the equation with your answer.- $\qquad$ $2x + 5 = 15$

$\qquad$ $(2 \times 5) + 5 = 15$

$\qquad$ $10 + 5 = 15$

$\qquad$ $15 = 15$

The solution to the equation $2x + 5 = 15$ is $x = 5$. (Globe Fearon, 2000, p. 406)

USING TECHNOLOGY

The Math Forum http://mathforum.org /students/index.htm Provides practice with problems and puzzles.

Because each word is essential, students must be able to read and follow directions with 100 percent accuracy. They must be able to read and know the meaning of *undo*, *operation*, *equation*, *variable*, and *replace*. They must also be able to monitor for meaning. They need to know when they are not able to follow directions because they have forgotten a part of the directions or have skipped a step. Monitoring for meaning also means that they have to check the math as well as the reading to make sure that the results of their operations make sense from a math point of view. Students must be able to use repair strategies if comprehension fails. Repair strategies involve rereading or using the example to check on the meaning of the directions. Retention is also involved; students must understand and remember the steps so that they can apply them to new problems.

Solving two-step word problems involves a more complex reading process. What literacy processes might a student use to solve the following word problem?

The cost to rent a car is $35 per day plus a fee of $20. Mr. Hillwig rented a car for $195. For how many days did he rent the car?

Struggling Readers

Analyze problems students are expected to solve and note at what point they might have difficulties. For instance, ask, Will they be able to read all the words and understand what is being asked?

Students need to know what information is given and what they are asked to solve for. Because reading is difficult for them, poor readers may just abstract the numbers from the problem without carefully reading it. Students need to focus on cost per day as the rate and realize that this is the figure that is divided and that a fee is referring to an initial payment. They also need to be able to translate the word problem into a series of steps. There are a number of systems for solving word problems. One such system is Read, Reread, Plan, Do, Check (Globe Fearon, 2000).

Read first to get an overview.

Reread more carefully to see what you need to find out.

For how many days did Mr. Hillwig rent the car?

Plan what you need to do.

Write an equation to solve the problem.

Cost + rate per day $\times$ number of days rented + fee

Put in the numbers from the problem.

Solve for cost.

Do the plan.

$$\text{Cost} = (35 \times d) + 20$$
$$195 = (35 \times d) + 20$$
$$195 - 20 = (35 \times d) + 20 - 20]$$
$$175 = 35 \times d$$
$$175/35 = (35 \times d)/35$$
$$5 = d$$

Check to see whether your answer makes sense.

From a literacy standpoint, students should also reread the problem to make sure that they were solving for the variable that the problem was asking for and that they followed the necessary steps and made all the correct substitutions. One method of helping students learn how to solve problems is to provide them with model problems that have been solved. To get the best results with this activity, alternate or interleave studying of model problems that have already been solved with solving problems on their own (Pashler et al., 2007). Students who alternate between studying solved sample problems and solving problems on their own do better than students who simply work a series of problems after having studied a series of similar problems. For homework, rather than having nine problems to solve, it would be more effective if students were given three sets that consist of a worked example and two problems to solve. Having the sample problem provides students with a guide that they are motivated to consider because it will help them solve their assigned problems. As students grow in expertise, they can spend more time working problems and less time studying them.

Building Metacognitive Awareness

Based on her work with students who had difficulty with both math and reading, Kresse (1984) recommends helping students become metacognitively aware of the processes that they use to solve word problems. This involves modeling the reasoning processes in think-alouds and gradually having students take over more of the procedure. The key is to have students become aware of their thought processes so they become better prepared to select the correct procedures.

Another procedure that helps students understand math problems is to have them create their own. When students compose their own problems, they see how problems are constructed. In the beginning, students might simply change textbook problems, but with increased understanding and confidence, they can begin to compose their own. In one study, the teacher gave the students, who were underachievers in math, the equation and the students created problems to fit the equation (Ferguson & Fairburn, 1985). The students then solved each other's problems and made significant progress in their ability to solve math problems.

CHECKUP

1. What techniques can be used to develop the ability to solve word problems?

Using Communication Skills to Foster Understanding

Just as discussion fosters learning in history, language arts, and other highly verbal subject matter areas, it also promotes learning in math. To foster increased understanding of the math text and also to help students learn the skills and vocabulary needed to comprehend math texts, discuss portions of the text with them. Types of questions you might pose include those that probe understanding of the concepts or operations being discovered, those that help students make connections between current concepts and past concepts, those that probe students' ability to apply the concepts or operations to other

 Struggling Readers

Noting that his geometry class composed of struggling students were falling for "misconceptions, pitfalls, traps," high school teacher Jason Mumford arranged for students to meet in small groups and discuss proofs as problems to be solved. With the help of Mumford's guidance when needed, the students were able to reason their way to appropriate solutions and achieve a basic understanding. As one student explained, "I finally got it." (Langer, 2011, p. 103)

Discussions can help students become aware of the processes they use to solve problems.

Source: Image Source/Alamy.

situations, along with metacognitive questions that probe students' awareness of their understanding of what they are reading and steps they might take to promote increased understanding. Questions used by Leah Casados (Tanner & Casados, 1998), a high school math teacher, included the following:

- What possible applications can you see for the law of sines and cosines?
- What are some different methods you can use to rotate a point 180 degrees and find the coordinates of the image?
- Are there any new ideas in this section? Is there anything in this section you have seen before?
- What steps/procedures did the author recommend following?
- What steps did you actually use? (p. 345)

The discussions helped. As Casados commented, discussion showed me that my students can become insightful, logical mathematical problem solvers by talking through ideas and taking ownership of them (Tanner & Casados, 1998, p. 396). Through discussion, students began articulating math concepts, started using the vocabulary of math, and shared strategies that they used to solve problems.

Using Writing to Foster Understanding

Writing can also be a valuable learning tool in mathematics. Through writing, students can reflect on and organize their thoughts and even simplify problems. Some types of writing that have been used to foster understanding include restatement and brief summaries. Restatement writing can be used to rephrase a problem in simpler terms, as in the following example.

Original: Find three positive, even, consecutive integers such that the product of the two smallest integers is equal to two-thirds the product of the two largest integers.

Rewrite: Find three even whole numbers. They must be in a row, like 2, 4, 6 or 10, 12, 14. If you multiply the two smallest and get your answer, it should be the same number as when you multiply the two largest and then take 2/3 times that answer. (Havens, 2001)

The rewrite could be a whole-class, group, or individual project. Through rewriting, students must achieve and demonstrate a concrete understanding of both the technical vocabulary and the math processes needed to solve the problem.

One-sentence summaries have also been shown to be helpful. Before turning in an assignment, students compose a one-sentence summary of a key concept, process, or term. If students are writing about a process that involves a series of steps, they can use a frame that contains the words *begins with*, *continues with*, and *ends with*:

Adding a series of decimal numbers *begins with* your writing the numbers one right under the other with the decimal points in each number lined up, *continues with* your adding the numbers in columns as if they were whole numbers, and *ends with* your bringing the decimal point straight down from the numbers above into the answer. (Havens, 2001)

As they read, students can use sticky notes to rewrite procedures or problems in their own words, devise their own examples, note where they are having difficulty and why, draw a comparison with materials read previously or in another source, or use pictures to illustrate concepts (Havens, 2001).

Learning Logs

Learning logs can be used to provide students an opportunity to reflect on their understanding of math. Students can explain processes they used to solve problems, reflect on what they have learned, or raise questions about puzzling concepts or procedures. Learning logs help students to become more thoughtful in math and to become more aware of their cognitive processes. When they are aware of their cognitive processes, students are better able to make full and effective use of them. The teacher can read the learning logs to gain insight into the students' understanding.

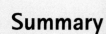 **Struggling Readers**

By checking learning logs periodically, you can get a sense of students' ongoing understanding of key concepts and procedures and take corrective steps when students indicate that they are confused.

Building on What Students Know

Through analyzing class discussions and students' writing, teachers can discover what students know about a topic and plan accordingly. Students are required to learn a variety of strategies for solving math problems and they also must learn when and where to use those strategies and which ones work best for them. When assessing students, note not only their grasp of math processes, but also the cognitive and language strategies they use to solve problems. Are they able to sift through the information to ascertain the major question being asked? Are they able to apply problem-solving skills? Are they able to monitor their work from both a math and a reading point of view?

C H E C K U P

1. How might discussion and writing be used to develop understanding in math?

Developing Higher–Level Thinking Skills

One way to help students develop higher-level thinking skills is to provide them with problems that can be solved in more than one way and then ask them to explain their reasoning processes. Here is an example of a problem: I have chickens and rabbits. I count 50 heads and 120 legs. How many of each type of animal do I have? Observe students as they discuss solutions in their groups (Oliver, 2009).

Summary

Reading in the sciences is inquiry based and constructive. Students construct their understandings based on what they know. Written in complex, precise language, science texts are challenging to read. Life science texts are primarily descriptive/technical. Physical sciences are more conceptual and theoretical. Both life and physical science texts contain a large number of technical terms. Science material is cumulative, with concepts building on each other. Reading in small doses, using visual aids, and checking one's comprehension through summarizing and self-questioning are recommended. Teachers can foster conceptual understanding by using think-alouds, building on what students know, using well-planned questioning techniques, and developing strategies such as using imagery.

Having created their own intuitive understanding of the way the world works, students often construct misconceptions. Teachers need to be aware of students' misconceptions, address them directly, and replace them with accurate concepts that students find acceptable because they see the logic of them and the concepts are credible. Students also need to be taught higher-level thinking skills so they can evaluate scientific information.

Science texts frequently require students to solve problems. Before being asked to solve problems, students should have conceptual understanding of the topic. Strategies for solving problems should be modeled, discussed, and practiced.

Learning math is also a constructive process in which students build understanding based on their prior knowledge and personal perspective. Word problems pose special difficulties for students. In addition to requiring careful reading and the ability to translate a series of written directions into mathematical operations, math problems also require knowledge of specialized symbols and the technical vocabulary of math. Students should be taught strategies for solving problems. Instruction should foster metacognitive awareness so students can better control their cognitive processes and also create problems of their own.

Both discussion and writing can be used to help students become more aware of their thought processes and of effective problem-solving strategies. In restatement writing, students rephrase a problem in simpler terms. Students can use sticky notes to rewrite procedures or problems in their own words, devise their own examples, note where they are having difficulty and why, draw a comparison with materials read previously or in another source, or use pictures to illustrate concepts. Learning logs can be used to provide students with an opportunity to reflect on their understanding of math.

Just as in science and math, career-technology subjects require the reading of complex texts. Skills and strategies taught should match the nature of each specific subject area.

Through analyzing class discussions and students' writing, teachers can discover what students know about a topic and plan accordingly. To help students attain conceptual knowledge, it is essential to find out what students know about a topic and then build on that knowledge. Metacognition is also an essential element in conceptual understanding. Students need to be aware of what they know and what they need to have clarified.

Reflection

Return to the Anticipation Guide at the beginning of this chapter. Respond once again to the items. Did your responses change? If so, how and why? Which content area seems most difficult to read? Why? Why might a student with good general reading skills still have difficulty reading in the sciences or in math?

Extension and Application

1. Examine a text from one of the sciences or from physical education or career-technology area. What reading skills does the text require? Does the text have any suggestions for reading it effectively? If so, what are they?
2. Examine a math text. What reading skills does the text require? Does the text have any suggestions for reading it effectively? If so, what are they? What suggestions does the text have for reading and solving word problems? Try out the suggestions. How easy to use and effective are they?
3. Every day for a week, read a portion of a challenging math, science, or career-technology text. In a journal or learning log, note the strategies you use, the difficulties you encounter, and how you deal with these difficulties.

Go to Topic 4: Writing, Topic 5: Comprehension, and Topic 6: Vocabulary in the MyEducationLab (www.myeducationlab.com) for your course, where you can:

- Find learning outcomes for Writing, Comprehension, and Vocabulary along with the national standards that connect to these outcomes.
- Complete Assignments and Activities that can help you more deeply understand the chapter content.
- Apply and practice your understanding of the core teaching skills identified in the chapter with the Building Teaching Skills and Dispositions learning units.
- Examine challenging situations and cases presented in the IRIS Center Resources.

Go to the Topic A+RISE in the MyEducationLab (www .myeducationlab.com) for your course. A+RISE® Standards2Strategy™ is an innovative and interactive online resource that offers new teachers in grades K–12 just-in-time, research-based instructional strategies that:

- Meet the linguistic needs of ELLs as they learn content.
- Differentiate instruction for all grades and abilities.
- Offer reading and writing techniques, cooperative learning, use of linguistic and nonlinguistic representations, scaffolding, teacher modeling, higher order thinking, and alternative classroom ELL assessment.
- Provide support to help teachers be effective through the integration of listening, speaking, reading, and writing along with the content curriculum.
- Improve student achievement.
- Are aligned to Common Core Elementary Language Arts standards (for the literacy strategies) and to English language proficiency standards in WIDA, Texas, California, and Florida.

CHAPTER 12

Using Technology,
Trade Books, and Periodicals
in the Content Areas

For each of the following statements, put a check under "Agree" or "Disagree" to indicate your opinion. Discuss your responses with classmates.

	Agree	Disagree
1. Trade books do a better job of presenting information than most textbooks do.	___	___
2. Most students are unable to use the Internet well to explore topics.	___	___
3. The Internet should be used sparingly in content classes.	___	___
4. The Internet should be used only under close supervision.	___	___
5. Periodicals are underused and undervalued in most content area classes.	___	___

H ow do you know what you know? All of us have learned from textbooks and lectures, but what are some other sources of information that have been valuable to you? How has the Internet added to your store of knowledge? How have you used the Internet to explore a topic or acquire information? How about periodicals and trade books? Did any of your teachers use periodicals in the classroom? Did any use trade books? How might these sources of information—technology, trade books, and periodicals—be used to foster increased knowledge in your content area?

Using What You Know

The Promise of Technology

Without leaving their desks, today's students can watch President Kennedy give his inaugural address, listen to songs of a whale, check up on the space station, view photos of the Civil War, read diaries of families heading West, talk to an expert on DNA, take a virtual tour of a rain forest, communicate with a friend across the street or across the continent, read any one of several million books, or read and print out any one of 2 million magazine articles. Through the Internet, today's students have access to a vast, rapidly expanding storehouse of information. They also have at their fingertips an array of tools for communicating. Through the Internet, they can present reports not just to classmates but also to other students around the world. Depending on their ability to use today's tools, they can complement their words with film clips, photos, music, speeches, and artwork. As Bransford et al. (2001) note,

> The new technologies provide opportunities for creating learning environments that extend the possibilities of "old"—but still useful—technologies—books; blackboards; and linear, one-way communication media, such as radio and television shows—as well as offering new possibilities. Technologies do not guarantee effective learning, however. Inappropriate uses of technology can hinder learning—for example, if students spend most of their time picking fonts and colors for multimedia reports instead of planning, writing, and revising their ideas. And everyone knows how much time students can waste surfing the Internet. (p. 206)

Increasing Importance of Digital Literacy

Recently, the venerable *New York Times* reduced the size of its pages. My hometown newspaper, *The Hartford Courant*, which is said to be the oldest continuously published paper in America, reduced both the size and the number of its pages. It is now a thin version of its former self. Figuratively and literally, print media is shrinking. The way we consume and produce information is undergoing a drastic change. Use of the Internet and other forms of digital communication is increasing, whereas TV viewing and newspaper reading are decreasing. Books, articles, maps, and other print and graphic materials are being digitized at a rapid pace. It has been predicted that by the year 2017 most scholarly articles will be available to anyone who has an Internet connection (Joint Information Systems Committee, 2008).

Although sometimes known as New Literacies, digital literacy relies heavily on the old literacies of activating prior knowledge, previewing, inferring, summarizing, and evaluating. However, as Coiro (2009) notes, online reading requires more complex applications of offline skills. There are some excellent offline readers who struggle when reading online. Online literacy requires the ability to "formulate online questions effectively; to generate effective search terms; to evaluate critically the relevancy, reliability, and stance of website information; to integrate information from multiple sources; and to use one or more online communications tools to share a response with others" (p. 447). Being adept navigators, adolescents may give the appearance of being competent Internet users; however, they tend to "power browse." "They scan through the site rapidly, glancing over a few pages, but not doing any 'real reading.'" (Joint Information Systems Committee, 2008). They also have difficulty planning a search. "There is no evidence in the serious literature that young people are expert searchers" (Joint Information Systems Committee, 2008, p. 22).

USING TECHNOLOGY

Thorough coverage of all areas of online learning, ranging from locating information to using it ethically is provided by the 21st Century Information Fluency Project (21CIF) http://21cif.com/aboutus/index.html. Many of CIF's resources are free, but some require a subscription.

Young people had difficulty creating search terms before the Internet and still do. Students need skills in creating search terms together with an understanding of how the Internet works. They may have difficulty creating search terms because they have little knowledge about a domain. They may not know which synonyms to use or may not be able to translate natural language into a search query. Students spend little time evaluating information. One group believed that if the site was indexed by Yahoo, it was authoritative. Because of their exposure to online media at an earlier age, today's adolescents may have developed parallel processing skills needed for multitasking. However, the "wider question is whether sequential processing abilities, necessary for ordinary reading, are being similarly developed" (Joint Information Systems Committee, 2008, p. 18).

Today's students, having grown up in a high-tech era, seem to have an almost innate grasp of digital tools and are sometimes referred to as "digital natives." However, they often lack the life experience and cognitive processing skills needed to make effective use of these skills. As Stephens and Ballast (2011) comment, "Digital natives are accustomed to using Facebook and Wikipedia, for instance, but these young writers may not have the social skills to communicate with clarity. In a time when teachers feel they are competing with games systems, iPods, and cell phones, it is comforting to know that you still play an important role in an adolescent's education" (p. 73). The teacher's role is even more important than in the past. Given the widespread usage of **Web 2.0** tools, chances are your students' writing will have a real impact on others, so it's more important than ever that students learn how to express themselves effectively—and that they have something of significance to say.

Today's literacy instruction needs to include systematic training in online literacy. As always, instruction should build on what students already know. Students need to understand how the strategies and skills they have been taught can be applied to online reading. Coiro (2009) suggests comparing online and offline reading, particularly text features. Point out features such as hyperlinks, digitized speech, embedded glossaries, and interactive questions that are present in online reading, but not offline reading. Also stress the increased importance of setting a purpose for reading, and reading to fulfill that purpose. It's easy to lose sight of one's purpose for reading when confronted with an excess of information. Skimming and scanning also take on a new importance. Think-alouds in which the teacher demonstrates and explains how she or he reads online are especially helpful. Students might also share their own effective techniques and strategies. An approach

■ **Web 2.0** refers to the use of the Internet to construct content and to interact with others on the Internet.

known as *Internet reciprocal teaching* uses a series of lessons to develop needed skills. For instance, students used the following reciprocal teaching strategies to investigate the reliability of Web sites (Internet Reciprocal Teaching, 2009).

Predict: Do you think your site is a reliable source of information?

Question: How do you know that a Web site has accurate information?

Clarify: How do you go about checking on the validity of Web sites?

Summarize: Which strategies were most useful? Which were not?

Although online literacy strategies can be taught separately, it is important that they also be embedded in the study of content topics so that students can see how the strategies are applied. Students should also be encouraged to share experiences that they have had with online literacy. They may have created their own Web sites, blogs, or **microblogs**, and it is highly likely that they participate in Facebook or other social networks, or they may have made YouTube videos. They may know of intriguing sites or be aware of useful software. One high school senior had helped his dad create daily blogs that included still photos as well as video clips during a 35-day, 8,000-mile cross-country trip.

Part of learning the new literacies is developing skills needed for collaborating. Online literacy lends itself to collaboration. Students bring their own unique skills, background knowledge, and perspectives to literacy tasks. Just as in literature circles, students need to learn to treat each other with respect and to adopt a cooperative, collaborative approach so that everyone contributes. In addition to learning traditional face-to-face collaborative skills, students need to learn how to use online communication tools in a respectful, cooperative manner as they may be collaborating online with classmates and students in other schools and other lands. Finally, students need to learn how to use digital technologies ethically. They need to know about property rights, copying, citing sources, and using information and online tools in an ethical manner. Given the increased complexity of online reading, students should be encouraged to reflect on and evaluate their ability to engage in key digital literacy tasks. Students may need help locating information or navigating sources, and they may have difficulty evaluating the quality of information (Coiro, 2009). Through reflection, students can build on their strengths and shore up their weaknesses. A general goal is to build students' sense of self-efficacy in using online resources. Students who are confident and competent are likely to be more engaged and more successful.

A More Active Environment

Online literacy is more active than traditional literacies. Through choosing sites to visit and hyperlinks to click on, students are more involved in the reading process. Students also are creators. They prepare entries for MySpace or Facebook, use Ning to start a social network group, produce presentations for YouTube or SchoolTtube, or create **blogs**, **wikis**, or their own Web pages. Technology can be used to enliven and extend traditional topics and to deepen students' learning. It can also motivate students who are disengaged. In their junior high literacy lab, O'Brien, Beach, and Scharber (2007) have used technology to motivate students to undertake and successfully complete projects that require extensive reading and writing. "Rather than considering technologies and innovation as replacements for more traditional instruction and learning, the technologies provide more effective ways to engage students" (p. 488). In addition, "the technologies enhance teaching and learning by providing access to media and enabling students to use various modalities

CCSS

Use technology, including the Internet, to produce and publish writing and to interact and collaborate with others.

 USING TECHNOLOGY

School Tube www2.schooltube .com
Provides teachers with channels that they and their students can use to upload and share videos. Has links to a number of resources, such as royalty-free music and graphics along with suggestions for creating videos.

■ **Microblogs** are brief blogs. "Tweets," as Twitter's microblogs are called are limited to 140 characters. Microblogs are used to send updates or concise comments

■ **A blog** (a combination of the words web and log) is a Web site on which the creator periodically adds content, with the latest content being placed first.

■ **A wiki** is a Web site which contains a database of pages that can be easily edited by visitors. For some wikis, content can be freely added. For moderated wikis, content is reviewed before being edited.

Exemplary Teaching

Using Wikis

Students at Westwood Middle School share their writing through wikis. Instead of writing for an audience of one, the students write for each other by posting their wikis. Students like the wikis because they can post their work immediately and get swift feedback from a variety of fellow students. In a sense, wikis increase participation. Students who might be reluctant to read their work in class don't mind posting on the wiki. As teacher Neil Kulick comments, "'The wiki is an equalizer in classroom participation, Everyone has a role. It's a way to showcase their comments and their give-and-take in a medium they take to like a duck to water" (Bolton, 2009). Wikis have had a lasting effect on the students' writing: They continue to post on the wiki site even after completing the course.

USING TECHNOLOGY

Google Search www.google.com /support/websearch/bin/answer.py?hl= en&answer=1095407 By using an advanced Google search, users can select articles that are estimated to be basic, intermediate, or advanced. Basic is about a middle school level.

to explore and publish ideas" (O'Brien & Dubbels, 2009, p. 488). For instance, in a lesson plan entitled "Using Microblogging and Social Networking to Explore Characterization and Style," students used a host of technology tools, including tweets (http://twitter.com/) and Ning to trace the development of characters, examine writing style, and share their findings while reading Jane Austen's *Emma* (Linder, 2009). After discussing how to write tweets, students sent tweets to each other as though they were characters in the novel.

Efficient Use of Internet Resources

One problem with using the vast resources of the Internet is locating and keeping track of pertinent information. A key skill that fosters handling information efficiently is tagging. In a sense tagging is an adaptation of categorizing that is a valuable Web 2.0 tool. Tagging is a keyword or phrase used for labeling a Web site, a blog, a video, or any other item. Students use tags when they conduct searches and devise tags when they identify information that they wish to retrieve or create content for the Internet. A number of Web sites allow users to create tags for their contributions.

The basic purpose of tags is to direct searchers to relevant content. Creators of tags need to think of what key words searchers might look under and use these to provide tags. Tags need to have the right level of specificity. Tags that are too general will yield too many hits. Tags that are too specific will yield too few. Tags should also be accurate. They should point to key concepts covered in the content.

CHECKUP

1. How is literacy changing?
2. What are some promises and problems resulting from the new literacies?
3. Why is tagging an important skill?

CCSS

Integrate and evaluate content presented in diverse formats and media, including visually and quantitatively, as well as in words.

■ **The Internet** is a network of interlinked but independent computer networks that allows the exchange of vast amounts of information.

Using the Internet in Content Classes

Web sites can be used to supplement and amplify textbook information. For instance, a middle school science text may contain just two pages of information on acid rain, but the Acid Rain Program (www.epa.gov/acidrain/what/index.html) sponsored by the EPA presents more than a dozen pages of information and describes nine easy-to-conduct experiments. Related Web sites are also noted.

Although the **Internet** has the potential to enrich learning in previously unimaginable ways, it demands a higher level of literacy. With vast sources of information available, much of it written on sophisticated levels, students must be able to decide what is important and useful for them. Students must also be able to synthesize large amounts of information and judge the reliability of information.

Social networking, e-mail, text messaging, and interactive sites require that students be able to communicate in writing and also have the ability to combine the visual and the verbal. Students need to be adaptable and able to learn new skills as today's technological wonders will soon be replaced. Just as students need to learn to read and write in the content areas, it is also essential that they have the ability to use technology to help them learn content and communicate what they have learned.

Source: Chris Pearsall/Alamy.

Carefully chosen Web sites can amplify information contained in texts.

Online Learning

Most states offer online courses. Florida Virtual School (http://flvs.net/), a leader in the field, offers a full range of secondary courses and memberhip in student organizations. Although designed originally for Florida residents, these courses are available to nonresidents for a fee. Private and charter schools also offer courses, as do state departments of education. Online courses vary in quality. Some are little more than correspondence courses, but others provide opportunities for interaction with classmates and the teacher. A number of universities offer courses for free. Through its Open Courseware (http://ocw.mit.edu/OcwWeb/hs/home/home/index.htm), MIT offers a wide range of courses and provides demonstrations on a number of topics, such as atomic physics and quantum effects, electromagnetism, and fluid mechanics.

Meanwhile, blended or hybrid courses are increasing in popularity (Schulte, 2011). Blended courses combine instruction by a live teacher with online learning. Through online learning, students can move at their own pace, spending more or less time on a topic or skill depending on their rate of learning. However, blended courses also have the benefit of a teacher to provide guidance, lead discussions, clarify confusions, help with goal setting, and foster higher-level thinking. According to recent research, the teacher is a key element in online learning (Means, Toyama, Murphy, Bakia, & Jones, 2010). Although students did slightly better when provided online instruction than they did with face-to-face instruction, they made almost twice the gains when provided with blended instruction. Blended learning was more effective than learning that was strictly online or strictly face-to-face.

CHECKUP

1. What role is technology, and especially the Internet, playing in content area instruction?

Teaching Students How To Use the Internet More Effectively

The Internet has been described as the greatest library in the world, but one in which all the books have been tossed onto the floor. The information is there, but it can be hard to find and overwhelming. Typing in key words such as *Martin Luther King* or *diabetes* can turn up thousands of sites. Mixed in with excellent sites are sites of limited value or too advanced for students.

USING TECHNOLOGY

A thorough but easy-to-understand explanation of techniques for searching on the Web is World of Searching at www.worldofsearching.org

Although students may be as digitally savvy as their teachers, or even more so, they may not know how to conduct an efficient search. Before embarking on lessons about how to do an Internet search, find out what students know about searching and which techniques they use. You might have them map out their search procedures by having them list the steps they take or snap screen shots of the steps (Mills, 2010). Use students' knowledge of search procedures as a starting point so that you build on what they know. An efficient search starts with a careful delineation of the topic and the questions the student hopes to answer and then moves to a determination of whether the information obtained is relevant and reliable. Whether the topic is assigned or selected, the student writer must formulate a thesis statement or question to be answered. With novice writers, a key skill is narrowing the topic so that it has reasonable limits. A student interested in the development of the automobile, for instance, might limit her topic to concept or prototype cars. On reflection, she might decide to focus on current concept cars as a way of predicting what the cars of the future might look like. Her question might be: What are the main features of current concept cars?

Selecting a Search Engine

Using Indexes

Search engines come in two forms: indexes and directories. After establishing a topic and a search question, the next step is to decide which search tool to use. Most search engines compile information in the form of indexes of key words arranged in alphabetical order. Directories, on the other hand, arrange information by categories. **Indexes** are more complete and up to date and so are used more frequently. The two most popular index search engines are:

> Google: www.google.com
>
> Yahoo: http://search.yahoo.com
>
> Google and Yahoo also have extensive directories.

Using Directories

Because their sites are arranged by categories, **directories** are better organized and less cluttered than indexes, but may not contain as many items. Directories are searched by examining and clicking on category names and are arranged in hierarchical fashion. For instance, in Yahoo's Directory (http://dir.yahoo.com), the topic *Auroras* is listed under *Astronomy*, which is listed under *Science*. Directories are most useful when a student wants to explore an area, but isn't sure what the area contains. A student who is planning a paper on *Insects* but isn't sure which one might click on *Insects* and see which ones are listed.

Goggle (www.google.com/dirhp?hl=en) can also be searched by category. Broad categories such as Art, Business, Health, and Reference are broken down into subcategories. Under Reference, Books are listed, under Books, Young Authors are listed, Under Young Authors, the writer Avi is listed. Additional directories can be found at www.dmoz.org/Kids_and_Teens/Directories.

Using Periodical and General Reference Searches

Computerized searches of periodicals and general references that include the text so that students can view the references and obtain the articles are also available. One such service is Infotrac, which has several versions designed specifically for students. The general

---

■ **A search engine** is a program used to search the Web.

■ **Indexes** are search engines that list Web sites alphabetically by key word. Searches are conducted by electronic devices.

■ **Directories** are search engines that organize Web sites by category. Some directories are put together by humans.

student edition contains nearly 9 million articles (www.gale.cengage.com/pdf/facts/itstu .pdf). Libraries subscribe to the service and then offer it to patrons. Patrons use their library bar codes or password to access the services from their home or school computer.

Subject Databases

Many school and public libraries subscribe to general and subject-specific databases. Directed especially to secondary students, the subject database Teen Health and Wellness (www.thwrlra.com) [Rosen] covers such areas as Nutrition; Mind, Mood, and Emotions; Eating Disorders; Friendship and Dating; Drugs and Alcohol; Green Living; and Fast Foods. Articles are about 6,000 words long. The database provides links to additional resources and sources as well as related topics. The database has an instant translator, which can translate articles into more than 50 languages; interactive polls and quizzes to keep users engaged; and an MLA citation generator. It is also aligned with state standards. Because Teen Health and Wellness offers topics of particular interest to teens and has a high-interest, teen-friendly format, this might provide an engaging introduction to databases and their uses. Similar databases on science and social studies are available from Rosen. In addition, there are dozens of other subject-specific databases available from other providers. If schools or local libraries subscribe to this or similar databases, students can usually access it at home by using their library card number or some other sort of access code.

Helping Students Get Started

Before students start their searches, discuss their topics and the key questions that they will be asking. After students have established their questions, they should determine which key or concept words will enable them to obtain answers to their questions. For instance, a student interested in the cars of the future might frame her question as: What will tomorrow's cars be like? Possible key words include *cars*, *autos*, *concept*, *dream*, *experimental*, *prototype*, and *future*. A sample worksheet for searching the Internet is presented in Figure 12.1.

Once students have located sources of information, they need to decide which sources are useful. Living in the information age, this is one of the most important literacy skills in all content areas and in life. Without it, we are in danger of drowning in trivia. Discuss with students the importance of selecting material that provides answers to their questions. Show how you might use titles or brief annotations or quickly skim articles to decide whether a

USING TECHNOLOGY

CultureGrams http://culturegrams.com/ has an extensive database on countries, states, and Canadian provinces. Also has individual reports.

USING TECHNOLOGY

Strategy Tutor www.cast.org /learningtools/strategy_tutor/index .html Strategy Tutor is a free Web-based tool designed to help students read and conduct research on the Internet. It provides a dictionary, text-to-speech capability, helpful comprehension strategies, and a worklog where students keep track of their work. It also allows teachers to plan lessons, check students' work and provide assistance.

FIGURE 12.1
Internet Search Plans

What question do you want answered?
What will cars of the future look like?

What are the key words for your concept? What are synonyms for your key words?

Key Word	Synonym
car	auto, vehicle
concept	experimental, prototype, dream, futuristic

How will you word your question for the Internet?
(car *OR auto) AND (concept OR dream OR experimental OR futuristic OR prototype)

Hints: Put parentheses aound synonyms and join them with OR. Put AND between key words. Use an asterisk to signal a search for different forms of the words.

CCSS

Gather relevant information from
multiple print and digital sources,
assess the credibility and accuracy of
each source, and integrate the information while avoiding plagiarism.

source is appropriate. Show how you quickly reject sites that merely describe auto shows. If you are investigating current concept cars, show how you reject sources that talk about concept cars of the past, or how, when you are reading an article, you skip descriptions of past cars and focus on current concept cars. Narrowing the topic and the search makes this stage of the process easier because students do not have as much material to wade through.

In addition to assessing the source to see whether it contains pertinent information, students must also evaluate the source to see whether the information is trustworthy. Students should evaluate sources for authority, objectivity, reliability, timeliness, and cover-age (Kentucky Virtual Library, 2002). To assess authority, students must ask, "Who is the author?" On some Web sites, the author is not identified. The site may have been put up by an organization, and the author's name may not be provided. The student must also ask, "What are the author's credentials?" Students should look to see what the author's education and experience are. Some authors may be experienced writers, but may not have experience in the field they are writing about. People who are experts in one field some-times speak out in a field in which they have little or no expertise. To assess objectivity, the student must ask, "Is the author unbiased? Does the author have anything to gain by taking a particular standpoint?" One way to assess the objectivity of a site is to see whether it is a commercial site. Commercial sites tend to favor a point of view that profits their interests. The students might also look at the language used and note whether it seems to be fair. Are all sides of the issue presented? The student should also note the author's purpose. Is it to inform, entertain, or persuade? Advertisements, editorials, and political addresses are designed to persuade.

Students should also assess the accuracy of information. For instance, one Web source describes John Boole, the famous mathematician, as being English. Another says he was Irish. One way to verify information is to use more than one source or to use a highly reli-able source to check facts contained in Web sites or other sources of unknown reliability.

Depending on the nature of the topic, timeliness is a concern. The information in a just-published book may be two or more years old. Information in a newspaper or online sources may be just hours old.

CHECKUP

1. How can students use the Internet more effectively?

Internet Sites

General Sites

One approach to making use of the Internet's vast resources is to use central sites rather than key word searches (Leu & Leu, 2000). In the best central sites, the links have been screened so that they are of high quality and appropriate for students. Here are some recommended general sites.

ALA Great Sites for Kids: Compiled by members of the American Library Associa-tion. Has sites designated for middle school students.
www.ala.org/greatsites

BJ Pinchbeck's Homework Helper: The site has been expanded to cover the high school and college years.
www.bjpinchbeck.com

IPL2 Information You Can Trust: has a wide-range of resources. Included are Teen-Space that includes links to numerous sites arranged by content area, tips for search-ing the Internet, tips for writing terms paper, and tips for overcoming procrastination. Also has a Teen Poetry Wiki.
www.ipl.org

Florida Virtual School Library: Has a wide range of links to sites for secondary school students. Exceptionally complete. Warns that the Virtual Library does not control the sites' content, some of which could be objectionable to some users.
library.flvs.net/home.htm

Kid Info: Arranged by subject area and linked to many of the best educational sites online.
www.kidinfo.com/school_subjects.html

Library of Congress: Along with wide range of resources, has a special page for teachers that includes a listing of primary source materials and suggestions.
www.loc.gov/teachers

Subject-Specific Sites

Although many sites have a general utility, some are more subject specific. In history, for instance, sites that contain primary documents are especially helpful. However, students need instruction both in locating primary documents and in interpreting them in the context of the times in which they were written. In science, students need to learn to become more critical readers. With some sites making doubtful claims, especially in the fields of health and medicine, students need to be able to tell the difference between reliable and questionable information. Along with the increase in the amount of information available comes the responsibility of using it wisely.

CHECKUP

1. What are some of the resources on the Internet that can help the content area teacher?

Content Lessons That Make Use of Internet Sites

Math and science lessons that make use of materials on the Internet are listed on the Illuminations sections of the National Council of Teachers of Math site (www.NCTM.org). Science lessons using the Internet can be found at Science Netlinks (www.sciencenetlinks.com). For instance, in one block of lessons created by Habits of Mind (Lessons: 9–12, Adolescent Sleep), students integrate science, math, and technology to examine the arguments for and against changing the starting time for high school students based on the findings of several scientific research studies on sleep and school achievement (AAAS, 2011). The teacher can download and print out studies, or direct students to the sites so that they can read and analyze them.

As students read summaries of the studies, they use the following prompts to guide their reading.

1. What was the purpose of the study?
2. Who were the subjects of the study?
3. Describe the methods used.
4. Summarize the findings of the study.
5. What evidence is presented to support the findings?
6. How would you assess the logic of the argument presented? Explain your reasoning. (AAAS, 2011)

After reflection and discussion, students apply language arts skills by composing an editorial in which they express their opinions regarding high school starting times. In keeping with the requirements for writing an effective persuasive piece, they present what they believe is the strongest evidence to support their opinion, as well as arguments to refute what they perceive is the strongest evidence against their position. As an extension and application of statistical math skills, students survey others in their school and community to find out how they would feel about a later starting time for high school. Opinions of the various groups are compared by age, gender, and occupation.

The Web can also be used to foster a better appreciation of literature. Possible projects include using Web sites to gather historical, social, and cultural information about a literary movement or period. For instance, as part of a unit about Harlem Renaissance writers, students might gather additional information about artists and photographers or jazz and blues singers and other musicians of that period. Students might also research the history of Harlem and gather photos of the time period, beginning with the Web site Harlem 1900–1940 at www.siumich.edu/CHICO/Harlem/tex/teachers.html (Claxton & Cooper, 2000). Students might work in small groups to investigate aspects of the topic and produce a Web site that displays the results of their efforts. In addition, the Harlem Renaissance project could be a joint venture for the history and English teachers.

With its riches of information and opportunities for collaboration, the Internet lends itself to inquiry projects (Bruce & Bishop, 2002). Inquiry begins with asking questions and includes investigating solutions, gathering information, discussing discoveries, and reflecting on newfound knowledge. On the Inquiry Page (http://inquiry.uiuc.edu), teachers and other professionals work together to create inquiry units. These units can be used as they are or revised. Many of the units are still being created. Visitors to the site are invited to add their expertise.

Thinkfinity

Thinkfinity provides the following free, Internet-based content across academic disciplines.

- Econedlink
  www.econedlink.org
  Provides lessons and a listing of high-quality links to economics sites, a guide for using the Internet to teach economics, and links to macroeconomic data.

- Edsitement
  http://edsitement.neh.gov
  Provides activities, lessons, and a listing of high-quality links to a wide array of sites in the areas of Art and Culture, Literature and Language Arts, Foreign Language, History, and Social Studies.

- Illuminations
  http://illuminations.nctm.org
  Provides math activities, lessons, a description of standards, and a lengthy listing of high-quality links to a wide array of math sites.

Exemplary Teaching

Using Technology to Bolster Learning

Chris Ludwig, a high school biology teacher at La Junta (Colorado) High School, uses laptops and a variety of other digital tools to bolster learning in his class (Ray, 2010). He uses Edmodo to share assignments and information. Edmodo is a microblogging system that maintains users' privacy and is designed for education. This fosters increased communication with students. More importantly, students have the tools to create digital content to complete assignments. Using Moodle, a course management system, Ludwig is able to more readily compose and deliver flexible assessments. Using their laptops and movie-making software such as Xtranormal and Domo Animate, students created animated cartoons that explained key concepts in the structure and function of muscles. They also made videos to explain various aspects of plant physiology. Students had to plan out their projects, create a story line to explain target concepts, and also create interesting but accurate dialogue. Summing up the value of laptops, Ludwig comments, "I think that students with laptops in class are more likely to contribute to class discussions and are able to engage course content in more meaningful ways. The most exciting change is the spontaneity and interactivity that laptops bring to classroom discussions."

- Read Write Think
  www.readwritethink.org
  Features an extensive listing of high-quality lesson plans in reading and the language arts. Under "Web Resources," it lists an extensive compilation of sites for students and teachers.

- Science NetLinks
  www.sciencenetlinks.org
  Science NetLinks provides a wealth of standards-aligned resources for K–12 science educators, including lesson plans, interactive features, and reviewed Internet resources.

- Xpeditions
  www.nationalgeographic.com/xpeditions
  Provides standards, activities, lessons plans, and maps for geography. Features a virtual museum that uses film clips to explore geographical concepts.

CHECKUP

1. What are some of the kinds of lessons offered on the Internet?
2. Which would be most useful to teachers in my discipline?

Safety in Cyberspace

In addition to providing valuable, worthwhile information, the Internet unfortunately also allows access to information and sites that are inappropriate and even harmful to students. The Internet can also be used to threaten or insult others and interfere with their work and privacy. Because of these factors, it is essential to put safeguards in place. Most schools now have acceptable-use policies and ask students and their parents to sign agreements by which they promise to abide by the school's policies. In addition, students should always be supervised when using the Internet. Some schools have taken the precaution of installing software that blocks objectionable sites or restricts access to the Internet.

Computer Software and Apps

In addition to providing a portal to the Internet, computers and other devices that provide access to the Internet are also widely used to run software. One of the most effective uses of software is as a learning or communication tool. Outstanding general software includes:

- Word processing software, such as Microsoft Word, which allows students to type and design reports
- Graphic organizer software, such as *Inspiration*, which allows students to create a variety of visual displays of data
- Presentation software, such as PowerPoint, which allows students to collect, organize, and manipulate data and prepare charts and graphs
- Spreadsheets such as Microsoft's Excel or Apple's Numbers (in iWorks), which allow students to organize and manipulate data.

In addition, there are hundreds of pieces of software that allow students to organize and manipulate data in specialized ways or provide simulations or carefully thought-out drill and practice. The Internet is also a rich source of tools, reference resources, and drill-and-practice programs. The richest supply of these programs comes in the form of Web applications (apps). Along with hundreds of games, **apps** include dictionaries, translators, calendars, news outlets, calculators, prep for AP exams, vocabulary builders, study aids, note taking aids, thesauruses, lab techniques, puzzles, search engines, and more. Apps can be activated on both computers and smart phones.

> ■ **Apps** is a short form for "applications" and refers to programs written for smart phone or computer use.

Exemplary Teaching

Using Technology

One teacher used a variety of media and technology to help students develop a deeper understanding of the office of President and some of the men who led the United States during the twentieth century. After watching the Discovery Channel School series *The Modern Presidency*, students in Michael Hutchinson's high school history classes researched one of the presidents who held office during the past century. They used both Internet sites and texts. In many instances, they were able to view film clips and examine primary documents. Students in senior classes used the presentation software PowerPoint to compose reports on the presidents they had studied. They also created a Web page to report their research. The reports were of such high quality that they have been used by other students who are studying the presidency. Presentations can be viewed at: www.vcsc.k12.in.us/staff/mhutch/modpres/mainpage.htm.

CHECKUP

1. What are some ways to use software and online tools in a content area class?

Using Sources of Professional Development for Teachers

One benefit of using technology is that teachers and students become learners together. Because the teacher is learning the new technology along with the students, the teacher can model how an experienced learner goes about obtaining and applying new skills. It also changes the nature of the teacher–student relationship from one in which the teacher is the dispenser of knowledge to one in which teacher and student are involved in a collaboration. This new relationship is often a self-esteem builder for students. Intrigued by the technology, some students may spend so much time with a topic or one aspect of technology that they learn more about it than anyone else, even the teacher, so they are in the position of being able to share their exclusive knowledge, sometimes for the first time (Bransford et al., 2001).

The Internet also provides teachers with a range of opportunities for professional development. Each major professional organization has a Web site, and these are excellent sources of information and encouragement. Many professional sites even have sample units and lesson plans, some of which are portrayed in film clips so that teachers can view segments of lessons.

The following are especially useful sites for professional development:

- International Reading Association
  www.reading.org
  Has many resources, including journals, books, position papers, reports on key topics, and lesson plans, podcasts, and other professional development activities.
- National Council of Teachers of English (NCTE)
  www.ncte.org
  Has many resources, including journals, books, position papers, reports on key topics, and NCTE Ning, a discussion group. NCTE also sponsors extensive online professional development.
- National Science Teachers Association
  www.nsta.org
  Has many resources including 32 Science Objects and Web Seminars. Science Objects are two-hour on line interactive inquiry-based content modules that help teachers better understand the science content they teach. NSTA Web Seminars are 90-minute,

live professional development experiences that use online learning technologies to allow participants to interact with national experts.

- National Council of Teachers of Mathematics
  http://nctm.org
  In addition to journals and papers, NCTM offers seminars and e-workshops. Also has Reflection Guides for key articles so they can be used in professional development discussions.

  - Math Forum
    http://mathforum.org
    Offers a wealth of problems and puzzles, online mentoring, research; team problem solving, collaborations; and professional development. Has an Ask Dr. Math feature in which students can pose questions.
  - TeacherLine
    www.pbs.org/teachers
    Offers more than 130 professional development courses in a variety of content areas.
  - iTunesU
    www.apple.com/education/itunes-u
    Contains a wide variety of lectures, educational film clips, labs, and sample lessons. Teachers can post information or whole lessons on iTunes U.

Using Trade Books in the Content Areas

In one U.S. history text, the Great Depression is covered in less than a page. Ireland's Great Famine and its impact on the United States are not covered at all. In a science text, Marie Curie is mentioned in passing. The reader is told of her important contributions, but there is little information on the brilliant, courageous scientist who should be greatly admired. With the information explosion, today's content area texts are more fact-packed than ever. There simply isn't enough room to explore topics in detail or to get a feel for what it was like to be jobless and have a family to support in the 1930s or to leave one's homeland for the promise of a better life in the United States, only to encounter signs that say, "No Irish Need Apply."

One solution to this problem is to use **trade books** in the classroom. Trade books can provide the depth of coverage missing in the core textbook. They can also bring ideas and people to life. Having more leeway than textbook writers, the authors of trade books can bring a richness of background, originality of style, and creativity that is often missing in textbooks. They can hook readers with interesting anecdotes and fascinating facts.

Trade books also offer another point of view. In fact, some trade books, such as a set of texts entitled *Perspectives*, are designed to portray a series of multicultural events and topics in U.S. history. In the *Perspectives on History* series (http://historycompass.com), American history is told from the perspective of people of color, ethnic minorities, poor whites, and women; as a result, the series provides a fuller description of key events in our history. History varies according to who's doing the telling. Immigration told from the immigrants' point of view will differ from immigration told from the perspective of those who faced the loss of jobs due to the influx of immigrants; this in turn will differ from the point of view of factory owners and railroad builders who used this fresh supply labor. Of course, the careful historian balances these perspectives.

From a comprehension point of view, contrasting perspectives leads to greater understanding and retention because it forces students to process information more deeply as they make comparisons and contrasts and attempt to synthesize information that is sometimes conflicting. From a social studies point of view, multiple perspectives bring students face to face with the work of the historian. Students are called upon to reconcile

FYI

The Literature for Youth Series (Scarecrow Press) assist students interested in exploring the literature dealing with key topics, such as World War II, the Great Depression, the Middle Ages, and Islam.

■ **Trade books** are books that are written for and sold to the general public and distributed through book stores and the libraries.

conflicting accounts. This introduces them to historical inquiry so that they "begin to understand and appreciate differences in historical perspectives, recognizing that interpretations are influenced by individual experiences, societal values, and cultural traditions" (National Council for the Social Studies, 1994, p. 22). As Palmer and Stewart (1997) note, "By using a variety of nonfiction trade books, students can explore a broad range of topics or examine a single topic in depth, while synthesizing information and applying critical reading/thinking skills" (p. 631).

In-Depth Concept Development

Trade books can also offer a greater depth of explanation. In textbooks, complex science concepts are often covered in a page or two. For instance, one high school biology text gave symbiosis less than a page of text. Trade books devoted to single concepts can develop them in depth and also explain the concepts in a more interesting and understandable fashion. In the *Science Concepts, Second Series*, the highly respected science writers Alvin and Virginia Silverstein and Laura Silverstein Nunn have written 14 sixty-four page books, each designed to develop one key concept—for instance, food chains, photosynthesis, and symbiosis. Woven into the explanation of each concept are interesting examples and little-known facts designed to maintain readers' interest. In the book on symbiosis, for example, notice how the authors entice readers into the text with intriguing questions and an interesting example of symbiotic behavior:

> Imagine a world where hungry sharks and tiny fish can live a peaceful existence together. How about man-eating crocodiles and tiny birds? These animal relationships may be hard to believe, but they actually occur. Some plants even have ants as bodyguards to attack intruders. In nature, there are many strange relationships where different kinds of animals, plants, and other organisms in the five kingdoms of life come together for the benefit of at least one partner. (Silverstein, Silverstein, & Nunn, 2008, p. 5)

The authors then explain how the honey guide, a small, delicate bird who likes honey but is unable to take honey from a beehive, finds honey and signals to the ratel, a member of the weasel family, who breaks open the nest and eats the bee grubs. The honey guide then eats the honey. The authors also explain how the honey guide is involved in two other relationships, one in which it uses bacteria in its intestine to help it digest food and the other in which it tricks other birds into hatching their eggs and rearing their young.

After creating reader interest and giving concrete examples of three kinds of symbiosis, the authors explain what symbiosis is and define the three major types. At this point, students are able to build the concept on the concrete example that the authors provided so that their understanding goes from the concrete to the abstract. With the help of many examples and interesting information, the rest of the text expands on the concept of symbiosis.

Trade books can even make a complex, abstract topic such as the periodic table both interesting and comprehensible. Along with explaining how gold is mined and some of the many interesting ways in which gold is used, *The Element: Gold* (Angliss, 2000) also discusses its special properties, including its location on the periodic table. The author also supplies an informative, easy-to-understand explanation of the periodic table. Other books in the *Elements* series investigate calcium, hydrogen, and magnesium.

Trade books that place concepts within the framework of a story have the power to make concepts both more understandable and more memorable. Based on carefully designed studies of how students learn content, Nuthall (1999) concluded that

> Our studies suggest that narratives provide powerful structures for the organization and storage of curriculum content in memory. Stories often contain a rich variety of supplementary information and connect to personal experiences, as well as being integrated and held together by a familiar structure. (p. 337)

USING TECHNOLOGY

HELP Read™ freeware is a program developed by the Hawaii Education Literacy Project (HELP) and distributed freely over the Internet at www.dyslexia.com/helpread.htm. This program uses a text-to-speech synthesizer and can read text files, Web pages, e-books, and text in the Windows clipboard.

Humanizing Learning

One of the goals of content area instruction is to lead students to think like a scientist, a mathematician, or an historian. Reading biographies of scientists can provide students with insight into the methods that scientists use. They also come to understand the social and historical context in which the discoveries were being made and the obstacles the discoverers had to overcome. For instance, *Fish Watching with Eugenie Clark* (Ross, 2000) is a fascinating account of the obstacles that Eugenie Clark overcame on her way to fame and accomplishments as one of the nation's best-known scientists. Readers are also introduced to methods of scientific experimentation and information about sharks and other fascinating sea creatures.

> Reading about the different experiments of scientists and their individual struggles with revolutionary ideas provides students with insights into the tentative nature of discovery. . . . Autobiographies, biographies, and fictionalized histories of scientists can serve to draw students into the personal world of the scientist and allow them to vicariously share the experience of exploration. (VanSledright & Frankes, 2000, p. 119)

An excellent source of biographies is *Profiles in American History* (Mitchell Lane Publishers). *Profiles* is an eight-volume series that provides an overview of key eras and events in American history, along with in-depth profiles of major historical figures. Each chapter focuses on one event, places it in historical context, and profiles two to seven figures who were major participants in the event. The series gives a human face to history.

Updated Information

Trade books can also offer information that is more up to date. Because of their expense, textbooks are often used five or even ten years before being replaced. Trade books can be used to update textbooks. Students who use trade books have the opportunity to learn more content than students restricted to a text (Guzzetti, Kowalinski, & McGTowan, 1992).

Motivation

Trade books can also be used to motivate students and launch a unit of study. As one social studies teacher comments, "Literature is a way to entice and engage students initially so they are motivated to discover the substance and the facts" (Lindquist, 1995, p. 89). Tarry Lindquist initiates a study of colonial life and the American Revolution by having her students read Scott O'Dell's (1980) *Sarah Bishop*:

> I like this book because both boys and girls find it engaging. It does a good job of bringing out multiple perspectives about the Revolutionary War and provides a setting for the more historically driven information the students will need to understand the Constitution and the Bill of Rights. (Lindquist, 1995, p. 88)

An excellent series for expanding on modern U.S. history is *A Cultural History of the United States: Through the Decades*. Each text tackles a decade in the twentieth century. Chapters are theme-based. The text devoted to the 1990s provides an overview of the 1980s and highlights key topics from the 1990s, such as changes in Washington, the end of the Cold War, violence in America, trends in family and education, gender and race conflict, pop culture, technology, medicine, and the environment.

Trade Books Can Be Easier to Understand

Written on a variety of levels, trade books can also be easier than textbooks. Recently, when I was taking a course in brain development, an area in which I had limited background and found the text tough going, I read a children's book on the subject and acquired some basic vocabulary and key concepts so that I was better able to cope with the assigned textbook. I have also used children's books to learn about the Internet, DNA, and other technical topics.

In its *English Explorer* series, Benchmark has a number of books on a wide range of science and social studies topics that are heavily illustrated and written on levels ranging from a first- to a fourth-grade level. These can be used to develop language skills and build background.

Rosen has an extensive catalogue of content-related books that range from a book on geometry's great thinkers to one on forensic science. For each book, correlation to state standards is available. Many of the books are written on a relatively easy level. ATOS readability levels are available for each book, and all of the titles are available as e-books.

Trade Books Can Be More Focused

Today's social studies textbooks attempt to convey not only the political history of the time but also the social and cultural history. As a result, students may lose sight of the essential events and movements. *The Drama of American History* series focuses on the political and institutional aspects so that students have a better sense of what happened and why. As the authors state, "The difference between this series and many standard texts lies in what has been left out. We are convinced that students will better remember the important themes if they are not buried under a heap of names, dates, and places" (Collier & Collier, 1998, p. 7). The texts are especially effective in establishing why events took place and what their impact was. This should make the information both more understandable and more memorable.

Trade Books Can Evoke Emotions

Using literature adds another dimension to the study of content area concepts. Most content areas involve the learning of information and concepts from a cognitive-logical point of view. Literature offers the possibility of complementing logic with emotion. Through literature, students can experience the feeling side of learning. Fred and Patricia McKissack, a husband-and-wife writing team, have created dozens of highly regarded books for young people in order to put some feeling into the events of the past. Fred McKissack explains,

> One of the reasons we write for children is to introduce them to African and African-American history and historical figures and to get them to internalize the information not just academically, but also emotionally. We want them to feel the tremendous amount of hurt and sadness that racism and discrimination cause all people, regardless of race (2001b).

Trade Books Can Make Concepts More Vivid

The writing in carefully chosen trade books is generally more vivid and can foster a deeper, more complete understanding. Helen Roney Sattler's (1995) figurative language creates a memorable picture of plate tectonics:

> The understanding of plate tectonics has helped scientists solve many of Earth's puzzling mysteries. Continents and oceans ride on the plates like passengers on a raft and move about Earth's surface. This explains how the Antarctic region could have had a warm climate at one time. It also explains why evidence of past glaciers is found in the Sahara Desert and why a coral reef lies under the topsoil of my backyard, five hundred miles from the nearest seashore. (p. 10)

DK (Dorling Kindersley) books such as Stephen Biesty's (1998) *Incredible Body* provide highly visual descriptions of the body's key systems. In *Stinkbugs, Stick Insects, and Stag Beetles and 18 More of the Strangest Insects on Earth* (Kneidel, 2001), the author uses the strange appearance and antics of twenty-one arthropods to convey key concepts about insects. *Grolier's New Book of Popular Science Series* (Grolier Educational) consists of six separate volumes or an online version that emphasize the basic information needed for scientific literacy. Although advertised for students in grades 5 and up, the books could provide a useful reference for older students who may have missed or forgotten key concepts.

Sources of Information about Trade Books

Titlewave (www.flr.follett.com) provides extensive information about books and other media, including interest level, readability level, book reviews, and awards that books have won. You can search by author, title, topic, grade level, subject area, curriculum standard, or even readability level. To get books on a certain level, include the readability level as part of your search. In a trial search, the database yielded 112 books on cells, with readabilities ranging from 4.3 to 8.6. A description of most books was provided, along with ATOS and Lexile levels and reviews and sample pages. Sample pages were especially valuable for judging the appropriateness of the book for a particular class or group of students. Books on this and most topics are available for struggling as well as advanced readers. A more complete listing of books is available from Google Books.

Google Books (http://books.google.com) lists millions of books, where they can be purchased and their prices, or where they can be borrowed from libraries. If the book is in the public domain or permission has been granted, a pdf version can be downloaded. Many of the books can be previewed. However, no reviews or readability levels are provided.

USING TECHNOLOGY

Center for the Study of Books in Spanish for Children and Adolescents http://csbs.csusm.edu/csbs/www.book.book_home?lang=SP features a recommended list of more than 3,000 books in Spanish. Books are listed by age, grade level, and country.

CHECKUP

1. What are some of the ways in which trade books can be used in content area classes?

Periodicals

Periodicals enable students to read about the latest space probe, new medicines, new inventions, national elections, and major events and issues in the nation and the world. They offer an excellent means for updating and complementing textbook content. Ebsco http://www2.ebsco.com/en-us/InfoProfs/k12schools/Pages/index.aspx lists more than 300 magazines that are frequently ordered by school libraries. Table 12.1 contains a list of periodicals produced specifically for schools and designed to foster learning in specific content areas.

In addition there are a number of online magazines of note.

In addition to news and special-interest periodicals produced for secondary school audiences, there are a number of general-interest online news sources. Three of the best known include:

- CNN.com
  www.cnn.com
  News, videos, in-depth reports, and other features. Can be read by text-to-speech features on most computers.
- The *New York Times* on the Web
  www.nytimes.com
  In addition to coverage of news and a variety of topics, it has links to video clips of news events.
- USA Today
  www.usatoday.com
  Has quiz features for some articles and links with Facebook, Reddit, Newsvine, Mixx, and other sites for sharing stories.

USING TECHNOLOGY

Newseum www.newseum.org/todaysfrontpages/default.asp Presents the front pages of approximately 800 newspapers from 80 countries. Good source for what's happening around the country and the world. Key events are archived so students can look at coverage of major events for the past ten years or so.

TABLE 12.1 **Social Studies Periodicals**

PERIODICAL	APPROPRIATE GRADES	CONTENT
Career World WR	7–12	Features descriptions of careers and advice on getting a job.
Current Events	6–10	Current events.
Junior Scholastic	6–8	Current events and general social studies topics.
News for You	High school & adult	News and general interest. Easy to read. At least one article on a 2–3 level.
New York Times Upfront	7–12	Current events, trends, and entertainment.
Teen Newsweek	6–10	Current events and general interest.

PERIODICAL	APPROPRIATE GRADES	CONTENT
Science Periodicals		
Current Health 2	7–12	Health.
Current Science	6–10	Various science.
World Science	7–10	General science.
Literature/Reading/Fine Arts Periodicals		
Action	7–12	Literature, current biographies. High-interest features. Easy to read: 3–5 reading level.
Literary Cavalcade	9–12	Classic and current literature and writing workshop.
Read	6–10	Literature selections, current issues, writing.
Scholastic Art	7–12	Art techniques, biography, and student art.
Scholastic Scope	6–8	Fiction, nonfiction, and poetry. Easy to read.

CHECKUP

1. What role might periodicals and supplementary materials play in content area classrooms?

Summary

Now that virtually all schools have Internet connectivity, today's teachers and students have access to rich resources. However, these rich resources demand a higher level of literacy.

Today's students must be better able to search for, select, assess, and synthesize large amounts of information and know how to combine the visual and the verbal in communication. To search the vast amounts of available information effectively, students must carefully formulate search questions and use strategies.

Both general and specific Web sites feature useful information and activities for a wide variety of topics. Unfortunately, the Internet also allows access to information and sites that could be harmful to students. Safeguards need to be put into place.

Computers are also widely used to run software. One of the most effective uses of software is as a learning or communication tool. Outstanding general tools include word processing software, graphic organizer creators, presentation software, and spreadsheet software. Apps, which can be run on computers or smart phones and other digital devices, offer a wide range of general and specific learning tools.

The Internet provides teachers with a range of opportunities for professional development. Each major professional organization has a Web site. Many professional sites even have sample units and lesson plans.

Trade books have a number of potential uses in the content areas. They offer other points of view, provide greater depth of development, humanize learning, supply updated information, and can provide motivation. In addition, trade books can be easier to understand, be more focused, add an emotional component to learning, and make science and other content areas more vivid.

Periodicals also offer an excellent means for updating and complementing textbook content. Online magazines offer the most current news and information. Databases of thousands of periodical articles are also available.

Reflection

Return to the Anticipation Guide at the beginning of this chapter. Respond once again to the items. Did your responses change? If so, how and why? What role might technology, trade books, and periodicals play in the teaching and learning of content area concepts? What new literacy skills must students learn in order to take full advantage of technology to help them learn content area material?

Extension and Application

1. Explore some of the Internet sites mentioned in this chapter. Maintain a file of useful Internet sites.
2. Start a database of titles of trade books that might be useful in the teaching of your content area.

3. Check out the site maintained by the professional organization for your subject matter area. What kinds of resources are available? How might you use these?

PEARSON
myeducationlab
Where the Classroom Comes to Life

Go to Topic 9: Integrating Technology in the MyEducationLab (www.myeducationlab.com) for your course, where you can:

- Find learning outcomes for Integrating Technology along with the national standards that connect to these outcomes.
- Complete Assignments and Activities that can help you more deeply understand the chapter content.
- Apply and practice your understanding of the core teaching skills identified in the chapter with the Building Teaching Skills and Dispositions learning units.

A+RISE

Go to the Topic A+RISE in the MyEducationLab (www.myeducationlab.com) for your course. A+RISE® Standards2Strategy™ is an innovative and interactive online resource that offers new teachers in grades K–12 just-in-time, research-based instructional strategies that:

- Meet the linguistic needs of ELLs as they learn content.
- Differentiate instruction for all grades and abilities.
- Offer reading and writing techniques, cooperative learning, use of linguistic and nonlinguistic representations, scaffolding, teacher modeling, higher order thinking, and alternative classroom ELL assessment.
- Provide support to help teachers be effective through the integration of listening, speaking, reading, and writing along with the content curriculum.
- Improve student achievement.
- Are aligned to Common Core Elementary Language Arts standards (for the literacy strategies) and to English language proficiency standards in WIDA, Texas, California, and Florida.

Evaluating Progress in the Content Areas

Evaluation is an integral part of content area learning. Evaluation is a judgment by teachers, students, parents, administrators, and the public as to whether instructional goals or standards have been met. It provides teachers with data so they can judge how well programs and individual students are doing and make changes as necessary. Self-evaluation gives students guidance so they can become more involved in their learning.

Using What You Know

What experiences have you had with evaluation? How was your schoolwork assessed in the content areas? Which assessments seemed to be the most effective? What role did assessment play in your learning?

Key Audiences for Assessment Data

The basic purpose of assessment is to provide feedback—an essential component for learning. Students need feedback to determine whether they are on the right track and to help clarify misunderstood information or procedures. Teachers need feedback so they can implement instruction based on students' current level of understanding. School boards and administrators need feedback to ascertain how well programs are working. The public needs feedback to evaluate how well local schools are doing.

Formative and Summative Assessment

Assessment can be thought of as being formative and summative. **Formative assessment** is ongoing assessment that can be used to plan lessons and offer additional instruction if needed. Formative assessment is often informal and can be done through observation, discussions, quizzes, or examination of lab reports and other assignments. Both individuals and groups are assessed. Frequent formative assessment fosters learning and transfer and teaches students the value of review (Bransford et al., 2001).

■ **Assessment** is the process of gathering data about an area of learning through tests, observations, work samples, or other means.

■ **Formative assessment** is ongoing, with the results of the assessment being used to make needed improvements.

Summative assessment occurs at the conclusion of a semester or unit of study. Its main purpose is to evaluate whether goals were reached. Because of its timing, summative assesment cannot be used to improve ongoing instruction, but might be used to rethink or replan future lessons. Summative evaluation can also be used by administrators and school boards to evaluate achievement over long periods of time. On a state and national level summative assessment can be used to assess the achievement of the nation's school children and to compare states or even nations with each other.

Combing characteristics of summative and formative tests is a type of test known as an "interim" test. Interim tests are often used to determine whether students are on track to reach key instructional goals or benchmarks or to predict how students will perform on the end-of-year state test or other high-stakes tests. They are given periodically: every quarter or month, for instance. Because they are given at intervals during the school year, they can be used to plan future instruction (Hamilton, Halverson, Jackson, Mandinach, Supovitz, & Wayman, 2009). Making use of technology, assessments for the Common Core State Standards will be given three times a year and will provide teachers with quick feedback so results can be used to plan instruction.

Embedded Assessment

Embedded assessment, which is a type of formative assessment, is built into instruction. For example, after being introduced to a concept, students discuss it. The teacher observes how well students grasp concepts and notes areas that need clarifying or expansion. As students are conducting lab experiments, for instance, the teacher observes how well they plan and implement their experiments and how familiar they are with lab procedures. Based on observations, the teacher provides on-the-spot help. In another example, after looking at rough drafts for an essay, the teacher notes common needs for the whole class or for groups of individuals and provides needed instruction. Learning logs, journals, exit slips, and portfolios also offer opportunities for ongoing assessment.

Assessing for Learning: Using Formative Assessments

The goal of assessing for learning is to provide all students with the skills and knowledge they need to succeed (Stiggins, 2006). Data is gathered on students and then instruction is provided based on what the assessment data reveals. The first step is to explain to students the standards they are expected to meet. The standards might need to be broken down into a series of subobjectives, or steps that will lead to meeting the standard. The standard is expressed in terms that the students can understand. For a writing standard, for example, students might be shown samples that meet the standard, so they have a clear idea of what is expected. Students are then assessed on an ongoing basis in relation to the standard to determine what they need to do to reach it. Assessments provide students with indicators of performance so they can monitor their progress. Self-assessment is also developed. Because formative assessments are geared to what students are learning, most students make substantial progress. And if they have difficulty, they are provided with whatever assistance is needed.

CHECKUP

1. What are formative, summative, interim, and embedded assessments?

2. What are some examples of formative and summative assessment?

3. How can formative assessment be used to foster learning?

■ **Summative assessment** is the final measure of progress toward meeting a goal.

■ **Embedded assessment** is a type of formative assessment in which assessment is a part of instruction.

Using Grade Portals for Formative Assessment

Assessment at Napa New Technology High School (California) includes content skills plus 21st Century skills. 21st Century skills consist of those capabilities necessary to be successful in today's and tomorrow's world. It means being well versed in core subjects such as English, reading or language arts, world languages, arts, mathematics, economics, science, geography, history, government, and civics. But students are also judged on 21st Century skills such as Creativity and Innovation, Critical Thinking and Problem Solving, Communication and Collaboration (Trilling & Fadel, 2009). Using the grade portal assessment system, which is a software program that allows continuous access by educators and students to assignments and assessments, teachers can check students' work on an ongoing basis (21st Century Skills, 2009a). In writing, for instance, they check students' initial drafts and provide suggestions for revision. For collaboration, they check to see how well students work with others. The teachers want to see what is going right and what is going wrong, so they can intervene if necessary. Feedback is put into a digital format known as a grade portal so students and teachers can refer back to it. A key to the effectiveness of the grade portal is that assessments are accompanied by suggestions for improvement, so that students know what they need to do in order to reach their goals.

The Starting Point

Evaluation starts with a set of goals. You cannot tell whether students are performing satisfactorily if you aren't quite sure what it is that you want them to learn. Calkins, Montgomery, and Santman (1998) recall observing a language arts teacher whose students were conducting an author study. The students were engaged in a number of interactive activities, but something seemed to be missing. The activities seemed to lack a focus. The researchers asked the teacher, "Why did you choose this author to study?" At first, the teacher seemed to be confused by the question. She seemed to feel that an author study was inherently beneficial. "It was something to do. And we had the books," the teacher responded. Further questioning revealed that she had no plans for assessing the effectiveness of the author study. Except for wanting her students to engage in a variety of reading and writing activities, the teacher had no clear goal. Lacking a goal, she had no way to assess the effectiveness of the author study. Goals need to be translated into objectives that are clear and observable. Some possible goals in this case could have been to study an author's development, to compare an author's earlier works with later works, to analyze an author's style, or to increase reading fluency by reading several books by the author.

Once you have established goals, you need to decide how you will ascertain whether students have reached them. The goal that students will conduct an author study might be translated into the objective that students will better understand Mark Twain's craft by comparing two of his books and creating a diagram showing similarities and differences in theme, style, plot, and characterization. It's important, that students have a role in setting goals or are, at least, aware of them and how they will be assessed.

The Standards Movement

Goals for all major content areas now exist in lists of standards. Standards are listings of the content and skills students are expected to acquire. Sometimes referred to as objectives, content standards form a foundation for a subject's curriculum. Because standards

■ **Evaluation** is the process of using the results of tests, observations, work samples, or other devices to judge the effectiveness of a program or students' learning.

vary widely from state to state, most states have adopted Common Core State Standards in both language arts and math. Curriculum materials and tests aligned with these standards are now being created.

Benchmarks

Broad content standards are typically translated into more specific objectives, which are sometimes known as **benchmarks**. Benchmarks articulate standards. For instance, the physical science standard "Understands the structure and properties of matter" has a series of seventeen benchmarks, the first of which is "Knows the structure of an atom (e.g., negative electrons occupy most of the space in the atom; neutrons and positive protons make up the nucleus of the atom; protons and neutrons are almost two thousand times heavier than an electron; the electric force between the nucleus and electrons holds the atom together)" (MCREL, 2009).

In addition to standards recommended by national organizations, states and local school districts have issued standards or curriculum frameworks. Ultimately, these national and state standards have to be translated, adapted, and revised so that they fit the needs of your students.

High–Stakes Testing

As the name suggests, the outcome of a **high-stakes test** determines the answer to an important question, such as whether the student passes or fails, is placed in a special program, or is awarded a diploma. In a position paper, the International Reading Association (IRA) announced its opposition to high-stakes testing. The IRA is not opposed to assessment. Rather, it is opposed to making critical decisions based on a single test. In addition, because of their importance in students', teachers', and administrators' lives, high-stakes tests have had an undue influence on what is taught in the schools. As the Board of Directors of the International Reading Association (1999) commented, "Our central concern is that testing has become a means of controlling instruction as opposed to a way of gathering information to help students become better readers" (p. 257). In other words, high-stakes tests have in some instances become the tail that wags the dog. Instead of being used to assess how well students are doing and providing information for program improvement, high-stakes tests dictate curriculum. Rather than teaching what their community has judged to be important, educators teach what will be included on the tests. This has the impact of narrowing the curriculum. In situations in which there are many students in danger of doing poorly on high-stakes tests, the focus on the test is intensified and the amount of time devoted to test preparation is increased.

Currently, about 80 percent of secondary school students also take either the ACT or the SAT test, which are high-stakes tests because of their role in college admissions. Although some colleges no long require SAT or ACT scores, most still do. A number of states also use the ACT as a proficiency test.

CHECKUP

1. What are standards and high-stakes assessment?
2. What impact do they have on assessment?

■ **Benchmarks** are more specific statements of general standards. They translate broad statements of standards into specific objectives. Benchmarks are standards of performance against which students' achievement might be assessed.

■ A **high-stakes test** is one in which the results are used to make important decisions such as passing students, graduating students, or rating a school.

Setting Goals

Assessment is conducted in terms of the goals that you set. National, state, and local standards will have an impact on your goals, as will assessments used

NORM-REFERENCED VERSUS CRITERION-REFERENCED TESTS **375**

to measure students' progress. However, your goals should also reflect the basic principles of learning presented in Chapter 1. Students need an in-depth understanding of key concepts. A basic goal of learning is that students should be able to transfer knowledge and skills to other topics in the domain, to other domains, and to the world outside school. Before knowledge or skills can be transferred, they must be mastered. Information that is thoroughly understood is far more likely to be transferred than information that has simply been skimmed or memorized. Focusing on broad themes and seeing how facts are interrelated fosters the necessary understanding. If your goals include a depth of knowledge and understanding, your assessment should reflect those goals. The assessment devices that you use need to reveal how well students can integrate or apply key concepts. Questions that require students to state the causes of the Great Depression should be complemented by items that require them to apply such concepts as supply and demand, business cycles, and the role of government in a market economy to today's world. In other words, if you teach for understanding, you need to assess to see how well students have achieved understanding. Not surprisingly, students tend to focus on the kinds of skills and knowledge that are being assessed.

A wide variety of measures are available to assess whether goals have been met, whether programs are effective, or how well students do when compared with national or international samples of students. Widely used assessment measures include norm- and criterion-referenced tests, book tests, teacher-created tests and quizzes, observations, rubrics, think-alouds, anecdotal records, questionnaires and interviews, and portfolios.

CHECKUP

1. What are some of the factors that should be considered when setting goals?

Norm-Referenced Versus Criterion-Referenced Tests

Norm-Referenced Tests

Tests are either norm referenced or criterion or standards referenced. In a **norm-referenced test**, students are compared with a representative sample of others who are the same age or in the same grade. The scores indicate whether students did as well as the average, better than the average, or below the average. The norm group is chosen to be representative of the nation's total school population and typically includes students from all sections of the country, from urban and nonurban areas, and from a variety of racial or ethnic and socioeconomic groups.

Norm-Referenced Reporting

Norm-referenced scores offer a variety of comparisons.

- *Raw score.* A **raw score** represents the total number of correct answers. It has no meaning until it is changed into a percentile rank or other score. However, it is important to check the raw score to see how many possible questions there were and how many the student got correct. If the student got all or almost all the answers correct, the test did not have enough ceiling room. The student may have done even better if the test had contained additional items at higher levels. If the student answered only a few items correctly, the test did not have an adequate floor and may simply have been too difficult for

> ■ With norm-referenced tests, students are compared with a representative sample of students who are the same age or in the same grade.

> ■ A raw score is the number of correct answers or points earned on a test.

FIGURE 13.1 **Normal Curve and Comparison of Norm-Referenced Scores**

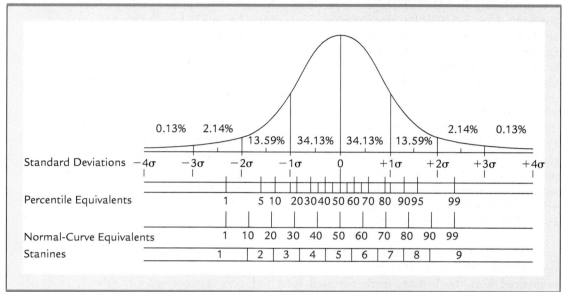

the student. If the test has a multiple choice format, the student may have a chance score. A chance score is one that can be achieved strictly by guessing. For instance, if the test has four answer options, the test taker has a one-in-four chance of getting an answer correct through sheer guessing. If the student did not get more than one out of four items correct of those that were attempted, the score can be attributed to chance and is invalid.

■ *Percentile rank.* A **percentile rank** tells where a student's raw score falls on a scale of 1 to 99. A score at the first percentile means that the student did better than 1 percent of those who took the test. A score at the fiftieth percentile is an average score and indicates that the student did better than half of those who took the test. A top score is the ninety-ninth percentile. Most norm-referenced test results are now reported in percentiles; however, the ranks are not equal units and should not be added, subtracted, divided, or used for subtest comparison. As you can see by looking at the normal curve in Figure 13.1, percentile ranks in the middle are closer together than they are at ends of the curve. This means that getting one or two more answers correct in the middle ranks will move an average percentile score more than it will move a very low or very high score. Getting two more answers correct might move a student from the fiftieth to fifty-fifth percentile, but move a student only from the ninety-fifth to the ninety-sixth percentile. Percentiles should not be confused with percentages. One mother complained that her son had done poorly because he had scored only in the eightieth percentile. She believed that he had gotten 20 percent of the answers wrong. Actually, he had done better than 80 percent of the norm group who had taken the test.

■ The percentile rank is the point on a scale of 1 to 99 that shows what percentage of students obtained an equal or lower score. A percentile rank of 75 means that 75 percent of those who took the test received an equal or lower score.

■ A grade equivalent score indicates the score that the average student at that grade level achieved. Grade equivalent scores have

been sanctioned by the International Reading Association and are relatively valid when pupils are tested on their instructional level and when extrapolations are limited to a year or two beyond the target grade level.

■ *Grade equivalent score.* The **grade equivalent score** characterizes a student's performance as being equivalent to that of other students in a particular grade. A grade equivalent score of 8.2 indicates that the student correctly answered the same number of items as the average student in the second month of eighth grade. Note that the grade equivalent score does not tell on what level the student is operating; that is, a score of 8.2 on a reading test does not mean that a student is reading on an eighth grade level. Grade equivalent scores are more meaningful when the test students have taken is at the right level and when the score is not more than a year above or a year below average. Grade equivalent scores are also more meaningful at the lower grades. It takes quite a bit of reading ability to move from a 3.2 to a 4.2. However, scores tend to flatten out as students move up through the grades, and so it doesn't take as much reading ability to move from a 9.2 to 10.2. Because grade equivalent scores are misleading and easily misunderstood, they should be used with great care or not at all.

■ *Normal curve equivalents.* **Normal curve equivalents** (NCEs) rank students on a scale of 1 through 99. The main difference between NCEs and percentile ranks is that NCEs represent equal units and so can be added and subtracted and used for comparing performance on subtests.

■ *Stanine.* **Stanine** is a combination of the words *standard* and *nine*. The stanines 4, 5, and 6 are average points, with 1, 2, and 3 being below average, and 7, 8, and 9 above average. Stanines are useful when making comparisons among the subtests of a norm-referenced test.

■ *Scaled scores.* **Scaled scores** are a continuous ranking of scores from the lowest levels of a series of norm-referenced tests—first grade, for example—through the highest levels—high school. They start at 000 and end at 999. They are useful for tracking long-term reading development through the grades. They are also useful for out-of-level testing. For instance, a ninth-grade student reading on a fourth-grade level should be given a fourth-grade test. For this student, a percentile score would be meaningless, as would a stanine or NCE because the scores would compare the ninth grader with fourth graders. However, the scaled score could be checked against ninth-grade norms and yield a valid score, even though the student had taken a fourth-grade test.

Scores reported on norm-referenced tests are not particularly helpful to teachers. Of what value is it to know that a student scored in the thirtieth percentile or fourth stanine? It indicates that the student is performing below average when compared to the norm group, but does not yield any information about what the student knows or is having difficulty with.

For additional information about tests, especially norm-referenced instruments, see the *Eighteenth Mental Measurements Yearbook* (Spies, Carlson, & Geisinger, 2010) or *Tests in Print VII* (Murphy, Spies, & Plake, 2006), which contain reviews of recent tests and suggestions for choosing and using tests.

Norm-referenced tests are available for virtually all subject matter areas. However, norm-referenced tests are more frequently given in reading and math. In checking norm-referenced scores in your subject matter area, take a look at the students' reading scores to get an estimate of their reading ability. A low score on the reading test may indicate that the results of the subject matter test are invalid. Unless students are reading close to grade level, they may have difficulty reading the subject matter portion of the test. A low score may reflect below-level reading ability rather than a lack of knowledge of science or history.

Norm-referenced tests are not particularly useful for gauging achievement. Their purpose is to sort students: to show who is average, who is above average, and who is below average. Test items are selected on the basis of the ability to discriminate. Thus, a question that assesses a key concept in a subject matter area might not be included because most students would be able to answer it and so it would have a low discriminatory value (Popham, 2000). A well-constructed criterion-referenced test will emphasize items that assess key concepts.

Norm-referenced tests may also be used to measure overall gains. But because they typically use a multiple

■ A **normal curve equivalent** is the rank on a scale of 1 through 99 that a score is equal to.

■ A **stanine** is a point on a nine-point scale, with 5 being average.

■ A **scaled score** is a continuous ranking from 000 to 999 of a series of norm-referenced tests from the easiest- to the highest-level test.

choice format, guessing becomes a factor, and skills and knowledge are not tested in the way in which they are used in and out of the classroom. In addition, group norm-referenced tests tend to be general in content and may have just a few items for key areas or skills, so they will probably not provide an adequate assessment of your subject.

Despite their disadvantages, norm-referenced tests are used extensively. For instance, in 61 percent of schools, norm-referenced tests are the primary tool for determining placement in secondary programs for below-level readers (Barry, 1997). In 58 percent of schools, norm-referenced tests are also used to determine progress made in these programs. Often, another form of the placement test is used as a posttest to measure gains. However, there is an encouraging trend toward using teacher observation, portfolios, and teacher-made tests to place students in intervention programs and to gauge progress. In pre-1950 programs, 90 percent of the schools relied on norm-referenced tests to place students, as opposed to today's figure of 61 percent.

CHECKUP

1. What are norm-referenced tests?
2. How are they used in content area programs?
3. In what ways are scores on norm-referenced tests reported?

Criterion-Referenced Tests

For content area teachers, **criterion-referenced tests** are more helpful than norm-referenced measures because they compare students' performance with some standard, or criterion. For instance, the criterion on a comprehension or a science test might be answering 80 percent of the questions correctly. The informal reading inventory is criterion referenced; a student must have at least 95 percent word recognition and 75 percent comprehension to be on the instructional level. Tests that accompany content area texts are generally criterion referenced. Many have a passing score, which is the criterion. The quizzes and tests that you construct for your students are also criterion referenced; you set the criterion for a passing score.

Performance on criterion-referenced tests is not reported in the same way as it is on norm-referenced tests. In norm-referenced reporting, a student's performance is compared with that of other students. In criterion-referenced reporting, a student's performance might be described in terms of a standard or expected performance, or in terms of the student's goals. One of the best known criterion-referenced tests in the content areas is the Advanced Placement Test. Students must meet certain criteria or get a certain number of items correct in order to pass the test. Standards-based tests are also criterion referenced; the criterion is meeting a certain standard. Many state tests are criterion referenced; students must achieve a certain score in order to reach the standard. One problem with criterion-referenced tests is that the criterion may be set arbitrarily or unrealistically. For instance, someone might set a criterion for reading comprehension of material at 90 percent. While a high level of comprehension is desirable, it may be unrealistic. Before setting a criterion, the test constructors should find out how students actually perform on the measure. In some states, for instance, the criterion for proficiency was set so high that more than half the students failed to meet the standard. This suggests that the standard has been set at an unrealistic level. Federal legislation now requires that scores be reported in three categories: advanced, proficient, and partly proficient. The third level allows states to track the progress of low-achieving students toward meeting state standards. On a national level, NAEP tests may have unrealistic standards since only about a third of students reach proficiency on most of them. Although no one would argue with creating challenging standards, setting standards that are unrealistically high is demoralizing to both students and educators; it also creates a false impression among the general public that schools are not doing very well.

■ In a criterion-referenced test, the student's performance is compared to a criterion or standard.

TABLE 13.1   Rubric for Web Site Creation

	NOVICE	APPRENTICE	PROFICIENT	ADVANCED
Content	Very little information.	Limited information. Main ideas not fully developed.	Adequate information. Main ideas well developed.	Very informative. Goes beyond giving basic details.
Style	Text is difficult to understand. Poorly written.	Text is not clear in some spots. Some portions are awkwardly written.	Text is clear and easy to follow.	Text is appealing and has voice.
Layout/Design	Little or no evidence of design.	Not all elements fit into the overall design.	Design is functional.	Design is eye-catching and highly effective.
Navigation/Links	Has no links or links fail to operate.	Has insufficient links. Some links do not seem relevant.	Has a sufficient number of key links.	Has more than enough links. Some links to hard-to-find sources.
Mechanics	A number of spelling, punctuation, capitalization, or usage errors.	A few mechanical errors.	No errors.	No errors.

Rubrics

One type of standard or criterion is the **rubric**. A rubric is a written description of what is expected in order to meet a certain level or performance. As such, it functions as a scoring guide so that the assessor can differentiate between below-average, average, and superior performance. Rubrics can be used to assess science experiments, social studies projects, artwork, musical performances, pieces of writing, and other products produced by students. A chief advantage is that they can be constructed to accommodate many of the content area standards. The sample rubric in Table 13.1 is designed to help with the creation of a Web site. Note the concrete description of four levels of achievement.

Rubrics for Constructed Responses   Rubrics can also be created for assessing responses to open-ended questions of the type that your students will be asked to answer, if these are not already available (see Figure 13.2). These assessments could be tests that you make up, tests from the reading program you are using, or state tests. Provide students with practice using the rubrics so that they understand what the expectations are. Distribute sample answers and have students use rubrics to assess them. Begin with correct, easily assessed answers so that students have some guidance, and then have them assess answers that receive no credit or partial credit. As a whole-group activity, you and the class can compose responses to open-ended questions, and then assess the responses with a rubric. Once students have some sense of how to respond to open-ended questions, ask them to compose individual responses and assess them with the rubric.

Rubrics have a number of advantages. First, they help objectify subjective judgment. They also lead the evaluator to decide what characterizes different levels of performance, and, when shared with students, provide them with a clear idea of what they must do in order to perform adequately. If students help develop the rubrics, they acquire a sense of ownership and a better understanding of the task's requirements. One researcher found that students who participated in the creation of rubrics for a writing assignment turned in better writing pieces than those who didn't (Boyle, 1996).

USING TECHNOLOGY

RubiStar http://rubistar.4teachers.org RubiStar provides generic rubrics in a format that can be customized and printed out. For each rubric, teachers can select from a variety of categories or add their own and change almost all suggested text in the rubric to make it fit their project. A number of the rubrics are in Spanish.

CHECKUP

1. What are criterion-referenced assessment measures?
2. What role do they play in content area programs?
3. What role might rubrics play in an assessment program?

■ A rubric is a description of the traits or characteristics of standards used to judge a process or product.

FIGURE 13.2   **Sample Scoring Rubric for Constructed Response to a Question about the Theme of a Short Story**

Score	3	2	1	0
Criterion	States a plausible theme. Gives ample evidence from the story to support answer	States a plausible theme. Gives partial evidence from the story to support answer	States an implausible or peripheral theme Or fails to give evidence from the story to support answer	Does not state a theme No response

Judging Assessment Measures

Reliability

To be useful, tests and other assessment instruments, whether criterion or norm referenced, must be both reliable and valid. **Reliability** is a measure of consistency, which means that if the same test were given to the same students a number of times, the results would be approximately the same. Reliability is usually reported as a coefficient of correlation and ranges from 0.00 to 0.99 or –0.01 to –0.99. The higher the positive correlation, the more reliable the test is. Reliability is tested in two major ways: through a mathematical calculation of internal consistency and through test-retest—that is, giving the same test a second time to see if relative performance stays approximately the same. Group tests should have an internal consistency of 0.85 and a test-retest of 0.70 or higher. For tests on which individual decisions are being based, reliability should be in the 0.90s. A test that is not reliable is of no value because the results of measurement could be different each time.

Validity

In general, **validity** means that a test measures what is says it measures: vocabulary knowledge or science knowledge, for instance. For content area teachers, the key validity is curricular or content validity, which means that the test measures the content that has been presented and assesses it in the way it has been taught or is typically used. To be valid, the assessment must also present useful information. Ultimately, it means that a particular test will provide the information needed to make a decision, such as whether to review misunderstood concepts or go on to the next level or whether to give a passing grade (Farr & Carey, 1986). To check for content validity, list the objectives or standards of the program and note how closely a particular test's objectives match them. The test's specific content should be examined, too, to see whether it reflects the type of material the students have covered. Also, determine how knowledge or skills are tested. If a test assesses skills or content that you do not cover or evaluates them in a way that is not suitable, the test is not valid for your class.

Closely tied to validity are the uses to which the assessment will be put. For instance, a statewide assessment that is tied to graduation will almost surely be used by teachers as a kind of curriculum guide. If the test assesses only a narrow part of the curriculum, it will be detrimental and thus invalid (Joint Task Force on Assessment, 1994). If a state's high-stakes test assesses persuasive writing, this area may be overemphasized, and other kinds of writing neglected.

Assessment measures should also be fair to all who take them. There

■ **Reliability** is the degree to which a test yields consistent results. In other words, if you took the test again, your score would be approximately the same.

■ **Validity** is the degree to which a test measures what it is supposed to measure, or the extent to which a test will provide information needed to make a decision. Validity should be considered in terms of the consequences of the test results and the use to which the test results will be put.

should be no biased items, and the content should be such that all students have had an equal opportunity to learn it.

CHECKUP

1. How are assessment measures judged?

Functional Level Assessment

The typical class will exhibit a wide range of reading ability. Just as students need appropriate levels of materials for instruction, they also should have appropriate levels of materials for testing. Unfortunately, many of the high-stakes tests may lack sufficient bottom. That is, they fail to include below-grade-level content appropriate for struggling learners. Approximately one student out of four is reading significantly below grade level. Thus if these students are given tests that are written on grade level, they will not be able to read most of the items. The poorest readers may not be able to read any of the items. In addition to being inhumane, such a test is also invalid for struggling learners. It yields no useful information except to indicate that the student is operating below grade level. This type of test is also potentially damaging to the struggling students' motivation. If students are unable to demonstrate what they have learned, a prime source of external motivation is taken away. One solution is to administer tests that have items at low levels as well as at average and above-average levels. A second solution is to use **functional level testing**, also known as *out-of-level testing*, in which students are given tests that are on their reading level rather than on their grade level. To ascertain students' reading level, you can use either your professional judgment or a test such as the GRADE Reading-Level Indicator and Spanish Companion (Pearson Assessments), a brief assessment designed to estimate the reading levels of students in grades 4 through 12. Although designed for students in grades 4 and above, the GRADE Locator Test has items on beginning reading levels as well as advanced reading levels. The test also has a Spanish component that provides an estimate of students' ability to read Spanish. Directions are provided in Spanish but may also be pantomimed.

As a general rule, if a student answers more than 90 percent of the items on a test correctly, he or she should be tested at a more difficult level (Touchstone Applied Science Associates, 2006). If a student answers less than 10 percent of the items correctly, she or he should be tested at an easier level. Giving students a test at the wrong level results in erroneous, invalid information. This is true whether a norm-referenced, criterion-referenced, or other type of assessment is being used. In addition, if teachers are being assessed on the basis of the progress that their students make, it is absolutely essential that accurate beginning and ending points be established. This requires functional level assessment.

Another possible way to assess struggling readers is to read items to the students so that the below-level readers are not penalized. This works for content areas, but not reading. The only solution for reading assessment is to give students tests that are on their level.

English Language Learners

According to current regulations, all public school students in grades 3 through 8 must be assessed in reading and math on a yearly basis and at least once during grades 10 through 12. An assessment in science is also required in one of the grades in each of the following ranges: 3–5, 6–9, and 10–12. Students with severe disabilities can be allowed to take out-of-level tests or alternate assessments; however, this group should not exceed 2 percent of the population. ELLs are required to be tested in English proficiency each

USING TECHNOLOGY

Some computerized assessments are adaptive. If the test taker gets a number of items wrong, the test taker is given easier items. If the test taker is getting almost all of the items correct, the test taker is given items on a higher level. Assessments being constructed for the Common Core State Standards will be adaptive.

■ **Functional level testing** is the practice of assigning students to a test level on the basis of their reading ability rather than their grade level.

year and in English reading after having completed 10 months of schooling in the United States.

Assessing English language learners is a complex issue. Testing ELLs in their native language seems to be a logical approach. This works best for students who are new arrivals. If students have been exposed to English for a period of time, then they will have learned some new terms in English, but not in their native language. On the other hand, students who have extensive experience with English should be tested in English. However, there may be terms and concepts that they know in their native language, but not in English. One solution to this dilemma is to test students in both languages (Cummins, 2001). The Bilingual Verbal Abilities Test (BVAT) is one instrument that accomplishes this task. The BVAT (Riverside) consists of three verbal tests derived from the Woodcock-Johnson-Revised: picture vocabulary, oral vocabulary, and verbal analogies. These tests have been translated into fifteen languages. Students take the tests in both languages so they are given credit for both responses in English and items answered in their native language that they were unable to respond to in English. When used with nonverbal tests, the BVAT offers a reasonably valid estimate of students' academic ability. Applying this principle to the content areas, the most effective assessment would allow students to be assessed in both English and their native language.

CHECKUP

1. What is functional level assessment?
2. How might functional level assessment be implemented in a content area program?
3. How should ELLs be assessed?

Measuring Growth

Struggling Readers

Given effective instruction, below-level students frequently perform at an above-average rate. However, efforts still have to be made to bring these students up to a proficient level.

In the past, most states reported performance in terms of what percentage of students met the state's proficiency level. These percentages are known as *threshold measures*. In addition to knowing what level students have achieved, it is also important to measure their growth. Threshold testing may mask growth. The results tell what percentage of students has met a certain standard, but not how much students' scores have changed. For instance, students' scores might be increasing, bringing them closer to meeting the standard, but this is not indicated in the results. Unless growth is measured, schools that have large numbers of struggling students might be misjudged. Many urban schools show below-level achievement and might be classified as low performing or in need of improvement. However, their students might be making better-than-average gains, but not enough to take them over the threshold. On the other hand, some students who score above the threshold might currently be making less than average progress, but their lack of progress is hidden because their scores exceed the threshold. Current emphasis is on measures of growth that are used to identify and help students who are not making adequate progress and teachers whose classes are not making at least average progress. National assessments aligned with Common Core State Standards are now being created that will measure growth and that will be given periodically during the school year so the results can be used to plan instruction.

Measuring growth is also known as **value added** assessment. Teachers are judged according to how much their students demonstrate growth above or below the average progress made by students in similar circumstances. High-performing teachers, for instance, might have students whose gain is three or fourth months above the average, Low-performing teachers might have students whose gain is three or four months below the average (Schochet & Chiang, 2010).

Regardless of how they are evaluated, teachers should be measuring the growth of their students so they can make sure all students are making adequate progress and make changes as necessary. Measures of growth can include quizzes, unit tests, observations,

■ **Value added** is a measure of how much growth above or below a school or district average a group of students demonstrate. Complex statistical formulas that factor in student and other variables are typically used to measure value added.

portfolios, and other measures as described in the next section. Even if formal measures are used by the school or district to measure growth, teacher-constructed and informal measures should be used to provide additional information.

Other Methods of Assessment

USING TECHNOLOGY

Supporting Instruction: Investing in Teaching www.gatesfoundation .org/highschools/Documents/ supporting-instruction.pdf Provides sample templates that can be used for instruction or assessment.

Performance Assessment

Performance assessment is just what its name suggests. Instead of showing what they know by answering multiple choice questions or filling in the blanks, students demonstrate knowledge through their performance (Popham, 2000). Students might write and put on a one-act play or plan a balanced diet. They might be given materials and asked to design an experiment—for instance, one designed to assess whether a sample of water is acidic. Or the teacher might set up stations in which students have to perform a variety of basic lab tasks or identify rock specimens.

Performance tasks potentially assess knowledge and skills in a more realistic way at the application level. In the sciences, performance assessments can be set up to show whether students can use scientific equipment and conduct measurements and other lab procedures. It's one thing to be able to answer questions about starches, sugars, protein, and oils in foods. It's quite another to measure the starches, sugars, protein, and oils in foods and plan a balanced diet based on these measurements. Students who will be assessed on a performance measure need to be more active learners and must be able to apply knowledge, not merely recite facts. Despite its obvious value, performance assessment does have some limitations. Performance assessment can be more expensive and more time-consuming. The assessments are also narrower in scope than paper-and-pencil tests, which are better at assessing a wide range of knowledge.

Sample Classroom Formative Performance Assessment

The Bill and Melinda Gates Foundation (2010a) has constructed templates, which are sample teaching tasks or assignments that address the Common Core State Standards. The template tasks require students to read, analyze, and comprehend materials described by the Common Core State Standards and then write arguments, explanations, or narratives specified by the template. Modules, courses, and assessments are also being constructed. The templates can be used as is or they can serve as building blocks for assignments or assessments. Here is a sample template.

> Task 1 TEMPLATE (argumentative/analysis L1, L2, L3):
>
> After researching (informational texts) on (content), write an (essay or substitute) that argues your position, pro or con, on (content). Support your position with evidence from your research. L2 Be sure to acknowledge competing views. L3 Give examples from past or current events or issues to illustrate, clarify, and support your position. Appropriate for: social studies, science

Think-Alouds

Think-alouds have been presented in previous chapters as a device for instructing students. Think-alouds can also be used to gain insight into the thought processes students use as they deal with difficult words, study, write reports, or attempt to understand a chapter in a content area text. During a think-aloud, the reader explains her thought processes while reading a text or writing. These explanations can come after each sentence, at the end of each paragraph, or

■ **Performance assessment** involves employing tasks in which knowledge, skills, or strategies are assessed in the way they are typically used.

■ **Think-alouds** are procedures in which students are asked to describe the processes they are using as they engage in reading or another cognitive activity.

at the end of the whole selection or while engaging in a particular task, such as deriving the meaning of an unknown word. Think-alouds reveal whether the reader is focused on individual words, phrases, sentences, or the integration of sentences. Think-alouds also show the types of inferences the reader is making and the kinds of memory processes he or she is using (Trabasso & Magliano, 1996).

According to data from think-alouds, readers engage in a variety of processes as they read. They summarize, paraphrase, make inferences, highlight essential details, integrate portions of the text, monitor for meaning, and react personally (Pressley & Afflerbach, 1995). Skilled readers and those who have more prior knowledge generally apply a greater variety of strategies as they read. As a result, they remember more (Goldman, 1997). Because think-alouds provide insight into students' use of strategies and cognitive processes, they are a valuable assessment tool and have the potential to reveal why students are having difficulty comprehending their content area texts. Think-alouds also can be used to plan instruction for students in strategies they are neglecting or not using effectively.

Before asking students to engage in think-alouds or using think-alouds to assess students, model the process. A variety of coding systems can be used to classify students' comments, or you can simply take informal notes.

An excellent example of the use of think-alouds with content area texts can be found in the Qualitative Reading Inventory-5 (Leslie & Caldwell, 2011). First a student reads a segment of text in the regular way. The student then reads the second section, but stops when the word *stop* appears. At that point, the teacher explains that she is going to demonstrate a think-aloud. After reading the section, she tells what she is thinking and invites the student to do the same. In the third section, the student reads, stops when the word *stop* appears, and then thinks aloud. The student's responses are recorded and coded. The following think-aloud responses indicate understanding:

- *Paraphrasing or summarizing.*
- *Making new meaning.* This includes drawing an inference or conclusion or reasoning about what has been read.
- *Questioning that indicates understanding.* The questioning generally shows that the student is seeking to figure out how a particular piece of information fits in with what has already been read or what its significance might be.
- *Noting understanding.* The student verbalizes that he understands what he has read.
- *Reporting prior knowledge.* The student explains how a passage agrees with what he already knows or explains how this passage has caused him to alter his thinking.
- *Identifying personally.* The student comments on how the text affects him personally or makes a personal judgment about text.

Some comments that indicate a lack of understanding include:

- *Querying the meaning of a word or phrase or asking a question about the content of the passage, which signals that he has not understood the passage.*
- *Noting lack of understanding.* The student comments that he doesn't understand a word or phrase or does not comprehend the passage (Leslie & Caldwell, 2001).

One study found that the type of responses made by students in think-alouds varied in type and quality. Students who engaged in summarizing or paraphrasing and making inferences had the highest level of comprehension. Some students showed a preference for one type of strategy, such as summarizing, whereas others used a variety of strategies. A number of students offered no comments at all (Leslie & Caldwell, 2001). Think-alouds are affected by the difficulty level, familiarity, and nature of the text being read. Students who are reading about an unfamiliar topic would probably use summarizing or paraphrasing in their attempt to simply retell what the author said. They would have more difficulty drawing inferences or conclusions. Students also are more likely to respond personally to literary selections than they are to science or social studies passages (Leslie & Caldwell, 2006).

As students think aloud, record and then analyze their responses. Note the behaviors listed below. Then come to conclusions about the effectiveness of the strategies that the student is using and the extent to which the student is monitoring for meaning.

- Made predictions or created hypotheses
- Revised prediction or conclusion based on new information
- Considered information previously read
- Made inferences
- Drew conclusions
- Made judgments
- Visualized or created images
- Paraphrased
- Summarized
- Constructed questions
- Reasoned about reading
- Made connections
- Monitored for meaning
- Noted difficult words
- Noted confusing passages
- Used fix-up strategies
- Reread section
- Used illustrations as an aid
- Used context or other decoding skills
- Used glossary
- Skipped difficult words. (Gunning, 2002)

A sample think-aloud is presented in Figure 13.3.

Think-alouds can be used to examine specific processes as well as general reading ability. In the think-aloud protocol quoted below, students were asked to locate difficult words in books that they were reading and discuss their thought processes as they tried to analyze the words. What does the brief interchange between researcher and student tell you about the student's strategies? How might you use the information to plan a program for the student?

The whole system could suddenly collapse. And that was what he said about Jurassic Park. That it had *inherent instability*. (Crichton, 1990, p. 243)

Researcher: What do you think this means?

Brady: Instant. You inherit it instantly.

Researcher: What gives you that idea?

Brady: Well, because the first word—instant, it looks like. . . uh . . . something.

Researcher: Does that make sense with the story?

Brady: Well, the sentence doesn't sound right to me though. That it had inherent . . . it sounds like it needs an *ed* at the end of inherent.

Researcher: What else?

Brady: I don't know.

Researcher: Does it bother you to keep on reading?

Brady: No. (Harmon, 1998a, p. 583)

In confusing the word *inherent* with *inherited* and *instability* with *instant*, Brady uses word analysis, rather than contextual clues, to derive a possible meaning for the word. The meaning doesn't fit the context, but Brady moves ahead anyhow. Brady obviously needs instruction in context clues, especially clues that might be found in other sentences. He also needs to keep on working at the word until he achieves a definition that makes sense. And he needs to use the dictionary or glossary when other strategies don't work. The think-aloud provides invaluable information about Brady's use of word analysis skills and needs.

FIGURE 13.3
Sample Think-Aloud

Teacher explanation: I would like you to read this section and then tell me what you were thinking as you read it. If I know what students are thinking as they read, it will help me better understand how they are reading their textbooks. Once I know how they are reading their textbooks, I can show them ways to get more out of their reading. Read the section silently as you normally would. Stop reading when you come to the word stop. Then I will ask you to tell me what you were thinking about as you read. I will show you what I mean. Then you can give it a try. [*Teacher demonstrates.*]

> Volcanic belts form along the boundaries of Earth's plates. At plate boundaries, huge pieces of the lithosphere diverge (pull apart) and reconverge (push together). Here, the lithosphere is weak and fractured, allowing magma to reach the surface. Most volcanoes occur along diverging plate boundaries, such as the mid-ocean ridge, or in subduction zones around the edges of ocean. But some volcanoes form at "hot spots" far from the boundaries of continental or oceanic plates. (Exline et al., 2001, p. 179) STOP

Teacher: What were you thinking as you read?
Student: It says that volcanoes form along the plate boundaries. It says that here is where pieces of lithosphere pull together and push apart. What is lithosphere? It says volcanoes occur where plates diverge or in subduction zones. Diverging plates are plates that pull apart. But I don't know what a subduction zone is. Sub means "under." Could it mean "under the ocean"? Part of this is in heavy black print. That means it's important. I better read that again.

[Additional helpful probing questions include: *Did you look at the map? If so, did the map help? How? What might you do to get the meanings of lithosphere and subduction? Do you ever use the glossary? What did you do before you started reading?*]

Volcanoes at Diverging Plate Boundaries

> Volcanoes form along the mid-ocean ridge, which marks a diverging plate boundary. Recall from Chapter 4 that the ridge is a long, underwater rift valley that winds through the oceans. Along the ridge, lava pours out of cracks in the ocean floor. Only in a few places, as in Iceland and the Azores Islands in the Atlantic Ocean, do the volcanoes of the mid-ocean ridge rise above the ocean's surface. (Exline et al., 2001. p. 179) STOP.

Teacher: What were you thinking as you read?
Student: It looks like volcanoes in the ocean pour lava out of cracks in the ocean floor. But some volcanoes actually come up from beneath the sea. Does that mean that volcanoes form islands?

Informal Think-Alouds

Think-alouds can be brief and informal. For instance, during a discussion of a selection, you might ask questions similar to the following:

- How did you figure out that difficult word?
- What do you do when you encounter a difficult word?
- What were you thinking about as you read the selection?
- What was going through your mind as you read the selection?
- Were there any parts of the selection that were confusing? How did you handle those parts?
- If you were going to be given a test on this selection, show me how you would go about studying for it.

Group Assessment of Text Processing

Obtaining think-alouds from large numbers of students would be prohibitively time consuming. However, it is essential that you obtain information about the way students process their texts, especially if they are having difficulty with them. In most content area classes, the text is a major source of information. To save time, think-alouds may be expressed in writing. Students can be asked to provide a written description of their thoughts as they read a selection in a context area text. In their learning logs, students can note the difficulties they encountered in confusing passages and describe the processes they used to comprehend the selections. In follow-up class discussions, they can compare their thought processes and strategies with those of other students (Brown & Lytle, 1988). Students can also be asked to attach sticky notes to passages that they find confusing. The class might list passages they found confusing and talk about the steps they took to resolve their confusions. If a number of students found the same passages confusing, you might analyze the reason for this and take steps to help students sort through the passages. The passage might be poorly written, or the students might not be using effective comprehension strategies.

Another way to obtain insight into the ways students process information in the text is to administer a group text processing assessment. The text processing assessment seeks two types of information: what the students understood and how they went about constructing meaning. Students read brief segments of text, generally a paragraph at a time. Text for the assessment could be segments from the textbook students are using with notations telling students where to stop reading and respond by thinking aloud. On a sheet of paper divided into two columns, they are asked, "Tell what the text was about in your own words. Summarize the main points." In a second column, students are asked, "Tell what was going on in your mind as you read the section. Tell what you were thinking or seeing in your mind. Tell about anything in the paragraph that was confusing to you." Model the process and work through a sample selection with students. As they work through the assessment, note how they go about reading it and responding to it. After students have completed the assessment, discuss it with them. This provides them with the opportunity to expand on their responses.

Observation

Observation is one of the best ways to assess students. Through observation, you can verify information gleaned from tests and assess behaviors that could not readily be evaluated in any other way. For instance, you can assess how well a student works with others and participates in class and hands-on activities such as experiments and presentations.

Observation can be supplemented by asking questions to gain insight into students' reasoning processes. Analyzing the kinds of questions that students ask is also good source of information about their understanding.

Observation is an invaluable tool. However, observations can be subjective and unreliable. Planning observations and keeping records adds to their reliability, validity, and overall usefulness. For instance, if you wish to assess students' work habits in a cooperative group, it would be more reliable if you observed several meetings. Otherwise, you might catch the students on a bad day or a good day and form an erroneous impression. It would also help if you have a checklist to guide your observations (see Table 13.2). A checklist notes the essential behaviors a task entails and provides a way of keeping a record of your observations.

To find out how students read their textbooks, provide them with some time to read them in class. Note how they go about this task: What do they do before they read? Do

USING TECHNOLOGY

Handheld computers or other digital devices can be used to take observational notes. Software such as *ThoughtManager for Education* (Hands High Software) can be used to organize these notes.

TABLE 13.2 **Checklist for Performance in a Cooperative Group**

Name _____ Date _____

	Never	Occasionally	Usually	Always
Completes assignments	___	___	___	___
Has needed materials	___	___	___	___
Helps others	___	___	___	___
Attends meetings	___	___	___	___
Joins in discussion	___	___	___	___
Respects opinions of others	___	___	___	___
Gets along well with other group members	___	___	___	___

FIGURE 13.4
Text Usage Interview

Before Reading
What do you do before you read?
Do you read the title and headings?
Do you look at the illustrations, charts, graphs, and maps?
Do you predict what the selection might be about?
Do you ask yourself what you know about the topic?
Do you plan how you are going to read the selection—fast, medium, or slow?
Do you have questions in mind that you plan to answer through your reading?

During Reading
What do you do while you're reading?
Do you think about what you're reading?
Do you stop every once in a while and ask yourself what you've read so far?
Do you picture in your mind the people, events, and places that you are reading about?
Do you make up questions in your mind as you read?

Do you try to answer those questions?
Do you imagine that you are talking to the author as you read?

What do you do if the passage is confusing?
Do you read it again?
Do you just keep on reading?
Do you try to get help from photos, charts, graphs, or maps?

What do you do if you run into a hard word?
Do you use context to try to figure it out?
Do you look for word parts that you know?
Do you use a dictionary or a glossary?

After Reading
After reading the selection, what do you do?
Do you think about what you've read?
Do you do something with the information that you've learned?
Do you compare what you've just learned from your reading with what you already know?

they survey the chapter, for instance? As they read, do they take notes? Do they use graphic aids? After observing their reading, administer a questionnaire or interview that inquires about the way they read their texts (see Figure 13.4). After students have completed their questionnaires, discuss with them how they go about reading their texts. Based on the information obtained, provide instruction for efficient use of texts.

Anecdotal Records

Another way of collecting observational data is to keep anecdotal records or take field notes. An **anecdotal record** is the recording of an event that sheds some light on the student's learning behavior. It may be very brief, but should contain a summary portrayal of the event, including time, date, names of persons involved, and a description of the setting.

Anecdotal records may be used to obtain data about students' learning processes, interests, attitudes, work habits, interaction with others, or other elements of the program. Records might be kept daily, weekly, or monthly. When making anecdotal records, include a number of observations to be sure conclusions are based on representative data. Also, take note of positive factors as well as negative ones. There is a tendency to stress the negative (Bush & Huebner, 1979).

An anecdotal record should be a neutral recording, not an evaluation of behavior. Tell what the student did; do not evaluate the behavior. For instance, the statement "Alexia was defiant today" is an evaluative statement, whereas the statement "Alexia refused to follow directions" is a neutral description of her behavior. Anecdotal records are most helpful when they shed light on a key behavior. In order for anecdotal records to be useful, they should be reviewed periodically and summarized. Teachers should look for patterns of behavior and ascertain what the information reveals about the student and how it can be used to plan her or his instructional program. See the sample anecdotal record in Figure 13.5.

■ An **anecdotal record** is the recording of the description of a significant incident in which the description and interpretation are kept separate.

■ A **questionnaire** is an instrument in which a subject is asked to respond to a series of questions on some topic.

■ An **interview** is the oral process of asking a subject a series of questions on a topic.

Questionnaires and Interviews

Questionnaires are useful devices for obtaining information about work and study habits, reading interests, and attitudes (see Figure 13.4). **Interviews** are

Student _____ Date _____

During Lab, Anya let her partner do much of the work. She observed as her partner dissected the sheep's brain. Anya's role was to hand her partner the dissecting tools and to check in the lab to make sure that procedures were being followed.

Student _____ Date _____

While completing the drawing of the dissected sheep's brain, Anya copied the illustration from the text rather than from the actual sheep's brain that her partner had dissected. Anya was focused on the drawing. She didn't even look when two students in the back of the room got into a brief argument.

FIGURE 13.5
Anecdotal Record

simply oral questionnaires. The advantage of an interview is that the teacher can probe a student's replies, rephrase questions, and encourage extended answers, thus obtaining a wide range of information. An interview can focus on such topics as a student's favorite activities in a class, favorite authors, or work habits. One kind of interview, the process interview, provides insight about the learning strategies students use. Because it helps students become aware of their processes, they can gain more control over them and use them more effectively (Jett-Simpson, 1990). The process interview can be conducted informally on a one-to-one basis, but if time is limited, you can hold sessions with small groups or seek written responses instead of oral ones. Possible process interview questions include the following, which are adapted from Jett-Simpson (1990). Only one or two or these questions should be asked at one sitting.

1. How do you choose something to read?
2. How do you get ready for reading?
3. How do you go about studying for tests?
4. When you come to a word you don't know, what do you do?
5. When a paragraph is confusing, what do you do?
6. How do you go about reading your science [history; geography] text?
7. What do you do to help remember what you've read?
8. How do you go about reading and solving a math word problem?

The Metacognitive Awareness of Reading Strategies (MARS) (Mokhtari & Reichard, 2002) is a carefully constructed questionnaire that can be used to assess reading strategy awareness. In addition to providing information about the students' use of strategies, the MARS or a similar instrument can be used to build students' awareness of strategies (Klingner, Vaughn, & Boardman, 2007).

Student Feedback Questionnaire

One way of improving classroom instruction is to get feedback from students. This can be done informally or through a questionnaire, such as the Tripod, which is designed to provide information about the quality of instruction in secondary schools. Questions obtain data about the Seven Cs: Care, Control, Clarify, Challenge, Captivate, Confer, and Consolidate. The two qualities most closely correlated with achievement are control [Our class stays busy and does not waste time.] and Challenge [My teacher pushes everybody to work hard.] (Bill & Melinda Gates Foundation, 2010a). Classes that had high scores on the Tripod questionnaire had higher achievement. Administer the Tripod or a similar questionnaire and be sure to include questions that can be used to improve your instruction so that the questionnaire becomes a formative assessment.

Unfortunately, questionnaires, interviews, and ratings have a common weakness. Their validity depends on students' ability and willingness to supply accurate, honest information. To find out if students actually do what they say they do, observations can be helpful (Klingner et al., 2007).

 **USING TECHNOLOGY**

Tripod Project www.tripodproject.org/
index.php/about/about_background
Provides additional information about
Tripod questionnaires.

Work Samples

Samples of student work are an excellent source of assessment information, especially if they shed light on the students' thought processes; this helps the teacher understand how students are conceptualizing information and figure out ways to clarify any misconceptions. For instance, concept maps have an excellent potential for revealing students' grasp of ways in which ideas are related. Semantic maps can also be used to assess comprehension of content and relationships. If students compose maps before and after a learning unit, concept maps can be used as pre- and postassessments. Essays, lab reports, projects, and completed math problems that show students' work also have high potential for yielding useful information about students' thought processes and understanding of content.

CHECKUP

1. What are some informal ways of assessing students' performance?
2. How can these approaches be used in a content area program?

▌Assessing Background Knowledge

More than almost any other factor, background knowledge will determine what students learn and, indeed, how well they understand their texts. In one study, conceptual knowledge was a better predictor of reading comprehension than reading ability (Leslie & Caldwell, 2006). The more students know, the more they are prepared to learn. In some instances, students' background knowledge is a potential barrier to learning because they have formed erroneous concepts. This is especially true in science. Students will be unable to form accurate concepts until their misconceptions have been corrected.

Background knowledge may be assessed in a number of ways: free recall, word association, structured questions, unstructured questions, and recognition. A quick and easy way to assess background knowledge is through free association or brainstorming. For instance, if you are a science teacher about to begin a unit on cells and are unsure of the extent of students' knowledge, place the word *cells* on the board and ask students to brainstorm it. Ask, "What comes to mind when you think of the word *cells*?" Jot down students' responses on the board. Then ask students to tell which words on the board go together and explain why. This will help you determine both the extent and depth of their knowledge and also its accuracy. If students are English language learners, note the extent of their academic English. They may have a relatively good command of everyday English, but be less familiar with the more formal academic language.

A fairly straightforward way to assess background is to have students survey a chapter and predict what it will be about. For instance, before students read a brief history of conflict in the Balkans, ask them to look at the title (The Balkan Powder Keg) and the subheads (A Region of Divided Loyalty, The East-West Tug-of-War, An Ethnic Patchwork, and The Nations Emerge in the Balkans). Also have them examine the accompanying illustrations. Based on a survey of these items, students predict what information the section will contain. Some students may make very general predictions: The section will describe difficulties in that part of the world. Others may be able to make a series of predictions: The section will tell that there was trouble in the region; it will tell about different ethnic groups; it will tell about the many countries in the Balkans. A few students may be able to integrate the information garnered from the survey with their background knowledge and predict that the section will explain that the region has had many conflicts because the people have different ethnic identities, religions, and languages, and have been split by a number of wars. Through students' responses, you can gauge the quality and quantity of their background knowledge. Another way to assess background knowledge is through PReP, which was explained Chapter 5.

Checking for Understanding

Content area and secondary school researchers and former classroom teachers Douglas Fisher and Nancy Frey (2007) confess to having asked students the question, "Does everybody understand?" and when a lone voice answered "Yes," proceeding with the lesson, only to find out through a quiz or discussion that understanding was not universal. It is vitally important to find out whether students are following along or are lost—or are somewhere in between. However, most students typically don't respond to the "Does everybody understand?" question. To elicit that kind of information, there are a number of steps you might take. You might call on a number of students, including those who don't usually raise their hands, or probe incorrect or incomplete responses to determine the nature of the misunderstanding and figure out ways to correct it. You might ask for thumbs up to indicate understanding or thumbs down to signal a lack of understanding. You might use every-pupil response cards. A physics teacher displaying various examples of energy via a PowerPoint presentation had students hold up cards labeled "kinetic energy" or "potential energy" to indicate their responses. This action, along with having students explain their choices when there was disagreement, allowed him to see how well students were grasping the concept and to remedy confusions immediately (Fisher & Frey, 2007). Listening in on student discussions, using a quick write, and observing students as they write or complete a lab assignment are also helpful checks to gauge students' understanding. An electronic interactive response system used in conjunction with an interactive white board enables teachers to administer quizzes via the white board at any point during the lesson. Students use remotes known as "clickers" to respond to multiple choice or true-false questions. Students can also respond with very brief responses of about 20 letters or fewer. The response can also be used to take a poll: How many ate breakfast this morning? Responses are checked and compiled immediately: 80 percent had breakfast. Quizzes or questions can be prepared by the teacher or can be purchased or obtained free from a learning community. Some measure of how well teachers engage in **checking for understanding** is a key characteristic assessed on evaluations of teacher effectiveness (iObservation, 2010)

Self-Evaluation

The most important evaluation is self-evaluation. Unless students can assess their own progress toward meeting goals, they are hampered in taking the steps necessary to reach them. The first step in self-evaluation is the setting of goals. At the beginning of the semester and periodically during the semester, students should be encouraged to set learning goals. They should then use their sense of how they are doing, quizzes, tests, assignments, work samples, and portfolios—if they have them—to assess their progress and make improvements in their work habits and effort as needed. Students need to ask themselves how they are doing so they can do better. Teachers might hold conferences in which they discuss content learned or skills mastered, as well as goals for the future and how those goals might be met. Portfolios, which are described later in this chapter, also offer opportunities for self-assessment.

Logs and Journals

Learning logs and response journals, as explained in Chapter 8, can be part of students' evaluations, as well as a source of information for the teacher. Learning logs or journals provide a record of topics covered, key concepts learned, and students' reflections on their learning. Response journals provide a record of students' reactions to their reading. Logs and journals offer opportunities for self-evaluation, especially if the teacher confers with

■ **Checking for understanding** is the practice of periodically assessing students' grasp of material being taught in a lesson.

Holding conferences with students helps them to evaluate their progress and set goals.

Source: Shutterstock.

students about them or encourages students to set learning goals and reflect on what the journals and logs show about their progress.

CHECK UP

1. *How might background knowledge be assessed?*
2. *How might teachers check for understanding?*
3. *What role can self-evaluation play in a content area program?*

Evaluating Writing

Because it is probably the most complex cognitive task in which students engage, writing is also one of the most difficult to assess. Two major approaches to assessing writing are holistic and analytic scoring.

Holistic Scoring

In **holistic scoring**, a teacher evaluates a composition in terms of a limited number of general criteria instead of noting specific strengths and weaknesses. The criteria are used "only as a general guide" in reaching a holistic judgment" (Cooper & Odell, 1977, p. 4).

The teacher does not stop to check the piece to see whether it meets each of the criteria, but simply forms a general impression. The teacher can score a piece according to the presence or absence of key elements. There may be a scoring guide, which can be a checklist or a rubric. (See Chapter 8 for information about constructing and using rubrics to assess writing.) A holistic scoring guide in the form of a rubric is shown in Table 13.3.

Applying Holistic Scoring

Before scoring the pieces, the teacher should quickly read them all to get a sense of how well the class did overall. This prevents setting criteria that are too high or too low. After sorting the papers into four groups—beginning, developing, accomplished, exemplary—the teacher rereads each work more carefully before confirming its

■ **Holistic scoring** is a process for sorting or ranking written pieces on the basis of an overall impression of the piece. Sample pieces (anchors) or a description of standards (rubric) for rating the pieces might be used as guides.

TABLE 13.3 **Holistic Scoring Guide**

	BEGINNING	DEVELOPING	ACCOMPLISHED	EXEMPLARY
Topic	Not relevant or appropriate.	Too broad or too narrow.	Appropriate.	Interesting and original.
Content	Little or no development.	Limited development.	Adequate development.	Fully developed; includes convincing details or examples.
Organization	Little or no organization.	Some evidence of organization but irrelevant details are included and some details are in the wrong place.	Has an obvious organization; details are relevant and appropriately placed.	Well organized.
Style	Lack of style.	Some parts are not clear.	Clearly written.	Appealing, convincing style.
Mechanics	Many errors in spelling, punctuation, usage, and sentence structure.	Some errors in mechanics.	Very few errors in mechanics.	Flawlessly written.

placement. If possible, a second teacher should also evaluate the papers, especially if the works are graded.

Analytic Scoring

Analytic scoring involves analyzing pieces and noting specific strengths and weaknesses. It requires the teacher to create a set of specific scoring criteria. Instead of overwhelming students with corrections, it is best to decide on a limited number of key features, such as those that have been emphasized for a particular writing activity. Key factors generally include content, organization, style, and conventions. Although more time-consuming than holistic scoring, analytic scoring allows the teacher to make constructive suggestions about students' writing. An analytic scoring guide is presented in Table 13.4.

It is important that students understand the rubric or criteria for assessing their written pieces. As Dahl and Farnan (1998) note,

> When writers lack specific standards and intentions, their ability to reflect on and evaluate their writing is severely compromised. It is not surprising that if writers do not know what they want to accomplish with a particular writing, it will be difficult for them to judge whether they have created an effective composition. (p. 121)

■ **Analytic scoring** is a type of scoring that uses a description of specific features to be considered when assessing the piece.

TABLE 13.4 Analytic Scoring Guide

	BEGINNING	DEVELOPING	ACCOMPLISHED	EXEMPLARY
Topic	Not relevant or appropriate.	Too broad or too narrow.	Appropriate.	Interesting and original.
Content	States an idea but fails to develop it.	Develops an idea with one or two details. Details are not fully explained.	Develops an idea with three or more details. Details are explained but not elaborated on. Details are fairly ordinary.	Develops an idea with three or more details. Details are elaborated but not overly so. Details are interesting and convincing and include one or more that are original.
Organization	Little or no organization.	Main idea is stated in a topic sentence. Some of the details support the main idea, but some do not. Main idea does not stand out. Important and unimportant details might be mixed in so it is difficult to tell which are the key details.	Main idea is stated in a topic sentence that clearly explains that this is the main idea. Supporting details follow. Concluding sentence sums up or restates main idea. Uses connecting words such as *next, so,* and *however* to show that ideas are related. Announces concluding sentence. Structure of the piece is apparent.	Main idea is emphasized through placement in beginning of report and is supported by details that follow. Uses placement of ideas rather than formal connecting words to show that ideas are related. Uses placement and flow of language to indicate main idea, supporting details, and conclusion. Has subtle but strong structure.
Style	Lack of style.	Some ideas are not clearly expressed.	Ideas are expressed in language that is plain and easy to understand. Limited use of varied vocabulary or varied sentence structure.	Ideas are expressed in language that is both clear and appealing. First sentence piques reader's interest. Intriguing details and examples keep reader interested. Varied vocabulary and varied sentence patterns make the writing flow.
Mechanics	Many errors in spelling. First word in the sentence and names of people and places are not capitalized. Failure to use end punctuation.	Some errors in spelling. Failure to capitalize some proper names. Some sentence fragments and run-on sentences.	Few errors in mechanics. No more than one or two misspelled words. May have an error or two in use of commas, colons, or semi-colons.	Virtually flawless. Uses semicolons, colons, dashes appropriately. Varied vocabulary is spelled correctly.

Teachers' Comments

When checking students' papers, resist the temptation to mark all errors. Focus your corrections and comments. Students do their best when comments are positive and when there is emphasis on one or two areas, such as providing a fuller explanation or combining choppy sentences. This is especially effective when instruction is geared to the areas highlighted and students are given the opportunity to revise targeted areas in their compositions (Dahl & Farnan, 1998).

CHECKUP
---

1. How can writing be assessed?

Portfolios

Although they were once the domain of artists, photographers, actors, and designers, **portfolios** are now used widely in education. Portfolios provide a broad sampling of work for assessment and demonstrate growth over time. More important, portfolios actively involve students in the assessment process and have the potential to help them become more reflective and more engaged learners. As science educators Baker and Piburn (1997) note:

> The process of putting together a portfolio results in a number of positive outcomes besides learning and the development of positive attitudes toward science and scientific dispositions. It builds a feeling of self-efficacy because students are participating in the assessment of their own progress and they are not being compared to others. It fosters motivation because it is not being used as a way to control behavior. It also fosters reflection and the development of metacognitive strategies as students evaluate their own progress. (p. 383)

The foundation of the portfolio is a statement of objectives or standards. The purpose of the portfolio is to show the extent to which these key objectives have been met. Work samples are included to document the degree to which each objective has been reached. The portfolio should contain a statement of key objectives, a listing of work samples or other items showing that objectives have been met, and an overall reflection in which the student discusses the progress he or she has made and considers future plans. The core of the portfolio should be the documentation. Each item should have a caption that briefly explains why it documents a particular objective.

Documentation varies depending on the subject area and objectives. Items might include field notes of observations, a recording or write-up of an interview with the town manager, photos of insects, a labeled rock collection, models, charts, an annotated listing of books read, a video of a skit on acid rain, the results of a questionnaire, lab reports, logs, journal entries, and so on.

In math, students might include a write-up of a statistical investigation, a reflection on processes used to solve a complex problem, and graphs and charts. A writing portfolio might include samples of the student's work. If process is being emphasized, samples from the beginning, middle, and end of the year might be included, along with the samples that show the whole process from preplanning notes through drafts to final copy.

Types of Portfolios

Portfolios vary according to purpose (Valencia & Place, 1994). The four major kinds of portfolios are the showcase, evaluation, documentation, and process portfolios. *Showcase portfolios* are composed of works that students have selected as their best. Students in work-study programs or in the graphic arts program might assemble showcase portfolios in order to document their abilities as they apply for additional schooling or work. The emphasis in the *evaluation portfolio* is on obtaining representative pieces of work from key areas. The

■ A **portfolio** is a collection of work samples, test results, checklists, or other data used to assess a student's performance.

samples included might be standardized; that is, they have to embrace a certain topic or task and must conform to a standard set of directions. A *documentation portfolio* contains elements of the showcase and evaluation portfolios and is designed to provide evidence of students' growth. As such, the documentation portfolio is more open-ended and allows for more student choice in the selection of items to be included. The purpose of the *process portfolio* is to show the learning processes that students use, so it includes documentation from various stages of a project. For a writing portfolio, rough drafts as well as final copies would be included.

Each artifact or document should have a brief caption that identifies the item and notes which goal it documents. Students must also explain why they chose a particular item—it shows their ability to draw logical conclusions from an experiment, for example. Through classroom discussions and in conferences, help students explore criteria for including items in their portfolios.

Portfolios are most effective when a rubric is created for assessing them. When students have a role in creating the rubric, they have a deeper understanding of the evaluation process as well as a sense of ownership (see Table 13.1). Students should write a cover letter or complete a statement in which they reflect on their portfolios. The reflection might include a description of goals they feel they have met, areas that need added work, and plans for the future.

The value of portfolios extends well beyond providing assessment data. When Liza, a teen enrolled in an alternative high school, was asked how portfolio conferences helped her, she replied, "By letting me know what I should work on more, and makes me and Ms. Young be more closer—like friends. Not just student and teacher" (Young, Matthews, Kietzmann, & Westerfield, 1997, p. 348).

In portfolio assessment, students become active participants in the learning process and get to know themselves as learners. Through assembling a portfolio, they become part of the evaluation process. However, in order to play an active role, students should assess their work before placing it in a portfolio. Using the rubric created for a particular essay, project, or other product, students should note its strengths and weaknesses as well as their plans for making improvements (Popham, 2000). They should also assess the overall portfolio periodically. By doing this, students might realize that they are writing only narratives and should branch out to dramatic or poetic pieces, or that they are doing a lot of reading in science but very few hands-on projects. Through examining and reflecting on the materials contained in the portfolio, they can gain insights into their strengths and weaknesses and see what they need to work on to improve their skills. In addition to helping students set goals, portfolios help students track their progress toward meeting those goals. A form for student evaluation of a portfolio is presented in Figure 13.6.

Reviewing Portfolios

To check on students' progress, periodically review their portfolios. Portfolio conferences might be held at the end of each unit of instruction or before the end of each marking period. Young (Young et al., 1997) held conferences every six weeks. As a result of those conferences and related classroom activities, students built a relationship with the teacher, started taking more responsibility for their learning, began setting more specific goals, and gained insight into what they needed to do to meet their goals.

Before you start to review a portfolio, decide what you want to focus on. It could be number of books read, changes in writing, or effort put into revisions. Your evaluation should, of course, consider the student's stated goals; it is also important to emphasize the student's strengths. As you assess the portfolio, consider a variety of pieces and look at the work in terms of how it has changed. Ask yourself, "What does the student's work show about his progress over the time span covered? What might he do to make continued progress?"

To save time and help organize your assessment of the portfolio, you may want to use a checklist that is supplemented with personal comments. A sample portfolio review checklist is presented in Figure 13.7. Because the objective of evaluation is to improve

FIGURE 13.6
Portfolio Self-Evaluation

Name _____ Date _____

Portfolio Self-Evaluation

What were my goals in writing for this period?

What progress toward meeting these goals does my portfolio show?

What are my strengths as a writer?

What are my weaknesses?

What are my goals for improving as a writer?

How do I plan to meet these goals?

What questions do I have about my progress as a writer?

(Gunning, 2003)

FIGURE 13.7
Sample Portfolio Review Checklist

	Not adequate	Adequate	Proficient	Advanced
Amount of writing				
Variety of writing				
Planning				
Revising				
Self-editing				
Content				
Organization				
Style				
Mechanics				

Strengths: _____

Needs: _____

Comments: _____

instruction, students should be active partners in the process. "It follows that assessment activities in which students are engaged in evaluating their own learning help them reflect on and understand their own strengths and needs, and it instills responsibility for their own learning" (Tierney, Carter, & Desai, 1991, p. 7).

Disadvantages of Portfolios

Portfolios are not without their shortcomings. Although using a rubric helps in making fair and consistent evaluations, creating effective rubrics is difficult and labor intensive. In addition, careful assessment of portfolios is time-consuming (Popham, 2000). Unless the purpose and nature of the portfolio is clearly stated and students are selective about what should be included, portfolios might become unwieldy collections of miscellaneous items.

> ## C H E C K U P
>
> 1. What are the advantages and disadvantages of portfolio assessment?
> 2. How might portfolio assessment be used in a content area program?

Screening, Benchmark, and Progress–Monitoring Assessments

Response to Intervention programs typically implement screening, benchmarking, and progress monitoring. **Screening tests** are designed to identify students who are at risk or who are falling behind. Screening assessments also monitor progress and provide an overview of the effectiveness of instruction. If whole groups of students are not making expected progress, this is an indicator that the program might need to be adjusted. If certain classes are not doing as well as others, this could be a sign that the teachers in those classes need assistance. The screening tests that you select should assess the key skills that students need to be successful. The most useful screening instruments in reading, for instance, are those that assess actual reading of the type in which students usually engage.

Often the screening instrument is also used for benchmarking. **Benchmark assessments** are typically based on grade-level performance standards. A benchmark might state that students should be able to read a grade-level passage with 95 percent accuracy and 70 percent comprehension, or read grade-level material at a rate of 150 words a minute.

Although benchmark assessments are frequently written on grade level, it is important to obtain an estimate of the students' reading levels. This is an essential piece of information for all content areas that use printed material. Knowing students' reading levels enables you to avoid providing materials that are too difficult. It also flags students who are reading below grade level and may need added help. If possible, obtain or construct benchmark or screening measures that have a wide enough range so that they have passages appropriate for below-level readers and so can be used to provide estimated levels of performance. As explained in Chapter 2, individual and group inventories can also be used to estimate students' reading levels. The group inventory can be a commercial one, such as the STAR, the DRP, or the Scholastic Reading Inventory. It can also be a group inventory that you construct using your texts or it can be a curriculum-based measure, such as an oral fluency test or a maze assessment.

Curriculum–Based Measures

Curriculum-based measures (CBMs) are actually curriculum independent and not tied to a particular curriculum or program. CBMs have been described as general outcome assessments. They measure overall indicators of proficiency rather than mastery of specific skills. Thus, the ability to read passages orally and to complete maze (fill-in-the-blank) passages are indicators of overall achievement in reading. CBMs are standardized and are quick, easy-to-administer probes of students' overall proficiency. They are designed so that multiple but equivalent versions can be created, allowing progress to be monitored frequently, in some cases as often as once a month or more (Hosp, Hosp, & Howell, 2007).

Fluency and Comprehension CBMs

Oral Reading Fluency The most widely used CBM is *oral reading fluency*, which measures how many words a student can accurately read in one minute. Oral reading fluency is a general outcome measure and is a rough indicator of a student's proficiency

Struggling Readers

Ideally, screening instruments should include below-grade-level as well as grade-level passages so that useful assessment data is obtained for all students.

■ **Screening** tests are assessments used to identify students who need additional assessment because they appear to be at risk.

with lower-level reading skills. It has been compared to a thermometer because it is a measure of general reading health. In one study, however, 15 percent of students who had good oral reading fluency had poor comprehension. Those students also tended to have low vocabulary scores (Riedel, 2007). Measures of oral reading fluency need to be complemented with measures of comprehension.

Maze Passages At the secondary level, **maze passages** are preferred to oral reading passages because they provide a measure of basic comprehension, can be administered to groups, and take very little time (Torgesen, Nettles, Howard, & Winterbottom, n. d.). Maze passages are 150 to 400 words in length. Every seventh word is deleted, but no words are deleted from the first or last sentences. Answer options include the word from the selection, an option that is not the same part of speech and does not make sense in the selection, and another option that may or may not be the right part of speech but doesn't fit the sense of the selection. The two distractors are usually chosen from other parts of the selection (see Figure 13.8). Students read for 3 minutes. Passages for grades 2 to 10 are available from *Core* (2008) and *iSteep* (2005).

Although they are not designed to yield reading levels, maze tests can provide that information. When being screened, students are given grade-level passages. As a general rule, students should be able to correctly identify 70 percent to 80 percent of the replacement words by the end of the year. Students whose scores are below the 70 to 80 percent level should be given lower-level selections until they are able to correctly replace at least 70 percent of the items. (If norms are available, use them instead of the percentage figure.) As a practical matter, you might give your students two lower-level selections at the same time that you give the on-grade selection, especially if you suspect that some of your students are reading below grade level. Another option would be to give only the grade-level passage, but to individually test those students scoring below 70 percent. Instead of or along with mazes or oral reading fluency, many secondary schools use state assessments and other measures, including norm-referenced reading tests, unit tests, department tests, and grades to screen and monitor progress.

Setting Benchmarks

Many screening and progress-monitoring measures have benchmarks, or expected levels of performance. Some benchmarks have been set because they are desired levels of performance. Others have been set by noting the relationship between students' performance on a benchmark and their later performance on an outcome measure. In mazes, replacements average .5 words a month, but for some studies they have been as low as .25 (Hosp, Hosp, & Howell, 2007).

Although screening and benchmark measures are frequently set at grade level, monitoring measures should be provided that are on the students' reading levels. Thus, a ninth grader reading on a third-grade level should be given a monitoring measure that is on a third-grade level. Students' growth is best measured with assessments that are on their reading level.

In general, it is recommended that all students be given benchmark or screening tests three times a year. That way, students who did well in the beginning of the year but fell behind can be identified and given help if necessary. Students who are identified as being at risk or who are placed in intervention programs are generally assessed more frequently. Some programs suggest weekly monitoring. However, the Florida Center for Reading Research (2009) recommends that general outcome measures such as mazes "should not be given more frequently than is necessary to establish a reliable estimate of growth. Giving them more frequently than that takes time away from instruction unnecessarily. In contrast, teachers should be constantly (hourly, daily, weekly) acquiring formative assessment data about their students' progress in mastering their specific lesson objectives." Formative assessments include quizzes, unit tests, work samples, and observations.

■ Maze passages are assessments, usually timed, in which every seventh word has been deleted and replaced by three or more answer options, one of which is the deleted word. The test task is to select the deleted word.

Creating Your Own Monitoring System

Because of the overemphasis on speed of responding and a possible lack of correspondence between what current progress-monitoring systems assess and what you teach, you might choose to construct your own system. First, decide what your key objectives are. Determine what students should know and be able to do by the end of the year. These objectives should, of course, include school and district standards, but they might also include additional goals that you have set for your students. Translate these standards into language that students can understand so they have a clear idea of what is expected of them. You might also list the steps needed to meet the standards. Then create or adapt measures that assess those objectives. For instance, for comprehension, you might use the maze passages. Graph performances so that you can see whether students are on track. Mark where you believe students should be by the end of the year. Then mark students' current status. Draw an **aimline** from students' current status to where it is expected they will be at year's end. The **slope** of the line gives you a sense of the rate of progress necessary for students to reach the end mark. Monitor students' progress at least three times a year and mark their progress. Monitor more frequently if students are struggling. If students fall below the aimline, provide added instruction and arrange for intervention, if necessary. If students are consistently scoring above the aimline, adjust the program to make it more challenging. Monitoring progress is one of the most effective steps you can take to help all students reach their full literacy potential.

Figure 13.8 shows ninth grader Alexia's progress on a maze assessment. The student was given passages at the third, fourth, and fifth grade levels from the Core (2008) assessment. Alexia is reading at the beginning fourth-grade level, so the goal was to demonstrate two years of growth. Since each point represents approximately two month's growth, the objective for Alexia was to increase her score by 10 points to 35. Alexia's beginning score is 25. Note that her progress was slow up until January, but then it accelerated. At that time, an extra session was added to her intervention each day. In June, Alexia scored 33, missing her goal by 2 points. She gained approximately 1.6 years. A summer program was recommended to maintain and extend her gain.

Monitoring Progress and Assessing for Learning

Assessing for learning requires monitoring of progress. However, some CBMs don't do much more than provide a general indication of students' current status. For instance, if a student has a low oral reading fluency, you need to determine why so you can provide an effective intervention. If you analyze the student's miscues, you might find that the student is reading slowly because he is having difficulty with multisyllabic words or with words containing complex vowels and needs instruction in word recognition. Assessing for learning requires information not provided by progress-monitoring assessments. Information from observations, discussions, work samples, daily or weekly quizzes, unit tests, and other sources is also required.

Exemplary Assessment

As its screening measure for secondary school students, Florida uses a computer-administered reading comprehension assessment. If students do poorly, they are given a maze test. If they do poorly on the maze test, they are given a word analysis test. The maze test is viewed as a measure of reading efficiency. It measures rate, accuracy, and low-level comprehension. Students who do well on the maze test but poorly on the reading comprehension test apparently possess basic decoding skills, fluency, and low-level comprehension skills, but they lack higher-level skills or the ability to deal with larger segments of text. Think alouds, observations and analysis of

USING TECHNOLOGY

Florida Center for Reading Research Assessment Programs www.fcrr.org/assessmentMiddleHighSchool.shtm Provides information about Florida's assessment programs for secondary students.

■ The **aimline** is the line on a graph that shows how much progress will have to be made in order to reach a goal.

■ The **slope** is the angle of an aimline. It shows the rate of progress that needs to be made in order to reach a goal.

FIGURE 13.8
Cumulative Mazes Screening Chart

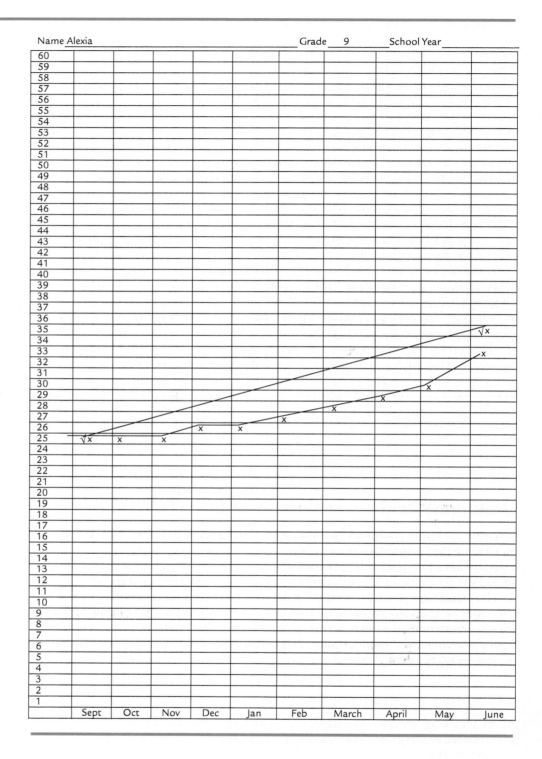

students' written and oral responses to their reading might be used to shed additional light on the students comprehension difficulties

---

CHECKUP

1. What are the purposes of screening and progress monitoring?
2. How might screening and progress monitoring be implemented in a secondary school?

Teacher Self–Assessment

Virtually all of the assessment measures used to evaluate students can be used by teachers to evaluate the effectiveness of their programs. However, the best assessment measures are those that are most fully aligned with the teacher's goals and curriculum. Teacher-created quizzes and unit tests provide a measure of the content students have learned. Portfolios provide a measure of content learned, but also offer insight into the effectiveness of assignments. In some classes, students complete exit slips on which they talk about what they have learned that day or ask questions that they did not have time to raise in class or were reluctant to bring up. Exit slips are composed in the last five or ten minutes of class. Students might read their slips and discuss them, or the teacher can read them over to get a sense of what students learned and what they might need help with. During the next class period, the teacher can answer questions that have been raised or clarify confusions. Entrance slips, in which students reflect on the previous day's class and/or home assignments, might be used instead of or along with exit slips. Learning logs and journals might perform a similar function (see Chapter 8). As an alternative, the teacher and the class might design a form on which students tell what they learned in a certain class and list questions that they still have. Exit slips and log and journal entries provide information about the quality and clarity of daily instruction as well as give insights into the quality of the classroom atmosphere. External tests, such as those mandated by the district or state, also provide a measure of student learning, but the validity of the data depends on the extent to which the tests measure what was taught. Through reflection on these measures, the teacher can judge the effectiveness and quality of instruction and, based on these reflections, decide what changes need to be made in the program and in instruction.

USING TECHNOLOGY

National Center for Research on Evaluation, Standards, and Student Testing www.cse.ucla.edu Provides information on assessment.

National Center on Educational Outcomes www.cehd.umn.edu/NCEO Features information on assessing students who have disabilities.

The Final Step: Improving Instruction

Evaluation begins with the setting of goals and ends with action. An essential component is improvement of instruction. Once strengths and weaknesses are noted, steps should be taken to build on the strengths and repair the weak spots. For example, if you find that students' ability to interpret graphs is weak, you should make plans to improve that area. If students are unable to synthesize data from two sources of information or solve word problems, you should work on those skills. As the Board of Directors of the International Reading Association (1999) commented, "Assessment involves the systematic and purposeful collection of data to inform actions. From the viewpoint of educators, the primary purpose of assessment is to help students by providing information about how instruction can be improved" (p. 258). The final step in evaluation is to improve the program and the achievement of each of your students.

Summary

The basic purpose of assessment is to provide feedback so that improvements can be made. Formative assessment is ongoing assessment that can be used to plan instruction. Summative assessment is designed to evaluate achievement over long periods of time. Interim assessment combines features of both formative and summative assessments. Evaluation starts with a set of goals. Goals now exist in lists of standards for each major content area.

In addition to standards recommended by national organizations, states and local school districts have issued standards or curriculum frameworks. Goals should reflect basic principles of learning.

Standards are often assessed with high-stakes tests on whose outcomes important decisions will be based. However, more than one source of assessment should be used to make such decisions. High-stakes testing has the potential to narrow the curriculum if educators allow tests to dictate what is taught. Despite being controversial, the amount of high-stakes testing is increasing. In addition, tests have become more inclusive. As much as possible and with modifications and accommodations if necessary, English language learners and students in special education programs are required to take part in state and national assessments.

Tests are either norm-referenced or criterion-referenced. In norm-referenced tests, test takers are compared to a representative sample of students who are the same age or in the same grade. Scores are reported in a variety of ways: raw scores, percentile ranks, grade equivalent scores, stanines, normal curve equivalents, and scaled scores. In criterion-referenced tests, students' performance is assessed in terms of a criterion or standard. Because they indicate whether students have mastered a particular skill or strategy, these tests tend to be more valuable than norm-referenced tests for planning programs. Rubrics are a type of criterion-referenced reporting that provides descriptions of both expected or desirable performances and unsatisfactory performances.

Tests should be reliable, valid, and fair. Students should also be given tests designed for the level on which they are reading. Tests that are too easy or too difficult are invalid and yield erroneous information. Assessment should measure both students' overall level of achievement and their growth, which is known as value added.

Informal means of assessment include think-alouds, which are designed to gain insight into the thought processes students use, observations, checklists, ratings, questionnaires, and interviews. Observations may include composing anecdotal records or field notes. An anecdotal record is the recording of an event that sheds some light on the student's learning behavior.

Because background knowledge is such an important element in learning, it should be carefully assessed. Background knowledge may be assessed through free recall, word association, structured questions, unstructured questions, recognition, brainstorming, and predictions. The most important type of evaluation is self-evaluation. Unless students assess their own progress toward meeting goals, they are hampered in taking the steps necessary to reach those goals. Tests and quizzes, exit and entrance slips, learning logs, and response journals can be a part of students' self-evaluation, as well as a source of information for the teacher. Portfolios also offer opportunities for self-assessment.

Writing can be assessed holistically or analytically. In holistic scoring, a composition is evaluated in terms of a limited number of general criteria. Analytic scoring involves analyzing pieces and noting specific strengths and weaknesses.

Portfolios provide a broad sampling of work for assessment and are effective in showing growth over time. They also actively involve the student in the assessment process.

Screening tests are designed to identify students who are at risk or who are falling behind. Monitoring measures are used to track progress. Informal reading inventories have been widely used to place and screen students and can be used to monitor progress. Curriculum-based measures (CBMs) such as oral reading fluency and mazes are also used to screen and monitor progress. CBMs measure overall indicators of proficiency rather than mastery of specific skills. Norm-referenced tests are also used to screen and monitor progress. Although screening and benchmarking measures are frequently set at grade level, monitoring measures should be provided that are on the students' reading levels so that progress can be adequately measured. Tests, quizzes, work samples, and informal measures, such as oral and written retellings, think-alouds, observations, anecdotal records, questionnaires, interviews, and ratings are frequently used to assess performance on an ongoing basis.

The final step in evaluation is to improve the programs and student achievement.

Reflection

Return to the Anticipation Guide at the beginning of this chapter. Respond once again to the items. Did your responses change? If so, how and why? Why is assessment such an important part of instruction? Which practices seem to lead to the most effective assessment? Why is high-stakes testing controversial?

Extension and Application

1. Maintain a file of rubrics, observation guides, checklists, sample tests, think-aloud protocols, questionnaires, and other assessment devices that might be useful. Try these out with students and reflect on their effectiveness.

2. Examine the assessment devices in texts in your content area. Which kinds of devices are available? Is there provision for observation and portfolios? Which devices would seem to be most useful? Are standards or goals clearly stated? Is assessment aligned with standards?

3. Construct a checklist for an important area in your subject: lab reports, study strategies, participation in class or cooperative learning groups, work habits, or a similar area. If possible, try out the checklist. Revise it, if necessary.

4. Try out the think-aloud technique with a classmate. What does the think-aloud reveal about your reading process? How might you use this assessment technique in your content area?

Go to Topic 2: Assessment in the MyEducationLab (www.myeducationlab.com) for your course, where you can:

- Find learning outcomes for Assessment along with the national standards that connect to these outcomes.

- Complete Assignments and Activities that can help you more deeply understand the chapter content.

- Apply and practice your understanding of the core teaching skills identified in the chapter with the Building Teaching Skills and Dispositions learning units.

Go to the Topic A+RISE in the MyEducationLab (www.myeducationlab.com) for your course. A+RISE® Standards2Strategy™ is an innovative and interactive online resource that offers new teachers in grades K–12 just-in-time, research-based instructional strategies that:

- Meet the linguistic needs of ELLs as they learn content.

- Differentiate instruction for all grades and abilities.

- Offer reading and writing techniques, cooperative learning, use of linguistic and nonlinguistic representations, scaffolding, teacher modeling, higher order thinking, and alternative classroom ELL assessment.

- Provide support to help teachers be effective through the integration of listening, speaking, reading, and writing along with the content curriculum.

- Improve student achievement.

- Are aligned to Common Core Elementary Language Arts standards (for the literacy strategies) and to English language proficiency standards in WIDA, Texas, California, and Florida.

Creating an Effective Content Area Program

The previous thirteen chapters have discussed methods, materials, and assessment measures that you might use in a content area program. Think back on your own content area teachers who were particularly effective. What made them effective? What techniques did they use? How did they make the material understandable and interesting? How did they organize their classes? What kinds of materials did they use? Based on the highly effective teachers that you have known, what you have read, and your own experiences, how would you set up the literacy dimension of the content area that you teach? As you read this last chapter, be prepared to add to, delete from, or modify elements of your current teaching approach.

Using What You Know

The overall intent of this text was to explore techniques, strategies, approaches, methods, materials, and organizational patterns that build literacy in the content areas—resulting in students understanding how to learn and communicate in the content areas, as well as mastering more content area material. Special attention was paid to students who have traditionally had a difficult time learning content area material. This final chapter summarizes the major points of previous chapters, provides practical ways of implementing key practices and principles, and addresses ways to set up a content area program that will result in maximum learning for all students.

Setting Goals

Organizing an effective content area program starts with a statement of goals. You need to decide what it is you want your students to know and be able to do. According to research, setting goals and providing feedback has a powerful impact on student learning. Two studies found that students gained an average of 23 to 25 percentile points when their teachers set goals and provided feedback as to whether goals were being met (Marzano, Gaddy, & Dean, 2000; Haystead & Marzano, 2009). To set goals, consider the standards set by your national professional organization. Also look at standards set by the state and the district in which you teach or plan to teach. Most states have adopted the Common Core State Standards, which have been noted throughout this text. The state and/or district may have a curriculum guide. Also take a look at the kinds of tests that your students will be asked to take. Goals should be adapted to fit the needs of the community in which you will be teaching and the needs of your students.

You could, of course, simply accept the district's or state's goals. In some instances, state or district goals are vague or presented in such general terms that they provide inadequate guidance. By adapting these goals to fit your situation, and possibly adding some of your own, you are reflecting on what is important from your professional point of view. When you make the goals your own, you will have a greater commitment to reaching them. Once goals have been set, you have a foundation for selecting materials and deciding on instructional approaches and techniques.

The next step is to build students' awareness of the goals, so they know what they are going to learn and why. To increase their motivation to learn, help students set personal goals based on your overall content goals or standards. For instance, the content goal in health might be to learn how to plan a balanced diet. A student who is member of the cross-country team might be interested in learning what kind of diet is best to build endurance and also what kind of meal she should eat on the day of a race. A budget-conscious student might want to determine which foods are both nutritious and inexpensive. Set both long-term and short-term goals, and determine ways of monitoring progress toward reaching these goals.

A key element in setting goals—and indeed in all instruction—is feedback. On the basis of analysis of hundreds of studies, one researcher concluded, that "the most powerful single modification that enhances achievement is feedback" (Hattie, 1992, p. 9). Tutoring is such an effective method of learning because students get immediate personal feedback (Bloom, 1976). However, not all feedback is created equal. Feedback given long after the test or project was completed is less effective than feedback given immediately or the next day. The best feedback lets the students know right away whether they are on the right track, and if they are not, it helps them to make needed corrections (Marzano et al., 2000).

CHECKUP

1. What role do goal setting and feedback play in a content area program?

Assessing Progress

In order to provide students the feedback they need, their work must be assessed on an ongoing basis. Assessment should be embedded in instruction so teachers know when review, reteaching, or a change in approach is needed. Teachers also should assess whether students have the necessary background skills and knowledge to master the material in their class. In an analysis of thousands of studies investigating dozens of factors involved in successful achievement, monitoring and charting students progress was the most effective. Using formative assessments to monitor progress and sharing this information with students so they could measure their progress toward reaching an instructional goal resulted in a percentile increase of 39 points (Haystead & Marzanno, 2009). Planning and implementing a content area literacy program requires the following assessment information:

- Students' instructional reading level
- Students' grasp and use of reading strategies in the target content area
- Students' grasp and use of study skills and strategies
- Students' background knowledge in the target content area
- Students' ability to do the kind of writing typically expected in the content area
- Students' interests and attitudes
- Difficulty level and reading demands of the texts that will be read. (Farr & Pritchard, 1996)
- Students' achievement in the content area

- Students' progress in meeting standards to prepare them for college and/or career requirements and, if applicable, high school graduation requirements
- Students' performance on state and district assessments and national assessments

USING TECHNOLOGY

Sharing Success www.sharingsuccess .org Provides information on various aspects of organizing programs to foster increased learning.

Quizzes, unit tests, logs and journals, rubrics, observations, checklists, students' self-assessments, think-alouds, and portfolios can be used to obtain both formative and summative information on students' progress. In addition, information can be obtained from the mandated district, state, and national assessments. Assessments aligned with Common Core State Standards are currently being constructed. To make major decisions, such as whether to pass or fail a student, several sources of information should be consulted. Recommended assessment measures include the following:

Placement: Informal or group inventories verified by students' actual performance in assigned materials.

Background knowledge: Quizzes, questionnaires, List-Group-Label, or other brainstorming techniques, and learning logs. Students might be given a list of key terms from an upcoming unit and asked to check those they are familiar with. Class discussions also provide insights into students' background knowledge.

Knowledge of comprehensive strategies: Group or individual think-alouds, placement inventories, quizzes, and observations of discussion responses after a selection has been read.

Knowledge and use of study strategies: Questionnaires, discussions, observations of students as they study, learning or study logs, and discussions of study approaches and habits.

Content area writing ability: Writing samples, observations of students as they write, and portfolios.

Difficulty level and demands of text: Readability formula, subjective analysis, checkists, inventories, and discussions with students after they have read a portion of text.

Students' interests and attitudes: Discussions, questionnaires, observations, journals, and conversations with students.

Progress monitoring: As part of Response to Intervention, many schools have put into place monitoring assessments that are administered three or four times a year to all students and more often to students judged to be at risk. For basic reading comprehension, the DRP or mazes might be administered. Progress might also be monitored with the assessments listed above.

CHECKUP

1. What elements should be assessed in a content area literacy program?
2. How might these elements be assessed?

Selecting Materials

Once you have set content goals and you have some idea about students' background knowledge and abilities, you can select materials. In most content area classes, the textbook is the basic source of printed information. In some instances, you may have the freedom to choose your own text. Note the kinds of learning aids and supplementary resources that the text offers, such as the availability of a Web site or audiovisual aids. Certain texts are available in recorded versions so that if some students are unable to read the words, they can read along with the spoken version or they may have an electronic text with text-to-speech capability. If some of your students are unable to read the selected textbook, try to find an easy-to-read text or trade books written on an easier level for them or make adjustments. Consider the text to be just one source of information. Also have available as resources a library of trade books, periodicals, computer software, CD-ROMs, and DVDs. You might also create a list of bookmarked Web sites and technology tools as resources.

Selecting Strategies

A number of learning experts (Haystead & Marzano, 2009; Marzano et al., 2000; National Reading Panel, 2000; Rosenshine et al., 1996) have identified learning strategies that research has demonstrated work particularly well. These highly effective strategies are listed in Table 14.1. Some of the most effective strategies are remarkably simple and easy to implement. For instance, the most effective practice was encouraging students to see similarities and differences in concepts. Each of the strategies has been tried out in a number of studies with experimental and control groups. The National Reading Panel concluded that seven of the sixteen strategies it studied were highly effective. (These are also noted in Table 14.1.) Other learning experts calculated the **effect size** of the strategies. The effect size is the degree to which the experimental group did better than a matched group of students. Effect sizes are typically expressed in standard deviations. A **standard deviation** is a measure of the variability of performance, and can be translated into percentiles or months of growth. One standard deviation is roughly equivalent to a year's growth. For instance, according to Table 14.1, summarizing and note-taking have an effect size of 1: This is equal to a percentile gain of thirty-four points. If students were at the fiftieth percentile (an average rank)

■ **Effect size** is a statistical technique used to determine how well an experimental group performed when compared to a control group. Effect sizes provided in this chapter are based on tests made up by the experimenter. Effect sizes yielded by standardized tests were much smaller.

■ **Standard deviation** is a statistical measure of how much scores vary from the average. In a normal distribution, 2/3 of the scores would fall above or below the standard deviation of the average score. Approximately 98 percent would fall within two standard deviations.

TABLE 14.1 Highly Effective Learning Strategies

STRATEGY	AVERAGE EFFECT SIZE	PERCENTILE GAIN
Identifying similarities and differences	1.61	45
Summarizing and note-taking	1.00 NRP top 7	34
Generating questions	.86	31
Combined predicting, questioning, summarizing, and monitoring	.85 NRP top 7	30
Creating graphic organizers and other nonlinguistic representations	.75 NRP top 7	27
Story grammar	NRP top 7	
Combined strategies used in cooperative learning	.75 NRP top 7	27
Generating and testing hypotheses	.61 NRP top 7	23
Activating prior knowledge	.59	22
Monitoring comprehension	NRP top 7	

before the treatment, they would be at the eighty-fourth percentile after the treatment. In other words, instead of doing better than 50 percent of students, they would be doing better than 84 percent.

Of course, this doesn't mean that if you teach one of these strategies, your students will achieve exactly the same gains. The authors of the study warn:

> The effectiveness of a strategy depends in part on the current achievement level of a student, in part on the skill and thoroughness with which a teacher applies the strategy, and in part on contextual strategies such as grade level and class size. (Marzano et al., 2000, p. 5)

An examination of the research indicates that the most effective strategies are those that have been highlighted in previous chapters of this book. (Table 14.2 lists key comprehension strategies presented in this text.) Strategies are especially effective if they activate prior knowledge; highlight, organize, and summarize information; engage students in generating hypotheses or questions; and involve students in monitoring their reading. Using graphic organizers is also highly effective. Although most strategies are taught individually, this doesn't mean that they are applied in that way. Note that two of the highly effective listings (in Table 14.1) are multiple (combined) strategies. As they read a selection, students apply a number of strategies. It makes sense to teach strategies one at a time, so that students don't become confused or overwhelmed. However, after students have learned a new strategy, they should be taught to integrate it with other strategies. Monitoring for meaning should be integrated with summarizing and other strategies. Not being able to summarize is a sign that a student hasn't understood a passage.

Some effective strategies explored in this text, such as imaging and inferring, are not included in the effective strategy list in Table 14.1. They have been studied enough so

TABLE 14.2 Recommended Comprehension Strategies

Preparational	**Study**
Activating prior knowledge	Rehearsing
Previewing/Surveying	Organizing information
Predicting	Seeking understanding
Setting goal/purpose	Creating images
	Making associations/Using mnemonics
Selecting/Organizing	Using narratives to organize information
Using text structures to organize information	Using SQ3R
Determining main ideas/essential information	Taking notes
Summarizing	Outlining
Using graphic organizers	Using metamemory
	Setting and keeping study schedules
Elaborational	Managing time
Making connections	Using self-talk
Connecting new information with background knowledge	Using test-taking strategies
Inferring	Adjusting rate of reading to purpose
Imaging	
Creating analogies	**Writing**
Generating questions	Brainstorming
	Freewriting
Monitoring for Meaning (Metacognition)	Rehearsing
Monitoring	Distancing
Regulating	Drawing
Checking	
	Word Recognition
Repairing/Reading difficult material	Using context
Looking back	Using morphemic analysis
Rereading	Using the dictionary/glossary
Using graphics	
Reading intensively step by step	
Reading out loud	
Paraphrasing	

Struggling Readers

When provided high-quality instruction, struggling learners often do as well as achieving students. Apparently, instruction helps struggling learners master the strategies that achieving students may have picked up on their own.

that they can be recommended with confidence, but the studies did not meet the high technical standards set by the National Reading Panel.

CHECKUP

1. Which strategies seem to be most effective?
2. What do effective strategies have in common?

Selecting Techniques

The late Ed Fry (1995), the creator of the Fry Readability Graph discussed in Chapter 2, tells the story of observing a teacher in Africa who was teaching reading to a group of students. The students were outside under a tree. They had no computers, no whiteboard, and no books. The teacher was writing a story in the dirt with a stick. The students then read the stick-written story. Despite the lack of materials, the students were learning—and learning well. Although materials are helpful, it is the teacher who is the key to what students learn. As the teacher, you will decide which approaches and techniques to use with your students, how to adapt them to your class, and when to switch them because a technique isn't working or the students are tired of it. A number of the techniques covered in this text are listed in Table 14.3, along with some of their advantages and disadvantages.

In addition to being taught strategies, students need to be provided with preparation in background and vocabulary. Instruction in strategies, background, and vocabulary are often combined in techniques that foster improved comprehension of content area knowledge. Reading assistance can be provided through a variety of techniques. For instance, a segment to be read might be presented through a DRA, DRTA, KWL Plus, ReQuest, Reciprocal Teaching, or Questioning the Author activity, or even a cooperative learning group. If students are reading on their own, they might use SQ3R. All of these approaches are designed to provide preparation before reading, guidance during reading, and discussion of or reflection on material that was read. Which approach is best? Each is best in particular situations. For example, the Directed Reading Activity works best when maximum preparation is needed, and Questioning the Author and Reciprocal Teaching are effective ways to help students work their way through dense text. Table 14.3 lists the key features, advantages, and disadvantages of each technique.

Combining Content and Strategy Instruction

Strategy instruction has the potential to become most effective when it is embedded within specific content. As Wilkinson and Son (2011) conclude "strategies supply the tools to help students make sense of content, and the content gives meaning and purpose to the strategies—in other words, the two inter-animate or inter-illuminate each other" (p. 367). One pitfall of strategy instruction is that the strategies are overemphasized to the point where comprehension of content is neglected. Strategies need to be kept in perspective: they are the means to better comprehension, not the end. The ultimate aim is construction of meaning, which is fostered by strategy use but is also fostered by individual reflection and classroom discussion.

Elements of Successful Techniques

Based on a careful analysis of instructional studies, Rosenshine, Meister, and Chapman (1996) identified a number of key elements that fostered success. These included:

- Providing prompts
- Modeling
- Anticipating potential difficulties
- Regulating the difficulty of the material

- Guiding student practice
- Providing feedback and corrections
- Assessing student mastery

As the researchers noted, most of these elements involved scaffolding. The purpose of scaffolding is to provide temporary support to students so that they can accomplish a task with assistance that they would be unable to complete on their own (Bruner, 1986).

Providing Prompts

Prompts can be used in all content areas, but they have been widely used in reading instruction. Prompts for reading comprehension include questions such as: What is the author trying to say here? What is the main point of this passage? What are the key details that back up the main point? How does what I just read relate to what I know about this subject? Prompts that are concrete and provide guidance are the most effective (Rosenshine et al., 1996). In a study in which students with learning disabilities made dramatic progress learning to summarize, the following prompts were used:

1. What's the most important sentence in this paragraph? Let me underline it.
2. Let me summarize the paragraph. To summarize, I rewrite the main idea sentence and add important details.
3. Let me review my summary statements for the whole subsection.
4. Do my summary statements link up with one another? (Wong, 1986)

Questioning the Author makes extensive use of prompts. For a list of possible prompts, see pages 168 to 169. Cue cards and checklists similar to the list of summarizing prompts above have also been a part of many successful comprehension programs.

Just as with any other procedure, prompts can be overused or used inappropriately. If the teacher overprompts, students may do very little cognitive processing; then they may not internalize the necessary procedures or achieve the understanding required to complete the task. Students may also come to overrely on prompts. Prompts should be faded so that students internalize the operations initiated by the prompts and begin to operate independently.

Modeling

Teachers should model strategies and use think-alouds as examples so that students gain insight into the cognitive processes required to apply a strategy. Printed copies of successful performances may also be used as models. Examples of well-constructed questions or summaries can be provided as models for students who are learning to generate this type of material. Models and think-alouds might be presented in the introductory stage, during guided practice so students can get help completing the task, and after completing the task so students can compare their performance with that of the model.

Anticipating Potential Difficulties

For many strategies, potential difficulties can be anticipated and dealt with before students experience them. For instance, students can be taught not to include too many details when summarizing. Students can be taught to avoid composing main idea statements that are too narrow when generating main ideas. In question generation, students can be taught to avoid questions that focus on unimportant details or that lack clarity.

Regulating the Difficulty of the Material

Successful programs start out with brief, well-structured passages and move into longer, more complex ones. Prompts might also be reduced as students become more independent in their use of strategies. The practice selections should be relatively easy so that students don't have to grapple with difficult vocabulary at the same time they are trying to apply a new strategy. Ultimately, students will apply their skills to the kind of reading that they will be expected to do in their content area subjects after they have become accustomed to the material.

Struggling Readers

Ironically, struggling readers are often provided fewer prompts than other students. Provide prompts that will help struggling learners build on what they know and that will also encourage them to respond.

Struggling Readers

Struggling learners often end up with materials that are well beyond their reading ability. Make sure that steps are taken to make the content area reading material accessible. See Chapter 9 for suggestions.

TABLE 14.3 Techniques for Building Literacy

COMPREHENSION	ADVANTAGES	DISADVANTAGES
Before-During-After Reading		
Instructional Framework	Carefully structured.	Mostly teacher directed.
Directed Reading Activity	Structured. Works well with students who need maximum preparation before reading.	Students may be passive participants.
Directed Reading-Thinking Activity	Involves students in making predictions.	Requires some background knowledge and ability to make predictions.
KWL-Plus	Builds background. Involves students in creating questions and finding answers to questions.	Requires some background knowledge.
ReQuest	Students are involved in both asking and answering questions. Is especially effective with students who have difficulty comprehending.	Students may have difficulty composing higher-level questions.
Reciprocal Teaching	Fosters four effective strategies: predicting, questioning, summarizing, and clarifying as students and teacher discuss selections.	Students may experience difficulty applying some of the strategies.
Questioning the Author	Students and teacher collaboratively build meaning of a selection section by section. Works well with material that is difficult and contains many new ideas.	Can be time consuming.
Cooperative Learning/Discussion Groups	Students work together on a project. Students are more fully involved and learn to work as members of a group.	Some students may not be accepted by the group. Students may be off task.
Collaborative Strategic Reading	Adds the structure of learning strategies to cooperative learning. Designed to help struggling learners.	Students may have difficulty coping with puzzling passages.
Before Reading		
Anticipation Guide	Involves students by having them agree or disagree with statements. Good for correcting erroneous concepts and considering controversial issues.	Requires background knowledge.
Structured Overview	Displays key concepts so students can see how they are interrelated.	Mostly teacher directed. Can be adapted to obtain added student input.
Prereading Survey	Involves students in surveying, selecting, and obtaining an overview.	Texts do not always lend themselves to a survey.
Drawing Before Reading	Works well with ELL students and students who are better at representing what they know graphically rather than verbally. Involves everyone in responding.	Requires background knowledge. Students who are not visually oriented may have difficulty.
Writing Before Reading	Gives students time to organize their ideas.	Requires background knowledge.
Strategy Guides/Glosses	Students are provided with questions and explanations to help them comprehend material as they read, view, and/or listen.	Students may become overly focused on answering questions.
Frame Matrix/Information Map	Students compare and contrast ideas.	Doesn't work with all kinds of writing.
Embedded Questions	Students respond to questions as they read.	Students may focus on sections covered by questions and fail to integrate information across sections.

(Continued)

TABLE 14.3 **Techniques for Building Literacy (*Continued*)**

COMPREHENSION	ADVANTAGES	DISADVANTAGES
After Reading		
Constructing Analogies	Helps students see how new ideas or processes are similar to familiar ideas or processes.	Analogies may be misleading. No two items are exactly alike. Students may fail to see how items being compared are different.
Constructing Graphic Organizers	Helps students organize ideas.	May oversimplify information.
Writing After Reading	Helps students summarize and reflect on new ideas.	Students may have difficulty articulating their ideas in writing.
Extending and Applying	Students build on new knowledge and put it to use.	Not all new knowledge can be put to immediate use.
Modeling/Think-Alouds	Reveals thinking processes.	Students may have difficulty relating to teacher's thinking processes.
Using Prompts	Develops students' thinking. Provides scaffolding.	Questions can become oral quizzes rather than invitations to discuss.
Quality Talk	Develops thinking, comprehension, and broadens students' perspective.	Teacher may take over discussion and fail to develop students' discussion abilities
Direct Instruction	Builds background and skill and provides practice and application.	Students may be too passive.
Reading Aloud to Students	Builds background and appreciation of language.	Selections may not be equally interesting to all students.
Sheltered English	Provides support for ELLs as they learn content and build language skills.	Requires much preparation.
Language Experience	Uses language of students to summarize content selections or compose stories or essays. Works well with struggling learners and ELLs.	Language may be too restricted.
Writing		
Modeling/Think-Alouds	Provides insight into processes writers use.	Models might be too advanced.
Using Models	Provides insight into craft of writing.	Models can be so advanced that students can't relate to them.
Brainstorming/Discussing	Builds topics for writing.	Students may become overly reliant on others' ideas.
Freewriting	Fosters fluency.	Students may get idea that writing without planning beforehand is an effective practice.
Minilessons/Strategic Writing Lessons	Direct instruction in needed skills.	Application may be neglected.
Writing Workshop	Opportunities for instruction, feedback, practice, and application.	May not provide enough guidance.
Conferences	Provides instruction, guidance, and encouragement.	Tendency for teachers to be overly directive.
Dialogue Journals	Can be used to model good writing and prompt extended responses.	Over time, journals may become routine.

Guiding Student Practice

Guided practice is an essential element in all successful programs. Most often, guided practice is teacher directed. In some instances, guided practice is provided in reciprocal teaching groups or in learning pairs or cooperative groups.

Providing Feedback and Corrections

Feedback and accompanying corrections are powerful factors in improving performance. Feedback and corrections can be provided in a variety of ways to the whole class or in small groups, orally or in written form. Self-checking materials, found in some computer software programs, also provide feedback. Students can also use checklists or other devices to obtain feedback and make corrections. Davey and McBride (1986) used the following checklist to help students assess and correct the kinds of questions they had generated:

- How well did I identify important information?
- How well did I link information together?
- How well could I answer my questions?
- Did my "think" questions use different language from the text?
- Did I use good signal words? (p. 206)

Assessing Student Mastery

The most effective programs assessed students' performance and provided additional instruction until students had achieved **mastery** of the strategy. In the summarizing program involving students with learning disabilities (Wong et al., 1986), students kept working on the learning activities until they achieved 90 percent accuracy for three days in a row. Some students needed two months before they could compose a summary correctly. However, the progress of the group was significant, especially considering that summarizing is one of the most difficult of the comprehension strategies to learn.

Using a Variety of Techniques

■ Mastery learning is based on the principle that just about all students will learn if given appropriate instruction and enough time.

Students benefit from using a variety of techniques and activities. Memory is both semantic and episodic. Semantic memory is our recall of facts and ideas. Episodic memory is our recall of events. One way to help recall an idea is to remember the setting in which

Exemplary Teaching

Providing Preparation for Reading

Dissatisfied with her traditional introduction of Faulkner's "The Bear", in which she gave students a brief introduction to the rather difficult short story, Lee Patton (1993), a high school teacher, decided to try an approach in which she increased students' preparation for reading the story. She began her introduction by asking students how many had ever gone hunting. Several had. A discussion ensued in which students voiced a variety of reactions, some positive, some negative, to hunting. There was talk of gaining confidence, showing courage, and of getting to know family members better as well as comments about the ethics of killing defenseless creatures. It was a period of "emotional activation of prior knowledge" (p. 131). Students had discussed some key issues before reading the story. Other classes discussed these same issues only after reading the story. To see whether before-story discussion worked better than after-story discussions, Patton compared the performance of two classes on a quiz. The before-story group outperformed the after-story group and also had a more productive discussion after reading the selection. They were better able to respond to the higher-level questions that were asked. More important, they seemed to be more deeply involved in the story. The results had profound implications for Patton's approach to teaching. She recognized that setting the stage for students' construction of meaning worked better than directing the interpretation of the story. And she realized that she should be more a guide and less the expert interpreter who is the only one who really knows what the story means.

it was learned. For instance, we may remember how mold forms by recalling an experiment in which slices of bread were exposed to different degrees of dampness. When students perform the same kinds of activities over and over again, the activities become difficult to distinguish from one another. Their value as episodic cues to help students recall the content contained within the activities is lost. Even the most effective techniques lose their value if they are repeated too often (Nuthall, 1999). Therefore, if the same content is presented within a variety of contexts and activities, it will be learned more completely and effectively. Different ways of representing content also lead to different memory connections.

Making a Commitment to Teach Strategies

Although previous chapters presented evidence that instruction in strategies pays off in increased learning, you may still feel hesitant to try out the content area strategies presented in this text. If so, you are not alone. Several studies suggest that content area teachers fail to implement strategies they have been taught. A primary reason is that we tend to teach the way we were taught. If we were taught by a one-book-fits-all lecture method, there is a good chance that we will teach that way. Another hindrance has to do with the way we learned about strategies. If we know strategies primarily through hearing and reading about them, but have never actually used them, we may not feel familiar enough to try them. An effective way to learn strategies is to test them out with our own reading, see how they work, and then try them out with students (Keene & Zimmerman, 1997). This tryout should be more than a one-shot attempt, because, as with any other new procedure, the presentation might be awkward the first time. Give yourself and your students time to work out the kinks and become familiar with the strategy or approach.

You may also believe that teaching literacy strategies eats into the limited time you have to teach your content area. As discussed earlier in the text, this may be true at first. But as students catch onto the strategies, you should be able to cover more content in greater depth because they will be able to take more responsibility for their learning and they also will remember more of what they read. Keep in mind that you are not being asked to be a reading and writing teacher. You are only asked to teach those reading and writing strategies that are essential to students' being able to understand, communicate in, and continue to learn in your content area.

You may also feel pressured by district, state, or even national tests to teach in such a way that students are well prepared to take those tests. Teaching strategies and teaching in depth provide the best preparation for just about any test that students will take.

USING TECHNOLOGY

The Knowledge Loom Adolescent Literacy in the Content Areas http:// knowledgeloom.org/adlit/media/meltzer_media.html Discusses the need for content area literacy instruction in the secondary school.

CHECKUP

1. What are the major instructional techniques?
2. What are the key elements of effective techniques?

Making Connections

Making connections and developing key concepts foster learning. As noted earlier, learning to see similarities and differences is a powerful strategy, as is the ability to derive generalizations. One organizational pattern that helps students see similarities and differences and construct generalizations is a **thematic approach**, in which content is studied in terms of broad ideas or questions. Themes help students build connections to other disciplines. For instance, although there are many topics in chemistry, they are related to nine overarching themes: energy, stability, patterns of change, systems and interactions, unity and diversity, scale and structure, form and function, models and organization, and evolution and adaptation (LeMay, Beall, Roblee, & Brower, 2000). In a popular chemistry

■ **The thematic approach** is the organization of instruction around themes or central ideas rather than around subject matter topics.

text, the concept of *energy* is developed in a number of chapters, as are the other major themes. The theme of energy can be related to physics, earth science, history, and geography. By seeing relationships, students form more connections among ideas and activities that might otherwise be isolated in separate chapters. The more connections that are formed, the deeper and broader is the students' understanding.

In a series of carefully conducted studies, Nuthall (1999) and his colleagues concluded that it takes four significant encounters with a concept before it is learned and passed into long-term memory. Encounters with concepts are multiplied when a thematic approach is taken. Observing a unit in which Antarctica was studied from both a science and a social studies perspective, Nuthall noted that the teacher introduced human interest materials from the social studies along with scientific information. Students were able to establish links between geological information about Antarctica and the hardships scientists endured collecting that information.

Subject matter can be presented through single disciplines, through **coordination** between or among disciplines, or through **integration** (Allan & Miller, 2000). Many schools follow a single discipline model in which chemistry is taught by one teacher, English by a second teacher, and history by a third teacher. However, on many occasions, teachers may point out connections between their subjects and other subjects. While discussing the makeup of the atom, the chemistry teacher might discuss the history of its exploration and the consequences of using nuclear energy. Coordination comes about when teachers work together to explore the same topics or themes. The math teacher might review problem-solving techniques while students balance atomic equations in chemistry. The physics teacher might discuss the particle and wave theories of the internal structure of the atom. These are all examples of coordination. Integration occurs when students use two or more of the disciplines to explore broad themes or topics. The theme of change, for instance, might be viewed through science, social studies, and the humanities.

At Rogers High School in Spokane, Washington, social studies teacher Peter Perkins and English teacher Jeri Giachetti teamed up to teach a full-year inter-disciplinary course called "It's My American History." In this two-period course, students used electronic technology, library resources, and human resources from the community to create portfolios relating their personal family history to the literature and history of twentieth-century America. Students also took part in a service-learning project at a local community center in which they individually interviewed and composed the personal history of a senior citizen for a multimedia CD-ROM presentation (Perkins, 2001). In other assignments, students used journal entries to compose a biography and a compare/contrast piece in which they compared the life of someone in the era between 1950 and 1970 with the life of someone in the 21st century. They also created a news show about the impact of immigration on Spokane and the nation.

Understanding by Design

In an approach known as Understanding by Design, the focus is on essential questions and teaching for understanding (Wiggins & McTighe, 2006). Planning begins by specifying the essential questions that students will be answering and the big idea that they will be considering. In a study of the presidency, for instance, the essential question might be: What qualities should a president have? For a literature unit, the essential question might be: How are conflicts resolved? As students gather information to answer the essential question, they make inferences, synthesize, and summarize. Most of important of all, they generalize. Based on their reading, writing, viewing, and discussions, they formulate specific conclusions that can be synthesized into an overall generalization. For the presidential unit, they might go beyond answering the essential question to a deeper

■ **Coordination** is the process of introducing the same concept or topic from different subject matter areas so that they are covered at the same time and reinforce each other, or using skills or topics in one subject to support the skills or topics in another content area.

■ **Integration** is an approach in which varied subject matter areas are drawn upon to solve problems, answer broad questions, or explore topics or themes.

question: What qualities should a good leader have? Students transfer their generalizations to real-life situations. As they explore essential questions, students engage in the six "facets of understanding": Students explain, interpret, apply, consider varied perspectives, empathize, and explore their own perceptions.

Understanding by design requires "continual opportunities for students to go beyond the content to make important generalizations, conclusions, and other inferences" (Wiggins, 2009). It also requires "opportunities to use high-level processes, e.g., research, scientific inquiry, strategic reading, writing, problem solving and decision making." The teacher provides prompts as necessary and uses techniques to organize and deepen thinking, such as graphic organizers and opportunities to engage in genuine discussions. Through scaffolding, students are led to higher levels of thinking. Wiggins and McTighe (1999) utilize the "WHERE" approach in this stage of the process.

- **W** stands for students knowing Where they are heading, Why they are heading there, What they know, Where they might go wrong in the process, and What is required of them.
- **H** stands for Hooking the students on the topic of study.
- **E** stands for students Exploring and Experiencing ideas and being Equipped with the necessary understanding to master the standard being taught.
- **R** stands for providing opportunities for students to Rehearse, Revise, and Refine their work.
- **E** stands for student Evaluation.

Exploring big ideas can aid retention as well as enable understanding. Buehl (2007) provides an example of the need for both understanding and retention in the following anecdote: An eleventh-grade social studies class was discussing Johnson's Great Society. The teacher asked the class, "When should government step in? When should people take responsibility?" One student responded by inquiring, "When did government start stepping in?" Since the student was a high achiever, the teacher was a bit taken aback. He gently asked, "Do you remember talking about the New Deal in ninth grade?" Pausing, the student responded, "We studied it." In ninth grade, the New Deal was a topic to be memorized but not understood in any deep way, so the student had either forgotten the material or failed to see that it was a form of government intervention.

Developing Thinking Skills

In one way or another, standards for all of the disciplines call for developing higher-level thinking skills. Making connections is an excellent device for developing a variety of thinking skills, including comparing and contrasting, classifying, constructing generalizations, and drawing conclusions. Based on extensive research into how students learn content area concepts, Nuthall (1999) concluded that

Tasks need to be set up that model and give students practice in activities that involve making connections between related pieces of information and identifying implications and potential differences and contradictions. As students practice these activities and become expert in the habits of mind involved in the activities, these habits become internalized and an unconscious but automatic part of the way their minds deal with new experiences. (p. 377)

Nuthall warns against restricting the opportunities for struggling learners to apply higher-level thinking skills:

Restricting the intellectual complexity of tasks (as is usual for students in low-track classes) results in a progressive lowering of scores on tests of academic aptitude (Oakes, 1992). The success of activities designed to increase students' facility with "habits of mind" such as questioning, explaining, and evaluating evidence has been demonstrated in studies such as those by King and Rosenshine (King, 1994; King & Rosenshine, 1993). (p. 337)

CHECKUP

1. Why is making connections important?
2. What are some ways connections can be made?
3. How does Understanding by Design develop connections and a greater depth of understanding?

Designing an Effective Classroom

Effective content area classrooms come in a variety of shapes and sizes. However, they share a number of characteristics. In a series of studies on effective instruction, Pressley and his colleagues discovered that motivation had a significant impact on students' learning (Boothroyd, 2001; Pressley, Wharton-McDonald, Mistretta-Hampston, & Echevarria, 1998). According to the researchers, motivation is best generated in a positive and encouraging, but challenging environment. Students get the feeling that they are valued and competent and that they are engaged in interesting, worthwhile learning activities. The following characteristics are also featured in effective classrooms:

- Cooperation rather than competition is emphasized.
- Hands-on activities are prominent. However, the activities are minds-on and have legitimate learning goals.
- A variety of techniques is used. Techniques are matched to students' needs.
- Routines and procedures are well established. The classroom is orderly.
- Effort is emphasized. Praise and reinforcement are used as appropriate.
- The teacher builds a sense of excitement and enthusiasm.

In his decade-long study, Ruddell (1995) concluded that **influential teachers**

- use highly motivating and effective teaching strategies,
- help students with their personal problems,
- create a feeling of excitement about the subject matter or skill areas they teach,
- exhibit a strong sense of personal caring about the students, and
- demonstrate the ability to adjust instruction to the individual needs of the student. (p. 455)

Ruddell also found that influential teachers had in-depth knowledge of both their content areas and methods of teaching, had well-formulated instructional plans, and appealed to intrinsic motivation rather than extrinsic motivation. In other words, students were motivated to learn because their curiosity was aroused, learning gave them a sense of personal control, and they were interested in the subject. Extrinsic motivation, such as learning in order to please the teacher or get high grades, played a relatively minor role. Influential teachers also fostered higher-level thinking skills and used probes and prompts to draw out students' responses in discussions. Their class discussions were instructional conversations in which students constructed meaning and made discoveries rather than oral quizzes directed by the teacher. In a more recent study, researchers found that teachers who foster deep conceptual leaning generally have higher value-added scores than teachers who take a test prep approach. As one researcher commented, "Teaching to the test makes your students do worse on the rest" (Dillon, 2010, p. 17). In the same study, students were asked to respond to Tripod, a questionnaire about instructional environment. The two qualities most closely correlated with achievement are Control (Our class stays busy and does not waste time) and Challenge (My teacher pushes everybody to work hard) (Bill & Melinda Gates Foundation, 2010a). Classes that had high scores on the Tripod questionnaire had higher achievement.

USING TECHNOLOGY
41 Key Strategies Identified by Research for Effective Teaching www.iobservation.com/files/WP_CAS_AppendixA.pdf Lists the key strategies identified by Marzano

Influential teachers are teachers who stand out in students' memories because they had a lasting, significant, positive impact on their learning.

Key Instructional Strategies Identified by Research for Effective Teaching

One of the most comprehensive collections of effective teaching techniques is one composed by Marzano (iObservation, 2010) as part of an instructional improvement system. Based on work conducted for more than three decades and that includes an analysis of thousands of studies, Marzano created a list of 41 instructional factors that account for an effective instructional program. The 41 factors fell into the following five categories:

- Communicating learning goals, tracking student progress, and celebrating success—includes helping individuals track their progress toward reaching goals
- Carefully teaching lessons—includes providing for in-depth instruction, review, and application and making use of groups to foster learning
- Engaging students—includes noting when students are not engaged and taking steps such as making the learning more active or involving to engage them
- Establishing and maintaining classroom rules and procedures
- Maintaining effective relationships with students—includes demonstrating that you respect and care for all students
- Communicating high expectations-includes providing extra help for underachieving students

Maximizing Time on Task

Effective teachers use their time well. One of the best predictors of academic achievement is the amount of **time** spent **on task**, assuming, of course, that the task is one that results in learning. Worksheets completed during class time, for instance, don't usually result in much learning. The key to learning, especially for students who are struggling, is active instruction. Observe students' responses to activities, and eliminate or revise those activities in which students have difficulty staying on task (Baker & Piburn, 1997). Also look for wasted time. In one study, content area teachers wasted as much as 30 percent of class time—at the beginning of the period, at the end, and during transitions between activities (Mitman, Mergendoller, Packer, & Marchman, 1984). Careful planning and effective management techniques, including having a useful activity for students to engage in as soon as they enter the room, should reduce lost time.

CHECKUP

1. What steps can be taken to design an effective content area literacy program?

Coping with the Quiet Crisis

In today's middle schools and high schools, there is a quiet crisis. The quiet crisis is the inability of many students to deal with their academic texts (Schoenbach et al., 1999). Although most of these students can read at a basic level, they can't currently achieve the higher-level comprehension demanded by many of their subject matter texts. They have hit a "literacy ceiling":

> We have come to refer to students' difficulty with reading and understanding subject area texts as the literacy ceiling—a ceiling that limits what students can hope to achieve both in the classroom and in their lives outside of school. (p. 5)

One reaction to the literacy crisis has been to assume that little can be done for these students, an idea that Schoenbach and colleagues termed "incorrect and destructive" (p. 7). In a carefully planned program implemented in a number of schools, they have shown that it is possible to help older students obtain the skills and positive attitude required to be strong, independent readers.

■ **Time on task** is a component of effective instruction. The term refers to the amount of class time that students actually spend on an activity.

For more information about the Strategic Literacy Initiative, see the WestEd Web site. http://www.wested.org/stratlit/

Strategic Literacy Initiative Approach

To help students caught in the quiet crisis, the Strategic Literacy Initiative (SLI) was created. Based on research and tryouts, the SLI adapted a reading apprenticeship model in which the classroom teacher functions as the master reader to the student apprentice readers. The program can be implemented in two ways: (1) as a supplementary literacy program, or (2) as a program integrated within an academic subject. The Strategic Literacy Initiative featured four dimensions:

1. *Social.* The class became a community of learners in which students helped each other and felt free to express their ideas and discuss their reading and writing difficulties.
2. *Personal.* Students' sense of their own identities and their academic self-confidence were built up.
3. *Cognitive.* Students' learning strategies and deeper thinking processes were developed.
4. *Knowledge building.* Students' background knowledge was expanded so that they had more to bring to the text and thus would learn more from it.

To build the social dimension, students read biographical selections that demonstrated the power of literacy and the role it played in the lives of famous people. Through discussions, they shared interpretations of texts and the strategies they used to construct meaning, as well as the difficulties they encountered and how they dealt with them.

To develop the personal dimension, students looked as themselves as readers. They discussed and wrote about their reading experiences, along with their reading likes and dislikes. They also explored the processes they used when reading and discovered ways to persist when the reading was difficult. To help students gain insight into themselves as readers, they were asked to keep metacognitive logs of their reading. Students were asked to think of themselves as scientists and to record what was going on in their heads as they read. In addition to teaching them more about themselves as readers, this activity gave students the opportunity to discover the particular problems they encountered during reading and to explore possible solutions.

To develop the cognitive dimension, students explored key strategies, such as monitoring for meaning, setting purposes, adjusting reading processes, and reading for main ideas and details. They also engaged in scaffolded practice and application.

To build knowledge, students shared information about key topics, developed essential vocabulary, and noted the kinds of writing and thinking used in major academic areas. They also looked at the kinds of questions that content areas explored and the kinds of language that each discipline used. Specially created units led them to think, read, and write as historians and scientists. More structured approaches for helping struggling secondary students include the Strategic Instruction Model, Content Enhancement Routines, and the Content Literacy Continuum.

Center for Research on Learning www.kucrl.org/sim Provides more information on SIM.

Strategic Instruction Model (SIM)

Although it was created to help students identified as having learning disabilities and other struggling students, SIM benefits all students. The learning strategies introduced in SIM follow an information-processing model of acquisition, storage and retrieval, and expression. Students are taught strategies that help them acquire information, store it and retain it in their long-term memory, and use it in their reading and writing. Strategies range from those designed to improve word recognition to those that improve comprehension and retention.

Content Enhancement

Content Enhancement

www.kucrl.org/sim/routines/course.shtml Describes 14 content enhancement routines.

Designed to be used alone or with SIM, Content Enhancement is a research-based framework for teaching curriculum content that was designed to assist struggling readers but also is useful with achieving readers (Center for Research on Learning, 2009a). Content Enhancement is instruction in which the teacher "models and guides students in learning how to learn" (Bulgren & Scanlon, 1997/1998, p. 293). Content Enhancement organizes and presents the curriculum in such a way that key concepts are easier to grasp and more readily learned. As history teacher Brian Rodriguez explained, Content Enhancement "makes me think about the way students will learn the materials rather than simply presenting material in masses of information" (2010). He was able to better organize the material, use a cognitive approach, and make difficult material easy to understand. He used the routine in AP classes as well as classes for students with learning disabilities and English learners. Steps for implementing Content Enhancement include:

Step 1: Compose two or three key questions that the unit should answer.

Step 2: Create a concept map of the key content for the unit.

Step 3: Based on an examination of the key questions, content map, and the text, note the difficulties that your students, especially the struggling readers, might experience.

Step 4: Based on the potential difficulties and the nature of the material to be learned, select Content Enhancement Routines. Content Enhancement Routines help learners understand key concepts by relating them to prior knowledge and noting defining characteristics. Content Enhancement Routines include lesson organizer routines in which students are shown how the key ideas in a lesson are related to each other, to past and future lessons, and to the unit of study. A framing routine helps students see how details and main ideas are related. And a survey routine highlights the most important content.

Step 5: Decide on key learning strategies that students will need to use.

Step 6: Incorporate the Content Enhancements and student strategies in your instruction.

Step 7: Monitor students' progress and make adjustments as necessary (Torgesesen, 2004).

Content Literacy Continuum

The Content Literacy Continuum (CLC) is a framework for implementing SIM. Depending on the extent of students' needs, it includes five levels.

Level 1: Teachers in general education classrooms try to ensure mastery of critical content by using Content Enhancement Routines.

Level 2: Teachers directly teach and embed instruction of selected strategies in the content area classes.

Level 3: Students experiencing difficulty receive explicit, intensive instruction in learning strategies from support personnel in the general classroom, a pull-out program, or through another course.

Level 4: Students receive decoding and language instruction from reading specialists and special education teachers, often using programs such as Corrective Reading or Language! These teachers assist the content teachers in making modifications for struggling readers.

Level 5: Speech-language pathologists, as well as other support personnel, deliver one-on-one intensive instruction in a clinical setting. They assist the content teachers in making modifications for students who are struggling readers. (Center for Research on Learning, 2009b)

Schools That Beat the Odds

The ACT & Education Trust (2005) studied nine U.S. schools that had a high percentage of minority and low-income students, but high ACT scores. The schools offered a sequence of courses designed to prepare students for college. Teachers used an exposition and questioning style of teaching—explaining material first and then asking questions to check for understanding and to involve students in the material. Big or foundational ideas were systematically developed. For example, in a biology course, during a study of the nature of lipids and their insolubility in water and solubility in other lipids, the teacher went beyond the physical description of lipids and led students to see the advantages of having a lipid membrane surrounding cells and of having transport vesicles encased in lipids. Students learned not only how lipids were constructed but why they were constructed that way. In English classes, teachers used a variety of whole works and made multiple connections between them. One teacher related African rites of initiation found in *The Dark Child* to students' coming-of-age experiences, such as proms and bar mitzvahs. Precalculus teachers drew examples from sports, consumer economics, music, and other areas of interest to teens. Textbooks were used as a major source of information or as a reference, along with supplementary materials and technology.

Student input was encouraged in classes. Students often had a hand in deciding upon and setting up experiments. Good work habits such as note taking were emphasized, with teachers monitoring and checking students' notes for effectiveness. Students followed the school rules and controlled their behavior. All teachers provided extra help outside the classes. "In general, through their obvious love of their academic discipline (English, mathematics, and science), their relations with the students, and their focus on the material in the curriculum, these teachers conveyed to the students the importance of what they were teaching and their expectations that the students could master the work and move to the next course" (ACT & Education Trust, 2005, p. 15).

J.E.B. Stuart High School

At J.E.B. Stuart High School in Falls Church, Virginia, 76 percent of students were reading below grade level before the principal instituted a literacy program. There was also high absenteeism. Automated wake-up calls, lots of persuasion, and a more engaging program helped reduce absenteeism. To attack the literacy problem, a literacy coach was hired and intensive professional development was initiated, with teachers being instructed on a core of strategies. Demonstrations and coaching helped teachers understand how to implement the strategies. Because standards had recently been introduced, many of the content teachers felt that they couldn't cover the standards and also teach literary strategies; they were shown how strategies could actually enable their students to learn more on their own. As students' achievement improved, the teachers became believers. One science teacher remarked, "We're all extraordinarily aware of literacy here" (Guensburg, 2006).

A program of assessment was also instituted. Incoming freshmen are now screened with the Gates-MacGinitie Reading Test. Those who score below the 40th percentile are administered an individual informal reading inventory to assess their reading skills. Data is used to plan instruction and also to determine what level of materials should be given to students (National Association of Secondary School Principals, 2005). Progress is also closely monitored and changes are made as needed.

All freshmen take a required literacy course. However, those who are behind are given a second course. Tutoring is also provided for those who need it. Spare-time reading and library use are also emphasized. On any given morning as many as 100 students might be using the school's 19,000-volume library before the school day officially begins (Guensburg, 2006). The percentage of students reaching proficiency on the state's high-stakes test increased from 64 to 94 percent.

Coordinating and Integrating Intervention

Struggling readers often receive reading instruction in intervention programs that are isolated from the learning demands expected of them in their content classes. Based on their analysis of secondary school programs, Buehl and Stumpf (2000) recommended that support for learning in content classes, such as tutoring assistance and skill development, be offered within a class, during study periods, or outside the school day. Ability plays a limited role in what students learn. Students classified as slow learners learn just as much as students classified as average or above average if the material is well taught. "If the

Exemplary Teaching

Turning Around a Failing School

Western High School (pseudonym) was about as needy as a school could be. Along with its reputation for violence, drug use, and gang activity, only 12 percent of the Western students scored at the proficient or advanced level on the state assessment in reading. The graduation rate for Western was 67 percent. The school had been officially designated as being "in need of improvement." Researchers Douglas Fisher, Nancy Frey, and Diane Lapp (2009) from San Diego State University provided professional development for the staff and helped them plan an intervention.

The first step was to have the staff elect a literacy leadership team (LLT) so that the staff's views would be represented. The main goal of the team was to make adequate yearly progress (AYP). Making AYP was translated into the pedagogical goal of developing the kinds of literacy habits that would enable students to complete assignments and be successful in high school and beyond. With this pedagogical goal in mind, the staff began planning an intervention. With dozens of techniques and approaches to choose from, they decided that the elements selected would have to meet the following criteria:

- A solid evidence base
- Usable across content areas
- High utility in college or adult life

Using those three criteria, the following components were chosen:

Cornell Note-Taking. The staff decided it would be helpful to have a common routine for taking notes, and Cornell's two-column note-taking system had been validated in a number of studies.

Think-Alouds. Since comprehension was a key concern, think-alouds seemed an effective approach for providing instruction in the processes used to understand text.

Writing to Learn. Initially some faculty members objected, but when they were assured that they would be using students' writing only to gauge understanding and plan instruction (and not implement process writing or check grammar, punctuation, and spelling),they agreed to include this component.

Dedicated Reading Time. The school already had optional time set aside for reading, but students had been given the choice of doing homework or talking quietly with friends. The committee decided that 20 minutes would be set aside strictly for reading.

Later, when it became clear that students were having difficulty taking notes because they lacked adequate summarizing ability, teaching summarizing was added.

One of the first changes that took place was that students started making good use of the time set aside for reading. Library circulation increased, and students were seen carrying books and reading them. The researchers believe that this early positive sign encouraged the staff and led to other positive changes. Over time, all four components were implemented across the school. After just six months, the percentage of proficient readers increased from 12 percent to 21 percent. After two and a half years, the percentage of proficient readers increased to 54 percent. The graduation rate increased from 67 percent to 73 percent. Although there is still lots of room for improvement, Western has demonstrated that dramatic progress can be made in the most difficult circumstances when a faculty takes a whole-school approach and makes a sincere, sustained, well-planned effort to make a difference.

appropriate number of learning experiences occur, without significant gaps between them, learning occurs regardless of the learning ability of the students" (Nuthall, 1996, p. 33).

One factor that does limit learning is students' knowledge of the culture of the school. Understanding the language of instruction (e.g., *paraphrasing, quality, quantity, essay*) and being able to carry out academic tasks has an influence on what students can learn.

Those who fail to acquire the implicit understandings that characterize the language of a classroom are those who do not share the cultural understanding and background of the majority of the students. They may end up working hard ... but the work is not valued by the teacher, or it results in critical learning experiences being missed. (Nuthall, 1996, p. 28)

Teachers must explain the purpose of assignments and provide thorough, clear instructions to help students who lack the knowledge of how academic tasks should be completed. Teachers should also make efforts to affirm students so that they feel valued and competent.

CHECKUP

1. What are some approaches to helping struggling learners?
2. What do the approaches have in common?

Working with Other Professionals

The most effective programs are those in which a whole department, or better yet, a whole school participates. The school agrees on overall goals, including strategies that students should know, assessment measures, and techniques. For instance, all teachers might agree to use SQ3R, KWL-Plus, or graphic organizers. In one urban high school in San Diego, the school's staff development committee agreed to focus on six instructional techniques: concept mapping, vocabulary instruction, KWL-Plus, writing to learn, structured note-taking, and reciprocal teaching, which includes four powerful student strategies: predicting, questioning, summarizing, and clarifying or monitoring for meaning. In addition to learning more content material, the students achieved significant gains in reading (Fisher, 2001). Having a whole school agree to focus on and use a common set of strategies in each class is highly effective because it enables students to become better strategy users. Teachers save time because they can build on what other teachers have already done; in addition, their efforts also are reinforced by other teachers.

In some instances, teachers weren't aware of techniques they could use to enhance students' performance. As one English teacher explained:

We used to think that they [the students] knew all the words in the book, but that they were lazy. Now we know that they have a lot of vocabulary to learn and that we better make that part of our teaching. Now I can't imagine asking students to read something at home without previewing the vocabulary. Can you imagine what it must have been like to start reading your homework and not knowing a whole bunch of the words on the page? (Fisher, 2001, p. 96)

Programs work best when teachers buy into them—participation in the San Diego program was voluntary—and when there is strong administrative support. It also helps if teachers are able to give input. Although pleased with their success, the teachers at the high school saw two major needs: writing across the curriculum and providing literacy instruction in after-school programs. The teachers also wanted a writing rubric that could be used in all classes. As once science teacher explained:

I wasn't trained to teach and evaluate student writing. I know it's important, but I need to know what the English teachers want me to look for. If we all use the same format to give students feedback about their writing, the consistency will have a positive impact. (Fisher, 2001, p. 99)

Perhaps the most important factor in the school's success was that teachers were working together to achieve common goals. When they became aware that students needed help reading content area materials and writing about content area topics, they were willing to try out new approaches. At the beginning of the program, a student teacher at the school asked, "Why do we have to teach them to take notes? Can't they figure it out on their own? It seems like we're babying them with all this" (p. 96). Two months later, she commented:

If we want them to understand the content of our class, we have to make sure that they know how to record information from the textbook, their research, and our lectures. How did I think they would learn this? Notetaking is really different in each class and grade. (p. 96)

Even if your school lacks an all-department or all-school approach, you can team up with others. Perhaps you can work with the colleagues who teach other sections of the same grade or who teach the same students that you do. Or, you can seek out other like-minded colleagues and work with them. You might start a study group in which you discuss common concerns and seek solutions. Since you have a certain amount of expertise in this area after taking a course in content area reading, you might agree to share your knowledge with others.

Working with Specialists

Take full advantage of the expertise of your school's specialists. Seek the advice of the learning disabilities specialist when working with struggling learners, the bilingual or ESL teacher when working with English language learners, and the reading specialist when working with struggling readers and writers. The reading specialist or literacy coach can assess the literacy capabilities of struggling readers in your class and also suggest materials and techniques you can use. The school's guidance counselor can provide recommendations on how to handle controversial issues, suggestions about what to do when students reveal information that suggests they are in some sort of danger from drugs or abuse, or advice on how to help a student who is undergoing a difficult time at home or at school.

USING TECHNOLOGY

For information on secondary literacy coaches, see Standards for Middle and High School Literacy Coaches at www.reading.org/downloads/resources/597coaching_standards.pdf This document was a collaborative effort among IRA, NCTE, NCTM, NSTA, and NCSS.

CHECKUP

1. What are some of the benefits of working with other professionals?

Developing Professionally

Much of the information in this textbook is based on research. There is a wealth of research, for instance, to show that strategies work, especially when they are combined with each other and integrated with content knowledge. Research has shed light on how students go about constructing meaning from text, and has shown that cooperative learning has a variety of positive payoffs. Much of the information in this textbook was derived from a personal research of an informal nature. For instance, suggestions for using morphemic analysis and context clues and cognates are based on my personal experience and informal tryouts with students. Formal research will never answer all the questions that teachers have about the best way to present a specific topic, handle a particular learning problem, or manage a problematic organizational issue. Instructional or action research should always be an essential part of the content area teacher's professional development.

Becoming a More Effective Teacher

Overall, that has been a shift in secondary education. In the past, emphasis was on seat time. Students were awarded credits and eventually a high school diploma based on the amount of time they put in. Today the emphasis is on learning. The question has shifted from, "Did the students complete the required courses?" to "Did the students meet the required standards?" Or to put it another way, "Did the student learn what the teacher taught?"

Implementing an effective technique or routine can result in a gain of 15 to 20 percentile points in measured student learning, as long as the technique is appropriate and well implemented. For instance, providing feedback is a highly effective technique. However, as Hattie (2009) warns, "One should not immediately start applying more feedback and then await the magical increases in achievement" (p. 4.). The total classroom environment has to be

Teachers multiply their effectiveness by collaborating with other professionals.

Source: dmac/Alamy.

TABLE 14.4 **Checklist for an Effective Content Area Literacy Program**

	NEVER	SELDOM	OFTEN	REGULARLY
Teaching Practices: General				
Provide in-depth exploration of key concepts.	____	____	____	____
Stress overall themes.	____	____	____	____
Help students relate new information to old and apply it to their lives.	____	____	____	____
Develop the vocabulary needed to understand my subject matter.	____	____	____	____
Foster intrinsic motivation and sense of self-efficacy.	____	____	____	____
Teaching Practices: Reading				
Teach preparatory strategies such as surveying and predicting.	____	____	____	____
Teach during-reading strategies such as summarizing, comparing, applying, and extending.	____	____	____	____
Teach morphemic analysis skills especially helpful in my subject area.	____	____	____	____
Make use of graphic organizers and encourage students to do the same.	____	____	____	____
Teaching Practices: Speaking				
Foster higher-level discussions with active student involvement.	____	____	____	____
Provide opportunities for student-to-student discussions.	____	____	____	____
Provide opportunities for students to communicate their knowledge about the content area.	____	____	____	____
Provide opportunities to use technology and presentation software.	____	____	____	____
Teaching Practices: Studying				
Directly instruct students in study techniques especially effective for my content area.	____	____	____	____
Foster helpful study habits. Teach note-taking techniques especially useful in my content area.	____	____	____	____
Teach how to use research techniques and materials, including the Internet.	____	____	____	____
Teaching Practices: Writing				
Use process and strategic instruction approach.	____	____	____	____
Teach skills necessary to communicate in my content area.	____	____	____	____
Assign essays, research papers, and other tasks that develop higher-level thinking skills.	____	____	____	____
Plan a variety of writing activities.	____	____	____	____
Give students choices of topics and tasks when possible.	____	____	____	____
Teaching Practices: Selecting and Using Materials				
Use high-quality materials that provide in-depth, accurate coverage.	____	____	____	____
Supplement texts with trade books, periodicals, Web sites, and other sources of information.	____	____	____	____
Provide materials that are user friendly and accessible.	____	____	____	____
Provide materials that are accessible to struggling readers by adapting them, acquiring easy-to-read materials, or providing added guidance.	____	____	____	____
Present skills and strategies needed to make use of materials.	____	____	____	____

	NEVER	SELDOM	OFTEN	REGULARLY
Evaluating				
Set goals and objectives based on accepted standards and help students set goals.	____	____	____	____
Align assessment with goals.	____	____	____	____
Continually monitor progress with formative and summative assessments.	____	____	____	____
Use informal as well as formal assessment measures.	____	____	____	____
Involve students in the assessment process. Encourage self-assessment.	____	____	____	____
Use rubrics.	____	____	____	____
Use portfolios.	____	____	____	____
Use formative and summative assessment data to improve the program.	____	____	____	____
Organizing/Managing				
Provide for individual differences.	____	____	____	____
Use varied ways to present information so that it is accessible to all.	____	____	____	____
Provide sheltered instruction for English language learners.	____	____	____	____
Make needed modifications and accommodations for students with special needs.	____	____	____	____
Challenge the gifted.	____	____	____	____
Help the undereducated catch up.	____	____	____	____
Maximize time on task and emphasize high-payoff activities.	____	____	____	____
Involve students in decisions.	____	____	____	____
Provide opportunities for various kinds of grouping, including cooperative learning.	____	____	____	____
Make sure that students are engaged in the learning process.	____	____	____	____
Convey high expectations.	____	____	____	____
Establish and maintain classroom rules and routines.	____	____	____	____
Build and maintain caring, effective relationships with students.	____	____	____	____
Professional				
Set up short- and long-term objectives for professional development.	____	____	____	____
Keep abreast of latest developments in my content area.	____	____	____	____
Keep abreast of latest developments in teaching techniques and technology.	____	____	____	____
Play an active role in professional organizations.	____	____	____	____
Attend professional conferences and meetings.	____	____	____	____
Try out and practice new methods and materials, especially thiose shown to be effective.	____	____	____	____
Assess the effectiveness of my teaching and make necessary changes.	____	____	____	____

considered. The classroom climate would need to be one in which "errors" were seen as opportunities for improvement. The feedback would need to presented in such a way that it was understood and accepted. Implementing techniques effectively also requires deliberate practice (Marzano, 2009). Once a teacher has identified a technique that she wishes to use or improve, then she should deliberately practice it. Feedback is important. Through self-evaluation, she can assess how well things are going and make changes as needed. It is also helpful to get feedback from a literacy coach or other knowledgeable peers or from students. As Marzano (2010) comments, "Every teacher can get better ... and have a positive impact, in some cases a dramatic impact, on student achievement."

Joining professional organizations, taking courses, attending conferences, reading professional journals and texts, obtaining professional information from the Internet, and joining a professional study group or a school committee, or consulting with the literacy coach or other specialist are some of the many other ways to develop professionally. You may find it helpful to compose a professional development plan. Fill out the Checklist for an Effective Content Area Literacy Program, found in Table 14.4. This will help you assess your strengths and weaknesses as a content area teacher. List steps that you can take to build on your strengths and reduce or eliminate weak areas.

Will the recommendations summarized in Table 14.4 work?

> Research shows...that students who receive intensive, focused literacy instruction and tutoring will graduate from high school and attend college in significantly greater numbers than those not receiving such attention.... Students require teachers who are knowledgeable in the subject they teach and can convey the subject matter effectively. (Joftus, 2002, p. 9)

What happens when secondary schools put in place an effective literacy program? As noted in Chapter 1, at Bullard-Havens, which implemented the SIMS program and Collins Writing, the percentage of students who achieved proficiency on the demanding state tests increased from 55 percent to 80 percent in the last three years. The secret at Bullard-Havens was that the professional development was high quality, intensive, and job-embedded, with universal implementation. Coaches visited classrooms to assist teachers with implementation; administrators visited classrooms to ensure implementation by every teacher; andteachers adopted the attitude that they believed that by teaching the literacy skills necessary for success in their disciplines, students would learn more. They also adopted a "we're-all-in this-together" attitude.

CHECKUP

1. What are some ways content area teachers can develop professionally?

Summary

Organizing an effective content area program starts with a statement of goals. It includes assessing progress toward reaching those goals and selecting appropriate materials, student strategies to be taught, and techniques to be used. Although strategies can be taught singly, students should learn how to use them in an integrated fashion. Effective instructional techniques include providing prompts, modeling, anticipating potential difficulties, regulating the difficulty of the material, guiding student practice, providing feedback and corrections, and assessing student mastery. Although strategies have been shown to increase student learning, content area teachers may be reluctant to present them because they feel insecure about teaching strategies, they don't feel it is their responsibility as a content area teacher, or they believe teaching strategies will take time away from teaching their subject matter. However, strategies should be taught as a means to an end and not as an end in themselves.

Because it helps students make connections, developing themes also fosters students' learning. When material can be presented through coordination between or among disciplines or through integration, learning is enhanced.

In an effective classroom, cooperation is emphasized, hands-on activities are prominent, varied effective techniques matched to students' needs are employed, routines are established, effort is emphasized, and a sense of excitement and enthusiasm are built by the teacher. Effective teachers also exhibit a strong sense of personal caring about the students and demonstrate the ability to adjust instruction to their individual needs. Effective teachers have in-depth knowledge of their content areas and appeal to intrinsic motivation. In effective classrooms, time on task is maximized and activities that have limited instructional value are minimized.

The quiet crisis facing many content area teachers is the large number of students who struggle to learn. Programs to help these students are varied, but they stress the teaching of strategies, building background, and fostering a sense of self-knowledge and competence. Finding out what obstacles stand in the way of students' learning and helping students overcome them is also effective. Having professional staff work together to help students is also a factor in effective teaching.

Reflection

Return to the Anticipation Guide at the beginning of this chapter. Respond once again to the items. Did your responses change? If so, how and why? What role do you think the content area teacher should play in the teaching of learning strategies? What is your attitude toward teaching learning strategies? What do you think is the content area teacher's role in helping struggling learners? Who was the most effective teacher that you have ever had? What made that teacher effective?

Extension and Application

1. Create a five-year plan for professional development. Include both short-term goals and long-term goals.
2. Select two or three key learning strategies and use them until you feel you have thoroughly mastered them. Then devise a plan for teaching them to your students.
3. Think of the characteristics of effective teachers. Which of these characteristics do you possess? In which areas do you feel you are lacking? What can you do to strengthen those areas?
4. Read and reflect on the following resource, which contains an excellent listing and discussion of the most effective elements in fostering student achievement. The listing is based on an analysis of 800 meta-analyses, which included more than 50,000 studies. (Atherton, J. S. (2011). *Teaching and learning: What works and what doesn't*. Available online at www.learningand teaching.info/teaching/what_works.htm)

 *Where the Classroom Comes to Life*

Go to Topic 7: Planning for Instruction in the MyEducationLab (www.myeducationlab.com) for your course, where you can:

- Find learning outcomes for Planning for Instruction along with the national standards that connect to these outcomes.
- Complete Assignments and Activities that can help you more deeply understand the chapter content.
- Apply and practice your understanding of the core teaching skills identified in the chapter with the Building Teaching Skills and Dispositions learning units.
- Examine challenging situations and cases presented in the IRIS Center Resources.

Go to the Topic A+RISE in the MyEducationLab (www.myeducationlab.com) for your course. A+RISE® Standards2Strategy™ is an innovative and interactive online resource that offers new teachers in grades K–12 just-in-time, research-based instructional strategies that:

- Meet the linguistic needs of ELLs as they learn content.
- Differentiate instruction for all grades and abilities.
- Offer reading and writing techniques, cooperative learning, use of linguistic and nonlinguistic representations, scaffolding, teacher modeling, higher order thinking, and alternative classroom ELL assessment.
- Provide support to help teachers be effective through the integration of listening, speaking, reading, and writing along with the content curriculum.
- Improve student achievement.
- Are aligned to Common Core Elementary Language Arts standards (for the literacy strategies) and to English language proficiency standards in WIDA, Texas, California, and Florida.

Appendix

Morphemic Elements for the Content Areas

Prefixes

ab: from; away; off

  abdicate, abduction, abnormal, abstain, abstract, absurd

ambi: both

  ambidexterous, ambiguous, ambilateral

amphi: around; on both sides; both

  amphibian, amphibious, amphipod, amphitheater

ante: before; earlier; in front of

  antebellum, antecedents, antedated, anterior, anteroom

anti: against; opposite

  anti-American, antibacterial, antibiotics, antibodies, anticlimax, anticoagulants, anticommunist, antidote, antifederalists, antigens, antinuclear, antioxidants, antipollution, antipoverty, antiseptics, antislavery, antisocial, antitoxin, antitrust, antiwar

bi: two; twice

  bicameral, biceps, bicuspids, bicycle, bilateral, bilingual, binary, bipedal

co: with

  coanchor, coarticulation, codiscoverer, coeditor, coeducation, coexistence, copilot

com: with

  commensurate, commingle, communication, community

contra: against; opposite

  contra-angles, contraband, contradict, contradistinction, contrariwise

counter: opposite

  counteract, counterarguments, counterattack, counterbalance, counterclockwise, counterculture, countermeasures, counteroffensive counteroffer, counterproductive, counterrevolutionary, counterweight

di: two; twice; double

  diagonal, diatoms, diodes, dioxide, diploid, divide

dia: passing through; opposed; thoroughly

  diabetes, diagram, dialect, dialysis, diameter, diaphragm, diathermy

em: form of *en* generally used before *b, m, p*

  embankment, embark, embitter, emboldened, embrace, empowered

en: in; cause to

  enable, enact, encased, encircled, enclosed, enclosure, encompasses, encounter, encouragement, endanger, engrossed, engulfed, enlarged, enlightened, enlist, enraged, enrich, enrolled, enslaved, entangled, entitled, entrenched, entropy, entrusted

epi: over; outer; near; beside

  epicardium, epicenter, epicuticle, epidemic, epidemiologist, epidermis, epiglottis, epimetheus, epiphytes

extra: outside; beyond

  extracellular, extract, extradition, extramarital, extraneous, extraordinary, extrapolate, extrasensory, extraterrestrial, extraterritorial, extravagance, extraverted

fore: before; front; superior

  forearm, forebode, forebrain, forecast, foredeck, forefather, forefinger, foregone, forehand, foreknowledge, foreman, foremast, forenoon, foreperson, forerunner, foreshadow, forewoman, foreword

hemi: half

hemialgia, hemiparesis, hemiplegia, hemisphere

hemo, hemato: blood

hematocycst, hematology, hematoma, hemoglobin, hemophilia, hemorrhage

hyper: above; beyond

hyperactive, hyperbole, hyperextension, hyperglycemia, hyperkinetic, hypersensitive, hypersonic, hyperspace, hyperstimulation, hypertension, hyperthyroidism, hypertonic, hyperventilation

hypo: under; beneath; below; below normal

hypoactive, hypoallergenic, hypochondria, hypocritical, hypodermis, hypogastric, hypoglycemia, hypokinetic, hypotension, hypothalamus, hypothermia, hypothyroid, hypoventilation

il: not; variant of *in* used before words beginning with *l*

illegal, illegible, illegitimate, illicit, illiterate

im: not

imbalance, immature, immeasurably, immobile, immoral, immortal, immovable, impartial, impassable, impatient, impenetrable, imperfect, impersonal, impolite, impossible, impractical, improbable, improper

in: not

incredible, indefinite, independence, indifferent, indirect, inefficient, inexpensive, informal, inorganic, insignificant, insoluble, insufficient, invariably, invertebrates, involuntary

inter: between; among

interalliance, interbank, interchangeable, intercirculation, intercorrelation, intercortical, interfamily, intergeneration, interlibrary, interlinear, intermediate, intermission, international

intra: within

intracellular, intramural, intramuscular, intrastate, intravenous

meta: beyond; after; along with; in chemistry: the least hydrated of a series

meta-antimonic, metabolic, metacarpal, metacognitive, metacomet, metamorphic, metamorphosis, metaphor, metaphysical, metaphysics

para: beyond; outside of; similar to

paralanguage, paramagnetic, paraphrase, paraprofessional, parapsychology, parasympathetic

peri: around; about; surrounding

pericardium, perigee, perimeter, peripheral, periphery, periscope

post: after; later than

postcranial, postdated, posterior, postgraduate, posthumously, post-industrial, postmortem, postnatal, postoperative, postpartum, post-school, postscript, post-season, postsecondary, postwar

pre: before; in front of

preamble, precambrian, precaution, preceded, precedent, preconceived, predetermined, prediction, predisposition, preface, prehistory, prejudice, premature, prenatal, prepaid, prerequisite, preschool, preset, preview

re: again; back

react, rebirth, rebuild, recall, recover, recycle, renaissance, renewable, repay, replace, rewrite

sub: under, below; not perfect

subarctic, subatomic, subcategories, subcommittee, subcommittees, subconscious, subcontinent, subculture, subdivided, subdivision, subfloor, subgroups, subheadings, submarine, submerged, subordinate, subphyla, subregion, subspecies, substrate, subsystems, subterranean, subtitle, subtropical

syn: with; together

asynchronous, idiosyncrasies, idiosyncrasy, idiosyncratic, synapse, synchronized, synchrotron, syncopated, syndicated, syndrome, synergy, synonym, synthesis, synthesize, synthetic

trans: across

transaction, transatlantic, transcend, transcontinental, transcribe, transcript, transducer, transfer, transform, transfusion, transgression, transience, transient, transistor, transition, translate, translucent, transmission, transmit, transmutation, transparent, transpiration, transplant, transponder, transport, transportation, transverse

un: not; opposite

unaided, unavoidable, unconscious, unconstitutional, uncontrolled, undigested, unemployment, unequal, unexplored, unfavorable, unfortunate, unhealthy, uninhabited, unlikely, unlimited, unnatural, unofficial, unpopular, unprecedented, unpredictable, unreliable, unrest, unsafe, unsaturated

uni: one

unicameral, unicellular, unicorn, unicycle, unidirectional, uniform, uniformity, unilateral, union, unique, unison, unitary, unitized, univalves, universe, university

Suffixes

able: capable of; able to; tending to

affordable, arable, biodegradable, disposable, distinguishable, durable, equitable, fashionable, favorable, flammable, habitable, honorable, impassable, impenetrable, impermeable, implacable, impregnable, inalienable, incurable, indescribable, indispensable, inflammable, inhospitable, insurmountable, malleable, measurable, memorable, navigable, negotiable, notable, objectionable, perishable, permeable, profitable, taxable, variable, venerable

age: collection; process; rate of; place of; charge

acreage, amperage, anchorage, assemblage, bandage, blockage, bondage, brokerage, coinage, heritage, mileage, mortgage, orphanage, parsonage, patronage, percentage, plumage, postage, sewage, steerage, suffrage, voltage

al: pertaining to; often makes adjectives of nouns

abdominal, aerial, agricultural, anatomical, ancestral, annual, architectural, asexual, astronomical, bilateral, biochemical, biographical, biological, bronchial, celestial, centrifugal, cerebral, chronological, classical, clinical, coastal, colonial, congressional, constitutional, continental, cylindrical, diagonal, dictatorial, digital, directional, dorsal, ecclesiastical, ecological, economical, editorial, electoral, electrical, electrochemical, elliptical, environmental, equatorial, experimental, fetal, fiscal, fractional, gastrointestinal, geographical, geological, geothermal, glacial, global, governmental, grammatical, gravitational, historical, horizontal, hormonal, hypothetical, international, intestinal, judicial, lateral, legal, liberal, mathematical, mechanical, nasal, naval, neural, numerical, nutritional, optical, orbital, physical, physiological, political, provincial, psychological, racial, radial, regional, skeletal, societal, spatial, spherical, spinal, statistical, subtropical, symmetrical, technical, tidal, tropical, transcontinental, tribal, umbilical, universal, vertical, viral, visual

an: forms adjectives from nouns

American, Puritan, Republican

ance: forms nouns from adjectives or verbs

abundance, appearance, assistance, brilliance, distance, elegance, entrance, ignorance, importance

ant: (forms nouns and adjectives from verbs): having or acting as; thing that carries out a certain action

abundant, buoyant, coolant, defendant, defiant, descendant, disinfectant, dominant, dormant, immigrant, inhabitant, malignant, migrant, militant, mutant, pollutant, predominant, radiant, reactant, recombinant, resistant, significant, stimulant, triumphant, tyrant, valiant

ar: forms adjectives

angular, circular, familiar, globular, lunar, muscular, popular, similar, singular, solar, stellar, triangular

ate: forms adjectives or verbs

advocate, approximate, dedicate, deviate, domesticate, educate, emancipate, evaporate, extricate, hesitate, illustrate, liquidate, locate, permeate

eer: one associated with

auctioneer, buccaneer, cannoneer, charioteer, engineer, harpooneer, mountaineer, musketeer, pamphleteer, pioneer, privateer, profiteer, puppeteer, volunteer

en: forms adjectives

ashen, brazen, frozen, golden

ence:

absence, abstinence, competence, conference, dependence, difference, incontinence, independence, influence, insistence, intelligence, residence, persistence

ent: forms nouns or adjectives from verbs

absent, accident, belligerent, confident, competent, dependent, different, independent, insistent, intelligent, persistent, resident

er: one who; one who has

astronomer, banker, builder, commander, commissioner, consumer, customer, designer, employer, explorer, laborer, lawyer, leader, manager, manufacturer, mariner, minister, observer, officer, owner, philosopher, photographer, pitcher, researcher, retailer, trader, voter, weaver, worker

ess: female

actress, countess, duchess, empress, governess, princess, waitress

etic: forms an adjective and occurs in some nouns

aesthetic, anesthetic, apathetic, cybernetic, diabetic, diuretic, eidetic, electromagnetic, esthetic, generic, kinesthetic, kinetic, magnetic, onomatopoetic, parasympathetic, photosynthetic, poetic, prophetic, prosthetic, synthetic

ful: full of; having; characterized by

boastful, bountiful, distrustful, doleful, dutiful, grateful, healthful, lawful, merciful, mournful, plentiful, powerful, resourceful, respectful, scornful, successful, thoughtful, truthful, uneventful, vengeful, wasteful

fy (–ify): make; cause to be

beautify, deify, dignify, glorify, horrify, liquefy, magnify, notify, signify, terrify

ian: variant of *an*

agrarian, amphibian, Asian, authoritarian, barbarian, Bostonian, centenarian, circadian, civilian, collegian, comedian, contrarian, crocodilian, custodian, diagnostician, disciplinarian, draconian, egalitarian, dietician, equalitarian, equestrian, Euclidian, guardian, historian, humanitarian, libertarian, librarian, mammalian, Martian, octogenarian, parliamentarian, pedestrian, plebian, proletarian, reptilian, ruffian, salutorian, sanitarian, sectarian, technician, theologian, thespian, tragedian, utilitarian, utopian, valedictorian, vegetarian, veterinarian

itis: inflammation of

bronchitis, gastritis, hepatitis, neuritis

ial: variant of –al

facial, fictional, filial, financial, imperial, industrial, influential, marital, martial, official, pictorial, presidential, terrestrial, territorial, trivial, tropical

ible: variant of *able*

audible, combustible, contemptible, credible, deductible, illegible, incomprehensible, incredible, indelible, indivisible, inflexible, intelligible, invincible, permissible, plausible, visible

ic: forms adjectives; used in some nouns; when used with chemical terms is used to show the one that has a high valence: ferric oxide

acidic, allergic, anesthetic, antibiotic, aquatic, aristocratic, atmospheric, atomic, autocratic, carcinogenic, climatic, cosmic, cubic, democratic, domestic, economic, electrolytic, electronic, electrostatic, endothermic, exothermic, galactic, gastric, generic, geographic, geologic, geometric, Germanic, hydraulic, hydrochloric, inorganic, isometric, kinetic, linguistic, magnetic, metabolic, metallic, microscopic, nucleic, numeric, Olympic, organic, Paleozoic, parasitic, periodic, photoelectric, pneumatic, poetic, prehistoric, republic, scientific, seismic, sulfuric, symbolic, synthetic, systematic, thermodynamic, toxic, tragic, ultrasonic, volcanic

ician: forms a noun indicating occupation

beautician, cosmetician, electrician, magician, mathematician, mortician, musician, obstetrician optician, pediatrician, physician

ide: used in the names of chemical compounds

bromide, carbide, chloride, cyanide, dioxide, disaccharide, disulfide, hydrochloride, hydroxide, iodide, monosaccharide, monoxide, nucleotide, oxide, peptide, peroxide, polypeptide, polysaccharide, sulfide, tetrachloride, triglyceride

ish: forms adjectives from nouns and other adjectives; belonging to; like; having the characteristics of

babyish, bookish, foolish, fortyish, Swedish, youngish

ism: state of; way of behaving; belief

authoritarianism, behaviorism, botulism, capitalism, colonialism, communism, confucianism, constitutionalism, consumerism, depotism, fascism, federalism, humanism, humanitarianism, imperialism, impressionism, industrialism, isolationism, liberalism, Marxism, mercantilism, metabolism, mutualism, nationalism, patriotism, pluralism, progressivism, puritanism, racism, romanticism, sectionalism, socialism, symbolism, terrorism, totalitarianism

ist: one who; one that

abolitionist, anthropologist, archaeologist, archeologist, audiologist, biochemist, biologist, capitalist, chemist, colonist, communist, conservationist, ecologist, economist, entomologist, fascist, federalist, feminist, geneticist, geologist, humanist, hygienist, imperialist, lobbyist, loyalist, meteorologist, nationalist, naturalist, neurologist, paleontologist, pathologist, physicist, populist, protagonist, racist, scientist, socialist, sociologist, terrorist

ite: native; follower of; part of

anthracite, bauxite, graphite, hematite, meteorite, nitrite, pyrite, satellite, sulfite, trilobite

ity: state or condition

ability, adversity, captivity, charity, civility, dignity, eternity, jollity, majority, reality, sensitivity, severity, sincerity, uniformity, university

ive: tending toward a certain action

active, corrective, supportive

ization: action; state

authorization, centralization, characterization, civilization, colonization, crystallization, decentralization, fertilization, hospitalization, immunization, industrialization, ionization, mechanization, mobilization, modernization, nationalization, naturalization, rationalization, socialization, specialization, stabilization, sterilization, urbanization, vaporization

ize: make; cause to

actualize, agonize, anesthetize, anodize, categorize, characterize, civilize, colonize, crystallize, energize, popularize

less: without; not having

> bloodless, boundless, cloudless, colorless, countless, heartless, heedless, jobless, landless, lawless, limitless, motionless, nameless, needless, numberless, odorless, penniless, stainless, timeless, weightless, wireless

ment (forms a noun): result; action; state

> amendment, announcement, bombardment, commandment, commitment, confinement, department, deployment, detachment, disarmament, discouragement, displacement, endorsement, enforcement, enlightenment, enlistment, environment, equipment, experiment, government, impeachment, imprisonment, improvement, indictment, installment, measurement, nourishment, replacement, requirement, resentment, retirement, sediment, settlement, shipment

ness: state of; having

> aggressiveness, awareness, bitterness, consciousness, greatness, hardness, heaviness, numbness, seriousness, unconsciousness, uniqueness, vastness, weakness, weariness, wilderness

oid: looking; having the form of

> amoeboid, arachnoid, asteroid, celluloid, haploid, hominoid, meteoroid, paranoid, sphenoid, steroid, tabloid, thyroid, trapezoid, typhoid

or: one that does; thing that does

> accelerator, aggressor, ambassador, ancestor, compressor, conductor, connector, conqueror, depositor, detector, dictator, generator, governor, incinerator, incubator, indicator, insulator, inventor, investor, legislator, liberator, mediator, microprocessor, monitor, navigator, proprietor, prospector, regulator, resistor, surveyor, translator, warrior

ose: having or being

> bellicose, comatose, fructose, glucose, lactose, morose, sucrose, varicose

osis: actions; disorders; states

> apotheosis, arteriosclerosis, cirrhosis, diagnosis, halitosis, hypnosis, metamorphosis, mitosis, multiple sclerosis, osmosis, tuberculosis

ous: having; full of

> amorphous, analogous, aqueous, autonomous, carnivorous, coniferous, contagious, deciduous, dubious, fibrous, gaseous, hazardous, heterogeneous, homogeneous, igneous, industrious, infectious, intravenous, melodious, mountainous, nervous, nonferrous, noxious, nutritious, poisonous, populous, porous, precious, thunderous, unanimous, victorious

sion: forms a noun

> admission, aggression, commission, concussion, convulsion, corrosion, dimension, dispersion, division, emission, emulsion, erosion, exclusion, excursion, expansion, extension, fission, fusion, hypertension, illusion, intermission, inversion, percussion, permission, propulsion recession, revision, secession, subdivision, submission, succession, suppression, suspension, tension, transfusion, transmission, vision

some: forms adjectives

> burdensome, irksome, quarrelsome

ster: forms nouns

> broadcaster, chorister, gamester, gangster, harvester, huckster, mobster, pollster, roadster, songster, teamster, trickster, youngster

tion: forms nouns

> absorption, acceleration, application, assassination, association, assumption, characterization, circulation, civilization, classification, colonization, combustion, communication, compensation, computation, condensation, confederation, conservation, constitution, declaration, digestion, distillation, elevation, equation, eruption, evaluation, evaporation, evolution, expedition, experimentation, extinction, fertilization, formulation, foundation, friction, function, immigration, industrialization, infection, integration, invention, investigation, ionization, irrigation, isolation, legislation, location, migration, moderation, modernization, multiplication, nation, navigation, nomination, notation, nutrition, occupation, operation, opposition, oxidation, pollination, pollution, population, precipitation, proclamation, proportion, radiation, reaction, respiration, revolution, rotation, sanitation, segregation, solution, starvation, taxation, transaction, transition, translation, transportation, urbanization, vaccination, variation, vegetation

ty: quality or state of

> Christianity, clarity, complexity, creativity, density, dynasty, equality, equity, fertility, gravity, heredity, humanity, humidity, minority, mobility, nobility, polarity, popularity, probability, productivity, prosperity, quantity, radioactivity, relativity, reliability, sovereignty, stability, superiority, utility, validity, velocity

ure: action; result of

> adventure, capture, creature, culture, departure, feature, legislature, literature, manufacture, mixture, nature, overture, pasture, pressure, puncture, signature, temperature, torture

Roots and Combining Forms

aero: air

aerobes, aerobic, aerobics, aerodynamic, aeromedics, aeronaut, aeronautical, aeronautics, aerosols, aerosol-sprayed, aerospace, anaerobic, anaerobes

anthrop, anthropo: human being

anthropoids, anthropological, anthropologist, anthropology, anthropomorphism, misanthropy, paleoanthropologists, philanthropic, philanthropists, philanthropy

aqua: water

aquaculture, aquafarm, aquanaut, aquarium, aqueducts

arthr, arthro: joint

arthritis, arthroplasty, arthropod, arthroscope

aud(i): hearing; sound

audible, audibly, audience, audiences, audio, audiologist, audiometer, audiovisual, audit, audition, auditions, auditor, auditorium, auditory

auto: self; same

autobiographical, autobiography, autocracy, autocratic, autograph, autoharp, autoimmune, autonomic, autonomous, autonomy, autopsy, autosome, autotroph, autotrophic, semiautonomous

bene: well

benediction, benefactor, beneficial, beneficiaries, beneficiary, benefit, benefiting, benevolence, benevolent

bi: two; twice

biannual, biceps, bicultural, bicuspid, bicycle, bilabial, bilateral, bimetalism, bimonthly, binary, binocular, binomial, biped, biplane, bipolar

bio: life

antibiotics, biochemical, biodegradable, biodiversity, biofeedback, biography, biological, biologist, biology, bioluminescence, biomass, biome, biomedical, biomolecules, biopsy, biorhythms, biosphere, biosynthesis, biotic, microbiologist, symbiosis

card(i): heart

cardiac, cardiologist, cardiopulmonary, cardiorespiratory, cardiovascular, electrocardiograms, electrocardiograph, endocarditis, myocardial, pericardium

centi: hundredth part

bicentennial, centauri, centennial, centigrade, centimeters, centipede, percentile

cephal, cephalo: head

cephalopod, cephalothorax, encephalitis, hydroencephalic

cerebro: forebrain and midbrain

cerebellum, cerebral cortex, cerebrospinal, cerebrum

chlor: green

chlorate, chloride, chlorides, chlorinated, chlorine, chlorophyll, chloroplast, hydrochloric, tetrachloride

chrom: color

chromatic, chromoplast, chromosome, chromotism

chron, chrono: time

chronic, chronically, chronicle, chronicler, chronological, chronology, chronometer, synchronized, synchrony

cide: kill

biocide, fungicides, herbicides, homicides, infanticide, insecticides, pesticides

corpus: body

corporal, corporate, corporation, corps, corpse, corpulent, corpus, corpuscles, incorporate

cred: believe

accreditation, credence, credential, credible, credit, creditor, credulous, incredible, incredulous

deca: ten

decade, decapod, decathlon, decimal

derm: skin

dermatologist, dermatology, dermatosis, epidermis

di: two; twice; double

dialogue, diatomic, dichotomy, digraph, diode, dioxide, dipolar

dict: to say

abdicate, benediction, contradict, contradiction, dictation, dictator, diction, dictionary, dictum, edict, indictment, jurisdiction, malediction, predict, predictive, valedictorian, verdict dys: bad; difficult

dysentery, dysfluency, dysfunction, dysfunctional, dyslexia, dystrophy

eco: ecology; environment; nature

ecohazard, ecological, ecology, ecosystem

ecto: outer; outside; external

ectoblast, ectoderm, ectogenous, ectomorph, ectopia, ectoplasm, ectotherm

ectomy: surgical removal of

appendectomy, tonsillectomy

endo: within

endocrine, endoderm, endogenous, endomorphism, endoskeleton, endosperm, endospore, endotherm

fidelis: faithful

affidavits, confidence, confident, confidential, fidelity

gastro: stomach

gastritis, gastrointestinal, gastropod, gastrovascular cavity

ge(o): earth; ground

geographic, geography, geologic, geologists, geology, geometric, geometry, geophysical, geothermal

gen: that which produces

antigen, carcinogen, endogen, hydrogen

gram: drawing, writing, record

monogram, telegram

giga: billion

gigabyte, gigacycle, gigahertz, gigawatt

graph: something written

autograph, climatograph, digraph, electrocardiograph, electroencephalograph, electromyograph, heliograph, histograph, micrograph, monograph, paragraph, phonograph, photograph, pictograph, polygraph, seismograph, sonograph, spectrograph, telegraph, thermograph

hepta: seven

heptachlor, heptagon, heptahedron

heter, hetero: other

heterogeneity, heterogeneous, heterosporous, heterotroph, heterozygote, heterozygous

hexa: six

hexachloride, hexafloride, hexagon, hexameter

hom, homo: same; similar

homogeneity, homogeneous, homogenized, homographs, homologous, homonyms, homophones, homozygous

hydr, hydro: water

carbohydrate, dehydrated, dehydration, hydrant, hydrated, hydration, hydraulic, hydrocarbon, hydrochloric, hydroelectric, hydrofoil, hydrogen, hydrogenated, hydrogens, hydrolysis, hydrometer, hydrophilic, hydrophobia, hydroplane, hydroponics, hydrosphere, hydroxide, hydroxyl

iso: equal

isobars, isobath, isochromatic, isodynamic, isometric, isotherm

jec(t): throw

conject, conjecture, deject, dejected, eject, ejection, inject, injection, interject, interjection, object, objection, project, projectile, projection, projector, reject, rejection, trajectory

jur: law

jurisdiction, jurisprudence, jury, perjury

kilo: thousand

kilocalories, kilogram, kilohertz, kilometer, kilowatt

leg: law

illegal, legacy, legal, legality, legislate, legislation, legislature, legitimate

lith(o): stone

lithium, lithography, lithosphere, megalith, mesolithic, monolith, monolithic, neolithic, paleolithic

logy: study of; science of

anthology, anthropology, archaeology, archeology, astrology, bacteriology, biology, chronology, cosmology, criminology, cytology, ecology, epidemiology, etymology, geology, gerontology, high-technology, ideology, immunology, meteorology, methodology, microbiology, mythology, paleontology, pathology, phonology, physiology, psychology, psychopathology, sociology, technology, terminology, theology, zoology

lumen: light

bioluminescence, illuminated, illumination, luminance, luminary, luminosity, luminous

macr(o): large

macroanalysis, macrocosmic, macroeconomic, macrominerals, macromolecules, macronucleus, macronutrients, macro-organization, macroscopic magna: great

magnification, magnificences, magnificent, magnificently, magnify, magnitude

mal: bad; abnormal

maladaptive, malady, malaise, malaria, malevolent, malfunction, malice, malicious, malignant, malnourished, malnutrition, malocclusion, malpractice

mania: great enthusiasm; madness

bibliomania, kleptomania, megalomania, pyromania

mar: sea

marina, marine, mariner, marines, maritime, submarine

mega: great; large, multiplied by a million

megacycles, megahertz, megalith, megalodon, megalomania, megalopolis, megalosaurus, mega-malls, megaphone, mega-predator, megaton, megatrends, megavitamin, megawatt

meso: middle

mesoblast, mesocephalic, mesoderm, Mesolithic, mesosome, mesosphere

meter: 39.37 inches; means of measuring

altimeter, ammeter, anemometer, audiometer, barometer, calorimeter, centimeter, chronometer, diameter, galvanometer, hydrometer, hygrometer, kilometer, micrometer, micrometers, millimeter, odometer, ohmmeter, perimeter, photometer, radiometer, spectrometer, speedometer, tachometer, thermometer, voltmeter

metry: process of measuring

allometery, asymmetry, audiometry, calorimetry, geometry, optometry, photogrammetry, spectrometry, symmetry, trigonometry

micro: very small; one millionth

microbes, microbiology, microclimate, microcomputer, microelectronics, microfilm, microfossils, micrometer, micronesia, microphones, microprocessor, microscope, microseconds, microsurgery, microwave

mon(o): one

monochromatic, monochrome, monocots, monocular, monograph, monolithic, mononucleosis, monoplane, monopod, monopolize, monopoly, monorail, monosaccharide, monosyllables, monotheistic, monotone, monotonous, monotony, monoxide

ne(o): new

neoclassical, neocolonialism, neoliberal, neolithic, neonates, neophyte

neur(o): nerve

neural, neuralgia, neurasthenic, neuroanatomy, neurological, neurologist, neuromuscular, neuron, neuroses, neurosis, neurosurgeon, neurotic, neurotransmitter

nona: nine

nonagenarian, nonagon, novena

octa, octo: eight

octachord, octagon, octameter, octave, octogenerian

omni: all

omnibus, omnibuses, omnidirectional, omnipotence, omnipotent, omnipresence, omnipresent, omniscience, omniscient, omnivores, omnivorous

ortho: straight; right; correct

orthodontics, orthodox, orthography, orthopedic

ovi: egg

oviduct, oviferous, oviparous, ovipositor

pale(o): very old

paleoanthropologists, paleocene, paleo-Indians, Paleolithic, paleontologist, paleontology, Paleozoic

pan: all

panacea, pan-American, pandemic, pandemonium, pandora, Pangaea, panorama

path(o): suffering, disease

pathetic, pathogen, pathology, psychopath, sympathy

ped, pod: foot

arthropod, centipede, cephalopod, impede, millipede, pedal, pedestal, pedestrian, pedometer, podiatrist, podiatry, podium

pel, pul: drive, push

compel, compulsory, dispel, expel, expulsion, impel, impulse, impulsive, propel, propeller, propulsion, repel

pent(a): five

pentagon, pentameter, pentathlon, pentecost, penthouse, pentoxide

phil(o): love of

philanthropic, philanthropy, philharmonic, philosophy

phobia: fear

agoraphobia, claustrophobia, gerontophobia, hydrophobia, photophobia

phon(o): sound; voice

homophones, hydrophone, megaphone, microphone, phonemes, phonics, phonograph, saxophone, symphony, telephone, Xenophon, xylophone

phot(o): light

photocell, photochemical, photocopy, photoelectric, photograph, photometer, photons, photosensitive, photosynthesis, photosynthetic, photovoltaic, telephoto

poly: many; much

monopoly, polychrome, polyester, polyglot, polygon, polygraph, polymers, Polynesia, polynomial, polypeptide, Polyphemus, polysaccharides, polystyrene, polytechnic, polytheistic, polyunsaturated, polyvinyl

port: carry

deport, export, import, portable, porter, support, transport

proto: first; earliest form

protoceratops, protococcus, proton, protoplasm, prototype, protozoa

pseud(o): false

pseudo-event, pseudomonas, pseudonym, pseudopods, pseudoscience

psych(o): mind; spirit; soul

psyche, psychiatry, psychic, psychobiography, psychology, psychomotor, psychotic

quad: four

quadrangle, quadrant, quadraphonic, quadratic, quadrennial, quadrilateral, quadriplegic, quadruped, quadruple

quasi: resembling

quasi-academic, quasi-favorable, quasi-official, quasi-scientific

quint: five

quinter, quintile, quintillion, quintuplets

scrib, script: write

ascribe, circumscribe, conscript, describe, description, inscribe, inscription, prescribe, prescription, proscribe, proscription, scribble, Scripture, subscribe, subscript, subscription, superscript, transcribe, transcription

sect: six

sextant, sextet, sextillion

some: body

autosome, chromosome

spec, spect: see

aspect, inspect, inspector, perspective, retrospect, retrospective, spectacle, spectacles, spectacular, spectator, spectroscope, spectrum, speculate

sphere: round body; surrounding layer of gas

biosphere, hemisphere, ionosphere, spherical, stratosphere

spira, spire: to breathe

aspirants, aspiration, aspire, cardiorespiratory, conspiracy, conspirators, conspire, inspiration, inspirational, inspire, perspire, respiration, respirator, spirited, spiritually, transpiration, transpired

stella: star

constellation, interstellar, stellar

terra: earth; land

extraterrestrial, terrace, terrain, terrarium, terrestrial, terrier, territories

therm(o): heat

ectothermal, endothermal, endothermic, exothermic, geothermal, hypothermia, isotherm, thermal, thermo-chemical, thermodynamic, thermograms, thermograph, thermometer, thermonuclear, thermoplastic, thermos, thermosetting, thermostat

tri: three

triacid, triad, triangle, triathlon, triceratops, trichromatic, tricycle, trifold, triple, tripod, triumvirate, trivet

ultra: beyond

ultrahigh-frequency, ultrahigh-speed, ultralow, ultramarine, ultramicroscope, ultramodern, ultranationalist, ultra-new, ultrapure, ultrasauraus ultrasensitive, ultrasonic, ultrasound, ultra-suspicious, ultrasweet, ultrathin, ultraviolet

uni: one

unicolor, unicorn, unicycle, uniform, unilateral, unipod, unison, unitary, universe

vert, vers: turn

aversion, avert, conversion, convert, convertible, controversy, diversify, diversion, divert, inversion, invert, reverse, reversion, revert, subversion, subvert, universe, versatile, versus, vertigo

vide, vis: see

evidence, evident, invisible, provide, provision, revise, supervise, supervision, video, videocassette, videotape, visa, visible, vision, visionary, visitation, vista

viv, vit: live

revival, revive, survival, survive, vital, vitality, vitalize, vitamin, vivid, viviparous, vivisection

voc: call

advocate, avocation, convocation, equivocal, evocative, evoke, invocation, invoke, irrevocable, provoke, revocation, revoke, vocabulary, vocal, vocalize, vocation, vociferous

References

Professional

AAAS (American Association for the Advancement of Science) (2011). Lessons: 9–12, *Adolescent sleep*. Science Netlinks.

Achievement First (2011). *The achievement gap.* Author. Available online at www.achievementfirst.org/our-approach/achievement-gap-and-mission

ACT. (2006a). *Ready for college and ready for work: Same or different?* Available online at www.act.org/research/policymakers/reports/workready.html

ACT. (2006b). *Reading between the lines.* Available online www.act.org/research/policymakers/reports/index.html

ACT. (2008). *The forgotten middle: Ensuring that all students are on target for college and career readiness before high school.* Available online at www.act.org/research/policymakers/reports/ForgottenMiddle.htm

ACT & Education Trust. (2005). *On course for success: A close look at selected high school courses that prepare all students for college and work.* Available online at www.act.org/research/policymakers/reports/success.html

Adams, A., Carnine, D., & Gersten, R. (1982). Instructional strategies for studying reading content area texts in the intermediate grades. *Reading Research Quarterly, 17,* 27–55.

Afflerbach, P., & VanSledright, B. (2001). Hath! Doth! What? Middle graders reading innovative history text. *Journal of Adolescent & Adult Literacy, 44,* 696–707.

Alexander, P.A., & Jetton, T.L. (2000). Learning from text: A multidimensional and developmental perspective. In M. L. Kamil, P. B. Mosenthal, P. D. Pearson, & R. Barr (Eds.), *Handbook of reading research* (Vol. III, pp. 285–310). Mahwah, NJ: Erlbaum.

Alfassi, M. (1998). Reading for meaning: The efficacy of reciprocal teaching in fostering reading comprehension in high school students in remedial reading classes. *American Educational Research Journal, 35,* 309–332.

Allan, K.K., & Miller, M.S. (2000). *Literacy and learning: Strategies for middle and secondary school teachers.* Boston: Houghton Mifflin.

Alley, G., & Deshler, D. (1979). *Teaching the learning disabled adolescent: Strategies and methods.* Denver, CO: Love.

Alliance for Excellent Education (2007). *Making writing instruction a priority in America's middle and high schools.* Available online at www.all4ed.org/files/WritPrior.pdf

Alliance for Excellent Education. (2009). *Elements of a successful high school.* Available online at www.all4ed.org/what_you_can_do/successful_high_school

Alliance for Excellent Education (2011).*Transforming high schools: Performance systems for powerful teaching.*Washington, DC: Author. Available online at www.all4ed.org/files/TransformingHSs.pdf

Alvarerz, M. (2009, May). *Promoting self-knowledge in adolescents.* Paper presented at the International Reading Association Convention. Minneapolis, MN.

Alvermann, D.E. (1991). The discussion web: A graphic aid for learning across the curriculum. *The Reading Teacher, 45,* 92–99.

Alvermann, D.E. (2009). Sociocultural constructions of adolescence and young people's literacies. In L. Christenbury, R. Bomer, & P. Smagorinsky (Eds.), *Handbook of adolescent literacy research* (pp. 14-28). New York: Guilford.

Alvermann, D.E., & Moore, D.W. (1991). Secondary school reading. In R. Barr, M.L. Kamil, P. Mosenthal, & P. D. Pearson (Eds.), *Handbook of reading research* (Vol. II, pp. 951–983). New York: Longman.

Alvermann, D.E., & Phelps, S.F. (2002). *Content area reading and literacy: Succeeding in today's diverse classrooms* (3rd ed.). Boston: Allyn & Bacon.

Alvermann, D. E., Phelps, S. F., & Gillis, V. R. (2010). *Content area reading and literacy: Succeeding in today's diverse classrooms* (6th ed.). Boston: Allyn & Bacon.

American Association for the Advancement of Science. (2001). *Designs for science literacy.* New York: Oxford.

American Council on the Teaching of Foreign Language. (2010). *Standards for foreign language learning: Executive Summary.* Alexandria, VA: Author.

American Federation of Teachers. (2008). *Sizing up state standards 2008.* Washington, DC: Author. Available on line at www.aft.org/pubs-reports/downloads/teachers/standards2008.pdf

American Psychological Association. (2002). *Developing adolescents: A reference for professionals.* Washington, DC: Author.

Anderson, R. C., Reynolds, R. E., Schallert, D. L., & Goetz, E. T. (1977). Frameworks for comprehending discourse. *American Educational Research Journal, 14,* 367–381.

Anderson, T. H. (1980). Study strategies and adjunct aids. In R. J. Spiro, B. C. Bruce, & W. F. Brewer (Eds.), *Theoretical issues in reading comprehension: Perspectives from cognitive psychology, artificial intelligence, linguistics, and education* (pp. 483–502). Hillsdale, NJ: Erlbaum.

Anderson, T. H., & Armbruster, B. (1984). Studying. In P. D. Pearson, R. Barr, M. L. Kamil, & P. Mosenthal (Eds.), *Handbook of reading research* (pp. 657–679). New York: Longman.

Anderson, V., & Roit, M. (1993). Planning and implementing collaborative strategy instruction for delayed readers in grades 6–10. *The Elementary School Journal, 94,* 121–137.

Anthony, A. (2008). Output strategies for English-language learners: Theory to practice. *The Reading Teacher, 61,* 472-482.

Applebee, A. N. (1984). *Contexts for learning to write: Studies of secondary school instruction.* Norwood, NJ: Ablex.

Applebee, A. N. (2000). Alternative models of writing development. In R. Indrisano & J. R. Squire (Eds.), *Perspectives on writing, research, theory, and practice* (pp. 90–110). Newark, DE: International Reading Association.

Applebee, A. N., Durst, R. K., & Newell, G. E. (1984). The demands of school writing. In A. N. Applebee (Ed.), *Contexts for learning to write: Studies of secondary school instruction* (pp. 55–77). Norwood, NJ: Ablex.

Applebee, A. N., Langer, J. A., Nystrand, M., & Gamoran, A. (2003). Discussion-based approaches to developing understanding: Classroom instruction and student performance in middle and high school English. *American Educational Research Journal, 40,* 685-730.

Applegate, D. (2001). Information organization. *Learning strategies database.* Muskingum College Center for Advancement of Learning. Available online at www.muskingum .edu/~cal/database/organization.htm

Archer, L. E. (2010, December). Lexile reading growth as a function of starting level in at- risk middle school students. *Journal of Adolescent & Adult Literacy, 55,* 281–290.

Armbruster, B. (1996). Considerate texts. In D. Lapp, J. Flood, & N. Farnan (Eds.), *Content area reading and learning instruction strategies* (2nd ed., pp. 47–57). Boston: Allyn & Bacon.

Armbruster, B. B., & Anderson, T. H. (1981). *Content area textbooks* (Tech. Rep. No. 23). Champaign, IL: University of Illinois, Center for the Study of Reading.

Aronson, E. (1978). *The jigsaw classroom.* Beverly Hills, CA: Sage.

Ashcraft, M. H. (1994). *Human memory and cognition.* New York: HarperCollins.

Atwell, N. (1987). *In the middle.* Portsmouth, NH: Boynton/Cook.

Atwell, N. (1990). *Coming to know: Writing to learn in the intermediate grades.* Portsmouth, NH: Heinemann.

Atwell, N. (1993). Foreword. In L. Patterson, C. M. Santa, K. G. Short, & K. Smith (Eds.), *Teachers are researchers: Reflection and action* (pp. vii–x). Newark, DE: International Reading Association.

Aud, S., Hussar, W., Planty, M., Snyder, T., Bianco, K., Fox, M., Frohlich, L., Kemp, J., & Drake, L. (2010). *The condition of education 2010*(NCES 2010-028). Washington, DC: National Center for Education Statistics, Institute of Education Sciences, U.S. Department of Education.

Baker, D. R., & Piburn, M. D. (1997). *Constructing science in middle and secondary school classrooms.* Boston: Allyn & Bacon.

Baker, L., & Brown, A. L. (1984). Metacognitive skills and reading. In P. D. Pearson, R. Barr, M. L. Kamil, & P. Mosenthal (Eds.), *Handbook of reading research* (pp. 353–394). New York: Longman.

Balfanz, R., McPartland, J. M., & Shaw, A. (2002). *Re-conceptualizing extra help for high school students in a high standards era.* Baltimore, MD: Center for Social Organization of Schools, Johns Hopkins University.

Ballator, N., Farnum, M., & Kaplan, B. (1999). *NAEP 1996 trends in writing: Fluency and writing conventions.* Washington, DC: National Center for Education Statistics.

Barron, B., & Darling-Hammond, L. (2008). Teaching for meaningful learning: A review of research on inquiry-based and cooperative learning. In L. Darling-Hammond, B. Barron, P. D. Pearson, A. H. Schoenfeld, E. K. Stage, T. D. Zimmerman, G. N. Cervetti, & J. Tilson, *Powerful learning: What we know about teaching for understanding* (pp. 3–15). San Francisco, CA: Jossey-Bass. Available online at www.edutopia.org/pdfs/edutopia-teaching-for-meaningful-learning.pdf

Barron, R. F. (1969). Research for the classroom teacher: The use of vocabulary as an advanced organizer. In H. L. Herber & P. Senders (Eds.), *Research in reading in the content areas: The first report* (pp. 28–47). Syracuse, NY: Syracuse University, Reading and Language Arts Center.

Barron, R. F. (1979). Research for classroom teachers: Recent developments on the use of the structured overview as an advanced organizer. In H. L. Herber & J. D. Riley (Eds.),

Research in reading in the content areas: Fourth report (pp. 171–176). Syracuse, NY: Syracuse University, Reading and Language Arts Center.

Barry, A. L. (1997). High school reading programs revisited. *Journal of Adolescent & Adult Literacy, 40,* 524–531.

Bateman, H. V. (2009). Adolescent peer culture - gangs, parents' role-overview. *Education Encyclopedia.* Available online at http://education.stateuniversity.com/pages/1738/Adolescent-Peer-Culture.html

Bean, T. W., Bean, S. K., & Bean, K. F. (1999). Intergenerational conversations and two adolescents' multiple literacies: Implications for redefining content area literacy. *Journal of Adolescent & Adult Literacy, 42,* 438–448.

Beck, I. L., & McKeown, M. G. (1983). Learning words well—a program to enhance vocabulary and comprehension. *The Reading Teacher, 36,* 622–625.

Beck, I. L., & McKeown, M. G. (2006). *Improving comprehension with questioning the author: A fresh and expanded view of a powerful approach.* New York: Scholastic.

Beck, I. L., McKeown, M. G., Hamilton, R. L., & Kucan, L. (1997). *Questioning the author: An approach for enhancing student engagement with text.* Newark, DE: International Reading Association.

Beck, I. L., McKeown, M. G., Sinatra, G. M., & Loxterman, J. A. (1991). Revising social studies text from a text-processing perspective: Evidence of improved comprehensibility. *Reading Research Quarterly, 26,* 251–276.

Bereiter, C., & Scardamalia, M. (1987). *The psychology of written composition.* Hillsdale, NJ: Erlbaum.

Berkowitz, S. J. (1986). Effects of instruction in text organization on sixth-grade students' memory for expository text. *Reading Research Quarterly, 21,* 161–178.

Biancarosa, C., & Snow, C. E. (2006). *Reading next—A vision for action and research in middle and high school literacy: A report to Carnegie Corporation of New York* (2nd ed.). Washington, DC: Alliance for Excellent Education. Available online at www.all4ed.org/publications/ReadingNext/ReadingNext.pdf

Bill & Melinda Gates Foundation. (2009). *College-ready-for-all education plan.* Available online at www.gatesfoundation.org/topics/Pages/high-schools.aspx aspx

Bill & Melinda Gates Foundation. (2010a). *Learning about teaching: Initial findings from the measures of effective teaching project.* Available online at www.gatesfoundation.org/college-ready-education/Documents/preliminary-findings-research-paper.pdf

Bill & Melinda Gates Foundation. (2010b). Supporting instruction: Investing in teaching. Available online at www.gatesfoundation.org/highschools/Documents/supporting-instruction.pdf

Bjorklund, B., Handler, N., Mitten, J., & Stockwell, G. (1998, October). *Literature circles: A tool for developing students as critical readers, writers, and thinkers.* Paper presented at the 47th annual conference of the Connecticut Reading Association, Waterbury.

Blachowicz, C. L. Z. (1986). Making connections: Alternatives to the vocabulary notebook. *Journal of Reading, 29,* 643–649.

Blakeslee, T. (1997). *Helping students with constructed response items on the HSPT and MEAPs.* Available online at miscience.org/Files/The_Why.doc

Bloom, B. (Ed.). (1957). *Taxonomy of educational objectives.* New York: McKay.

Bloom, B. (1976). *Human characteristics and school learning.* New York: McGraw-Hill.

Board of Directors of the International Reading Association. (1999). High-stakes assessments in reading. *The Reading Teacher, 53,* 257–264.

Bolton, M. M. (2009, December 3). Their words, unleashed by wiki, Web tool opens brave new world for young writers. *Boston Globe*. Available online at www.boston.com/news/local/articles/2009/12/03/young_writers_in_westwood_unleash_their_best_words_with_web_tool

Bookshelf (2010). *Graphic storytelling and the new literacies: An interview with NCTE educator Peter Gutiérrez*. Available online at www.diamondbookshelf.com/public/default.asp?t=1&m=1&c=20&s=182&ai=74165&ssd

Boothroyd, K. (2001, December). *Being literate in urban third-grade classrooms*. Paper presented at the annual meeting of the National Reading Conference, San Antonio, TX.

Bormuth, J. R. (1971). *Development of standards of readability: Report of development* (Project No. 9–0237). Chicago, IL: University of Chicago. (ERIC Document Reproduction Service No. ED 045–233).

Bousfield, W. A. (1953). The occurrence of clustering in the recall of randomly arranged associates. *Journal of General Psychology, 30*, 149–165.

Bower G. H., Clark, M. C., Lesgold, A. M., & Winenz, D. (1969). Hierarchical retrieval schemes in recall of categorical words lists. *Journal of Verbal Learning and Verbal Behavior, 8*, 323–343.

Boyle, C. (1996). *Efficacy of peer evaluation and effects of peer evaluation on persuasive writing*. Unpublished master's thesis, San Diego State University, San Diego, CA.

Boyle, J. R. (2007). The process of note-taking: Implications for students with mild disabilities. *The Clearing House, 80*, 227–230.

Brady, P. L. (1990). *Improving the reading comprehension of middle school students through reciprocal teaching and semantic mapping strategies*. doctoral dissertation, University of Oregon, Eugene.

Bransford, J. D., Brown, A. L., & Cocking, R. R. (2001). *How people learn: Brain, mind, experience, and school*. Washington, DC: National Academy Press.

Bristow, P. S., Pikulski, J. J., & Pelosi, P. L. (1983). A comparison of five estimates of reading instructional level. *The Reading Teacher, 37*, 273–279.

Brock, C. (2000, May). *Serving English language learners in English dominant classroom: Important issues and considerations*. Paper presented at the annual conference of the International Reading Association, Indianapolis, IN.

Brown, A. L., & Day, J. D. (1983). Macrorules for summarizing text: The development of expertise. *Journal of Verbal Learning and Verbal Behavior, 22*(1), 1–14.

Brown, C. S., & Lytle, S. L. (1988). Merging assessment and instruction: Protocols in the classroom. In S. M. Glazer, L. W. Searfoss, & L. M. Gentile (Eds.), *Reexamining reading diagnosis: New trends and procedures* (pp. 94–102). Newark, DE: International Reading Association.

Bruce, B. C., & Bishop, A. P. (2002). Using the Web to support inquiry-based literacy development. *Journal of Adolescent & Adult Literacy, 45*, 706–714.

Bruner, J. (1963). *The process of education*. New York: Vintage.

Bruner, J. (1986). *Actual minds, possible worlds*. Cambridge, MA: Harvard University Press.

Buehl, D. (2001). *Classroom strategies for interactive learning* (2nd ed.). Newark, DE: International Reading Association.

Buehl, D. (2007). Panel Discussion. *Reading and writing are more than elementary: A summit on adolescent literacy instruction*. Available online at www.all4ed.org/node/926/print Madison, WI.

Buehl, D., & Stumpf, S. (2000). *Developing middle school and high school programs for struggling readers*. Paper presented at the annual meeting of the International Reading Association, Indianapolis, IN.

Bulgren, J. A., Hock, M. F., Schumaker, J. B., & Deshler, D. D. (1995). The effects of instruction in a paired associates strategy on the information mastery performance of students with learning disabilities. *Learning Disabilities Research and Practice, 10*(1), 22-37.

Bulgren, J.A., & Lenz, B.K. (1996). Strategic instruction in the content areas. In D. D. Deshler, E.S. Ellis, & B.K. Lenz (Eds.), *Teaching adolescents with learning disabilities: Strategies and methods* (2nd ed., pp. 409-473). Denver, CO: Love Publishing.

Bulgren, J., & Scanlon, D. (1997/1998). Instructional routines and learning strategies that promote understanding of content area concepts. *Journal of Adolescent & Adult Literacy, 38,* 372–376.

Bush, C., & Huebner, M. (1979). *Strategies for reading in the elementary school* (2nd ed.). New York: Macmillan.

Butler-Nalin, P. (1984). Revisions patterns in students' writing.>In A. N. Applebee & J. N. Langer (Eds.), *Contexts for learning to write: Studies of secondary school instruction.* (pp. 121-215). Norwood, NJ: Ablex.

Cadeiro-Kaplan, K. (2002). Literacy ideologies: Critically engaging the language arts curriculum. *Language Arts, 79,* 372–381.

Calder, L., & Carlson, S. (2002). *Using "think alouds" to evaluate deep understanding.* Policy Center on the First Year of College. Available online www.brevard.edu/fyc/listserv/remarks/calderandcarlson.htm

California Department of Education. (2007). *Reading/Language Arts Framework for California Public Schools.* Sacramento, CA: Author. Available online at www.cde.ca.gov/ci/cr/cf/documents/rlafw.pdf

Calkins, L. M., & Mermelstein, L. (2003). *Nonfiction writing: Procedures and reports. Units of study for primary writing: A yearlong program.* Portsmouth, NH: Heinemann.

Calkins, L., Montgomery, K., & Santman, D. (1998). *A teacher's guide to standardized reading tests.* Portsmouth, NH: Heinemann.

Carey, S. (1986). Cognitive science and science education. *American Psychologist, 10,* 1123–1130.

Carlson, N. R., & Buskist, W. (1997). *Psychology: The science of behavior* (5th ed.). Boston: Allyn & Bacon.

Carpenter, S. K., Pashler, H., Cepeda, N. J., & Alvarez, D. (2007). Applying the principles of testing and spacing to classroom learning. In D. S. McNamara & J. G. Trafton (Eds.), *Proceedings of the 29th Annual Cognitive Science Society* (p. 19). Nashville, TN: Cognitive Science Society.

Carver, R. (1990). *Reading rate: A review of research and theory.* New York: Academic Press.

Carver, R. (1992). What do standardized reading comprehension tests measure in terms of efficiency, rate, and accuracy? *Reading Research Quarterly, 27,* 346–359.

Carver, R. P. (1975–76). Measuring prose difficulty using the rauding scale. *Reading Research Quarterly, 11,* 660–685.

CAST. (2009). *Research & development in universal design for learning.* Wakefield, MA: Author: http://cast.org/research/index.html

Caverly, D. C., & Orlando, V. P. (1991). Textbook study strategies. In D. C. Caverly & V. P. Orlando (Eds.), *Teaching reading and study strategies at the college level* (pp. 86–165). Newark, DE: International Reading Association.

Caverly, D. C., Orlando, V. P., & Mullen, J. L. (2000). *Textbook study reading.* In R. F. Flippo & D. C. Caverly (Eds.), *Handbook of college reading and study strategy research* (pp. 105–147). Mahwah, NJ: Erlbaum.

Center for Research on Learning. (2009a) *Content enhancement.* Lawrence, KS: University of Kansas. Available online at www.kucrl.org/sim/brochures/CEoverview.pdf

Center for Research on Learning. (2009b). *Learning strategies brochure.* Available online at www.ku-crl.org/sim/strategies.shtml

Chadwell, G. B. (2002). *Developing an effective writing program for the elementary grades.* West Newbury, MA: Collins Education Associates.

Chall, J. S., Bissex, G. L., Conrad, S. S., & Harris-Sharples, S. H. (1996). *Holistic assessment of texts: Scales for estimating the difficulty of literature, social studies, and science materials.* Cambridge, MA: Brookline.

Chall, J. S., & Dale, E. (1995). *Readability revisited: The new Dale-Chall readability formula.* Cambridge, MA: Brookline.

Chamot, A. U., & O'Malley, J. M. (1994). Instructional approaches and teaching procedures. In K. Spangenber-Urbschat & R. Pritchard (Eds.), *Kids come in all languages: Reading instruction for ESL students* (pp. 82–107). Newark, DE: International Reading Association.

Chinn, C. A., & Brewer, W. F. (1993). The role of anomalous data in knowledge acquisition: A theoretical framework and implications for science instruction. *Review of Educational Research, 63,* 1–49.

Christenbury, L., Bomer, R., & Smagorinsky, P. (2009). Introduction. In L. Christenbury, R. Bomer, & P. Smagorinsky (Eds.), *Handbook of adolescent literacy research* (pp. 1–13). New York: Guilford.

Christenbury, L., & Kelly, P. (1983). *Questioning: A path to critical thinking.* Urbana, IL: National Council of Teachers of English.

Claxton, M. M., & Cooper, C. C. (2000). Teaching tools: American literature and the World Wide Web. *English Journal, 90,* 97–103.

Coiro, J. (2009). Promising practices for supporting adolescents' online literacy development. In K. D. Wood & W. E. Blanton (Eds.), *Literacy instruction for adolescents* (pp. 442–471). New York: Guilford.

Colburn, A., & Echevarria, J. (1999). Meaningful lessons. *The Science Teacher, 66*(2), 36–39.

Coleman, E. B. (1971). Developing a technology of written instruction: Some determiners of the complexity of prose. In E. Z. Rothkopf & P. E. Johnson (Eds.), *Verbal learning research and the technology of written instruction* (pp. 155–204). New York: Teachers College Press.

Collins Education Resources. (2009). *Research results.* Available online at www.collins educationassociates.com/research.htm

Collins, J. J. (2004). *Selecting and teaching focus correction areas.* West Newbury, MA: Collins Education Associates.

Collins, J. J. (2010). *Improving student performance through writing and thinking across the curriculum.* West Newbury, MA: Collins Education Associates.

Collins, P., & Scarcella, R. (2007). *Effective literacy and English language instruction for English learners in the elementary grades: A practice guide* (NCEE 2007-4011). Washington, DC: National Center for Education Evaluation and Regional Assistance, Institute of Education Sciences, U.S. Department of Education. Available online at http://ies.ed.gov/ncee

Conard, S. S. (1990, May). *Change and challenge in content textbooks.* Paper presented at the annual conference of the International Reading Association, New Orleans, LA.

Conley, M. R. (1997). *Content reading instruction* (2nd ed.). New York, NY: McGraw-Hill.

Conley, M. (2008). Cognitive strategy instruction for adolescents: What we know about the promise, what we don't know about the potential. *Harvard Educational Review, 78,* 84-106.

Connecticut Technical High School System. (2009). *Connecticut Technical High Schools Receive Strategic Instruction Model Impact Award.* Hartford, CT: Author. Available online at www.cttech.org/central/main-news/SIM-Award-10-09/index.htm

Cook, L. K., & Mayer, R. E. (1998). Teaching readers about the structure of scientific text. *Journal of Educational Psychology, 80,* 448–456.

Cooper, C. R., & Odell, L. (1977). *Evaluating writing: Describing, measuring, judging.* Urbana, IL: National Council of Teachers of English.

Coppola, J. (2002, May). *Creating opportunities to learn: Literacy instruction for English language learners in a fifth-grade, all English classroom.* Paper presented at the annual meeting of the International Reading Association, San Francisco, CA.

The Council of Chief State School Officers and The National Governors Association Center for Best Practices. (2009). *Common core state standards initiative.* Available online at www.corestandards.org

Council of the Great City Schools. (2009). *Urban indicator: High school reform survey, school year 2006-2007.* Available online at www.cgcs.org/publications/achievement.aspx

Countryman, J. (1992). *Writing to learn mathematics: Strategies that work.* Portsmouth, NH: Heinemann.

Coxhead, A. (2000). A new academic word list. *TESOL Quarterly, 34,* 213–238

Crago, M. B. (1992). Communicative interaction and second language acquisition: An Inuit example. *TESOL Quarterly, 26,* 487–505.

Craik, F. I. M., & Lockhart, R. S. (1972). Levels of processing. *Journal of Verbal Learning and Verbal Behavior, 11,* 671–684.

Crawford, A. N. (1993). Literature, integrated language arts, and the language minority child: A focus on meaning. In A. Carrasquillo (Ed.), *Whole language and the bilingual learner* (pp. 61–75). Norwood, NJ: Ablex.

Cummins, J. (1981). The role of primary language development in promoting educational success for language minority students. In C. F. Leyba (Ed). *Schooling and language minority students: A theoretical framework* (pp. 3-49). Los Angeles, CA: Evaluation, Dissemination and Assessment Center, California State University, Los Angeles.

Cummins, J. (1994). The acquisition of English as a second language. In K. Spangenberg-Urbschat & R. Pritchard (Eds.), *Kids come in all languages: Reading instruction for all ESL students* (pp. 36–62). Newark, DE: International Reading Association.

Cummins, J. (2001). Assessment and intervention with culturally and linguistically diverse learners. In S. R. Hurley & J. V. Tinanjero (Eds.), *Literacy assessment of second language learners* (pp. 115–129). Boston: Allyn & Bacon.

Cunningham, A. E., & Stanovich, K. E. (1998). What reading does for the mind. *American Educator* (Spring/Summer), 1-8.

Curtis, M. E. R., & Longo, A. M. (1999). *When adolescents can't read: Methods and materials that work.* Boston: Brookline.

Dahl, K., & Farnan, N. (1998). *Children's writing: Perspectives from research.* Newark, DE: International Reading Association & National Reading Conference.

Dale, E., & O'Rourke, J. (1971). *Techniques of teaching vocabulary.* Chicago, IL: Field.

Daly, J. A., & Hailey, J. L. (1984). Putting the situation into writing research: State and disposition as parameters of writing apprehension. In R. Beach & L. Bridwell (Eds.), *New directions in composition research.* New York, NY: Guilford Press.

Daniels, H. (1994). *Literature circles: Voice and choice in the student-centered classroom.* York, ME: Stenhouse.

Daniels, H. (2002). *Literature circles: Voice and choice in book clubs and reading groups.* York, ME: Stenhouse.

Daniels, H. (2008). *What's new with literature circles?* Paper presented at the Annual Conference of the Connecticut Reading Association. Cromwell, CT.

Dave, R. H. (1964). *The identification and measurement of environmental process variables that are related to educational achievement.* Unpublished doctoral dissertation, University of Chicago.

Davey, B., & McBride, S. (1986). Effects of question-generation training on reading comprehension. *Journal of Educational Psychology, 78,* 256–262.

Department of Psychology, University of Memphis. *Readability formulas.* (2009). Available online at http://cohmetrix.memphis.edu/cohmetrixpr/readability.html readability formulas

Deshler, D., & Ehren, B. (2008). *Literacy pearls are not all alike: Differential discipline-specific requirements.* Paper presented at the SIM Conference. Lawrence, Kansas. Available online at www.ku-crl.org/conferences/sim/2008con/downloads/Handout.doc

Deshler, D. D., Schumaker, J. B., Bui, Y., & Vernon, S. (2006). High schools and adolescents with disabilities: Challenges at every turn. In D. D. Deshler & J. B. Schumaker (Eds.), *Teaching adolescents with disabilities: Accessing the general education curriculum* (pp. 1–34). Thousand Oaks, CA: Corwin Press.

Devine, T. G. (1987). *Teaching study skills: A guide for teachers* (2nd ed.). Boston: Allyn & Bacon.

Diaz-Rico, L. T. (2004). *Teaching English learners: Strategies and methods* (2nd ed.). Boston: Allyn & Bacon.

Diaz-Rico, L. T., & Weed, K. W. (2002). *The cross-cultural, language, and academic development handbook: A complete K–12 reference guide.* Boston: Allyn & Bacon.

Dillon, J. T. (1983). *Teaching and the art of questioning.* Bloomington, IN: Phi Delta Kappa.

Dillon, S. (2010, December 11). What works in the classroom? Ask the students. *The New York Times,* p. A15.

Dole, J. A., Sloan, C., & Trathen, W. (1995). Teaching vocabulary within the context of literature. *Journal of Reading, 38,* 452–460.

Dolly, M. R. (1990). Integrating ESL reading and writing through authentic discourse. *Journal of Reading, 33,* 360–365.

Draper, R. J. (2008). Redefining content-area literacy teacher education: Finding my voice through collaboration. *Harvard Educational Review, 78*(1), 60–83.

Dreher, M. J., & Guthrie, J. T. (1990). Cognitive processes in textbook chapter search tasks. *Reading Research Quarterly, 25,* 323–339.

Duffelmeyer, F. A., Baum, D. D., & Merkley, D. J. (1987). Maximizing reader-text confrontation with an extended anticipation guide. *Journal of Reading, 31,* 146–150.

Duffy, G. G., & Roehler, L. R. (1987). Improving reading instruction through the use of responsive elaboration. *The Reading Teacher, 40,* 514–520.

Duffy, H. (2007). *Meeting the needs of significantly struggling learners in high school: A look at approaches to tiered intervention.* National High School Center. Available online at www.betterhighschools.org/docs/NHSC_RTIBrief_08-02-07.pdf

Duffy, T., Higgins, L. Mehlenbacher, B., Cochran, C., Wallace, D., Hill, C., Haugen, D., McCaffrey, M., Burnett, R., Sloane, S., & Smith, S. (1989). Models for the design of instructional text. *Reading Research Quarterly, 24,* 434–457.

Dupin, J. J., & Joshua, S. (1987). Conceptions of French pupils concerning electric circuits: Structure and evolution. *Journal of Research in Science Teaching, 24,* 791–806.

Durst, R. K. (1984). The development of analytical writing. In A. N. Applebee (Ed.), *Contexts for learning to write: Studies of secondary school instruction* (pp. 79–102). Norwood, NJ: Ablex.

Dutro, S., & Moran, C. (2003). Rethinking English language instruction: An architectural approach. In G. G. García (Ed.), *English learners* (pp. 227–258). Newark, DE: International Reading Association.

Dwyer, D. C. (1995, July). *Finding the future in the past: Readying schools for the 21st century.* Proceedings of the Australian Computers in Education Conference, Perth, Australia. Available online on www.tdd.nsw.edu.au/resources/papers/info_skills.htm

Early, M., & Sawyer, D. J. (1984). *Reading to learn in grades 5 to 12.* New York: Harcourt Brace Jovanovich.

East Bay Educational Collaborative (2010), *Scientist's notebook toolkit.* Warren, RI: Author. Available online at http://ebecri.org/content/toolkit

Echevarria, J., Vogt, M., & Short, D. J. (2000). *Making content comprehensible for English language learners: The SIOP model.* Boston: Allyn & Bacon.

Edugreen. (2001). *What you can do to reduce air pollution.* Available online at http://edugreen.teri.res.in/explore/air/ucan.htm

Eeds, M., & Cockrum, W. A. (1985). Teaching word meanings by expanding schemata vs. dictionary work vs. reading in context. *Journal of Reading, 28,* 492–497.

Egan, M. (1999). Reflections on effective use of graphic organizers. *Journal of Adolescent & Adult Literacy, 42,* 641–645.

Eggen, P., & Kauchak, D. (2001). *Educational psychology: Windows on classrooms* (5th ed.). Upper Saddle River, NJ: Merrill Prentice Hall.

Eisenberger, J., Conti-D'Antonio, M., & Bertrando, R. (2000). *Self-efficacy: Raising the bar for students with learning needs.* Larchmont, NY: Eye on Education.

Electronic Journal of Combinatories. (2001). *Who was John Venn?* Available online at: www.combinatories.org/Surveys/ds5/VennJohnEJC.html

Emig, J. (1971). *The composing process of twelfth-graders.* Urbana, IL: National Council of Teachers of English.

Escamilla, K., & Cody, M. (2001). Assessing the writings of Spanish-speaking students: Issues and suggestions. In S. R. Hurley & J. V. Tinajero (Eds.), *Literacy assessment of second language learners* (pp. 43–63). Boston: Allyn & Bacon.

Fagella-Luby, M. N., Ware, S. M., & Capozzoli, A. (2009). Adolescent literacy—Reviewing adolescent literacy reports: Key components and critical questions. *Journal of Literacy Research 41,* 453–475.

Fairbanks, C. M., Roser, N. L., & Schallert, D. L. (2008). The role of textbooks and tradebooks in content area reading. In D. Lapp, J. Flood & N. Farnan (Eds.), *Content area reading and learning: instructional strategies* (3rd ed., pp. 19–34). New York: Taylor & Francis.

Farr, R., & Carey, R. F. (1986). *Reading: What can be measured?* Newark, DE; International Reading Association.

Farr, R., & Pritchard, R. (1996). In D. Lapp, J. Flood, & N. Farnan (Eds.), *Content area reading and learning instructional strategies* (2nd ed., pp. 383–402). Boston, MA: Allyn & Bacon.

Ferguson, A. M., & Fairburn, J. (1985). Language experience for problem solving in mathematics. *The Reading Teacher, 38,* 504–507.

Ferguson, R. F. (2002). *What doesn't meet the eye: Understanding and addressing racial disparities in high-achieving suburban schools.* Cambridge, MA: Harvard University, John F. Kennedy School of Government. (ERIC Document Reproduction Service No. ED 474 390)

Fisher, D. (2001). "We're moving on up": Creating a schoolwide literacy effort in an urban high school. *Journal of Adolescent & Adult Literacy, 45,* 92–101.

Fisher, D., & Frey, N. (2007). *Checking for understanding, Formative assessment techniques for your classroom.* Alexandria, VA: ASCD.

Fisher, D., Frey, N., & Lapp, D. (2009). *In a reading state of mind.* Newark, DE: International Reading Association, 2009.

Fleischman, H. L., Hopstock, P. J., Pelczar, M. P., & Shelley, B. E. (2010). *Highlights from PISA 2009: Performance of U. S. 15-year-old students in reading, mathematics, and science literacy in an international context* (NCES 2011-004). Washington, DC: U. S. Department of Education, National Center for Education Statistics. U. S. Government Printing Office.

Flexner, S. B., & Hauck, L. C. (1994). *The Random House dictionary of the English language* (2nd ed., rev.). New York: Random House.

Freedman, T. (2010). *Web 2.0 for rookies: What is tagging?* The Educational Technology Site. Available online at www.ictineducation.org/home-page/2010/1/1web-20-for-rookies-what-is-tagging.html?utm_source=twitterfeed&utm_medium=twitter

Freeman, Y., & Freeman, D. (2002, May). *Teaching language through content themes and literature.* Paper presented at the annual meeting of the International Reading Association, San Francisco, CA.

Fry, E. (1995). African reading stories (Reading around the World). *The Reading Teacher, 48,* 444–445.

Fung, I. Y. Y., Wilkinson, I. A. G., & Moore, D. W. (2003). L1-assisted reciprocal teaching to improve ESL students' comprehension of English expository text. *Learning and Instruction 13*(1) 1–31.

Fusaro, J. (1988). Applying statistical rigor to a validation study of the Fry Readability Graph. *Reading Research and Instruction, 28,* 44–48.

Gallagher, K. (2003). *Reading reasons.* Portland, ME: Stenhouse.

Gallagher, K. (2006). *Teaching adolescent writers.* Portland, ME: Stenhouse.

Gambrell, L. B. (1980). Think time: Implications for reading instruction. *The Reading Teacher, 34,* 143–146.

Gambrell, L. B., & Bales, R. J. (1986). Mental imagery and the comprehension monitoring performance of fourth- and fifth-grade poor readers. *Reading Research Quarterly, 21,* 454–464.

Gambrell, L. B., Kapinus, B. A., & Wilson, R. M. (1987). Using mental imagery and summarization to achieve independence in comprehension. *Journal of Reading, 30,* 638–642.

Gambrell, L. B., Wilson, R. M., & Gantt, W. N. (1981). Classroom observations of good and poor readers. *Journal of Educational Research, 24,* 400–404.

Gans, R. (1940). *Study of critical reading comprehension in intermediate grades: Teachers College contributions to education, No. 811.* New York, NY: Bureau of Publications, Teachers College, Columbia University.

Gardner, H. (1983). *Frames of mind: The theory of multiple intelligences.* New York: Basic Books.

Garner, R. (1994). Metacognition and executive control. In R. B. Ruddell, M. R. Ruddell, & H. Singer (Eds.), *Theoretical models and processes of reading* (4th ed., pp. 715–732). Newark, DE: International Reading Association.

Gaskins, I.W. (2005). *Success with struggling readers: The Benchmark School approach*. New York: The Guilford Press.

Gaskins, I. W., & Elliot, T. (1991). *Implementing cognitive strategy instruction across the school*. Cambridge, MA: Brookline.

Gates, A. I. (1917). Recitation as a factor in memorizing. *Archives of Psychology, 40*, 65–104.

Gaudrey, E., & Spielberger, C. D. (1971). *Anxiety and educational achievement*. Sydney, Australia: John Wiley & Sons.

Gerrity, K. (2004). Strategic reading in music. In R. Billmeyer (Ed.), *Strategic reading in the content areas, Practical applications for creating a thinking environment* (pp. 161–168). Omaha, NE: Dayspring Printing.

Gersten, R., & Baker, S. (2000). What we know about effective instructional practices for English-language learners. *Exceptional Children, 66*, 454–470.

Gersten, R., Compton, D., Connor, C.M., Dimino, J., Santoro, L., Linan-Thompson, S., & Tilly, W.D. (2008). *Assisting students struggling with reading: Response to Intervention and multi-tier intervention for reading in the primary grades. A practice guide* (NCEE 2009-4045). Washington, DC: National Center for Education Evaluation and Regional Assistance, Institute of Education Sciences, U.S. Department of Education. Retrieved from http://ies.ed.gov/ncee/wwc/ publications/practiceguides

Giles, J. (2005, December 15). Special report: Internet encyclopaedias go head to head. *Nature, 438*, 900–901.

Gleason, M. M. (1999). The role of evidence in argumentative writing. *Reading and Writing Quarterly, 15*, 81–106.

Glynn, S. M. (1994). *Teaching science with analogies: A strategy for teachers and textbook authors* (Reading Research Report No. 15). Athens, GA: National Reading Research Center.

Goldenberg, C. (2008). Teaching English language learners: What the research does—and does not—say. *American Educator*, 8-23.

Golding, W. (1954). *Lord of the flies*. London: Faber & Faber.

Goldman, S. (1997). Learning from text: Reflections on 20 years of research and suggestions for new directions of inquiry. *Discourse Processes, 23*, 357–398.

Gonzales, O. (1999). Building vocabulary: Dictionary consultation and the ESL student. *Journal of Adolescent & Adult Literacy, 43*, 264–270.

Gottlieb, R. (2001, January 8). Dropout rate falls in city. *Hartford Courant*, pp. A1, A8.

Graham, S., & Perin, D. (2007). *Writing next: Effective strategies to improve writing of adolescents in middle and high schools—A report to Carnegie Corporation of New York*. Washington, DC: Alliance for Excellent Education.

Graves, M. F. (1987). Roles of instruction in fostering vocabulary development. In M. G. McKeown & M. E. Curtis (Eds.), *The nature of vocabulary acquisition* (pp. 165–184). Hillsdale, NJ: Erlbaum.

Grigg, W., Donahue, P., & Dion, G. (2007). *The nation's report card: 12th-grade reading and mathematics 2005* (NCES 2007-468). Washington, DC: U. S. Department of Education, National Center for Educational Statistics. U. S. Government Printing Office.

Grunwald Associates. (2001). *Children, families and the Internet*. Available online at www.grunwald.com/survey/survey_content.html

Guensburg, C. (2006, February). Reading rules: The word of the day Is 'literacy.' At JEB Stuart High, students can't wait to hit the books. How'd that happen? *Edutopia*. Available online at www.edutopia.org/reading-rules

Gunning, T. (2003). *Creating literacy instruction for all children* (4th ed.). Boston: Allyn & Bacon.

Gunning, T. (2006). *Closing the literacy gap.* Boston: Allyn & Bacon.

Gunning, T. (2010). *Assessing and correcting reading and writing difficulties* (4th ed.). Boston: Allyn & Bacon.

Guthrie, J. T. (2004). Teaching for literacy engagement. *Journal of Literacy Research, 36,* 1–28.

Guthrie, J. T., Alao, S., & Rinehart, J. M. (1997). Engagement in reading for young adolescents. *Journal of Adolescent & Adult Literacy, 40,* 438–446.

Guzman-Johannessen, G. (2006, May). *Stages of second-language acquisition.* Paper presented at the International Reading Association Conference, Chicago, IL.

Guzzetti, B. J., Kowalinski, B. J., & McGowan, T. (1992). Using a literature-based approach to teaching social studies. *Journal of Reading, 36,* 114–122.

Haggard, M. R. (1982). The vocabulary self-collection strategy: An active approach to word learning. *Journal of Reading, 27,* 203–207.

Hague, S. (1987). Vocabulary instruction: What L2 can learn from L1. *Foreign Language Annals, 20,* 217–225.

Hall, L. A. (2008/2009). Research Connections: Understanding youth who struggle with middle school reading. *Journal of Adolescent & Adult Literacy, 52,* 353–355.

Halliday, M. A. K. (1994). *An introduction to functional grammar* (2nd ed.). London: Edward Arnold.

Hamilton, L., Halverson, R., Jackson, S., Mandinach, E., Supovitz, J., & Wayman, J. (2009). *Using student achievement data to support instructional decision making* (NCEE 2009-4067). Washington, DC: National Center for Education Evaluation and Regional Assistance, Institute of Education Sciences, U.S. Department of Education. Retrieved from http://ies.ed.gov/ncee/wwc/publications/practiceguides

Hampton, S., & Resnick, L. B. (2009). *Reading and writing with understanding: Comprehension in fourth and fifth grades.* Washington, DC: National Center on Educational and the Economy; Newark, DE: International Reading Association.

Harklau, L., & Pinnow, R. (2009). Adolescent second-language writing. In L. Christenbury, R. Bomer, & P. Smagorinsky (Eds.), *Handbook of adolescent literacy research* (pp. 126–139). New York: Guilford.

Harmon, J. M. (1998a). Constructing word meanings: Strategies and perceptions of four middle school learners. *Journal of Literacy Research, 30,* 561–599.

Harmon, J. M. (1998b). Vocabulary teaching and learning in a seventh-grade literature-based classroom. *Journal of Adolescent & Adult Literacy, 41,* 518–529.

Harouni, H. (2009). High school research and critical literacy: Social studies with and despite Wikipedia. *Harvard Educational Review, 79,* 473–494.

Harris, A. J., & Sipay, E. R. (1990). *How to increase reading ability* (9th ed.). New York, NY: Longman.

Hart, C., Mulhall, P., Berry, A., Loughran, J., & Gunstone, R. (2000). What is the purpose of this experiment? Or can students learn something from doing experiments? *Journal of Research in Science Teaching, 37,* 655–675.

Harvey, S. (1998). *Nonfiction matters: Reading, writing, and research in grades 3–8.* York, ME: Stenhouse.

Hatano, G., & Inagaki, K. (1996). *Young children's thinking about the biological world.* New York: Psychology Press.

Hattie, J. A. (1992). Measuring the effects of schooling. *Australian Journal of Education, 36*(1), 5–13.

Hattie, J. A. (2009). *Visible learning: a synthesis of over 800 meta-analyses relating to achievement.* London: Routledge.

Hattie, J A., Biggs, J., Purdie, N. (1996). Effects of learning skills interventions on student learning: A meta-analysis. *Review of Educational Research, 66*, 99-136.

Havens, L. (2001). *Daily writing in mathematics and science helps students become metacognitive and improves their problem solving skills.* Paper presented at the annual conference of the International Reading Association, New Orleans, LA.

Haystead, M. W., & Marzano, R. J. (2009). *Meta-analytic synthesis of studies conducted at Marzano Research Laboratory on instructional strategies.* Englewood, CO: Marzano Research Laboratory.

Hawkins, E., Stancavage, F., Mitchell, J., Goodman, M., & Lazer, S. (1998). *Learning about our world and our past: Using the tools and resources of geography and U. S. history—a report of the 1994 NAEP assessment.* Washington, DC: National Center for Education Statistics.

Head, M. H., & Readence, J. E. (1986). Anticipation guides: Meaning through prediction. In E. K. Dishner, T. W. Bean, J. E. Readence, & D. W. Moore (Eds.), *Reading in the content areas* (2nd ed., pp. 229–234). Dubuque, IA: Kendall/Hunt.

Heiman, M., & Slomianko, J. (1986). *Methods of inquiry.* Cambridge, MA: Learning Associates.

Heller, M. F. (1997). Reading and writing about the environment: Visions of the year 2000. *Journal of Adolescent & Adult Literacy, 40*, 332–341.

Heller, R., & Greenleaf, C. (2007). *Literacy instruction in the content areas: Getting to the core of middle and high school improvement.* Washington, DC: Alliance for Excellent Education.

Hennings, D. G. (1993). On knowing and reading history. *Journal of Reading, 36*, 362–370.

Herber, H. L. (1970). *Teaching reading in content areas.* Englewood Cliffs, NJ: Prentice-Hall.

Herber, H. L., & Herber, J. N. (1993). *Teaching in content areas with reading, writing, and reasoning.* Boston: Allyn & Bacon.

Hersch, P. (1999). *A tribe apart: A journey into the heart of American adolescence.* New York: Ballantine Books.

Holt, T. (1990). *Thinking historically.* New York, NY: College Entrance Examination Board.

Hopkins, G., & Bean, T. W. (1998–1999). Vocabulary learning with verbal-visual word association strategy in a Native American community. *Journal of Adolescent & Adult Literacy, 21*, 274–281.

Horowitz, R. (1985). Text patterns. *Journal of Reading, 28*, 534–542.

Hosp, M. L., Hosp, J. L., & Howell, K. W. (2007). *The ABCs of CBM: A practical guide to curriculum-based measurement.* New York, NY: Guilford.

Hotchkiss, P. (1990). Cooperative learning models: Improving student achievement using small groups. In M. A. Gunter, T. H. Estes, & J. H. Schwab (Eds.), *Instruction: A models approach* (pp. 167–184). Boston: Allyn & Bacon.

Huffman, L. E. (1998). Spotlighting specifics by combining focus questions with K-W-L. *Journal of Adolescent & Adult Literacy, 41*, 470–472.

Huitt, W. (2003). The information processing approach to cognition. *Educational Psychology Interactive.* Valdosta, GA: Valdosta State University. Available online at http://chiron.valdosta.edu/whuitt/col/cogsys/infoproc.html

Hulme, C., & MacKenzie, S. (1992). *Working memory and severe learning difficulties.* Hillsdale, NJ: Erlbaum.

Hurst, D. (2001). Notetaking. *Learning strategies database.* Muskingum College Center for Advancement of Learning. Available online at www.muskingum.edu/~cal/database/notetaking

Hyerle, D. (2001). Visual tools for mapping minds. In A. L. Costa (Ed.), *Developing minds: A resource book for teaching thinking* (3rd ed., pp. 401-407). Alexandria, VA: Association for Supervision and Curriculum Development.

Hynd, C. R. (1999). Teaching students to think critically using multiple texts in history. *Journal of Adolescent & Adult Literacy, 42, 428–436.*

International Reading Association. (1999). *High stakes assessments in reading: A position statement of the International Reading Association.* Newark, DE: Author.

International Reading Association. (2010). *Standards for reading professionals—revised 2010.* Author.

International Reading Association, National Council of Teachers of English, National Council of Teachers of Mathematics, National Science Teachers Association, and National Council for the Social Studies. (2006). *Standards for middle and high school literacy coaches.* Newark, DE: International Reading Association. Available online at www.reading.org/downloads/resources/597coaching_standards.pdf

Internet Reciprocal Teaching. (2009). *Internet reciprocal teaching strategies for critically evaluating websites.* Available online at ctell1.uconn.edu/somers/quag.htm

iObervation (2010). *Marzano collection, the leading framework for expert teaching.* Available online at www.iobservation.com/files/Brochure_Marzano_Suite.pdf8

Ivey, G., & Broaddus, K. (2007). A formative experiment investigating literacy engagement among adolescent Latina/o students just beginning to read, write, and speak English. *Reading Research Quarterly, 42,* 512.

Jensen, S. J., & Duffelmeyer, F. A. (1996). Enhancing possible sentences through cooperative learning. *Journal of Adolescent & Adult Literacy, 39,* 658–659.

Jett-Simpson, M. (Ed.). (1990). *Toward an ecological assessment of reading progress.* Schofield, WI: Wisconsin State Reading Association.

Jiménez, R. T. (1997). The strategic reading abilities and potential of five low literacy Latina/o readers in middle school. *Reading Research Quarterly, 32,* 224–243.

Joftus, S. (2002). *Every child a graduate: A framework for an excellent education for all middle and high school students.* Washington, DC: Alliance for Excellent Education.

Johns, C. (2009). *RTI in high school.* Webinar. Available online at www.ilprincipals.org/professional-development/webinars/on-demand-webinars

Johnson, D., & Steele, V. (1996). So many words, so little time: Helping college ESL learners acquire vocabulary-building strategies. *Journal of Adolescent & Adult Literacy, 39,* 348–357.

Johnson, D. D., & Pearson, P. D. (1984). *Teaching reading vocabulary* (2nd ed.). New York, NY: Holt, Rinehart & Winston.

Johnson, D. W., & Johnson, R. T. (1994). *Learning together and alone: Cooperative, competitve, and individualistic learning* (4th ed.). Boston: Allyn & Bacon.

Joint Information Systems Committee. (2008). *Information behaviour of the researcher of the future.* Available online at www.jisc.ac.uk/media/documents/programmes/reppres/gg_final_keynote_11012008.pdf

Joint Task Force on Assessment. (1994). *Standards for the assessment of reading and writing.* Newark, DE: International Reading Association and Urbana, IL: National Council of Teachers of English.

Jones, M. S., Levin, M. E., Levin, J. R., & Beitzel, B. D. (2000). Can vocabulary-learning strategies and pair-learning formats be profitably combined? *Journal of Educational Psychology, 92,* 256–262.

Jorgenson, G. W. (1975). An analysis of teacher judgments of reading levels. *American Educational Research Journal, 12,* 67–75.

Josel, C. A. (1997). Abbreviations for notetaking. *Journal of Adolescent & Adult Literacy, 40,* 393–394.

Kamil, M. L., Borman, G. D., Dole, J., Kral, C. C., Salinger, T., & Torgesen, J. (2008). *Improving adolescent literacy: Effective classroom and intervention practices: A practice guide* (NCEE #2008-4027). Washington, DC: National Center for Education Evaluation and Regional Assistance, Institute of Education Sciences, U.S. Department of Education. Available online at http://ies.ed.gov/ncee/wwc

Kastberg, D., Arafeh, S., Williams, T., & Tsen, W. (2000). *Pursuing excellence: Comparisons of international eighth-grade mathematics and science achievement from a U. S. perspective, 1995 and 1999.* Washington, DC: National Center for Education Statistics.

Keene, E. O., & Zimerman, S. (1997). *Mosaic of thought: Teaching reading comprehension in a reader's workshop.* Portsmouth, NH: Heinemann.

Kentucky Virtual Library. (2002). *Why evaluate information sources?* Available online at www.kyvl.org/html/tutorial/research/whyeval.shtml

Keys, C. W. (2000). Investigating the thinking processes of eighth grade writers during the composition of a scientific laboratory report. *Journal of Research in Science Teaching, 37,* 676–690.

Kibby, M. W., Rapaport, W. J., & Wieland, K. M. (2004). *Contextual vocabulary acquisition: From algorithm to curriculum.* Paper presented at the International Reading Association Convention, Reno, NV. Available online at www.cse.buffalo.edu/?rapaport/CVA/cvaslides.html

King, A. (1994). Autonomy and question asking: The role of personal control in guided student-generated questioning. *Learning and Individual Differences, 6,* 163–185.

King, A., & Rosenshine, B. (1993). Effects of guided cooperative-questioning on children's knowledge construction. *Journal of Experimental Education, 6,* 127–148.

Kintsch, W. (1994). The role of knowledge in discourse comprehension: A construction-integration model. In R. B. Ruddell, M. R. Ruddell, & H. Singer (Eds.), *Theoretical models and processes of reading* (4th ed., pp. 951–995). Newark, DE: International Reading Association.

Kintsch, W., Kozminisky, E., Streby, W. J., McKoon, G., & Keenan, J. M. (1975). Comprehension and recall of text as a function of content variables. *Journal of Verbal Learning and Verbal Behavior, 14,* 196–214.

Kist, W. (2010). *The socially networked classroom, Teaching in the new media age.* Thousand Oaks, CA: Corwin.

Kittle, P. (2008). *Write beside them.* Portsmouth, NH: Heinemann.

Klein, J. D. (1997). The national longitudinal study on adolescent health: Preliminary results-great expectations. *Journal of the American Medical Association, 278,* 864-865.

Kletzien, S. B. (1991). Strategy use by good and poor comprehenders reading expository text of differing levels. *Reading Research Quarterly, 26,* 67–86.

Knoester, M. (2009). Inquiry into urban adolescent independent reading habits: Can Gee's theory of discourses provide insight? *Journal of Adolescent & Adult Literacy, 52,* 676–685.

Krashen, S. D. (1985). *The input hypothesis: Issues and implications.* New York: Longman.

Krashen, S. D. (1993). *The power of reading.* Inglewood, CO: Libraries Unlimited.

Krause, C. (2001). Information organization. *Learning strategies database.* Muskingum College Center for Advancement of Learning. Available online at www.muskingum.edu/~cal/database/organization.html.

Kresse, E. C. (1984). Using reading as a thinking process to solve math story problems. *Journal of Reading, 27,* 598–601.

Krueger, W. C. F. (1929). The effect of overlearning on retention. *Journal of Experimental Psychology, 12,* 71–78.

Kwak, M. (2002). *Think pair share secondary level.* Film clip. Rockville, MD; Montgomery County Public Schools. Available online at www.montgomeryschoolsmd.org/departmets/developmet/resources/strategies/think_pair_share.html

Laflamme, J. G. (1997). The effect of the multiple exposure vocabulary method and the target reading writing strategy on test scores. *Journal of Adolescent & Adult Literacy, 40,* 372–381.

Lake, J. H. (1973). The influence of wait time on the verbal dimensions of student inquiry behavior. *Dissertation Abstracts International, 34,* 6476A (University Microfilms No. 74-08866).

Lalas, J., Solomon, M., & Johannessen, G. (2006). *Making adaptations in content area reading and writing: A gateway to academic language development for English language learners.* Paper presented at the International Reading Association convention, Chicago, IL.

Landsberger, J. (2001). *Study guides and strategies.* University of St. Thomas' ISS-Learning Center. Available online at www.iss.stthomas.edu/studyguides.

Langer, J. A. (1981). From theory to practice: A prereading plan. *Journal of Reading, 25,* 152–156.

Langer, J. A. (1990). Understanding literature. *Language Arts, 67,* 812–816.

Langer, J. A. (1995). *Envisioning literature: Literary understanding and literature instruction.* New York: Teachers College Press.

Langer, J. A. (1999). *Beating the odds: Teaching middle and high school students to read and write well.* Albany, NY: National Research Center on English Learning and Achievement. (ERIC Document Reproduction Service No. ED-435-993.)

Langer, J. (2011). *Envisioning literature: Literary understanding and literature instruction.* New York: Teachers College Press.

Langer, J., & Applebee, A. N. (1987). *How writing shapes thinking.* Urbana, IL: National Council of Teachers of English.

Langer, J. A., Applebee, A. N., Mullis, I. V. S., & Foertsch, M. A. (1990). *Learning to read in our nation's schools: Instruction and achievement in 1988 at grades 4, 8, and 12.* Princeton, NJ: Educational Testing Service.

Langer, J. N. (1984). Where problems start: The effects of available information on responses to school writing tasks. In A. N. Applebee (Ed.), *Contexts for learning to write: Studies of secondary school instruction* (pp. 135–148). Norwood, NJ: Ablex.

Lapp, D., & Fisher, D. (2009). Commentary: It's all about the book: Motivating teens to read. *Journal of Adolescent & Adult Literacy, 52,* 556–561.

Lapp, D., Flood, J., & Hoffman, R. P. (1996). Using concept mapping as an effective strategy in content area instruction. In D. Lapp, J. Flood, & N. Farnan (Eds.), *Content area reading and learning instructional strategies* (2nd ed., pp. 291–305). Boston: Allyn & Bacon.

LaPray, M., & Ross, R. (1969). The graded word list: Quick gauge of reading ability. *Journal of Reading, 12,* 305–307.

Larson, C. O., & Dansereau, D. F. (1986). Cooperative learning in dyads. *Journal of Reading, 29,* 516–520.

Lee, J., & Weiss, A. (2007). *The nation's report card: U. S. history 2006* (NCES 2007-474). U. S. Department of Education, National Center for Education Statistics. Washington, DC: U. S. Government Printing Office.

Lenz, B. K., Deshler, D. D., with Kissam, B. (2004). *Teaching content to all: Evidence-based inclusive practices in middle and secondary schools.* Boston: Allyn & Bacon.

Leslie, C. W., & Roth, C. (2003). *Nature journal: Discover a whole new way of seeing the world around you.* (2nd ed.) Pownal, VT: Storey Books.

Leslie, L., & Caldwell, J. (2001). *Qualitative reading inventory-3.* New York: Addison Wesley Longman.

Leslie, L., & Caldwell, J. (2011). *Qualitative reading inventory-5.* Boston: Allyn & Bacon.

Lester, J. H., & Cheek, E. H. (1997–1998). The "real" experts address textbook issues. *Journal of Adolescent & Adult Literacy, 41,* 282–291.

Leu, D. J., & Leu, D. D. (2000). *Teaching with the Internet: Lessons from the classroom* (3rd ed.). Norwood: MA: Christopher-Gordon.

Levin, J. R., Johnson, D. D., Pittelman, S. D., Hayes, B. L., Levin, K. M., Shriberg, L. K., & Toms-Bronowski, S. (1984). A comparison of semantic and mnemonic-based vocabulary-learning strategies. *Reading Psychology, 5*(2), 1–15.

Light, N. (2004). Strategic reading in art. In R. Billmeyer (Ed.), *Strategic reading in the content areas: Practical applications for creating a thinking environment* (pp. 116–122). Omaha, NE: Dayspring Printing.

Linden, M., & Wittrock, M. C. (1981). The teaching of reading comprehension according to the model of generative learning. *Reading Research Quarterly, 17,* 44–57.

Linder, S. (2009). *Study guide to Kurt Vonnegut, Jr.'s* Slaughterhouse Five. Available online at www.k-state.edu/english/baker/english220/sg-Vonnegut-Slaughterhouse_5.htm

Linder, S. (2009). Using microblogging and social networking to explore characterization and style. Read•Write•Think. Available at http://readwritethink.org/lessons/lesson_view.asp?id=1171

Linderholm, T., Gaddy Everson, M., van den Broek, P., Mischinski, M., Crittenden, A., & Lindquist, T. (1995). Why and how I use historical fiction. *Instructor, 105*(3), 46–50, 52, 80.

Long, L., MacBlain, S., & MacBlain, M. (2007). Supporting students with dyslexia at the secondary level: An emotional model of literacy. *Journal of Adolescent & Adult Literacy, 51,* 124-134.

Lycke, K. L. (2010, December). *Adolescent literacies across school contexts: Teachers and students negotiate communal school activities.* Paper presented at Literacy Research Association Conference, Forth Worth, TX.

Lyman, F. (1981). The responsive classroom discussion. In A. S. Anderson (Ed.), *Mainstreaming digest* (pp. 109–113). College Park: University of Maryland, College of Education.

Madden, N. (2000, February). Meeting the expository challenge with SFA. *Success Story,* 6. Available online at www.successforall.net/current/successstories_2_00.pdf

Many, J., Fyfe, R., Lewis, G., & Mitchell, E. (1996). Traversing the topical landscape: Exploring students' self-directed reading-writing research processes. *Reading Research Quarterly, 31,* 122–135.

Manzo, A. V. (1969). The ReQuest procedure. *Journal of Reading, 13,* 123–126.

Manzo, A. V., & Manzo, U. C. (1993). *Literacy disorders: Holistic diagnosis and remediation.* Fort Worth, TX: Harcourt Brace Jovanovich.

Manzo, A. V., Manzo, U. C., Albee, J. J. (2004). *Reading assessment for diagnostic-prescriptive teaching* (2nd ed.). Belmont, CA: Thomson Learning.

Manzo, K. K. (2010). Whiteboards' impact on teaching seen as uneven. *Education Week.* Available online at www.edweek.org/dd/articles/2010/01/08/02whiteboards.h03 .html

Maria, K. (1990). *Reading comprehension instruction: Issues and strategies.* Parkton, MD: York Press.

Marian, R., Sexton, C., & Gerlovich, J. (2001). *Teaching science for all children* (3rd ed.). Boston: Allyn & Bacon.

Marshall, J. D. (1984a). Process and product: Case studies of writing in two content areas. In A. N. Applebee (Ed.), *Contexts for learning to write: Studies of secondary school instruction* (pp. 149–168). Norwood, NJ: Ablex.

Marshall, J. D. (1984b). Schooling and the composing process. In A. N. Applebee (Ed.), *Contexts for learning to write: Studies of secondary school instruction.* Norwood, NJ: Ablex.

Martin, M. O., Mullis, I. V. S., & Foy, P. (with Olson, J. F., Erberber, E., Preuschoff, C., & Galia, J.). (2008). *TIMSS 2007 international science report: Findings from IEA's trends in international mathematics and science study at the fourth and eighth grades.* Boston: TIMSS & PIRLS International Study Center, Lynch School of Education, Boston College. Available online at www.timss.bc.edu/TIMSS2007/sciencereport.html

Marzano, R. J., Gaddy, B. B., & Dean, C. (2000). *What works in classroom instruction?* Aurora, CO: Mid-continent Research for Education and Learning.

Mastery Charter Schools. (2009a). *Mastery charter schools 2008-2009 overview.* Philadelphia, PA: Author. Available online at www.masterycharter.org/.../Mastery%20Charter% 20Overview%202009.pdf

Mastery Charter Schools. (2009b). *Mastery model.* Philadelphia, PA: Author. Available online at www.masterycharter.org/MasteryModel.html

Mastropieri, M. A., & Scruggs, T. E. (1989). Reconstructive elaborations; Strategies for adapting content area information. *Academic Therapy, 24,* 391–406.

Mastropieri, M. A., & Scruggs, T. E. (1991). *Teaching students ways to remember: Strategies for learning mnemonically.* Cambridge, MA: Brookline.

McCabe, D. (2009). *Sequential spelling.* Available online at www.avko.org/sequential spelling.html

McConnell, S. (1992–1993). Talking drawings: A strategy for assisting learners. *Journal of Reading, 34,* 184–186.

McCormick, S. (1987). *Remedial and clinical reading instruction.* Columbus, OH: Merrill.

McDonald, H. (2011). *Geologic puzzles: Morrison formation.* Available online at http://serc.carleton.edu/introgeo/interactive/examples/morrisonpuzzle.html

McKenna, M. C., & Robinson, R. D. (1990). Content literacy: a definition and implications. *Journal of Reading, 34,* 184-186.

McKenna, M. C., & Robinson, R. D. (2006). *Teaching through text: A content literacy approach to content area reading* (4th ed.). Boston: Pearson.

McKeown, M. G., Beck, I. L., & Blake, R. K. (2009). Rethinking reading comprehension instruction: A comparison of instruction for strategies and content approaches. *Reading Research Quarterly, 44*, 218-253.

McKeown, M. G., Beck, I. L., & Sandora, C. A. (1996). Questioning the author: An approach to developing meaningful classroom discourse. In M. F. Graves, P. Van den Broek, & B. M. Taylor, (Eds.), *The first R: Every child's right to read* (pp. 97–119). New York: Teachers College Press.

McKissack, P., & McKissack, F. (2001a). A biographical sketch of Frederick Douglass. *Biography writing with Patricia and Frederick McKissack.* Available online at http://teacher.scholastic.com/writewit/biograph/biography_sketch.htm

McKissack, P., & McKissack, F. (2001b). Brainstorming. *Biography writing with Patricia and Frederick McKissack.* Available online at http://teacher.scholastic.com/writewit/biograph/biography_brainstorming.htm

McNamara, D. S., Crossley, S. A., & McCarthy, P. M. (2010). Linguistic features of writing quality. *Written Communication, 27*(1), 57–86.

McNamara, T. P., Miller, D. L., & Bransford, J. D. (1991). Mental models and reading comprehension. In R. Barr, M. L. Kamil, P. Mosenthal, & P. D. Pearson (Eds.), *Handbook of reading research* (Vol. II, pp. 490–511). New York: Longman.

MCREL. (2009). *A compendium of content standards and benchmarks for K–12 education in both searchable and browsable formats.* Available online at www.mcrel.org/standards-benchmarks

MCREL. (2009). *Content knowledge, List of benchmarks for science.* Available online at www.mcrel.org/compendium/standardDetails.asp?subjectID=2&standardID=8

McTighe, J., & Lyman, F. T., Jr. (1988). Cueing thinking in the classroom: The promise of theory-embedded tools. *Educational Leadership, 45*(7), 18–24.

Means, B., Toyama,Y., Murphy. R., Bakia, M., & Jones, K. (2009). *Evaluation of evidence-based practices in online learning: A meta-analysis and review of online-learning studies.* Washington, DC: U. S. Department of Education.

Meltzer, J. (2002). *Adolescent literacy resources: Linking research and practice.* South Hampton, NH: Center for Resource Management.

Meltzer, L. J., Roditi, B. N., Haynes, D. P., & Biddle, K. (1996). *Strategies for success: Classroom teaching techniques for students with learning problems.* Austin, TX: ProEd.

Metametrics. (2010). *Lexile-to-grade correspondence.* Durham, NC: Author.

Meyer, B. J. F., & Rice, G. E. (1984). The structure of text. In P. D. Pearson, R. Barr, M. L. KIamil, & P. Mosenthal (Eds.), *Handbook of reading research* (pp. 319–351). New York: Longman.

Miller, G. A. (1956). The magical number seven, plus or minus two: Some limits on our capacity for processing information. *Psychological Review, 63*, 81–97.

Miller, J. S., & Levine, K. (2009). *Miller & Levine biology.* Upper Saddle River, NJ: Pearson Education.

Mills, K. A. (2010). Shrek meets Vygotsky: Rethinking adolescents' multimodal practices in schools. *Journal of Adolescent & Adult Literacy, 54*, 35-45.

Milone, M. (2008). *The development of atos: The renaissance readability formula.* Wisconsin Rapids, WI: Renaissance Learning.

Mitman, A., Mergendoller, J., Packer, M., & Marchman, V. (1984). *Scientific literacy in seventh grade life science.* San Francisco, CA: Far West Laboratory.

Moje, E. (1996). "I teach students, not subjects": Teacher-student relationships as contexts for secondary literacy. *Reading Research Quarterly, 31*, 172–195.

Moje, E. B., & Luke, A. (2009). Literacy and identity: Examining the metaphors in history and contemporary research. *Reading Research Quarterly,44* , 415–437.

Moje, E. B., Overby, M., Tysvaer, N., & Morris, K. (2008). The complex world of adolescent literacy: Myths, motivations, and mysteries. *Harvard Educational Review, 78*, 107–154.

Mokhtari, K., & Reichard, C. A. (2002). Assessing students' metacognitive awareness of reading strategies. *Journal of Educational Psychology, 94*, 249–259.

Moore, D. W., & Moore, S. A. (1986). Possible sentences. In E. K. Dishner, T. W. Bean, J. E. Readence, & D. W. Moore (Eds.), *Reading in the content areas: Improving classroom instruction* (2nd ed., pp. 174–179). Dubuque, IA: Kendall/Hunt.

Moore, D. W., Moore, S. A., Cunningham, P. M., & Cunningham, J. W. (1992). *Developing readers and writers in the content areas* (2nd ed.). New York: Longman.

Moore, D. W., Readence, J. E., & Rickelman, R. J. (1989). *Prereading activities for content area reading and learning* (2nd ed.). Newark, DE: International Reading Association.

Moreno, R., & Mayer, R. E. (1999). Multimedia-supported metaphors for meaning making in mathematics. *Cognition and Instruction, 17*, 215–248.

Mosenthal, J. H. (1990). Developing low-performing, fourth-grade, inner-city students' ability to comprehend narrative. In J. Zutell & S. McCormick (Eds.), *Literacy theory and research: Analyses from multiple paradigms* (Thirty-ninth Yearbook of the National Reading Conference) (pp. 275–286). Chicago, IL: National Reading Conference.

Mower, P. (2003) *Algebra out loud: Learning mathematics through reading and writing activities.* San Francisco, CA: Jossey-Bass.

Moyer, R. S. (1973). Comparing objects in memory: Evidence suggesting an internal psychophysics. *Perception and Psychophysics, 13*, 180–184.

Murphy, L. L., & Spies, R. A., & Plake, B. S., (Eds.).(2006). *Tests in print VII.* Lincoln: University of Nebraska Press.

Muth, K. D. (1987). Teachers' connection questions: Prompting students to organize text ideas. *Journal of Reading, 31*, 254–259.

Nagy, W. E. (1988). *Teaching vocabulary to improve reading comprehension.* Newark, DE: International Reading Association.

Nagy, W. E., & Anderson, R. C. (1984). How many words are there in printed English? *Reading Research Quarterly, 19*, 304–330.

Nagy, W. E., & Herman, P. A. (1987). Breadth and depth of vocabulary knowledge: Implications for acquisition and instruction. In M. G. McKeown & M. E. Curtis (Eds.), *The nature of vocabulary acquisition* (pp. 19–35). Hillsdale, NJ: Erlbaum.

Nation, P. (2001). *Learning vocabulary in another language.* Cambridge, England: Cambridge University Press.

National Assessment Governing Board. (2010). *Writing Framework for the 2011 National Assessment of Educational Progress.* Washington, DC: Author.

National Association of Secondary School Principals. (2005, October 12). *Fairfax County, VA principal named national high school principal of the year.* News release. Available online at www.principals.org/s_nassp/sec_news.asp?TrackID=&SID=1&DID=52917&CID=35&VID=167&RTID=0&CIDQS=&Taxonomy=&specialSearch=

National Center for Educational Statistics. (2002). *The nation's report card: 2001 U. S. history results.* Available online at http://nces.ed.gov/nationsreportcard

National Center for Education Statistics. (2010). *The nation's report card: Grade 12 reading and mathematics 2009 national and pilot state results* (NCES 2011–455). Washington, D.C.: Institute of Education Sciences, U.S. Department of Education.

National Commission on Writing. (2006). *Writing and school reform.* New York: College Board. Available online at www.writingcommission.org/report.html

National Council for the Social Studies. (NCSS). (1994). *Expectations of excellence: Curriculum standards for social studies.* Available online at www.ncss.org/standards/stitle.html

National Council of Teachers of English. (2008). *The NCTE definition of 21st century literacies.* Available online at www.ncte.org/positions/statements/21stcentdefinition

National Governors Association Center for Best Practices and the Council of Chief State School Officers. (2010). *Common core state standards initiative.* Available online at www.corestandards.org

National Governors Association, Council of Chief State School Officers, & Achieve. (2008). *Benchmarking for success: Ensuring U.S, students receive a world-class education.* Achieve. Available online at www.achieve.org/BenchmarkingforSuccess

National Joint Committee on Students with Learning Disabilities. Available online at www .ldonline.org/about/partners/njcld#reports

National Reading Panel. (2000). *Report of the National Reading Panel: Teaching children to read: An evidence-based assessment of the scientific research literature on reading and its implications for reading instruction: Reports of the subgroups* (NIH Publication No. 00–4754). Washington, DC: U. S. Government Printing Office.

National Science Board. (2001). *Science and engineering indicators 2001.* Arlington, VA: National Science Foundation.

NCSS. (2008). *Expectations of excellence, curriculum standards for social studies, draft revision.* National Council for the Social Studies Available online at www.socialstudies.org/ standards/taskforce/fall2008draft

NCTE. (2001, May). On the Net: Teaching reading at the high school level. *The Council Chronicle, 10*(4), pp. 10–11.

Nelson-Herber, J. (1986). Expanding and refining vocabulary in content areas. *Journal of Reading, 29,* 626–633.

Neubert, G. A., & Wilkins, E. A. (2004). *Putting it all together: The directed reading lesson in the secondary content classroom.* Boston: Pearson.

Newmann, F. M., & Wehlege, G. G. (2000). *Successful school restructuring.* Madison, WI: Center on Organization and Restructuring of Schools.

Nichols, W. D., Jones, J., Wood, K., & Hancock, D. (2000, November). *Exploring the relationship between teacher reported instructional design and students' perceptions of how they learned: Why are students task oriented learners?* Paper presented at the National Reading Conference, Scottsdale, AZ.

Nilsen, A. P., & and Donalsen, K. L. (2009). *Literature for today's young adults* (8th ed.). Boston: Allyn & Bacon.

Nist, S. L., Hogrebe, M. C., & Simpson, M. L. (1985). The relationship between the use of study strategies and test performance. *Journal of Reading Behavior, 7,* 15–28.

Nist, S. L., & Simpson, M. L. (1989). PLAE, a validated study strategy. *Journal of Reading, 33,* 182–186.

Noble, C. E. (1952). The role of stimulus meaning in serial verbal learning. *Journal of Experimental Psychology, 43,* 437–446.

Northwest Regional Educational Laboratory. (2003). *Overview of second language acquisition theory.* Available online at www.nwrel.org/request/2003may/overview.html

Noyce, R., & Christie, J. F. (1989). *Integrating reading and writing instruction in grades K–8.* Boston: Allyn & Bacon.

Nuthall, G. (1996, December). *What role does ability play in classroom learning?* Paper presented at the meeting of the New Zealand Association for Research in Education. Nelson, New Zealand (ERIC Document Reproduction Service No. ED 414 042).

Nuthall, G. (1999). The way students learn: Acquiring knowledge from an integrated science and social studies unit. *The Elementary School Journal, 99,* 303–335.

Oakes, J. (1992). Can tracking research inform practice? Technical, normative, and political considerations. *Educational Researcher, 21,* 12–21.

O'Brien, D. (2003). Juxtaposing traditional and intermedial literacies to redefine the competence of struggling adolescents. *Reading Online.* Available online at www.readingonline .org/newliteracies/lit_index.asp?HREF=/newliteracies/obrien2

O'Brien, D. G., Beach, R., & Scharber, C. (2007). "Struggling" middle schoolers: Engagement and literate competence in a reading writing intervention class. *Reading Psychology, 28*(1), 51–73.

O'Brien, D. G., & Dubbels, B. (2009). Technology and literacy, current and emergent practices with student 2.0 and beyond. In K. D. Wood & William E. Blanton (Eds.), *Literacy Instruction for adolescents* (pp. 472-494). New York: Guilford.

O'Byrne, B. (2001). Needed: A compass to navigate the multilingual English classroom. *Journal of Adolescent & Adult Literacy, 44,* 440-449.

Ogle, D. M. (1989). The know, want to know, learn strategy. In K. D. Muth (Ed.), *Children's comprehension of text.* (pp. 205–223). Newark, DE: International Reading Association.

Ogle, D. M. (1996). Study techniques that ensure content area reading success. In D. Lapp, J. Flood, & N. Farnan (Eds.), *Content area reading and learning instructional strategies* (2nd ed., pp. 277–290). Boston: Allyn & Bacon.

Ollmann, H. E. (1996). Creating higher level thinking with reader response. *Journal of Adolescent & Adult Literacy, 39,* 576–581.

Olson, C. B. (2007, February). The challenge of achieving academic literacy for ELLs. *California English Journal.* Available online at www.cateweb.org/california_english/ ce_2007_february.htm

Olson, C. B., & Land, R. (2007). *The pathway project demonstrates success with cognitive strategies for reading and writing for English language learners.* National Writing Project. Available online at www.nwp.org/cs/public/print/resource/2487

O'Mara, D. A. (1981). The process of reading mathematics. *Journal of Reading 25,* 22–30.

Paivio, A. (1971). *Imagery and verbal process.* New York: Holt.

Palincsar, A. S., & Brown, A. L. (1986). Interactive teaching to promote independent learning from text. *The Reading Teacher, 39,* 771–777.

Palincsar, A. S., Winn, J., David, Y., Snyder, B., & Stevens, D. (1993). Approaches to strategic reading instruction reflecting different assumptions regarding teaching and learning. In L. J. Meltzer (Ed.), *Strategy assessment and instruction for students with learning disabilities: From theory to practice* (pp. 247–292). Austin, TX: Pro-Ed.

Palmer, R. G., & Stewart, R. A. (1997). Nonfiction trade books in content area instruction: Realities and potential. *Journal of Adolescent & Adult Literacy, 40,* 630–641.

Parker, D. (2002, May). *Accelerated literacy for English language learners (ELLS): A field-tested, research-based model of training and teaching.* Paper presented at the annual meeting of the International Reading Association, San Francisco, CA.

Parker, W. C. (2001). *Social studies in elementary education* (11th ed.). Upper Saddle River, NJ: Merrill Prentice Hall.

Parker, W. C., & Jarolimek, J. (Eds.). (2001). *A sampler of curriculum standards for social studies: Expectations of excellence.* Upper Saddle River; NJ: Merrill Prentice Hall.

Pashler, H., Bain, P., Bottge, B., Graesser, A., Koedinger, K., McDaniel, M., & Metcalfe, J. (2007). *Organizing instruction and study to improve student learning* (NCER 2007-2004). Washington, DC: National Center for Education Research, Institute of Education Sciences, U.S. Department of Education. Available online at http://ncer.ed.gov.

Patton, L. (1993). *In the woods: The impact of prereading activities.* In L. Patterson, C. M. Santa, K. G. Short, & K. Smith (Eds.), *Teachers are researchers: Reflection and action* (pp. 130–136). Newark, DE: International Reading Association.

Pauk, W. (1989). *How to study in college* (4th ed.). Boston: Houghton Mifflin.

Pearson 21. (2009). *California Proposition Public Service Announcements Project* [Video]. Available online at https://thepartnershipfor21stcenturyskills238.educision.tv/default.aspx

Pearson 21. (2009). *The culture of 21st century skills.* Available online at https://thepartnershipfor21stcenturyskills238.eduvision.tv/default.aspx

Pearson, B. Z. (1993). Predictive validity of the Scholastic Aptitude Test (SAT) for Hispanic Bilingual students. *Hispanic Journal of Behavioral Sciences, 15,* 342-356.

Pearson, J. W., & Santa, C. M. (1995). Students as researchers of their own learning. *Journal of Adolescent & Adult Literacy, 38,* 462–469.

Pearson, P. D., & Camperell, K. (1994). Comprehension of text structures. In R. B. Ruddell, M. R. Ruddell, & H. Singer (Eds.), *Theoretical models and processses of reading* (4th ed., pp. 448–568). Newark, DE: International Reading Association.

Pearson Education Limited. (2008). *The Longman dictionary of American English.* New York: Author.

Penner, D. E. (2000). Explaining systems: Investigating middle school students' understanding of emergent phenomena. *Journal of Research in Science Teaching, 37,* 784–806.

Perfetti, C. A., Britt, M. A., & Georgi, M. C. (1995). *Text-based learning and reasoning.* Hillsdale, NJ: Erlbaum.

Perkins, P. (2001). *It's my American history: Compendium of practices: Models of contextual teaching and learning in K–12 classrooms and preservice teacher preparation programs.* Washington State Consortium for Contextual Teaching and Learning Compendia. Available online at http://depts.washington.edu/wctl/itsmyamhist.htm

Peters, C. (1979). The effect of systematic restructuring of material upon the comprehension process. *Reading Research Quarterly, 11,* 87–110.

Phillips, L. M., Norris, S. P., & Korpan, C. A. (2000). *Texture and structure of media reports of science: University students' interpretations and their need to understand the metadiscourse of science.* Paper presented at the National Reading Conference, Scottsdale, AZ.

Pitcher, S. M., Albright, L. K., DeLaney, C. J., Walker, N. T., Seunarinesingh, K., Mogge, S., Headley, K. N., Ridgeway, V., Peck, S., Hunt, R., & Dunston, P. J. (2007). Assessing adolescents' motivation to read. *Journal of Adolescent & Adult Literacy, 50,* 378–396.

Planty, M., Hussar, W., Snyder, T., Kena, G., Kewal Ramani, A., Kemp, J., Bianco, K., & Dinkes, R. (2009). *The condition of education 2009* (NCES 2009-081). Washington, DC: National Center for Education Statistics, Institute of Education Sciences, U.S. Department of Education.

Popham, W. J. (2000). *Modern educational measurement: Practical guidelines for educational leaders*. Boston: Allyn & Bacon.

Powers, C. (2010, January 8). Beyond teacher chalk talk [Video] *Education Week*. Available online at www.edweek.org/dd/articles/2010/01/08/02whiteboards.h03.html

Pressley, M., & Afflerbach, P. (1995). *Verbal protocols of reading: The nature of constructively responsive reading*. Hillsdale, NJ: Erlbaum.

Pressley, M., Ross, K. A., Levin, J. R., & Ghatala, E. S. (1984). The role of strategy utility knowledge in children's strategy decision making. *Journal of Experimental Child Psychology*, *38*, 491–504.

Pressley, M., Wharton-McDonald, R., Mistretta-Hampston, J., & Echevarria, M. (1998). Literacy instruction in 10 fourth- and fifth-grade classrooms in upstate New York. *Scientific Studies of Reading*, *2*, 159–194.

Probst, R. (1992). Five kinds of literary knowing. In J. A. Langer (Ed.), *Literature instruction: A focus on student response* (pp. 54–77). Urbana, IL: National Council of Teachers of English.

Prochaska, J. O., Norcross, J. C., & DiClemente, D. C. (1994). *Changing for the good*. New York: Avon.

Rampey, B. D., Dion, G. S., & Donahue, P. L. (2009). NAEP 2008 *Trends in academic progress* (NCES 2009-479). Washington, DC: National Center for Education Statistics, Institute of Education Sciences, U.S. Department of Education.

Raphael, T. E. (1984). Teaching learners about sources of information for answering questions. *The Reading Teacher*, *28*, 303–311.

Raphael, T. E. (1986). Teaching question/answer relationships, revisited. *The Reading Teacher*, *39*, 516–522.

Raphael, T. E., & Englert, C. S. (1990). Writing and reading: Partners in constructing meaning. *The Reading Teacher*, *43*, 388–400.

Ratney, J. J., & Hagerman, E. (2008). *Spark, the revolutionary new science of exercise and the brain*. New York: Little, Brown.

Ray, B. (2010, January 21). Guest blog: 1:1 Laptop programs: shifting the way students learn. *Edutopia*. Available online at www.edutopia.org/1-to-1-laptop-programs-edchat-chris-ludwig

Readence, J. E., Moore, D. W., & Rickelman, R. J. (2000). *Prereading activities for content area reading and learning* (3rd ed.). Newark, DE: International Reading Association.

Reeves, D. (2000). *The 90/90/90 schools: A case study*. Available online at www.making standardswork.com/Downloads/ainA%20Ch19.pdf

Reeves, D. B. (2010). Getting ready for national standards. *ASCD Express January 21, 2010*. Available online at www.ascd.org/ascd_express/vol5/508_reeves.aspx

Reninger, K. (2007). *Intermediate-level, lower-achieving readers participation in and high-level thinking during group discussions about literary texts*. Unpublished doctoral dissertation, The Ohio State University, Columbus.

Reninger, K. B., & Wilkinson, I. A. G. (2010). Using discussions to promote striving readers' higher level comprehension of literary texts. In J. L. Collins & T G. Gunning (Eds.), *Building struggling students' higher level literacy, practical ideas, powerful solutions* (pp. 57–83). Newark, DE: International Reading Association.

Richardson, J. S., & Morgan, R. F. (1997). *Reading to learn in the content areas* (3rd ed.). Belmont, CA: Wadsworth.

Richgels, D. J., & Hansen, R. (1984). Gloss: Helping students apply both skills and strategies in reading content texts. *Journal of Reading*, *27*, 312–317.

Rideout, V. J., Foehr, U. G., & Roberts, D. F. (2010). *Generation M2: Media in the lives of 8- to 18-year-olds. A Kaiser Family Foundation study.* Available online at www.kff.org/entmedia/upload/8010.pdf

Rinehart, S. D., Stahl, S. A., & Erickson, L. G. (1986). Some effects of summarization training on reading and studying. *Reading Research Quarterly, 21,* 422–438.

Robinson, D. H. (1998). Graphic organizers as aids to text learning. *Reading Research and Instruction, 37,* 85–105.

Robinson, F. P. (1970). *Effective study* (4th ed.). New York: Harper & Row.

Rodriguez, B. (2010). *Content enhancement film clip* [Video]. KU Center for research on learning Lawrence: University of Kansas. Available online at www.kucrl.org/sim/content.shtmlat

Roe, M. F., & Stallman, A. C. (1995). *A comparative study of dialogue and response journals* (Tech. Report No. 612). Champaign, IL: University of Illinois, Center for the Study of Reading.

Roehler, L. (1996). The content area teacher's instructional role: A mediational view. In D. Lapp, J. Flood, & N. Farnan (Eds.), *Content area reading and learning instructional strategies* (2nd ed., pp. 141–152). Boston: Allyn & Bacon.

Rohrer, D. and Pashler, H. (2010). Recent research on human learning challenges conventional instructional strategies. *Educational Researcher, 39,* 406-412

Rolling Meadows High School. (2010). *RMHS model to student achievement.* Available online at http://rmhs.d214.org/RMHSModel/index.p

Romero F., Paris S. G., & Brem S. K. (2005, November). Children's comprehension and local-to-global recall of narrative and expository texts. *Current Issues in Education* [On-line], *8*(25). Available: http://cie.ed.asu.edu/volume8/number25

Rosenblatt, L. (1978). *The reader, the text, the poem.* Carbondale, IL: Southern Illinois University Press.

Rosenblatt, L. (1991). Literature—S. O. S.! *Language Arts, 68,* 444–448.

Rosenblatt, L. M. (1982). The literary transaction: Evocation and response. *Theory into Practice, 21,* 268–277.

Rosenblatt, L. M. (1990). Retrospect. In E. S. Farrell & J. R. Squire (Eds.), *Transactions with literature: A fifty-year perspective* (pp. 97–107). Urbana, IL: National Council of Teachers of English.

Rosenblatt, L. M. (1994). The traditional theory of reading and writing. In R. B. Ruddell, M. R. Ruddell, & H. Singer (Eds.), *Theoretical models and processes of reading* (4th ed., pp. 1057–1092). Newark, DE: International Reading Association.

Rosenshine, B., & Meister, C. (1994). Reciprocal teaching: A review of research. *Review of Educational Research, 64,* 479–530.

Rosenshine, B., Meister, C., & Chapman, S. (1996). Teaching students to generate questions: A review of the intervention studies. *Review of Educational Research, 66,* 181–221.

Rosenthal, J., & Ehri, L. (2008). The mnemonic value of orthography for vocabulary learning. *Journal of Educational Psychology, 100,* 175–191.

Roseth, C. J., Fang, F., Johnson, D. W., & Johnson, R. T. (2006, April). *Effects of cooperative learning on middle schools students: a meta-analysis.* Paper presented at the Annual Meeting of the American Educational Research Association.

Rothenberg, S. S., & Watts, S. M. (1997). Students with learning difficulties meet Shakespeare: Using a scaffolded reading experience. *Journal of Adolescent & Adult Literacy, 40,* 532–539.

Rowe, M. B. (1969). Science, silence, and sanctions. *Science for Children, 6*(6), 11–13.

Rubenstein, R. N. (2000). Word origins: Building communication connections. *Mathematics in the Middle School, 5,* 493–498.

Ruddell, M. R. (1992). Integrated content and long-term vocabulary learning with the vocabulary self-collection strategy. In E. K. Dishner, T. W. Bean, J. E. Readence, & D. W. Moore (Eds.), *Reading in the content areas: Improving classroom instruction* (3rd ed., pp. 190–196). Dubuque, IA: Kendall/Hunt.

Ruddell, R. B. (1995). Those influential literacy teachers: Meaning negotiators and motivation builders. *The Reading Teacher, 48,* 454–463.

Rumelhart, D. (1984). Understanding understanding. In J. Flood (Ed.), *Understanding reading comprehension* (pp. 1–20). Newark, DE: International Reading Association.

Saddler, B., & Andrade, H. (2004). The writing rubric. *Educational Leadership, 62 (2),* 48–52.

Sadowski, M., & Paivio, A. (1994). A dual coding view of imagery and verbal processes in reading comprehension. In R. B. Ruddell, M. R. Ruddell, & H. Singer (Eds.), *Theoretical models and processes of reading* (4th ed., pp. 582–601). Newark, DE: International Reading Association.

Salahu-Din, D., Persky, H., & Miller, J. (2008). *The nation's report card: Writing 2007* (NCES 2008-468). Washington, DC: National Center for Education Statistics, Institute of Education Sciences, U.S. Department of Education.

Salomon, G., Globerson, T., & Guterman, E. (1989). The computer as a zone of proximal development: Internalizing reading-related metacognitions from a reading partner. *Journal of Educational Psychology, 81,* 620–627.

Salsovic, A. R. (2009). Designing a webquest. *Mathematics Teacher, 102,* 666-671.

Samuels, C. (2009, January 28). *Schools try out RTI. Education Week's Spotlight On Response To Intervention.* Available online at www.edweek.org/ew/articles/2009/01/28/19rti_ep.h28.html

Santa, C. (1994, October). *Teaching reading in the content areas.* Paper presented at the International Reading Association's Southwest Regional Conference, Little Rock, AR.

Santa, C., Havens, L., & Maycumber, E. M. (1996). *Creating independence through student-owned strategies* (2nd ed.). Dubuque, IA: Kendall/Hunt.

Santa, C. M., Abrams, J., & Santa, J. (1979). Effects of notetaking and studying on the retention of prose. *Journal of Reading Behavior, 11,* 247–260.

Santangelo, T., Harris, K. R., & Graham, S. (2007). Self-regulated strategy development: A validated model to support students who struggle with writing. *Learning Disabilities: A Contemporary Journal, 5*(1), 1–20.

Schallert, D. L., & Tierney, R. J. (1980). *Learning from expository text: The interaction of text structures with reader characteristics.* Washington, DC: U. S. Department of Education. National Institute of Education. (ERIC Document Reproduction Service No. ED 221-833).

Schifini, A. (1994). Language, literacy, and content instruction. In K. Spangenberg-Urbschat & R. Pritchard (Eds.), *Kids come in all languages: Reading instruction for all ESL students* (pp. 36–62). Newark, DE: International Reading Association.

Schifini, A. (1996). Discussion in multilingual, multicultural classrooms. In L. Gambrell & J. F. Almasi (Eds.), *Lively discussions! Fostering engaged reading.* Newark, DE: International Reading Association.

Schifini, A. (1999). *Successful strategies for your older struggling readers.* Torrance, CA: Staff Development Resources.

Schnorr, J. A., & Atkinson, R. C. (1969). Repetition versus imagery instructions in the short- and long-term retention of paired associates. *Psychonomic Science, 15*, 183–184.

Schoenbach, R., Greenleaf, C., Cziko, C., & Hurwitz, L. (1999). *Reading for understanding: A guide to improving reading in middle and high school classrooms.* San Francisco, CA: Jossey-Bass.

Schochet, P. Z., & Chiang, H. S., (2010). *Error rates in measuring teacher and school performance based on student test score gains* (NCEE 2010-4004). Washington, DC: National Center for Education Evaluation and Regional Assistance, Institute of Education Sciences, U.S. Department of Education.

Schule, B. (2011). Hybrid schools for the iGeneration. *Harvard Education Letter, 27* (2), 1–4.

Schwartz, R. M. (1988). Learning to learn vocabulary in content area textbooks. *Journal of Reading, 32*, 108–118.

Schwartzman, S. (1994). *Words of mathematics: An etymological dictionary of mathematical terms used in English.* Washington, DC: Mathematical Association of America.

Scott, T. (1998, May). *Using content area text to teach decoding and comprehension strategies.* Paper presented at the annual meeting of the International Reading Association, Orlando, FL.

Scruggs, T. E., Bennion, K., & Lifson, S. (1985a). An analysis of children's strategy use on reading achievements tests. *Elementary School Journal, 85*, 479–484.

Scruggs, T. E., Bennion, K., & Lifson, S. (1985b). Learning disabled students' spontaneous use of test-taking skills on reading achievement tests. *Learning Disability Quarterly, 8*, 205–210.

Scruggs, T. E., & Mastropieri, M. A. (1990). The case for mnemonic instruction: From laboratory investigations to classroom applications. *Journal of Special Education, 24*, 7–32.

Scruggs, T. E., & Mastropieri, M. A. (1992). *Teaching test-taking skills: Helping students show what they know.* Cambridge, MA: Brookline.

SERP (Strategic Education Research Partnership) (2009). *An introduction to word generation.* Boston: Author. Available online at www.serpinstitute.org/tools-an-resources/word-generation.php

Shanahan, C. (2005). *Adolescent literacy intervention programs: Chart and program review guide.* Naperville, IL: Learning Points Associates.

Shanahan, T., & Shanahan, C. (2008). Teaching disciplinary literacy to adolescents: Rethinking content-area literacy. *Harvard Educational Review, 78*(1), 40–61.

Shearer, B. (1999). *The vocabulary self-collection strategy (VSS) in a middle school.* Paper presented at the 49th Annual Meeting of the National Reading Conference, Orlando, FL.

Shearer, B. A., Ruddell, M. R., & Vogt, M. E. (2001). Successful middle school reading intervention: Negotiated strategies and individual choice. In J. V. Hoffman, D. L. Schallert, C. M. Fairbanks, J. Worthy, & B. G. Maloch (Eds.), *Fiftieth yearbook of the National Reading Conference, 50* (pp. 558–571). Chicago, IL: National Reading Conference.

Shefelbine, J. (1990). A syllabic-unit approach to teaching decoding of polysyllabic words to fourth- and sixth-grade disabled readers. In J. Zutell & S. McCormick (Eds.), *Literacy theory and research: Analyses from multiple paradigms* (39th yearbook of the National Reading Conference) (pp. 223-229). Chicago, IL: National Reading Conference.

Silver, E. A., Kilpatrick, J., & Schlesinger, B. (1990). *Thinking through mathematics: Fostering inquiry and communication in mathematics classrooms.* New York: College Board. Available online at www.eric.ed.gov:80/ERICWebPortal/search/detailmini.jsp?_nfpb=true&_&ERICExtSearch_SearchValue_0=ED387350&ERICExtSearch_SearchType_0=no&accno=ED387350

Simonsen, S. (1996). Identifying and teaching text structures in content area classrooms. In D. Lapp, J. Flood, & N. Farnan (Eds.), *Content area reading and learning instructional strategies* (2nd ed.) (pp. 59–75). Boston: Allyn & Bacon.

Simpson, M. L. (1986). PORPE: A writing strategy for studying and learning in the content areas. *Journal of Reading, 29,* 407–414.

Singer, H. (1975). The SEER technique: A non-computational procedure for quickly estimating readability levels. *Journal of Reading Behavior, 3,* 255–267.

Singer, H., & Donlan, D. (1989). *Reading and learning from text* (2nd ed.). Hillsdale, NJ: Erlbaum.

Sippola, A. E. (1995). K-w-l-s. *The Reading Teacher, 48,* 542–543.

Slater, W. H., & Graves, M. F. (1989). Research on expository text: Implications for teachers. In K. D. Muth (Ed.), *Children's comprehension of text* (pp. 140–160). Newark, DE: International Reading Association.

Slavin, R. E. (1987). Cooperative learning and the cooperative school. *Educational Leadership, 45*(3), 7–13.

Slavin, R. E. (1996). A cooperative learning approach to content area reading. In D. Lapp, J. Flood, & N. Farnan (Eds.), *Content area reading and learning instructional strategies* (2nd ed., pp. 369–382). Boston: Allyn & Bacon.

Smith, P. L., & Tompkins, G. E. (1988). Structured notetaking: A new strategy for content area readers. *Journal of Reading, 32,* 46–53.

Smith, W. L. (1978). Cloze procedure as applied to reading. In O. K. Buros (Ed.), *Eighth mental measurements yearbook* (*Vol. II,* pp. 1176–1178). Highland Park, NJ: Gryphon Press.

Snow, C. E., Burns, M. S., & Griffin, P. (1998). *Preventing reading difficulties in young children.* Washington, DC: National Academy Press.

Spandel, V. (2008). *Creating writers through 6-trait writing assessment and instruction* (5th ed.). Boston: Allyn & Bacon.

Spies, R. A., Carlson, J. F.., & Geisinger, K. F. (Eds.). (2010).*The eighteenth mental measurements yearbook.* Lincoln: University of Nebraska Press.

Spillane, J. P., & Callahan, K. A. (2000). Implementing state standards for science education: What district policy makers make of the hoopla. *Journal of Research in Science Teaching, 37,* 401–425.

Stahl, S. A. (1986). Three principles of effective vocabulary instruction. *Journal of Reading, 29,* 662–668.

Stahl, S. A., Hynd, C. R., Britton, B. K., McNish, M. M., & Bosquet, D. (1996). What happens when students read multiple source documents in history? *Reading Research Quarterly, 31,* 430–456.

Stahl, S. A., & Kapinus, B. A. (1991). Possible sentence: Predicting word meanings to teach content area vocabulary. *The Reading Teacher, 45,* 36–43.

Stauffer, R. G. (1969). *Directing reading maturity as a cognitive process.* New York: Harper & Row.

Stauffer, R. G. (1970, January). *Reading-thinking skills.* Paper presented at the annual reading conference at Temple University, Philadelphia, PA.

Steinberg, J. (1999, September 9). Free college notes on the Web: Aid to learning, or laziness. *The New York Times,* p. A1.

Stephens, L. C., & Ballast, K. H. (2011). *Using technology to improve adolescent writing, Digital make-overs for writing lessons.* Boston: Allyn & Bacon.

Sternberg, R. J. (1987). Most vocabulary is learned from context. In M. G. McKeown & M. E. Curtis (Eds.), *The nature of vocabulary acquisition* (pp. 89–105). Hillsdale, NJ: Erlbaum.

Sternberg, R. J., & Powell, J. S. (1983). Comprehending verbal comprehension. *American Psychologist, 38*, 878–893.

Stewart, R. A., & Cross, T. L. (1993). A field test of five forms of marginal gloss study guide: An ecological study. *Reading Psychology, 14*, 113–139.

Stiggins, R. (2006). Assessment for learning: A key to motivation and achievement. *Edge, 2*(2), 3–19.

Stotsky, S. (1984). Commentary: A proposal for improving high school students' ability to read and write expository prose. *Journal of Reading, 28*, 4–7.

Strauch, B. (2003). *The primal teen: What the new discoveries about the teenage brain tell us about our kids.* New York: Doubleday.

Street, B. (2009). Hidden features of academic paper writing. *Working Papers in Educational Linguistics.* Philadelphia, PA: University of Pennsylvania. Available online at www.thinking writing.qmul.ac.uk/.../Street%20Hidden%20features%20of%20AW%20Aclits%202009.doc

Strommen, L. T., & Mates, B. F. (2004). Learning to love reading: Interviews with older children and teens. *Journal of Adolescent & Adult Literacy, 48*, 188–200.

Sutton, C. (1989). Helping the nonnative English speakers with reading. *The Reading Teacher, 42*, 684–688.

Swain, M. (2005). The output hypothesis: Theory and research. In E. Hinkel (Ed.), *Handbook on research in second language teaching and learning* (pp. 471–484). Mahwah, NJ: Erlbaum.

Swain, M., & Lapkin, S. (1998). Interaction and second-language learning: Two adolescent French immersion students working together. *Modern Language Journal, 82*, 371–391.

Swanborn, M. S. L., & de Glopper, K. (1999). Incidental word learning while reading: A meta-analysis. *Review of Educational Research, 69*, 261–285.

Taba, H. (1965). The teaching of thinking. *Elementary English, 42*, 534–542.

Tanner, M. L., & Casados, L. (1998). Promoting and studying discussions in math classes. *Journal of Adolescent & Adult Literacy, 41*, 342–350.

Teachscape (2006). *Supporting English language learners: Building literacy skill in high school.* San Francisco: Author.

Technorati. (2010). *Tag page.* Available online at http://technorati.com/tag

Thomas, E. L., & Robinson, H. A. (1972). *Improving reading in every class: A sourcebook for teachers.* Boston: Allyn & Bacon.

Thompson, M. (2008). Multimodal teaching and learning: Creating spaces for content teachers. *Journal of Adolescent and Adult Literacy, 52*, 144-153.

Thonis, E. (1983). *The English-Spanish connection.* Compton, CA: Santillana.

Tierney, R. J., Carter, M. A., & Desai, L. E. (1991). *Portfolio assessment in the reading-writing classroom.* Norwood, MA: Christopher-Gordon.

Tierney, R. J., & Readence, J. E. (2005). *Reading strategies and practices: A compendium* (6th ed.). Boston: Allyn & Bacon.

Tonjes, M. J. (1991). *Secondary reading, writing, and learning.* Boston: Allyn & Bacon.

Torgesen, J., Nettles, S., Howard, P., & Winterbottom, R. (n.d.). *Brief report of a study to investigate the relationship between several brief measures of reading fluency and performance on the Florida Comprehensive Assessment Test-Reading in 4th, 6th, 8th, and 10th grades.* FCRR Technical Report #6. Tallahassee, FL: Florida Center for Reading Research. Available online at www.fcrr.org/science/scienceTechnical Reports.shtm

Touchstone Applied Sciences Associates. (1994). *DPR handbook.* Brewster, NY: Author.

Touchstone Applied Science Associates. (2006). The DRP model of reading. *TASA Talk.* Available online at www.tasaliteracy.com/tasatalk/tasatalk-main.html

Tovani, C. (2000). *I read it but I don't get it: Comprehension strategies for adolescent readers.* Portland, ME: Stenhouse.

Trabasso, T., & Magliano, J. P. (1996). How do children understand what they read and what can we do to help them? In M. F. Graves, P. Van den Broek, & B. M. Taylor, (Eds.), *The first R: Every child's right to read* (pp. 160–188). New York: Teachers College Press & International Reading Association.

Trees, A. R., & Jackson, M. R. (2007). The learning environment in clicker classrooms: Student processes of learning and involvement in large university-level courses using student response systems. *Learning, Media & Technology, 32* (1), 21–40.

Trilling, B., & Fadel, C. (2009). *21st century skills, learning for life in our times.* San Francisco, CA: Jossey-Bass.

Tulving, E. (1962). Subjective organization in free recall of "unrelated" words. *Psychological Review, 69,* 344–354.

21st Century Skills. (2009a). *California propositions public service announcement skill-by-skill development* [DVD]. In B. Trilling & C. Fadel (2009), *21st century skills.* San Francisco, CA: Jossey-Bass.

21st Century Skills. (2009b). *Example of project-based learning, science lab (biology).* [DVD]. In B. Trilling & C. Fadel (2009), *21st century skills.* San Francisco, CA: Jossey-Bass.

University of Houston. (2010). *The educational uses of digital storytelling. 7 elements of story telling.* Available online at http://digitalstorytelling.coe.uh.edu/7elements.html

U. S. Bureau of the Census. (2010). *Small area income and poverty estimates (SAIPE): 2009 highlights.* Washington, DC: Author. Available online at www.census.gov/did/ www/saipe/data/highlights/files/saipe_highlights_2009.pdf

U. S. Department of Education. (2001). *No child left behind: Moving limited English proficient students to English fluency* (Title III). Available online at www.ed.gov/offices/DESE/ esca/nclb/part7.html

U. S. Department of Education. (2002). *The No Child Left Behind Act of 2001.* Available online at www.ed.gov/legislation/ESEA02.

U. S. Department of Education. (2009). *Striving readers.* Available online at www.ed .gov/programs/strivingreaders/index.html

U. S. Department of Education. (2009). *What Works Clearinghouse: Intervention: Read 180.* Available online at adolescent_literacy/read180/index.asp

U. S. Department of Education. (2010). *A Blueprint for reform: The reauthorization of the Elementary and Secondary Education Act.* Available online at www2.ed.gov/policy/elsec/ leg/blueprint.

Unsworth, L. (1999). Developing critical understanding of the specialized language of school science and history texts: A functional grammatical perspective. *Journal of Adolescent & Adult Literacy, 42,* 508–521.

Vacca, R. T., & Vacca, J. L. (1986). *Content area reading* (2nd ed.). Boston: Little Brown.

Vacca, R. T., & Vacca, J. L. (2002). *Content area reading: Literacy and learning across the curriculum* (7th ed.). Boston: Allyn & Bacon.

Valencia, S. W., & Place, N. A. (1994). Literacy portfolios for teaching, learning, and accountability: The Bellevue literacy assessment project. In S. W. Valencia, E. H. Hiebert, & P. P. Afflerbach (Eds.), *Authentic reading assessment: Practices and possibilities* (pp. 134–156). Newark, DE: International Reading Association.

van den Broek, P., & Kremer, K. E. (2000). The mind in action: What it means to comprehend during reading. In B. Taylor, M. F. Graves, & P. van den Broek (Eds.), *Reading for meaning: Fostering comprehension in the middle grades* (pp. 1–31). New York: Teachers College Press.

Van der Meij, H., & Dillon, J. T. (1994). Adaptive student questioning and students' verbal ability. *Journal of Experimental Education, 62,* 277–290.

VanSledright, B. A., & Frankes, L. (2000). Concept- and strategic-knowledge development in historical study: A comparative exploration in two fourth-grade classrooms. *Cognition and Instruction, 18,* 239–283.

Vaughn, S., Klinger, J., & Schumm, J. (n.d.). *Collaborative strategy instruction: A manual to assist with staff development.* Miami, FL: University of Miami.

Vogt, M. E. (2001, May). *Strategic approaches to engage struggling readers.* Paper presented at the annual conference of the International Reading Association, New Orleans, LA.

Wade-Stein, D., & Kintsch, E. (UD). *Summary street: Interactive computer support for writing.* University of Colorado, Institute of Cognitive Science. Available online at ics.colorado.edu/techpubs/pdf/03-01.pdf

Wagner, M., Marder, C., Blackorby, J., Cameto, R., Newman, L., Levine, P., & Davies-Mercier, E. (with Chorost, M., Garza, N., Guzman, A., & Sumi, C.). (2003). *The achievements of youth with disabilities during secondary school. A report from the national longitudinal transition study-2* (NLTS2). Menlo Park, CA: SRI International. Available at www.nlts2.org/reports/2003_11/nlts2_report_2003_11_complete.pd

Walczyk, J. J., & Griffith-Ross, D. A. (2007). How important is reading skill fluency for comprehension? *The Reading Teacher, 60,* 560–569.

Walker, M. L. (1995). Help for the "fourth-grade slump": SRQ2R plus instruction in text structure or main idea. *Reading Horizons, 36,* 38–58.

Walpole, S. (1998–1999). Changing texts, changing thinking: Comprehension demands of new science textbooks. *The Reading Teacher, 52,* 358–369.

Wark, D. M., & Flippo, R. F. (1991). Preparing for and taking tests. In R. F. Flippo & D. C. Caverly (Eds.), *Teaching reading and study strategies at the college level* (pp. 294–338). Newark, DE: International Reading Association.

Warner, L. A., Bierer, L. K,, Lawson, S. A., & Cohen, T. L. (1991). *Life science: The challenge of discovery.* Lexington, MA: Heath.

Waters, K. (2010). Literacy initiatives in the urban setting that promote higher level thinking skills in an urban middle school classroom. In J. Collins & T. Gunning (Eds.), *Building struggling students' higher level literacy, Practical ideas, powerful solutions.* Newark, DE: International Reading Association.

Weinstein, C., & Mayer, R. (1986). The teaching of learning strategies. In M. C. Wittrock (Ed.), *Handbook of research on teaching* (pp. 315–327). New York: Macmillan.

Weir, C. (1998). Using embedded questions to jump-start metacognition in middle school remedial readers. *Journal of Adolescent & Adult Literacy, 41,* 458–467.

Weisberg, R., & Balajthy, E. (1990). Development of disabled readers' metacomprehension ability through summarization training using expository text: Results of three studies. *Journal of Reading, Writing, and Learning Disabilities International, 6*, 117–136.

Wiggins, G. (2009). *Understanding by design textbook adoption criteria.* Available online at www.pearsonubd.com/programs.html

Wiggins, G., & McTighe, J. (1999). *Understanding by design.* Alexandria, VA: Association for Supervision and Curriculum Development.

Wiggins, G., & McTighe, J. (2006). *Understanding by design, expanded 2nd edition.* Alexandria, VA: ASCD.

Wilhelm, J. D. (1997). *"You gotta BE the book": Teaching engaged and reflective reading with adolescents.* New York, NY: Teachers College Press.

Wilkinson, I. A. G. (2009, February). *Quality talk about text to promote high-level reading comprehension.* Invited paper presented at the Research Conference of the International Reading Association, Phoenix, AZ.

Wilkinson, I. A. G, & Son, E. H. (2011). A dialogic turn in research on learning and teaching to comprehend., M. L. Kamil, P. D. Pearson, E. B. Moje, & P. P. Afflerbach (Eds.), *Handbook of reading research* (Vol. IV, pp. 359–387). New York: Routledge.

Wilkinson, I., Soter, A. & Murphy, P. K. (2009). *Quality talk web, Group discussion project.* Available online at www.quality-talk.org

Wilkinson, I. A. G., Soter, A.. & Murphy, P. K. (2010). Developing a model of quality talk about literary text. In M. G. McKeown & L. Kucan (Eds.), *Bringing reading research to life.* New York: Guilford Press.

Willingham, D. T. (2009). *Why don't students like school?* San Francisco, CA: Jossey-Bass.

Willner, L., Rivera, C., & Acosta, B. D. (2009). Ensuring accommodations used in content assessments are responsive to English-language learners. *The Reading Teacher, 62,* 696–698.

Wolk, S. (2009). Reading for a better world: teaching for social responsibility with young adult literature. *Journal of Adolescent & Adult Literacy, 52,* 664–673.

Wong, B. Y. L. (1986). The efficacy of a self-questioning summarization strategy for use by underachievers and learning disabled adolescents in social studies. *Learning Disabilities Focus, 2*(1), 20–35.

Wood, E., Willoughby, T., McDermott, C., Motz, M., Kaspar, V., & Ducharme, M. (1999). Development differences in study behavior. *Journal of Educational Psychology, 91,* 527–536.

Wood, K. D., Lapp, D., Flood, J., & Taylor, D. B. (2008). *Guiding readers through text: Strategy guides for new times* (2nd ed.). Newark, DE: International Reading Association.

Writing across the Curriculum. (2010). *How to write a narrative.* Northern Illinois University. Available online at www.engl.niu.edu/wac/personass.html#narr

Wylie, J., & McGuinness, C. (2004). The interactive effects of prior knowledge and text structure on memory for cognitive psychology texts. *British Journal of Educational Psychology, 74,* 497–514.

Young, J. P., Mathews, S. R., Kietzman, A. M., & Westerfield, T. (1997). Getting disenchanted adolescents to participate in school literacy activities: Portfolio conferences. *Journal of Adolescent & Adult Literacy, 40,* 348–360.

Zakaluk, B. L., & Samuels, S. J. (1988). Toward a new approach to predicting comprehensibility. In B. L. Zakaluk & S. J. Samuels (Eds.), *Readability: Its past, present, and future* (pp. 121–144). Newark, DE: International Reading Association.

Zinsser, W. (1988). *Writing to learn.* New York: Harper & Row.

Zolman, M. F., & Wagner, H. (2002, May). *Professional development plan for secondary teachers on strategies for struggling readers.* Paper presented at the annual meeting of the International Reading Association, San Francisco, CA.

Zoss, M. (2008). Visual arts and literacy. In L. Christenbury, R. Bomer, & P. Smagorinsky (Eds.) *Handbook of adolescent literacy research* (183–196). New York: Guilford.

Zwiers, J. (n.d.). *The third language of academic English, five key mental habits help English language learners acquire the language of school.* Available online at www.makassed.org.lb/Article/the third lang all.pdf

Zwiers, J. (2008). *Building academic language, Essential practices for content classrooms.* San Francisco, CA: Jossey-Bass.

Zywica, J., & Gomez, K. (2008). Annotating to support learning in the content areas: Teaching and learning science. *Journal of Adolescent & Adult Literacy, 52* 155–165.

Trade Books and Textbooks

Akre, J. B., Gray-Wilson, N., & Wilkin, D. (2009). *CK-12 bology.* Palo Alto, CA: CK-12 Foundation. Available online at http://about.ck12.org/about/ca/freetextbooks

Angliss, S. (2000). *Gold (The Elements).* New York: Benchmark Books.

Badders, W., Bethel, L. J., Fu, V., Peck, D., Sumners, C., & Valentino, C. (1999a). *Discovery works 4.* Parsippany, NJ: Silver Burdett Ginn.

Badders, W., Bethel, L. J., Fu, V., Peck, D., Sumners, C., & Valentino, C. (1999b). *Discovery works 6.* Parsippany, NJ: Silver Burdett Ginn.

Beldsoe, L. J. (1994). *Fearon's biology* (2nd ed.). Paramus, NJ: Globe Fearon.

Biesty, S. (1998). *Incredible body.* New York: Platt.

Boorstin, D. J., & Kelley, B. M. (2002). *A history of the United States.* Upper Saddle River, NJ: Prentice Hall.

Brimblecombe, S., Gallannaugh, D., & Thompson, C. (1998). *QPB science encyclopedia.* New York: Helicon.

Brown, G. W., Syukys, P. A., & Anderson, L. H. (1993). *Understanding business and personal law* (9th ed.). Lake Forest, IL: Glencoe.

Butler, L. (2007). *The Longman academic writing series.* White Plains: Longman.

Cather, W. (1900). The sentimentality of William Tavener. In V. Faulkner (Ed.). (1970). *Willa Cather's collected short fiction, 1892–1912* (pp. 353–357). Lincoln: University of Nebraska Press.

Clay R. (1997). *Ukraine, A new independence.* New York: Benchmark Books.

Cleary, B. (1983). *Dear Mr. Henshaw.* New York: Morrow.

Collier, C., & Collier, J. L. (1998). *The American Revolution.* New York, NY: Marshall Cavendish Benchmark Books.

Collier, C., & Collier, J. L. (1999). *The Jeffersonian Republicans: The Louisiana Purchase and the War of 1812.* New York: Marshall Cavendish Benchmark Books.

Crane, S. (1985). The red badge of courage. In A. Mellors & F. Robertson (Eds.), (1998) *The red badge of courage and other stories*. New York: Oxford.

Crichton, M. (1990). *Jurassic Park*. New York: Random House.

Cuevas, M. M., & Lamb, W. G. (1994). *Holt physical science*. New York: Holt, Rinehart, and Winston.

Dickson, T. R. (1995). *Introduction to chemistry* (7th ed.). New York: Wiley.

Dixon, D. (1992). *The practical geologist*. New York: Simon & Schuster.

Dolan, E. (1995). *The American Revolution: How we fought the War of Independence*. Brookfield, CT: Millbrook Press.

Duncan, L. (1977). *Summer of fear*. Boston: Little, Brown.

Ellis, E. G., & Esler, A. (2001). *World history: Connections to today*. Upper Saddle River, NJ: Prentice Hall.

Ellison, R. (1952). *The invisible man*. New York: Random House.

Exline, J. D., Pasachoff, J. M., Simons, B. B., Vogel, C. G., & Wellnitz, T. R. (2001). *Earth science*. Upper Saddle River, NJ: Prentice Hall.

Garcia, J. R., Gelo, D. J., Greenow, L. L., Kracht, J. B., & White, D. G. (1997). *The world and its people*. Parsippany, NY: Silver Burdett Ginn.

Gloag, A., Gloag, A., & Kramer, M. (2010). *CK-12 basic algebra*. Palo Alto, CA: CK-12 Foundation. Available online at www.ck12.org/flexbook

Globe Fearon. (1994). *Basic mathematics* (3rd ed.). Paramus, NJ: Author.

Globe Fearon. (1994). *The Latino experience in U. S. history*. Paramus, NJ: Author.

Globe Fearon. (2000). *Basic mathematics* (4th ed.). Paramus, NJ: Author.

Goldstein, M. (1999). *Weather guide for complete idiots*. New York: Alpha Books.

Grolier. (1997). *Grolier multimedia encyclopedia*. Novato, CA: Mindscape.

Grolier Educational. (2000). *Grolier's new book of popular science series*. Danbury, CT: Grolier.

Hakim, J. (1993). *Oxford history of US: Making thirteen colonies*. New York: Oxford.

Hakim, J. (1994). *Oxford history of US: An age of extremism*. New York: Oxford.

Heiserman, D. L. (1992). *Exploring chemical elements and their compounds*. New York: McGraw Hill.

James, N. (1979). *Alone around the world*. New York: Coward, McCann & Geoghegan.

Kallen, S. A. (1999). *The 1950s*. San Diego, CA: Lucent.

King, D. C. (1996). *First facts about American heroes*. Woodbridge, CT: Blackbirch.

King, W., & Napp, J. (1998). *Our nation's history*. Circle Pines, MN: American Guidance Service, p. 524.

Klag, M. J. (1999). *Johns Hopkins family health book*. New York: HarperCollins.

Kneidel, S. (2001). *Stinkbugs, stick insects, and stag beetles and 18 more of the strangest insects on earth*. Boston: John Wiley.

Lapsansky-Werner, E. J., Levy, P. B., Roberts, R. & Taylor, A. (2010). *Prentice-Hall United States history*. Upper Saddle River, NJ: Pearson.

LeMay, H. E., Beall, H., Robblee, K. M., & Brower, D. C. (2000). *Chemistry: Connections to our changing world*. Upper Saddle River, NJ: Prentice Hall.

LeVasseur, M. L., Schaleman, Jr., H. J., Sheldon, S., & Gleason, H. M. (2002). *World geography*. Upper Saddle River, NJ: Prentice-Hall.

Litwin, L. B. (1999). *Benjamin Banneker, astronomer and mathematician*. Springfield, NJ: Enslow.

Malam, J. (1999). *Mesopotamia and the fertile crescent, 10,000 to 539 B. C.* Austin, TX: Raintree Steck Vaughn.

Massa, R., (1998). *Ocean environments*. Austin, TX: Steck Vaughn.

McKeever, S., & Foote, M. (1998). *The DK science encyclopedia*. New York: DK Publishing.

McKissack, P., & McKissack, P. (1986). *The new true book of the Maya*. Chicago, IL: Children's Press.

Morgan, S. (1996). *Weather*. Syndney, Australia: Allen & Unwin.

Moss, J., & Wilson, G. (1998). *Profiles in American History: Civil Rights movement to the present*. Detroit, MI: UXL.

Neff, M. M. (1990). Legends: How Gordie Howe was a hockey star in his youth and also when he was a grandpa. *Sports Illustrated for Kids, 2*(2), p. 48.

Nishi, D. (1998). *Life during the Great Depression*. San Diego, CA: Lucent Books.

O'Dell, S. (1980). *Sarah Bishop*. New York: Scholastic.

Parker, S. (1999). *An ant's life by Ant, with help from Steve Parker*. Pleasantville, NY: Readers Digest.

Press, P. (1999). *The 1930s*. San Diego, CA: Lucent.

Roberts, P. C. (1997). *Ancient Rome*. New York: Time Life.

Rodriguez, L. J. (1993). *Always running: La vida loca, gang days in L. A.* Willimantic, CT: Curbstone Press.

Ross, M. E. (2000). *Fish watching with Eugenie Clark*. Minneapolis, MN: Carolrhoda.

Sager, R. J., & Helgren, D. M. (2008). *Holt's Word Geography today*. Boston: Holt McDougall.

Sattler, H. R. (1995). *Our patchwork planet: The story of plate tectonics*. New York: Lothrop, Lee & Shepherd.

Sauvain, P. (1996). *Oceans*. Minneapolis, MN: Carolrhoda.

Schaaf, F. (1998). *40 nights to knowing the sky*. New York: Holt.

Silverstein, A., & Silverstein, V. (2008). *Symbiosis*. Brookfield, CT: Millbrook Press.

Simon, S. (1993). *Weather*. New York, NY: Morrow.

Simon, S. (1998). *Now you see it, now you don't: The amazing world of optical illusions*. New York: Morrow.

Smith, M. (1996). *Living earth*. New York: Dorling Kindersley.

Snedden, R. (1999). *Earth and beyond*. Des Plaines, IL: Heinemann.

Speare, E. (1958). *The witch of Blackbird Pond*. Boston: Houghton Mifflin.

Spiegelman, A. (1990). *Maus: A survivor's tale*. New York: Pantheon.

St. George, J. (2001). *John & Abigail Adams*. New York: Holiday.

Sullivan, A., & Sheffrin, S. M. (2010). *Prentice Hall economics*. Upper Saddle River, NJ: Pearson Education.

Suter, J. (1994). *World history*. Paramus, NJ: Globe Fearon.

Uschan, M. B. (1999). *The 1950s: Cultural history of the United States through the decades*. San Diego, CA: Lucent Books.

Wiesel, E. (1955, 2006). *Night*. New York: Hill and Wang.

William, K. (1986). *Sweet Valley High: Winter carnival*. New York: Bantam.

Yolen, J. (1992). *Encounter*. Orlando, FL: Harcourt.

Zeman, A., & Kelly, K. (1994). *Everything you need to know about science homework*. New York: Scholastic.

Index

Credits